Chile and Argentina
THE BRADT TREKKING GUIDE

THE BRADT STORY
Hilary Bradt

The first Bradt travel guide was written by Hilary and George Bradt in 1974 on a river barge floating down a tributary of the Amazon in Bolivia. From their base in Boston, Massachusetts, they went on to write and publish four other backpacking guides to the Americas and one to Africa.

In the 1980s Hilary continued to develop the Bradt list in England, and also established herself as a travel writer and tour leader. The company's publishing emphasis evolved towards broader-based guides to new destinations – usually the first to be published on those countries – complemented by hiking, rail and wildlife guides.

Since winning *The Sunday Times* Small Publisher of the Year Award in 1997, we have continued to fill the demand for detailed, well-written guides to unusual destinations, while maintaining the company's original ethos; that adventurous travel is more enjoyable if the wishes of the local people are taken into consideration.

Travel guides are by their nature continuously evolving. If you experience anything which you would like to share with us, or if you have any amendments to make to this guide, please write; all your letters are read and passed on to the author. Most importantly, do remember to travel with an open mind and to respect the customs of your hosts – it will add immeasurably to your enjoyment.

Happy travelling!

19 High Street, Chalfont St Peter, Bucks SL9 9QE, England; tel: 01753 893444; fax: 01753 892333; email: info@bradt-travelguides.com; web: www.bradt-travelguides.com

Chile and Argentina

THE BRADT TREKKING GUIDE

Fifth Edition

Tim Burford

Bradt Travel Guides Ltd, UK
The Globe Pequot Press Inc, USA

First published in 1980 by Bradt Publications
This fifth edition published in 2001 by Bradt Travel Guides Ltd
19 High Street, Chalfont St Peter, Bucks SL9 9QE, England
Published in the USA by The Globe Pequot Press Inc,
246 Goose Lane, PO Box 480, Guilford, Connecticut 06437-0480

British Library Cataloguing in Publication Data
A catalogue record for this book is available from the British Library
ISBN 1 84162 036 X

Library of Congress Cataloging-in-Publication Data
Burford, Tim
    Chile & Argentina : the Bradt trekking guide / Tim Burford. -- 5th ed.
    p. cm.
    Rev. ed. of Chile & Argentina. 4th ed. c1998
    Includes bibliographical references and index
    ISBN 1 84162 036 X
    1. Backpacking--Chile--Guidebooks. 2. Backpacking--Argentina--
    Guidebooks. 3. Chile--Guidebooks. 4. Argentina--Guidebooks.
    I. Title: Chile and Argentina. II. Burford, Tim. Chile and Argentina.
    III Title.

GV199.44.C44 B87 2001
918.204'64--dc21   2001033149

Photographs
Front cover Cerro FitzRoy, Aguja Poincenot & Aguja St Exupery (Kathy Jarvis)
Illustrations Hilary Bradt
Maps Alan Whitaker
Inside front cover Mountain High Maps™ © 1995 Digital Wisdom Inc

Typeset from the author's disc by Donald Sommerville
Printed and bound in Italy by Legoprint SpA, Trento

Authors/ Acknowledgements

This edition of *Chile and Argentina: The Bradt Trekking Guide* is the latest stage in an evolutionary process: its ancestor was written in 1980 by John Pilkington and Hilary Bradt and formed one of the six core guides to hiking in South America that launched Bradt Enterprises, which later became Bradt Travel Guides Ltd. Since then each edition has been revised by travellers or expatriates who updated and added to the hikes. For the fourth edition we wanted to start again with a new author, so Tim Burford, with the assistance of Kathleen Ladizesky and John Pilkington, painstakingly rewalked the old trails and found some new ones. For this fifth edition he has had help from Kathleen Ladizesky and Kathy Jarvis. Tim has, however, often kept much of the original description because it was still accurate and 'if it ain't broke, don't fix it'. Below, then, are the authors of, and contributors to, earlier editions whose words still form the basis of many of the trail descriptions: Elizabeth Allison, Rick Ansell, J M Bibby, Hilary Bradt, Sebastian Cooper, Nick Cotton, Andrew Dixon, Simon Elms, Hamish Galpin, Clare Hargreaves, John and Christine Myerscough, John Pilkington, Patrick Symington and Graham Youdale. Their names have been removed from 'their sections' except when their words are completely unchanged.

In addition Tim Burford would like to thank the following: Arnie & Veronica Cotton, Simon Hosking, Jo Medina, Jaime Utreras, Jorge, Cristian, Claudio & Pato, Albrecht & Sabina, Jurgen & Madelon, Matthias Holzmann, Adrian Turner, Cathy Berard, Francisco Valle, Scott Altenhof, Jo Duncan, Jessamie Simpson, Graham Hornsey, Keith Tuckwell, Debbie Butland, Sergio Herrera, Sam Esmiol, Alberto de Castillo, Mike Gooley, Scott Sheldon, the Sato family, Jim Harding, Carolina Morgada, Gerardo Niklitschek, John Ashford, Paul Barmey, Sergio Sandoval, Ivan Vigoureux, Nick, Jo, Jane, Marie, and their Raleigh International groups, Paola at Niko's, Fernando Viveros of Onas Patagonicas, Christine Fox, Catherine Kenrick, Sophie Hooper, John Burton, Martin Wierzbicki; and readers Glenn Ord, R Steffen, Dick van Oordt, Sarah Booth & Brad McCartney and C Walker.

Special thanks to Kathleen Ladizesky and Kathy Jarvis, and as ever, many thanks to Donald Sommerville, Alan Whitaker and all at Bradt, notably Tricia Hayne.

TIM BURFORD

Tim Burford studied languages at Oxford University. In 1991, after a brief career as a publisher, he began writing guidebooks for Bradt Publications, firstly for hiking in East-Central Europe and then for backpacking and ecotourism in Latin America. He has now written six books for Bradt, as well as the Rough Guide to Romania.

Contents

LIST OF MAPS

Introduction

Ever since Magellan first explored the coastline of Chile and Argentina in 1520, these vast countries, at the southernmost extremity of the world, have been a source of fascination for travellers. Darwin left a superb account not only of the area's fauna, flora and geology, but also of its people. In his footsteps followed George Musters, a naval officer who roamed 2,000 kilometres across the windswept Patagonian plains with a band of Tehuelche Indians; the naturalist William Hudson, who devoted his life to studying the birds of the Río Negro; Lady Florence Dixie, daughter of a Scottish Marquis, who traipsed through southern Patagonia with her brother, Lord Queensberry and a retinue of servants, hunting guanaco and 'wild ostrich' for food. More recently Patagonia has won a place on the literary map through Bruce Chatwin's travels, inspired by a piece of Patagonian 'brontosaurus' which adorned his grandmother's living room.

Whichever kind of landscape or climate is for you, you can find it in Chile and Argentina. You can swelter on the high, parched plateaux of northwest Argentina, or freeze on the fringe of Antarctica in Tierra del Fuego, where the Andes take a final plunge into the sea. You can watch elephant seals and southern right whales calving off the Valdés Peninsula, or laze in the alpine meadows of the Lakes District. All these areas are covered in this guide, concentrating unashamedly on the territory south of Santiago and Aconcagua, which offers the most accessible hiking. However, there is also a summary of possibilities further north.

If you are expecting to ride in rickety buses and rub elbows with brightly clad Indians in bowlers and ponchos, you will be disappointed; both Chile and Argentina have all but eradicated their indigenous populations, and today the majority of the people have more in common with Europeans and North Americans than with the former native inhabitants. The standard of living is far higher in Chile and Argentina than elsewhere in Latin America. Hotels, restaurants and transport are also far more sophisticated in both countries than elsewhere – as are their prices. In fact, the only real discomfort you need to experience will be due to the elements – particularly if you opt for a boat trip to the shipwreck-studded rocks of Cape Horn.

Nevertheless, ancient traditions remain in the countryside. In Argentina you will still see leather-faced *gauchos* careering across the *pampas* on horseback, looking as if they have charged straight out of a Western movie. And everything they ever told you about Argentine steak is true: between midday and four in the afternoon, any self-respecting Argentine will be found gorging himself on huge hunks of the stuff, a pound (half a kilo) at a time, washing it down with a few glasses of red Argentine wine and then sleeping it off. Vegetarians will not feel at home in these countries, although there is plenty of pizza and pasta around.

Around the Chilean city of Temuco, you may well encounter some of the last remaining pure-blood Indians, many of whom still use traditional agricultural methods. As in Darwin's day, Chileans are renowned for their hospitality. You will almost certainly be invited to stay in people's homes, however poor, and be treated to a *cazuela* (stew) and a bottle of very drinkable Chilean wine. Enjoy this hospitality, but be careful not to abuse it.

WALKING

Chile and Argentina offer some of the most spectacular walking opportunities in South America. Perhaps the best-known hiking area is around the magnificent peaks of the Torres del Paine in southern Chile. However, equally fine possibilities can be found in Argentina around Mount FitzRoy (named after the captain of the *Beagle*) and on Tierra del Fuego. For those who prefer walking in warmer climes, the Lakes District offers countless hikes past deep-blue lakes, smouldering volcanoes and lush forests. Further north, towards the borders with Peru and Bolivia, is one of the most primitive backpacking areas, where the people and terrain are similar to those of Peru and Bolivia to the north.

Chile and Argentina are a paradise for mountaineers, too, as well as practitioners of all sorts of other sports. Many mountaineers have been tantalised by the sheer, granite spires of the Paine and FitzRoy massifs or the glaciated peaks of the Cordillera Darwin. However, since this is primarily a walking guide, we cover climbs which would be suitable for a reasonably fit and properly equipped walker and which do not require specialist expertise. This is true even of Aconcagua, the highest mountain outside the Himalayas, which needs careful acclimatisation to altitude and attention to the weather, but little technical expertise.

Almost all the trails described in this guide are through national parks. Along many routes you will find *refugios* (mountain huts), maintained by the local Club Andino (walking club), where you can sleep, often free of charge. Many of the hikes are waymarked with splashes of paint, daubed onto trees, rocks or anything convenient. We have tried to add accurate latitudes and longitudes to our maps, but mapping is an inexact science in Latin America and you should not follow your GPS slavishly. Normally you have to pay a small fee when you enter a national park, but this never amounts to more than a few US dollars.

TELL US ABOUT YOUR TRIP

The readership of any travel guide will collectively experience the countries it covers in far more depth than the author can, and will personally test a far greater number of hotels, campsites, restaurants and tour operators.

So, whether you want to make my day with a blow-by-blow account of your off-the-beaten-track adventures, or spoil it by letting me know that I'm wrong about absolutely everything, your time and effort in writing to me about your trip will be greatly appreciated. Every letter will help make the next edition even better, enhancing the experiences of those who follow in your footsteps. The more detail the better, though even one hot tip about a new hotel or restaurant will not only help me and future travellers, but also be of benefit to the owners of the establishment.

Every correspondent will be acknowledged in the next edition, so do print your name clearly if your letter is handwritten. The best contributors will receive a Bradt travel guide of their choice. Letters can be addressed to Tim Burford, Bradt Travel Guides, 19 High Street, Chalfont St Peter, Bucks SL9 9QE, UK. Alternatively email me at tim@owlstone.demon.co.uk with a copy please to info@bradt-travelguides.com.

Part One

General Information

TOP TEN HIKES

From north to south

Geography and Climate

Chile is famous as that absurdly long, thin country squeezed between the Andean *cordillera* (range) and the Pacific Ocean, while Argentina is for most the land of the prairie-like *pampas*, although there is far more to the country than that. The southern parts of both countries form Patagonia, perhaps more a concept or a state of mind than a specific place; indeed there is no agreement on just where it begins – at the Río Colorado or the Río Negro in Argentina, at the Río Biobío in Chile, or at the 40th parallel which passes between the Colorado and Negro and just south of Valdivia in Chile. It doesn't seem to matter, as a Patagonian knows that he is a Patagonian, and that suffices.

GEOLOGY

The Pacific coastal ranges of Chile are ancient and almost worn away, but the Andes and the rest of Chile were created relatively recently as the South American plate moved west and drove the Nazca and Antarctic plates under the edge of the continent. This process is continuing – Araucanía and the Lakes District are dotted with volcanoes and are particularly susceptible to earthquakes.

In Argentina, the *pampas* and Patagonia are covered with thick deposits of eroded rock removed by wind, rain and ice from the Andes, although older granite protrudes in places. The Andes have also been subject to glaciation. At its maximum, the Antarctic ice sheet covered the Chilean Andes and the coasts as far north as Puerto Montt and Río Gallegos. At the last glacial maximum, 28,000–19,000 years ago, the basins of Lakes General Carrera/Buenos Aires, O'Higgins/San Martín, Viedma, Argentino and Fagnano, as well as marine enclosures such as Skyring and Otway Sounds and the Straits of Magellan, were eroded by huge glaciers flowing east from the Andes. Glaciers also flowed west and south to cut the fjords.

GEOGRAPHY
Chile

Embracing almost 40 degrees of latitude (or over 70 degrees if you include its claim to part of Antarctica), Chile encompasses more climates, landscapes and ways of life than any other country of its size in the world. Your impressions will depend very much on which part you visit. Chile is over 4,300km long, but averages only 180km wide; its total area is 748,800km² (without Antarctica), making it one of the smaller countries of South America.

From north to south, the country falls into five sharply contrasting zones:

- Gran Norte ('Great North'), with its virtually rain-free desert and huge deposits of nitrate and copper, occasional oases and the port of Antofagasta.

- Norte Chico ('Little North'), a semi-desert with irrigated valleys, and the city of La Serena.
- The Heartland, where most of Chile's population live. Huge farms and vineyards cover this exceptionally beautiful area, which includes the country's three largest cities: Santiago, Valparaíso and Concepción, as well as the Central Valley, Chile's most fertile land.
- Araucanía and the Lakes District – the area of forests, mountains and lakes between Concepción and Puerto Montt. Its main centres are Temuco, Valdivia and Puerto Montt.
- The islands, forests, fjords, mountains and icecaps between Puerto Montt and Cape Horn. This sparsely populated area offers some of the country's finest and wildest scenery.

In addition there are two further areas not covered in this book:

- The Pacific islands of Juan Fernández and Rapa Nui (Easter Island), home to all sorts of endemic species.
- And finally, the Chilean claim to a chunk of Antarctica, stretching to the South Pole.

You will also meet contrasting peoples as you travel around Chile; the majority of the 14.8 million population is *mestizo* (mixed Hispanic and indigenous blood), but there are 15,000 Aymara Indians in the north, and up to a million Mapuche around Temuco. In a country whose present-day population is overwhelmingly urban, the Indians are unusual in being largely rural. There are many Chileans of German origin in the Lakes District, and in the far south many are of Croatian or British descent. These are descendants of 19th-century immigrants and many still speak their mother tongue (which may help if you do not speak Spanish). Their influence can also been seen in the architecture and atmosphere of the towns and villages.

GEOGRAPHY
Argentina
At over 2.8 million km² in area (plus a claimed million more in Antarctica), Argentina is much larger than Chile, with higher peaks, such as Aconcagua and Pissis, but equally contrasting landscapes – from the sub-tropical climate of the northeast and the Andean aridity of the northwest to the subantarctic wastes of Tierra del Fuego. In Buenos Aires you could be in any European city, but fly a couple of hours south to the barren steppes which make up a third of the country's area, and you could be in the Wild West.

Argentina is an enigma in terms of its economic development. Although it is undoubtedly one of the richest countries in Latin America for natural resources, its economic problems have brought unprecedented hardship to a traditionally prosperous people. Argentines say that there are four types of country: the developed ones; the undeveloped ones; Japan, because it has nothing and has become very rich; and Argentina, because it has everything and wastes it all. As the French statesman Georges Clemenceau said, Argentina is 'a country with a wonderful future, and it always will be', hinting at the Argentine tendency to dream rather than work.

From a walker's point of view, Argentina offers almost inexhaustible possibilities. Broadly speaking the country can be divided into four main physical areas:

- The Andes, high and parched in the northwest on the border with Bolivia, and eroded by glaciers in the Patagonian south, where the mountains plunge into the sea. The oases stretching along the eastern foot of the Andes – Jujuy, Salta, Tucumán and Mendoza – were the first places to be colonised by the Spaniards and retain much of their architecture.
- The north and Mesopotamia, containing the vast plains of the Chaco and the floodplain between the Paraná and Uruguay rivers.
- The *Pampas*, south of the Chaco, east of the Andes and north of the Río Colorado, covering about 650,000km². These are divided into the humid and the dry *pampas*; over a metre of rain a year falls on Rosario, while Bahía Blanca has just 535mm.
- Patagonia, an area of windswept plateaux south of the Río Colorado rising up to the snow-capped peaks of the Andes. This covers around 780,000km².

In contrast to Chile, the Argentine population is 95% white, due to the virtual extermination of the indigenous people and massive immigration in the late 19th and early 20th centuries. Almost 40% of its 36 million inhabitants live in Buenos Aires city and province; under 3% live in Patagonia, where there is less than one inhabitant per square kilometre.

CLIMATE

The northern parts of Chile and Argentina have the distinct rainy and dry seasons also found in Peru and Bolivia. The rainy season, known as the *invierno boliviano* (Bolivian winter) is from November to March (the southern hemisphere's spring and summer), and the driest months are from May to October. Corrientes and Misiones provinces, in northeastern Argentina, are at their wettest in September.

Further south the climate is temperate, with four distinct seasons whose timing is the exact reverse of those in Europe. Spring is roughly November and December, summer January and February, autumn April and May and winter May to October. Spring is usually wet, summer is clear and sunny with occasional rainy days, autumn is crisp and cool, and winter is cold and damp. As you travel south, summers become cooler and a persistent wind blows, but winters are never really cold anywhere, except in the far south.

Northwest Argentina and northern Chile are good for hiking in winter (May–October) since the summer rains wash out the trails. The best times to visit the other areas in this guide are late spring, summer or early autumn, ie: November–April. In high summer (January and February) the towns do get a bit crowded for comfort, but the children go back to school at the beginning of March, so you will then have many places completely to yourselves. In April, facilities start to shut down and public transport is reduced, but in July and August everything springs to life again in the Lakes District for the winter sports season. However, only the main roads are kept open at this time, and you will find most of the hikes impassable.

In Patagonia and Tierra del Fuego, summer temperatures reach a maximum of 15°C. The region is notorious for relentless winds and rain, and at high altitudes it may snow even in January or February. One advantage, however, is that during this season the days are very long and it does not get dark until nearly midnight. Autumn (late February and March) is a good time to visit Paine, as there will be less wind and rain than in the summer.

Southern Chile and Argentina lie directly beneath an ozone hole (or more accurately an area of ozone depletion), which is at its worst from September to

EL NIÑO

El Niño (or scientifically ENSO, the *El Niño* Southern Oscillation) is the name of a sporadic weather system, usually occurring in the southern hemisphere's summer, when the cold waters which usually flow north from Antarctica up the west coast of South America are diverted to the west, and a transient body of warm water reaches the Pacific coast. Seas up to 8°C warmer than usual produce more evaporation, therefore more cloud and more rain. When you hear this has happened (roughly every four to seven years), you would do well to reconsider plans to hike in the north of Chile and Argentina, which will generally be battered by heavy rains.

The phenomenon was first identified on Christmas Eve in 1982 (hence its name – '*El Niño*' is 'the Christ Child'), but it is nothing new. In 1925 almost 2m of rain fell on Lima (compared with its usual 5cm), and in 1965 27 million seabirds died when anchoveta fish stocks crashed after *El Niño* had struck. After three years of drought, Chile received three times its usual average rainfall from the 1997–8 *El Niño*. Buenos Aires received 7cm in under four hours in early 1998, closing down ATMs nationwide.

However, in other areas *El Niño* can lead to the rains failing. Fires lit by settlers to clear trees in the Brazilian state of Roraima blazed out of control in early 1998, when the wet season failed to extinguish them. Over 60,000km^2 were burned, including large areas of virgin Amazonian rainforest, home to the Yámana and other indigenous peoples.

mid-October. This leads to an increase in ultra-violet radiation, and, coupled with altitude and dry, unpolluted air, in the risk of cataracts and skin cancer; be specially sure to wear a sun hat and sunglasses at these times. Chilean scientists say that the situation is now improving, and over the next 30 to 50 years it should return to that of the 1960s.

A separate aspect of man-made climate change is the 'Greenhouse Effect' (*el efecto invernadero*), which is expected to reduce rain in the centre and south of Chile and Argentina (which will reduce crops); to increase the effect of the *invierno boliviano* (and extend it southwards); and to increase average temperatures by 2°C (in the north) and 5°C (in the south). The southern icecap has already shrunk by 500km^2 in the last 50 years; between 1896 and 1995 the O'Higgins glacier retreated no less than 14km. In the wine-growing areas of Central Chile 1996 was the driest year on record, and 1997 was the wettest, thanks to *El Niño*.

Natural History

Hilary Bradt

'These goslings are black and white and have feathers over their whole body of the same size and fashion, and they do not fly, and live on fish… The sea wolves have a head like that of a calf and small round ears. They have large teeth and no legs, but feet attached to their body resembling a human hand. And they had nails on these feet and skin between the toes like the gosling. And if they could have run they would have been truly fierce and cruel; but they do not leave the water, where they swim wondrously and live on fish.'

> Diary entry by Magellan's chronicler Antonio Pigafetta
> during their voyage down the Patagonian coast, 1520

To the 16th-century explorers Magellan and Pigafetta, the penguin and sea lion were animals 'the like of which no Christian man had e'er set eyes on' and to 20th-century travellers they are still fascinating, if more familiar. Inland there is also much to interest backpackers. The flora and fauna you are most likely to come across in the Lakes District, Patagonia and Tierra del Fuego are described below (see also pages 112–4 for sketchier details of wildlife elsewhere in Argentina and pages 129–131 for wildlife in Chile's Norte Grande).

Given Chile's position, squeezed in between the Andes to the east, the Pacific to the west, the arid *puna* (high-altitude desert covered with patchy grasslands) and Atacama to the north, and the ice-caps to the south, it is not surprising that there are lots of endemic species – and of course the Pacific islands are even more isolated, so there are even more endemic species there. Some species are accepted as 'endemic' even though they also appear in contiguous areas of Argentina – in fact, Argentina shares much of its wildlife with the countries to its north. Species diversity declines towards the south – in the temperate zone, rodents (including introduced hares and rabbits have begun to dominate), partly as a result of human action which has decimated their predators, notably the puma.

Man has transformed the landscape to a vast extent, with alien species now found in the most unlikely places. The *puna* in the north and the sub-antarctic zones in the far south are relatively untouched, but everywhere in between you will find European herbs as well as broom, wild roses and brambles. The characteristic sign of settlement in Argentina's Patagonia is a line of poplars or willows, while large areas of Chile are covered with plantations of pine and eucalyptus. The first horses and cows were brought to the River Plate in 1537 and left to run free when the colony was abandoned for a time. Their population exploded, and by 1580 horses had reached the Straits of Magellan! The Mapuche soon mastered the skills of horsemanship, enabling them to beat off the Spanish in Chile and spread to the Atlantic. Similarly, European hares and rabbits are now omnipresent, and form the core diet of many native predators such as pumas.

VEGETATION

In the **far north**, on the borders with Bolivia, the *puna* is drier than the *paramo* further north. What precipitation there is comes mostly in January and February, usually as snow, sleet or hail, but there is time for most animals to give birth. The scrub forests of queñoa (*Polylepis tarapacana*), which may have covered the *puna* until the 16th century, are now only to be found in damper gullies. The llareta (*Laretia gummifera*) is like brain coral (ie: coral in the shape of a brain), a mound up to 1m high and 30m² in area, comprising many thousands of tiny rosette leaves. It can be several thousand years old, growing just 1.5mm per year. Beneath the surface is dead material which makes good fuel. At lower levels there are cacti and huarango (*Prosopis* spp.), with tussock grass.

South of the Atacama desert, the **Norte Chico** and **central Chile** are dominated by sclerophyllous shrubs adapted to conserve water, with some *Nothofagus* (see box) at higher altitudes in the coastal ranges. In most areas, hot, dry summers and cool, moist winters produce a Mediterranean scrub (*matorral*) with low evergreen trees such as litre (*Lithraea caustica*), boldo (*Peumus boldus*), peumo (*Cryptocarya alba*) and lingue (*Persea lingue*). In the damper southern part of this region, you will find Maulino forest between 100m and 900m, dominated by hualo (*Nothofagus glauca*), with ruil (*N. alessandrii*), pitao (*Pitavia punctata*), as well as queule (*Gomortega keule*), the only species in its genus, which is found only on the coast of the 8th Region (Biobío).

The forest zone which hikers are most likely to see is also biologically the richest – the **Valdivian Forest**, a temperate rainforest extending through Araucanía, the Lakes District and Aysén to the Northern Patagonian Icefield and to Los Alerces in Argentina. At lower levels, mostly south of Puerto Montt, this is mostly evergreen forest dominated by the tall coihue (or coigüe; *Nothofagus dombeyi*), with tepa (*Laurelia philippiana*), ulmo (*Eucryphia cordata*) and tineo (*Weinmannia trichosperma*), and with a very dense understorey. In the wettest areas thrives a cypress, the ciprés de las Guiatecas (*Pilgerodendron uvifera*).

There is little low-level forest left to the north of Puerto Montt; higher levels are covered by a largely deciduous forest, dominated by lenga (*Nothofagus pumilio*); a tree which flourishes in exposed sites is ñirre (*N. antarctica*). High, dry areas are home to Andean cypress (ciprés de la cordillera; *Austrocedrus chilensis*), and to the pehuen or monkey-puzzle tree (*Araucaria araucana*). There used to be huge stands of the latter throughout southern Chile, but it is now confined mostly to the Lakes District, Nahuelbuta and the upper Biobío, though you may see scattered examples elsewhere, with many planted in towns from Santiago to Punta Arenas. Its seeds are eaten by the Mapuche, as well as by the choroye parakeet, and about 70 species of insects are found only on the monkey-puzzle. It lives for up to 3,000 years, and can grow to 50m in height and 3m in diameter. Further south is the similarly long-lived alerce (*Fitzroya cupressoides*), which seeds only when 200 years old and lives for up to 4,000 years, second only to the bristle-cone pine. Both of these have unfortunately been heavily logged and now survive mainly in national parks.

The understorey is dense and, from our point of view, a great impediment to hiking; *Chusquea* bamboos (mainly quila; *C. quila* to the north and the more flexible caña colihue; *C. coleou* to the south) form dense thickets, together with arrayán and other shrubs. Many have red flowers, to attract hummingbirds, such as the aptly named 'fire bush' (notro or ciruelillo; *Embothrium coccineum*), and fuchsia (chilco; *Fuchsia magellanica*).

THE SOUTHERN OR FALSE BEECHES

There are ten Chilean species of *Nothofagus*, a genus also found in Australia and New Zealand. Three are evergreen: coihue (or coigüe; *N. dombeyi*), coihue de Magallanes (or guindo; *N. betuloides*) and coihue de Chiloé (*N. nitida*). These normally grow at lower altitudes or in milder climates. The deciduous species flourish at higher elevations, further south and in harsher conditions, although they may appear in almost unrecognizable stunted forms. In good conditions they can be massive trees, up to 40m in height. In April and May their leaves turn gold, giving autumn hiking a special tinge. Of these, the most widespread are lenga (*N. pumilio*), a beautiful, tall tree with a copper tinge to its leaves. and ñirre (*N. antarctica*), spelt ñire in Argentina, a small, often stunted tree with characteristically crinkled and irregular leaves. Others are roble (or roble pellín; *N. obliqua*), hualo (*N. glauca*), raulí (*N. alpina*), ruil (*N. alessandri*) and roble maulino (*N. nervosa*); in addition there is huala (*N. leonii*), now thought to be a hybrid of roble and roble maulino.

Chile's national flower (as seen on matchboxes) is the copihue (*Lapageria rosea*), a creeper with deep-pink, elongated, bell-shaped flowers, which clings to the larger trees and bushes. You can see it on Cerro Ñielol in Temuco. Look also for the lovely red ourisia (*Ourisia alpina*), which grows in the spray of waterfalls. By the water you will also see nalca (*Gunnera chilena*), similar to rhubarb (and equally edible), which produces huge leaves that can serve as umbrellas. Canelo (*Drimys winteri*), known as 'Winter's bark' or 'cinnamon tree', also likes water; it is a large tree (a shrub towards its northern limit), sacred to the Mapuche, which has branchlets with elongated, green leaves, and white flowers at their tips from September and November.

In spring, the meadows are a mass of colour: wild gentian, daisies, vetch, larger lupins, fragrant sweet maidens, the woods violet (*Viola maculata*), and the yellow orchid (*Gavilea lutea*).

To the south of Lago General Carrera/Buenos Aires, the species-poor **Magellanic Forest** is dominated by coihue de Magallanes (or guindo; *Nothofagus betuloides*), an evergreen with tiny leaves, with lenga and ñirre the second and third most common. Except in the inaccessible parts of the Pacific coast, the forest is generally open, with herbs and over 400 species of moss – far too many to describe here. In more open areas, there are many small, flowering trees and bushes, such as the various barberries (calafate; *Berberis* spp.) with their yellow flowers and edible berries (see page 18).

On the eastern side of the Andes, almost entirely in Argentina, there is a semi-desert steppe of coirón grass (*Stipa* spp.), thorny 'saltbush' mogote or mata barrosa (*Mulinum spinosum*) and mata guanaco (*Anartrophyllum desideratum*).

Finally, in the sub-antarctic climes of the **far south**, little grows except for these low bushes and bogs of sphagnum mosses. In fact one could argue that the most successful plant in this area is kelp, the fastest growing plant on earth, which can be up to 100m in length (from a depth of 50m) in sheltered waters. Like rainforest, it is a highly stratified habitat for an amazing quantity of marine crustacea and other creatures that are very little known.

BIRDS

There are over 450 species of birds in southern Chile and Argentina. The following covers some of the more interesting or conspicuous. Keen bird-watchers should get hold of a field guide (see *Appendix 2*).

Three birds that are omnipresent in the areas in which you are likely to spend most time are the buff-necked ibis (bandúrria; *Theristicus caudatus*), southern lapwing (tero or queltehue; *Vanellus chilensis*) and the chimango caracara (tiuque; *Milvago chimango*). These three species have benefited greatly from man's clearing of fields, but paradoxically the first two take great exception to human intruders – the honk of the ibis and the squawk of the lapwing will be the soundtrack accompanying much of your walking. The tiuque and other types of caracara are frequent visitors to campsites and car-parks. Surprisingly, the ibis is listed as vulnerable and the lapwing and caracara are also protected in Chile. Other birds are quite unperturbed by humans, and it is easy to get within five metres of Magellanic woodpeckers and pygmy owls.

Waterfowl are also very noticeable. You will come across beautiful geese (in fact *Ashy-headed goose* sheldgeese, closer to ducks than to true geese, and almost inedible), including the kelp goose (canquén blanca; *Chloephaga hybrida*), the upland goose (canquén de Magallanes; *C. picta*), the ashy-headed goose (canquén real; *C. poliocephala*) and the ruddy-headed goose (canquén colorado; *C. rubidiceps*), and a variety of ducks (patos), some sporting plastic-looking blue bills. The Andean or ruddy duck (*Oxyura jamaicensis*) is the most common. You will probably see torrent ducks (pato cortacorrientes; *Merganetta armata*) by fast-flowing rivers up to 3,600m. These attractive, small ducks, with vertical black-and-white stripes on the neck of the male, feed on stonefly larvae which can only exist in highly oxygenated water, hence the birds' reckless dives into the rushing torrents. Equally distinctive are the two species of steamer duck, one flightless and in saltwater only (also known as the 'flapping loggerhead duck'; pato vapor or quetru no volador; *Tachyeres pteneres*), and the other flying and in both fresh and saltwater (pato vapor volador; *T. patachonicus*). When alarmed (increasingly rare, as far as I can see), they depart on the surface in a cloud of spray, from whence their name, but the myth (dating back to Darwin) that they beat their wings alternately has been disproved by filming. Black-necked swans (cisne de cuello negro; *Cygnus melancoryphus*) are also frequently seen, from sea level to over 4,000m, although the white coscoroba swan (cisne coscoroba; *Coscoroba coscoroba*) is rare. Along rivers, you are likely to see the ringed kingfisher (martín pescador; *Ceryle torquata*).

Ruddy-headed goose

In the southern forests, look for the Magellanic woodpecker (carpintero negro or gigante; *Campephilus magellanicus*), the Araucanian woodpecker (carpinterito; *Picoides lignarius*), the Chilean flicker (piteo; *Colaptes pitius* – also a woodpecker),

Spine-tailed rayadito

and the tiny Austral pygmy owl (chuncho; *Glaucidium nanum*). In the dense Valdivian forest there are quite a few birds that you are more likely to hear than see. The thorn- or spine-tailed rayadito (*Aphrastura spinicauda*), a tiny orange and brown bird with a strange, spiky tail, which often hangs upside-down like a treecreeper, has particularly strong views about its territorial rights. The chucao (*Scelorchilus rubecula*) is a ventriloquist with a musical chuckle from which it takes its name; if it calls from the right side of the path it is said to portend good luck, while a call from the left portends bad luck. The huet-huet (*Pteroptochus albicollis*), almost black with a red cap and breast, also takes its name from its call; due to its erect tail, it is known as 'tapaculo', translated by Darwin as 'cover your posterior'. It is related to the black-throated huet-huet (*P. tarnii*), which Darwin called the 'barking-bird', and to the turco (*P. megapodius*), found further to the north, which resembles a fieldfare.

Rhea

Small birds which you are bound to notice are the rufous-collared sparrow (chincol; *Zonotrichia capensis*), and in the south the Patagonian yellow-finch (chirihue austral; *Sicalis lebruni*).

The most distinctive large bird is the flightless rhea (ñandú), South America's version of the ostrich. The Darwin's or lesser rhea (ñandú petiso, or in Argentina the choique; *Pterocnemia pennata pennata*), which inhabits the Patagonian steppes, is smaller than those found further north (the puna rhea or suri cordillerano; *P. pennata tarapacensis*, and on the *pampas*, the greater rhea; *Rhea americana albescens*). Female rheas are thoroughly liberated, playing no part in the raising of their family. The male has the responsibility of mating with a variety of females, collecting the 20 or so eggs that they lay haphazardly around his chosen nest site, incubating them entirely unaided, and then caring for the lively chicks or charitos. The adults can run very fast, and swim to escape predators such as pumas. Also on the steppes, the martineta tinamou (martineta; *Eudromia elegans*) scurries about wearing a ridiculous pointed hat, and is much prized as a game bird. The loica (*Sturnella loyca*), grey-hooded sierra-finch (cometocino; *Phrygilus gayi*) and cinnamon-bellied ground-tyrant (dormilona rufa; *Muscisaxicola capistrata*) are also common here.

Martineta tinamou

Even in Tierra del Fuego you will see two members of bird families normally associated with tropical climates: hummingbirds (picaflores) and parrots (loros). The green-backed fire-crown (*Sephanoides galeritus*) is a brilliant green hummingbird with an iridescent red crown, and the Austral parakeet (cotorra austral or cachaña; *Enicognathus ferrugineus*), the only parrot found at this southerly latitude, is dark green with a reddish belly and tail. In araucaria forests the slender-billed parakeet (choroye; *E. leptorhynchus*) uses its specially adapted beak to probe for nuts in monkey-puzzle trees; also in Araucanía there is the burrowing parrot (loro tricahue; *Cyanoliseus patagonus*). Although the green-backed fire-crown is the most southerly, there are six other species of hummingbird in Chile and Argentina, including the dove-sized Chilean giant hummingbird (*Patagona gigas*).

Birds of prey are very common, the largest being the Chilean grey eagle or black-chested buzzard-eagle (águila mora; *Geranoetus melanoleucus*) which feeds on rodents and small birds. Ospreys are summer visitors, and the small red-tailed buzzard (aguilucho de cola roja; *Buteo ventralis*) is often seen. Carrion eaters include caracaras and turkey vultures (jote; *Cathartes aura*) which hang around sheep stations. But the most impressive carrion eater is the Andean condor (cóndor; *Vultur gryphus*). This huge bird is quite common in the southern Andes and all the way to Cape Horn, and may come to look at hikers. It can be recognized in flight by its white, fluffy neck ruff and the 'fingering' of the primary wing feathers. The Andean condor has the largest wing area of any bird (almost 2m²), but the 3m span is not as great as that of the wandering albatross (albatros errante; *Diomedes esculana*) which has the largest wing span of all. These marvellous birds are occasionally seen near the shore during their wanderings in the southern seas. Two other species of albatross can also be seen in Chile. The sooty albatross (*Phoebetria fusca*) spends much of its time at sea, while the black-browed albatross (albatros de ceja negra; *Diomedea melanophris*) is commonly seen in the channels around Tierra del Fuego.

Condor

You may also see the great skua (salteador skua; *Cathara cathara chilensis*) which resembles a large, brown gull. These are opportunists and scavengers, ever ready to grab an egg or young bird. Skuas are fiercely territorial; woe betide the unprotected head of the backpacker who inadvertently wanders near a skua nest!

The penguin found around the southern coast is the Magellanic or 'Jackass' penguin (*Spheniscus magellanicus* – not the true Jackass, found only in South Africa, but with the same donkey-like bray) – the least dignified of all the penguin species. They nest in burrows near the shore, and when alarmed they run on all fours, using their flippers as an extra pair of legs and achieving remarkable speeds with no apparent concern for physical safety. Once in the shelter of their burrows, they glare at you first from one eye, then the other, wagging their heads from side to side. The Humboldt penguin (*S. humboldtii*) overlaps with the range of the Magellanic penguin in the region of Chiloé, and in addition, seven species of penguin are found in the part of Antarctica claimed by Chile, of which the rockhopper penguin (pingüino de penacho amarillo; *Eudyptes crestatus*) is also common on the Isla de los Estados (Staten Island) and occasionally reaches the shores of Tierra del Fuego and Cape Horn.

ARGENTINE FOSSILS AND DINOSAURS

The first fossil to be recognised as an extinct species was a *Megatherium*, found in 1785 in Argentina by Spanish soldiers, and now in the Madrid Museum of Natural History. Darwin found many fossils of all kinds in the 1830s, and Florentino Ameghino (with his brother Carlo) collected 6,000 species and developed ever-more eccentric theories about the origins of life until his death in 1911. Of the wealth of fossils in Argentina, it is the dinosaurs that are currently attracting most attention. New species are being discovered all the time (one a year on average in one location alone), and small towns in deserts that produce nothing else are hoping, probably in vain, for salvation through dinosaur tourism.

The South American dinosaurs could be the most 'authentic' (ie: primitive) of all. They include what are currently the oldest reptile yet found (*Lagosuchus*); probably the oldest raptor (*Herrerasaurus*; 225 million years old); and the largest raptor yet (*Gigantosaurus carolinii* – up to 9 tonnes and 14m long, dethroning *T. rex*); and what may be the largest land animal to have lived, a still unnamed herbivore 100 tonnes in weight and 40m in length, which lived in Río Negro province 87 million years ago. The smallest known dinosaur, just 50cm long, was also found in Patagonia.

There is also a great deal of popular interest in Cenozoic mammals that may have co-existed with man. These include *Hoplophorus* (a toothed herbivore, like an armadillo, 1.8m long and 0.7m high), *Macrauchenia patachonica* (like a guanaco, though not related), the above-mentioned *Megatherium americanum* (a 5m-long herbivore that survived until 8,500 years ago), and of course the *Mylodon* (see page 271).

Triassic fossils are found mainly in the northwestern provinces of Salta, La Rioja and San Juan, and more recent Jurassic and Cretaceous ones to the south in Neuquén, Chubut and Santa Cruz. Fossils are also being found in the area of Argentina claimed by Antarctica, including a duck-billed platypus (70 million years old), a *Plesiosaurus* with a shark's tooth embedded in it, and araucaria trees. The town which is perhaps pinning most hope on its dinosaurs is Plaza Huincul (between Zapala and Neuquén), which has built a new museum (tel: 0299 465 486).

MAMMALS
Land mammals

Seventy million years ago the only mammals in South America were ungulates, marsupials (including sabre-toothed 'cats') and palaeanodonta, such as the taxodont, a hippo-sized guineapig. Sloths, anteaters and armadillos evolved (including now-extinct variants such as 6m-long ground sloths and the heavily-armoured 2m-long glyptodont). About 40 million years ago rodents and monkeys suddenly arrived by the island chain from North America, and 2–3 million years ago the Panama landbridge was completed, allowing a free interchange of species between North and South America. Animals moving north from South America included the sloth, opossum, capybara, toxodontes, porcupine and anteater, while the raccoon, deer, mastodon, weasel, tapir, skunk, peccary, dog and bear moved south from North America.

The camelids were among those moving from North America and are now extinct there. Of the four surviving in South America, the guanaco (*Lama guanacoe*) is the largest and most successful, feeding both by grazing and browsing, and ranging from the high-altitude deserts of the north to Tierra del Fuego. It is a slender, elegant animal, golden brown in colour fading to white on the belly and inner legs. Guanacos live in family groups with one male guarding from four to 12 females. The young, called chulengos, are adorable animals and often kept as pets, but they tend to become vicious as they grow up. Like all the camelids, guanacos are very inquisitive and give passing backpackers their full attention. Its domesticated cousin is the llama (*L. glama*) of which 40,000 live on the Chilean puna, and many more to the north. It works as a pack animal, carrying 40–50kg with a body weight of just 55kg, and also provides meat and competes in races. The vicuña (*L. vicugna*) is superbly adapted for its life on the arid *puna*. It is the only ungulate with continuously growing lower incisors (like rodents), allowing it to eat the hard festuca (bunchgrasses), and it has 14 million red corpuscles per mm^3 of blood (man has 5–6 million), helping it to cope with the low oxygen levels between 3,700m and 4,800m. The wool of the bib below its neck is the finest on earth, just 10 microns in diameter, compared to 30 microns for the best merino, but it produces only 500g of wool a year, against the 30kg of its domesticated cousin the alpaca. Unfortunately it is easier just to shoot the vicuña and sell the skins, so between 1954 and 1969 its population fell by 96%. This shooting activity was illegal, but was only stopped by import controls in developed countries. From perhaps two million at the time of the Conquest, the Chilean population of vicuña fell to around 1,000 in 1969, but has now recovered to over 12,000, most in the Lauca National Park. The alpaca (*L. paca*) produces a relatively rough wool and also meat; it will not work as a pack animal and breeds relatively slowly, so it has often been replaced by sheep or cattle, leading to erosion. It is similar to the llama but with a shorter nose, legs and ears.

Three species of deer can be found in Chile and Argentina, plus the swamp, pampas and red brocket deer in northeastern Argentina. The pudú (*Pudu pudu*) is a dwarf deer that lurks in the thickest parts of the Valdivian forest, and the huemul (*Hippocamelus bisculus*) is a desperately endangered deer, of which perhaps only 2,000 survive on the higher and more remote slopes between Chillán and Paine. To the north, the Peruvian or northern huemul (taruca; *H. antisensis*), discovered only in 1944, is now classified as a separate species.

Three species of fox can be found in Chile and southern Argentina. The small grey or Patagonian fox (zorro chilla; *Dusicyon griseus*) is common from the Río Negro and La Serena south to the Magellan Straits, and has been introduced into Tierra del Fuego, threatening the habitat of the Fuegian fox, one of the five sub-species of the rarer and much larger red or Andean fox (zorro culpeo or colorado; *D. culpaeus*), which has reddish tints to its grey coat. There is also the Chilote fox (*D. fulvipes* or Darwin's fox) found in Chiloé, and for some reason in Nahuelbuta, and in northern Argentina there are the crab-eating and pampas foxes and the maned wolf (aguará-guazú; *Chrysocyon brachyurus*). Smaller predators include the lesser grison (hurón; *Galictis cuja*) and Patagonian skunk (chingue or zorrino; *Conepatus humboldti*). In addition to the puma (*Felis concolor*), wild cats include Geoffroy's cat (gato montes; *Leopardus geoffroyi*), and the Chilean forest cat (huiña or kod-kod; *L. guigna*). There are two otters, the Chilean marine otter (chungungo; *Lutra felina*) and the Patagonian river otter (huillín; *L. provocax*). The steppes are home to several types of armadillo.

Rodents are plentiful, the most interesting being the Patagonian hare (mara;

Dolichotis australis). These strange inhabitants of the Patagonian plains look as though they were designed by a committee. They have box-like faces, longish ears, spindly legs and a horizontal, white stripe across their bottom. Despite the name they are not true hares, but members of the agouti family. Even so, they can move at 80km/hr; as John Cleese said in the film *Fierce Creatures*, 'we all hate it, because it only has two modes of operation – one is coma and the other is panic. Rather like one of my recent wives, actually… '. In the wetlands of northeastern Argentina lives the world's largest rodent, the water hog (carpincho or capybara; *Hydrochaeris h.*), which can weigh up to 65kg. The mountain vizcacha or chinchillón (*Lagidium viscacia*), like a rabbit with a long tail, is related to the chinchilla (see page 135), and can be seen from Patagonia to Peru. Its cousin, the pampas vizcacha (*Lagostomus maximus*) builds cairns over its burrows, incorporating anything you may have lost anywhere in the neighbourhood. There are half a dozen species of tuco-tuco (*Ctenomys* spp.), a burrowing rodent like a large rat.

There are three marsupial species in Chile: the Chilean mouse opossum (yaca; *Marmosa elegans*) in the north, with big eyes and enormous ears; the Chilean shrew opossum (comadrejita trompuda; *Rhyncolestes raphanurus*), the rarest mammal in Chile, discovered in the 1920s in the Valdivian forests; and the Chilean opossum (monito del monte; *Dromiciops australis*), also to be seen in the Valdivian forests, including the Argentinian lake district. There are others in Argentina such as the Argentine opossum (*Didelphis crassicaudata*) and Virginia opossum (*D. virginiana*), whose range now extends from Canada to northern Argentina.

Reptiles, amphibians etc

There are no venomous snakes in Chile, but the brown recluse spider has a bite which is rarely fatal but can turn gangrenous; and the vampire bat (*Desmodus rotundus*), which can carry rabies, is found to the north of Chiloé. In Argentina there are coral snakes, rattlesnakes and pit vipers, mainly in the north, but extending their range southwards. The tiny Darwin's frog (ranita de Darwin; *Rhinoderma darwinii*), found by the great man in the Valdivian forest, is an oddity: the males guard the eggs, and when they begin to move appear to eat them. In fact they are safely held in the male's vocal sac, which extends right down the underside of his body, and are later born through his mouth. This frog can also float like a dead *Nothofagus* leaf to escape predators. There are plenty of lizards, and the biggest, fluffiest bees you will ever see.

The seal family

Seals evolved some 30 million years ago, and can be divided into two groups: *Otariidae* (eared seals), descended from a bear-like animal; and *Phocidae* (true seals), whose ancestors were otter-like carnivores. Seals are far more at home in the sea than on land, and all species share special adaptive features: hind limbs which have evolved into tail-like appendages, forelimbs like flippers and about 5cm of blubber beneath their skin to insulate them from the cold of the seas.

In Chile and Argentina you may see southern sea lions, fur seals and elephant seals, which share the same seasonal timetable. In spring the bulls arrive on shore to establish their territories, then the cows join them, and those that are pregnant give birth within days. As soon as the pups are independent, the parents return to the sea to feed, and come back to shore in the autumn again to moult. This accomplished, they leave until the following spring.

Sea lions

Southern sea lions (lobo común or lobo marino de un pelo; *Otaria byronia*) are seals with small, clearly visible external ears. They are much more mobile on land than true seals, being able to rotate their rear flippers sideways to propel their bodies forward. Sea lions can move quite fast in this manner, something to remember if you meet an angry bull. A fully grown male southern sea lion is much larger and more impressive than his northern cousin, the Californian sea lion. This massive animal measures well over 2m long, and weighs up to half a tonne. His enormous neck is adorned with a shaggy mane, hence the name 'sea lion', which also refers to his roar.

Southern sea lions

The elegant limpid-eyed females that make up his harem weigh only a quarter of his great bulk, but then they expend less energy. From the time he comes ashore in December to when he leaves in March, the bull sea lion neither eats nor sleeps for more than a few minutes at a time. Guarding his harem is a full-time job.

The black, furry pups are born in early January. They are not fully weaned for six months, but the females return to the sea for feeding before this time, leaving a nursery or 'pod' of pups to gain safety in numbers. In fact they have few land predators, and the high juvenile mortality rate is largely through the clumsy actions of fighting males.

Fur seals

Only their golden brown fur and upturned noses distinguish southern fur seals (lobo fino austral or lobo marino de dos pelos; *Arctocephalus australis*) from sea lions. This luxurious coat almost led to their extinction through hunting, but now they are fully protected and their numbers are increasing. The fur seal has two layers of fur: a soft, dense undercoat, and an outer layer of coarse hair which traps bubbles of air to increase insulation. In fact, fur seals often seem to get too hot, and you will see them wave their flippers around in an attempt to cool off. There are marvellous 'rookeries' of these animals on Península Valdés. Try to visit in January when there is plenty of action; you will hardly be able to tear yourself away. The Juan Fernández fur seal (*A. philippi*) was believed to be extinct (it is estimated that three million were killed between 1797 and 1804), until it was rediscovered in 1965.

Elephant seals

These massive animals regularly measure as much as 6m long and weigh around three tonnes (the record is nearly 7m long and four tonnes). The bull southern elephant seal (elefante marino del sur; *Mirounga leonina*) has an elongated nose which can be inflated and extended, although the bulls only give this spectacular display when in rut. Normally they content themselves with letting it overhang their mouths as they roar a warning to another bull or a tiresome human.

Although you could never call a female elephant seal elegant, they have endearingly placid expressions, with huge, dark eyes designed for deep-sea fishing.

They are half the size of the bulls, with no 'trunk'.

These true (or earless) seals have great difficulty heaving themselves overland since their hind limbs are useless for propulsion. Consequently both bulls and cows are loath to stir themselves and can be easily approached (where permitted), although they may give vent to their annoyance by emitting a roar. An angry bull adds to the effect by rearing upright so that only his tail end remains on the ground. They have remarkably supple spines and can even touch their head with their tails. When forced to move they undulate along the beach like giant maggots.

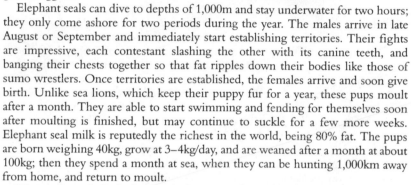

Elephant seal

Elephant seals can dive to depths of 1,000m and stay underwater for two hours; they only come ashore for two periods during the year. The males arrive in late August or September and immediately start establishing territories. Their fights are impressive, each contestant slashing the other with its canine teeth, and banging their chests together so that fat ripples down their bodies like those of sumo wrestlers. Once territories are established, the females arrive and soon give birth. Unlike sea lions, which keep their puppy fur for a year, these pups moult after a month. They are able to start swimming and fending for themselves soon after moulting is finished, but may continue to suckle for a few more weeks. Elephant seal milk is reputedly the richest in the world, being 80% fat. The pups are born weighing 40kg, grow at 3–4kg/day, and are weaned after a month at about 100kg; then they spend a month at sea, when they can be hunting 1,000km away from home, and return to moult.

Like sea lions, bull elephant seals do not eat during this period on shore. Once the parents are relieved of the cares of mating and child rearing, they return to the sea to feed, coming back in the autumn to moult. They lie morosely on the beach, looking like sun-burned tourists with their skin hanging off in strips, and do little else but wallow in the mud and scratch. During this season you can observe the transformation of their forelimbs from ugly flippers to nimble 'hands', able to deal with a nasty itch as daintily as a dowager.

Until the arrival of man, elephant seals had but one enemy: the orca (killer whale). Their future was then threatened when sealers found that one elephant seal would yield 360 litres of oil. However, since 1893 they have been protected, and their numbers are now recovering.

Cetaceans

The only whale easily seen off the coasts of Chile and Argentina is the southern right whale (see page 296). Dolphins and porpoises are far more common, of which the most attractive is the Commerson's dolphin (tonina overa; *Cephalorhynchus commersoni*), which can be seen off Valdés, but is usually found around Tierra del Fuego. The black or Chilean dolphin (delfín chileno; *C. eutropia*), ranging from Concepción to Cape Horn, is little known but seems to be endangered. Also very rare and very attractive is the hourglass dolphin (*Lagenorhynchus cruciger*), seen only to the south of Cape Horn. Peale's dolphin (delfín austral; *L. australis*) is also found around Tierra del Fuego, where it is still illegally used for bait by centolla (king crab) fishermen. The River Plate dolphin (delfín franciscana; *Stenodelphis blainvillei*) has up to 250 teeth, more than any other living animal.

Of the porpoises, Burmeister's porpoise (marsopa espinosa; *Phocoena spinipinnis*) is the most widespread, from Buenos Aires to Peru, while the spectacled porpoise (marsopa de anteojos; *P. dioptrica*) is very rare in general, but seems to be common in the Beagle Channel.

EATING WILD

Devotees of wild food will be in seventh heaven here. The temperate zones of South America have such an abundance of edible berries, greenery, fungi, eggs and seafood that even people who have never sampled the fruits of the trail before will probably succumb to temptation.

As in any country, you should not eat wild food until you have positively identified it. Here are a few of the tastier possibilities.

Berries

Calafate

The barberry (*Berberis* spp.) grows in great profusion in Patagonia and Tierra del Fuego, above all the box-leafed barberry (calafate; *B. buxifolia*) and holly-leafed barberry (michay; *B. ilicifolia*), which produce fruit similar to the blackcurrant or blueberry. In Patagonia there is an old saying '*Quien come el calafate vuelve por más*' – 'Whoever eats the calafate berry will come back for more' – which just shows how addictive this berry – not to mention the landscape – can be. The calafate grows on spiny bushes and ripens between January and March. Its dark purple juice stains the lips and tongue a beautiful colour, and it also happens to be a good laxative. As the berries are full of pips, it is best to gather a quantity and stew them in a little water and sugar. Then strain off the juice (we used some spare mosquito netting) and you will have a thick syrup which will keep for a few days and can be diluted as you need it. It is especially good poured over porridge, or as dessert with yoghurt or custard.

The wild strawberry or rainberry (frambuesa silvestre or frutilla (de Magallanes); *Rubus geoides*) grows from Ñuble to the south, most abundantly in Tierra del Fuego. With its tiny lumps, it looks like a small raspberry and tends to grow in tree mould or moss; delicious with sugar and cream. The lahueñe (frutilla silvestre; *Fragaria chiloensis*), which grows with aruacaria, also produces reddish edible fruit; but do not confuse them with the false strawberry (frutilla del diablo; *Gunnera magellanica*).

The blackberry (mora; *Rubus* spp.) was introduced to Chile by the early settlers as hedging, and soon spread throughout the Lakes District. There are masses of blackberries there in March and April.

The Magellanic blackcurrant (parrilla de magallanes; *Ribes magellanicum*) grows extensively in Tierra del Fuego and Patagonia. It is unwise to eat a huge quantity as it is an effective laxative.

The diddle-dee berry (sepisa; *Empetrum rubrum*), found in many parts of Tierra del Fuego, is rather bland compared with the rainberry. There are two types: the bright red berries are bitter, but the black ones are sweeter.

The murtilla (*Gaultheria caespitosa*, *G. pumila*, *Ugni molinae*) has small red berries, with a sweet, slightly perfumed flavour, which make delicious jam. If you visit the Lakes District around Easter, you will almost certainly see people selling them from buckets at the roadside. You will find them growing wild, among other places, on the lower slopes of Volcán Osorno.

Greenery

If you are accustomed to eating sorrel, wild garlic, wild celery, cress or mint at home, you will enjoy being able to do the same here. You can also eat the inner stem of the tussock grass or the tangy leaves of the scurvy grass. Wild celery and cress grow in damp areas, sorrel in sunny meadows and mint everywhere. Try some mint tea. Also in damp areas of the Valdivian forest is the huge rhubarb-like nalca (see above), which can be eaten as you would rhubarb – strip back the peel with a knife and then stew the stalks.

Fungi

The climate of southern Chile and Argentina seems ideal for fungi. Never have we seen so many varieties – but it is frustrating if you do not know what they all are. The ones we recognised were field mushrooms, giant puffballs, shaggy ink caps and coral mushrooms. If you are a mushroom enthusiast we strongly recommend that you bring your field guide. Most of the fungi in this part of the world are the same as those you find in Europe or North America.

We can particularly recommend the giant puffballs that are common in Torres del Paine National Park. We ate them in a variety of ways: fried in sardine oil, mixed with soup, and thinly sliced and dried in the sun, after which they were as crunchy and tasty as potato crisps. Similar yellow-orange fungi (llao-llao or pan del indio; *Cyttaria darwini*) are found in Tierra del Fuego. They were a mainstay of the indigenous people, but are generally considered to be pretty tasteless.

Seafood

The seafood available includes river and lake trout, if you are lucky or skilful enough to catch one. There is one native species, but the rest were introduced in the mid-19th century and have flourished (the story is that a harsh skipper was marooned by his crew, who allowed him three barrels of provisions; he took one,  plus two of fertilised trout eggs). Chile and Argentina offer some of the best trout fishing in the world, and few backpackers can pass through areas such as the Lakes District without being infected by the fishing bug. We tried the local method, using bait or lures and a tin can for casting. We had many bites, but we had not anticipated the size and strength of these monsters, and most got away.

The type of seafood which stays still for the picking is tempting but dangerous. The red tide (*marea roja*) is an algal bloom that makes seafood terminally poisonous, and in much of southern Patagonia it is usually forbidden to gather shellfish (although crabs and so on are safe). If you are absolutely sure that it is safe, you will find extensive mussel beds in Tierra del Fuego National Park and many other places. Just steam the mussels in a little wine for about ten minutes or until they open. Accompany them with wild garlic for an unforgettable experience. The

deep-water mussel (cholga; *Aulacomya ater*) is highly prized, although you are unlikely to find it for yourself. Clams are even harder to find, but well worth the effort. Empty clam shells on a sandy beach should be evidence enough to encourage you to look for their holes. They live 10–15cm below the surface and can be dug out with a stick or tent pole. They can then be steamed like mussels.

If, amazingly, you have acquired a taste for sea urchins (erizo; *Loxechinus albus*), you can eat their orange roe raw or steamed, using a mussel shell as a container and setting it on a bed of seaweed. All crabs are edible. The most highly prized is the southern king crab (centolla; *Lithoides antarticus*, see page 49), although this has been over-fished and is now protected for most of the year.

Getting There and
What to Take

AIRLINES AND FLIGHTS

Travel to South America is currently as cheap as it ever has been, and with the economic growth of Chile and Argentina and booming tourism, the quantity and range of flights is ever greater. Chile and Argentina both have national flag-carrier airlines which fly to Madrid and to North America, and many of the world's other leading carriers fly to Santiago and Buenos Aires, carrying passengers for their alliance partners.

The leading airline grouping is the STAR Alliance, of United, bmi British Midland, Lufthansa, the Austrian Airlines Group, Air Canada, Varig, Mexicana, SAS, Thai Airways International, Air New Zealand, Ansett Australia, Singapore Airlines and All Nippon Airways. This means that, for example, in addition to Lufthansa's 747 from Frankfurt to Santiago via Buenos Aires (six nights a week), it is also possible to take its daily flight from Frankfurt to Miami and fly on with United or Varig. In fact, given the mysteries of code-sharing, you could be on a United plane throughout. Varig flies four times a week from London Heathrow to São Paolo, connecting to Buenos Aires (ten times a day), Córdoba and Santiago. It might be a better deal to buy a return flight to Brazil and then use a Mercosur Airpass, which includes Santiago, Iquique, Puerto Montt, Iguazú, Buenos Aires, Mendoza, Bariloche, Trelew and Ushuaia.

The second grouping is the 'oneworld' alliance of American Airlines, British Airways, Iberia, Qantas, Cathay Pacific, Aer Lingus, Finnair and LanChile. When LanChile joined in June 2000 BA ceased to fly to Santiago, instead using LanChile's Buenos Aires–Santiago flights for codeshared connections out of BA's five non-stop flights a week from London Gatwick. Equally you could change at Miami to American Airlines. Similarly, Iberia and LanChile codeshare their daily flights (one each) between Santiago and Madrid, with Iberia providing connections to London, Paris, Amsterdam and elsewhere. Both airlines use new A340 Airbuses, for one of the world's longest non-stop flights (10,000km, in 13½ hours); LanChile also uses A340s from Santiago to New York and Los Angeles.

From the USA, American Airlines flies to Buenos Aires once a day from New York, and twice from Miami, with connections from other points.

Although the Spanish government owns a majority share in Aerolíneas Argentinas, it is up for sale and has not joined any alliance. However, it still has a codeshare with Iberia, with Aerolíneas flying twice daily between Madrid and Buenos Aires (in slightly antiquated 747-200s) and Iberia providing connections to London and elsewhere, as well as flying its own A340s to Buenos Aires four times a week. Aerolíneas also flies every night to Miami and New York, and three times a week to Los Angeles.

Rapidly developing as the third global alliance is SkyTeam, formed by Delta, Air

France, Aeromexico, Korean Air and CSA Czech Air. Air France flies from Europe to Santiago via Buenos Aires (although cheap fares are rare), and Aeromexico serves Santiago from North America. In addition Delta began flying daily from Atlanta to Santiago in 2000 and to Buenos Aires in April 2001. Similarly Continental has a daily 767-400 from Newark to Santiago via Lima, and will serve Buenos Aires from December 2001, as well as codesharing with COPA via Panama. In addition Continental connects with the Argentinian private airline LAPA, which flies three times a week non-stop from Atlanta to Buenos Aires, and with the Chilean domestic carrier Avant.

For the Europe-based Qualiflyer group, Swissair flies from Zurich to Buenos Aires and Santiago (three times each per week). KLM flies to Buenos Aires four times a week but has pulled out of Santiago (no loss given their current reputation for losing baggage). South African Airways flies twice a week from Johannesburg to Buenos Aires, as does MAS en route from Kuala Lumpur.

The only Latin America airline to fly direct from London to South America is Avianca, which offers connections in Bogotá to most countries in the continent; it is also often the cheapest option.

Chile's national airline, **LanChile** (www.lanchile.com), is replacing its long-range Boeing 767s, only three years old, with Airbus A340s (and its 737s with A320s for internal flights, with Ladeco); cabin service does not quite match the high technical standard, although it is not at all bad and certainly better than on Aerolíneas Argentinas. LanChile flies daily from Frankfurt to Santiago via Madrid; connecting flights can be included in the price, and there are also cheap flights with easyJet from Britain to Madrid.

From North America, LanChile flies daily from New York, Miami and Los Angeles (for Asian connections) to Santiago and (cheekily) on to Buenos Aires. It also codeshares with American Airlines, which flies daily from Dallas and Los Angeles to Santiago; and twice daily from Miami for connections from all its other US destinations. It is also possible to fly across the South Pacific, although this is an expensive route, even as part of a round-the-world ticket; you fly with Qantas or Air New Zealand to Tahiti, and continue with LanChile to Santiago, with the option of a stopover on Easter Island (Rapa Nui).

Regionally, LanChile flies nine times daily to Buenos Aires, twice to Mendoza, and daily to Montevideo; in addition its partner, TAM (Transportes Aéreos del Mercosur), flies to Asunción from Santiago and Iquique, and its subsidiary LanPerú flies to Lima. On Saturdays, LanChile flies to the Falklands/Malvinas, the only useful connection from South America. LanChile offers an internal airpass (with subsidiary Ladeco) at US$150 for three flights in a month, and just US$50 each for up to three more flights. Easter Island and the Falklands/Malvinas are excluded. Prices rise to US$350/US$80 if you do not travel to Chile with LanChile.

Aerolíneas Argentinas (www.aerolineas.com.ar) uses relatively aged Boeing 747-200s for its double-daily flights to Madrid, but it also has new A340 Airbuses which fly non-stop to Rome, Los Angeles and Auckland (and on to Sydney); it will soon have the A340-600, which will be the world's longest passenger jet. Service is not as slick as with LanChile, but smoking has finally been banned. It offers the only single-airline route from London to Australia via South America (from £581 one way). The Argentina Airpass (with Austral and Kaiken) costs US$299 (arriving with Aerolíneas or Iberia) or US$339 (with other airlines) for three flights in 60 days, and US$105 for extra flights. It must be pre-routed, but dates may be left open.

LAPA (Lineas Aereas Privadas Argentinas) also has an airpass, at US$339 for three flights in 60 days, and US$100 for extra flights. Aerolíneas, Austral and LAPA co-operate in the Mercosur Pass, along with Varig, Vasp, Transbrasil, Lapa, Pluna, and Lineas Aereas Paraguayas. LAPA also has a link with LanChile, allowing Patagonian circuits via Punta Arenas, Ushuaia, Río Gallegos, Bariloche and Trelew.

If you are visiting both Chile and Argentina, the Buenos Aires–Santiago route is one of the few in South America with genuine competition and reasonable prices, with around 16 flights a day (one daily with Aerocontinente, Lufthansa and Air France, as well as those of LanChile and Aerolíneas). There are also short hops from Santiago to Mendoza, and from Punta Arenas and Puerto Montt to towns in Argentinian Patagonia, as well as buses. However, there is talk of LanChile and Aerolíneas sharing planes and codes, which may reduce this competition.

The specialists in cheap fares to this area are **Journey Latin America** (JLA), whose best low-season return fares are currently £415 to Santiago or Buenos Aires. The direct route with British Airways from London to Santiago costs £685, while their non-stop flight from London to Buenos Aires costs £666. 'Open-jaw' routes can easily be arranged by specialists; in fact JLA can book you to fly in to Buenos Aires and out of Santiago for £415 as well. High-season fares generally apply in December/January and July/August. South America is now within reach for short breaks: JLA offers five nights for £740 in Santiago, and £836 in Buenos Aires. A North American equivalent to JLA is **eXito** (see listings below).

Airlines

Aerolíneas Argentinas 54 Conduit St, London W1R 9FD; tel: 020 7494 1001; fax: 7494 1002; aerolineas_arg@compuserve.com; and 630 Fifth Avenue, Suite 1658, New York, NY 10111; tel: 212 698 2080; 1800 333 0276; www.aerolineas.com.ar

LanChile Oak House, County Oak Way, Crawley, West Sussex RH11 7ST; tel: 01293 596 606; reservations: 596 607; fax: 596 658; and Leganitos 47, 1 planta, Plaza España, Madrid, Spain; tel: 01 559 7295; fax: 542 3157; and 9700 South Dixie Highway, Miami, FL 33156, USA; tel: 305 670 1961, 1800 488 0070; fax: 305 670 9553; www.lanchile.com

American Airlines 45 Piccadilly, London W1 9AJ; tel: 020 8572 5555, 0845 778 9789; and PO Box 619616 MD 5398, Dallas/Fort Worth Airport, TX 75261-9616, USA; tel: 1800 433 7300, 817 967 1234; fax: 817 967 4318; www.aa.com

British Airways Waterside, PO Box 365, UB7 0GB; tel: 0845 779 9977; www.britishairways.com

Iberia 27 Glasshouse St, London W1R 6JU; tel: 0845 601 2854, also 020 7413 1201; fax: 7413 1263; marketing@iberiaairlines.co.uk; and 6100 Blue Lagoon Drive, Miami, FL 33126, USA; tel: 1800 574 8742; www.iberia.com/ingles/

United Airlines 7 Conduit St, London W1R 9TG; tel: 0845 844 4777; fax: 020 8276 6680; www.unitedairlines.co.uk; and PO Box 66100, Chicago, IL 60666, USA; tel: 1800 241 6522; www.united.com or www.ual.com

HOLIDAY COMPANIES
Agents
UK

Journey Latin America 12 Heathfield Terrace, Chiswick, London W4 4JE; tel: 020 8747 3108; fax: 8742 1312; sales@journeylatinamerica.co.uk, and 28 Barton Arcade, Deansgate, Manchester M3 2BH; tel: 0161 832 1441; fax: 832 1551; man@journeylatinamerica.co.uk

Flightbookers 34 Woburn Place, London WC1H 0TA; tel: 020 7757 2320; www.ebookers.com

North-South Travel Moulsham Mill, Parkway, Chelmsford CM2 7PX;
tel/fax: 01245 608 291; brenda@northsouthtravel.co.uk
Scott Dunn Latin America Fovant Mews, 12 Noyna Rd, London, SW17 7PH;
tel: 020 8767 8989; fax: 8767 2026; latin@scottdunn.com
South American Experience 47 Causton St, London SW1P 4AT; tel: 020 7976 5511;
fax: 7976 6908; info@southamericanexperience.co.uk
Steamond 23 Eccleston St, London SW1W 9LX; tel: 020 7730 8646.
For tours, 278 Battersea Park Rd, London SW11 3BS; tel: 020 7738 0285;
fax: 7730 3024; www.easyticket.com
STA has offices across the UK (London; tel: 020 7361 6145); 0870 160 6060;
www.statravel.co.uk
Trailfinders 194 Kensington High St, London W8 7RG; tel: 020 7938 3939; fax: 7937
9294; www.trailfinders.com; also in five other English cities, plus Glasgow and Dublin.

North America
Council Travel 205 East 42nd St, New York, NY 10017; tel: 1800 226 8624,
212 661 1414; fax: 212 972 3231; cts@ciee.org; www.counciltravel.com
eXito 1212 Broadway, Suite 910 Oakland, CA 94612; tel: 1800 655 4054, 510 655 2154;
fax: 415 704 3255; exito@wonderlink.com
STA 5900 Wilshire Boulevard, Suite 2110, Los Angeles, CA 90036, USA;
tel: 1800 777 0112; fax: 213 937 2739; or 10 Downing St, New York, NY 10014;
tel: 1800 777 0112, 212 627 3111; www.sta-travel.com
TravelCUTS 187 College St, Toronto M5T 1P7, Canada; tel: 1800 667 2887,
416 979 2406; fax: 416 977 4796; www.travelcuts.com

Group tours
A number of tour operators offer trekking in the southern Andes. Some also
include riding, cycling or rafting. Here are a few:

UK
Alpine Mountaineering Unit 5b, Southwest Centre, Troutbeck Rd, Sheffield S7 2QA;
tel: 0114 258 8508; fax: 255 1603
Andean Trails The Clockhouse, Bonnington Mill Business Centre, 72 Newhaven Rd,
Edinburgh EH6 5QG; tel/fax: 0131 467 7086; info@andeantrails.co.uk;
www.andeantrails.co.uk
Exodus 9 Weir Rd, London SW12 0LT; tel: 020 8675 5550; fax: 8673 0779;
sales@exodus.co.uk
Explore Worldwide 1 Frederick St, Aldershot GU11 1LQ; tel: 01252 760 000;
fax: 760 001; info@exploreworldwide.com
Field Studies Council Overseas Montford Bridge, Shrewsbury SY4 1HW;
tel: 01743 850 522; fax: 850 599, www.fscOverseas.mcmail.com.
Footprint Adventures 5 Malham Drive, Lincoln LN6 0XD; tel: 01522 690852;
fax: 501396; sales@footventure.co.uk
Mountain Travel Sobek 67 Verney Avenue, High Wycombe, Bucks HP12 3ND;
tel: 01494 448 901; fax: 465 526; sales@mtsobekeu.com
Outdoor Odyssey Strone Cottages, Dores, Inverness-shire, Scotland IV2 6TR;
tel/fax: 01463 751 230; smiler@outdoor-odyssey.co.uk
Pura Aventura 18 Bond St, Brighton BN1 1RD; tel: 01273 676 712; fax: 676 774;
enquiries@pura-aventura.com
Ramblers Holidays PO Box 43, Welwyn Garden City, Hertfordshire, AL8 6PQ;
tel: 01707 331 133; fax: 333 276; info@ramblersholidays.co.uk

Worldwide Journeys & Expeditions 27 Vanston Place, London SW6 1AZ; tel: 020 7386 4646; fax: 7381 0836; wwj@journex.demon.co.uk

North America

Adventure Center 1311 63rd St, #200, Emeryville, CA 94608, USA; tel: 1800 227 8747, 510 654 1879; fax: 654 4200; tripinfo@adventurecenter.com

KE Adventure Travel 1131 Grand Avenue, Glenwood Springs, CO 81601, USA; tel: 1800 497 9675, 970 384 0001; fax: 384 0004; ketravel@rof.net; www.keadventure.com

Mountain Travel Sobek 6420 Fairmount Avenue, El Cerrito, CA 94530, USA; tel: 1888 687 6235, 510 527 8100; fax: 525 7710; info@mtsobek.com

Outer Edge Expeditions 4830 Mason Rd, Howell, MI 48843-9697, USA; tel: 1800 322 5235, 517 552 5300; fax: 552 5400; adventure@outer-edge.com

Southwind Adventures PO Box 621057, Littleton, CO 80162, USA; tel: 1800 377 9463, 303 972 0701; fax: 972 0708; info@southwindadventures.com

Tread Lightly 37 Juniper Meadow Rd, Washington Depot, CT 06794, USA; tel: 1800 643 0060; fax: 860 868 1718; info@treadlightly.com

Trek Holidays 8412-109 St, Edmonton T6G 1E2, Canada; tel: 1800 661 7265, 403 439 0024; fax: 433 5494

Wilderness Travel 1102 Ninth St, Berkeley, CA 94710, USA; tel: 1800 368 2794, 510 558 2488; info@wildernesstravel.com

Wildland Adventures 3516 NE 155th St, Seattle, WA 98155-7412, USA; tel: 1800 345 4453, 206 365 0686; fax: 363 6615; info@wildland.com

Worldwide Adventures 36 Finch Avenue West, Toronto M2N 2G9, Canada; tel: 1800 387 1483, 416 221 3000; fax: 221 5730; travel@worldwidequest.com

Climbing trips

These companies concentrate mainly on Aconcagua:

Andes 93 Queen St, Castle Douglas, Dumfries and Galloway, Scotland, DG7 1EH; tel: 01556 503 929; john@andes.com (also Ojos del Salado, other peaks, and trekking)

Camp 5 Expeditions 9 Exchange Place, Suite 900, Salt Lake City, Utah 84111, USA; tel: 1800 914 3834; fax: 0801 534 0515; info@camp5.com

Gane and Marshall International 98 Crescent Rd, New Barnet, Hertfordshire, EN4 9RJ; tel: 020 8441 9592; fax: 8441 7376; holidays@ganeandmarshall.co.uk

High Places Globe Centre, Penistone Rd, Sheffield S6 3AE; tel: 0114 275 7500; fax: 275 3870; highpl@globalnet.co.uk; www.highplaces.co.uk

KE Adventure Travel 32 Lake Rd, Keswick, Cumbria CA12 5DQ; tel: 01768 773966; fax: 774693; keadventure@enterprise.net; www.keadventure.com

Peak International Bwlch y Gwynt, Capel Uchaf, Clynnog Fawr, Caernarfon LL54 5DH; tel: 0845 458 4440; fax: 127 4439; wilderness-adventure@talk21.com; www.wildernessadventure.co.uk

World Expeditions 4 Northfields Prospect, Putney Bridge Rd, London, SW18 1PE; tel: 0800 074 4135, 020 8870 2600; fax: 8870 2615; enquiries@worldexpeditions.co.uk; also 3rd Floor, 441 Kent St, Sydney, NSW 2000, Australia; tel: 02 9264 3366; fax: 9261 1974; enquiries@worldexpeditions.com.au; and Level 6, 580 Market St, San Francisco, CA 94104, USA; tel: 1888 464 8735, 415 989 2212; fax: 989 2112; contactus@weadventures.com

Cycling trips

Saddle Skedaddle Ouseburn Building, Albion Row, East Quayside, Newcastle Upon Tyne NE6 1LL; tel/fax: 0191 265 1110; info@skedaddle.co.uk. Cycle-camping in Isluga and Lauca (to 5,000m) and from Coyhaique to Cochrane.

Backroads 801 Cedar St, Berkeley, CA 94710-1800, USA; tel: 1800 462 2848, 510 527 1555; fax: 527 1444; www.backroads.com ; in the UK book through **Country Lanes**, 9 Shaftesbury St, Fordingbridge, Hampshire SP6 1JF; tel: 01425 655 022; fax: 655 177; bicycling@countrylanes.co.uk; http://dspace.dial.pipex.com/countrylanes/

Horseback trips
In the Saddle Baughurst Rd, Ramsdell, Tadley, Hampshire RG26 5SH; tel: 01256 851 665; fax: 851 667; rides@inthesaddle.com
Last Frontiers Fleet Marston Farm, Aylesbury, HP18 0QT; tel: 01296 658 650; fax: 658 651; info@lastfrontiers.co.uk
Ride World Wide Staddon Farm, North Tawton, Devon EX20 2BX; tel: 01837 82544; fax: 82179, RideWW@aol.com; www.rideworldwide.com

Rafting trips
Adrift (UK) Wessex House, 127 High St, Hungerford RG17 0DL; tel: 01488 684 509; fax: 685 055; raft@adrift.co.uk
Adventure-Whitewater 20 The Cobbins, Waltham Abbey EN9 1LH; tel: 0870 443 240; info@adventure-whitewater.com
Water By Nature Rafting Journeys Ltd Wessex House,127 High St, Hungerford, Berks RG17 0DL; tel: 01488 680 825; fax: 685 055; www.waterbynature.com; also 1975 South Xenon St, Lakewood, CO 80228, USA; tel: 303 989 7194; fax: 989 7193; usa@waterbynature.com

Skiing trips
PowderQuest Tours USA; tel: 1888 565 7158; 804 285 4961; fax: 240 209 4312; info@powderquest.com

Wildlife and birdwatching trips
Animal Watch Granville House, London Rd, Sevenoaks, Kent, TN13 1DL; tel: 01732 741 612; fax: 455 441
Avian Adventures 49 Sandy Rd, Norton, Stourbridge DY8 3AJ; tel: 01384 372 013; fax: 441 340; aviantours@argonet.co.uk
Blue Travel c/o Whale and Dolphin Conservation Society, Alexander House, James St West, Bath BA1 2BT; tel: 01225 334 511; fax: 480 097; bluetravel@wdcs.org; www.bluetravel.co.uk
Eagle-Eye Tours Inc PO Box 94672, Richmond BC, V6Y 4A4, Canada; tel: 1800 373 5678, 604 948 9177; fax: 948 9085; birdtours@eagle-eye.com
Naturetrek Cheriton Mill, Cheriton, Alresford, Hants SO24 0NG; tel: 01962 733 051; fax: 736 426; info@naturetrek.co.uk
Neotropic Bird Tours 38 Brookside Avenue, Livingston, NJ 07039, USA; tel: 1800 662 4852; fax: 201 884 2211
Ornitholidays 1/3 Victoria Drive, Bognor Regis, West Sussex PO21 2PW; tel: 01243 821 230; ornitholidays@compuserve.com; www.ornitholidays.co.uk
Travelling Naturalist PO Box 3141, Dorchester, Dorset DT1 2XD; tel: 01305 267994; fax: 265506; www.naturalist.co.uk
Wildlife Worldwide 170 Selsdon Rd, South Croydon, Surrey, CR2 6PJ; tel: 020 8667 9158; fax: 8667 1960; sales@wildlifeworldwide.com
Wild Oceans International House, Bank Rd, Bristol, BS15 2LX; tel: 0117 984 8040; fax: 961 0200; wildinfo@wildwings.co.uk

VOLUNTEER PROGRAMMES

Raleigh International 27 Parsons Green Lane, London SW6 4HZ; tel: 020 7371 8585; fax: 7371 5116; info@raleigh.org.uk; runs youth development programmes, and has a large presence in Coyhaique (Chile), as has **NOLS** (National Outdoor Leadership School), 288 Main St, Lander, WY 82520-3140, USA; tel: 307 332 5300; www.nols.edu.

Earthwatch 57 Woodstock Rd, Oxford OX2 6HJ; tel: 01865 318 838; fax: 311 383; info@uk.earthwatch.org; runs conservation trips, usually working with scientists on research projects. **Caledonian Languages Abroad** is a language school with homestay and volunteer programmes; tel: 0131 621 7721; fax: 621 7723: info@caledonianlanguages.co.uk; www.caledonianlanguages.co.uk.

Overland trips (in trucks or public transport)

Adventures Abroad 20800 Westminster Hwy #2148, Richmond BC, V6V 2W3, Canada; tel: 1800 665 3998, 604 303 1099; fax: 604 303 1076; info@adventures-abroad.com; also Australia: tel: 1800 890 790; info@adventures-abroad.org; and in New Zealand: tel: 0800 800 434; adventures-abroad@xtra.co.nz; and in the United Kingdom: tel: 0114 247 3400; info@adventures-abroad.co.uk

The Adventure Centre 25 Bellair St, Toronto, M5R 3L3, Canada; tel: 1800 267 3347, 416 922 7584; fax: 416 922 8136; with Trek Holidays (see *Groups, North America*)

Dragoman 94 Camp Green, Debenham, Stowmarket, Suffolk IP14 6LA; tel: 01728 861 133; fax: 861 127; info@dragoman.co.uk; with Adventure Center (see *Groups, North America*), Trek Holidays (see *Groups, North America*), & Adventure World, 73 Walker St, North Sydney, NSW 2060, Australia; tel: 02 9956 7766; fax: 9956 7707; email: infao@adventureworld.com.au

Exodus (see *Groups, UK*)

GAP 264 Dupont St, Toronto M5R 1V7, Canada; tel: 1800 465 5600, 416 922 8899; fax: 416 922 0822; adventure@gap.ca; www.GAPadventures.com; in the UK through

Guerba Wessex House, 40 Station Rd, Westbury, Wilts BA13 3JN; tel: 01373 826 611; fax: 858 351; info@guerba.co.uk

Journey Latin America (see *Agents, UK*)

Journeys International 107 April Drive, Suite 3, Ann Arbor, MI 48103, USA; tel: 1800 255 8735, 734 665 4407; fax: 665 2945; info@journeys-intl.com

Kumuka Expeditions 40 Earls Court Rd, London W8 6EJ; tel: 020 7937 8855; fax: 7937 6664; sale@kumuka.co.uk

Overland Latin America Pleck House, Middletown, Moreton Morrell, Warks CV32 5AA; tel/fax: 01926 650 166; fax: 650 120; info@ola-adventure.com

Travelbag Adventures 15 Turk St, Alton GU34 1AG; tel: 01420 541 007; fax: 541 022; info@travelbag-adventures.com

Trips Worldwide 9 Byron Place, Bristol BS8 4JT; tel: 0117 311 4400; fax: 311 4401; info@tripsworldwide.co.uk

Tucan Ealing House, 33 Hanger Lane, London W5 3HJ; tel: 020 8810 8844, 8896 1600; fax: 8810 8833; matt@tucantravel.com

Tailormade/bespoke trips

Chile Tours 62 Fenchurch St, London EC3M 4AQ; tel: 020 7481 4466; fax: 7480 5510; www.chiletours.uk.com

Journey Latin America (see *Agents, UK* above)
Last Frontiers (see *Horseback trips* above)
Muir's Tours Nepal House, 97A Swansea Rd, Reading RG1 8HA; tel: 0118 950 2281;
info@nkf-mt.org.uk
Roxton Bailey Robinson Worldwide 25 High St, Hungerford RG17 0NF;
tel: 01488 689 701; fax: 689 730; latinamerica@rbrww.com
Sunvil Sunvil House, Upper Sq, Old Isleworth TW7 7BJ; tel: 020 8758 4774;
fax: 8758 4770; latinamerica@sunvil.co.uk; www.sunvil.co.uk/latinamerica

WHAT TO TAKE

As Saint-Exupéry said, 'He who would travel happily must travel light'. You should
take the standard 20kg airline allowance as your absolute maximum, bearing in
mind that you gain a kilogram when you put a litre of water into your bottle. Start
by disposing of as much packaging as you can before departure; I find that a 60ml
Body Shop plastic bottle carries enough shower gel for a month or two, and if you
want solid soap as well this can be carried in a film canister.

Essentials

Specifically for hiking, you will need the six essentials of map, compass, matches
(and maybe a firelighter) in a waterproof box, first-aid kit, extra food and extra
clothing. A knife, spoon and plastic mug or bowl are also pretty important. Wood
fires are cheerful, warming, and increasingly environmentally unacceptable; if you
want to cook, take a stove. Kerosene (known locally as *parafina azul*) is usually
available, and it is getting easier to find Camping Gaz (which is forbidden on
aeroplanes). Stove alcohol or white gas is known as *bencina blanca* in Chile (where
it is used for dry-cleaning and sold in pharmacies) and as *solvente (para quemar)* in
Argentina. Personally I don't bother with cooking on three- to five-day trips in
warm climes.

Clothing

Cold will not be a problem in summer except in the far south, or if you plan to go
high. In the Lakes District, you will more often be too hot than too cold, so bring
lightweight clothes, and remember the key principle of layering; take T-shirts and
long-sleeved shirts, an insulation layer (a light pullover or a fleece jacket) and a
shell layer (waterproof jacket and trousers). Wind is your main enemy, and it is vital
that your outer layer is windproof. In Patagonia a duvet (down) parka is handy, as
well as thermal underwear. Hats are essential, a cotton hat (more practical than a
straw one) against the sun, and a wool or fleece one to keep you warm. Remember
a swimsuit for those lovely thermal pools!

Shirts and trousers (pants) should be mostly cotton; jeans are not suitable, as
they are heavy, hot, hard to wash, and take ages to dry. It is always been inadvisable
to dress outlandishly in Latin America. Officials generally treat travellers who look
dirty and penniless with suspicion and hostility, and if you look (to them) like a
drug user you may have drugs planted on you. So short hair and trimmed beards
for men, and reasonably conventional clothing for women are sensible.

Argentina and Chile are Roman Catholic and it is offensive to the local people
to wear shorts in churches, or for women to be conspicuously bra-less. In addition
the latter invites attention from all those macho men. Also bear in mind the
problems of getting to your money-belt if you are wearing a dress.

Comfortable hiking boots with good ankle support and shock absorption are essential. If hiking on volcanoes, 'Vibram' soles or the like are the only ones that will not be cut up by the lava. Padded insoles may be useful for long walk-outs on rocky roads. Take a spare pair of bootlaces, and use them as a laundry line. You will also need to waterproof your boots from time to time.

Backpacking equipment

To carry all this you need a backpack or rucksack with a padded hipbelt, and preferably also with a so-called 'internal frame'. This is less likely to be caught on jungle creepers, and is handier for travelling on trucks and buses. At airports wrap the hipbelt backwards around the pack, do it up in reverse and tuck away or tie up any strap ends, both to stop them getting caught in conveyor belts, and to delay anyone wanting to sneak a look inside; a small padlock is also useful (and for some hotel rooms), although more as a deterrent than as a real barrier. No rucksack is ever totally waterproof, so you should keep clothes and other important items in plastic bags. Ideally you should carry 50% of your load on the hips – any more and you slip out of your shoulder straps, even with a chest strap. Nowadays there are also likely to be straps to adjust the balance of the load for uphill or downhill work, away from the body going uphill, and closer to the body downhill.

A hiking pole (or two) is invaluable: for establishing a rhythm on level ground, for extra security and confidence downhill, crossing scree, bogs and log bridges, for leverage uphill, for fending off dogs and wet or spiky foliage, for digging toilet holes, and of course essentially for playing noughts and crosses in the sand.

Tent and equipment

You are also likely to need a tent – do not wait until you get there to buy one. It will need to be waterproof, and as light as possible – no more than 2.5kg for a two-person tent. Make sure it can take a pounding from those Patagonian winds; it is worth spending a bit more to make sure you have a tent which will last. In the north ventilation will be a problem, but elsewhere condensation is more of an issue, though most tents are made of permeable nylon which allows some moisture to escape. A cotton inner tent, under a separate flysheet, is more effective against condensation, but is heavier. Light tents (such as those made by Doite and Cacique) can be bought cheaply enough in Buenos Aires and Santiago, but they are not of high quality. In some places you will find tents for hire, but these tend to be ancient and leaky.

Some sort of insulation and protection from the cold, hard ground is essential; closed-cell 'ensolite' foam mats are the most efficient, providing good insulation and tolerable comfort even when less than a centimetre thick. The most comfortable mat of all, though, is the combination of air-mattress and foam-pad made by Thermarest, available in three-quarters or full length.

Rather than a conventional torch (flashlight), use a headtorch, which frees your hands and is ideal for cave exploration and for putting up your tent after dark. Remember a spare bulb. Alternatives are a candle-holder or a Camping Gaz-fuelled lantern.

Useful items

See *Health and Safety* on page 33 for the contents of the definitive first-aid kit. Other useful items include a sewing kit (with heavy thread and needles for tent repairs), safety pins, pencils or ball-point pens, a notebook and paper, travel alarm clock, penknife (preferably Swiss Army type), a few 'zip-loc' plastic bags, a universal bath

PHOTOGRAPHY

Chile's and Argentina's dramatic scenery make them a photographer's dream, and it only takes a small amount of forethought and care to come home with something more appealing than blurred snapshots.

Film

For landscapes and people, low-speed films (50, 64 and 100 ASA) are ideal. For close-up shots of animals, faster speeds such as 400 ASA will be better, provided that you are working with print film (slide films of 200 ASA or greater tend to produce very grainy results). Print film, usually 100 ASA, is available in major cities, but if you use slide film or have other specific requirements, you should bring what you need with you.

Equipment

If you are buying a camera to travel with, bear in mind that the simpler it is, the less there is to go wrong. This is not much of a concern on a short holiday, but may be a consideration for a longer, rougher trip, since complex gadgetry is highly sensitive to rain and dust, and zoom lenses can be destroyed by vibration on rough roads. A simple manual-focus camera with a 50mm lens will be adequate for most purposes. A solid and reliable camera for long trips is the Pentax K1000; a good second-hand one should not cost more than £100 in London. Keep your camera bag on your lap off the main roads, or wrap your gear in a towel or clothing for protection. Do not forget to bring a spare lens cap and enough batteries.

plug (or punctured squash-ball), clothes-pegs, scrubbing brush, dental floss (excellent for running repairs, as well as teeth), toilet paper, and a Latin-American Spanish dictionary or phrasebook.

It is very useful to bring a small daypack; you can leave things in a hotel while you are backpacking, and in any case you invariably end up coming home with more luggage than you started with (see also *Leaving luggage* on page 40). A lightweight nylon bag with a lockable zip is ideal, or a stuffsack for your sleeping bag (with compression straps) can double up.

Camera

A camera should be as robust as possible (I have destroyed several in the past by travelling on rough roads; remember not to sit behind the rear axle of a bus). Simple, practical cameras are the best in tropical climates, particularly mechanical Nikons and Leicas (if you can afford them). It may be worth putting tape over flash and motordrive sockets, when not in use. It is also worth remembering that if the sun shines directly into the lens it can warp delicate camera innards – keep that lens cap on. Nature-lovers will probably want a macro lens for close-ups of all those wonderful flowers and insects, and also a telephoto lens for shots of birds and animals (this can also replace binoculars or a telescope), but otherwise a 35mm compact camera is the most practical; even those incorporating a small zoom lens are now pretty affordable.

You will need a spare battery for a long trip, and plenty of film; in both Chile and Argentina film is expensive and there is a limited range. Slide film is hard to find, as is film of ASA 400 and faster, which you will need in the jungle, as there is little light there.

Portraits

The question of photographing people is a sticky one, and the first rule at all times is to ask permission and accept gracefully if it is refused, no matter how much it hurts. When somebody does agree to let you photograph them, your next question will be how to go about this without every nearby kid leaping into the frame. If you have a point-and-shoot camera, the answer is to take the picture as quickly as you can. On the other hand, if you have a camera that requires a certain amount of fiddling around, then you may have to compromise by first taking a group photo, then trying to clear the frame of extraneous kids, bearing in mind that, if they then decide to line up behind you, there is a good chance that the photograph will be spoiled by their shadows.

Another thing to bear in mind is that people often pose very stiffly when you point a camera at them and relax only when the flash goes off, so it may help to take two shots in quick succession, hoping that the second one will capture a more natural pose.

Sensitivity

Military paranoia has largely evaporated, but it remains illegal to photograph defence installations of any kind. Technically this includes bridges and railway facilities, but photographing these is now likely to cause only amusement. If in doubt, ask.

Insurance

Baggage insurance is well worth having. Things can get lost even when you take all the care in the world, and it does ease the grief somewhat if it is insured. Read the small print carefully. If something is stolen you must report the theft to the police and get a *certificado*, which you will need to make your claim.

Documents

It is a good idea to keep a strong rubber band around your passport to hold in your tourist card. Another one is to stick a coloured dot of paper or even a gold star on to the front of your passport. Then you will be able to recognize it if it is taken from you and given back by calling out an unintelligible version of your name, for example when crossing a Latin American border by bus. Your passport, air ticket, most of your travellers' cheques and so on should be kept in a money belt; keep a separate note of their numbers, and email this to yourself as a Hotmail (or similar) message.

Health and Safety

With Dr Felicity Nicholson

GENERAL HEALTH
Before you go

Chile and Argentina have modern medical facilities and excellent doctors. No vaccinations are required, but make sure you are up to date with your typhoid, hepatitis A and tetanus injections. Yellow fever and polio have now been eradicated in Chile and Argentina, and malaria will only be a problem in the extreme north of Argentina. In general, your best protection is to be fit and well before you set off on a hiking trip. Have your teeth checked, carry your prescription (or leave it as a Hotmail message) if you wear glasses, and be sure to take out appropriate medical insurance.

Many drugs available only on prescription in the UK and US are sold over the counter in South America, and they are often cheaper, so do not worry about replacing your basic medical supplies. You are, however, advised to check expiry dates, and to bring your own first-aid kit, in particular some sterilized needles. In Britain you can buy specially designed Sterile Equipment Packs from the Medical Advisory Service for Travellers Abroad (see *Travel clinics* on page 38).

Malaria prevention

There is a risk of malaria only in the far north of Argentina. It is crucial to avoid being bitten by mosquitoes, which may bite from dusk to dawn. If you will be in an affected area for more than three days then it is worth taking chloroquine pills, starting a week before arriving there. Telephone the Malaria Reference Laboratory

SUGGESTED MEDICAL KIT
- Elastoplast (Band-Aids)
- butterfly closures
- micropore tape
- bandages
- tubular bandages
- Melolin dressings
- Vaseline (for cracked heels and removing ticks)
- blister packs (Compeed)
- antifungal foot powder
- scissors
- safety pins
- tweezers
- earplugs
- sterile hypodermic needles
- drugs
- malaria pills
- aspirin or paracetamol/ Tylenol (for fever and toothache)
- a more powerful pain-killer/anti-inflammatory such as ibuprofen (Nurofen/Advil)
- diarrhoea medicine (Diocalm, Imodium)
- antihistamine tablets such as Clarityn or Zirtek
- antibiotics (ciprofloxacin, tinidazole, ampicillin)
- antiseptic and wipes
- travel sickness pills

in London for the latest advice; tel: 0891 600 350, or in the USA the Centers for Disease Control in Atlanta; tel: 877 394 8747. (See also page 38–9.)

Inoculations

Hepatitis A is common throughout the continent. The majority of travellers are advised to have immunisation against hepatitis A with eg: Havrix Monodose or Avaxim. One dose of vaccine lasts for one year and can be boosted to give protection for up to ten years. The course of injections costs about £100. The vaccine can be used even close to the time of departure. This is always preferable to gamma globulin which gives immediate but only short-term and partial protection; there is also a theoretical risk of new variant CJD (the human form of mad cow disease) with this blood-derived product.

The newer typhoid vaccines last for three years and are about 75% effective. They should be encouraged unless the traveller is leaving within a few days for a trip of a week or less when the vaccine would not be effective in time.

Vaccinations for rabies are advised for visits to more remote areas. Ideally three injections should be taken over a period of four weeks prior to travel. The timing of these doses does not have to be exact and a schedule can be arranged to suit you. Rabies is transmitted from bites of warm-blooded mammals or from contact with animal saliva in an open wound. Whether pre-exposure vaccines have been taken or not, if bitten by a possibly rabid animal, you should wash the wound in soap and water, apply an antiseptic and seek medical help as soon as possible. Always tell the doctor if you have been vaccinated as this will affect subsequent treatment.

Hepatitis B vaccination should be considered for longer trips (say two months or more) or for those working in situations where the possibility of contact with blood is increased, or with children. Three injections are ideal, which can be given over a period of four to eight weeks prior to travel. The only vaccine licensed in the UK for the latter more rapid course at the time of writing is Engerix B. The longer course is always to be preferred as immunity is likely to be longer lasting.

Cholera is not a great problem at the moment (although there have been recent outbreaks in San Pedro de Atacama in Chile and Santiago del Estero in Argentina), but *ceviche* (uncooked shellfish) should be avoided. There is currently no effective cholera vaccine available in the UK, but cholera is rarely serious in the well-nourished and is treatable with antibiotics.

COMMON MEDICAL PROBLEMS

Many of the ailments that beset travellers are caused by poor toilet practice, eating contaminated food and drinking unclean water, so you can do much to avoid illness by taking a few simple precautions: wash your hands after using the toilet (to remove other people's germs, not your own); do not eat raw vegetables, salads or fruit you have not peeled yourself; boil water or purify it with chlorine (Sterotabs, Puritabs or Halozone) or better still with iodine tablets eg: Potable Aqua (which kill amoebae). Compact water purifiers are now available to filter out and kill amoebae, viruses and bacteria. Tea and coffee are usually made with hot rather than boiling water, and ice is also unsafe. But do not spoil your trip by never eating in wayside restaurants or from street stalls. Just be cautious at first while your system adjusts, and do not eat food that has been sitting around cooling.

Diarrhoea

Although Chile and Argentina are a good deal more hygienic than some of their northern neighbours, you have to face the fact that almost everyone comes down

SUNGLASSES AND SUNBURN

With thanks to Dr Bob Vinton

Depletion of the ozone layer, coupled with dry, unpolluted air, has led to increased levels of ultraviolet radiation in southern Chile and Argentina, causing sunburn and increasing the risk of cataracts and skin cancer. A broad-brimmed hat reduces eye damage to a certain extent, but sunglasses should also be used, especially at altitude or when light is reflected off water or snow. Together they can cut UV exposure by 95%; buy sunglasses which block 95–100% of UVB rays and at least 60% of UVA rays. The ability to absorb UV radiation is not determined by lens colour or darkness, although they should be dark enough for you not to see your eyes in a mirror. Grey and green lenses distort colours least; brown-amber improves contrast in haze or fog, but causes other colour distortions. Polarised lenses reduce reflected glare off glass and water, but have no UV protection. The best sunglasses are large, curved to fit the face and with opaque or UV-blocking side-shields.

Remember that even on hazy or cloudy days you can still receive 70–80% of a clear day's radiation. Prevent sunburn by using sunscreens, which come in two main kinds. Reflectors such as zinc oxide and titanium oxide reflect and scatter UV wavelengths; because they are thick and messy, they are used only in high-risk areas such as the nose and lips. Absorber sunscreens, such as PABA (para-aminobenzoic acid), cinnamates, benzophenones and parsol, absorb UV waves.

Soak mild to moderate sunburn in cold water, give ice massages, and take painkillers if needed. Solarcaine and other anaesthetic creams may cause allergic reactions. Severe sunburn with blisters should receive medical treatment.

Sunburn leads to rough, sagging skin with liver spots, wrinkles and increased skin-cancer risks; these effects are cumulative, irreversible, and begin at an early age. By the time wrinkles appear, the damage is done. To avoid any of the above, take preventative action all the time.

with diarrhoea somewhere in South America. 'Travellers' trots' is usually caused by the enterotoxic forms of the bacteria *Escherischia coli* which everyone has naturally in their intestines. The problem is that each area has its own strain of *E. coli*, and alien strains cause inflammation of the intestine and diarrhoea. On a long trip you will aquire a nice collection of the local *E. coli* in your gut and be troubled no more, but the first few weeks can be tough. Everyone has a favourite remedy, but most people agree that it is best to let nature take its course rather than rushing off to the pharmacy for antibiotics at the first signs of *turista*. It is far better to rest and drink plenty of tea, *manzanilla* (camomile tea) or *maté de coca* (coca tea – only in the far north) without milk. Don't eat any greasy or fatty food for 24 hours, then for a few days stick to a bland diet with plenty of mashed potatoes or rice and bananas. Avoid alcohol, fatty and spicy foods and milk products, and take plenty of fluids. Replace the lost salts and minerals by sipping a solution of half a teaspoon of salt and four teaspoons of sugar or honey in a litre of (clean) water; if possible add baking soda (half a teaspoon) and potassium chloride (a quarter teaspoon), or a little orange or lemon juice. You can buy this (Electrolade is a common brand) or make up some of this 'electrolyte replacement' formula before leaving home. You need to take in at least three litres of liquid a day, and more if the diarrhoea is really bad.

There will be times when you will want to block the symptoms of diarrhoea: before setting off on a long bus ride, for instance, or when you are camping in heavy rain. Probably the best 'chemical cork' is loperamide (Diocalm or Imodium), but codeine-based blockers can also be effective.

Dysentery

If you have diarrhoea with a fever, bad gut cramps and blood in your stool, you may have bacterial (bacillary) dysentery. Amoebic dysentery is similar but starts more gradually, and the diarrhoea is persistent but not dramatic. Giardiasis presents with gut cramps, greasy bulky yellow stools and sulphurous burps. Get your stool analysed and take the result to a doctor, who will probably prescribe a week's course of Flagyl (metronidazole or preferably tinidazole) for amoebic dysentery or giardia, or an antibiotic such as ciprofloxacin for the bacterial variety.

Fever

If you develop a fever for any reason, you should rest and take aspirin or paracetamol/Tylenol. You should also bring with you a supply of antibiotics, such as ciprofloxacin or tetracycline, in case you are struck by some more serious infection in a hopelessly inconvenient place. If this happens, take antibiotics as instructed on the packet and see a doctor as soon as possible. For gut infections, a single dose of 500mg of ciprofloxacin should suffice. However if a three-day course of 500mg of ciprofloxacin twice daily fails, then seek medical help.

Injury

Many of the hikes described in this book take you well away from civilisation, so you should be prepared for trouble. If you are not familiar with mountain first-aid, carry a booklet on the subject, and pack an appropriate medical kit. If there are only two of you and one has an accident, the other should stay with the injured one and wait for help to arrive. The temptation is to rush for help, but being injured, worried and alone could have a disastrous effect on the patient. So, except for the rare cases when you know the trails are little used, wait for someone to come along, and keep the injured person warm and comfortable. In general, do not hike when you are tired, and do not take risks.

Heat-related problems

It takes up to two weeks for the body to adjust to hot weather, but you can help by drinking lots of water (at least three litres a day), avoiding alcohol, and taking extra salt in your diet. Avoid hiking during the hottest part of the day and do not wear or carry too much. Dehydration occurs faster at altitude, and can be brought on even by travelling in air-conditioned buses or on the wind-swept back of a pick-up truck.

Mountain health
Altitude sickness

Altitude sickness (*soroche*) is more likely to affect you on the *altiplano* of Peru or Bolivia than in Chile or Argentina. However, you are certain to feel the effects of altitude if you climb Aconcagua, and may do so if you walk in northern Chile or northwestern Argentina, where the hikes take you above 2,400m. Most people will

HANTA FEVER

Hanta fever (or hantavirus pulmonary syndrome) crossed from Argentina to Chile in 1995 and caused a degree of panic; for a while campsites were even kept clean. In 2000 it reached the Santiago Metropolitan Region. The fever is carried by a virus which has been common for some time in the USA, where it has a fatality rate of over 40%. The symptoms are flu-like fever, muscle pains, headache and fainting, followed by breathing difficulties. Hanta fever is not responsive to drugs, so treatment, even in hospital, is 'supportive', controlling symptoms until the body fights off the infections.

It is transmitted mainly by the long-tailed mouse (ratón colilargo; *Oligoryzomys longicaudatus*), which is about 10cm long with a tail of the same length. Do not touch food that has been chewed or defecated on by a rodent, and do not leave it where this might happen. The Chilean Ministry of Health has produced lots of posters and even an English-language leaflet, which unfortunately suggests burying garbage rather than packing it out. Hiking etiquette is now to remove all rubbish rather than bury or burn it. 'Pack it in, pack it out' is the generally accepted rule.

need to do little more than rest for an hour or two for the usual symptoms of thumping heart and gasping breath to pass. However, some will experience other symptoms including headaches, fatigue, dizziness, loss of appetite and nausea (similar to a hangover). Take plenty of fluids and carbohydrates (up to 70% of your diet), and perhaps aspirin or paracetamol, and if it fails to clear up overnight, consider descending at least 500m and then returning in shorter stages. If you know that the ascent will be rapid, consider taking Diamox (acetazolamide) 250mg twice daily for three days before reaching 3,500m, then continue for a further two days. Do not use this drug if allergic to sulphur compounds. It is always best to try Diamox out for two days at sea level at least two weeks before travel.

Two dangerous varieties of altitude sickness – cerebral oedema and pulmonary oedema – cause a rapid collapse with coughing, frothing and blue lips; the only solution is immediate and rapid descent. The key symptom of both types is a loss of coordination, accompanied in the case of cerebral oedema by illogical thought processes, loss of interest in events and surroundings, and even hallucinations, and in pulmonary oedema (water in the lungs) by a dry cough, breathlessness and a rapid heartbeat.

Hypothermia

Sometimes referred to as exposure, this is a simple but effective killer. Simply put, it means the body loses heat faster than it can produce it. It is the combination of wet and cold that is lethal, with mountain winds chilling you even if the air temperature is well above freezing; fatigue is also often a contributory factor. Symptoms include lethargy, shivering (initially only), numbness (especially of fingers and toes), staggering, slurred speech and irrational perceptions and behaviour. The loss of rationality is particularly dangerous as it means the sufferer often fails to recognise his condition and to take necessary measures. Further exercise is exhausting and soon results in worse hypothermia. As soon as possible get the victim out of the wind and into dry warm clothing or a sleeping bag, and give high-energy food and warm, non-alcoholic drinks. If the situation becomes

WESTERN MEDICINE AND LOCAL PEOPLE
One of the by-products of well-equipped trekkers permeating every mountain stronghold is that local people will beg medicines above any other consumable. Even the most culturally sensitive trekker or backpacker feels it would be cruel to deny them this easing of the harshness of their lives, yet there are good reasons to say no. Apart from the risks to them of inappropriate dosage, it adds to the belief that Western medicine is good and traditional remedies are bad, despite the advantages of the latter in availability and cost. In short, do not dabble in other people's health!

more serious, climb into the sleeping bag, too, and use your naked body as a radiator.

It is extremely unlikely that long-distance hikers will succumb to hypothermia because they carry their weather protection with them. Inadequately equipped day hikers are in more danger, so if you are going above 2,000m or so, be sure to carry a good sleeping bag (keeping it dry), a light sweater or fleece jacket, and, most important, a thoroughly waterproof jacket and trousers. There are various ways of keeping warm without relying on heavy or expensive clothing: wear a hat to prevent heat loss from your head, and make sure your collar fits snugly, or use a scarf. Turn back if the weather looks threatening, and get under cover before becoming soaked.

TRAVEL CLINICS
UK
British Airways Travel Clinic and Immunisation Service 156 Regent St, London W1, tel: 020 7439 9584. This place also sells travellers' supplies and has a branch of Stanford's travel book and map shop. There are now BA clinics all around Britain and three in South Africa. To find your nearest one, phone 01276 685040.
Fleet Street Travel Clinic 29 Fleet Street, London EC4Y 1AA; tel: 020 7353 5678
MASTA (Medical Advisory Service for Travellers Abroad) Keppel St, London WC1 7HT; tel: 09068 224100. This is a premium-rate number, charged at 50p per minute.
NHS travel website www.fitfortravel.scot.nhs.uk, provides country-by-country advice on immunisation and malaria, plus details of recent developments, and a list of relevant health organisations.
Nomad Travel Pharmacy and Vaccination Centre 3-4 Wellington Terrace, Turnpike Lane, London N8 0PX; tel: 020 8889 7014.
Thames Medical 157 Waterloo Rd, London SE1 8US; tel: 020 7902 9000. Competitively priced, one-stop travel health service. All profits go to their affiliated company InterHealth which provides health care for overseas workers on Christian projects.
Trailfinders Immunisation Centre 194 Kensington High St, London W8 7RG; tel: 020 7938 3999. Also 254–284 Sauchiehall St, Glasgow G2 3EH; tel: 0141 353 0066.

Irish Republic
Tropical Medical Bureau Grafton Street Medical Centre, Grafton Buildings, 34 Grafton Street, Dublin 2. Tel: (353-1) 671 9200. This organisation has a useful website specific to tropical destinations: www.tmb.ie.

USA

Centers for Disease Control 1600 Clifton Road, Atlanta, GA 30333;
tel: 877 394 8747; 800 311 3435; web: www.cdc.gov/travel. This organisation is the
central source of travel information in the USA. Each summer it publishes the invaluable
Health Information for International Travel which is available from the Division of
Quarantine at the above address.
Connaught Laboratories PO Box 187, Swiftwater, PA 18370; tel: 800 822 2463.
They will send a free list of specialist tropical-medicine physicians in your state.
IAMAT (International Association for Medical Assistance to Travelers) 736 Center St,
Lewiston, NY 14092. A non-profit organisation which provides lists of English-speaking
doctors abroad.

Canada

IAMAT (International Association for Medical Assistance to Travellers) Suite 1, 1
287 St Clair Avenue West, Toronto, Ontario M6E 1B8; tel: (416) 652 0137;
web: www.sentex.net/~iamat
TMVC (Travel Doctors Group) Sulphur Springs Rd, Ancaster, Ontario;
tel: (905) 648 1112; web: www.tmvc.com.au

Australia and New Zealand

TMVC tel: 1300 65 88 44; website: www.tmvc.com.au.
TMVC has 20 clinics in **Australia**, **New Zealand** and **Thailand**, including:
Auckland Canterbury Arcade, 170 Queen Street, Auckland City; tel: 373 3531
Brisbane Dr Deborah Mills, Qantas Domestic Building, 6th floor, 247 Adelaide St,
Brisbane, QLD 4000; tel: 7 3221 9066; fax: 7 3321 7076
Melbourne Dr Sonny Lau, 393 Little Bourke St, 2nd floor, Melbourne, VIC 3000;
tel: 3 9602 5788; fax: 3 9670 8394
Sydney Dr Mandy Hu, Dymocks Building, 7th floor, 428 George St, Sydney,
NSW 2000; tel: 2 221 7133; fax: 2 221 8401

South Africa

There are six **British Airways travel clinics** in South Africa:
Johannesburg, tel: (011) 807 3132; Cape Town, tel: (021) 419 3172; Durban, tel: (031)
303 2423; Knysna, tel: (044) 382 6366; East London, tel: (043) 743 7471; Port Elizabeth,
tel: (041) 374 7471
TMVC (Travel Doctor Group) 113 DF Malan Drive, Roosevelt Park, Johannesburg;
tel: +27 (011) 888 7488. Consult their website www..tmvc.com.au for addresses of other
clinics in South Africa.

Switzerland

IAMAT (International Association for Medical Assistance to Travellers) 57 Voirets,
1212 Grand Lancy, Geneva; web: www.sentex.net/~iamat.

SECURITY

When an elderly couple suggested that their driver/guide lock the car before going
into a Patagonian restaurant, he asked, 'Why?'. There is little casual crime in Chile
and Argentina, but you should take sensible precautions, especially in cities. Avoid
looking like a wealthy tourist: leave your jewellery and other such valuables at
home. If you carry a bag in addition to your pack, never put it down. Keep it under
your arm or over your shoulder. Do not keep valuables in it: not only can it be

DANGER: TOURISTS

Tourism need not be a destructive force for tribal peoples, but unfortunately it frequently is. We at Bradt Travel Guides totally support the initiative of the charity Survival in protecting the rights of tribal peoples.

Recognise land rights
- Obtain permission to enter
- Pay properly
- Behave as if on private property

Respect tribal peoples
- Don't demean, degrade, insult or patronise

Don't bring in disease
- Diseases such as colds can kill tribal peoples
- AIDS is a killer

Survival (11–15 Emerald St, London WC1N 3QL, UK, tel: 020 7242 1441; fax: 020 7242 1771; survival@gn.apc.org) is a worldwide organisation supporting tribal peoples. It stands for their right to decide their own future and helps them protect their lives, lands and human rights.

Tourism Concern (Stapleton House, 277 Holloway Rd, London N7 8HN; tel: 020 7753 3330; fax: 7753 3331; info@tourismconcern.org.uk) aims to promote awareness of tourism's impact on people and their environment.

snatched, but it can be picked, slit or slashed open. The same applies to a 'bum bag', although this is a handy way to carry a compact camera.

For cash, travellers' cheques, passport and air tickets, use a money belt, neck pouch or secret inside pocket. Alternatively you can sew a false pocket into the front of trousers or shorts. If your passport is too bulky to carry comfortably and safely, keep handy some other form of identification, such as a driving-licence, or photocopies of the key pages of your passport. Keep the numbers of your travellers' cheques, passport, credit cards and air tickets separate from other valuables, so that if they are lost you can replace them more easily; it is also smart to leave them as a Hotmail (or similar) message to yourself. Divide your money and travellers' cheques between at least two different places, in your baggage and on your body.

Leaving luggage

Most travellers finish a trip with far more luggage than when they started, and packs become quite unpackable. And of course you need space for several days' food when you go hiking. It is a good idea to get accustomed to finding a safe place to leave unwanted baggage – a hotel will nearly always keep it for you, usually free. Even if they charge, it is not much. Bring a lockable bag for this purpose, and make sure it is put somewhere safe, preferably also locked. Avoid leaving luggage in hotels frequented by other budget travellers. They are not all as honest as you are, and the policy of claiming your own bag invites theft. If you have to do this, try to chain your bag to something solid, or at least put your passport number, name and return date on it with instructions not to give it to anyone else.

On the Road

MONEY

The Argentinean peso is tied to the US dollar at parity, and the two currencies can be used interchangeably. At the time of writing there were about 500 Chilean pesos to the US dollar (about 840 to the pound sterling). You can bring in as much money as you want to either country, although it will normally be easier to keep it in your account at home and withdraw it from an ATM (cash machine) as needed.

The US dollar is the only foreign currency that is easily exchanged outside the capitals, although you will find a few banks and exchange offices that may change pounds sterling and other currencies. You should carry some dollars as cash (some in small denominations) and some in travellers' cheques, as a security reserve. The trick is not to cash the travellers' cheques, at least not until near the end of the trip, but when the time comes, remember that American Express or Thomas Cook travellers' cheques can be changed in their respective offices without commission; otherwise you will pay at least 2% (either declared as a commission or just massaged from the exchange rate), as well as the 1–1.5% paid when you bought the cheques. If buying cash in Britain, Thomas Cook offices give a notoriously bad rate.

ATMs can be found in modern bus stations and supermarkets as well as at banks; in addition RedCompra swipe-card terminals are beginning to appear in shops. There are two systems, Cirrus, linked to Mastercard, and Plus, linked to Visa; both the issuing bank and Visa or Mastercard take a fee of 1-2%. You can also use ATMs to draw cash on your credit card, but this is horrendously expensive (in Argentina there is often a surcharge on credit card purchases as well). The real advantages are in being able to get cash at any time, without queues, with English instructions, and in small quantities, just to last you to the border. In Argentina, some ATMs also dispense US dollars. In small towns the only bank is likely to be the Banco del Estado; this may have an ATM, but these tend not to accept any foreign cards.

If you want to have money sent to you, plan this in advance with your bank, which will have a partner bank in Chile or Argentina. Then all you have to do is cable your bank and wait for the cash. It will take a few days, and actually collecting the cash is a hassle, but it works. LBSA (Lloyds Bank South America) in Argentina is part of Britain's Lloyds-TSB, while the American Citibank is present in both Chile and Argentina, as is Western Union.

TRANSPORT

> 'I asked the sleeping car attendant what was up. The tracks, he said.'
> Paul Theroux *The Old Patagonian Express*

Chile and Argentina are big places, with lots of empty space. In fact you could drop the whole of western Europe on the two countries and still have thousands of hectares round the edge. This means that getting from one place to another by road or rail can take not hours, but days. Some sample distances: Arica to Puerto Montt, 2,900km; Buenos Aires to Ushuaia, 3,200km; Salta to Ushuaia, 4,700km.

Air

Both Chile and Argentina have excellent, reasonably priced domestic air services, operated by state and private airlines. If you are thinking of doing a lot of your travelling by air, it is certainly worth considering an airpass. These can only be bought outside the country and prices vary depending on whether you buy your ticket into the country at the same time (see page 22). In the holiday months of January and February, flights get very full so you need to book well in advance.

Chile

In Chile, naturally, all travel is essentially along one north–south axis; **LanChile** and its subsidiary **Ladeco** (originally Linea Aerea del Cobre – the Copper Airline) are increasingly merging their operations as the SuperRuta Nacional (tel: 600 526 2000); south of Santiago they serve Concepción, Temuco, Valdivia, Osorno, Puerto Montt, Balmaceda and Punta Arenas, as well as seven cities in the north; competition comes from Avant (owned by TurBus) which took over the bankrupt Nacional and serves Los Angeles, Concepción, Temuco, Valdivia, Osorno, Puerto Montt, Balmaceda and Punta Arenas, and six northern cities. A new competitor since 2000 is **Aerocontinente**, serving the biggest cities. It is not possible to fly from Coyhaique/Balmaceda to Punta Arenas, and no flights currently serve Puerto Natales. In addition **DAP** operates local services between Punta Arenas and both sides of Tierra del Fuego. Air travel has increased from 1.9 million passengers in 1990 to 6 million in 1997 (3.1 million of them internal); likewise cargo doubled between 1994 and 1997.

Argentina

In Argentina, too, traffic is booming; in 2000 there were 7 million passengers, and there are expected to be 15 million by 2025. Air services in Argentina were first developed to carry mail around the immense expanses of Patagonia. The first pilots were mostly French, including Antoine de Saint-Exupéry, who arrived in 1929, and drew on his experiences to write *Vol de Nuit*. Another of them, Leonardo Servetti, remembers the dreadful weather conditions: 'Winds were of a speed that almost stopped the plane and blew it backwards. I remember that in order to land we had to nose-dive at full power and stick the plane to the soil. We had to fly close to sea level so the ice would melt on the wings. On the other hand, the snow blurred the windshield and we had to lean out of the window to see. Then our goggles blurred and when we took them off we had tears which froze on our faces'.

In 1936, Aeroposta Argentina began flying to Ushuaia, taking six days from Buenos Aires; in 1937 three German Junkers 52s (one of which is still preserved at the Aeroparque) took over, cutting the journey to three days, and after World War II, these were replaced by DC-3 Dakotas. In 1950, Aeroposta was transformed into **Aerolíneas Argentinas**. The country's second airline, Austral, was founded in 1971, saved from bankruptcy by Aerolíneas in 1980, and privatised in 1987. Aerolíneas was also privatised in 1990, and both are now owned by SEPI, a Spanish government holding company, which is trying to get rid of them. There is now lots of competition, with airlines such as Kaiken, Dinar, LAPA (*Lineas Aereas Privadas Argentinas*), TACA (*Transportes Aéreo Costa Atlántica*), TAN (*Transporte Aéreo*

Neuquén), LAER (*Lineas Aéreas Entre Ríos*), and Southern Winds, which flies stylish little Regional Jets. And the airports are now also privatised, with Aeropuertos Argentina 2000 committed to investing US$2bn over a 30-year concession. After the two Buenos Aires airports, the most important is Córdoba, being developed as a hub for internal flights; Aerolineas and Austral operate the *Córdoba Shuttle* from the Buenos Aires Aeroparque every 90 minutes (every 30 minutes in the peaks, in co-operation with Dinar and Southern Winds).

In addition, the Argentine Air Force has an airline of its own, Líneas Aéreas del Estado (LADE). If you want to go somewhere, such as Perito Moreno, not reached by the commercial airlines the chances are that you can get there once a week with LADE. This is an experience not to be missed, especially as it is sometimes actually cheaper than going by bus. Again, you will need to book well in advance, but even when a flight is fully booked, there tend to be some no-shows, so it is always worth turning up at the airport on the off-chance.

Buses

Long distance buses in Chile and Argentina are comparable to those in North America (particularly Mexico), and better than many in Europe. Fast, reliable and comfortable, they could hardly be more different from the rustic vehicles of the Andean countries further north. Regular inter-city buses are known as Pullmans, and often come with reclining seats, toilets, videos and drink service. Even so, it is possible to pay almost twice as much for bigger seats that fold down into virtual beds (*salón-cama*).

Buses are better value in Chile than Argentina. The trip from Buenos Aires to Bariloche, for example, costs about US$70, about two-thirds of the airfare (and takes 22 hours); but from Puerto Montt to Santiago the fare is just US$25 (*cama* US$40), a sixth of the airfare. In any event, buses are very popular, and during the main holiday period of January and February may be booked up weeks in advance. At other times there is lots of competition, so you should always ask for a student discount or a *promoción*, which may be as much as a third off close to departure time – **TurBus** are said to be especially helpful (air fares are also cut in the 24 hours before departure). Buses may not run on backroads nor to national parks in winter.

Long-haul buses are fitted with alarms that go off when they go over the speed limit (100km/hr in Chile and 90km/hr in Argentina). In Patagonia your baggage is usually loaded without charge, but in Santiago and northern Argentina you may have to tip a dollar or so. In either case you will usually be given a baggage tag, which you will have to return to get your baggage back. Likewise a control tab may be torn off your travel ticket when you get off. It is best to sit on the right, not so much to keep an eye on your baggage as to avoid being dazzled by oncoming headlights.

A new development is the **Backpackers' Bus** (casilla 24D, Talca, 7th Region, Chile; tel: 071 231 157, or mobile 09 452 5680; fax: 071 224 611) which follows a circuit of tourist sights and budget hotels in southern Chile.

Trains

A cheap and civilised way to travel, where possible, is by train. Both Chile and Argentina have extensive railway systems, but unfortunately most lines are now open for freight only. In Chile EFE passenger trains operate only between Santiago and Temuco, and suburban trains in Concepción and between Valparaíso, Viña del Mar and Limache. In 1993 the Argentine government withdrew federal funding for the railways, leaving it to provinces to decide on subsidies. As a result there are reasonable passenger services in Buenos Aires province, but few elsewhere (although the Buenos Aires–Tucumán service is useful for reaching the northwest). In Chile, there are no railways south of Chiloé, for the very good reason that the mountains, fjords and ice-caps make it impossible. In Argentina, the extreme sparsity of settlement in the vast *pampas* of the south meant that railways were never an economic proposition there, except for a few special lines such as that from the Río Turbío coal mines to the sea, and the line to Esquel, made famous through Paul Theroux's *The Old Patagonian Express* (see page 348).

You will usually have a better view of landscape and wildlife from a train than a bus, and if you have 18 hours to spare, we highly recommend the overnight journey between Santiago and Temuco. It is like travelling inside an antique – which is in effect what the sleeper carriages are, built in Germany in 1929–31. For around US$40 you can sleep in a spacious, velvet-lined bed with starched, white sheets, after dinner in the dining car – perfectly edible, though the choice is limited and a bit pricey. For less than the bus fare you can travel on a hard seat. The only drawback is that timetables do tend to be elastic and the ageing hardware of track and rolling stock is subject to all kinds of unlikely mishaps.

Hitch-hiking

If you have got time to spare, hitch-hiking (*hacer el dedo* – 'doing the thumb') will more than repay the effort. On the main roads of both Chile and Argentina there is plenty of traffic, particularly in the summer months, and hitch-hiking is common and accepted. However, on the back roads of Patagonia and Tierra del Fuego it is recommended only for the very patient. Authors of previous editions of this book waited two days or more for a lift.

In Chile it is easy enough to get a ride without fuss; in Argentina, where few people go out without all living grandparents and grandchildren, you wait longer, but once you get a ride, they are far more likely to go out of their way to help you. In Chile, it is technically illegal to ride on the back of a pick-up truck, but not only have I been through *carabineros* (police) checkpoints without problem, I have even been given a ride by *carabineros* on the back of their official *camioneta*.

Car hire

This is an expensive means of transport, particularly in Chile where you are not likely to want to return to where you hired the car. You will have to pay extra to take a hire car across the border. Both international and local car-hire companies are easy to find. You will need an International Driving Permit, and you may prefer to hire a pick-up (*camioneta*) if you are intending to spend a lot of time on *ripio* (dirt) backroads.

Large amounts of money are being spent in both countries on paving roads, and Argentina is also building new bridges across the Río Uruguay to Brazil as well as planning a 42km bridge, the world's longest, from Punta Lara (Buenos Aires) to Colonia Sacramento (Uruguay), which will cost almost US$1 billion (to be raised by tolls). The busiest 10,000km of Argentina's roads have been handed over to concessions, and in Chile the PanAmerican Highway is being converted into a dual-carriageway toll-road all the way from La Serena to Puerto Montt; you will also pay about US$4 on the main roads north, south and west of Santiago. Chilean cars are mostly sensible Japanese models, including a lot of pick-ups. In Argentina there are many ancient, domestically-built Renaults, Peugeots and Ford Falcons, now seemingly powered by rubber bands, as well as much bigger and more macho pick-ups than in Chile, with bull bars and dark windows. Not surprisingly, the roads are far more dangerous in Argentina, with an average 29 deaths per day (that's 10,000 a year; plus 1,400 cyclists a year); there is talk of requiring cars to use their headlights in the daytime. In both countries, it is acceptable to ride motorbikes without helmets, and signs marking one-way streets are discreet, just a small arrow on a wall.

Cycling

Cycling is a good way to get around, although you may wish to take a bus for long stretches of road north and south of Santiago and in much of Argentina. There are many unpaved roads, so a mountain bike may be a better choice than a tourer. These can be rented by the day in Pucón and San Pedro de Atacama, but otherwise you should bring your own. The Carretera Austral, in particular, is one of the best mountain-bike tours in the world, although by 2005 it will be largely paved. Further south it is too windy for cycle-touring, as a rule. There are a few cycle lanes, on the outskirts of Pucón and Coyhaique, and the Puerto Montt and Río Grande *costaneras* (seafront promenades), for instance, and major roads have shoulders, but Santiago is not a good place to ride. Cycles are taken by truck through the Cristo Redentor tunnel between Chile and Argentina, though at quiet times you can persuade the truck to follow you with its lights flashing.

See pages 246–7 for **ferry travel**.

COMMUNICATIONS

Chile has an efficient **postal service**; unfortunately it is also ruthlessly efficient in returning or throwing out poste restante (*Lista de Correos*) after 30 days. Argentina's is less good, but is being privatised, and there are already private companies competing in the domestic market. Letters take about two weeks to reach Europe or North America.

As elsewhere in the world, letters for poste restante should be clearly addressed with initials rather than forenames, or the recipient's surname underlined; in addition Chile lists men, women and companies separately, so make sure *Señor* or *Señora* is clearly indicated.

Chile has one of the most competitive **telephone** systems in the world, with a dozen companies operating, of which the largest are CTC and Entel. The cost savings possible with modern technology are so great that, rather than using cast-off equipment from the northern hemisphere, the Chilean companies all use the very latest kit, often before it is established in the northern hemisphere. Phonecards are common, but not useable in other companies' phones. Note that the phone code for Santiago is 02, followed by seven digits; other numbers are six digits.

The Argentinian telephone system has been privatised, but instead of Chile's highly competitive system, the country was simply divided in two, with Telecom Argentina taking over the north and Telefónica the south. Buenos Aires was similarly split. The two companies' charges are the same, and their phonecards are interchangeable. Now CTI and Movicam-Bell South are introducing some real competition. Telecom Argentina now has a totally digital system, having invested US$6 billion over seven years, has doubled the number of household phones and linked up another 1,136 villages. Argentine phone codes now begin with 011 for Greater Buenos Aires, 02 for Buenos Aires and Mendoza provinces and those further south, and 03 for the northern provinces. Additionally every local number is now prefixed with 4, making them six or seven digits, or eight for Buenos Aires. Cheap rates operate 22.00– 08.00, with peak rates 10.00–13.00 Monday–Friday.

Calling from abroad, the code for Argentina is 54 (eg: from Britain dial 00541 for Buenos Aires), and for Chile 56 (eg: from Britain dial 00562 for Santiago). Calling home from Chile or Argentina you need to begin with the international access code 00 and then the appropriate country code (eg: 0044 for the UK or 001 for the USA).

Call centres (*Locutorios* or *Centros de Llamados*) are widespread in both countries, and often open until midnight. Mobiles are well established in both countries, but with patchy reception in most hiking areas, except high on some volcanoes where reception may be better. It is much cheaper to phone and fax abroad from Chile, but the **internet** is better established in Argentina, with more websites and email than Chile. There are not many cybercafés (certainly compared to Peru and Bolivia), but Entel, Telecom Argentina and Telefónica offices often have internet access, as do some *hospedajes*, especially in places like Bariloche and Pucón.

An alternative is to use a direct access number to your home telecom company, billing either your chargecard or the number you are calling.

Direct Access numbers:
Chile
BT Direct 800 360 066, 800 800 044
AT&T 800 225 288
MCI WorldPhone 800 207300 (CTC), 800 360 180 (Entel)

Argentina
BT Direct 0800 555401 (Telecom), 0800 6664400 (Telefónica)
AT&T 0800 555 4288 (Telecom), 0800 222 1288 (Telefónica)
MCI WorldPhone 0800 555 1002 (Telecom), 0800 222 6249 (Telefónica)

ACCOMMODATION
Accommodation in Chile and Argentina, like transport, has more in common with Europe or North America than with the rest of Latin America. This means that water usually comes out of taps, and toilets generally work in the manner to which you are accustomed (although in Chile you have to use a basket for used toilet paper). It also means that, as in Europe and North America, the price of accommodation has risen steeply in recent years. This is especially true of Argentina, where prices match or exceed those in Europe.

In both countries you will come across a bewildering variety of names to describe a place where you can sleep: *hotel, hostal, hostería, hospedaje, residencial*. On the whole, budget travellers will want to opt for one of the last two, or for a room in a private house, although *hoteles* are found in all price ranges. *Cabañas* (wooden chalets) are a Chilean institution. Occasionally you may decide to splash out on a really nice hotel, such as in the Torres del Paine National Park, in Chilean Patagonia.

In Chile, where you will find many places run by elderly ladies of German ancestry, breakfast is usually excellent and often included in the price of the room. In Argentina (and along the Carretera Austral), breakfast is almost always extra. In both countries prices rise noticeably as you move south, and are at their most

MATÉ

The Guaraní of northern Argentina have been drinking infusions of *Ilex paraguarensis* for centuries, and now it is a national obsession across Argentina (and Paraguay and Uruguay), with 300,000 tonnes a year being consumed. It is not popular in Chile, except in the far south; while the Argentinians believe that life is about sitting about with your friends, the Chileans prefer to get on with things. It was no surprise to hear an Argentinian techno song: *Quiero maté-té-té-té*. Maté was also used as a treatment for rheumatism in Edwardian England, but is now utterly forgotten there.

Maté is drunk from a gourd through a shared *bombilla* (silver straw). The gourd will be passed in order around a group. When it is your turn you should drink all that you are given and then pass it back to whoever is in charge of the hot water; only say 'thank you' when you have had enough. It is usually served bitter, although sugar can be added for beginners. Vacuum flasks have been a godsend to *maté* addicts, who can now get their fix on buses or planes, too.

exorbitant in the fashionable tourist resorts such as Calafate and San Martín de los Andes. Places more accustomed to backpackers, such as Bariloche, Puerto Natales and Pucón, offer cheap accommodation in shared rooms.

Official HI (Hostelling International – formerly IYHF) youth hostels are spreading fast in both Chile and Argentina. In most cases these are existng *hospedajes* that give a discount for HI card-holders. Contact the Red Argentina de Alojamiento para Jóvenes, Florida 835, Of. 319B, (C1005AAQ) Buenos Aires; tel: 011 4511 8712; fax: 4312 0089; raaj@hostels.org.ar; or the Asociación Chilena de Albergues Turísticos Juveniles, Hernando de Aguirre 201, Of. 602, Santiago; tel: 02 233 3220; achatj@hostelling.cl. There is also a network of less official hostels in Chile – see www.backpackersbest.cl, and ask for Scott's list if you stay at SCS Habitat in Santiago.

There is quite a range of possibilities for **camping**. In Argentina, where there are fewer cheap rooms, it is easy to camp for about US$4, while conversely in Chile, where rooms are cheaper, campsites are usually charged by the site or carload, discriminating against lone backpackers.

EATING AND DRINKING

In both Chile and Argentina, the main meal is usually at midday (after which everyone takes a couple of hours to sleep it off); this is when fixed-price menus will be available, so it is more economical to have your main meal then (in any case the evening meal is ridiculously late in Argentina). On the other hand, it is very difficult to find a snack on the move, especially if you are vegetarian. There is no sandwich culture, and even if you do find a cheese sandwich, it is usually with *jamón* (ham) or *ave* (chicken). You may just have to grab a few *pancitos* (bread rolls).

Breakfast consists of *pancitos*, jam and coffee; in Chilean *hospedajes* in particular, tea is usually available, with water kept hot in vacuum flasks. There is good coffee in Argentina, but in Chile it is always instant except in a few Santiago cafés.

A great treat is *dulce de leche*, a sort of liquid toffee/fudge spread (like the filling of banoffee pie) which can be eaten with bread and cheese or on its own. In Chile it is known as *manjar*. It was supposedly discovered accidentally by overcooking a milk and sugar rice pudding. Other typical sweet things include *dulce de batata* (sweet potato preserve), *dulce de zapallo* (pumpkin in syrup), and *dulce de membrillo* (quince jelly), eaten with cheese.

Jam, mayonnaise and *manjar* are sold in Chile in plastic refill sachets, while in Argentina jam comes in 1lb (450g) glass jars and there are no refills. Milk is UHT; only *chocomilk* and the yoghurty *leche cultivada* come in decently small quantities.

Most people do their shopping in **supermarkets** (which account for 65% of grocery sales in Argentina); the second largest branch of Walmart is in Buenos Aires, and Carrefour has 24 hypermarkets in Argentina and is moving into Santiago. Most supermarkets are open on Sundays, and you will find a free *guardería* for your luggage at the entrance. Remember to get your bread and fruit weighed before you get to the checkout. There will usually be a child to pack your purchases at the checkout, but you will not persuade them not to use lots of plastic bags. In Chile, in-store bakeries produce a range of bread and *pancitos*, including healthy *pan integral* and *pan centeno*; in Argentina it is hard to find anything but fluffy, white bread. In Chile almost everything is made by Nestlé, and they are also present, although not dominant, in Argentina. Argentine supermarkets have excellent cafeterias (where smokers are kept in glass cages) and toilets.

Vegetarians

Unusually for South America, Argentine salads are excellent and generally safe. And lovers of Italian food will be pleased to know that the pizzas of Buenos Aires are among the best in the world; pasta is also good here – paradoxically, vegetarians can fare better in the carnivore's paradise of Argentina than in Chile. Cannellini beans (or white kidney beans, fluffier, softer and juicier than haricots) were first cultivated in northern Argentina.

Local dishes
Chile

Seafood is the speciality here and the variety is enormous. Farmed fish can be a bit tasteless, but the wild seafood is superb. Our best recommendation is to try

OTHER CHILEAN DISHES	
Locos	abalones (giant shellfish)
Caldillo de congrio	conger eel soup
Paila chonchi	bouillabaisse or fish stew
Paila de huevos	scrambled eggs
Ostras	oysters
Mejillones or cholgas	mussels
Almejas	clams
Camarones	shrimp
Lomo	loin, steak in general
Pastel de choclo	casserole of meat, onions and olives with polenta (maize-meal mash) on top
Prieta	blood sausage stuffed with cabbage leaves
Parillada de mariscos	grilled mixed seafood
Curanto	typical Chilote stew of seafood, chicken, potatoes, beef, vegetables and pork

everything. *Congrio* (conger eel) is probably the most common type of fish; do not be put off by the name. Hilary Bradt recommends you beware of *erizos* (sea urchins), saying she has tasted nothing more disgusting; others find them delicious. A seafood dish that never fails to be scrumptious is *chupe de mariscos* (a thick shellfish soup often topped with cheese).

Of non-seafood dishes perhaps the most typical is *cazuela de ave*, a nutritious stew containing large chunks of chicken, potatoes, rice and maybe onions and green peppers. Also tasty are *empanadas*, turnovers or pasties with raisins, olives, meat, onions and peppers inside (or with cheese or apple). These can also be found in Argentina, where they are barely bite-sized.

In Punta Arenas and Tierra del Fuego you should definitely try *centolla* (southern king crab; *Lithodes antarcticus*). This enormous creature can measure a metre from leg to leg and weigh as much as 2kg, and tastes sublime.

You will find some fascinating fruits, such as *chirimoya* (custard apple), *alcayota* (which looks like melon but is more like a squash), and *nalca* (a rhubarb-like plant that you will see while hiking in the Lakes – see page 19). In Chiloé you might care to taste seaweeds such as *chochuyoyu*.

Argentina
The basis of the Argentine diet is *asado*, barbecued beef or (in the south, as in Chile) lamb. No fiesta or family gathering is complete without one, and even street workers regularly set up their charcoal fires for a lunchtime steak. In the northwest you will find ancient maize-based dishes such as *humitas* and *tamales*. In Buenos Aires you will find a highly cosmopolitan range of cuisines, and in Bariloche there are Germanic influences, and wonderful chocolates.

OTHER ARGENTINE DISHES

Puchero	pot-au-feu of meat, maize, potatoes and squash
Carbonada	ground beef with onions and tomatoes
Churrasco	thick cut beef steak
Parrillada	mixed grill
Milanesa	wienerschnitzel
Bife de chorizo	rump steak
Locro	a thick soup of maize, white beans, meat, pumpkin and herbs
Fiambre and matambre	fancy cold-cuts, especially good for picnics

Backpacking food
Food is a crucial factor in the enjoyment of a holiday. Contrary to what many people might think, meals for hiking and camping do not have to consist of crunchy pasta served with a half-hearted tomato sauce. With a bit of imagination and a few local ingredients picked along the way, a camping dinner, while simple, can be every bit as tasty as it would be back home, if not more so.

For backpacking it is best to take dehydrated food (about 0.5kg per day per head), which you can supplement with fresh fruit, bread and vegetables. If you are coming from home, it is a good idea to buy some provisions before leaving as there is likely to be more variety. You can also buy dried food in larger supermarkets in

Chile and Argentina. Useful items include dried vegetables (peas, peppers, mushrooms, onions and potatoes); porridge oats and/or muesli; dried prawns (also from Chinese stores); packet soups; pasta, rice or noodles (noodles cook fastest, using less fuel); milk and custard powder; tea, coffee and hot chocolate; powdered fruit drinks; muesli/granola bars; tubes of tomato puree; and dried fruit such as apricots, prunes and peaches (great for nibbling along the way, but heavy). Take empty film canisters filled with pepper, salt and mixed herbs.

If you like jams, you will find an incredible variety made from local fruits in the Lakes District, together with excellent honey (*miel*). Make sure you have a leakproof container. Remember that even at rest you should drink two litres of water a day. (See also page 18 for food that can be gathered for free.)

Wine
Chile

If you are not yet aware of Chilean wines, I don't know where you have been hiding. They are excellent and rapidly gaining international recognition. The first grapes, planted in the 1550s, were Muscatel and Pais varieties, producing a very rough wine for communion; then, just before *Phylloxera* infected the European vineyards in 1863, French varieties were introduced, especially Cabernet Sauvignon and Sauvignon Blanc. These produced most export wines until recently, while the domestic market had to be satisfied with Pais. Now stainless-steel technology (with oak ageing) is capturing fresh fruit flavours and producing typical 'New World' wines that leap out of the glass – full fruity wines at a good price – leading to a boom in exports.

Chile's reputation was based in the past on red wines (*vino tinto*); now elegant, but good-value Chardonnay and Sauvignon Blanc whites (*vino blanco*) are gaining the same recognition. New red wine varieties (Merlot and Pinot Noir) are improving with every vintage, producing reviews such as 'pure pungent gum-staining fun', and taking over from Cabernet Sauvignon. Winemakers are likely to deal with the current boom better than last time, when quality plummeted as production was stretched to meet demand. Instead Santa Carolina, Concha y Toro, San Pedro and Santa Rita (who together account for 80% of Chile's wine production) are investing in Argentine vineyards, at a quarter of Chilean land prices, as are multinational drinks giants Pernod-Ricard, Diageo and Allied-Domeq. However, domestic consumption is falling dramatically, from 60 litres a year to 28 litres (just three bottles a month).

From north to south the wine districts are: the Aconcagua valley (north of San Felipe), the Casablanca valley (northwest of Santiago, known for fine whites), the Maipo valley (southwest of Santiago), the Rapel valley (Rancagua to San Fernando), the Curicó valley (Curicó to Talca), and the Maule valley (south of Talca). Most of the more prestigious houses (Concha y Toro, Cousiño-Macul, Santa Carolina, Errázuriz) are based near Pirque in the Maipo valley, just south of Santiago, but most of their grapes are now actually grown to the south in the Rapel, Curicó and Maule areas. Harvest time is February and March, which is the best time to visit.

Argentina

In Argentina, red wine is a standard accompaniment to any meat dish. However, it is rarely taken in large quantities, and often mixed with mineral water to make a refreshing, long drink. White wine is good, but less common. Argentina is the world's fifth (until recently the third) largest producer by volume, about 95% of it for domestic consumption; of the other 5%, three-quarters goes to Spain. It is mostly old-fashioned, 'aged to within an inch of extinction in ancient wooden barrels' and not exportable, although now 'flying winemakers' and new technology, such as temperature-controlled stainless-steel vats, are producing modern, fruity styles. As in Chile, consumption is falling, from 25 litres/year in the 1960s to 10 litres/year in 1999.

Argentina has greater climatic diversity than Chile and probably has more potential to produce really great wines. The Tupungato area, south of Mendoza, has new cool-climate vineyards that may start to produce really good Sauvignons Blancs and Chardonnays. Some distinctive varieties are Malbec, Criolla (similar to the Chilean Pais), the Spanish Tempranillo and Torrontes (producing an aromatic white almost like sherry), and Italian Sangiovese. The centre of the Argentine wine industry is Mendoza, producing 10 million hectolitres a year, 70% of national output. The huge *bodegas* (processing plants) can be visited.

Other drinks

Pisco and *aguardiente* are both clear brandies. *Pisco*, made with grapes from the Illapel-Copiapó area (especially the Elqui valley variety), is the Chilean national drink, and available in supermarkets. *Pisco Sour* is made with egg white, icing sugar and lemon juice, and can be found ready-mixed in supermarkets. *Aguardiente* is less good, but is used in *colo de mono* (monkey's tail), a Christmas liqueur like Irish coffee, made with milk, coffee and cinnamon. *Chicha* is partly fermented grape juice made and consumed locally.

Beer (*cerveza*) is the most popular alcoholic drink in both countries, with almost all those available of the lager family; *malta* is a brown beer, but it is rather sharp and gassy. Draught beer is known as *Schopp* (from the French *une chope*), and is cheap and refreshing. Chile's largest brewery is Cerveceras Unidas, now expanding into Argentina, too; its most ubiquitous product in Chile is *Cristal*. Argentina's national brew (15% owned by Heineken) is *Quilmes*.

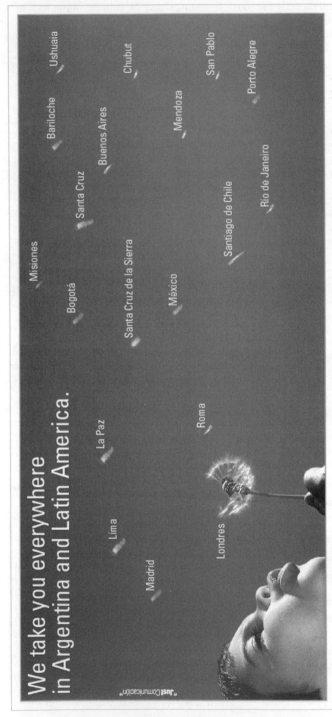

Chile: Background

HISTORY

It has long been supposed that humans first crossed into North America over the Bering Strait landbridge about 60,000 years ago, and headed south, crossing into South America around 15,000 years ago and reaching Tierra del Fuego approximately 4,000 years later. However, remains about 12,500 years old (about a thousand years older than expected) have now been found in Chile, and there may be much older remains. This has led some to suppose that there was an earlier crossing of the landbridge, or that Polynesian seafarers were the first to settle here. Even so, it is clear that the indigenous population is essentially descended from those who came overland. By 5,000 years ago they were cultivating maize, beans and squash, and then moved to higher altitudes where they cultivated potatoes and domesticated llamas and alpacas. Other groups lived along the coast by fishing the immensely rich Humboldt Current. By the 15th century, the far north was settled by the Aymara people, with the Atacameños to the south of the Río Loa, while south of present-day Santiago were the Araucanian peoples, of whom the most important were the Mapuche. To the south of the icefields lived various small groups, such as the Kaweshkar, Yámana and Selk'nam (see page 339 for further details). The Inca invaded in the second half of the 15th century and conquered the northern half of Chile (although they left few traces), but they were unable to defeat the Mapuche, who were not finally absorbed into Chile until the 19th century.

Facts become a bit more certain from 1520 when Fernão de Magalhães (Ferdinand Magellan) discovered the straits that bear his name en route to the Spice Islands of Asia. The first attempt to settle Chile, however, came from the north, when Diego de Almagro led what might be called a military exploration in 1535–7. In 1540, Pedro de Valdivia led a more serious invasion, founding the city of Santiago in 1541, although the Mapuche destroyed the city later that year, and rebelled again in the 1550s (killing Valdivia in 1553) and 1598–1608. In 1641 the Parlamento de Quilín established a frontier along the Río Biobío, south of which the Mapuche were left alone until the 19th century. Colonial society was based on ruthless exploitation of the continent's gold and silver reserves as well as of its native populace. The native peoples were swiftly decimated by Old-World diseases such as measles, smallpox and influenza, but a mestizo (mixed-blood) population rapidly replaced them, boosted by settlers from the Basque country and elsewhere. Spain's empire fell apart because mestizos and criollos (native-born Hispanics) resented the systematic exploitation of the colony, and above all the way its economy was stifled and prevented from developing. Things came to a head after Napoleon's invasion of Spain in 1808, which left the colonies uncertain who was supposed to be ruling them. Independence was declared on September 18 1810 and after minor scraps, José de San Martín led his Army of the Andes across the mountains in 1817, drove out the Royalists, and left his second-in-command,

Bernardo O'Higgins, to found the new nation, formally created in 1818. The socio-economic system remained largely unchanged and the 1833 constitution, which survived until 1925, led to a highly centralised and amazingly stable state. The national territory was consolidated, extending by 1879 nearly to Antofagasta in the north, and to Chiloé in the south.

The key event in Chile's development was the War of the Pacific from 1879–83, which arose from the mining of nitrates (used in fertilisers) in Bolivia's Atacama province by Anglo-Chilean companies. A tax dispute led to Chile declaring war on both Bolivia and Peru and trouncing them both; Chile took the Atacama from Bolivia, and Tarapacá, Arica and Tacna provinces from Peru, eventually returning Tacna in 1929.

Control of the world's nitrate reserves, and foreign (largely British) investment led to rapid economic growth and the rise of a new, wealthy middle class. Railways, roads and ports were built, together with an excellent education system. The national myth is of a Nordic (rather than Latin) people, living in a temperate climate, well educated, organised and disciplined, but this is only partially true. German colonists arrived in the second half of the 19th century, but almost all settled in the south; the climate is, of course, extremely hot and dry in the north and extremely wet and windy in the south, and in fact education was not compulsory until the 1920s, before which the literacy rate was not at all impressive. Those who did well did very well indeed, but the gap widened steadily between them and the rest of the population, and attempts by presidents such as José Manuel Balmaceda (1886–91) and Arturo Alessandri Palma (1920–25) to spread the benefits of economic success were blocked by the conservative congress.

The opening of the Panama Canal in 1914 led to Chile losing a great deal of passing trade, and the development of synthetic fertilisers during World War I undermined the nitrates business; copper mining (funded by North Americans) replaced it, but the following decades are generally seen as a period of stagnation and political turmoil, fueled by left-wing demands for land reform. Chile was the only Latin-American country not to declare war on the Axis during World War II, a fact perhaps not unrelated to its significant German population, while increased demand for copper boosted the economy. In 1958 the Socialists, led by Salvador Allende, and reformist Christian Democrats, headed by Eduardo Frei, both did well in elections, splitting the vote and allowing the conservatives to win with less than a third of the vote. In 1964 Frei won the election and began to introduce reforms. He raised hopes he could not meet, while doing enough to infuriate the upper classes; an increasingly bitter and polarised society elected Allende president in 1970.

Allende nationalised the copper, banking, railway, telephone and other industries, and raised public spending to boost the economy. However, industrialists, afraid of nationalisation, refused to co-operate, while peasants seized land, leading to a similar response from landowners. Meanwhile the US blocked foreign investment and capital fled abroad, the economy collapsed (aided by CIA subversion and general strikes), inflation soared, and left-wing guerrilla groups (founded by upper-middle class students in Concepción) agitated for more sweeping changes. It was no surprise to anyone when the military overthrew Allende on September 11 1973, but the savagery of the coup and the repression that followed was breathtaking. Allende probably committed suicide as his palace was bombed, 3,000–5,000 suspected leftists were killed and between 40,000 and 95,000 were imprisoned (and usually beaten or tortured) at some point over the next three years. The army's leader, General Augusto Pinochet, became president of a so-called 'authoritarian democracy', presiding over a repressive regime which quelled the guerrillas, banned political activity and trade unions and adopted rigorous free-market economic policies, slashing state spending, taxes and tariffs. In 1982, a debt crisis and high oil prices led to economic collapse, in which the peso fell by 40%, GDP by 14%, and unemployment rose by 33%; the banks were bailed out, and with the help of the IMF and the AFPs (private pension funds – see page 58) the economy recovered.

POLITICS

Having introduced Thatcherite economics before Thatcher, Chile then returned to democracy before the Soviet satellites and South Africa made the same transition. In a plebiscite in 1988, Pinochet's bid for a further eight years as president was rejected and an election was held the following year. The election was won by the Christian Democrat, Patricio Aylwin of the Concertación (Coalition of Parties for Democracy), and in 1990 he became president in a peaceful transfer of power, thanks to all kinds of guarantees to the military and restrictions on rapid change. Pinochet remained as commander-in-chief of the military, and finally retired in March 1998, becoming a life senator, guaranteeing immunity from prosecution. Even now the civilian president must choose the commander-in-chief from a list drawn up by the military, in effect the retiring

FRONTIER DISPUTES

In order to beat Peru and Bolivia without interference, Chile had to renounce its claims to much of Patagonia to Argentina. Their 1881 treaty stated that the frontier 'shall run over the highest summits of the cordillera which divide the waters, and shall pass between the sources of streams flowing on either side to the 52nd parallel' (south of Puerto Natales). Chile was given a thin strip along the northern shore of the Magellan Straits, and the Isla Grande of Tierra del Fuego was split north-south between Chile and Argentina. The islands to the east of Tierra del Fuego went to Argentina, and those to its west and those south of the Beagle Channel to Chile.

In fact, however, the watershed is well to the east of the line of the highest peak and it was not defined whether the Beagle Channel continued eastwards from the east end of Isla Navarino, north of Picton, Nueva and Lennox islands, or swung southwards, to the west of the islands. In 1896 Britain's Queen Victoria was asked to arbitrate and sent the vice-president of the Royal Geographical Society, Sir Thomas Holdich, to have a look; his compromise of 1902 favoured Argentina to the north and Chile to the south.

This was accepted until the possibility of oil and fishing rights came up. In the 1950s, with oil being produced in Tierra del Fuego, Argentina raised its claim that the Beagle Channel swung south, which would give it a large chunk of the Southern Ocean; in 1965 a Chilean border guard was shot dead, and events escalated to a near-war in 1968. In 1971 Britain's Queen,

commander-in-chief himself. A Commission for Truth and Reconciliation (*Comisión para la Verdad y Reconciliación*) was set up to document human rights abuses under Pinochet, but an amnesty law passed in 1978 means that the military has immunity from prosecution, with one exception. This concerned the murder in 1976 of Allende's foreign minister, Orlando Letelier, in Washington DC, for which Pinochet's right-hand man, the head of the notorious DINA secret police, Manuel Contreras, and his deputy Pedro Espinosa have been imprisoned. In addition the Argentines have jailed a former DINA agent for life, for his part in the murder in Buenos Aires of Allende's army chief Carlos Prats and his wife.

In 1994 Aylwin was succeeded by Eduardo Frei Ruiz-Tagle, son of the 1960s president Eduardo Frei Montalva, who continued the same policies of free-market economics, though with a boost in social spending, and a gradual transition to an open society. He was a member of the Christian Democrats, the largest party within the Concertación, but the Socialists had their turn in the 1999 elections, with the Blairite Ricardo Lagos (Minister of Public Works) becoming the Concertación's candidate. His campaign was very complacent, but he just beat Joaquin Lavin of the right-wing Alianza por Chile in a run-off in January 2000.

In October 1998, while in London for medical treatment, Pinochet had been arrested on a Spanish warrant for extradition on charges of being responsible for the deaths of Spanish citizens after the coup. He was held in comfortable house arrest while a long legal wrangle (which made legal history in Britain too) dragged on. The right wing was obsessed with the Pinochet issue, but Lagos kept his distance and campaigned mainly on economic issues. In March 2000 Pinochet was this time Elizabeth II, was again asked to arbitrate, and in 1977 the decision went against Argentina, which promptly refused to accept it. In the 'Six-Day Crisis' of December 1978 the two countries came even closer to war, and this time the Pope was asked to judge. Again he decided in favour of Chile, but south of the islands the border now swung back to the west, giving Argentina more of the Southern Ocean. In 1985 this was accepted by both countries.

In 1991 presidents Menem and Aylwin decided to settle all 24 remaining border disputes; 22 were decided by a bilateral commission, and in 1996 a Latin-American tribunal gave the Laguna del Desierto (see page 323) to Argentina. Only the Southern Patagonian Icecap (known in Argentina as the Hielos Continentales and in Chile as the Campos de Hielo Sur) remained, and a split was agreed along a straight line, giving 1,238km² to Argentina and 1,057km² to Chile, as it was of course impossible to locate the highest peaks under the ice. However, neither country's congress ratified the deal – the Chilean military being particularly nationalistic after the 'defeat' on the Laguna del Desierto.

The FACh (Chilean Air Force) sets up a base every summer on the disputed area of ice, near Cerro FitzRoy, and the Chilean IGM has produced a map which has increased the heights of the Mariano Moreno range. Nevertheless the politicians are creeping towards a settlement, as their economies and societies become more integrated, and in mid-1997 there were even joint Chilean-Argentine military exercises.

released on medical grounds and flew home to a grand reception from the army. While he was held in Britain, the official Chilean position, stated by both Frei and Lagos, had been that cases against him should be dealt with in Chile, and when he returned the dam burst, and there are now over 200 suits against Pinochet, including various requests for extradition. Judge Juan Guzmán has pursued an implacable investigation of the 'caravan of death' (a mobile squad held responsible for 76 deaths immediately after the coup), holding Pinochet responsible. Pinochet was eventually stripped of his immunity by the Supreme Court, but few believe he will be ever face trial, on health grounds (he has diabetes, a pacemaker, and mild senility, and has suffered several strokes). However, the power of the army has been broken and Chile's democracy has ultimately been strengthened.

The right-wing Renovación Nacional party is pro-Pinochet, but is split over reform of the 1980 constitution, above all the provisions for designated senators-for-life, chosen largely from retired generals, admirals and Supreme Court judges, thus building in a right-wing bias, at least until all of Pinochet's appointees have died. Although Chilean society is in many ways conservative, this issue may keep the right-wing from power for many years.

ECONOMICS

The government has stuck with neo-liberal, free-market economic policies, with great success. Since 1984, growth has averaged at least 6% per year, with low inflation and unemployment; the proportion of the population in poverty has fallen from 40% in 1990 to 28% in 1997, even though the gap between rich and poor has continued to grow. The two keys to the Chilean boom are the AFPs (private pension funds), introduced in 1981 and now worth US$29 billion, which have invested heavily in Chilean industry, making big profits and encouraging yet higher investment; and the huge reserves of minerals, above all copper.

In 1997 foreign investment (principally Canadian) in copper mining rose to about US$1 billion and copper exports rose almost 9% to an estimated 3.4 million tonnes, worth US$7 billion. In 1995 the private sector produced 1.37m tonnes, overtaking the state-owned Codelco for the first time; by 1999 production had risen to 4.4m t (40% of world output), only a third of it from Codelco. The state takes almost US$1 billion in tax from the copper industry, and since 1980, the military has taken 10% of copper revenues, making it the best equipped in the hemisphere. World copper consumption has risen 10% in five years, while Chile's output has risen 57%, so that over-production may depress world prices. Mining accounts for 8% of GDP and 10% of exports (worth US$8bn) and roughly a million jobs in all, at an average salary of US$1,000 a month, over twice the national average. Codelco runs the four mines nationalised by Allende, at Chuquicamata (the world's largest open-cast pit, 4km by 2km and 600m deep), El Teniente (including the Esmeralda mine, opened in 1997), Andina, and El Salvador.

Gold mining is also important, with the El Indio mine in the Elqui valley and the new Pascua deposit both producing around 380,000oz a year. Cerro Casale, at the southern end of the Atacama, produces 190,000oz a year, set to grow to 500,000oz, and El Refugio produces 300,000oz.

In 1995 12% of Chilean trade was with the Mercosur common market (set up in 1995) of Argentina, Brazil, Uruguay and Paraguay, and in 1996 Chile signed an association agreement, joining its free-trade zone but not its customs zone. It is estimated that this will create 100,000 new jobs, but the huge, flat estates of the other Mercosur countries are far more efficient than Chile's farms. Chile is also keen to join NAFTA, but as the US Congress has blocked fast-track entry Chile has negotiated separate deals with Canada and Mexico, as well as with the European Union, and is negotiating with Panama, Peru and Costa Rica. In 1997, tariffs on imports from other countries were in any case cut from 11% (already the lowest in Latin America) to 4%. Globalisation works both ways, with Chilean industry investing abroad, above all in Argentina.

Tourism is growing fast (about 12% pa) and is also crucial to the economy, producing 4% of GDP and 7% of foreign trade. From 624,000 foreign visitors in 1988, numbers have risen to 1.74 million in 2000, yielding just over US$1 billion. Over half the foreign tourists come from Argentina, but the fastest-growing sector is from Europe, now 10% of the market. In addition there are between three and four million domestic tourists per year. Other so-called 'non-traditional exports' include fruit (worth US$1.56 billion in 1997), flowers, and salmon (US$650 million in 1997); farming in floating cages was introduced in 1979, and Chile is now the world's second exporter of salmon after Norway. Most of it goes to Japan, although Chilean salmon has 45% of the US market. Wine exports have also boomed, from under US$10 million in the early 1980s to US$412.2 million (216.2 million litres) in 1997; exports to the UK doubled in 1995 and 1996, accounting for about 10% of exports and 2.8% of the UK market.

In 1997 inflation was 5%, unemployment fell to 6.1%, and GDP grew by 6.8%; however, Chile was especially vulnerable to the Asian slump, which forced the price of copper down by a third. Exports crashed, unemployment rose to 11.5%

and GDP shrank in 1999; However, there has since been a strong recovery. By January 2000 unemployment was down to 8.4%, and GDP grew by 5% in 2000 and is expected to grow by 5.5% in 2001.

CONSERVATION AND NATIONAL PARKS

Forestry protection has a long history in Chile: the araucaria (monkey-puzzle tree) has been protected since the 18th century, originally in order to ensure a supply of timber for the Spanish navy. Nevertheless, other trees have been mercilessly logged and burnt; the last scented sandalo tree (on Juan Fernández) had been felled by 1908. The first forestry reserve was created at Villarrica in 1912, and the Vicente Pérez Rosales National Park was created in 1926. The national park system is to this day part of Conaf, the National Forestry Corporation, which produces some distortions – there is no forestry north of Santiago, after all, but there are eight national parks in this area. Due in part to the boom in tourism (60% of foreign tourists visit a national park) and in part to a growth in environmentalist pressure domestically, there are now moves towards the creation of a dedicated parks service. The ecologists of Deproden, the Natural Resource Protection Department of the Agriculture and Livestock Service (SAG), are based at Bulnes 140 in Santiago, close to Conaf's new Unidad de Gestion de Patrimonio Silvestre, and they are working more closely together.

The country's various types of protected area are classified within the National System of State-Protected Wilderness Areas (SNASPE), and includes 33 national parks, 47 forestry reserves, and 13 natural monuments, a total of over 14.3 million hectares, 19% of the area of continental Chile (ie: excluding Antarctica). In 1980 there were in fact 51 national parks and 52 reserves; since then ten national parks and 20 reserves have been abandoned and eight national parks reclassified as natural monuments; but the area of national parks has increased by 22% to 8.38 million hectares, and the area of forestry reserves has decreased by 23% to 5.47 million hectares. More to the point, there is a better spread of protected ecosystems, but even so, 83.6% of protected land is in the 11th and 12th Regions, where no-one else particularly wants the land. Over half of Chile's evergreen forest is protected, but only 0.9% of Chile's desert (170,237ha), and 0.6% of its sclerophyllous (drought-resistant) scrub and woodland. In 1984, of 85 ecosystems in Chile, 28 were not included in SNASPE (and nor were seven of Chile's 11 endangered species of tree). This led to the creation between 1993 and 1996 of new national parks protecting such specific ecosystems as *desierto montano de la cordillera de Domeyko* (montane desert of the Domeyko range, in Llullaillaco), *estepa arbustiva de la pre-puna* (shrubby pre-puna steppe, in Licancábur), *estepa desértica de los salares andinos* (desert steppe of the Andean saltpans, in Nevado de Tres Cruces), and *desierto costero de Huasco* (Huasco coastal desert, in Llanos de Challe), and also of ten new reserves. In the south the only gap is now *bosque patagónico de coníferas* (Patagonian forest with conifers, around Futaleufú).

These are, of course, welcome developments, but totally inadequate as long as they remain so woefully underfunded; of Conaf's total budget of about US$40 million, just US$2.1 million is designated for national parks. The immense Laguna San Rafael National Park (1.7 million hectares) has just two rangers, and others are equally understaffed, with just 375 actual staff against a need for 533. Thus when Conaf bosses talk grandly of a 'minimum impact policy', what they mean is that they are unable to keep paths open beyond those to the most obvious and popular lakes and waterfalls. One response to this is the policy of contracting services such

GIVING SOMETHING BACK

If you are interested in voluntary work in Chile, the bodies listed below will be pleased to offer guidance:

Pressure groups

Chile's oldest and best-established environmental pressure group is:

Codeff (*Comité Nacional pro Defensa de Flora y Fauna*), the local arm of Friends of the Earth, at Bilbao 691, Providencia, Santiago (casilla 3675; tel: 02 251 0262; fax: 251 8433; info@codeff.mic.cl; www.netup.cl/~codeff). In addition to campaigning, Codeff owns some reserves such as Alto Huemul, near Chillán.

CIPMA (*Centro de Investigación y Planificación del Medio Ambiente*), at Holanda 1109, Providencia, Santiago (casilla 16362; tel: 334 1091; fax: 334 1095; info@cipma.cl) is more political and academic than Codeff and less concerned with public awareness. It produces three publications, and organises a conference every three years.

Defensores del Bosque Chileno (Defenders of the Chilean Forest), Diagonal Oriente 1413, Nuñoa, Santiago (tel: 204 1914; fax: 209 2527; bosquech@entelchile net; www.bosquechile.cl) works to protect native forest.

Casa de la Paz (House of Peace), Antonia López de Bello 024, Bellavista, Santiago (tel: 737 4280, fax: 777 5065; casapaz@netup.cl; www.casapaz.cl), houses *Acción Ciudadana por el Medio Ambiente* (Citizen's Action for the Environment) which welcomes volunteers for clean-ups and other work parties.

Ecocentro, Seminario 774, Ñuñoa, Santiago – this houses a variety of bodies, such as the *Instituto de Ecología Política* (tel: 274 6192; fax: 223 4522;

as kiosks, campsites and boat-hire to outside concessions, which both frees Conaf staff and brings in revenue (US$117,000 in 1992, compared to US$460,000 in entry fees, and far more by now). Conaf is becoming more decentralised, with parks being allowed to manage their own concessions and keep more of their own revenue. Unfortunately, this currently means bad managers are given more power, but there will no doubt be a shakeout before long.

Entrance fees already vary considerably, but are generally reasonable; what is unfair to *mochileros* (lone backpackers) is the Chilean habit of charging by the site or carload for camping. Given that some of the back-country trails are increasingly overgrown and blocked by fallen branches and trees, you may even prefer to find areas outside the national park system where roads are half built (such as the Exploradores and San Lorenzo areas in Aysén) and explore them before they get developed.

Conaf established an ecotourism unit in 1996 (defining it as (*sic*) 'the search contact with natural environments little altered by man, respecting what is indigenous to and representative of the country'), but it still seems to be thinking largely in terms of business concessions. It remains to be seen how this develops.

In Santiago, Conaf has a shop at Paseo Bulnes 291 (open Mon–Thur 09.30–17.30, Fri 09.30–16.30), where you can buy leaflet maps for 100 pesos iep@reuna.cl; www.iepe.org); *Observatorio Latinoamericano de Conflictos Ambientales* (tel: 274 5713, fax: 223 4522; oca@rdc.cl; www.relca.net/olca); *Programa Chile Sustentable* (tel: 209 7028; fax: 2640 4721; chilesus@rdc.cl; www.chilesustentable.cl); and *Renace* (*Red Nacional de Acción Ecológica*; tel: 223 4483; fax: 225 8909; renace@rdc.cl; www.renace.cl).

Greenpeace Eleodoro Flores 2424, Ñuñoa, Santiago (tel: 343 7788; fax: 204 0162; www.greenpeace.cl) welcomes volunteers.

Government bodies

Conaf Bulnes 291, Santiago (tel: 390 0125; www.iusanet.cl/conaf) The National Forestry Corporation, in charge of national parks (see above); contact the *Patrimonio Silvestre* (Natural Heritage) department on: 390 0000.

Conama (*Comisión Nacional del Medio Ambiente*), Obispo Donoso 6, Santiago (tel: 240 5600, fax: 244 1262; www.conama.cl) is essentially a bureaucratic body which contracts out field investigation to academics; it has a useful *Centro de Documentación* (open Mon–Thur 10.00–12.30, 15.00–17.30). It was seen as pro-industry, but since Adriana Hoffman (founder of *Defensores del Bosque Chileno*) took control it has played a more positive role.

Conicyt (*Comisión Nacional de Investigación Científica y Tecnológica*) is a research body, publishing excellent books such as *Diversidad Biologica de Chile* (ed. Javier A Simonetti, 1995).

The **Consejo de Defensa del Estado** (State Defence Council), under the redoubtable Clara Szczaranski, is a sort of ombudsbody, which is now extending its remit to cover ecological crimes.

(US$0.25), and a guidebook to the national parks (US$11); this is also available in English (US$14), but only covers the major parks. There is also a small library downstairs.

A few private reserves are appearing outside the SNASPE system: these include the Pumalín Park (page 249), Cañi (page 172), Alto Huemul (page 156), Seno Otway (page 269) and Yendegaia (page 326). Another is planned at Palos Quemados, west of the Cuesta El Melón (on the PanAmerican north from Santiago towards La Ligua). A new legal category, Santuario de la Naturaleza, has been devised for these private reserves. In addition, the government has granted its first conservation concession, for the management of part of Isla Magdalena, north of Puerto Aysén (not the Isla Magdalena penguin reserve off Punta Arenas), to Doug Tompkins of Pumalín; Codeff (see *Pressure groups* above) is also managing part of the Río Simpson reserve as a huemul sanctuary. Chile's first marine parks are now being created off Chiloé and Isla Choros. Conama is leading the **Sendero de Chile** project, for a high-quality trail (for cyclists and horses as well as hikers) from Visviri (on the Bolivian border) to Tierra del Fuego, along the precordillera; the pilot stretch opened in 2001 in the Conguillío National Park. Thankfully, the many minefields laid along the borders during various frontier disputes are being cleared anyway.

FORESTRY

Forestry is booming in southern Chile, another aspect of the country's highly 'successful' exploitation of its natural resources (in 1998 the WWF ranked Chile third worst in the world for depredation of natural resources). There are two aspects to this, on the one hand the logging of native forest and on the other the spread of plantations of exotic species. Perhaps 15m hectares (ha), a third of the original area of native forest, had been lost by 1955; another 700,000ha was lost in 1984–94. A survey in 1998 put the total of native forest at just over 13.4 million ha (17.8% of the national area, and 76.5% of the total forested area) rather than the previous assumption of 8.47 million ha; 70% of this is in the 10th and 11th Regions. In 1997 Codeff claimed that 120,000ha of native woodland is being lost every year, and it is clear that the rate is accelerating, perhaps doubling in the last decade. This is almost entirely due to the boom in the export of *astillas* (woodchips), largely to Japan, for the production of computer paper; this is highly controversial because Chile is the only country in the world to make its lowest-value product from its highest-quality wood, rather than as a by-product. Woodchip exports were 76,000m^3 in 1986, all from pine plantations, but rose to 2.5 million m^3 in 1995, worth US$136.3 million, and 62% of it from native forest. Production rose but the price fell so that in 1999 woodchips accounted for US$135m of a total US$2bn forestry exports; in that year tourism brought in just over US$1bn, a rather specious comparison that leads some to assume that forest tourism could replace logging. Certainly Chile should export only value-added products from its native forest.

Plantations of exotic species cover 2.2 million hectares, which is set to double in the next 20 years, thanks to generous subsidies; currently at least 60,000ha is planted per year, about half of the area cleared. About 90% of this is Monterrey pine (pino insigne; *Pinus radiata*), which was introduced in the 1880s and grows faster here than anywhere else (in the Lakes it is ready for harvesting in 15 years), and covers a far greater area than in its native California. There is also eucalyptus (8%), which is suited to the drier land to the north of Araucanía, and Oregon pine, which can cope with snow, to the south, and Conaf is now planning to plant large areas of poplars further to the north. This is the truly productive sector of the industry; forestry produces 3% of Chile's GDP and 2% of employment (0.1% in native forestry). Forest products are Chile's third most valuable export (11.8% of total exports), increasing by 22% each year over the last decade, and expected to increase from US$2bn in 1999 to US$3bn in 2010.

This area is home to many Mapuche, whose villages have become islands in exotic forest of pine which acidifies and dries the land (and seems to absorb less CO$_2$ than native forest); this is the poorest area in Chile, with 36% living in poverty. Not surprisingly there is increasing activism for indigenous land rights, fuelled not just by plantation forestry but also by dam-building on the Biobío (see pages 161–2).

The greatest recent controversy was the Río Condor project of the US Trillium Corporation to log subantarctic woodland for woodchips. They own 300,000ha in southern Tierra del Fuego, most in Chile, of which they intend to log 103,000ha, supposedly 'in order to protect' the rest better. This was opposed by an alliance of pressure groups, who succeeded in having the project's initial authorisation by CONAMA (National Environment Commission) declared illegal. This was taken to the Supreme Court and eventually approved by the Lagos government (though a similar plan in Chiloé was rejected). Trillium had appointed a Scientific

Committee including most of Chile's leading biologists (Mary Kalin Arroyo, Claudio Donoso, Edmundo Pisano), who not surprisingly reported against the project; Dr Jerry Franklin, one of the most respected US forestry ecologists, was appointed *fideicomisario* (a sort of environmental ombudsman), and has persuaded Trillium to reduce the annual cut, produce more lumber rather than *astillas*, and bought the disused Magallánica de Bosques mill, in Bahía Catalina, near Punta Arenas. Unfortunately they damaged a listed *conchal* (indigenous shell-pile, up to 5,000 years old) building an access road, which created quite a fuss. Trillium is also talking of ecotourism in the areas opened up by them, though any true ecologist will wish the roads had never been built. Now it has been revealed that the Chilean state sold the land to Trillium for just five dollars a hectare, less than half the fair price; Trillium agreed to pay the balance as a "donation" to the town of Puerto Porvenir, but the payment has not been made.

However, an even more disastrous forest project has now appeared: the Cascada Chile scheme, which will devastate the Lakes District. Half-owned by Boise Cascade (already notorious in the USA), it proposes the world's largest woodchip mill at Ilque, on the coast near Puerto Montt. Rather than buying forest, it will rely on private land-owners to supply it with wood, to produce 700,000m³ pa of oriented-strand board, for home-building in the USA. The Camino Costero Sur, about 200km of new road from Corral to Maullín, is bound to lead to logging anyway, and is controversial due to the government undertaking Environmental Impact Assessments only for the short stretches where the road passes through protected areas.

There is further controversy over the effects of planned cellulose plants in the Valdivia area, due to the effects of toxic effluents on fishing and tourism. Forest fires are a problem, increasing three-fold between 1994 and 1998 to an average 23,000ha per year, mostly in the pine plantations of Arauco province, where Mapuche land-rights activists are blamed. Some of it is still due to arson by forest owners who would rather sell fire-damaged alerce wood than have protected trees growing on their land. Desertification, partly due to deforestation, has become a major environmental problem, affecting 40m ha (over half of Chile's area), of which 33m are highly eroded.

Pinochet's constitution guarantees the right to a clean environment, but the free-market ethos of the government and business has meant that this has been ignored. The mining industry has been one of the worst offenders; copper smelters produce 12 times as much sulphur dioxide pollution as in the US. Codelco are to spend US$360m over five years on environmental measures at Chuquicamata and El Teniente; everyone living at Chuqui' is to be moved to Calama by 2002, and the mine itself is to close in about 20 years. In Arica there is a lot of lead and arsenic contamination, and 20% of children are affected by lead poisoning. There is also massive use of pesticides (12,000t/yr), producing birth defects in seasonal workers and very high levels of DDT (2,788ppb) and lindane (773ppb) in fish in the Biobío. There is a growing rubbish-disposal problem, with Santiago producing 6,000 tonnes a day (over 1kg per head); even Antarctica produces 127 tonnes a year.

One of the world's leading environmental economists is Manfred Max-Neef, who stood as presidential candidate in 1993 for the green political grouping *Gente en Movimiento* and took 400,000 votes, 7% of the total. It cannot be said that there is mass support for green politics (there is not even much interest in recycling), but public awareness is growing (in one poll 89% of those asked said environmental issues should be tackled), and Max-Neef has now been appointed senator, and chancellor of Valdivia's Universidad Austral.

The founder of Defensores del Bosque Chileno, Adriana Hoffman, was recognised in 1999 as one of the world's 25 leading protectors of the ecosystem. She is pretty high-profile, writing a weekly column in *El Mercurio de Santiago* until Lagos put her in charge of Conama, equivalent to Minister for the Environment. Development is still the priority in Chile, but there are signs that a more sustainable approach may now be followed.

Chile: Practical Information

INFORMATION

The national tourism agency is **Sernatur** (www.sernatur.cl), which has offices in Santiago (see below) and in most other cities. Many towns have their own tourist offices. Tourism promotion abroad is handled by the **Chile Tourism Promotion Corporation**, Santa Beatriz 84B, Santiago (tel: 02 235 0105; fax: 235 3384; www.prochile.cl); most embassies have an office, known as ProChile. In addition you can usually get information from LanChile, and on the internet. The best general guidebook on Chile is the annual Turistel publication (no author named), which has excellent maps and lots of information; it is available in Spanish in three volumes (or in English, in one rather dated volume), plus a camping supplement.

RED TAPE

Only a few people (from Guyana, Haiti, Kuwait, Cuba, Korea, India, Poland, Russia, Jamaica, Thailand and other African and ex-communist states) need to obtain a visa in advance for Chile. Others will receive a tourist card (keep this safe) and permission to stay for 90 days, renewable once. In theory, a ticket out of Chile is required, though in practice it is never asked for, but you must have a full passport with at least six months validity remaining.

There are no restrictions on the amount of currency you can bring in or out. Carrying fruit, vegetables, dairy products or meat is far more of a problem (seriously), and travellers entering from Bolivia or Peru may be searched for drugs.

MAPS

In common with most Latin-American countries, Chile has an **Instituto Geográfico Militar (IGM)**, a rather more military version of the USGS or the British Ordnance Survey. Maps rarely extend beyond the Argentine border, so some are largely blank, which is useful if you run out of loo paper, but not if you are planning an international hike! You will find the IGM sales office in Santiago at Dieciocho 369, south of the Alameda (open Jan–Feb Mon–Fri 08.30–14.00; March–Dec Mon–Fri 09.00–17.30). Maps can be viewed at the Mapoteca (Diecicho 407; open Mon–Fri 10.00–12.00, 14.00–17.00) but it is actually easier to look at the display volumes in the sales office. Their 1:50,000 series is excellent and useful, especially if you are going to the Lakes District, but quite an investment at US$12 a sheet; luckily they accept credit cards. Also available, at about US$18, are 1:250,000 and 1:500,000 maps (and a few at 1:100,000). (The sheets needed are given in the text for each hike.)

A cheaper option is to go to the *mapoteca* of the National Library (open Jan–Feb Mon–Fri 09.00–17.30; March–Dec Mon–Fri 09.00–18.30, Sat 10.00–12.30), on the Alameda at the Santa Lucía metro station; here you can photocopy part of any

IGM map. If you want to buy maps before you go, Stanfords (12–14 Long Acre, London; tel: 020 7836 1321) sells some IGM maps, as, apparently, does the Chilean Embassy in Israel!

Far more up-to-date and user-friendly maps are produced by **Mapas JLM**, General del Canto 105, #1506, Providencia; tel/fax: 02 236 4808, 225 1365; jmattassi@interactiva.cl; and Chiloé 406, Punta Arenas; tel: 061 221 132, which now cover the whole of Chile at a variety of scales, and the San Martín de los Andes/Bariloche area of Argentina. These are available in shops throughout the country, particularly in tourist areas.

The best maps for driving and general navigation are those in the Turistel guides, available from larger newspaper kiosks as well as bookshops; Esso, Shell and JLM also produce good road maps. The International Travel Maps series from World Wide Books and Maps, 736A Granville Street, Vancouver BC, V6Z 1G3, Canada; tel: 604 687 3320; fax: 604 687 5925, are the best of those published abroad (also available at Stanfords).

OPENING HOURS AND PUBLIC HOLIDAYS

In Santiago, shops are generally open Mon–Fri 10.00–20.00 and Sat 10.00–14.00. Some shopping centres in the residential districts open on Sundays, and some shops, particularly outside the cities, tend to close at lunchtime. Offices, particularly in Santiago, are usually open 09.00–18.00 without closing for lunch. Banks open Mon–Fri 09.00–14.00.

Shops and banks are closed on the following public holidays: January 1 (New Year's Day), Holy Thursday (the day before Good Friday), Good Friday, Easter Sunday, May 1 (Labour Day), May 21 (Navy Day), Corpus Christi (in May or June), June 29 (Saints Peter and Paul), August 15 (Assumption), the first Monday of September (National Reconciliation Day), September 18 (Independence Day), September 19 (Army Day), October 12 (Discovery of America), November 1 (All Saints' Day), December 8 (Immaculate Conception) and December 25 (Christmas Day).

One of Chile's best fiestas is that of the Virgen del Rosario, in Andacollo, north of Ovalle, December 24–28 (with its climax on December 26), when 150,000 people camp on the hills around the village and its enormous basilica. Dances, music and costumes are pre-Hispanic in feel, and some even say that there are East Asian influences.

SANTIAGO

Opinions are divided on Chile's capital city: some love it, some hate it. Most agree that the architecture is singularly uninspiring, but the setting magnificent (when the smog does not obscure the view of the Andes). It is also a metropolis of 5 million people (fifth largest in South America) and those who do not like big cities will probably pass on as quickly as they can. Nevertheless it is a friendly enough place. The pace of life is less frenetic than in most Latin-American capitals, and people still seem to have time to stop and chat.

Santiago lies at an altitude of 543m in a valley between the Andes (commonly referred to as the *cordillera*) and a lower coastal range. Whilst the *cordillera* provides a magnificent backdrop, it unfortunately traps the smog which regularly rivals that of Los Angeles and Mexico City. Fortunately, you do not have to travel far in any direction to find fresh air. To escape, the capital's inhabitants (*santiagueños*), head for the ski resorts in winter and to Viña del Mar in the summer.

In summer, the climate is hot and dry with temperatures often reaching 30°C. To compensate, the winters are cool and wet. Spring and autumn are the most pleasant times to visit.

The axis of the city is the east–west Alameda (Avenida O'Higgins), which stretches west to the central station and the airport and east to Providencia and Las Condes, the modern business districts which could almost be anywhere in North America. The old city centre lies between the Alameda and the Mapocho River, near which are the **Estación Mapocho**, a former rail station converted into an arts centre, and the **Central Market**, a wrought-iron structure made in England. Here you will find plenty of interesting foodstuffs and seafood, including the huge *congrios* (conger eels) which feature on most restaurant menus. Heading east, beside the river, is the **Parque Forestal**, a popular promenade where you will find the imposing *Museo de Bellas Artes* (Museum of Fine Arts).

Across the pungent Mapocho River is **Bellavista**, the bohemian area of Santiago, with many restaurants, galleries, theatres and a street market on Friday and Saturday evenings along Avenida Pío Nono. The great poet, Pablo Neruda, lived in a house known as '**La Chascona**' at Márquez de la Plata 0192, which is perhaps the most fascinating sight in the city (open Tue–Sun 10.00–13.00, 15.00–18.00). It is in a dead-end abutting Cerro San Cristóbal (in the Parque Metropolitano) from which, however short your stay, you should try to watch the sunset. You can walk to the top of **Cerro San Cristóbal** (880m), take the funicular, or ride up in a cable-car from the far side. To the east the Andes, with their 6,000m snow-capped peaks, will, smog and rain permitting, be in full view – a truly magnificent sight. The peaks that stand out most clearly are Cerros San Ramón and Provincia in the pre-cordillera (see *Around Santiago*, page 138). The botanical gardens are here, as is the zoo, which is depressing rather than illuminating but is to move to the southern suburb of La Pintana.

Santiago has a **youth hostel**, at Cienfuegos 151 (tel: 02 671 8532; fax: 672 8880; histgoch@entelchile.net; www.hostelling.cl) just west of the ugly scar of the Via Norte-Sur; this area, known as the Barrio Brasil, is a studenty area poised for gentrification. As you walk up Cienfuegos from the metro or the airport bus, look out for the gargoyles on the right/east side, eg: at No.41, the ColoColo youth club. From the city centre, Huérfanos is a relatively unpolluted street, ending in a new footbridge across the Via Norte-Sur; there are no cycle-ramps, but a cycle route does run west from the bridge. Other recommended places to stay include **SCS Habitat**, San Vicente 1798, south of the Estación Central; tel: 683 3732; and the **Hotel Caribe**, San Martín 851; tel: 696 6681. The nearest **campsites** are in the Maipo Valley.

To the west of the Barrio Brasil, the **Museo Nacional de Historia Natural** (National Museum of Natural History) (open Tue–Sun 10.00–18.00; US$1) is in the Parque Quinta Normal, north of the central station, together with the **Museo de Ciencia y Tecnología** (Museum of Science and Technology) and the **Parque Museo Ferroviario** (Open-air Railway Museum). Just southwest of the centre, the **Parque O'Higgins** (open Tue–Sun 08.00–21.00) contains a pool with reedbeds and palms, the municipal aquarium and museums of Insects and Snails, Taxidermy and the *Huaso* (Chile's cowboys, see page 63), all of which cost less than a dollar. Nearby in Estación Central municipality, the **Parque Padre Hurtado** is the only green area in Santiago planted wholly with native trees.

The best arts and crafts in Santiago can be found in the **Los Dominicos** market (open Tue–Sun 11.00–around 20.00; in winter it closes a little earlier). Although

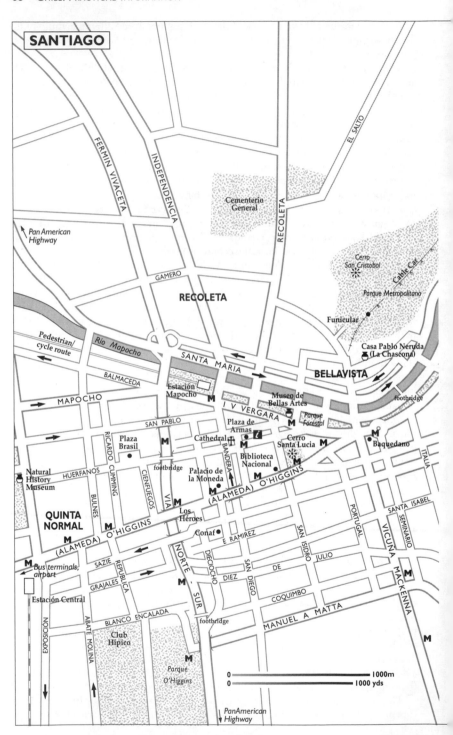

SANTIAGO

FERMIN VIVACETA

INDEPENDENCIA

EL SALTO

Cementerio
General

RECOLETA

Pan American
Highway

GAMERO

RECOLETA

Cerro
San Cristobal

Cable Car

Parque Metropolitano

Pedestrian/
cycle route

Río Mapocho

SANTA MARIA

Funicular

Casa Pablo Neruda
(La Chascona)

BALMACEDA

Estación
Mapocho

I V VERGARA

BELLAVISTA

footbridge

MAPOCHO

SAN PABLO

Museo de
Bellas Artes

Parque
Forestal

Plaza de
Armas

Plaza
Brasil

Cathedral

Cerro
Santa Lucia

Baquedano

RICARDO

CUMMING

CIENFUEGOS

footbridge

BANDERA

Biblioteca
Nacional

Natural
History
Museum

HUERFANOS

VIA

Palacio de
la Moneda

O'HIGGINS

ITALIA

BULNES

(ALAMEDA)

QUINTA
NORMAL

O'HIGGINS

Los
Héroes

PORTUGAL

SANTA ISABEL

(ALAMEDA)

Conaf

E RAMIREZ

SAN ISIDRO

JULIO

VICUNA

SEMINARIO

Bus terminals,
airport

SAZIE

REPUBLICA

GRAJALES

NORTE - SUR

DIECIOCHO

DIEZ

SAN DIEGO

DE

MACKENNA

Estación Central

EXPOSICION

ABATE MOLINA

BLANCO ENCALADA

COQUIMBO

footbridge

MANUEL A MATTA

Club
Hípico

Parque
O'Higgins

0 ———————— 1000m
0 ———————— 1000 yds

PanAmerican
Highway

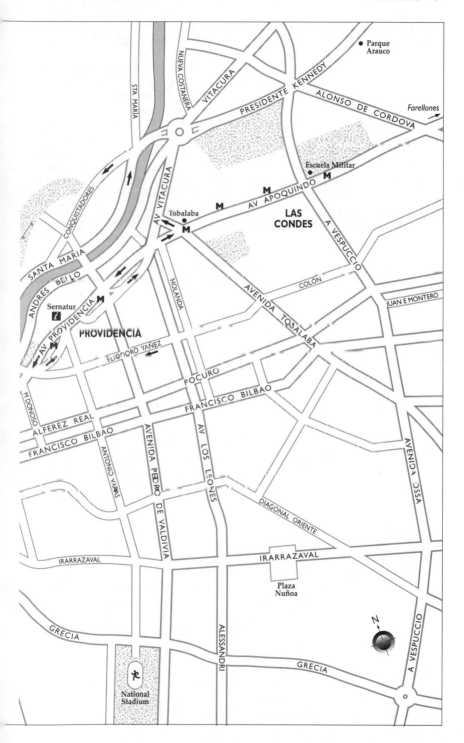

the quality of items is excellent, they can be expensive. To get there, take a Los Dominicos bus eastwards on the Alameda or from the Escuela Militar metro station.

Pollution is worst in winter, particularly in July, when there is little wind. At this time it is equivalent to smoking 60-plus cigarettes a day. In 1994 the air quality was better than it had been for a decade, as old buses were replaced, the metro expanded, and private cars were banned one a day a week in winter (determined by the last digit of the number plate). However, in June 1996 came the city's first pollution emergency, when a hundred factories were closed down temporarily. Now cars without catalytic converters are banned for two days a week, keeping 80,000 cars a day off the road. Catalytic converters have been fitted on all new cars since 1993; unfortunately these cars actually cause more ozone pollution than those without converters, and are also to be restricted. Every year, more than one million Santiago residents miss work because of pollution-related health problems, and Conama reported in 2000 that Santiago's pollution costs US$700 million per year (US$445 million due to transport). Now buses and taxis (and Hertz rental cars) are to be converted to natural gas, although President Lagos has extended the timescale from eight to ten years. In addition nickel levels are three times the safe limits, and traffic noise at schools is double international norms. Partly because of this, the World Health Organisation regards Santiago as the most stressful city in the world.

Information

Sernatur, Avenida Providencia 1550 (metro Manuel Montt/Pedro de Valdivia; open Mon–Fri 09.30–20.00, Sat/Sun 09.30–18.30; tel: 02 236 1420, 731 8300; fax: 236 1417; info@sernatur.cl). There are also offices at the airport, the San Borja bus terminal and in most major cities. The **municipal tourist office** is in the Casa Colorada (the city museum), Merced 860 (open Mon–Fri 10.00–18.00; tel: 632 7785).

Transport

Transport in Santiago hinges on the spotless and highly efficient **metro**, which has three main lines, one running east–west under the Alameda, and the others north–south. The newest line is *Linea 5*; lines 3 and 4 are to use railway tracks, and there are also plans to introduce through north–south rail services from Til-Til to Rancagua and Melipilla, as **suburban trains** currently only run south to Rancagua.

Metro ticket prices depend on the time of day, not distance; Monday–Friday peak rate (US$0.50) is 07.15–09.00 and 18.00–19.30, mid rate 09.00–18.00 and 19.30–21.00, and low rate (US$0.25) 06.30–07.15 and 21.00–22.30. The mid rate applies all day at weekends and on holidays; services do not start until 08.00 on Sundays and holidays. If you are making several trips, it is easier and cheaper to buy a *valor red*, a 'smart' multi-ride ticket from which value is debited as you pass through the barrier. You can also buy a through ticket for the **MetroBus** (a two-tone blue midi-bus; US$0.70) that runs from some metro stations to the suburbs. However, these are virtually swamped by the **yellow buses** that run until around 02.00 on a bewildering variety of routes throughout the city, 75% of them passing along the Alameda at some point (a thousand an hour at peak times). This is an amazing sight: the three right-hand lanes are for buses only, and are permanently jammed solid, the next is *preferencia buses*, and the two outer lanes are open to all.

Buses currently cost US$0.60, or just US$0.15 with an ISIC student card; pay the driver but take your ticket from the new machines.

Taxis are relatively cheap (and there is no need to tip), but do not expect the drivers to know every street or to have a street directory. In the suburbs you will also find *taxi-colectivos*, carrying up to five passengers on fixed routes.

Amazingly, people do **cycle** in Santiago, though mainly at weekends in the prosperous eastern suburbs; in the centre cyclists stick to the outside lane to avoid the mad bus drivers. There is now a bike route from Parque O'Higgins up República and Bulnes, linking to Huérfanos and to cycle tracks through the Parque Forestal and west of the Estación Mapocho. Although there is just a narrow lane on the west side of the road, this is in fact two-way.

Getting away
Leaving Santiago, you will usually find yourself travelling **by bus**. Services to the north use the Terminal San Borja, on the west side of the Estación Central, and those to the south and the coast use the Terminal de Buses Santiago (or Terminal Sur) about three blocks west, at Alameda 3878; TurBus and Pullman Bus have their own Terminal Alameda at Alameda 3712 (metro: Universidad de Santiago). Some companies also use the Terminal Los Héroes, on Jiménez just northeast of the Los Héroes metro station. Competition between bus companies is fierce, so it is always worth asking for a *promoción* or a youth discount, particularly out of season (April to November).

Trains run overnight from Santiago to Temuco all year round; day trains go south as far as Chillán, with a suburban service as far as Rancagua. Be warned – maintenance of the line does not seem to be the government's top priority!

Airport
The **Aeropuerto Internacional Arturo Merino Benítez** (SCL) is about 20km northwest of the city centre, just off the ring road (Américo Vespucio). The best way to get there is by blue-and-yellow Centropuerto buses from the island in the middle of the Alameda at the Los Héroes metro station, from 06.00–22.30 (US$1.60); this will also pick up passengers along the Alameda at the rail and bus stations, and at the Pajaritos metro station. The rival Tour Express service has been taken over by TurBus and now leaves from their terminal; it is slightly pricier. There are also shuttle buses to collect you from your hotel, such as Navett; tel: 695 6868. A taxi should cost around US$15.

There are two terminals at the airport, for domestic and international traffic; both have ATM cash machines and other key services.

Shops
Supermarkets
These account for 90% of food sales in Santiago, the highest rate in Latin America; however, most are out in the affluent eastern suburbs, notably Chile's largest, the Jumbo at Alto Las Condes and Bilbao 4144 (open daily 09.00–22.00), and the massive Parque Arauco mall (Avenida Kennedy 5413). There are two good supermarkets on either side of Exposición by the Estación Central; *Lider* is a big mall on the north side of the Alameda immediately west of the Terminal Sur. In Las Condes, the most convenient supermarket is the Unimarc opposite the Tobalaba metro station on Avda Apoquindo.

Bookshops

The best bookshops in Santiago are the Librería Universitaria in the Universidad de Chile on the Alameda (with a smaller branch at Providencia 2108), and the Feria Chilena del Libro, at Huérfanos 623 and Goyenechea 3162; the latter has armchairs and coffee (open Mon–Sat 11.00–20.00, Sun 11.00–17.00). The Unión de Ornitólogos de Chile, Providencia 1108, local 32 (tel: 236 8178) sells birding guides and its monthly *Boletin Chileno de Ornitologia*; the Gaia shop at Orrego Luco 054, Providencia (shared with the excellent El Huerto vegetarian restaurant) also has a few wildlife guides. The Librería Chile Ilustrado, at Providencia 1652, has some wildlife books as well as a good choice of old books. Second-hand English-language books can be found next door at Books. English-language books can also be found at Librería Inglesa, Huérfanos 669 and Pedro de Valdivia 47, and at Librería Anglo-Americana, 11 de Septiembre and Guardia Vieja in Providencia. For travel books, try Librería Catalonia at San Sebastían 2837, El Bosque.

Camping supplies

There are a number of stores in Santiago where you can buy and sell new and used equipment. The Patagonia Sportshop (open Mon–Fri 11.00–13.00, 17.00–20.00) is in the same building as the Federacíon de Andinismo, Almirante Simpson 77. It has a good range of new equipment and local maps, but is quite expensive. For outdoors gear, try Outdoors & Travel, Encomenderos 206, Las Condes (tel/fax: 02 335 7104; fhoyt@ctcreuna.cl), or Patagonia, the mountain clothing company, at Helvecia 210 (at Ebro), Las Condes (tel: 335 1796; fax: 242 8666).

The 800 and 900 blocks of Calle San Diego, south of the Alameda, are known for **bike shops**; there are also repair shops at Cerrito 288, Bellavista; tel: 738 0603 (near La Chascona) and Vitacura 102.

Communications

The main **post office** is on the north side of the Plaza de Armas, at Agustinas 1137. The best places for **internet** are near República metro station: Punto.con, Sanfuentes 2150 (open Mon–Sat 10.00–23.00); Nine Internet, Cifuentes 117 (open Mon–Sat 10.00–22.00); and others at Cifuentes 67 and Echaurren 127. There is also access (no longer free) at Entel at Morandé 315 (open Mon–Fri 09.00–18.00) and CTC in the basement of the TurBus terminal. The Spanish language daily **newspaper** *El Mercurio* (www.elmercurio.cl) lists evening entertainment and events.

ADVENTURE SPORTS IN CHILE
Skiing

Chile's most famous (and expensive) downhill ski resort is Portillo (see pages 123–4; www.skiportillo.com), north of Santiago on the main road to Mendoza. More popular are the four resorts just east of the capital: Farellones, Colorado, La Parva, and Valle Nevado (see page 143). Also within reach of Santiago are Chapa Verde (a new resort inland from Rancagua, 139km from Santiago), Termas de Chillán, and Volcán Antuco (inland from Los Angeles). Further south, the summer playgrounds of Araucanía and the Lakes also have winter resorts on volcanoes; the main ones are Villarrica and Antillanca, but there are others, such as La Burbuja (on Volcán Osorno), Lonquimay, and Llaima. Further south, the mountains are lower, and the weather is wetter and windier, but skiing is possible, for instance at Cerro El Fraile (Coyhaique) and Cerro Mirador (Punta Arenas).

The Lakes District is also ideal for cross-country skiing and snow-shoeing: ask at the resorts, or at ¡Ecole! in Pucón.

Climbing

There is too wide a range of opportunities for **climbing** to list them all here, but you will notice many possibilities both in the hiking descriptions and from the ski resorts listed above. The highest mountains are in the north, but this is very dry, uninhabited country, and it goes without saying that you may have altitude problems. Access would be a great problem for many of these peaks if it were not for the activities of mining companies, particularly those digging sulphur high on the volcanoes.

The Chilean Frontier Law is very old, but should soon be revised; technically half of the country is classified as a border zone, requiring **permits** for any 'expedition of a technical, scientific or sports nature'. These are issued by Difrol, the Dirección Nacional de Fronteras y Límites, Bandera 52, 4th Floor, Santiago (tel: 02 671 4110; fax: 697 1909; difrol2@minrel.cl; www.minrel.cl/test/difrol). You can apply through a Chilean embassy before leaving home, or print the form from their website and fax it.

There is a legal requirement of 90 days' notice, but in practice, pending the reform of the law, there is a list of 46 peaks for which a rapid authorisation process applies. This includes peaks such as Volcáns Llaima, Villarrica and Osorno, which are climbed by thousands of people every year and where the *guardaparques* would, I think, be surprised to hear that a permit was officially required. A revised law may reduce the border zone to a thin strip and allow permits to be issued in regional capitals.

Difrol can also arrange for expeditions to cross the border other than at the regular crossing points, but they will need a lot of persuading. The official Chilean view is that the circuit on ice around Cerro FitzRoy (page 321) is on Chilean territory, and you should carry your passport just in case the military are rattling their sabres in the area. The crossing from Villa O'Higgins, at the southern end of the Carretera Austral, by boat to the Argentine *gendarmería* at Cocoví on Lago San Martín is not a regular crossing, but apparently the *carabineros* (police) on the spot are happy for people to come and go this way.

For **information** on climbing, contact the Federación de Andinismo de Chile, two blocks south of the Baquedano metro station at Almirante Simpson 77, Casilla 2239, Santiago (tel: 02 222 0888, fax: 222 6285; open Mon–Fri 11.30–13.30, 15.30–19.00 – but you are more likely to find friendly faces in the early evening, when the library is open till 21.30 (Mon–Fri). On the same premises is the Patagonia Sportshop where you can buy local maps and guidebooks and expensive gear; upstairs is the Escuela Nacional de Montaña (tel: 222 0799), which arranges rock- and ice-climbing classes.

Weekend excursions to the mountains are organised by **local clubs**; most cities will have a Club Andino, which may own a hut or even a ski resort. In Santiago try Club Aguila Azul, Almirante Simpson 3, and Club Andino Wechupun, Avda Viel 1560. There is rock-climbing at Las Chilcas, 85km north on the PanAmerican Highway (buses for Llay-Llay), and at Las Palestras and Piedra Romel, at El Manzano in the Cajón del Maipo; for the first you will have to walk for 30 minutes, and for the second you will have to pay US$4 entry to the campsite. There are walls at Climbing Planet, Avda Condell 703, Providencia (tel: 02 634 6391; fax: 635 4516) and at GeoExpediciones (see below). For some reason the

Unión Panamericana de Asociaciones de Montañismo y Escalada is at the seaside, at Ecuador 80–K, Viña del Mar; tel: 032 882 602/187.

Not surprisingly, climbing is popular in Chile, and the country's most successful climber, Mauricio Purta, who has climbed the highest peak of each continent and four 8,000m peaks, has a regular column in *El Mercurio*. He is also behind a series of TV programmes, now released on video, which describe the major peaks of Chile. You can also buy two accompanying booklets, *Cumbres de Chile I & II*, at the Patagonia Sportshop and elsewhere.

For **mountain rescue** the Club de Socorro Andino is at Avda Ricardo Cumming 329; tel: 02 699 4763; for **weather forecasts** call: 02 601 9001.

Rafting

White-water rafting began in Chile in 1980, initially by *gringo* residents of Santiago on the nearby Río Maipó. Commercial trips spread to the Río Trancura, near Pucón, while hardnut expeditions discovered the joys of the Biobío and the Futaleufú rivers. These being Class V rivers, there were not enough Chileans experienced enough for tours to be viable for the domestic market, but gradually in the late 1980s the Biobío was discovered by the international market. It was actually ideal for tourism, with volcanoes and hot springs, and restful pools between the amazing rapids; but it is now dammed and virtually finished as a rafting river, despite frenzied protests (pages 161–2). The Biobío averages about two-thirds of the Colorado's flow but its gradient is five times as steep.

The Río Futaleufú is too testing for commercial rafting with novices, too hard to reach, and not really long enough, but commercial companies are developing it anyway, helped by coverage of the 2000 world championships. Otherwise it is ideal, with a steady flow of 260–280m³/second from the dam just inside Argentina, and an even gradient. Paddle rafts are used only with experienced crews; otherwise it is oar-rigged rafts rowed by staff. March is the best time of year to go. From a put-in at the Gélves bridge 3km east of the town, the Upper Futaleufú section of the river passes through a basalt gorge (the Gates of Hell), containing three Class V rapids (Wall Shot, Orgasm and Exit) where two people died in 1993, then along the Las Escalas valley to Zeta (V+), Throne Room (V+) (these two both have portage trails), and Wild Ride (or Wild Mile; IV) to a takeout at the Río Azul; the Middle Futaleufú section is in two parts, firstly from here to the Pasarela Zapata, via Terminator (V), Kyber Pass [*sic*] (IV+), Himalayas (III but with huge waves), and Mundaca (V), and then (the most popular section, the Corazón del Futa'), on to the Puente Futaleufú via Entrada, Tobogán, Rodeo Hole, Pillow, Cara de Indio, Mundaca, Pudú, Puma, Wiña, Cazuela, and Tiburon (all IV or IV+); and the Lower Futa' section continues via Más o Menos (IV), Casa de Piedra (V), and six III/III+ rapids. (See page 254 for the parallel hike.) The Puente Futa' is at km11.5 on the road, and the Río Azul *pasarela* is at km18, ie: 37.5km and 31km west of Futaleufú.

The nearby Río Espolón is for beginners, with a put-in at a bridge below the Cascada del Espolón (Class VI+), then four Class II/II+ rapids before Tres Enamorados (III) and the Puente Espolón takeout; the Lower Espolón has three Class III rapids between a couple of IIs, with a takeout before the confluence with the Futa'.

The Río Maipo (page 145) is still the most popular, and can be crowded at summer weekends; there are world-grade Class III rapids in the 16km from Las Animas to San José, but it is still accessible to beginners. There is also the Maipo

Alto, 16km from San Gabriel to San Alfonso, with the right-angled La Pirámide (IV+), La Calavera (IV), El Tobogán (IV+), El Túnel (IV+) and Curva del Francés (V), which is usually portaged; Cascada run trips on Saturday mornings from March to November.

The Río Trancura, near Pucón, flowing through a wonderful forest of mañío, ulmo and laurel, is immensely popular, and trips, from October to March, are remarkably good value. The rapids are Chucho (III+), Feo (IV), Ultima Sonrisa (IV+), Las Gemelas (III), La Lavanderias (II), De La Isla (II), Del Pescador (III) and La Leona (III). The lower section takes an hour and can cost as little as US$8; the upper Class IV section costs US$18–25, including an *asado*. Nearby, the rivers Fuy and Maichín are both Class IV+. Near Puerto Varas, the Río Petrohué offers a 17km run from Los Patos with 13 Class III+ rapids, taking an hour and a half, to the confluence with the Río Hueño-Hueño. Nearer Santiago, the Río Teno, just north of Curicó, is a little-known Class III/IV river (used by Grado Diez), and the rivers Maule and Cachapoel are also raftable. In Aysén, in addition to the Futaleufú, the Río Cisnes is Class III, and the Río Baker, which has the greatest flow of any river in Chile, has stretches of Class V. Other possibilities in this area are the Yelcho, Corcovado and Palena rivers. Finally, in Paine (pages 271–2) the rivers Tyndall and Serrano can be rafted, although there is no road access at either end and motored rafts are needed.

Kayaking

Kayaking is possible on the rivers described above and others, notably the Río Claro at Siete Tazas (see page 156), but the greatest potential for the future is in sea-kayaking in the southern fjords and the eastern side of Chiloé. Altué operates year-round at its base at Dalcahue, and from November to April in the fjords near Llanchahue; is also has exciting plans to take a support vessel to the Laguna San Rafael area. AlSur does supported trips to Fiordo Comau (in Pumalín), and Kayak Austral does the same to the east of Chiloé. The Paine/Ultima Esperanza area is scenically ideal but rather strenuous, due to the Patagonian winds and lack of shelter.

In Santiago, gear can be bought at Ocean Kayak, Av Colón 5328, Las Condes (tel. 02 202 3680), which is linked to Sur Kayak Hostería, Antonio Duce 849, Niebla, near Valdivia (tel: 063 282 228); and Nautisport, Av Las Condes 8606 (tel: 02 229 4093) sells mainly windsurfing gear.

Horses

In rural Chile, particularly in the south, many people seem to have grown up on **horses**, and the *huaso* (see box on page 85) tradition survives. It is particularly nice to see young men riding out in their finery on a Saturday night to visit their girlfriends.

Many tour companies can arrange for a few hours riding, but it is harder to organise multi-day trips. Some people have decided simply to buy horses and sell them back at the end of their trip; if you do this, you can rely on the *carabineros* for help and stabling. Exceptions are Pared Sur, which offers an eight-day trip south of Coyhaique, and Cascada, which has trips of up to 14 days from San Alfonso, as well as in Cañi and Paine; OpenTravel Andes Patagonicos (see page 199) offers horse-riding in the Puelo valley.

Caving

There is next to no organised **caving** in Chile as yet, but there is exciting potential in the almost inaccessible islands of the far south, the remnants of the massive coral reefs (1km thick) that ringed Gondwanaland 250 million years ago. Expeditions to the islands of Diego de Almagro and Madre de Dios, not far northwest of Paine, have found the world's southernmost sinkhole, the Perte de l'Avenir, 50m deep, and others up to 350m deep.

Wing sports

Para-gliding (*parapente*) and **hang-gliding** (*alas delta*) are trendy new sports that have not yet achieved wide popularity. They can both be practised around Santiago, but the best terrain is in the far north, especially on the coast near Arica and Iquique, where 30–35km/hr winds can be relied on in spring and summer. There is also a parapente centre at Antillanca. Near Santiago the best spots are La Pirámide, Cerro del Medio (La Dehesa), El Arrayán, Lagunillas, Colina and Rancagua, and at the Valle Nevado ski station (tel: 02 206 0027; info@vallenevado.com). For hang-gliding, contact Alas Delta (tel: 02 248 4591, 694 6152); for para-gliding contact Brisa Sur, at the El Colorado ski station (tel: 02 362 0565; fax: 362 0566; brisa@ia.cl); ProPilot (tel: 02 335 7304, 09 233 0349; www.parapente.cl); Sky Sports (tel: 02 223 0048, 09 821 2087; vuelouno@hotmail.com); and in Iquique Manutara; tel: 057 418 280. Off The Ground, Padre Mariano 70C, Santiago (tel: 02 264 2457, 09 441 5204) has what it calls 'power kites'. SportsTour, Moneda 970, piso 14, Santiago (tel: 02 549 5200; fax: 698 2981; mailbox@sportstour.cl) can arrange gliding and ballooning.

Chilean companies

CATA (Chilean Adventure Tourism Association), La Concepción 56, of. 203, Providencia, Santiago; tel: 02 377 1954; cata_aventura@123click.cl, is an association of the larger adventure tourism companies formed in 1994 to regulate their smaller competitors. The companies listed below mostly offer hiking, rafting and horse-riding (see also listings for Pucón, Puerto Varas etc):

ACE Turismo O'Higgins 949, piso 16, Santiago; tel: 02 240 9500, 696 0391; fax: 245 0360; acetur@entelchile.net. This is the senior adventure travel company in Chile, founded in 1987.

Adriazola Expediciones Santa Rosa 548, Puerto Varas; tel/fax: 065 233 477. Organises rafting, as well as climbs on Volcán Osorno.

Adventura Sports Viña del Mar; tel/fax: 034 423 9160. Organises rafting, kayaking, hydrospeed (boards down rapids), hiking, mountain-biking, skeet, archery.

Alpi Exploraciones Mercedes Marin 7103, Las Condes, Santiago; tel/fax: 02 229 3874. Offers mountain training.

AlSur Del Salvador 100, Puerto Varas; tel/fax: 065 232 300; alsur@telsur.cl. Offers rafting and expeditions to Pumalín.

Altué Expediciones Encomenderos 83, Las Condes, Santiago; tel: 02 232 1103; fax: 233 6799; altue@entelchile.net; www.chileoutdoors.com, www.altueseakayak.co.cl. Does hiking, rafting, horse-riding, and sea-kayaking.

Andes Trek Viña del Mar; tel/fax: 032 956 052. Has hiking and horse-riding.

AquaMotion Imperial 0699, Puerto Varas; tel/fax: 065 232 747; aquamotn@telsur.cl. Offers rafting, canyoning, hiking and horse-riding.

Azimut 360 Arzobispo Casanova 3, Bellavista, Santiago; tel: 02 737 3048; fax: 777 2375; azimut@reuna.cl; www.azimut.cl. Has hiking, rafting and riding.

CHILE ON HORSEBACK

It was a dream come true: we were trekking on horseback in Chile! Five days into our journey, autumn had set in among the mountains and the lenga trees were turning flame red against the yellowing grasses as we rode through Jeinimeni National Park. Overhead, parakeets swirled in a green, chattering cloud, and higher still condors circled. We set up camp before the rain turned to snow, with the horses tethered and Brown Dog fed and curled up under the largest bush. Already we felt the horses were working well as a team; Salsa, the little mare, was the natural leader, then came Rupert, bravely carrying the heavy packs, and finally Alazan bringing up the rear – not the brightest horse but with a very open, trusting nature.

We began our journey in Cochrane, a small town in the 11th Region in the south, and travelled north along the Carretera Austral to Puerto Montt, through the Lakes District and many of the national parks, to reach the 7th Region near Talca some ten months and 2,500km later. Chile being such a long country, the scenery and climate varied greatly. We travelled from glacier, through arid *pampas*, temperate rainforest, lush dairy pastures and dry mountain landscapes – but never far away were the snow-capped peaks of the Andes.

In Chile the pace of life is slow; many people still work the land, machinery is expensive and labour is cheap. While most people of the *campo* have very little money, they do have that precious commodity: time: time to have a few words, time to show you the right trail and where best to ford the rivers or cross the mountains. The door is always open. The people were the most welcoming and generous we have ever met. Often they would ask why we had chosen to travel by horse – surely we could afford the bus? – but they soon understood when we explained that, this way, we had so much more contact with the people and could really experience the country. That winter in Chile was one of the worst on record, with unprecedented rainfall, and many times we were forced down from the mountains, but the warmth and hospitality of the people more than compensated for the bad weather.

We had many ups and downs, in more than one sense. Perhaps the worst was when our unexpected but welcome companion, Brown Dog, was killed by a car, but we also had to contend with the anxiety of Salsa lamed by an infection in her hoof, and then parting with her when she foaled; tying the horses between two lorries for a ten-hour ferry journey, and crossing high passes in the snow. There were unforgettable moments of happiness, too: swimming with the horses in Lago Villarrica, racing full tilt through the trees along mountain trails, or listening to our companions munching the lush grass outside our tent. But our most enduring memories are of the people and the many friends we made. Our horses are now running free in 40,000 acres of woodland thanks to Roberto. We hope one day to return and maybe continue the journey – if we can find them!

Kate Wadley and Padraig Queally rode this journey in two parts, April–November 1997, and March–May 1998. Kate is a pony-trekking instructor and Padraig is a vet.

Cascada Expediciones Orrego Luco 040, Providencia, Santiago; tel: 02 234 2274, fax: 233 9768; info@cascada-expediciones.com. Has rafting, hiking, climbing, horse-riding and kayaking, and wildlife programmes.

Chile Eco-Adventure tel: 234 3439, 236 1325; fax: 234 3438; mountain services@chilnet.cl. Hiking, rafting and riding.

Earth River Expeditions Villanueva 95, Santiago; tel/fax: 204 2702; US tel: 1800 643 2784; www.earthriver.com. Offers rafting.

¡Ecole! General Urrutia 592, Pucón; tel: 045 441 675; fax: 441 660; ecole@asis.com; www.asis.com/ecole. ¡Ecole! is a *hospedaje* which arranges hiking trips and the like to support conservation projects. In the US, contact **Lost Forest Treks**, PO Box 2453, Redway CA 95560; tel/fax: 707 923 3001; 1800 447 1483.

ECO Travel Avenida Costanera, Puerto Varas; tel/fax: 065 232 303. Hiking, rafting and riding.

GeoExpediciones Camino al Volcán 07910, Laz Vizcachas, Puente Alto, Santiago; tel/fax: 02 842 4771; geoexpediciones@mail.com. Climbing, mountain-biking, trekking.

Grado Diez Avda Andres Bello 2239A, Santiago; tel: 02 234 4130, 234138.

Hot River Rafting Comercio 18896, San José de Maipo; tel: 02 861 1389.

Kayak Austral c/o Casa Perla, Trigal 312, Puerto Montt; tel: 065 254 600; kayakaustral@hotmail.com; www.angelfire.com/mt/kayakaustral.

Lys Miraflores 541, Santiago; tel: 02 633 7600; www.lys.cl. Mountain-bike excursions into the precordillera, and MTB hire (US$18/day).

Mountain Service Santa Magdalena 75, Of. 306, Providencia, Santiago; tel: 02 234 3439, 334 6636; fax: 234 438. Climbing and hiking trips.

Pared Sur Juan Estéban Montero 5497, Las Condes, Santiago; tel: 02 207 3525; fax: 207 3159; paredsur@paredsur.cl. Organises mountain-biking, rafting, horseback riding and hiking.

Rock Side Expeditions Moneda 2570, Santiago; tel: 02 681 6761, 682 0353. Kayaking trips offered.

travelArt Imperial 0661, Puerto Varas; tel: 065 232 198; fax: 234 818. Does mountain-biking down Volcán Osorno.

Travellers Avda Angelmó 2456, Puerto Montt; tel/fax: 065 258 555; info@travellers.cl.

Yak Expediciones Nocedal 7135, Santiago; tel/fax: 02 227 0427; info@yakexpediciones.cl. Kayaking.

Argentina: Background

HISTORY

Humans probably first crossed into North America over the Bering Strait landbridge about 60,000 years ago, and headed south, crossing into South America around 15,000 years ago and reaching Tierra del Fuego approximately 4,000 years later. The oldest remains yet found in Argentina, dating from approximately 12,900 years ago, are in Pico Truncado, Santa Cruz province. The Mapuche people, now found almost entirely in Chile, once dominated clear across to the Atlantic, and repelled the Incas; to their south, Patagonia was inhabited by the Tehuelche, divided from north to south into three groups, the Gununa'kena, Mecharnuekenk and Aonikenk. These were all semi-nomadic hunter-gatherers, numbering perhaps 300,000 when the first visitors from Europe arrived in 1516.

The first Spanish settlers were driven out, and it was not until 1573 that Santa Fe was established, followed by Buenos Aires in 1580. No great reserves of gold or silver were found in Argentina, and it was of interest to the Spaniards only as a supplier of food, animals and materials to Peru, from where it was governed. Huge areas of land (*estancias*) were given to Spanish settlers, and worked by the local Indians under the *encomienda* (forced-labour) system.

Nevertheless, despite Argentina's great potential, it was never allowed to develop fully under colonial rule. After Napoleon's invasion of Spain, the colonies were left to fend for themselves, and on May 25 1810 a *criollo* (native-born) government took power in Buenos Aires. Following Napoleon's defeat, the Spanish attempted to seize their colonies back but were driven off by José de San Martín, with a formal Declaration of Independence on July 9 1816.

Society was left largely unchanged by independence, although the freedom to export brought huge profits to the cattle-ranchers. In 1827 the reformist president, Rivadavia, was overthrown after attempting land reform, and in 1829 Juan Manuel de Rosas, a leader of the ranchers, took power, and was only overthrown in 1852, after over 20 years of rule by terror; he died in Britain.

Cattle were now joined by the more profitable sheep, which led to the Indian wars of the 1880s, under Colonel Julio Roca, who virtually exterminated the indigenous peoples in order to take their land. From 1857 the vast distances of the interior were tamed by railways, mostly built with British financial backing, and from 1877 the vast distances to European markets were tamed by refrigerated ships, producing a rich and conservative land-owning class. In the first decade of the 20th century alone 1.1 million immigrants entered a country of four million people; the population is now 40% of Italian origin and 30% Spanish, with Arabs, Jews and Britons also figuring. Gradually an urban middle class developed, which brought about universal male suffrage in 1912 and the election of their leader Hipólito Irigoyen as president in 1916. His Radical Party held power until 1930, when a military coup brought the conservatives back to power.

During World War II, industrialisation advanced, but its overwhelmingly

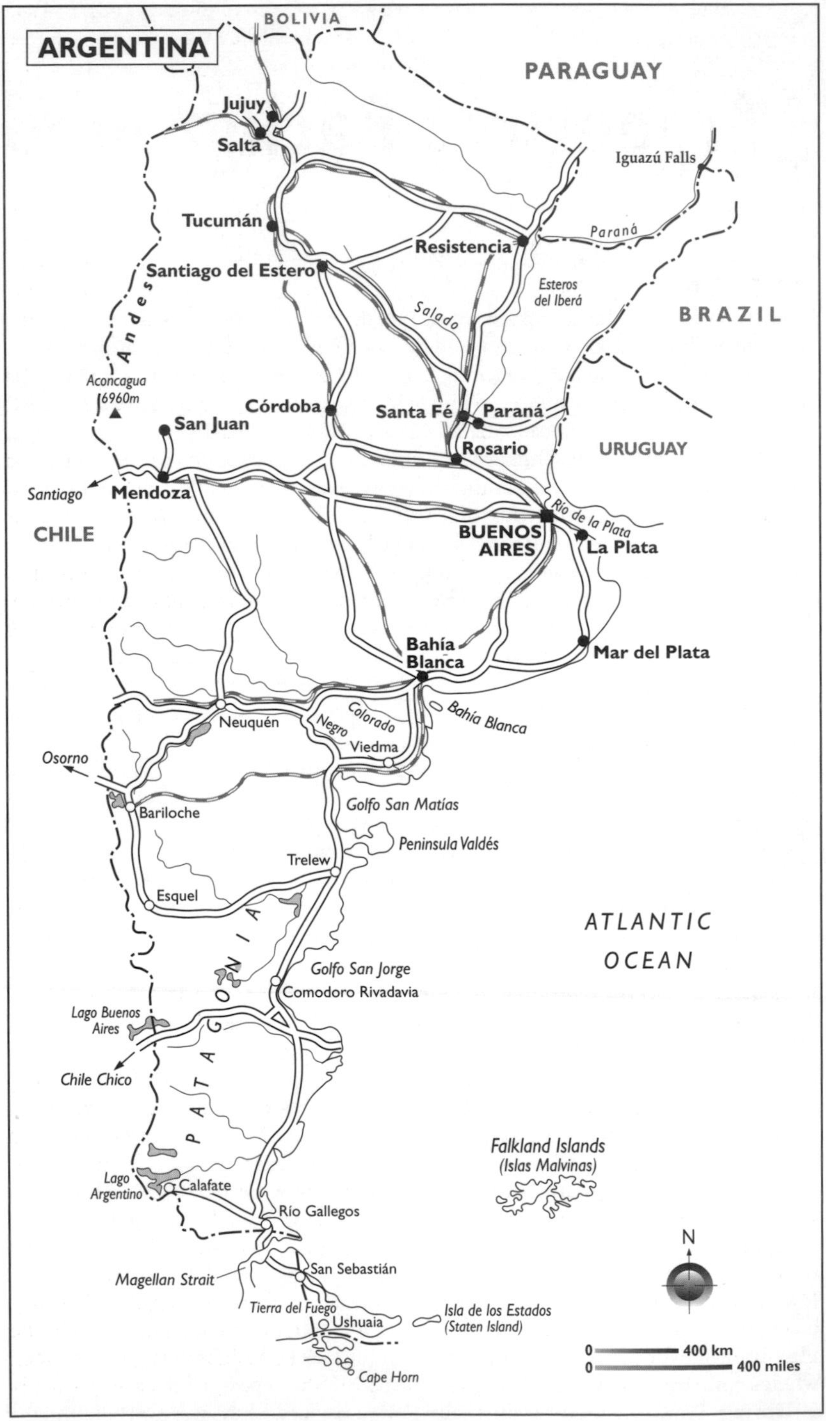
ARGENTINA
BOLIVIA
PARAGUAY
Jujuy
Salta
Iguazú Falls
Tucumán
Paraná
Resistencia
Santiago del Estero
Esteros del Iberá
Salado
BRAZIL
Andes
Aconcagua 6960m
Córdoba
Santa Fé
Paraná
San Juan
Rosario
URUGUAY
Santiago
Mendoza
Río de la Plata
CHILE
BUENOS AIRES
La Plata
Bahía Blanca
Mar del Plata
Colorado
Bahía Blanca
Neuquén
Negro
Viedma
Osorno
Bariloche
Golfo San Matías
Peninsula Valdés
Trelew
Esquel
ATLANTIC OCEAN
Golfo San Jorge
Comodoro Rivadavia
PATAGONIA
Lago Buenos Aires
Chile Chico
Falkland Islands (Islas Malvinas)
Lago Argentino
Calafate
Río Gallegos
N
Magellan Strait
San Sebastián
Tierra del Fuego
Ushuaia
Isla de los Estados (Staten Island)
0 400 km
0 400 miles
Cape Horn

foreign ownership led to an increase in nationalist feelings; a military coup in 1943 was supported by the workers, and in 1946 Colonel Juan Perón was elected president with over half the vote. He continued with labour reforms and improvements in the living conditions of working people, and pursued a popular nationalist policy, nationalising the railways in 1948. His second wife, María Eva (Evita) was a controversial figure, but helped greatly with his relations with women and the workers. She died at just 33 in 1952.

Economic problems led Perón to introduce a wage freeze and to woo foreign investment in the 1950s, and the military, wary of the rise in union power, deposed him in 1955. He had ruled in an undemocratic manner, deploying a secret police and press censorship, but this was nothing to what followed. Civilian governments were formed twice, but the military were clearly in charge, and guerrilla groups began to campaign against them. In 1973 elections were held and won by a Peronist, Hector Campora; Juan Perón returned from exile at the age of 78 to take over, but died the next year. His third wife, María Estela (or Isabela) succeeded him, but as chaos grew she was overthrown in 1976 by the army.

Left-wing guerrillas, known as the *Montoneros*, waged a campaign of bombings and murders, countered by a bloody repression known as the 'Dirty War', in which between 10,000 and 30,000 people were killed, mostly by the security forces. Not only real or suspected terrorists, but anyone who had vaguely sympathetic ideas was liable to 'be disappeared', tortured and killed, often by being thrown from a plane into the sea. The guerrillas were broken by 1977, but military rule continued, and economic mismanagement sent unemployment and inflation soaring.

As a distraction, the military *junta*, now led by General Leopoldo Galtieri, occupied the Falklands (Malvinas) Islands in 1982, but were, to their surprise, driven out by the British. Just as Germany and Japan 'won the peace' in 1945, it could be said that Argentina did better out of the war than Britain. The Thatcher government was re-elected, while the Argentine *junta* surrendered its power, with elections being held in October 1983.

POLITICS

The 1983 elections were won by the *Unión Cívica Radical* (UCR), with Raúl Alfonsín elected president. In 1985, the military leaders were put on trial, and five were jailed; however, military revolts in 1987 brought an abrupt end to further trials. *Las Madres de Los Disparecidos* (Mothers of the Disappeared) still gather in the Plaza de Mayo, outside the presidential palace, every Thursday afternoon, demanding justice, or at least information on the fate of their loved ones. In 1997 they were offered US$220,000 compensation each, to be raised by a bond on the stock exchange, but this was scornfully rejected. The Alfonsín government survived for a time, although economic problems were unsolved, but the 1989 elections were won by Carlos Saúl Menem and the Peronist *Partido Justicialista* (PJ). Although Menem pursued populist policies, he left expectations unfulfilled, and again had to buy off the military by releasing Galtieri and the other generals in 1990. He did, however, have the good sense to appoint a determined economy minister, Domingo Cavallo, in January 1991, and to support him when he tackled entrenched interests.

In July 1996, Cavallo was sacrificed by Menem after bitter in-fighting and was replaced by Roque Fernández, Governor of the Central Bank, who maintained the same tight grip on fiscal policy. The justice minister also resigned and was replaced by Elías Jassan, who in turn resigned in June 1997 after a scandal over his allegedly corrupt interest in post-office privatisation, as well as his ties with Alfredo Yabrán, a businessman linked to the murder of photo-journalist José Luis Cabezas, who was taking too close an interest in him. Yabrán committed suicide in 1998.

Unfortunately Menem did nothing to restrain corruption, and his very public battles with his wife, Zulema Yoma, did nothing to help his reputation. In late 1996 general strikes were staged against the '*flexibilización*' of labour laws, to free industry from the Peronist legacy of strong trade unions. Severance costs are particularly high, so around 40% of jobs are unofficial. Sales tax was raised to 22% (and extended to bus and taxi fares, medical insurance, and cable TV charges), but evasion is currently estimated at US$10 billion per year, of a total US$24 billion of tax evasion in all (of *c* $300 bn GDP). In addition, customs corruption is estimated to cost US$4 billion a year.

A new centre-left party, Frepaso (*Frente para un País Solidario*) was formed in late 1994, and took 29% of the votes in the May 1995 elections, which saw Menem re-elected. However, in June 1996 the UCR recovered to win the first election for the mayor of Buenos Aires city; Frepaso came second, and the PJ polled just 18.7%, in a huge protest vote against corruption. Another new grouping, *Nueva Dirigencia* (led by Gustavo Béliz, a Peronist defector) polled 13%, and later formed an alliance with *Acción para la Republica*, formed by Cavallo, whose feud with Menem and the corrupt elements of the PJ became ever more bitter and public.

Menem had just 9% support in a poll in early 1997; the Peronists were still backed by the poorest sectors of society, but were unlikely to defeat a united opposition. In August 1997, the two main opposition parties, the UCR and Frepaso, formed the *Frente para la Justicia* (Alliance for Justice) for the October 1997 congressional elections (when the government lost control of Congress) and the October 1999 presidential contest. Menem was unable to run for a third consecutive term of office under the terms of the constitutioin (although he aims to return as president in 2003); in his place the PJ's candidate for president was Eduardo Duhalde, Governor of Buenos Aires province and a former vice-president. He had gained popularity by purging the notoriously corrupt and brutal provincial police, who were implicated in the bombing of a Jewish community centre in 1994, in which 86 died.

The most notorious torturer of the Dirty War, Captain Alfredo Astiz, was sentenced to life *in absentia* by a French court for the disappearance in 1977 of two nuns. He was dismissed from the navy in 1996 just before Menem visited France, but a scandal broke in 1997 when he was found to be back at work at Naval Intelligence, and he was dismissed again. His extradition is also sought by Spain, which also wants Galtieri's extradition in connection with the disappearance of about 300 Spaniards. Menem said the case was closed and refused to budge. Also in 1997 Switzerland froze the bank accounts of various generals.

In the face of this international pressure, Argentina made much of its 'strategic alliance' with the USA, and has taken part in UN peace-keeping operations and contributed 100 troops during the 1998 Gulf Crisis. However, in 1996 ships off Angola had to be called home when the navy ran out of money. Operations in Croatia were compromised by the revelation that Argentina had illegally sold arms to Croatia at the height of the civil war. Diplomatic relations with Britain were restored in 1990, and British and Argentine troops worked together in Cyprus, and British companies invested US$2.2 billion in Argentina, largely through privatisation.

Menem's stock sank further as he struggled to make cuts demanded by the IMF;

two ministers resigned and he came close to losing the Economy Minister, Roque Fernandez, too. In the 1990s the economy had grown by 5% per year, but public spending had increased by almost 50% and public debt had doubled. In mid-1999 a trade dispute led to Brazil blocking imports from Argentina, which was forced to back down and ended up in its second deep recession in four years.

In October 1999 Fernando de la Rua, UCR mayor of the city of Buenos Aires, took 48% of the vote, beating Duhalde who polled 40%. De la Rua became possibly the weakest president in Argentinian history, with the opposition PJ controlling both chambers of Congress and most of the provincial governorships and dominating the trade unions and judiciary. He appointed José Luis Machinea (governor of the Central Bank under Alfonsín) as Economy Minister, who proposed emergency measures to raise taxes and cut tax evasion, blocked by the PJ who kept the congress inquorate. Further reform of labour law was required, but the bill had to be watered down and then in April 2000 a scandal erupted when it turned out that it was only passed thanks to US$10m in bribes to PJ senators. In October 2000 de la Rua reshuffled his cabinet, with his brother Jorge becoming Justice Minster and Alberto Flamarique, the former Labour Minister at the centre of the bribery scandal, replacing him (briefly) as presidential chief of staff; the vice-president, 'Chacho' Alvárez, resigned the next day, dealing a crippling blow to de la Rua's prestige. In November the Christian Democrat party also pulled out of the governing coalition. Since then the coalition has been pretty well dead in the water, with the Radicals governing more or less alone, with abysmal poll ratings. Also in November 2000 the third general strike in a year was backed by all four trade union groups, and was the first in 17 years to combine a strike with pickets, and roads and railways blocked.

In May 2000 Aníbal Ibarra of Frepaso was elected mayor of Buenos Aires, becoming arguably the most powerful member of his party once Chacho resigned. In March 2001 Machinea resigned, taking the blame for economic stagnation. His successor Ricardo Lopez Murphy proposed an austerity programme, leading three Frepaso ministers to resign in protest, and then resigned himself after just two weeks in office. Cavallo then returned as Economy Minister, proposing a more acceptable austerity package. Meanwhile, in May 2001, Menem married a Chilean ex Miss Universe, the lovely but unfortunately named Cecilia Bolocco; this is generally reckoned to be a political gimmick, part of his come-back campaign. However, days later he was arrested over allegations concerning illegal arms sales.

ECONOMICS

A temporary currency, the *Austral*, was replaced in 1991 by a new *Peso*, exactly equal in value to the US dollar. Inflation, which had peaked at 3,080% in 1989, fell to 3.9% in 1994, and GDP growth averaged 7.5% per year from 1991 to 1994. However, in 1994 it became clear that tax avoidance and increased unemployment due to privatisations were leading to a fiscal crisis, and the 'tequila crisis' triggered by the collapse of the Mexican *peso* led to panic and the withdrawal of 18% of bank deposits in the first three months of 1995. Unemployment rose to 18% and public-sector wages went unpaid.

The Southern Cone Common Market or Mercosur came into effect on January 1 1995; exports, also helped by a crash in the Brazilian exchange rate, rose by 33%, but even so GDP fell by 2.5% in 1995. The IMF insisted on sweeping cuts in spending and rises in tax, which, coupled with a drought, led to some rioting. The situation stabilised, and GDP grew by 4% in 1996, and 8.5% in 1997, with unemployment falling to 13.8% by the end of the year. However, inequality continued to increase, with the richest 10% taking 37% of income in 1997, and the top 20% taking 53%, while the poorest 30% got 8.2%.

The Asian crisis of 1997, the Russian debt moratorium of 1998, and Brazilian devaluation in January 1999 triggered one crisis after another. Industrial production fell 7% in 1999 and GDP by 3%, and unemployment rose to 15%. The worst was past by mid-1999, but the Menem government was still thrown out at the end of that year. The economy remained stagnant in 2000, with GDP rising just 0.5% and unemployment staying above 15%. However, exports rose 13% in 2000, and consumer prices hardly rose.

In 2001 the economy should grow by about 2.5%; a US$39.7bn IMF package will cover US$21.8bn of debt repayments in 2001 and then some. The federal deficit doubled to US$7.1bn in 1999, but must be eliminated by 2003 under the IMF deal. Over a third of the population is now living in poverty (and almost half of all children), against 22% in Chile. The fixed link to the US dollar may have to be abandoned, as external fluctuations have too great an effect on the economy. The provinces are also in financial crisis, with a deficit of US$2.9bn in 1999, and public servants frequently going unpaid.

Tourism is growing almost as fast as in Chile, although 85% is internal and 70% of the balance comes from the neighbouring countries of Brazil and Uruguay; there were 1.1 million arrivals in 1981, 2.9 million in 1991, and 5 million in 2000, bringing in US$5.5bn (4% of GDP). However, there is a tourism deficit overall, as 25,000 Argentines own second homes in Punta del Este and neighbouring resorts in Uruguay.

Mining, although not as developed as in Chile, is set to boom, with gold as important as copper. La Alumbrera, an open-pit copper and gold mine at 2,600m in Catamarca province, which opened in 1997, produces 600,000oz of gold per year, making it the world's 14th largest gold mine, as well as the 9th largest copper mine; the Pascua-Lama mine in San Juan will open in 2003, producing 800,000oz of gold a year, to rise to over one million ounces, as well as 35 million ounces of silver; nearby Veladero will produce 500,000oz of gold a year for ten years, as well as copper and silver, and Cerro Vanguardia (in Santa Cruz) opened in 1998 and produced 300,000oz of gold in 1999. Mining exports in 1999 were US$700 million in 1999, and may reach US$3 billion by 2005.

CONSERVATION AND NATIONAL PARKS

The *Administración de Parques Nacionales* was set up in 1934, but even now only 1% of the country's area has legal protection. Only 3% of the *pampas* is unspoilt, and just 0.3% is protected. Even so, Argentina's national parks are better run and funded than Chile's. You will pay a higher entry fee (around US$5) but will then have good free camping and properly maintained and signposted trails. There are 160 private-sector concessions in the national parks, which are largely left unsupervised; it is estimated that 70% of their buildings have just been flung up without blueprints. The APN's headquarters is at Santa Fe 680, (1059) Buenos Aires; tel: 0114311 0303, 4312 0783 (open Mon–Fri 10.00–17.00); you can get leaflets on major parks and further information from the library (closed Mon). In addition there are plenty of provincial parks and reserves. November 6 is National Parks Day, which helps to raise public awareness of environmental issues.

There are few private reserves in Argentina, but see page 302 for Cerro Pirque and the Proyecto Lemu. Doug Tompkins of Pumalín Park (page 249) has set up a

GAUCHOS AND HUASOS

Hilary Bradt

The horse played the same role in the shaping of Chile and Argentina as it did in the American West. The vast Argentine pampas were tamed by *gauchos* riding Spanish horses, and these cowboys played a decisive part in the bitter internal struggles following independence.

Gauchos were usually of Spanish/Indian descent, and the name derives from a Quechua word meaning 'orphan' or 'abandoned one'. It was a lonely life on the *pampas*, and the *gauchos* were fiercely independent men whose home was the open range. They lived almost entirely on beef, which they roasted in an open pit and then washed down with draughts of *yerba mate*, a herb tea. They drank heavily of *aguardiente* (sugar brandy) and spent much of their free time playing cards. The main tools of their trade were *boleadoras* or *bolas*, stones attached to cords which were thrown to bring cattle down from a distance by tangling around their legs. Their dress, still worn by their descendants today, included a thick, woollen poncho over the shoulders, a *rastra* (broad belt studded with silver coins) around the waist, and long, pleated trousers called *bombachas* which were gathered at the ankles and covered the tops of their high leather boots. Like the North American cowboy, the *gaucho* became something of a folk hero, symbolising the freedom and pioneer spirit of 19th-century Argentina. He was immortalised in José Hernandez' epic poem, *Martin Fierro*.

The Chilean *huaso* lacked the glamour of the *gaucho*. This may be because his historic role was more utilitarian and had to do with herding cattle rather than fighting wars, or perhaps because the limited space west of the Andes confined the spirit of these men and failed to ignite the proud arrogance which symbolises the Argentine *gaucho*. Darwin noted that 'The gaucho may be a cut-throat but he is a gentleman; the huaso is an ordinary, vulgar fellow'. Nowadays however, while the *gaucho* tradition has turned into bombastic humbug, the *huaso* survives as a straightforward salt-of-the-earth type.

similar project in Iberá and is said to be buying land in southern Patagonia, as are Ted Turner, Sylvester Stallone and the Benetton company – but these purchases are of course for their own private purposes rather than for conservation proper. Following the declaration of a South Atlantic whale sanctuary, there is now a campaign, led by Lucas Chiappe of Proyecto Lemu, for a moratorium on logging south of 40°S and ultimately for a Gondwanaland park, so called because the forests of the far south can all trace their origins back to the original supercontinent.

Argentina is also playing a part on the international environmental stage: the Kyoto Climate Change Conference of 1997 was chaired by a 'feisty Argentine' who was apparently very good at banging heads together; the next conference was held in Buenos Aires in November 1998.

As any traveller can confirm, Patagonia is one of the windiest places on earth, and it is estimated that Argentina could generate 5,000mW from the wind, 30% of its total needs and equal to the controversial new Yacireté dam on the Río Paraná and the Atucha and Embalse nuclear power stations. However, the country's first

GIVING SOMETHING BACK

If you are interested in voluntary work in Argentina, the bodies listed below will be pleased to offer guidance:

Fundación Vida Silvestre Argentina Defensa 251, 6th floor, (1065) Buenos Aires; tel: 011 4331 3631, 4343 4086; email: fusad@ibm.net; www.vidasilvestre.org.ar, which runs a bookshop (at Defensa 245) selling its own and other publications on wildlife and sponsors lectures and other educational programmes; also in Bariloche.

Fundación Patagonia Natural Marcus A. Zar 760 (9120) Puerto Madryn, Chubut; tel: 02965 474 363, 472 023; fax: 474 363; email: informacion@patagonianatural.org which has somehow managed to sell to Mattel the right to use the southern right whale in a Barbie doll competition.

Asociación Ornitológica del Plata 25 de Mayo 749, Buenos Aires; tel: 011 4312 8958; email: aop@aorpla.org.ar, which has a useful library and organises tours.

Greenpeace Mansilla 3046, (1425) Buenos Aires; tel: 011 4962 0404; fax: 4962 3090; email: gp@wamani.apc.org; www.greenpeace.org.ar

Finis Terrae Ushuaia; 02901 434 122; fax: 433 302 which aims to protect the environment of Tierra del Fuego, mainly by opposing logging.

'wind park' only opened in 1997, outside Comodoro Rivadavia, producing all of 10mW.

There are also plans to compete with Chile in forestry. Argentina presently has 60 million hectares of forest, and the intention is to add 200,000ha per year (as opposed to the present 20–30,000ha per year). As opposed to Chile's pine plantations, Argentina's will be largely eucalyptus, poplar and willow, in the hot, wet lowlands of the Plata (Plate) and Paraná Rivers, and of Misiones, where pine grows as much in ten years as in a century in Finland, and forestry accounts for 50% of provincial GDP. Jujuy province is specialising in making paper from sugarcane cellulose, as well as organic production of traditional varieties of potato.

Argentina: Practical Information

INFORMATION

Limited information can be obtained from embassies abroad, as well as from Adenauerallee 52, Bonn, Germany; tel: 228 228 910; Piazza della Rotonda 2–3 p.6 Roma, Italy; tel: 06 6830 0677; 12 West 56th Street, New York, NY, USA; tel: 212 603 0443; 5055 Wilshire Blvd, Suite 210, Los Angeles, CA, USA; tel: 213 930 0681; and 2655 Le Jeune Road, Ph 1, Suite F, Miami, FL, USA; tel: 305 442 1366. The *Secretaría de Turismo de la Nación* (Ministry of Tourism), Suipacha 1111, piso 21, Buenos Aires; tel: 011 4312 5611, 4312 8471; fax: 4313 6834; cvodovosoff@ turismo.gov.ar; www.sectur.gov.ar, can supply information; as can the *Cámara Argentina de Turismo*, Tucumán 1610, piso 5, (1050) Buenos Aires; tel: 011 4374 1699; fax: 4343 2245; http://turismo.gov.ar.

RED TAPE

No visitors from Western or first-world nations need **visas**; they do need a full passport with six months' validity remaining. Entry is permitted for three months, and the easiest way to extend your stay is simply to cross the border and return.

OPENING HOURS AND HOLIDAYS

In Buenos Aires, shops usually open at 09.00 and in many cases stay open until 19.00 Monday to Friday; on Saturdays they generally open only in the morning. Outside the capital, shops will often close for a siesta from 14.00 until 17.00. Dinner is served from 21.00, and few evening activities get going before 22.00 or 23.00.

There are many **banks** on Corrientes and San Martín; most now have cash machines. Exchange offices (*casas de cambio*) are generally open from 08.30–16.30, Mon–Fri, and some operate on Saturday mornings. Banks tend to have shorter hours, 10.00–16.00 Mon–Fri only.

Shops and banks are closed on the following public holidays: January 1 (New Year's Day), Holy Thursday, Good Friday, April 2 (Malvinas Day), May 1 (Labour Day), May 25 (Independence Day), June 20 (National Flag Day), July 9 (Declaration of Independence), August 17 (Anniversary of San Martín's death), December 8 (Immaculate Conception) and December 25 (Christmas Day).

BUENOS AIRES

More than any other capital city in Latin America, Buenos Aires ('BA' to its *gringo* friends, but 'BsAs' to bus companies and so on) dominates the country culturally, economically and psychologically. With Buenos Aires province, it is home to a third of the population, and this is where everything happens. It is possibly also the world capital of psychotherapy and plastic surgery. Along with Rio de Janeiro,

Buenos Aires is easily the most cosmopolitan city on the continent, with communities of Italian, Spanish, Portuguese, Jewish, Armenian, German and British origin, and a large shifting population of more temporary visitors. The British community built Argentina's railways in the second half of the 19th century, introduced wire fencing from the UK and thus made large-scale cattle ranching big business. They have somehow also managed to give the Spanish language an Oxbridge accent. Most stayed put during the Falklands/Malvinas War.

People born in the city of Buenos Aires are called *porteños* (those born in the surrounding province of Buenos Aires are *bonaerenses*) and their culture historically centres on the **Boca**, a maze of narrow streets with luridly coloured houses clustered around the old port, where the tango was born. It is dominated by a massive transporter bridge over the famously filthy Río Riachuelo (a cartoon: "'It's a stick-up!" "But that's a water pistol!" "Yes, but I filled it in the Riachuelo.'"). This strange mixture of working people's homes and cafés, gentrified townhouses and 'ethnic' tourist joints is still worth seeing, though you should see it soon before the last of its original inhabitants sell out, and watch out for muggers. **San Telmo**, slightly nearer the city centre, is developing as a new bohemian district, with its antique shops and market, while **Recoleta**, to the north, is the city's smartest and most expensive area.

To the east of San Telmo, beyond the docks of Puerto Madero (now revitalised by yuppy loft-living and tourism, with two preserved sailing ships, the frigate *Presidente Sarmiento* and the corvette *Uruguay*), the Reserva Ecológica del Costanera Sur is an immensely successful **wildlife reserve**. Best entered at Avda Tristán Achaval Rodríguez 1550 (free, open daily Apr–Oct 08.00–18.00, Nov–Mar 08.00–19.00, guided tours Sat, Sun & hols 09.30 & 17.30; tel: 011 4315 1320), it has been created on land reclaimed and then abandoned as marshland, where a pampa (prairie-like) ecosystem is being created. Not only is it visited by 25,000 people every weekend, but it is also home to large numbers of coipu and over 200 species of birds. There are now plans to open up more of the riverfront with new *bicisendas* (cycletracks) and *miradores* (viewpoints), notably at the Costanera Norte (by the Aeroparque), Ciudad Universitaria and Parque Frente al Río.

Accommodation

The so-called **youth hostel** at Brasil 675 (tel: 011 4362 9133) has been disowned by the official HI federation, but is still a reasonable place to stay; an official International Hostel is planned. There are also **private hostels**: the San Telmo, Carlos Calvo 614 (tel: 4300 6899, fax: 4300 9028; elhostal@satlink.com), two blocks from bus 86 (for Ezeiza) and 45 (for Retiro/Aeroparque); V&S Backpackers, Viamonte 887 at Suipacha (tel: 4322 0994, 4327 5131; hostels@vsyhbue.com.ar); Che Lagarto, Combate de los Pozos 115 (tel: 4304 7618; chelagarto@hotmail.com) at the Entre Rios Subte' stop; and the Milhouse Hostel, H. Yrigoyen 959 (tel/fax: 4345 9604; info@milhousehostel.com), a block from the Avenida de Mayo Subte' stop. Better, but still affordable, are Hotel La Giralda, Tacuari 17 (tel: 4345 3917; fax: 4342 2142); and Hotel O'rei, Lavalle 733 (tel: 4393 7186).

Information

The **national tourist office** is at Santa Fe 883 (09.00–17.00 Mon–Fri; free tel: 0800 50016, 4312 2232), with branches at the airports. The **municipal office** is at Pellegrini 217 (open 10.00–18.00 daily; tel: 4372 3612; www.buenosaires.gov.ar), with kiosks on Florida at Diagonal Roque Sáenz Peña (open 09.00–17.00 Mon–Fri)

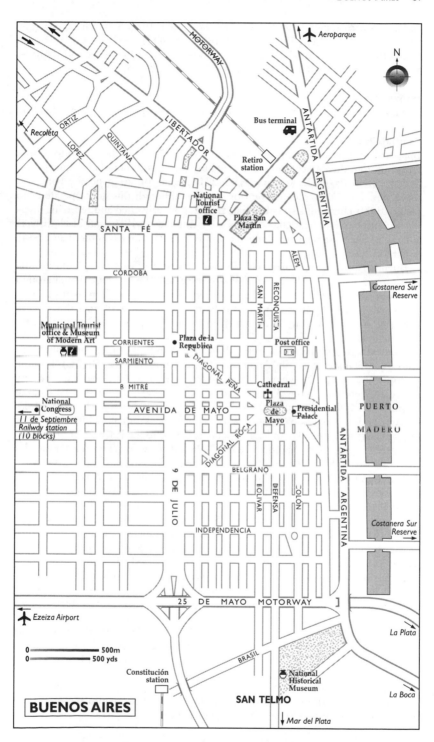

MOTORWAY

Aeroparque

N

Recoleta

ORTIZ

LOPEZ

QUINTANA

LIBERTADOR

Bus terminal

ANTARTIDA

Retiro
station

National
Tourist
office

Plaza San
Martín

SANTA FÉ

ARGENTINA

ALEM

CÓRDOBA

RECONQUISTA

SAN MARTIN

Costanera Sur
Reserve

Municipal Tourist
office & Museum
of Modern Art

CORRIENTES

Plaza de la
República

Post office

SARMIENTO

DIAGONAL PEÑA

B MITRE

Cathedral

National
Congress

AVENIDA DE MAYO

Plaza
de
Mayo

Presidential
Palace

PUERTO
MADERO

11 de Septiembre
Railway station
(10 blocks)

DIAGONAL ROCA

9 DE JULIO

BELGRANO

BOLIVAR

DEFENSA

COLON

ANTARTIDA ARGENTINA

Costanera Sur
Reserve

INDEPENDENCIA

25 DE MAYO MOTORWAY

Ezeiza Airport

La Plata

0 ══════ 500m
0 ══════ 500 yds

Constitución
station

BRASIL

National
Historical
Museum

La Boca

BUENOS AIRES

SAN TELMO

Mar del Plata

and at Córdoba (open 10.00–19.00 Mon–Fri, 11.00–19.00 Sat); Sarmiento 1551 (open 10.00–17.00 Mon–Fri; tel: 4371 1856; fax: 4374 7533); Retiro bus term (open 10.00–18.00 Mon–Fri); La Boca (open 10.00–17.30 daily); and dique 4, Puerto Madero (open 11.00–19.00 Mon–Fri, 10.00–20.00 Sat, Sun).

Newspaper

The *Buenos Aires Herald* (www.buenosairesherald.com) is published daily in English.

Transport

Buenos Aires has an efficient **metro** system known as the Subte', with four lines radiating from the city centre and one linking them (and more being built). This operates from 05.00–22.00 (Sun 08.00–22.00), and you are generally better off using this rather than the chaotic **bus system**, although this does operate from 04.00–01.00. There are also **suburban trains**, now privatised and receiving long-overdue investment. The 60,000 **taxis** are a distinctive yellow and black; drivers and their meters are not always reliable, but you should not pay more than US$45 to get to Ezeiza Airport.

Buenos Aires has two **airports**, although there has been talk of closing the Aeroparque, in the docklands, in 2005 – strange, at a time when cities all around the world are opening new docklands airports for use by modern 'whisper jets'. However, the latest plan is to rebuild it (with a 3km runway) across the *costanera* (riverside road) on land to be reclaimed from the Plata, with spoil from the new Subte' tunnels.

Domestic flights and those from Montevideo (and other international flights with intermediate stops in Argentina – known as *cabotaje* flights) use the **Aeroparque** (Jorge Newbery Airport; AEP), which is 4km north of the city centre and served by buses 33, 37C and 45. International flights use the **Ezeiza airport** (or Ministro Pisarini; EZE), 32km southwest of the city, where all airlines except Aerolíneas use a spanking new US$138m check-in hall. This is served by city bus 86 (the *diferencial* is an express service, US$4) to the Plaza de Mayo, and by two private companies, Manuel Tienda León and Ecuador. The former is a bit more costly (US$14; 05.00–23.00), but does also operate buses direct to Aeroparque for US$15. If you are connecting to Aerolíneas or Austral, they will provide a free transfer. A taxi from Ezeiza to the centre or Aeroparque will cost about US$35, plus tolls; or you could call 4583 8787 or 4633 7943 for a *remise* (radiotaxi), wait half an hour and pay US$20. It is also possible to reach Ezeiza is by taking a train (4 per hour, 44min trip) from Constitución station to the suburb of Ezeiza and then (one block away at Ramos Mejia & Paso de la Patria) bus 502 to the airport – under an hour and a half in all, costing US$1.65.

Long-distance **trains** are few and far between, due to lack of subsidy, and in any case are generally slower and more expensive than buses. It is worth considering the train to reach Mar del Plata and other destinations in congested Buenos Aires province, but not for destinations further afield, apart from the odd overnight service. The modern long-distance **bus terminal** is at Retiro, Avda Ramos Mejía 1880, adjacent to a major rail and Subte' station. There is plenty of competition on most routes, so it is worth asking for discounts with student or youth hostel cards.

Communications

The central **post office** (*correo central*) is at the corner of Sarmiento and Alem, and is open Mon–Fri 08.00–20.00 and Sat 08.00–13.00.

Argentina's twin telecommunications companies have split Buenos Aires between them just as they have split the country. Their phone cards are, however, interchangeable (and the same system applies for Direct Access international calls). Telefónica Argentina has a 24-hour phone centre at Corrientes 707, and Telecom has one at San Martín 640.

Books

Useful **bookshops** for English-language and wildlife books include: LOLA, Viamonte 976, 2nd Floor (open Mon–Fri noon–19.00); Librería del Turista, Florida 937; Librerías Turísticas, Paraguay 2457; and the Fundación Vida Silvestre and Asociación Ornitológica del Plata (page 85).

Specialist shops

For **camping gear**, try Aventura Cámping, Ecuador 1361 (tel: 4821 6421; fax: 4824 5915; aventuraoutdoors@arnet.com.ar); Bilbao Camping, Guatemala 5451; Campamento Base; Paraná 141; Camping Center, Blas Perera 3145, Olivos (tel: 4794 5534; fax: 4790 0581; email: consultas@camping-center.com); Deporcamping, Av Santa Fe 4830 (tel: 4772 0534; deporcamping@unetc.com); El Galleganez, Paraná 152; El Mochilero, San Juan 1231 (tel: 4304 8187; email: elmochilero1992@yahoo.com.ar); Eurocamping, Paraná 761 (tel: 4374 5007), Libertador 4062 (at Paraná), and Rojas 448 (Plaza San Martín); Oberón, Echeverría 2474; and Rupal, 11 de Septiembre 4555 (tel: 4702 9017; fax: 4702 1445; email: info@rupalnet.com). The manufacturers Cacique Camping have an outlet at Juan Justo 3326.

For **maps**, try the Instituto Geográfico Militar, Cabildo 301 (Subte' station Ministro Carranza) (open Mon–Fri 08.00–13.00). There is now no bureaucratic requirement to show a passport.

ADVENTURE SPORTS IN ARGENTINA

Skiing

Argentina's most prestigious ski resort is Cerro Catedral, just outside Bariloche. In 1997 new snow-making equipment was installed and chairlifts extended in order to bring it to the same level as Portillo in Chile. Other resorts discussed later in this guide include La Hoya (Esquel), Cerro Piltriquitrón (El Bolsón), Cerro Bayo (Villa La Angostura), Cerro Chapelco (San Martín de los Andes) and Penitentes (165km west of Mendoza). In addition there is great skiing at Las Leñas (west of San Rafael, served by charter flights to Malargüe), the slickest resort in the southern hemisphere, with great powder and lots of terrain to explore.

You can also ski at Parque Caviahue (360km from Neuquen), Valle de Chalhuaco (Río Negro), and in Tierra del Fuego, although this is largely cross-country, with added attractions such as husky and snow-cat tours. Downhill skiing is possible on Cerro Martial, on the outskirts of Ushuaia, and a new resort on the highway to the east.

Climbing

Climbing of all kinds is popular, and Argentines have reached the summits of both K2 (1994) and Everest (1995). In the 1960s the Sierra de la Ventana (Buenos Aires province) and Los Gigantes (Córdoba) developed as training areas; now Bariloche, Mendoza and Córdoba are all centres of climbing – contact the relevant Club Andino for information (see regional chapters for details). To climb in border areas, you should have a **permit** from the National Parks Administration (APN); tel: 011 4311 0303, 4393 5746.

In the capital, contact the Centro Andino Buenos Aires, Rivadavia 1255 (tel/fax: 011 4381 1566; centro_andino_buenos_aires@hotmail.com), or the Escuela Argentina de Escalada Deportiva (Argentinian School of Sports Climbing), Perú, Acassuso (tel: 4793 5986; fax: 4805 1418; info@escalando.com.ar). There is a wall and climbing school at Sarmiento 3391, Castelar; tel: 4481 0901.

Rafting

Rafting in Argentina does not reach the level it does in Chile, but it is still popular as a mass-market entertainment, especially in the Mendoza area. Most of the companies listed are general adventure sports' outfits who can also supply mountain bikes and horses. For operators on the Río Mendoza see page 121. In San Martín de los Andes (see page 206) there is rafting on the Río HuaHum, and also the Meliquina and Aluminé. Near Bariloche (see page 219), rafting is mainly on the Río Manso: the Manso Medio (from Lago Steffen to El Manso) is Class III–IV; the Lower Manso is Class II–III; and towards the border is again Class III–IV; this last stretch is pretty inaccessible and you may have to return by horse. There is also rafting on the Class III Río Azul near El Bolsón (page 299).

Horses

The *gaucho* culture is one of the selling points of Argentina, although it is largely humbug (see page 85). Almost any tourism agency will fit you up with an afternoon's riding, although a few hours on the dry, windswept steppes of Patagonia will be enough for most people. For more serious horse-trekking, contact Ride World-Wide, In The Saddle or Last Frontiers (see page 26).

Paragliding

Affluent young Argentines love to show off, so paragliding is very popular! The best spots are Mendoza, Bariloche, San Martín de los Andes, Mar del Plata, and in La Rioja, San Luis and Córdoba provinces. Contact the *Federación Argentina de Vuelo Libre*; tel: 02944 427 558; fax 425 095.

Argentine companies

Ecology and Adventure Argentina/Adventure Centre Talcahuano 736 #1, (1391) Buenos Aires; tel: 011 4374 9639/6848; fax: 4372 9956. For hiking, Aconcagua climbing groups, and birding.

Fairways Travel and Tourism Maipu 712, Buenos Aires; tel: 011 4322 9897; fax: 4322 1771; and in Esquel, Trekways, tel: 02945 453 380; trekways@cybersnet.com.ar.

Patagonia House Suipacha 963, 3rd Floor, #26, (1008) Buenos Aires; tel: 011 4313 6600; fax: 4313 5911. For 'adventure holidays', meaning dove/duck shooting, trout fishing, polo, golf, and estancia visits.

Rotrek Patagonia Mountain Trekking Solis 238, B1834HNF Temperley, prov. Buenos Aires; tel: 011 4244 1864; fax: 4292 3310; also Futa Lonco, Los Coihues s/n, Villa Campanario, Bariloche; tel: 02944 448 155; rosina@rotrek.com; www.rotrek.com. For trekking groups in the Bariloche area.

Sur Turismo Avda Cordoba 807, #9B, (1054) Buenos Aires; tel: 011 4311 7265/8335; fax: 4313 7205; surturismo@teletel.com.ar. Offices in Patagonia. Good for cruises.

Trekking Argentina Paraguay 542, (1057) Buenos Aires; tel: 011 4313 6853; fax: 4311 1807. For trekking, overlanding, horses, rafting, yachting, birding and safaris.

Part Two

Regional Guide

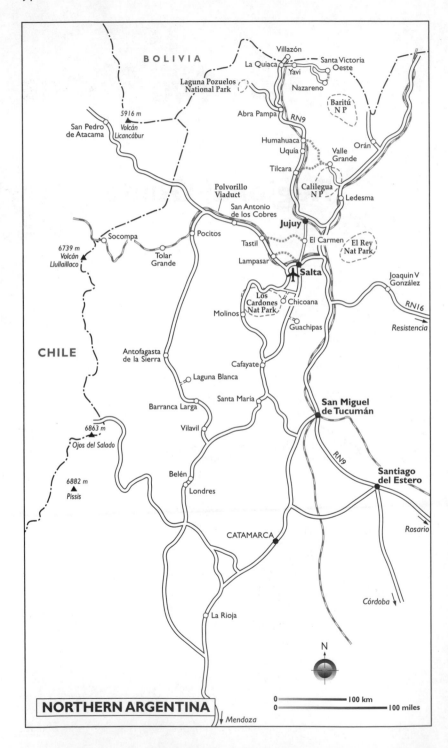

NORTHERN ARGENTINA

| 0 | 100 km |
| 0 | 100 miles |

Northern Argentina

NORTHWEST ARGENTINA

Kathleen Ladizesky

The provinces of Salta, Jujuy and Catamarca in northwestern Argentina provide some of the most primitive and remote backpacking in the country. Interesting trekking circuits can be made in the Andes, but it is harder to make long treks in the high desert terrain of the *puna* due to the scarcity of water. Nevertheless, the little-publicised salt lakes and volcanoes of the area offer the possibility of extremely rewarding daywalks and other explorations, with striking views of distant peaks covered by eternal snows.

The mountains are crossed by trails, many of which date back to the time of the Incas. Other well-worn paths branch off them, often making it necessary to backtrack to rejoin the main route. Andean churches, many of them ancient national monuments, are frequently encountered and a focal point of local life, with religious festivals celebrated throughout the year. The local people, like their homeland, are similar to those of Bolivia and the other northern Andean countries; they grow some crops such as potatoes and maize and raise sheep and goats for milk and meat, and llamas for their wool. They are very friendly and will be happy to help with directions, but it is important that you treat them with respect. Remember that you are a visitor in territory that they maintain and on which they depend for their livelihood. When you meet a pack train, stop and allow it to pass, and you will find the horsemen only too pleased to stop and talk. In this way you can glean a wealth of local knowledge.

Travelling up from the foothills, the natural **vegetation** ranges from lush, subtropical trees and bushes to giant cacti, small, thorny plants and shrubs. In some areas there is cloud forest where the trees are laden with epiphytic plants that have no contact with the ground. Above the treeline is stubby grass, while some areas of the plain are quite barren. The local *campesinos* (peasants) are great users of medicinal herbs, and you will also notice the bulge of a few coca leaves rolled into a ball and held in the cheek, a mild stimulant that helps them to walk for long distances at high altitude. The plant, grown in Peru and Bolivia, is not strictly legal in Argentina, but is commonly sold. The abundant **wildlife** of the mountains includes condors, guanaco, vicuña, llama and ñandú. In certain salty lagoons, various species of flamingo (see page 129) can also be seen.

The *puna* is a continuation of the Bolivian *altiplano*, which will give an idea of its nature. This block of very old crystalline rocks, elevated to around 3,800m, is split by faults through which erupted dozens of volcanoes, some of them among the highest on earth. Large *salares* (salt lakes) have formed in basins from which there is no drainage. The climate is very dry and hot in the daytime, and extremely cold once the sun sets. There is occasional rain in summer, and even less frequent snow in winter. However, some snowstorms can last several days, killing animals whose carcasses, due to the dry climate, do not rot but become dessicated and preserved. The *puna* is very sparsely populated, with less than one inhabitant per square kilometre in the province of Salta, and even fewer in Catamarca.

Hikes in the Andes of northwestern Argentina are best tackled in the southern winter (May–October) as any rain falls in summer. However, the *puna* can be visited at any time.

Salta and district
Salta city
The city of **Salta**, at an altitude of 1,187m, makes a useful base for treks in northwestern Argentina. Founded in 1582, this, of all Argentina's provincial capitals, is the one which has best conserved its Spanish-colonial architecture and atmosphere. Several large, **colonial houses** survive, notably the casas Hernandez, Arias Rengel and Leguizamon, all of which are near where the Peatonal Florida crosses Alvarado and Caseros streets. Other interesting buildings include the **Uriburu Museum**, Caseros 317, dating from the 18th century and, opposite, the 19th-century **church and convent of San Francisco**. The Museo de Altura is a new history museum opening in 2001. The life of the city centres on Plaza 9 de Julio, with its tall palm trees, to one side of which is the cathedral, constructed at the end of the 19th century.

From Avenida Yrigoyen near the bus terminal, a *teleférico* (cable-car) runs up Cerro San Bernardo, providing both a panoramic view of the area and a cool place to go on a hot day. In the pedestrian streets of Florida and Alberdi, vendors often sell local weaving and jewellery in the evenings; there are also food and clothes markets at the junction of Calles Alberdi and Urquiza where some local products are available.

Accurate information and leaflets can be obtained from the **tourist office** at Calle Buenos Aires 93 (tel: 0387 431 0950; fax: 431 0716; www.turismosalta.com).

How to get there
Several bus lines come to Salta from Buenos Aires, notably La Veloz del Norte (four services a day, taking around 22 hours, from US$60 *común*, US$66 *cama*). Planes fly from the Aeroparque in Buenos Aires; it is possible to fly one way with Dinar and take a TAC bus the other way, from US$170.

Accommodation
At the budget end of the market, there are two good **youth hostels**: Backpackers (Buenos Aires 930; tel/fax: 0387 423 5910; salta@hostels.org.ar); and Terra Oculta, (Cordoba 361; tel: 421 8769; terraoculta@ciudad.com.ar; www.terraoculta.com). There is also a municipal **campsite** 3km south by bus 13. Residencial San Jorge (Esteco 244; tel/fax: 421 0443; hotelsanjorge@arnet.com.ar) is about ten blocks from the centre; it is inexpensive and friendly, with cooking facilities. Some people use this as a base for an extended visit in the area. Two typical colonial **hotels** in the mid-price range are Residencial Elena (Buenos Aires 256; tel: 421 1529) and Residencial España (España 319; tel: 432 0898). Both provide accommodation but no food and are situated near the city centre.

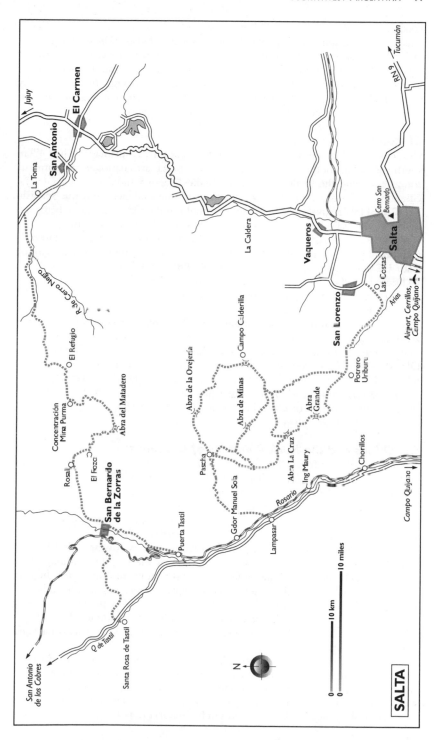

SALTA

Food

Baked *empanadas* and other regional specialities such as *humitas, tamales* and *locro* (all maize-based dishes) can be bought in many places, notably La Criollita, near the centre at Zuviria 326. On the same block at Zuviria 380 is the homely *comedor* (diner) of the Sociedad Italiana, which serves liberal helpings of economically priced food. There are several good ice-cream shops, including Rosmari, not far from the square on the corner of Pueyrredon and Belgrano.

Chicoana

Chicoana is a bustling colonial village set amidst tobacco plantations just 47km south of Salta. Both the church and the plaza are national monuments commemorating the battle of 1814 when the Diaguita Indians joined General Güemes and his *gauchos* in the struggle to gain independence from the Spanish. Many local folk festivals take place here throughout the year, the biggest being the mid-year *gaucho Fiesta de la Doma y el Tamal* (Festival of Rodeo and Tamal).

Local archaeologist and tourist guide Martin Pekarek owns the Hostería Chicoana on the plaza (tel/fax: 0387 490 7009; martinpek@impsat.co.ar), charging from US$25 (single) to US$48 (quadruple). The Finca Los Los, 3km away, is a traditional ranch offering day excursions with barbecues and trail rides in the surrounding hills and valleys, bookable in advance (tel: 0387 431 7258, 422 2959). It is usually possible to camp there.

There are several reliable restaurants around the plaza. Sunday lunch is often accompanied by music in a restaurant on Calle 25 de Mayo, when a local folk singer comes in from the country. On Calle El Carmen Simona Cornejo's 'The Old Market' bar and restaurant also houses an information centre which hires bikes and horses or arranges excursions further up the *quebrada* (gorge).

Chavez buses run hourly from Salta's bus station (US$2). It is also possible to share a *remise* (taxi) from Calle Pellegrini 481 for US$2.50, taking 40 minutes, about half an hour less than the bus.

Guachipas and the Rock Paintings of Las Juntas

From El Carril, 3km from Chicoana, the Salta–Guachipas road continues south for 95km passing through the well preserved colonial Spanish villages of Moldes, Ampascachi and La Viña. Guachipas ('flying arrows') no doubt describes the welcome that outsiders would have got if they wandered into the area in the heyday of Indian civilisation. As yet this is not a well known tourist area but the gentle rolling sierras of the pre-Andes are well worth a visit.

The *arte rupestre* (rock paintings) of the caverns of **Las Juntas**, 24km beyond Guachipas, were recently added to UNESCO's World Heritage List, although they remain virtually unknown. They offer a splendid insight into the life of the pre-Columbian inhabitants of this region, who saw spiritual meaning in some hill sites. Las Juntas was a religious site where paintings in caves and rock overhangs show the agrarian lifestyle and warlike nature of the people. Later paintings clearly depict the different clothing worn by different levels of the society, some very ornate and others more simple.

Parallel lines of dots are said to relate to the economy of the time. A set of observation points carved in the rocks allows the sun to shine through at certain times of the year onto certain paintings, somewhat in the manner of sundials. Many of the best preserved paintings are seen by lying down under an overhanging rock and looking up. A self-appointed guide, Victoria López, rides for two hours

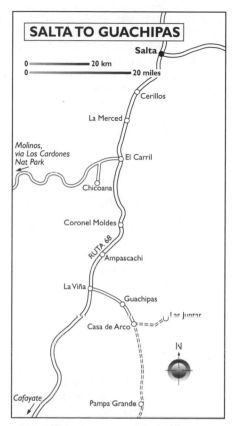

SALTA TO GUACHIPAS

0 ▬▬▬▬ 20 km
0 ▬▬▬▬▬ 20 miles

Salta
Cerillos
La Merced
Molinos,
via Los Cardones
Nat Park
El Carril
Chicoana
Coronel Moldes
RUTA 68
Ampascachi
La Viña
Guachipas
Las Juntas
Casa de Arco
Cafayate
Pampa Grande
N

by horse most days to explain the paintings to visitors. She is unpaid but grateful for any donations.

How to get there

Take the El Indio bus from Salta to Pampa Grande at 06.00 on Wednesdays which should reach Guachipas by 09.00 and Casa del Arco by 10.00; from here it is a 3km walk to the paintings. The bus returns at 16.20; it also runs on Saturday but does not return until Sunday, although anyone with a tent and provisions can find a place to camp, and there is water at the Casa del Arco bus shelter. Several El Indio buses daily run as far as Guachipas, 24km from Las Juntas over easy walking terrain. Alternatively it may be possible to hire a horse or take a taxi, but getting a lift in a passing vehicle would require patience. From Chicoana you will need to backtrack to El Carril to catch a bus, or maybe find a shared *remise* to Guachipas.

Tour guides

While mainstream agents in Salta do not visit this area, several adventure tour guides do, such as Hernán Uriburu and Martin Pekorek (see overleaf).

Los Cardones and El Rey national parks

It is worth mentioning a couple of national parks near Salta. **Los Cardones** is on Ruta 33 southwest of Salta beyond the Cuesta del Obispo (3,260m – although a sign claims 3,620m) towards the Valle Encantado. The park covers 65,000ha of terrain from 2,700m to as high as 5,000m. The 6m-high cardoon cactus *Trychocereus pasacana*, which gives the 65,000ha park its name, grows up to 3,400m altitude; it has edible fruit, and its trunk is used for making drums. Wildlife includes 100 species of birds, including condors, puna hawk, green-cheeked parakeet and tropical parula; and fox, puma, vicuña and taruca (northern huemul). The park is still very new, and has no facilities for tourists.

El Rey, 80km east of Salta, lies between the *yungas* (mountain woodland) and lowland Chaco. In the transition zone are huge trees such as cedro, tarco, tipa and nogal; above 800m is laurel cloudforest of *Myrtaceae* such as palo barroso, alpamato, mato, chal-chal and güilli, with a huge variety of epiphytes (including many orchids) and mosses; and above 1,500m is pino del cerro (*Podocarpus parlatorei*, the only conifer in northwestern Argentina) and then queñoa (*Polylepis australis*) and in the highest parts grass. Wildlife includes tapir, two species of peccary, puma, otter, foxes and coatí, and birds such as Chaco chacalaca, turquoise-fronted parrot, blue-hooded euphonia, sayaca tanager, rust-and-yellow tanager, picui ground dove, ruddy ground dove, eared dove, as well as red-fronted coot, grebe and ducks at Laguna de los Patitos, off the entry road south of the *Intendencia*.

The best season is winter, May–October; the unpaved RP20 north from Paso de la Cruz (48km) is often washed out in summer. You can camp near the *Intendencia*, and there is a one-hour vehicular interpretation trail to the Río Popayén. The road which leads west from the *Intendencia* for 12km to Pozo Verde continues as a 4km path to Cerro Chañar, where myrtles and pine give way to grass.

In addition the Chaco Woods, to the east of Salta, are a magnet for bird watchers, who base themselves in the village of Joaquín V González.

Trekking guides in the Salta Region

Martín Pekorek Calle España 45, (4423) Chicoana; tel/fax: 0387 490 7009; martinpek@impsat.com.ar.

Puna Expediciones (Luis and Maru Aguilar), PO Box 230, Braquiquitos 399, (4400) Salta; tel: 0387 434 1875; fax: 431 3341.

Overland (Federico Norte), Los Juncos 173, (4400) Salta; tel: 0387 439 6957; email: fedenorte@salta-argentina.com; www.salta-argentina.com/nortetrekking.htm.

Hernán Uriburu Leguizamon 446, (4400) Salta; tel/fax: 0387 431 0605; email: hru@salta-server.com.ar.

Puerta Tastil to El Carmen

Hernán Uriburu, a local trekking and horse-riding guide, has provided information on a hard, five-day trek in the mountains just north of Salta.

From Salta, take the El Quebradeño bus leaving at 15.00 (except on Sundays) and ask to be set down at Puerta Tastil, which is about 3½ hours from Salta and some way after Chorrillos and Lampasar. Because you arrive at around 18.30, it is necessary to camp here. The first day's hiking is mainly in the Quebrada, which is humid, with vegetation and small farms, ending up at San Bernardo de Los Zorros, near where you can camp. The next two days are spent climbing, with the going smooth in places and harder in others. It is very arid and reaches over 5,000m on the third day at Abra del Matadero. The second night is spent at El Pozo, and the third night at Concentración Mina Purma, where, although there is no longer a road, you will find (at 4,800m) an abandoned lorry, a relic of earlier days when the mine was working and there was vehicular access to the area. From here there is a long, smooth descent to the fourth camp at El Refugio and then El Carmen, where you can catch a bus back to Salta. You can also rest nearby at Hugo Macedo's Finca Las Pircas. Although it is not cheap, you may like to take a look at life on a *finca* after five days hard trekking.

This trek can also begin with a night at the Inca site (*c* 1200AD) of Santa Rosa de Tastil, just beyond Puerta Tastil, which was recently declared a national monument. There is a dormitory here, and the museum has an unusual musical instrument used by the Indians, consisting of a set of stones each producing a different tone when struck. Spectacular giant cacti stand among the ruins spread over the hillside. It is an easy half-day's walk from here to San Bernardo de Las Zorros for the second night, continuing as outlined above.

You can also make an easier four-day trek from Lampasar (half an hour before Puerta Tastil) to San Lorenzo, with overnight stops in Pascha, Campo Calderilla and Potrero Uriburu; this is an arid zone with many giant cacti, as well as guanaco.

Train to Socompa

A well-publicised tourist operation, the *Tren a las Nubes* runs on Saturdays all year round for 214km from Salta to the amazing La Polvorilla viaduct, a few kilometres beyond San Antonio de los Cobres – returning to Salta the same day. Little is heard about the **freight train** which leaves Salta on Friday mornings throughout the year, crosses La Polvorilla and heads on to Socompa on the Chilean border, a distance of 571km. The great beauty of the mountains and the desert landscape (complete with salt lakes and volcanoes) which unfolds after San Antonio is seldom reported, but this virtually unknown journey gives travellers a glimpse of this very faraway region of the world.

The train's main purpose is to carry drinking water and provisions from Salta to outposts on the railway line and to bring borax down from mines in the mountains to a processing plant at Campo Quijano, near Salta. One pullman-class (ie: with padded seats) passenger carriage takes customs' officers, soldiers and police to and from the border post. Other travellers can buy tickets shortly before departure time, at a cost of around US$30 for the return journey (taking 2½ days), as opposed to US$95 for the *Tren a las Nubes*.

The single-track metre-gauge line, built between 1921 and 1948, is an engineering masterpiece. It is possible to find rails marked with the stamp of the Camel foundry of Sheffield, England. Interestingly, one of the foremen engaged in its construction was a certain Josip Broz; it is often claimed that he later returned to Yugoslavia and ended up taking power as Marshal Tito, but this is now considered to be a picturesque myth – not one, but two workers of that name in fact died in Argentina. In the early section, hairpins, loops, 21 tunnels and 13 viaducts are used to tackle the steep climb to the *puna*; in ten hours the train climbs from 1,187m to the Abra Muñano at 3,952m, passing through the mountain pastures and giant cacti fields. After La Polvorilla (km217, at 4,190m) the scenery of the high, desert volcanic region of the *puna* begins and the journey continues across the salt lakes of Salar Pocitos and the Salar de Arizaro to Socompa (3,865m). Arizaro is the third largest salt lake in the world, but being covered with a thin layer of dust, it lacks the pristine whiteness of Pocitos.

Some isolated adobe houses and churches can be observed along the route, but settlements, concerned with railway and mining activities, are relatively new. There is little in the way of wildlife, although sharp eyes may spot the occasional guanaco, vicuña or flamingo.

It should be remembered that nights can be cold here and you should carry a sleeping bag or blankets. It is also advisable to take provisions, although there is a usually a small bar selling hot and cold drinks and simple cooked food. As the train reaches an altitude of 4,475m you are also likely to notice a lack of oxygen.

Although the track continues into Chile, there is no connecting passenger train and it is necessary to return to Salta on the same train. The continual variations of light and shade produce a landscape which is constantly changing. There are also two places in which you could break the journey to walk and explore this area. One is **Salar Pocitos** (3,666m), where a day can be spent wandering amongst the attractive formations in the salt lake and enjoying the silence. The white surface can be very bright, and you should use good sunglasses and keep the skin well protected. We understand that the good, but basic lodging formerly provided by Señora Dora Pintos is no longer available, but water can be obtained from the train station.

The other place where a stop could be made is **Tolar Grande** (3,525m), a railway encampment which now boasts a satellite telephone link. Here you can spend a pleasant day walking in a collection of red-sand hills, with views over the *salares* (salt pans) to the snow-capped mountains on the Chilean border. On the outward journey, the train arrives at both places at night, so you should expect to camp and be quite self-sufficient, although there may be accommodation in the municipality of Tolar Grande, where there is also a shop with basic provisions.

Although the train usually leaves from and returns to Salta as scheduled, the intermediate timings can vary. If stopping along the way, you should therefore check the expected return time. If you miss it, it is a week until the next train, and although there may be an occasional truck from Salar Pocitos to Salta, there is less likely to be any transport from Tolar Grande.

Bus trips

The same El Quebradeño bus mentioned on page 100, leaving Salta Mon–Sat at 15.00, runs parallel to the first part of the railway and reaches San Antonio de los Cobres (3,475m) at 21.00. It returns the next day at 09.00, passing the Inca site at Santa Rosa de Tastil around midday and arriving in Salta at 14.00 (taking an hour less in the downhill direction). You will need to spend two nights in San Antonio to make the trip (16km each way) to La Polvorilla viaduct, for a splendid view from below. An El Quebradeño bus goes to Salar Pocitos on Thursdays, leaving Salta at 09.00 and arriving at 18.00; it returns the next day at 13.00, arriving in Salta at 21.00.

Antofagasta de la Sierra

When travelling in northwestern Argentina, the small village of **Antofagasta de la Sierra** (Antofagasta for short, but not to be confused with the city of Antofagasta in Chile) is worth a visit. The village of 900 inhabitants, situated at 3,365m by the Río Punilla and overlooked by a large rock known as *El Torreón*, is the meeting place for the small local communities of the arid, desert-like region of Catamarca. This can be clearly seen around Easter each year when the descendants of Diaguita Indians gather at the artesanal fiesta with its array of local goods. Sunny days in this little basin among volcanic hills can seem quite perfect.

This part of Argentina shows traces of life from the earliest Stone Age through to the last days of the Inca empire. The carvings to be seen near Antofagasta have been built up progressively and demonstrate different styles and periods of the pre-Columbian civilisations. The remoteness of the area is a big factor in the good state of preservation of these sites, as well as deterring visitors.

How to get there

The sure way to get there is to travel the 582km from Catamarca on the weekly El Antofagasteño bus (tel: 03833 453 600), leaving at 04.00 on Friday for the 16-hour journey to Antofagasta, where it stays for the weekend, returning to Catamarca on Monday. This bus provides the local people with a lifeline to the world outside the *puna*, which offers tourists an insight into local life at grassroots level. From Catamarca, some people travel to Belén on the Thursday, stay the night and pick up the bus when it arrives at around 10.00, thus avoiding the early start. In Belén there are guest houses and the Hotel de Turismo, where camping is also allowed.

Coming from Salta take the El Indio bus which leaves at 07.00 on Wednesdays, arriving at Santa Maria at 13.00, and continue at 14.00 with the connecting Perra bus, arriving in Belén at 18.00, leaving Thursday free.

Where to stay

A *hostería*, with a good restaurant, opened in 2000; a double room costs US$25. Several cheaper guesthouses can be found in the centre of the village, including those of Darío Real and Pascuala Vasquez.

Information

For tourist information, ask at the Municipalidad of Antofagasta de la Sierra

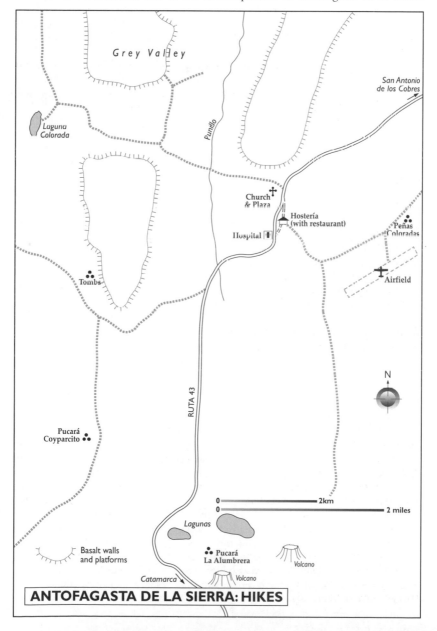

ANTOFAGASTA DE LA SIERRA: HIKES

(tel: 0835 471 001/2), or the House of Antofagasta de la Sierra in Catamarca (Republica 119; tel: 03833 422 300), or the House of Catamarca in Buenos Aires (Avda Cordoba 2080; tel: 011 4374 6891/93/95).

Hiking circuits

The road leads 6km south from the village to two *lagunas* backed by two volcanos with extensive black lava fields. Just beyond the lakes you will find the well preserved Indian site, **Pucará La Alumbrera**, with many artefacts still lying around in the soil. There is abundant birdlife in the lakes, including pink flamingos relishing the salty water at certain seasons. From the hill behind the church in the village there is a nice panorama of these sites.

An easy 5km walk eastwards from the village takes you to **Peñas Coloradas** where five big outcrops display a fine array of rock carvings. Herdsmen still work the land and animals are often housed amidst these precious historic relics, which in many parts of the world would be cordoned off even to the public.

Taking the road south from Antofogasta, beyond the Río Pumillo a track leads west to a site where, as well as good carvings, there are several well-preserved tombs. Unfortunately, the relics inside have long since disappeared. Following to the base of the hills south for a few kilometres further, you will come to the hill of Coyparcito, crowned with ruins of an Inca settlement, **Pucará Coyparcito**, and a few minutes further the old Indian mine of the same name. There are also many interesting geological formations giving an effect of a lunar landscape.

Taking a track north-westwards from Antofagasta you will soon be amongst impressive basalt walls and platforms. On the right-hand side of the track, above one of these platforms, is the Grey Valley with elaborate rock formations and a splendid panorama down the valley over Antofagasta and the plains to the volcanoes and *lagunas* in the south. Returning to the track, it is about 3km further west to **Laguna Colorada**, a small salt lake with a glimmering white surface. Nearby, there is an abandoned military factory and a warm spring.

Belén to Antofagasta de la Sierra

A free day in **Belén** can be spent climbing a nearby hill, in the archaeological museum, or visiting the town of Londres, 15km south.

Founded in 1558, **Londres** (London) was named in honour of the venue of the wedding of Philip II of Spain to Mary Tudor of England. It has been destroyed several times by Indian attacks and there are many archaeological sites in the area, the largest being the Inca **El Shinkal**.

For those with more time, breaks can be made along the road to Antofagasta using Pino Villagra's minibus (tel: 03835 461 067) which runs north from Belén to Laguna Blanca on Monday, Wednesday and Friday. From **Villavil** (80km from Belén) you can cross the river and walk 2km to a very comfortable hot spring at about 2,500m, where you can spend the day in waters which are supposed to be beneficial for kidney, liver and digestive problems. Local people wash clothes downstream of the water hole. In Villavil there is accommodation in a *hostería* and in a private house where the landlady has a big loom on which she weaves fine blankets. Further up the road passing travellers stay at the ranch of Barranca Larga, which is not shown on any maps. You are likely to meet traders who sell merchandise to the *campesinos* and also buy their woven textiles for sale in the city. There are easy walks along the riverbed and to the cross on a nearby hillock. After Barranca Larga there are no settlements on the road, and there is no public

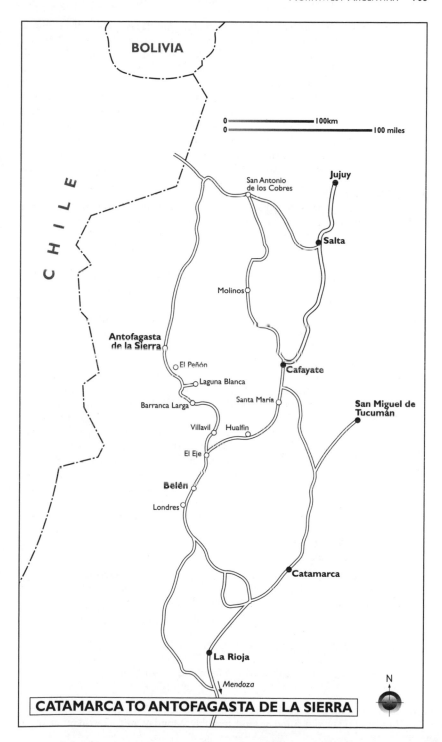

BOLIVIA

0 _____ 100km
0 _____ 100 miles

CHILE

Jujuy

San Antonio
de los Cobres

Salta

Molinos

Antofagasta
de la Sierra

El Peñón

Laguna Blanca

Cafayate

Barranca Larga

Santa María

San Miguel de
Tucumán

Villavil   Hualfin

El Eje

Belén

Londres

Catamarca

La Rioja

Mendoza

N

CATAMARCA TO ANTOFAGASTA DE LA SIERRA

transport north of the turning about 120km before Antofagasta where the minibus turns off to Laguna Blanca, 20km east. Nearby is the provincial Cattle Research Station and vicuña reserve, where the caretaker, Alejandro Villagra and his wife Simona can provide lodging and food in their home. Flamingo and ñandú are sometimes seen in the area. Indian ruins close by are being researched at present by the University of Catamarca. There is also a lovely small white Andean church with a cactus-wood ceiling on the plaza at Laguna Blanca. Other than the church, school, plaza and cemetery the village comprises four or five family houses. The last inhabited place before Antofagasta is El Peñón, 60km away. Travellers can stay here in the modest lodging of Carmelo Guzman or in the new municipality building which has two beds (contact Elina Ramon, tel: 03835 454 001).

Jujuy Province

The mountainous province of Jujuy (pronounced 'hoo-huey'), 100km south of the Bolivia/Argentina border, is one of the most primitive backpacking areas in Argentina. Its friendly, hardworking people and terrain are very similar to those of Peru or Bolivia. The inhabitants depend on sheep for a living and survive on a humble diet of potatoes and maize. They will be more than glad to tell you which way to go when you come to a fork in the trail. Well-worn side paths often lead to small *ranchos*, so you may have to backtrack occasionally to stay on the main track.

In many ways this part of the Andes resembles the desert of the southwest United States. In lower areas there are small, thorny trees and shrubs, then as you go above the treeline there is just stubby grass. As you approach the Quebrada de Humahuaca this is replaced by different types of cacti. Local people are very knowledgeable about the different types of medicinal herbs, such as *rica rica*, a dry shrub with a delicious flavour for tea that calms the stomach. At higher altitudes, there is a plant whose small leaves, if crushed between the fingers and inhaled, will cure headaches and nausea caused by the altitude. Wildlife is abundant here and you may well spot condors riding the thermals in search of carrion. Other animals include the vicuña and the vizcacha, a larger version of the chinchilla which lives near the highest passes and utters shrill whistles as it jumps from rock to rock.

There are two hikes in the area, which can be linked in a loop: from Valle Grande, north of Ledesma (also known as 'Libertador General San Martín', or 'Libertador'), to Tilcara, and back from Uquía; or Humahuaca to Valle Grande. Buses run from Jujuy to Ledesma (1½ hours), Uquía (3 hours) and Humahuaca (3½ hours). From Salta, you can take an Atahualpa bus to Ledesma, 2½ hours away.

Valle Grande to Tilcara
Getting to the trailhead

Distance	88km
Altitude	Between 1,600m and 4,000m
Rating	Difficult
Time	4 days
Start of trail	Valle Grande
End of trail	Tilcara
Maps	1:250,000 map of Salta and Jujuy (2566-11)

From Ledesma, Empresa 23 de Agosto operates a bus to Valle Grande, 93km north, on Tuesday, Friday and Sunday (and possibly Monday and Thursday) at 08.30

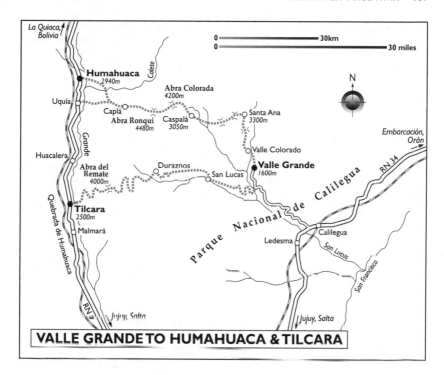

VALLE GRANDE TO HUMAHUACA & TILCARA

(returning the same day); in addition *colectivo* pick-ups run every day. The road can be in terrible condition during the summer rains.

The road to Valle Grande turns off the main Ruta 34 at Calilegua, 5km north of Ledesma, and runs through **Parque Nacional Calilegua**, 76,320ha of mountain forest which has the highest biodiversity in Argentina. It is sub-tropical, with a dry winter (average temperature 17°C) and a wet summer (average 28°C, and 2m of rain, with 60–85% humidity). In the deep gorges, between 350m and 500m above sea level, there is forest of palo blanco, palo amarillo, tipa and pacará. From 550 to 1,600m this becomes a Yungas cloud forest with an impenetrable tangle of lianas, vines, ferns and epiphytes, on trees such as cedar, laurel, horco molle, and nogal; above this, where snow falls, there is pine, aliso and queñoa, and grasslands above. Mammals include tapír, otters, yaguareté (a wild cat), and the taruca or northern huemul. The 260 species of birds include toucan, hummingbirds, woodpeckers, torrent duck, vultures, condors, eagles and the red-faced guan. In addition there are endemic reptiles and amphibians. Camping is possible at the Aguas Negras *guardería*, from where you can hike into the park. The road on to Valle Grande is outrageously beautiful, as it skirts canyons that seem bottomless.

Detour

Likewise, if you continue up Ruta 34 to Orán and continue 70km to the northwest you will reach the **Parque Nacional Baritú**: 74,439ha of virgin cloud forest receiving 2m of rain a year (mostly November–April). At lower levels, this is dominated by big trees such as timbo, viraró, peteribí, cevil/carril, tipa blanca, jacarandá (and in wetter areas piño del cerro with myrtaceae such as mato and guayabo), with tree ferns and the epiphytic maroma (*Ficus maroma*). Above this is forest of lapacho amarillo and laurel, and at the highest levels cedar and nogal. Wildlife includes yaguareté, ocelot, tapir, collared peccary, montane fox, otter, monkeys, parrots, toucans, the yapu (a thrush that builds hanging nests), and a fish-eating bat.

There are no services for visitors, and the park is threatened by plans for a dam on the Río Bermejo and for a gas pipeline which would cut the link between Calilegua and Baritú.

Route description
A third of this hike is below the treeline, which makes it easy to find shade, but even so heat exhaustion is a real possibility here in summer, and there are few settlements along this hike to offer help. Take everything you need.

In **Valle Grande** (1,600m) you can buy last-minute provisions, or a brimmed hat hand-made from local wool. Walking back south from the village, ask where the dirt road to Pampichuela turns off to the right/west (it can be seen across the canyon to the southwest); this continues as the trail to San Lucas and Tilcara. If you manage the steep, dusty ascent up the numerous hairpins, you will survive the rest of the hike. Near the end of the 5km climb, you will reach an abandoned hut to the right of the trail. This is an excellent place to rest, but the spring, hidden in the trees about 200m south, is a bit difficult to find.

After about 13km you will reach San Lucas (10 hours from the Ledesma road), which consists of a string of scattered houses. There are plenty of good grassy camping spots. If you camp near someone's *rancho*, be sure to meet the family with some sign of friendship, as they may not realise your good intentions. After another 26km of hiking up the San Lucas valley (10–12 hours) you will reach Duraznos, a few buildings including a small school hugging the side of the mountain. From here it is a 2-day walk (35km) to the 4,000m pass called Abra del Remate; it is then 3 hours (14km) downhill to the pretty village of **Tilcara**. The last stretch, from Alfarcito, is on a dirt road with occasional buses. Tilcara is in the narrow valley of the Río Grande, along which run the main road and railway from Jujuy to the Bolivian border at La Quiaca. Known as the **Quebrada de Humahuaca** (Humahuaca Gorge), this is a stunningly beautiful area with a variety of coloured rocks. Tilcara (at 2,500m) offers a handful of hotels, a youth hostel (Albergue Malka, on San Martín; tel/fax: 0388 495 5197; tilcara@hostels.org.ar), which rents out mountain bikes and horses, and a couple of campsites. There is also an archaeological museum and botanic garden, and an Inca *pucará* (fortress) 1km away. Buses run north to Uquía and **Humahuaca** (2,940m), which boasts five museums, a church dating from 1631, and craft shops; there are also hotels and a youth hostel at Buenos Aires 447 (tel: 03887 421 064).

Humahuaca to Valle Grande
Getting to the trailhead
It is actually easier to start this hike from Uquía (around 11km/3½ hours south of Humahuaca and 3 hours from Jujuy), which has a church, built in 1691, with fascinating old paintings. Uquía and Humahuaca are both served by all buses from Jujuy to La Quiaca.

Route description
It can be very cold at night, and there is very little water, but this difficult hike is superb and rewarding. From Uquía, cross the bridge, turn right and head up the

Distance	95km
Altitude	Between 2,600m and 4,480m
Rating	Difficult
Time	4 days
Start of trail	Uquía (11km south of Humahuaca)
End of trail	Valle Grande
Maps	1:250,000 map of Salta and Jujuy (2566-II)

embankment to pick up a path that follows the south side of a fenced field until it rejoins the dirt road through the canyon to Capla, a nearly deserted village at 3,400m (3–4 hours from Uquía). Starting from Humahuaca, cross the bridge near the market, turn right at a signpost with many pointers and head southeast; it should take about 2 hours over the hill to reach the road up the Calete valley. Follow this to the left for about 1km, then turn right to drop down to the river at 3,000m (the river may be dry, but there is water in an irrigation channel for at least a few hours a day). Continuing, head slightly upstream to find the path, which joins the road from Uquía and brings you to Capla in 2 hours.

From Capla follow the road up the valley, sometimes replaced by the (dry) riverbed, and then take the clearly visible trail uphill to your left (there are a couple of springs and campsites in this area). This climbs steeply, is level for about 2km, then climbs from a valley to the pass of Abra Ronqui, the highest point on the hike at 4,480m, 3–4 hours from Capla. It should take 1½ hours to descend to Abra Colorado (4,200m), the nicest camping spot on this route, with water and plenty of short grass on which to pitch a tent; however, it can freeze at night, even in high summer. It is also a good place to see vizcacha and vicuña. Further down, just before Caspalá, there are some postage-stamp-size camping spots which are considerably warmer than the higher sites.

It is another 2–3 hours' descent from Abra Colorado to **Caspalá** (3,050m), a picturesque village nestling in a deep valley where every flat space is put to some use, for a home, crops or livestock, so you will have to ask permission to pitch camp in someone's yard or pasture. All you see initially is a small, white church, as the surrounding houses blend in perfectly with the mountainside. From here the trail continues downhill for 1–1½ hours to a fast-flowing stream at about 2,900m, then ascends a steep, seemingly endless, slope known as Las Lajutas to reach (after 2–3 hours) a 3,550m pass, about 10km from Caspalá. From here it drops into a valley at 3,300m and climbs to another pass (3,550m), where you should swing right and descend with a canyon on your right to the village of **Santa Ana**, 2 hours from the first pass. This is a quaint, sleepy adobe village 3,300m above sea level, with one main street. Many people have moved down to the lowlands for better jobs, but about a hundred remain here to care for the family sheep. To the southwest of the village you can see the remains of a small copper mine which closed many years ago due to transport problems. Santa Ana is a good place to stop as there are many places near the river to camp, and the communal water supply is nearby. You can buy the barest essentials at the small general store, but the shop in Caspalá is much better stocked. Santa Ana has an occasional bus service to Humahuaca, allowing you to loop back from here.

The trail continues briefly up the Santa Ana valley to a pass with a cross, at which you should turn right, enjoying splendid views of the canyons. It takes about 5 hours to drop down to the small village of Valle Colorado (at about

2,600m), from where you follow the road down the valley for 2½ hours to Valle Grande (see above).

The Bolivian border
Getting to the trailhead
From Salta, both La Internacional and Balut lines offer six buses a day to La Quiaca (8 hours, US$23). If waiting for transport here, it is worth taking a bus or truck to Yavi (18km) to visit a very old Andean church where services are held one Sunday

Distance	60km
Altitude	4,100m at the highest point
Rating	Moderate
Time	3 days
Start of trail	Nazareno
End of trail	Santa Victoria Oeste
Maps	1:250,000 map of Salta and Jujuy (2566-II)

a month. It is pleasant to walk around the village, where there are several other interesting buildings.

Neither Nazareno nor Santa Victoria Oeste (described below) is served by bus, and in consequence they have been little publicised as trekking sites. However, it is not too difficult to obtain lifts, and information about transport can be obtained from the ACA petrol station near the frontier in La Quiaca, where the attendants know about local traffic movements. Around twice a week a scheduled truck goes to Nazareno (costing around US$15), and occasional trucks cover the 116km to Santa Victoria (for around US$10). Return trips can be arranged with local drivers from either place. Although both villages are in the province of Salta, they can only be reached by road from La Quiaca, in the province of Jujuy.

The mountainous region around La Quiaca, at 3,442m on the border with Bolivia, is a delight for hikers, and also offers pleasant sightseeing. The short walk over the border to Villazón in Bolivia is fun, and as prices in Bolivia are lower than those in Argentina, there is a constant stream of people and vans crossing to buy clothes and household goods. For western travellers, the many silver and woven items may be of interest, especially the well-known maroon Bolivian ponchos.

Nazareno
The area around Nazareno is full of footpaths in all directions, so that several days could easily be spent walking there. The road through the village follows the riverbed along the mountainside. If taking this road early in the morning, you may find yourself, after about an hour's walk, suddenly standing above masses of clouds lying in the valley, caused by the sudden rise in temperature as the sun has risen. These clouds can also disappear in a few seconds as the sun further heats the air. It is possible to find accommodation in the municipality in Nazareno, where there are also several grocers and a very interesting old church.

Nazareno to Santa Victoria Oeste
Luis and Maru Aguilar, of Puna Expediciones in Salta, have provided details of a 3-day trek from Nazareno to Santa Victoria Oeste (not to be confused with Santa Victoria Este, also in Salta province, but lying in the plains near the border with

Bolivia and Paraguay). You should walk for around 6 hours a day, with overnight stops at Poscaya and Trigo Huaico, where you may be able to sleep in the schools if the teachers are there; donations of pencils and other school materials would be appreciated.

From the village of Nazareno, the trek begins through a green valley where potatoes and maize are cultivated on mountainside terraces. This is followed by a climb to Poscaya, where the inhabitants are very cordial and there is a little school and a chapel. On the second day, the walk continues uphill to the source of the Río Nazareno and over the Mono Abra pass at 4,100m, then crosses a path to the old but still working Mina de Baritina, and descends to the hamlet of Trigo Huaico.

There is a remarkable solitude and silence in the last part of the trek. Remains of a path made from rock tiles by the first inhabitants of the area can be seen, and further down the mountain you will reach the last of the typical hamlets, Acoyte, site of an important battle in the war for independence from Spain. This essentially consists of a picturesque square surrounded by the church and houses. It was impressive to find four locals walking up the riverbed carrying a wardrobe which they had bought cheaply in Villazón in Bolivia.

About 3 hours beyond Acoyte, the suspension bridges over the Río Huerta mark the entrance to **Santa Victoria Oeste**. This is a captivating village with pebbled streets, a pretty square and a church. The municipality has a dormitory and there are about 30 food shops for the 300 inhabitants and others who walk great distances (sustained by their supply of coca leaves) through the surrounding hills to obtain provisions.

The best time to come here is April to November; at other times there are heavy rains and electric storms. There are springs of drinkable water throughout the trek, but you should carry a water bottle. It is suggested that you check the route with the villagers as there are many paths branching in all directions.

Laguna Pozuelos Natural Monument

Not far from the Bolivian border, **Laguna Pozuelos** (3,700m) covers an area of approximately 15,000ha (although this fluctuates with the seasons and its average size seems to have been shrinking in the 1990s). Here you can see up to 50,000 birds, notably three of the world's six species of flamingo, as well as ñandú, woodpeckers, Andean avocet, ducks, Andean, horned and giant coot and other species of waterbirds, and animals including vicuña. Precipitation is under 200mm per year, falling mostly in summer. While days are hot, at night the temperature falls below zero and early in the morning flamingos can be seen anchored to the lake with their legs frozen in place. As the ice melts, a spectacular scene ensues as the birds break free and take flight. A fascinating day can be spent watching their activities; especially impressive is the sight of their mass take-off when their leader decides to make a move.

The *laguna* is 50km northwest of Abra Pampa (reached by Salta–La Quiaca buses) where you can find the *guardaparque* (Raul Angerami, at Rivadavia esq. Alberdi, Barrio 31 de Agosto; tel: 03887 491 048). From here three local buses a week go to Rinconada, passing the park guard's hut at Pozuelos, near which you can camp. Water is available there, but you should take everything else you will need. There are easy walks on flat ground around the *laguna*, and also to a very nice adobe church to the southwest of the *laguna*.

NORTHEAST ARGENTINA

Northeast Argentina is not obvious hiking country, but nevertheless there are sites of ecotouristic interest, notably the national parks that protect representative chunks of the country's original ecosystems.

Just 56km east of Buenos Aires is the city of **La Plata**, where you should visit perhaps Latin America's best Museum of Natural Sciences (open daily 10.00–19.00; US$3); 12km north (bus 275) is the Punta Lara Nature Reserve, a small area of subtropical coastal forest with 270 bird species recorded. Near **Magdalena**, about 100km south of La Plata, the Costero del Sur Biosphere Reserve and the private El Destino reserve protect coastal marshland with plenty of birdlife. Heading south towards Mar del Plata, Argentina's leading resort, the **Bahía Samborombón** reserve is the flagship project of the Fundación Vida Silvestre, the country's leading conservation group. This is home to one of just three remaining populations of pampas deer (venado de las pampas or guazú-ti; *Ozotocerus bezoarticus*), the country's most threatened mammal, with only 1,300 left (of perhaps 40 million prior to colonisation). They have been driven out of virtually all their natural habitat by cattle ranchers; in San Luis province, to the west, 300,000ha of relict semi-xerofile *pampas* grassland is home to perhaps 1,000 pampas deer, but this area is threatened by a road project, although there are also plans to create the Los Venados National Park here. The third tiny group is in Corrientes province, between the Esteros del Iberá and the Río Aguapey.

Just northwest of the city of Buenos Aires (by Ruta 9, or 400m from Otamendi station on the Mitre railway to Zarate) the **Reserva Natural Otamendi** protects 2,600ha of almost sub-tropical wetlands, riverside forest and *pampas* grassland. A road leads 5.5km to the Río Paraná, and the El Talar trail leads 1km to a viewpoint. The **Parque Nacional Pre-Delta** (formerly the Reserva Diamante), 44km south of Paraná, covers 2,458ha of marsh and riverine forest, with trees such as native willow, timbó blanco and ceibo, and carpincho (waterhog), coipo, otter, water snakes and turtles, as well as 140 species of birds. Check in first with the *guardaparque* at Yrigoyen 396, Diamante (6km north of the park) to arrange a boat, the only way to see much.

To the north of the capital, 54km south of Concordia on Ruta 14 near the Uruguayan border, the **Parque Nacional El Palmar** protects 8,500ha of savanna grassland, groves of yatay palms (*Syagrus yatay*) up to 12m high and 800 years old, and gallery forest of native willow and laurel, with plenty of creepers and epiphytes. Mammals include vizcacha (near the Arroyo Los Loros campsite), carpincho, coipo, fox, raccoon, otter, yaguarundi and Geoffroy's and pampas cats; and birds include three types of woodpecker, ñandú and *cotorras* (monk parakeets), in communal nests 2m across that weigh 200kg. However, the park is afflicted both by introduced species such as European wild boar, and by the pressure of 79,000 visitors per year – one solution is to develop bicycle facilities. An unmade road leads 12km from Ruta 14 to the *Intendencia* (in the former *casco* or estate owner's house); there is a campsite nearby.

The **Esteros del Iberá**, in Corrientes province (just south of the controversial Yacyretá hydroelectric plant), have recently begun to attract a lot of attention from birdwatchers. This is 1.2 million hectares (about 15% of the province's area) of wetlands, of which 700,000ha owned by the province is protected. There is a new visitor centre by Laguna Iberá (53km² in area) at Carlos Pellegrini (110km northeast of Mercedes, reached by three buses a week or minibus, from Juan Pujol 1166; tel: 0376 492 9598). However, Doug Tompkins (see page 249) has in recent years bought almost 100,000ha here, and plans to have perhaps 400,000ha by 2010; he has ambitious plans for ecological restoration, and does not intend to allow access to visitors.

Its name comes from the 'Shining Waters' (Guaraní 'i', water, and 'bera' shining or brilliant) on which drift *embalsados* or floating islands of vegetation; on drier land there are five species of palm (palmera yatay, palma blanca, pindó, mbocayá, and pygmy yataypoñí), laurel, ceibo, curupí, timbo (or oreja de negro), lapacho, guayabo, with many lianas, bromeliads and epiphytes. The area is inhabited by about 370 species of birds (such as savanna hawk, monk parakeet, smooth-billed ani, giant wood-rail, semi-collared nighthawk, golden-breasted woodpecker, field flicker, yellowish pipit, grassland yellow-finch, rusty-coloured and double-collared seedeaters, red-winged tinamou, scissor-tailed nightjar, white-headed marsh-tyrant, white-banded mockingbird, black and white monjita, tropical screech-owl, southern screamers, three species of kingfisher, jabirú, anhinga, plumbeous and white-faced ibis, herons, ducks, gulls, flamingos, roseate spoonbill and ñandú), as well as mammals such as carpincho, capybara, maned wolf, otters, swamp and brocket deer, howler monkey, anteaters, tapir, peccary and jaguar; reptiles such as caimans, yellow anaconda, tegú lizard, and turtles; and fish such as dorado, shad, mojarra and piranha.

The 15,060ha **Parque Nacional Mburucuya**, just west (southeast of Corrientes City), also protects palmeras de yatay; there are maned wolves, howler monkeys, otters and caimans here as well as fish such as dorado and surubí. It is possible to arrange trips by boat or horse, or on foot with local tourist agencies.

The **Parque Nacional Chaco**, established in 1934, covers 150km² of the million-plus square kilometres of the Chaco. Specifically, this is sub tropical Eastern Chaco habitat, 130km northwest of Resistencia. Wetlands are home to lily-trotters, jabirú, herons, ducks and frogs; on seasonally flooded savanna there are palm trees, together with white woodpecker, red hawk, ñandú, puma and maned wolf. On the hillsides to the north is woodland of quebracho and other trees with bromeliads, cacti, and deer, carpincho, howler monkeys, jays, ovenbirds and parrots. Buses run daily from Resistencia to Capitán Solari, from where it is 6km to the park; there is a campsite, from which run various paths.

Iguazú Falls

In the extreme northeastern corner of Argentina (at the borders with Brazil and Paraguay, and best reached by air) are the **Iguazú Falls**, one of the great tourist sights of South America. Rightly named by the Guaraní 'The Great Waters', there are 275 falls spread over 3km, pushing an average 1,300m³ per second over a drop of 70m, and up to 6,500m³ per second at peaks. The best panorama is from the Brazilian side, but you can get closer on the Argentine side, particularly from boats to the seriously frightening *Garganta del Diablo*; helicopter trips are only allowed on the Brazilian side, and cause serious environmental disturbance.

Hourly buses take you to the excellent information centre below the falls (where you will pay a US$5 entry fee), and on to Puerto Canoas (a natural-gas-powered railway is being built to handle the 6–15,000 visitors per day, and all other vehicles will be banned). From Puerto Canoas a boardwalk leads across to the islands above the *Garganta del Diablo*; this may be damaged by floods, in which case (usually) you will be taken across by boat. This costs US$4, while there is a free boat service below the falls to the Isla San Martín. There is also the 4km Macuco Trail from the information centre, and a bird recuperation centre 1km from the information centre, with walk-through aviaries; inside are birds being prepared for release, while their wild brethren are attracted outside.

In addition to the incredible spectacle of the falls, there is also a **national park** protecting a large tract of sub-tropical rainforest. It is hot and humid here, with an average temperature of about 20°C, 2m of precipitation, and 75–90% humidity; the best time to visit is July–November. The rainy season, when the flow is highest, ends in July, but the weather is often cloudy and chilly then; by March, the flow is reduced by a third.

There are 2,000-plus species of plants (including 200 trees); emergents such as timbó, up to 30m high, rise above the canopy, while tree-ferns and shrubs form the mid-level, along with flowers, lianas, orchids and bromeliads. In the wettest areas near the falls thrive trees such as curupay, cupay, laurel de río, laurel blanco, aguay and ingá, as well as seibo (the national flower), and the grass *Paspalum lilloi*; elsewhere the 40m-high palo rosa grows in association with palmito palm trees. The 400-plus species of birds (120 of them present all year) include five species of toucan and toucanet, tanagers, trogons, tropical parula, red-ruffed fruitcrow, blue-naped chlorophonia, purple-throated euphonia, solitary tinamou, black-fronted piping guan, violaceous quail-dove, squirrel cuckoo, river warbler, tufted antshrike, waterfall and great dusky swifts, white-eyed and reddish-bellied parakeets, rusty-barred owl, plush-crested jay, white-necked puffbird, blue dacnis, lineated, blond-crested and yellow-fronted woodpeckers, red-rumped cacique, collared forest falcon, great black hawk, plumbeous kite, plush-crested jay and hummingbirds. The 76 mammal species are largely nocturnal, but include coatí (very common on the boardwalks), white-eared opossum, paca, agouti, anteaters, tapir, collared peccary, brocket deer, ring-tailed and howler monkeys, yaguareté (or tigre) and ocelot, as well as *Tropidurus* tree lizards, 60 species of frog, amazing butterflies, and, alas, mosquitoes and sandflies. It is best to get into the forest early, as the birds are quieter after 10.00, and the crowds flood in from then on.

Iguazú is at the heart of the once vast Paranaense Rainforest (*Selva Paranaense*, also known as *Bosque Atlántico Interior* or *Selva Atlántica*), only 7% of which survives. However, there are ambitious projects to create Green Corridors to link it with areas of forest in Brazil and Paraguay as well as in other parts of Misiones Province.

Near **Almirante Brown** in northeastern Misiones the Yacutinga Wildlife Reserve is 550ha of *Corredor Verde* surrounding the luxurious Yacutinga ecolodge (www.yacutinga.com). In the same area the 75,000ha Yabotí reserve is near the 3km-long Moconá falls, and the San Antonio Strict Natural Reserve protects one of the last natural populations of paraná pine trees (pino paraná or curí-y; *Araucaria angustifolia*), also found in the Cruce Caballero and Araucaria Provincial Parks. The pines, up to 30m high, are associated with yerba mate, laurel negro and guatambú blanco, birds such as coludito de los pinos and parrots, and red howler monkeys.

Formosa
Kathleen Ladizesky
Formosa Province in northeastern Argentina is one of the least known areas of the country. It is largely wild and uncultivated, and thought should be given to timing of visits, as in summer it is hot and many of the unpaved roads are impassable due to rains, although this is a good time for fishing from boats for huge surubí. There are few trekking circuits, but the province, with its uncultivated wildness and abundant ethnic population, has great potential for the traveller.

The city of Formosa is easily reached by bus from all parts of Argentina, passing

THE INDIGENOUS PEOPLES OF WESTERN FORMOSA

By minibus from Formosa it takes eight hours along the long straight Route 81 to reach Ingeniero Juárez. This is the territory of the aboriginal Wichi, Toba and Pilagas, each with its own distinct language (although most can speak Spanish). A big influx of missionaries of varying sects has widely implanted the Christian doctrine and people may show you handwritten cards from their house reading *Casa de Dios*, or an identity card given by their church.

While changing with the times and to some extent merging into the mainstream Argentine way of life, the Indians have retained a distinctiveness of their own. They seem a shy people who keep very much to their family groups and do not enthuse over outsiders. Some villages have been modernised but many people still live in mud houses, sitting crosslegged on the ground, cooking pots of stew on wood fires, or producing their traditional weavings. Although they may be reluctant to perform for onlookers, people here can make music very much like that of a bamboo pipe just by cupping their hands and blowing into them. Few have much chance of moving further than the next town; one man said he had been asked by his pastor to visit Buenos Aires and had been most impressed with the train that went underground, although he had been lost for three days in the city.

Along the River Bermejo main roads are paved, but most are sunbaked mud and may be impassable in the summer rains; even in winter it is a very hot region. The Scorpio bus travels one such track linking Ing. Juárez to the boundary with Salta Province, starting around 10.00 on Tuesday, Thursday and Saturday. The track is lined with dense vegetation, with many different cacti and trees, spiny bushes and parasitic plants completely covering many trees. The bus often stops at isolated dwellings in clearings in the bush. The three-hour journey ends along the Bermejo river with its wide flood plains and occasional fishermen punting their small wooden coracles. The skill of fishing with spears has largely disappeared and been replaced by lines and hooks. Fish here are gigantic *surubí*, which can be as much as 1.25m long, 0.6m across and 60kg in weight. On the return bus journey several seats may be taken up by large fishes in sacks going to the market. There is such a surfeit of fish that fishing is no longer very profitable, but those fishing for sport will be well rewarded.

through Resistencia. Onward travel can be made with one of the several reliable Formosa-based minibus operators or in a shared taxi, all of which offer door-to-door service, which is very convenient for travellers with luggage. An added attraction in this area is the **easy entry to Paraguay** through the boundary town of Clorinda to Asunción, or by boat across the Río Paraguay from Formosa. Many people go over to Paraguay for a day's cheap shopping and can bring back duty-free as much as they can carry by hand. Paraguayan vendors are commonly seen on the streets selling home-made bread from flat baskets on their heads.

The **Río Pilcomayo National Park**, on the Paraguayan border just west of Asunción, is a Ramsar wetland site of close to 60,000ha. With a sub-tropical climate with maximum temperatures of 45°C and 1,200mm of precipitation per year, tall-

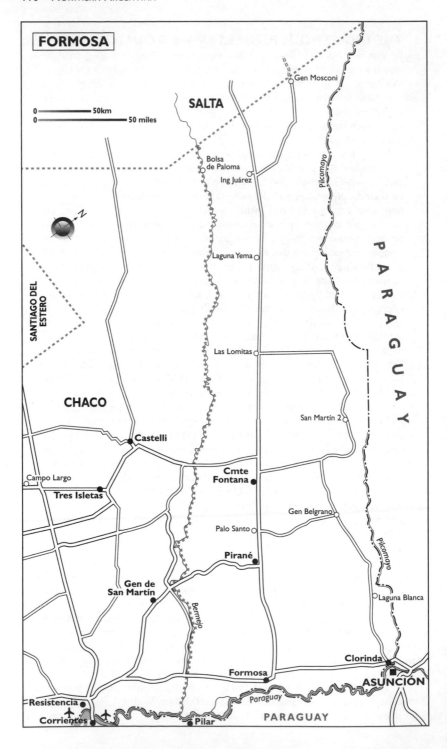

FORMOSA

0 ——— 50km
0 ——— 50 miles

SALTA

Gen Mosconi

Bolsa
de Paloma

Ing Juárez

Laguna Yema

Las Lomitas

Pilcomayo

PARAGUAY

SANTIAGO DEL
ESTERO

CHACO

Castelli

San Martín 2

Campo Largo

Tres Isletas

Cmte
Fontana

Gen Belgrano

Palo Santo

Pirané

Gen de
San Martín

Bermejo

Laguna Blanca

Pilcomayo

Clorinda

Formosa

ASUNCIÓN

Resistencia

Corrientes

Paraguay

Pilar

PARAGUAY

grass savanna is dominant here, with 14m caranday palms. By the rivers, there is a gallery forest of willow, and in higher and drier areas there is a forest dense with lianas, epiphytes, ferns and orchids. Birds to be seen here include parrots, woodpeckers, ñandú, spoonbills, herons and jabirú; and mammals include puma, maned wolf, anteater, carpincho, deer, and all three Argentinian species of monkey. There are also two species of caiman, both endangered, the boa curiyú, and lots of mosquitoes.

The base for the park is the small town of **Laguna Blanca**, four hours from Formosa by minibus; stay at the delightful colonial Residencial Guaraní. Nearby are two fastfood places where you can get reasonable meals. The Estero Pói sector of the park, 8km from Laguna Blanca, seems surprisingly lacking in wildlife, apart from huge ant colonies which the University of Würzburg in Germany is studying. Well-trodden paths extending from the anthills are filled with a constant stream of ants carrying proportionately enormous pieces of foliage back into the nests as food for the fungi which the ants themselves eat. In the recreational sector of the park, 16km from the town, there are pleasant viewing platforms over the Laguna Blanca where it is possible to swim. There are good camping facilities here.

Cabalgatas (horse-riding treks)
For those who wish to venture further off the tracks this is excellent terrain for horse-trekking, as walking is difficult due to the thorny bush. Apart from providing information on the National Park, the park warden in Laguna Blanca, Sr. Nestor Sucunza (tel: 03718 470 045) can help you find a reliable guide for horseback treks in the area. In Villa Belgrano Sr. Julio Silvera, manager of the Hotel Orlando (tel: 03716 491 003), is the best contact for hiring guides and horses.

Wetlands near Villa Belgrano
An hour away by bus, a track links Villa Belgrano with Route 81, and makes up for the lack of visible fauna in the park. Here there are marshes with an abundance of birdlife including several species of stork, large eagles and numerous other bird species; rare animals such as armadillos can often be seen. Wooden carts pulled by long horned oxen are still used on the land, and the small rivers are popular with local fishermen.

Boat trips
S.t.a.F Paraguay 520, Formosa; tel: 03717 420 780; offers several trips along these wide, serene rivers such as parts of the Bermejo or Monte Lindo Grande near Villa Belgrano.

Further Information
Carlos Arnedo Casa de Formosa, Yrigoyen 1429, Buenos Aires; tel: 011 4381 0721; tourismo@casadeformosa.gov.ar.
Dirección de Turismo Uriburu 820, (3600) Formosa; tel: 03717 420 442/426 502.
Instituto de Communidades Aborigenes Casa de la Artesanía, San Martín 802, Formosa

Minibuses from Formosa
Vilsa Maipú 864; tel: 03717 435 587; to Ing. Juárez US$20; Gral. Belgrano US$8 via Laguna Blanca.
Emmanuel Fontana 756; tel: 03717 435 761; to Palo Santo US$7; Clorinda US$7; Riacho He-He US$8.

Fede Av. Gonzalez Lelong 875; tel: 03717 424 430; to Laguna Blanca US$8; Güemes US$10; S. Martín Dos US$15.
Independencia Av. Independencia 17; tel: 03717 435 704; to Clorinda US$7; Riacho He-He US$10; El Colorado US$8.
Mercotur Av. Gonzalez Lelong 899; tel: 03717 431 469; to Espinillo US$10; Riacho He-He US$8.
Vega El Bagual or **Leki's** Moreno 715; tel: 03717 424 500; to Pirane US$5.
Via Libre Fotheringham 243; tel: 03717 420 943; to Las Lomitas US$10.
Zayas Sta. María de Oro 1470; tel: 03717 433 945; to Ibarreta US$7; Las Lomitas US$10.

Formosa National Reserve
The **Formosa National Reserve** is nowhere near the city of Formosa, on the Paraguayan border, but an area of sub-tropical semi-desert with drought-resistant species typical of the western Chaco. Wildlife includes puma, peccary, giant anteater and the carreta (an endangered armadillo) and birds like storks and herons.

Córdoba Province
Finally it is worth mentioning a few places in Córdoba province, where a north–south range of hills rises just to the west of the **city of Córdoba**. Immediately west of the city, Cerro Los Gigantes (2,374m) is the site of the Centro Nacional de Instrucción de Montaña (National Centre for Mountain Training) and of a refuge owned by the Club Andino de Córdoba. It is proposed to create a nature reserve of 12,000ha here. It can be reached by changing buses in Tanti. The highest peak of the Sierra de Córdoba is Cerro Champaqui (2,854m), southwest of the city. It is a Natural Monument (12,000ha), and offers good rock-climbing.

Further south, the arid granite plateau of the Pampa de Achala is protected by the 125,000ha **Reserva Natural Provincial Pampa de Achala** and the **Parque Nacional Quebrada del Condorito**, 37,000ha of upland grassland and *Polylepis* woods, reached by a trail from La Pampilla, 7km from the village of El Cóndor. Here you can see condors at their eastern limit as well as tabaquillo woodlands at their southern limit. Two reptiles and two amphibians are endemic to the Pampa de Achala, as well as a sub-species of red fox. On the far, western, side of the sierra the **Natural Monument Volcanes de Pocho**, 15km from Taninga, is connected to the **Parque Natural y Reserva Natural Chancaní**, a 4,960ha remnant of western Chaco forest.

Seven hours southwest of Córdoba is the city of **San Luis**, 120km northwest of which is the **Parque Nacional Sierra de las Quijadas**, covering 150,000ha of thorny scrub with dry woods in gullies and temporary watercourses, with cacti and bromeliads, as well as fossils and the Potrero de Aguada, an immense natural amphitheatre of weirdly eroded sandstone. Fauna consists largely of nocturnal burrowers (mara, guanaco, skunk, grison) as well as puma and birds such as elegant-crested tinamou, crested gallito.

To the west of Córdoba are the *pampas*. Gerald Durrell was once told: 'But the pampa is just a lot of grass... nothing, my dear fellow, absolutely nothing but grass punctuated by cows'. In fact the *pampas* are alive with wildlife, above all with birds – burrowing owls, black-and-white spur-winged plovers, Swainson's hawks, rhea, screamers, spoonbills, vulture, caracara, kingbirds, fork-tailed flycatchers, black-necked swans and ducks – as well as puma, deer, guanaco, skunks and armadillos.

Aconcagua

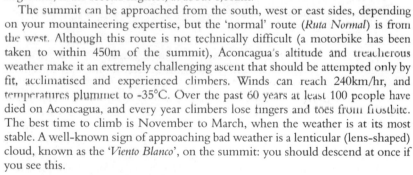

With its altitude of 6,962m, Aconcagua, just inside Argentina, is the highest mountain outside the Himalayas. Its claim to be the king of America's mountains, however, has not been undisputed.

For a long time its altitude was thought to be 7,021m, but a Chilean expedition to a remote part of the Andes east of Copiapó, reported that they had found a mountain, Ojos del Salado, rising to 7,087m on the Chilean-Argentine border. Feverish surveying followed until in 1956 an expedition led by H Adams Carter established the altitude of Ojos as 6,885.5m, as opposed to Aconcagua's 6,959.7m.

Modern technology has reduced Ojos del Salado to 6,863m, and raised Aconcagua to 6,962m. What is more, it is now clear that Pissis, 80km to the south of Ojos del Salado and wholly in Argentina, is the second highest, at about 6,882m.

The summit can be approached from the south, west or east sides, depending on your mountaineering expertise, but the 'normal' route (*Ruta Normal*) is from the west. Although this route is not technically difficult (a motorbike has been taken to within 450m of the summit), Aconcagua's altitude and treacherous weather make it an extremely challenging ascent that should be attempted only by fit, acclimatised and experienced climbers. Winds can reach 240km/hr, and temperatures plummet to -35°C. Over the past 60 years at least 100 people have died on Aconcagua, and every year climbers lose fingers and toes from frostbite. The best time to climb is November to March, when the weather is at its most stable. A well-known sign of approaching bad weather is a lenticular (lens-shaped) cloud, known as the '*Viento Blanco*', on the summit: you should descend at once if you see this.

Information and permits

Information can be obtained from the Aconcagua website www.aconcagua.org (www.aconcagua.com, www.cerroaconcagua.com and www.aconcaguaonline. com.ar are less use), the South American Explorers' *Aconcagua Information Packet*, and *Aconcagua, a climbing guide* by R J Secor, Uma Kukathas and Crystal Thomas (Mountaineers/Douglas & MacIntyre/Cordee, 2nd edition 1999). Thomas Taplin's *Aconcagua: the Stone Sentinel* (Eli, Santa Monica CA, 1992) is a highly entertaining account of the package trip from hell, but also includes a lot of practical information.

Good maps can be bought in Mendoza from shops and from the kiosk on the corner of Boulogne and Civit, opposite the provincial parks office. You can enquire at the Club Andino Mendoza at Beltrán 357, Gillén (tel: 0261 431 9870; open

CLIMBING HISTORY

The first recorded ascent of Aconcagua was by Matthias Zurbriggen of Edward Fitzgerald's expedition, in January 1897. However, it is clear that Araucanian and Aymara peoples lived on the mountain's slopes centuries ago, later to be invaded by the Incas from Peru, who called the great peak Acken Cahuac ('Stone Sentinel' in Quechua). In 1985 the mummy of an Inca child, complete with colourful poncho, was found at 5,300m. From this find and others, archaeologists believe that the Inca chiefs offered children as sacrifices to their gods in these high places.

Zurbriggen took an approximation of the present *Ruta Normal*, and in 1934 a Polish team climbed the Polish Glacier, now the second most popular route, in what was one of the earliest alpine-style ascents of a major peak. In 1953 an Argentine expedition took mules to 6,000m and conquered the southwest ridge, and in 1954 a French team made it up the south face, still the most difficult route.

Until 1980 the area was controlled by the Argentine Army, which imposed many restrictions, but did at least provide free mules! In 1983 the Aconcagua Provincial Park was created, and in 1983–4 the climb was attempted by 346 people; now there are over 2,000 a year, 70% on the *Ruta Normal*. The park became severely degraded, but in 1990, eight tonnes of rubbish were removed from the Horcones valley (mules were taken all the way to Refugio Independencia!), and there is now tight control of the tourist impact. In addition to the climbers, there are ever increasing numbers of hikers at lower levels, with numbers at Plaza de Mulas up by 274% in seven years; now everyone must hire 'an ecological or private bathroom service' at Plaza de Mulas.

Mon–Fri 20.00–22.00), and you can write to them at casilla 400, 5500 Mendoza. Note, however, that Aconcagua is not their prime interest, as they have huts in the Cordón del Plata, to the east of Tupungato (see below).

You need a **permit** to enter the Aconcagua park (but not for Tupungato, Vallecitos or the Cordón del Plata). The climbing season runs from November 15 to March 15; 20-day climbing permits for foreigners cost US$80 until December 9 and February 21 to March 15, US$120 December 10–14 and February 1–20, and March 15, and US$160 for the peak season from 15 December to 31 January. In addition trekking permits are available at US$20 for 3 days or US$30 for 7 days (US$20 and US$40 in peak season). All prices are halved for Argentinians. Permits must be obtained from the Subsecretaria de Turismo, San Martín 1155, Mendoza (open Mon–Fri 08.00–18.00, Sat & Sun 09.00–13.00); for information contact the Dirección de Recursos Naturales Renovables, Av Los Platanos, Parque San Martín (tel/fax: 0261 425 2090, aconcagua@mendoza.gov.ar).

Clothing and equipment

Adequate clothing and equipment are vital. Because of the intense cold generated by the high winds, no climber should attempt Aconcagua in single boots. Plastic double boots are best. Duvet (down-filled) trousers and parka are also strongly recommended. You will also need a tent capable of withstanding high winds. Crampons, an ice-axe and ropes are advisable, though not essential. You will usually find spare food left by others at the higher huts, and expeditions often give away their leftover supplies at Plaza de Mulas base camp, so it is more important to carry plenty of fuel than food. All supplies should be bought in Mendoza. Diamox tablets can help to prevent altitude sickness.

MENDOZA

Recommended **places to stay** in Mendoza include the Residencial Savigliano, Palacios 944 (tel/fax: 0261 423 7746; savigliano@hotmail.com), at the exit from the underpass from the bus station; and Campo Base, Mitre 946 (tel: 429 0707; info@campo-base.com.ar, www.campo-base.com.ar), which is a good place to make enquiries about climbing, as they have links with muleteers and the Vieja Estación in Puente del Inca. Another official HI hostel is the Hostel Internacional Mendoza, Av España 343 (tel: 424 0018; info@hostelmendoza.net), which charges slightly more but has smaller rooms.

The **provincial tourism office** is at San Martín 1143 (tel: 0261 420 2800; fax: 420 2243; subturism@lanet.com.ar; www.turismo.mendoza.gov.ar), and the **municipal office** is at Garibaldi and San Martín (tel: 420 1333; munimuza@supernet.com.ar; www.mendoza.com.ar), with a couple of other offices at 9 de Julio 500 (tel: 449 5185; fax: 438 1387) and Las Heras and Mitre (tel: 429 6298).

Mendoza is the centre of the Argentine wine industry and hosts a **wine festival** in the first week of March – a perfect time to finish the climb!

Mendoza has a complex network of fume-belching **buses**; there is next to no route information, and you have to pay 50% more than in Buenos Aires. Another oddity is that routes are grouped, so that you see first that a bus is, for instance, a 60, and then look more closely to see that it is in fact a 63 for the Aeropuerto (incidentally, this runs along San Juan, Alem, Salta, Urquiza, and San Martín streets).

Cheap **bikes** can be rented at Campo Base, and repaired at Bicicletería Bambino, at the junction of J F Moreno and Alberdi; Travesia (tel: 0261 448 0289; travesiabike@yahoo.com) are mountain-bike specialists.

Buy **supplies** at a hyper-market such as the WalMart Super-Center, by the freeway south of the terminal, or Plaza Mendoza, on the eastern outskirts; there are virtually no food shops in the city centre. For **equipment**, try Tienda de Montaña José Orviz, J B Justo 536 (tel/fax: 0261 425 1281; orviz@lanet.com.ar, www.orviz.com) or Mountain Sport, Arizu 502, Godoy Cruz (tel: 0261 424 5017; ulises@lanet.com.ar).

Do not forget to visit the **Parque San Martín**, on the western edge of the city; at its far side is the Cerro de la Gloria, where there are 700 species of trees and 110 animals (native and exotic) in the city zoo. The city's plazas also have both native and exotic trees labelled with their scientific names.

Adventure sports

There has been an explosion of companies offering all sorts of adventure sports around Mendoza. All of these offer **rafting** at Uspallata, on the way to Aconcagua, but almost all can offer something else too. Prices are very steep compared to Pucón or indeed anywhere else in Chile; rafting and mountain-biking cost from US$30 for an hour.

Argentina Rafting km53 (opposite the ACA campsite), Potrerillos; tel: 02624 482 037; arg_rafting@hotmail.com; www.argentinarafting.com; rafting, kayaking, trekking, rappel, mountain-biking, horse-riding.

Aymará Turismo 9 de Julio 1023, (5500) Mendoza; tel: 0261 420 0607, 420 5304; info@aymara.com.ar; rafting, trekking, mountain-biking, riding, parapente and hang-gliding.

Betancourt Rafting Lavalle 35, Galería Independencía, loc. 8, Mendoza; tel: 0261 429 9665; info@betancourt.com.ar; & Panamericana 2129, Barrio Trapiche Godoy Cruz; tel: 0261 390 229, 986 329; fax: 391 949; rafting, trekking, riding, parapente, 4WD driving.

Desnivel Rafting Ejercito de los Andes, Uspallata; tel: 02624 420 293; rafting.

Huentata Las Heras 680, Mendoza; tel: 0261 425 3108; fax: 425 7444; huentata@slatinos.com.ar; www.huentata.com.ar; rafting, trekking, mountain-biking, riding, rappel, parapente.

Ríos Andinos km50, Potrerillos; tel: 0261 496 3848, 0156 581 459; rafting@riosandinos.com.ar; rafting, river boarding, trekking, mountain-biking, riding, rappel.

There is good **rock-climbing** (October–April) at El Salto (1,800m), 75km west of Mendoza at the foot of the Cordón del Plata, which is reached by a TAC bus daily at 08.00. The Camping El Salto is just west of the village, and the climbing cliffs are 3 hours' hike from the village, beyond the eponymous waterfall. There are 25 routes, up to French grade 8a+.

There is more good climbing at Los Arenales, 135km southwest of Mendoza in the Cordón Portillo – take Ruta 40 south to Tunuyán, then Ruta 94 west for 42km via Vista Flores and Los Sauces to El Manzano Historico (The Historic Farm; 1,500m), from where a rough road continues west up the Arroyo Grande for 12.5km to the Refugio Portinari (2,500m), where there is a police post; the Club Andino also has a refuge here. A trail continues west over the Piuquenes pass (4,200m) to the Yeso valley in Chile (see page 146). ECLA buses at 15.00 on Fridays and 07.00 and 13.00 on Saturdays and Sundays will take you to the Samay Huasy Hotel 4.5km west of the Manzano (returning at 18.00 on Fridays and 11.00 and 18.00 on Saturdays and Sundays). The book *Escaladas en Mendoza* by Mauricio Fernández gives details of climbs.

Summit tel: 0261 496 4177; info@summit-mza.com.ar; are rock climbing specialists.

OUTFITTERS AND MULES

The leading outfitter is Fernando Grajales (who climbed the Grajales Couloir on the southwest ridge in 1953), who can be contacted at J F Moreno 898, (5500) Mendoza (tel/fax: 0261 429 3830; expediciones@grajales.net) or at the Hotel Ayelén, Los Penitentes (tel: 0261 425 9990, mobile 15 500 7718). The *South American Explorer* reported in 1993 that:

> '... there is such a demand for mules during the peak climbing season that Grajales can maximise his revenues by having his mules take one party's stuff up to Mulas in one day, returning that same day to Puente with another party's stuff. He is no longer willing (without considerable persuasion) to have his mules accompany a party up to the half-way point at Confluencia, spend the night there (which is good for the group's acclimatisation) and proceed the rest of the way up to Mulas the second day. Instead, he or his assistant Andreas García will insist on the mules taking your stuff all the way while you spend the night at Grajales' camp at Confluencia – sleeping in his tents, on his foam pads, buying a meal from his cook tent, etc. This works equally well for your acclimatisation but not for your wallet. We heard that this coerced hospitality comes with a tab of US$50 per person.'

At that time the cheapest price they were able to negotiate for the round trip was US$150 per mule (carrying 60kg each). Nowadays, due to increased competition, prices have come down to US$120 for the first 60kg, and US$60 for each extra 60kg.

However, this is misleading, as Grajales is well respected, and he and rivals such as Inka Expediciones (Juan B Justo 345, Mendoza; tel/fax: 0261 425 0871; inka@aconcagua.org.ar; www.inka.com.ar) provide an excellent service, with full back-up and radios for emergencies, while the cheaper operators simply provide mule transport and little else. These are mostly based at Los Puquios (where you can camp), 1.5km east of Puente del Inca, opposite the Cementerio de los Andinistas: Rudy Parra, who can be contacted at either Güiraldes 246, (5519) Dorrego, Guaymallén, Mendoza (tel/fax: 0261 431 7003; aconcagua@ rudyparra.com), or Tienda de Montaña José Orviz, Juan B Justo 536, Mendoza (tel/fax: 0261 425 1281; orviz@lanet.com.ar, www.orviz.com); Los Gateados, also at Los Puquios (mobile: 0290410 391 080; fax: 380 367); and Huera Pire Expediciones, Suarez 171, Maipú, (5515) Mendoza (tel: 0261 497 3393; fax: 497 2866). For a guide, contact the Asociación Argentino de Guias de Montaña, Caseros 1053, (5501) Godoy Cruz (tel: 0261 452 0641).

ACCLIMATISATION

It is recommended that climbers spend a day or two acclimatising before setting out from Puente del Inca to Plaza de Mulas, a climb of 1,500m in 37km. One possibility is to hike up to the Cristo Redentor (Christ the Redeemer) statue at the roughly 3,850m pass, now disused, above the tunnel of the same name to Portillo and Santiago. The old road starts at Las Cuevas, where it passes through an archway and swings right; it takes a minimum of 4 hours up and down, with views of the summit of Aconcagua. Equally you could acclimatise by carrying your equipment towards base camp, always returning to sleep at lower altitude. The hike to Plaza de Mulas can be done in 10 hours by fit and acclimatised people, but it is best to take 2 or 3 days to help you to adjust to the altitude. Plaza de Mulas, at the head of the Horcones valley, is the base camp for the *Ruta Normal*, and the destination of most non-climbers. A smart hotel, the Refugio Plaza de Mulas, has been built here, which charges luxury prices and has a helicopter if you cannot face haggling over the cost of mules! There is also a small hut which gets very crowded in peak season.

The **Cordón del Plata** is handy for acclimatisation, and not too hard to get to. A transfer bus can be organised by Ricardo Zajur Transfer (tel: 0261 429 0170: fax: 425 2884; mobile 155 633 901), or through the Residencial Savigliano; or email: transfer@trivu.com. This takes about two hours and costs US$80 return; a taxi will cost US$50 each way; regular buses will leave you 12km away. Heading south from Potrerillos for 21km you will come to the **Vallecitos ski resort** at 2,900m, below Pico Vallecitos (5,750m) with its huge east face. Cerro Plata (6,300m) is at the southern end of the range; base camp is at 4,200m and the next at 5,100m. From here the *Ruta Normal* goes via the Rincón, a 45° snow couloir, and traverses to a camp at 5,800m; then it is a big summit day, 12 hours of sustained non-technical climbing.

It is also worth mentioning the Chilean ski resort of **Portillo**, just west of the Cristo Redentor tunnel, as this can also offer handy acclimatisation hikes for Aconcagua. This is where the 200km/hr barrier was broken in 1978, and a world record of 217.67km/hr was set in 1987. The lifts will usually operate on summer weekends. The blue-and-yellow hotel is hard to miss on the north side of the road opposite the restaurant La Posada. Like all winter-sports centres, it looks pretty awful without snow. From the hotel (2,885m) you can hike to the three peaks known as Los Tres Hermanos (4,595m); a precipitous path leads 4km along the west side of the Laguna del Inca, and can be reached by going to the left/south of some private houses (signed 'No Entry') by the chairlift, and then right.

It takes 4 hours up the valley to reach a camping spot at 3,200m; from here it is 2 hours up the moraine, then 4 to 6 hours up to the central, highest, peak (of which the last 1½ hours is spent scrambling). There is just one *TAC* bus a day from Los Andes to Portillo, and the international buses pass by; otherwise, coming from the west, there is an hourly bus from Los Andes to the Saladillos turning, just east of Río Blanco (1,370m), from where you can hitch (eastbound trucks only cross the pass overnight). Incidentally, there is a copper mine further up the Río Blanco valley, and a Codelco-sponsored condor conservation project, which explains any orange tags you may see on their wings.

CLIMBING ACONCAGUA

Altitude	2,718m to 6,962m (from Puente del Inca)
Rating	Difficult
Time	15–18 days to reach the top
Start of trail	Puente del Inca
End of trail	Plaza de Mulas, then Puente del Inca
Maps	Aconcagua is at the southeastern corner of the IGM 1:50,000 map 3369-7-4 *Cerro Aconcagua*. Map 3369-14-1 covers Puente del Inca.

Getting to the trailhead

The climb starts near Puente del Inca, 174km west of the provincial capital of Mendoza. This can be reached by local buses (Empresa Uspallata; US$10) from Mendoza at 06.00 and 10.00 daily. If you miss these you will have to haggle with one of the many international buses, which will leave you at the Los Horcones border post just west of Puente del Inca. It is equally possible to take one of these buses directly from Santiago, but unless there are truly exceptional circumstances, you will all have to go to Mendoza to collect a permit.

Mendoza (750m) is at km1043 on Highway 7, which heads west through Cacheuta (km1085, 1,245m), where there are hot springs, Potrerillos (km1098, 1,354m), centre of a burgeoning adventure sports industry, and Uspallata (km1148, 1,900m), 2 hours away by bus. This is the only town on the way, with good hotels and a campsite. A poorer road runs to the north from Mendoza to Uspallata via Villavicencio (km47, 1,700m), where Darwin found a petrified forest, and the **Reserva Nacional El Leoncito**, a zone of 76,000ha created in 1994 to protect the environment of the El Leoncito astronomical observatory, on a peak of 4,366m. This can be visited (open daily 10.00–18.00; tel: 0264 421 3653, nocturna@castec.edu.ar), but the rest of the reserve is closed. Puna rhea can usually be seen near the observatory, and there are also plenty of guanaco, as well as chinchillón and lizards.

Running parallel to the Transandine Railway (and along the line of an Inca road) through gorges and bare mountains with spectacularly patterned sedimentary strata, Ruta 7 passes Punta de Vacas (km1201, 2,325m; start of the hiking routes to the east side of Aconcagua and to Tupungato, which can soon be seen to the south), and the small ski resort of Los Penitentes (km1210, 2,580m), where the Gente de Montaña hostel (tel: 02624 490 132; juanpedro@lanet.com.ar) offers B&B for US$10. From **Puente del Inca** (km1217, 2,718m) the highway continues into Chile by the Cristo Redentor tunnel from Las Cuevas (km1230, 3,151m).

At Puente del Inca there are hot springs, various snackbars and three places to stay, the pricey Hostería Puente del Inca (tel: 0261 438 0480, 02624 420 266), and the Parador del Inca and Refugio La Vieja Estación (cellular: 155 696 036), which charge about US$10 for bunks. The latter is linked to Campo Base in Mendoza (see above). Mules can be rented anywhere in Puente del Inca for carrying climbing gear and food to the base camp at Plaza de Mulas; the prices can be extortionate.

Route description

From Puente del Inca you can either follow the road uphill past the big new border post (2,800m) to the turning to the Aconcagua Provincial Park, or follow the disused railway track. After 10 minutes you will cross a bridge over the Arroyo Horcones, then pass through three *cobertizos* (snow galleries, clearly used for stabling the mules) and over another bridge after 15 minutes more; turn right after another 5 minutes, at the entrance to the fourth gallery, to reach the road at a sign to the Aconcagua *mirador*, 3km above Puente del Inca. It is a couple of minutes further up the road to the junction to Aconcagua; cars can go about 2km to the Guardería Pioneros (2,950m), from where people walk 300m further to Laguna Horcones, in fact three pretty nondescript pools – but the views more than compensate!

You must check in here, and will be given a rubbish bag which must be returned, with rubbish. Continue following the mule tracks to rejoin the disused road, which ends at an excellent suspension bridge at the Arroyo El Durazno in about 25 minutes. On the far (left/east) bank, there is space to camp. The path continues up the valley, climbing pretty steadily for almost an hour and then reaching the edge of the gorge of the Horcones Inferior in about 20 minutes more. Dropping down into this gorge, you will come in a couple of minutes to the path right to Plaza Francia, and in a couple more to a bridge; you can continue straight on up the valley, but most people will turn left to reach the **Confluencia** campsite (3,368m) after another 5 minutes, on the far side of the Horcones Superior, by a very unimpressive bridge. Another path leads directly up the valley from here, on the right bank. In summer there are rangers here, plus a tent where you can buy drinks and snacks. Confluencia is about 8km from Laguna Horcones, which can be done in under 2 hours, depending very much on your load and state of acclimatisation.

The next stage is a total of 22km to Plaza de Mulas, taking 6 to 8 hours. It is a broad valley in which the river wanders, and you may have to ford it; it is best to keep to the true right/west side of the valley where you have a choice. After 12km you will pass the Quebrada Sargento Mas; in another 4km the ruins of the Refugio Ibáñez (3,960m), and in another 4km the ruins of the old Plaza de Mulas (4,050m). From here there is a 2km climb known as the Cuesta Brava to the present **Plaza de Mulas** (4,230m). The hotel is 1km to the west at 4,370m; there is a doctor here from November 15 to March 15 each year, but there is no rescue service above the Plaza. Most people spend a few days here going on day-hikes to build up strength;

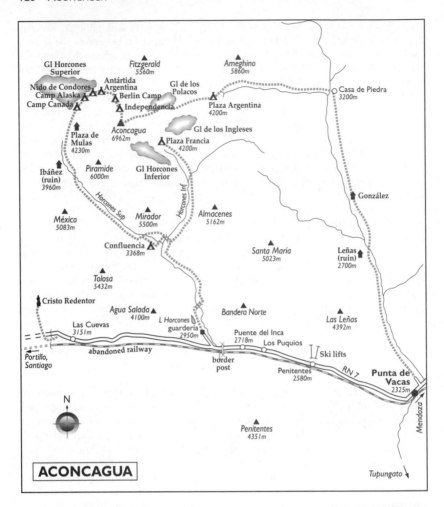

ACONCAGUA

there are some nice glaciated peaks (such as Cerro El Manso, 5,500m) which can be done in about 2 days as training climbs. Fill up with clean water from the streams above the camp; further up the water tends to be a chocolate colour, although it is OK to drink once it has settled. At this altitude you should drink between three and five litres a day to prevent dehydration. Further up there are good camping places, but you will have to melt snow to drink.

The **Ruta Normal**, easily visible, ascends a steep scree slope in broad switchbacks beside the large Horcones Superior glacier. Camp Canada (4,877m) is about 500m south of the trail, which makes it more pleasant, with less loo-paper about. You will also pass Camp Alaska (5,212m), just above the Cambio de Pendiente (5,150m), where the steep section ends and you turn to the right/east. After 5 to 7 hours you will pass the Nido de Condores (5,365m), a camping spot by a pond, and in another hour or so you reach the ruined Refugio Antártida Argentina (5,560m). You can camp here, or you may prefer to continue to the squalid trio of ruined huts known as Campamento Berlin (5,950m). This is above the *Gran Accarreo* ('Long Haul') scree field, which is best avoided by going east then south and following a ridge to the Berlin camp.

It is best to spend two nights here, carrying a load up to your next camp and returning to sleep. With 'only' 1,000m to go to the summit (a mere vertical kilometre!) it is tempting to make this the last camp, but only exceptionally strong and well-acclimatised climbers make the summit in one long day from here. It is possible to make your last camp another 200m above the Berlin camp. However, most would be well advised to go as far as the Refugio Independencia (6,546m), about 6 hours further up. This hut, reputedly the highest in the world, is also in ruins, but lies at a convenient point to make a summit bid.

Start early for the top, although you should wait until daylight if it is windy, as strong winds cause the body to lose heat. The route is straightforward, but you will find the last 300m very tiring. Go up and to the right along the *Cresta del Viento*, across the top of the *Gran Acarreo* to enter the notorious 45° couloir called the *Canaleta*. Keep on the right side of the gully, on the snow if possible, as the scree in the middle is very loose and steep and will wear you out. Concentrate on your footing and breathing.

Reaching the saddle between the north and south summits, continue left to the north summit along the *Cresta del Guanaco*, named after the remains of an animal found in 1947 and presumably sacrificed here by the Incas. Circle the summit block to the left and follow the trail to the top. Allow 6 to 9 hours from Independencia to the summit, more if conditions are bad or if you are suffering from the altitude. You should get back to Plaza de Mulas by the same route in 2 days.

Other routes on Aconcagua

From Confluencia, the Horcones Inferior valley leads northeast for 13km to the Plaza Francia (4,200m), base camp for the south face route. You probably will not want to climb it, but the hike to Plaza Francia is ideal for acclimatisation. The south face (*Pared Sur*) is almost 3km high and 7km across; its huge vertical seracs and hanging glaciers can be seen from the highway. It is a fearsome climb; Reinhold Messner climbed it solo in 3 days in 1974, and his route is now the preferred variant of the French route.

The second most popular route is by the Polish glacier, to the east-northeast. This is reached by the Vacas valley, from Punta de Vacas; it is 8km to the ruined hut and *guardaría* at Pampa de Leñas (2,700m), 18km more past the Refugio González to Casa de Piedra (3,200m), and then 15km west up the Arroyo Relinchos to Plaza Argentina (4,200m). The river has to be crossed by mule as a rule, which limits the route's suitability for hiking. To the west of the Plaza Argentina basecamp are two glaciers; to the north, with its base at 5,900m, is the *Glaciar de los Polacos*, and to its south the *Glaciar de los Ingleses* (or *Glaciar Este*), a more difficult route first attempted by Britons and finally achieved by Argentines in 1978.

PEAKS AND ROUTES NEARBY

To the south of Punta de Vacas is the valley of the Río Tupungato. Matthias Zurbriggen came this way after the first ascent of Aconcagua and (with Stuart Vines) made the first ascent of **Cerro Tupungato** (6,550m). This is also a provincial park (170,000ha), and access is usually from the east, by Ruta 89 to Digue Las Tunas, and then to estancia Gualtallary.

The **Laguna del Diamante** is another popular park, high in the Andes on the Chilean border. Take Ruta 40 south from Mendoza to San Rafael, and turn right south of Pareditas along a dirt road to the Laguna (3,250m) beneath Volcán Maipo (5,323m). This basalt peak is on the border and can also be reached from Fundo Cruz de Piedra in Chile's Maipo valley (page 148).

Northern Chile

The far north of Chile offers totally different experiences to the centre and the south. Here there are vast areas of *puna* beneath some of the continent's highest mountains. Biologically and culturally this area is closer to Peru and Bolivia than to the rest of Chile. Equally, in terms of climate, this area is best visited when winter is gripping the south, as the *invierno boliviano* can bring foul weather during the southern summer. However, these areas are arid and largely unpopulated, leaving you with little choice in many areas other than to rent a four-wheel drive vehicle or to take an organised trip.

THE FAR NORTH
Parque Nacional Lauca
Perhaps the most attractive of the northern parks, particularly for unsupported hiking, is also the furthest from Santiago, almost on the border with Peru. This is **Parque Nacional Lauca**, straddling the paved highway from Arica to Bolivia, which covers 137,883ha of *puna* between 3,200m and 6,342m (although 43,000ha may be excised from the park to allow mining). It receives just 280mm of precipitation per year (as rain in summer and snow in winter), and temperatures range from 20°C to -10°C at night. There are some woods of queñoa (*Polylepis tarapacana*) below 3,800m, but above this altitude there are only wet and dry *praderas* (grasslands) and *bofedals* (damp, marshy areas). There are few animals, other than the four camelid species, pumas, tarucas, vizcachas and the red fox (zorro culpeo). Only two reptiles live here, a lizard (*Liolaemus multiformis*) and a non-venomous snake.

There is a greater variety of birds (at least 120 species), especially at the lakes: most notably giant and horned coots, various ducks, the black-crowned night-heron (huairavo; *Nycticorax nycticorax*), and all three Chilean species of flamingo. Of these, the largest (up to 1.2m in height) is the Andean flamingo (parina grande; *Phoenicoparrus andinus*), which lives for up to 25 years; the James' flamingo (*P. jamesi*; parina chica) is the rarest in the world (and was thought extinct until 1957) but there are around 3,500 in this region. The Chilean flamingo (flamenco rojo; *Phoenicopterus chilensis*) ranges from the *puna* to Argentinian Patagonia and Paine; the others are only in this area. They feed on small molluscs and crustacea such as brine shrimps, *Aphanocapsa* algae and diatoms (which stain the lakes red); the three species have differently sized filters in their beaks so that they do not compete for the same food. The total Chilean population of flamingos was about 73,000 in 1986 and fell to 13,000 in 1994; it has recovered to 17,500, but they are still vulnerable. The Andean avocet (*Recurvirostra andina*) also feeds on fly larvae in

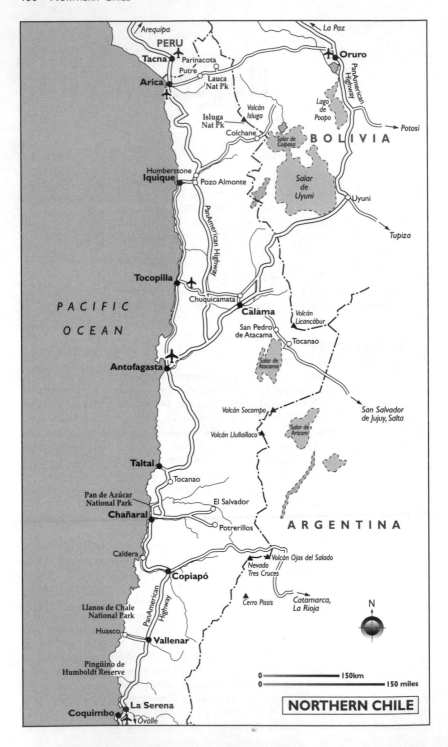

NORTHERN CHILE

these salt lakes. On dry land you may find the puna rhea (*Pterocnemia pennata tarapacensis*, much reduced by egg poaching), puna plover, puna tinamou (*Tinamotis pentlandii*), condor and black-chested buzzard eagle, among other raptors, and plenty of passerines (perching birds).

Unless you are already well acclimatised, it is well worth stopping in **Putre** (3,500m), 146km east of Arica (5km north of the highway to La Paz), which has hotels, shops and a church dating from 1670. Here Barbara Knapton from Alaska runs Birding Alto Andino, providing tours of Lauca and the other protected areas, and also Casa Barbarita, offering accommodation at Baquedano 299 (tel: 058 300 013, fax: 222 735; www.birdingaltoandino.com). Two walks are recommended here for acclimatisation and watching wildlife; firstly by a gravel track up past the Hotel Las Vicuñas, reaching the highway in 2–3 hours, and secondly the paths up the valley behind the church. There is a friendly Conaf office in Putre, where it is worth asking for a lift to Parinacota. Buses La Paloma (also known as Flota Paco) run daily from Arica to Putre. Buses Humire (in the eastern, Tacna, part of the Arica terminal) go on Tuesdays and Fridays at 10.30 to Parinacota and Visviri, and international buses will also take you to and from the park. Various tour companies in Arica also run tours of Lauca and the *altiplano*.

The Las Cuevas *guardería* is 5km from the park entrance, at 4,000m, here there are hot springs and a 9,000-year-old archaeological site, as well as plenty of vicuña. From here the road continues east, to the south side of the Bofedal de Parinacota (the Río Lauca flows south from the *bofedal* and then heads east into Bolivia) to Chucuyo (where beds are available). **Parinacota** lies 5km to the north at 4,392m; this is the only village in the park, but most houses are only opened for fiestas. There is a 17th-century church, and a Conaf *refugio* with two small dormitories (US$9 with a hot shower). From here the Sendero Cotacotani leads to the Laguna de Cotacotani, 8km east, and there are also shorter paths with information signs or leaflets. This is actually a connecting set of *lagunas*, 600ha in total, held behind dams of lava through which water filters to the Bofedal de Parinacota. Volcán Parinacota, on the border to the east, is the *altiplano* peak most commonly targeted by climbers.

Continuing towards the border, the highway passes to the southwest of Lago Chungara (21.5km² in area); this is home to many birds, including 8,000 odd giant coots, which make floating islands to support their nests, and all three Chilean species of flamingo. There is a *guardería*, *refugio* and campsite, very cold at night at 4,517m. Luckily, local women often sell excellent (and cheap) woollens here. It is not much further to the Chungara frontier post, at the 4,678m Portezuelo Tambo Quemado.

Reserva Nacional Las Vicuñas

Immediately to the south of Lauca is the **Reserva Nacional Las Vicuñas**, covering 209,131ha at between 4,300 and 5,600m; this is rather wilder, with roads open only March to November, and even then best tackled with four-wheel drive. Conaf's administration, with another *refugio*, is at Guallatiri, 84km from Putre, turning off the main highway 2km east of Las Cuevas. From here the rough road continues south to the **Monumento Natural Salar de Surire**, 11,298ha around a salt pan populated by three species of flamingo, rhea and vicuña. Just about the only drinkable water is at the Conaf *refugio* at Surire. Tours can continue south into the Isluga National Park, but you should check with the *carabineros* first.

Parque Nacional Isluga

The **Parque Nacional Isluga** can be reached by the highway from Iquique to Bolivia via the Colchane border crossing (3,750m); apart from the international buses, there is a bus to Colchane that leaves Iquique at 22.00 on Tuesdays and Fridays. The road passes the amazing Atacama Giant, a huge geoglyph (figure created with stones on the ground) on the side of Cerro Unita, 13km east of the PanAmerican Highway; it may be worth stopping to acclimatise at Chumiza (3,200m, 3km off the highway at km77), although the bus drops you off after midnight. From Colchane it is 6km northwest to the village of Isluga (like Parinacota, there is a 17th-century church here and houses which are opened up only at fiesta-time); the park entrance is a couple of kilometres on, and it is another 10km to the park administration at Enquelga, just below 4,000m. There is a *refugio* here, and a campsite 2km south at Aguas Calientes; you can hike west from Enquelga to Laguna Arabilla and Laguna Parinacoya. The park covers 174,744ha of *estepa de altura*, dominated by volcanoes such as the smoking peak of Volcán Isluga (5,218m), which can be climbed from Enquelga. Receiving all of 200–350mm of rain per year, the terrain is largely covered by a scrub of queñoa, with cushion plants (llareta; *Laretia compacta*) and marshy bofedals. Isluga is far less visited than Lauca, so it is quieter but with fewer facilities.

THE ATACAMA

Heading south from Iquique towards the 2nd Region, many buses now use the recently paved coastal highway, which is very attractive. However, if you take the PanAmerican Highway you will come to the main portion of the **Reserva Nacional Pampa del Tamarugal**, named after the tamarugo tree (*Prosopis tamarugo*) which once blanketed this area but was almost entirely cleared for fuel during the nitrates boom. In this arid area the re-growth has not been natural, but as a result of planting and irrigation by Conaf. The most common animal is the lauchón (*Phyllotis magister*), a small rodent; and the American kestrel (*Falco sparverius*) can be seen here all year. There is an Environmental Information Centre and campsite 24km south of Pozo Almonte; another 20km south is the turning to the Pintados geoglyphs, 7km west of the highway.

Chile's 2nd Region is dominated by the Atacama desert, so arid that some weather stations have never recorded rainfall. The world's best-known coastal deserts, the Atacama and Southern Africa's Namib, are possibly also its oldest and driest. At its northern edge is the mining city of Calama, on the Loa river, and another 103km southeast, across the Cordillera de Domeyko, is the oasis of **San Pedro de Atacama** (2,440m), the touristic centre of the region. This is jammed full with travellers' hangouts, tour companies, and the excellent Museo LePaige, which explains the archaeology and anthropology of the Atacama. It is anthropologically interesting to watch the *gringos* in their indigenous gear, interacting with *indigenas* in jeans.

Around San Pedro, in seven separate sectors totalling 73,987ha, is the **Reserva Nacional Los Flamencos**, which protects saltpans, lagoons and desert landforms. The flora is dominated by drought-resistant plants such as coirón amarga, paja amarilla and grama salada; mammals include foxes, vicuña and southern mountain cavy (cuy de la puna; *Microcavia australis*), and birds include rhea, tinamou, all three Chilean species of flamingo, coots, condors, and the Gay's seed-snipe (*Attagis gayi*), which is found from 5,000m-plus to Tierra del Fuego. The only area you can easily visit under your own steam, on foot (fortunately, the minefields are being lifted!)

or by mountain bike (easily rented in San Pedro), is the Valle de la Luna, 12km southwest of town; here wind-blown sand has produced weirdly shaped rock formations reminiscent of The Arches and similar parks in the western USA. Sunsets are great here, but thereafter it soon gets pretty chilly.

Sixty kilometres south of San Pedro is the Soncor sector, around Laguna Chaxa, the best site for seeing flamingos in this area. The Tambillo sector, on the main road 27km south of San Pedro, protects another tamarugo wood. Another flamingo site is Laguna Miscanti (4,350m), 126km south of San Pedro, beyond Socaire on the road to the Paso Sico border crossing (4,079m) and Salta.

Although not part of the Reserva Nacional, **Laguna Lejía** (4,190m) is well known for its birds, notably the horned coot (*Fulica cornuta*) which nests on a mound of stones about 50cm high, as well as flamingos, Andean gulls and Andean geese; it lies on the north side of the road to the closed border crossing of Paso Guaitiquina (4,296m), to the north of Paso Sico. Further north is the road to Jujuy via the Paso Jama (4,200m), now being paved to link northern Chile with Paraguay and Brazil.

There are several other tourist destinations close to San Pedro that are not part of the *reserva nacional*; the most obvious, in at least one sense, is the massive bulk of **Volcán Licancábur**, rising to 5,916m immediately east of town. The world's largest radio telescope, the MMA or Millimeter Array, is to be built by 2006 on Licancábur, and it is already possible to get to the top (where there is an Inca shrine) by four-wheel-drive vehicle or mountain bike. Tours are available, with guides who may even carry oxygen. The easiest access for hiking is from the Portezuelo del Cajón (4,480m), on the Bolivian border just to the east; tours from San Pedro to the Bolivian *salares* (salt lakes) use this pass, and there is a *refugio* at Laguna Verde, northeast of Licancábur.

In addition to the many tours available in San Pedro, the Altué company offers trekking to the north of San Pedro through the villages of Machuca, Puritama and Guatin. Mountain Service specializes in climbing peaks such as Licancábur and **Llullaillaco** (6,720m) – the latter is well to the south, beyond the Paso Socompa (3,858m), where the Antofagasta–Salta road and railway cross the border. The Llullaillaco National Park (262,000ha) was created in 1996. See pages 76–8 for company details.

You are bound to pass through **Antofagasta** itself, from where it is easy to visit the **Reserva Forestal La Chimba**, just 3km east of the coastal highway Ruta 1, 15km north of the city. This is 2,583ha of hills and canyons, with a flora supported by the *camanchaca* (sea mist), as well as guanacos, foxes and surprisingly many birds. On the coast slightly further north the **Monumento Natural La Portada** is an arched stack, which makes a pleasant day-out (reached by *micro 15*).

THE NORTE CHICO

Continuing south on the PanAmerican, the **Parque Nacional Pan de Azúcar** (Sugar Loaf National Park), just north of Chañaral, protects 43,774ha, almost all that is left of the *desierto costero de Taltal*, with 259 species of flora of which 134 are endemic, including a new *Tillandsia* identified only in 1991. There are 26 types of cactus, notably of the *Copiapoa* genus, as well as *Neoporteria*; lichen on the cacti condense water from the *camanchaca* sea mist, thus supporting the whole ecosystem (there is only 1.9mm of rain per year). There are geckos, living only in dead cacti. There are also rare and threatened animal sub-species, such as the peregrine falcon (*Falco peregrinus anatum*), the Chilean mouse opossum (yaca; *Marmosa elegans* *coquimbensis*) and a frog (*Bufo atacamensis*), as well as 200 guanaco. There are 103 species of birds, above all marine and coastal birds such as Humboldt penguins, cormorants, pelicans, gulls and oyster-catchers, and also raptors such as eagles and condors. Look out also for foxes, sea otters and sea lions. Seventy years ago the population of the Peruvian diving petrel (pato yunco; *Pelecanoides garnotii*) was half a million; now there are just 1,500 in Peru and 5,000 in Chile, found only on Isla Pan de Azúcar and the Islas Choros, to the south just before La Serena.

The Conaf administration and Environmental Information Centre are at Caleta Pan de Azúcar, best reached by a road following the coast north for 28km from Chañaral. Another, much rougher, road runs 20km west to Caleta Pan de Azúcar from the PanAmerican Highway 45km north of Chañaral. About halfway along this road, there is a junction north to Las Lomitas, where there is a *refugio rustico* and mist-catchers, to collect water. There is a 30km self-guided nature trail (for cars) from the Caleta to Las Lomitos, reaching a maximum altitude of 700m, and foot trails that continue north from here. Another path runs up the Quebrada del Castillo, just north of the park boundary on the road from Chañaral. Rather than walking, most visitors take a boat trip from the Caleta to Isla Pan de Azúcar, 2km offshore, to see birds without landing.

From Copiapó, 167km south of Chañaral, a very poor road heads inland to the Argentine border at Paso San Francisco (4,747m), where Diego de Almagro entered Chile in 1536, along an Inca road. This passes through a huge tract of some of the most desolate terrain in Chile, covered by the 59,082ha **Parque Nacional Nevado Tres Cruces**, formed in 1994. Apart from some flamingo lagoons, its chief feature is **Ojos del Salado**, the world's highest volcano, although the fumarole near the summit is currently inactive. In fact it was thought at one time that Ojos might be higher than Aconcagua, but in 1956 an expedition disproved this; modern technology has reduced Ojos still further to 6,863m. Nearby is Tipas (6,660m), the third-highest active volcano in the world and virtually unknown. It is not difficult to reach the summit of Ojos, as long as you consider the lack of oxygen and water, and a climate that can bring temperatures of -40°C and winds of 150km/hr. The best time is January to March. From the site of the former Hostería Murray (4,400m; now burned down, although you can still get water there) four-wheel-drive vehicles can reach the Refugio Universidad de Atacama at 5,200m (about 6 hours' hike), where two shipping containers provide rudimentary shelter for about eight people. An obvious zigzag path leads in about 3 hours to the larger Refugio Tejos at 5,750m, from where it is 10–12 hours to the summit, with a bit of technical climbing required on the final 50m. Santiago-based companies such as Altué and Mountain Service run trips here, and guides can be found in Copiapó.

SOUTH OF CHAÑARAL

From Chañaral virtually to Viña del Mar is a transition zone from desert to the Mediterranean vegetation to the south. This is marked by open *matorral* or scrub with low shrubs and cacti. After particularly heavy spring rains, the ground bursts into flower in September and October, bringing forth many insects that spend the rest of the year underground. This phenomenom, the *desierto florido*, is at its best around Vallenar and Huasco, in particular in the **Parque Nacional Llanos de Challe** (45,708ha), 50km north of Huasco. From km550 on the PanAmerican Highway, just south of Huasco (75km north of La Serena), a dirt road leads 45km west to Punta de Choros, headquarters of the **Refugio Forestal Pingüino de Humboldt**. This protects three islands, Chañaral (507ha), Choros (292ha), and

Damas (60ha). These are home to Humboldt penguins and the diving petrel, and also red-billed tropic birds, black and white-breasted cormorants, burrowing owls, pelicans, turkey vultures, sea lions and sea otters. From boats you can see fifty-odd bottle-nosed dolphins (one of just three fixed communities in the world and the only one in Chile), and occasionally marine turtles and whales (near Isla Chañaral, Sept–Dec). There is only 30mm of precipitation per year, largely in the form of mists; this supports *desierto costero de Huasco*, dominated by *Copiapoa* and *Neoporteria* cacti and *Atriplex saladillo* bushes. From Punta de Choros you can take a boat (for US$90) to Isla Damas, where you can camp, though you will need to bring all your water. Permission is needed from the administration or from Conaf in **La Serena** (ColoColo 1090; tel: 051 213 565, 223 333).

Just inland from here (and visible from the PanAmerican Highway) are two astronomical observatories, the European Southern Observatory at La Silla and the Carnegie Institute's site at Las Campanas; just to the south, near Vicuña, is the Interamerican Obervatory at El Tololo. These can be visited with permission on certain Saturdays, which gives the opportunity to enjoy a bit of mountain scenery at the same time – the observatories are all at between 2,200 and 2,500m altitude.

Still on the PanAmerican heading south, 110km beyond La Serena (which has now overhauled Viña del Mar to become Chile's largest holiday resort) is the **Parque Nacional Fray Jorge**, one of the most unexpected ecological havens you are likely to come across. In the semi-desert of the north an island of Valdivian forest survives here, with trees such as olivillo, canelo, and arrayán, as well as plentiful epiphytes, ferns and creepers. These flourish thanks to the *camanchaca* that provides up to 1m of precipitation on the higher parts (up to 667m altitude), as opposed to about 113mm on the coast. Of the park's 9,959ha, only 400ha are still covered by this forest, while the rest is covered by a xerophile scrub dominated by guayacán with cacti. In wetter areas, such as by the Quebrada Las Vacas near the campsite, you will find the willow-like maitén. There are around 80 species of birds, including partridge and quail, hummingbirds and the odd visiting condor.

The park is only open at weekends, and Thur–Sun in high summer. From km389 on the PanAmerican a road leads 22km west to the park's Environmental Information Centre (still half-built) and then either 3km south to the Administration (in a century-old *casco* or estate house; apparently a good spot to see owls) or 5km west to the Arrayancito campsite, where it is possible to see both local species of fox. From Arrayancito it is another 6km west by the Camino El Mineral to the forest, where a 1km path leads past various labelled trees. There is also a coastal track which runs north from Sector Desembocadura, at the mouth of the Río Limari, where there is a *refugio*, as well as wild ducks to watch. It is possible to make your way from the forest down to this track by following a fire break parallel to the Quebrada la Quesería.

The Chilean, coastal or long-tailed chinchilla (*Chinchilla lanigera*) has been protected since 1929, having been virtually wiped out in pursuit of its amazingly fine fur. It now survives only in two reserves, one in Quebrada Honda, near La Higuera, north of La Serena, and in the **Reserva Nacional Las Chinchillas**, near Auco, 18km northwest of Illapel, where there is a population of at most 6,000 chinchillas, in addition to their main predators, the red fox and the great horned owl. The chinchillas (and related species) can be viewed in the *nocturama*, a room with day and night reversed; there are rooms and a campsite here. Their cousin, the Andean chinchilla (*C. brevicaudata*) persists in far greater numbers through the mountains of north Chile and northwest Argentina, as well as in Bolivia and Peru.

Around Santiago

If, after several days in the smog and bustle of Santiago, you are hungry for peace and fresh air, a pleasant alternative to heading for the coast is to make for the mountains and valleys to the east. Within an hour or two you can be winding along a clear, rushing river up in the Andean foothills or dangling your feet in a soothing thermal pool; there is also a wide choice of peaks and cliffs for climbing, and opportunities for rafting, horse-riding and other outdoor sports.

There are two main axes for exploration, along the Mapocho valley to the northeast, and along the Maipo valley (the Cajón del Maipo) to the southeast.

ALONG THE MAPOCHO VALLEY

From the northeastern outskirts of the city rises **Cerro Manquehue** ('Place of the Condor', 1,638m), shaped like a volcano with its cone knocked off. This can be climbed in a few hours and, smog permitting, affords wide views of the city and the *cordillera* to the east. There are various routes up, although the one from La Pirámide, passing a microwave station, is supposedly officially discouraged. This starts from the terminus of bus 652 (Maipú–La Pirámide), by a small obelisk at a viewpoint, just north of the bridge where Avda Américo Vespucio (the ring road) crosses the river and Avda Sta María. Take the steep path uphill to the north (signed *Zona de Vuelo Libre*), with a fence on your right, and after almost ten minutes (just above the small microwave tower) turn right by a water channel. After five minutes fork left just after the sluices, and head up, away from the channels. The path heads northeast via Cerro El Carbón (1,366m) to Cerro Manquehue.

Alternatively, take bus 611 or 612 from the Escuela Militar metro station and Avda Apoquindo to the Lo Curro terminal at the southern end of Gran Via in La Dehesa (where Pinochet lives), or shared taxi 62 (Escuela Militar–Lo Curro). Head up Gran Via and then Via Roja, which winds in long zigzags up to below Cerro Manquehue, and then the path which passes along the southern side of Cerro Manquehue Chico (or Manquehito) and northwest to the summit. Another path leads from the end of Avda Agua del Palo in Barrio Santa María de Manquehue, joining the Via Roja path.

On this southern side of Cerro Manquehue there is scrubby woodland of peumo (*Cryptocarya alba*), with quillay and litre; a 180ha estate was given to the city almost a hundred years ago, and for a long time was used to rest stressed animals, such as lions and gazelles, from the zoo; now the Darwin Environmental Education Centre has been built here and the area is being reforested with native species (quillay, peumo, bollen, tralhuen and molle). To be known as the Bosque de Santiago, it will provide a wildlife corridor between the Parque Metropolitano (Cerro San Cristobal, created in 1917) to the Manquehue range. Already rodents such as ratoncito lanudo and degú, as well as foxes, eagles and condors, have been found here.

To the east of the Cordón del Manquehue is the valley of the Estero Arrayán, protected since 1973 by the **Santuario de la Naturaleza del Cajón del Arrayán** (or Camino del Cajón). This is owned by the Municipality of Las Condes rather than by Conaf, but you will still have to pay a couple of dollars to enter. The track follows the El Arrayán River past cacti and shrubs; it is worth looking out for fossils, too. You can bathe in the river which, although cold, is clean and invigorating after a few hours' walk. You can in fact continue northwards for 2–3 days, but it also makes a perfect day out with a picnic. From the Escuela Militar metro station, or from the Alameda, take any bus for Barnechea via Las Condes; it will fork left at the YPF petrol station (at Avenida Las Condes 14272), cross the river and turn left. You should get off here and continue along Camino Refugio del Arrayán, turning right after 100m and again after 500m on El Remanso to cross back to the left/southeast bank. After 5 minutes turn left on Pastor Fernández, then after 2 minutes head to the left up Camino El Cajón del Arrayán. This is lined with expensive houses for almost the whole 4.5km to the Sanctuary's gate (at 880m; open daily 09.00–20.00), where you will have to pay US$4. Alternatively get off the bus before the bridge at Plaza San Enrique and take a shared taxi straight up Pastor Fernández from here almost all the way to the gate.

The next turning left off Pastor Fernández (after Camino El Cajón del Arrayán) is Camino El Alto, from the end of which a path leads up Cerro Pochoco (1,805m), perhaps the most popular weekend walk near Santiago (about 3 hours return). Shared taxis take you from Plaza San Enrique to the Observatorio at the end of the road for US$2. Cars parked here may be broken into. The path, through spiney bushes and cacti, is badly eroded, so take a pole and gloves, as well as water.

The main road up the Mapocho valley forks to the right at the YPF filling station, and soon heads out of the city as El Camino Farellones. There are no public buses on this route, but hitching is not too hard, especially at weekends. Almost at once you will pass the Las Puertas checkpoint, which controls traffic to the ski resorts in winter, when there is a one-way regime and chains have to be fitted. Immediately before the Puente Ñilhue at km6 (where the paved road crosses to the right/north bank, at 970m) signs indicate the start of the Camino del Naranjo hiking route south to **Cerro Provincia** (2,751m) and **Cerro San Ramón** (3,249m). These peaks form the precordillera which is the backdrop to the east of Santiago, when the smog allows you to see anything. Climb to the top of these peaks and you will appreciate how bad *el esmog* really is. It does, however, have one advantage in that it produces blazing red sunsets.

This walk is best done between September and May, although it can be done in winter with the appropriate equipment. Cerro Provincia can be climbed in about 8–10 hours with backpacks, 5–7 hours without. Allow another 3 hours for the descent. It takes another 4–5 hours to reach Cerro San Ramón, with backpacks.

About 300m along the dirt road to the right, a path heads off to the right and climbs steeply along the ridge, which it follows all the way to the top; there are some yellow paint marks to guide you. After about an hour you will cross a small covered water channel; go to the left of the ridge if you want to fill a water bottle. After about another half hour of walking, you will reach a large tree which is an excellent place to camp if you have set off late in the day. The path from here is

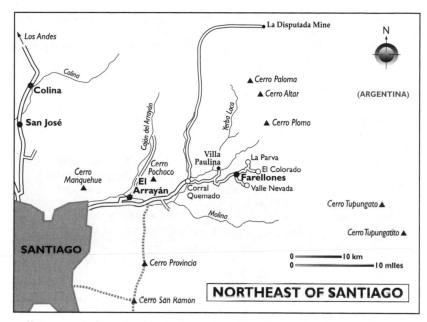

Map labels:
- La Disputada Mine
- Los Andes
- N
- Colina
- Colina
- Cerro Paloma
- Cerro Altar
- (ARGENTINA)
- San José
- Yerba Loca
- Cajón del Arrayán
- Cerro Plomo
- Villa Paulina
- La Parva
- Cerro Pochoco
- El Colorado
- Cerro Manquehue
- El Arrayán
- Farellones
- Corral Quemado
- Valle Nevada
- Cerro Tupungato
- Molina
- Cerro Tupungatito
- SANTIAGO
- 0 —— 10 km
- 0 —— 10 miles
- Cerro Provincia
- Cerro San Ramón
- **NORTHEAST OF SANTIAGO**

well worn, winding slowly up along the ridge for another hour and crossing another water channel. To the right you may see the odd condor soaring in the currents that also carry the noises of the bustling city below. The path then starts to climb more steeply up to the peak of Cerro Provincia, which you will reach in a further 3–4 hours. If you wish to continue to Cerro San Ramón, continue south along this same ridge, which climbs up and down and is quite rocky in parts. Nevertheless it is an easier route than the steep slopes below. Until early summer there is often a snow bank below an unnamed peak of 2,972m, about 2½ hours from Cerro Provincia, where you should be able to obtain some water, but do not rely on it being there. About another 2 hours of walking takes you to the top of Cerro San Ramón (3,249m).

There are various other routes from the west. From the stadium in San Carlos de Apoquindo a wide 4WD track heads east from the car park; after 15 minutes go left at a wooden post, cut back to the right and carry on up the zigzag path. There is water after an hour total, after another hour you will reach the main trail, and it takes another couple of hours to the top of Cerro Provincia. The *ruta clásica* up Cerro San Ramón via the Quebrada de Peñalolen starts at the end of Avda Grecia (about 1,000m), from where you should go diagonally north towards a pyramid peak to pick up a path by a stream (near some rugby pitches). It takes about 3 hours through native woodland to the Casa de Piedra, a rock shelter at 1,700m with room for three people. From here the path zigzags for 15 minutes to Casa de Piedra Alemana (by a stream), then up scree to Cerro Abanico, from where it is another 3 hours following the rocky ridge to the summit. In summer it is possible to do this as a day-trip if fit and strong. However, in the last couple of years it has been necessary to obtain permission the previous day from the Fundo Antupirén, at the end of Calle Antupirén. Other routes follow the Quebrada de Macul, immediately south of this route, and the Estero El Manzano, from the Cajón del Maipo (see page 146).

You will need warm clothing and a good sleeping bag if camping; in high summer it is dry enough to manage without a tent, but you will find it cold. Your greatest problem will be carrying the quantity of water needed, as the only water supplies are in the first two hours of the hike.

YERBA LOCA

Distance	18km, Villa Paulina to Cerro La Paloma
Altitude	Between 1,700m and 5,222m
Rating	Moderate
Time	7–8 hours return to Refugio Casa de Piedra Carajaval, or 9–10 hours to get to the foot of the glacier and back, or 3–4 days return to Cerros La Paloma and Altar
Start of trail	Villa Paulina
End of trail	Villa Paulina
Maps	The area is largely covered by IGM 5-04-05-0059-00 (Farellones) and 5-04-05-0052-00 (La Disputada) in the 1:50,000 series, and 3300-6900 (San José de Maipo) in the 1:250,000 series.

The main road (signposted to Farellones) continues up the right/north bank of the Mapocho, with a hikeable track linking the bases of electricity pylons above the left bank. The road crosses back to the south at Puente Lilen, and at km16 (Corral Quemado) most traffic continues north up the Maipo valley to the Disputada de las Condes copper mine, while the paved road to the ski resorts turns right to climb in a series of tight zigzags. This then follows a ridge for a period before starting to climb again. On the left at *Curva 15* (the most extreme hairpins are marked with numbered signs) is the Palco Chico gate to the **Santuario de la Naturaleza Yerba Loca**, which protects a couple of valleys heading deep into the *cordillera* and providing access to glaciers and peaks over 5,000m. The Estero de la Yerba Loca (Crazy Grass Stream) takes its name from a native grass which, if eaten, reportedly can cause a permanent state of delirium. So it is advisable not to nibble the local flora, although there is plenty of fresh water to quench your thirst.

Getting to the trailhead
From the gate (1,700m), where you have to pay US$3, a dirt road leads 4.2km to Villa Paulina (1,930m), site of the Santuario's administration and campsite; the von Kiesling family, who gave the estate to the Municipalidad of Las Condes in 1971 (it was transferred to Conaf in 1983), planted trees such as cypress, poplar, elm and pines, and re-introduced llamas and alpacas, not seen in this area for many years. Above 2,000m the vegetation is classified as *estepa alto andina* (high Andean steppe), dominated by shrubs such as hierba blanca, pingo-pingo, coirón and the threatened llaretilla; below Villa Paulina is a transitional zone dominated by olivillo de la cordillera, and below 1,300m (below the Disputada junction) is *matorral esclerófilo andino*, a scrub of spiny bushes and trees such as peumo, litre, quillay and bollón.

Day-walkers can do the return trip to Refugio Casa de Piedra Carajaval in between 7 and 8 hours, plus another 2 hours if you wish to climb to the foot of the glacier; this hike can be done all year round. Weather permitting, it is possible to climb Cerro La Paloma (4,910m) in 3 days return. Allow an extra half day to continue to Cerro Altar (5,222m). The best season for climbing these peaks is November to April.

Route description

From Villa Paulina follow the road (closed to vehicles) on the left/east bank of the western valley (the valley to the right/east is the Estero La Leonera – see below). This soon degenerates into a well-worn foot track, marked occasionally by red splashes of paint and not hard to follow. It climbs gradually, meandering through a number of small meadows, any of which are ideal for camping, although you might find yourself spending the night with wild horses or llamas.

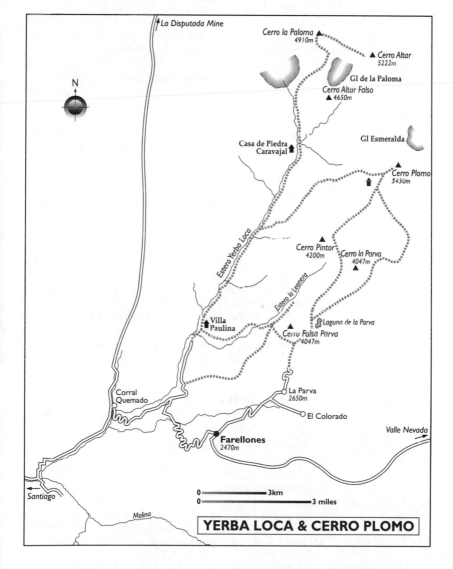

After about 3½ hours, you will arrive at a rocky plain where the river, tinged by mineral deposits, has coloured the rocks bright orange. The path now begins to climb more steeply and crosses two small streams rising on some spectacular peaks to the right, the highest of which is Cerro Altar Falso (4,650m). Shortly after crossing the second of these streams, the path zig-zags up over a rock wall. Near the top of this rise the path splits; the right-hand fork leads up the Estero Los Chorrillos del Plomo towards Altar Falso, and the left-hand one continues up the Yerba Loca valley to Refugio Casa de Piedra Caravajal, on the true right bank of the river at the top of this rise (3,240m). As the name suggests, this is a stone *refugio*, with a tin roof and even a small makeshift stove. It is very basic, but provides some shelter from the wind. Nevertheless, you will find it warmer in a tent.

From here it takes an hour to reach the foot of the glacier, or 2 days to Cerros La Paloma and Altar. The path on is less well worn and, therefore, somewhat easier to mistake. Follow it back over to the true left bank of the river and continue up the valley. After climbing past some cascades, the path will begin to head left. At this point, cross the river again and head for the left-hand side of the glacier. Early in the season no path exists because the river washes it away every spring.

To the right a path leads to a more difficult route up Cerro Altar. This is the last source of running water, so if heading for the peaks you will have to fill up here. Higher up water can only be obtained by melting snow. Shortly after crossing the river you will come across some ruins of the wooden Refugio Federación (3,500m) and a number of camping spots. From the base of the glacier the normal route up Cerro La Paloma takes between 15 and 20 hours return. It is therefore necessary to camp for at least one night before making it to the top. Follow the valley to the left of the Glaciar del Rincón, passing below a rocky formation known as El Morro Negro, then climb quite steeply up to the right, to the east–west ridge formed by Cerros Altar and La Paloma (reached in 5–6 hours). The best location to camp before proceeding to the peak is on the far, northern, side of this ridge. From this campsite, cross the La Paloma glacier and follow the ridge east up to the peak, taking another 5 hours. You can continue along the ridge to Cerro Altar in another 2 hours. Return by the same route to Villa Paulina.

To cross the glacier you will need crampons, ice-axe and a rope. The crossing is not technically difficult, but you should take care. Even day-walkers should carry warm clothing and long trousers, as there can be a very cold wind off the glacier, irrespective of season.

It is possible to climb these peaks from the northern side, starting at the La Disputada mine, at an altitude of 3,300m. Check at the Federación de Andinismo, or phone CMD (the Companía Minera Disputada) on 02 223 3037.

LA PARVA TO CERRO PLOMO

Distance	15km
Altitude	Between 2,650m and 5,430m
Rating	Moderate
Time	3–4 days (4 days will allow for acclimatisation)
Start of trail	La Parva
End of trail	Cerro Plomo
Maps	The area is covered by IGM 1:50,000 maps 3315-7015, 3315-7000 and 3300-7000, and 1:250,000 map 3300-6900 (San José de Maipo).

Getting to the trailhead

From the Yerba Loca gate, the road to the ski resorts dips slightly to Puente Manzanito and then climbs again. At bend 18 you will see waterfalls in an impressive rocky gully to the left, which is the only home of the toad *Alsodes tumultuosus*. There is some enjoyable climbing and scrambling here, best reached from bend 20. The road climbs to Farellones, entered at bend 40 where a road turns right to **Valle Nevada** (3,205m), the most modern of the ski resorts, about 9km east.

Farellones (2,470m/51km from Santiago) was the first of the Mapocho valley ski stations, but it is now more of a residential base for the resorts higher up the hill. There are great sunsets here, and in the mornings you can actually see Santiago, before the smog comes in! The road continues for 5km to **La Parva** (2,650m), turning left about half a kilometre before; to the right the road leads in a kilometre or so to the fourth of the ski resorts, **El Colorado** (2,430m), which does not offer much for walkers.

Looking east from Santiago, beyond the precordillera ridge of Cerros Provincia and San Ramón, one peak stands out – the rounded white mass of Cerro Plomo. At 5,430m, this is the highest peak easily accessible from Santiago, and it is not a technically difficult one to climb; the only problems you are likely to have will be due to the altitude. Cerro Plomo is also famous because the mummy of an Inca child-sacrifice was found just below the peak in 1954. Still in very good condition, it (or, as rumour has it, a replica – a dummy-mummy) is displayed in the Museo Nacional de Historia Natural in Santiago's Quinta Normal Park. So while you climb to the top with your space-age rucksack, super snug sleeping bag and Goretex and fleece clothing, give some thought to the Incas who walked these trails centuries before with little more than colourful ponchos.

There are also possibilities for daywalks from La Parva. The best season is November to April; from May to September you will need cross-country skis or snowshoes, as you will be walking in snow at least 1m deep. Supplies should be purchased in Santiago, as very little is available in Farellones or La Parva, especially in summer. A sturdy tent and good sleeping bag are essential as it can become extremely cold and windy at night. It can snow even in mid-summer, so you should be prepared for all conditions. Crampons, an ice-axe and perhaps a rope are needed for crossing the glacier near the summit.

Route description

From the top of the ski resort of La Parva, just below a small microwave tower, you can either take a dirt road running up to the left, or, if feeling fit and acclimatised, go straight up following two parallel chairlifts. The road zigzags up to their upper station at 3,100m (after roughly 40 minutes), from where other chair-lifts and ski-drags continue up the hill. The road also continues, zig-zagging up between two streams, and heads right at a junction after 10 minutes. After 15 minutes more it reaches a false horizon, and just beyond it the lower terminal of a ski-drag that runs virtually up to the pass. The road goes on up to the left, and in 5 minutes forks left where some red arrows mark the hiking route. This takes various shortcuts crossing the road, and reaches the Portezuelo San Francisco (3,570m) in 20 minutes. To the left is Cerro Falsa Parva (3,740m), rocky crags rising out of scree slopes, and ahead of you is Laguna de la Parva, just a couple of minutes below (1½–2 hours from La Parva), where you can camp.

From here you can either follow the ridge to the left, formed by Cerros Falsa

Parva, La Parva (4,047m) and Pintor (4,200m), or along the flanks of the mountains to the Cajón del Cepo. The advantage of the former is that it is more direct and will give you more time to acclimatise to the altitude; its disadvantage is that there is no running water until you reach the refuge, in 7–8 hours. You will pass Cerro La Parva on the west side (overlooking Santiago) and climb over Cerro Pintor to the plateau known as the Cancha de Carreras (4,200m). From here you will have to climb back down a scree slope into the Cajón del Cepo. (An alternative excursion is to swing left to Cerro La Leonera, 4,954m.) This route is relatively easy to follow except for finding where to climb back down. At the bottom you will find a small orange *refugio* close to the river.

The lower route is well used and easy to follow; it is also described in the *Cumbres de Chile* booklet. It is relatively easy walking with plenty of water along the way. However, it is longer, requiring some 8–10 hours to reach the same *refugio* from the Laguna de la Parva. If you started the day in Santiago, you might want to camp at Piedra Numerada (3,350m, 3–4 hours from the *laguna*), a huge rock covered in numbers, by the river, where there are good grassy sites.

From the *refugio* it is 5–6 hours to the peak, but you should only set off from here to the top in fine weather. The path climbs up a scree on the left bank of the river to La Olla, at the foot of the Esmeralda glacier (about 4,400m), another good camping spot with spectacular views of the glacier. Be careful to camp on high land as this basin floods on a hot day. The path continues up on the true left side of the glacier, and after another hour you will come to the Agostini *refugio* (4,600m), largely destroyed by the elements. No running water is available here, but you should be able to find snow to melt. From here the path zig-zags up a steep scree to a false summit where the path turns to the left. A little further on, at 5,140m, you will come to La Pirca del Inca, the tomb of the Inca (mummified by the dry climate rather than by the Incas themselves). From here only very experienced climbers, equipped with crampons, should continue to cross the glacier to the north; take great care as there are a number of crevasses into which you might fall. Finally follow the ridge up to the peak of Cerro Plomo (5,430m), and return by the Piedra Numerada route.

From the Portezuelo San Francisco, above the Laguna de la Parva, day-walkers might choose to return via the Estero La Leonera and Villa Paulina, to the west. A good new road heads west (to the right as you descend) beyond the stream and the top of a ski-lift and the Piuqenes ski-run; this curves around the shoulder of Falsa Parva and ends in 10 minutes at a large barrier. You can walk around this and drop down on scree for 15 minutes to reach a low stone windbreak, from where you can see the three ski resorts. This area seems arid, but in fact there are many wonderful alpine plants at your feet. Continuing down to the right, if you follow the natural line to pass just below a rocky shoulder, you will detect that you are not the first to have come this way, and beyond the shoulder you will briefly be on something that is almost a path, rising slightly to reach a ridge after another half hour. Here there is a view into the Estero La Leonera. You can continue to the right on steeper looser scree, or go a little to the left to pick up a path from La Parva. This has a few paint markings on rocks, but you are soon on your own as you descend the scree to reach the bottom of the valley in about half an hour. There is any number of lizards here, as well as big raptors including condors.

On the far, right, bank a path leads to Villa Paulina. On the left bank, orange poles mark the line of a water pipeline, just below which is a path on which, heading downstream, to the left, you soon find yourself high above the stream.

Better suited to mules than humans, but marked occasionally with red paint, it soon climbs steeply to reach the pipeline after 20 minutes. Following the pipeline, after 15 minutes you will glimpse El Colorado ahead, and then a house to the right. Turn right across country to the valley to the left of this house, ie: straight towards the Mapocho valley and Santiago. Keep to the left as a stream emerges, cross a path from the house and head on down to meet another which you should follow to the left to reach a viewpoint towards Farellones and the Yerba Loca gate, after 25 minutes. The path continues easily around to the left, reaching a good stream in 5 minutes, and then an abandoned shepherd-type hut and, after 10 more minutes, a junction at a post on a ridge. To the left it is quite a long way around a valley to reach Farellones, while to the right the path follows the ridge, with views left into the Manzanito gully, reaching the road just above the Yerba Loca gate in about 45 minutes. The upper part of the Leonera valley, leading to the west flank of Cerro Plomo, is well worth exploring, too, and is most easily reached by the path from La Parva – especially as at the Yerba Loca gate you will have to pay the full entry fee for every day you plan to stay in the Santuario.

CAJÓN DEL MAIPO AND EL MORADO NATIONAL PARK

The indigenous inhabitants of Chile walked through this and other valleys to cross the Andes into what is now Argentina, but because of the arid terrain they never made permanent settlements. As a result, unlike in the Central Valley, the names of the attractive villages which, thanks to irrigation, dot the Maipo valley today are Spanish rather than indigenous. Many are named after local trees and fruits, such as the peach and almond, whose blossom is spectacular in spring. This continued to be the main route into Argentina until the opening of the Portillo Pass, and a notorious smuggling route after that. During Pinochet's years in power, these valleys were used as escape routes for dissidents fleeing his secret police. In 1986 Pinochet himself was almost killed when his car was ambushed here by the FPMR guerrillas.

You can reach **San José de Maipo**, 48km southeast of Santiago, in a little over an hour (1½ hours by bus); this is the main town in the Maipo valley, and most day-trippers come this far and no further. However, it is well worth continuing to the end of the road, to the thermal pools of **Baños Morales** and the **El Morado National Park**. In fact the whole valley offers an amazing range of opportunities for hiking and climbing, as well as rafting trips and fossil hunting. Along the valley are many cliffs that are popular with Santiago's climbers, while to the east near the Argentine border are high peaks that are often used for acclimatisation before climbing Aconcagua, although they are actually more difficult than the big one. See JLM map 6 *Andes Centrales, Cajón del Maipo*.

Getting there

Buses Cajón del Maipo (tel: 02 850 5769, 697 2520) leave every 30 minutes for San José del Maipo, from just northwest of the Parque O'Higgins metro station (also picking up at Bellavista de la Florida, the southern terminal of metro line 5); one per hour continues to San Gabriel. At 07.00 on Saturdays, Sundays and holidays (daily in January and February) a bus runs all the way to Baños Morales (US$3), returning at 18.00. Others leave for El Volcán at 12.30 and 18.00 daily. Buses Manzur (tel: 211 7165) also operates a bus to Baños de Colina at weekends, leaving the south side of Plaza Baquedano at 07.30, returning at 18.30. If driving, head south on Avda Florida and follow signs east to San José de Maipo. It is a pleasant journey, on paved roads all the way to San Gabriel. On the way you will see large, outdoor earth-ovens and stalls selling traditional *empanadas*, popular stopping-off points for day-trippers.

Along the Cajón del Maipo

The lower part of the valley is irrigated, but the slopes and the upper part of the valley are *matorral esclerófilo andino*, with trees such as boldo, litre, guayacán and maitén, rodents such as chinchilla, cururo, coipo and native mice, as well as wild cats, rabbits and hares; birds include condor, thrushes, giant and Andean hummingbirds, doves, sparrows and ducks.

After **El Manzano** (889m, 37km from Santiago) the Maipo valley swings to the south, while the valley of the Río Colorado heads northeast, giving views of Tupungato and Tupungatito (page 127). A good road runs past a campsite and the Los Maitenes hydroelectric power-station to El Alfalfal (1,330m, 23km up the valley), giving access to little-touched peaks such as Cerro Pirámide (5,484m) and Punta del Paraíso (3,976m), as well as to Tupungato. Above El Manzano to the northwest of the junction, the cliffs of the Torrecillas del Manzano offer a good choice of climbing routes.

The main road continues to **San José de Maipo** (967m, 48km from Santiago), a colonial town dating from 1760 when a silver mine opened here. Its church, built in 1798, is now a National Historical Monument, as is the former railway station, now housing the town library. A narrow-gauge military line from Puente Alto to El Volcán opened in 1908, and is now disused, although you will see its remains parallel to the road and could indeed hike along parts of it. The town's fiesta is held on July 16; there is also a Semana de la Montaña in the last week of February. The town also has the nearest campsite to Santiago.

Three kilometres east of town is the junction to **Lagunillas**, the oldest and simplest of the ski resorts around Santiago, 17km north at 2,250m; nowadays it is also the base of CEAL (*Centro de Educación en Aire Libre*/Open-Air Education Centre).The Posada Chalet de Piedra (tel: 02 861 1243), 500m up the Lagunillas road, is a good cheap base for walking, riding and rafting.

At **Puente El Toyo** (977m, 54km) the much quieter road along the south bank of the Maipo ends; from here and El Melocotón (1,014m, 57km) rafting groups set off for the relatively unexciting 10km run to Guayacán. The **Cascada de las Animas** is a private nature reserve (owned by the Cousiño-Macul family; tel/fax: 02 861 1303); Cascada (see page 78) has an Outdoor Centre here, offering rafting, kayaking, horse-riding and trekking.

The pleasant town of **San Alfonso** (1,106m, 59km) has plenty of hotels and restaurants, and roadside stalls sell local delicacies such as walnuts and marzipan; there are fine views of the *cordillera*, as well as good climbing on the peaks to the north. Passing through the Tinoco gorge, the former railway runs through tunnels to the left, before a side road crosses the river to the right to El Ingenio, a good spot to hire horses, as the village is known for its saddlers. There is good climbing (and a good hostería-restaurant) at El Boyenar, before reaching San Gabriel (1,233m, 70km), where the asphalt ends and the road splits at a police checkpoint. One road heads north for 35km to Laguna Negra (2,680m) and the Embalse El Yeso (2,800m), which supply much of Santiago's water; from here there is access to the south sides of Tupungato and Tupangatito, and the Piuquenes pass (closed without special permission, although Darwin passed this way) to Tunuyán in Mendoza province, Argentina.

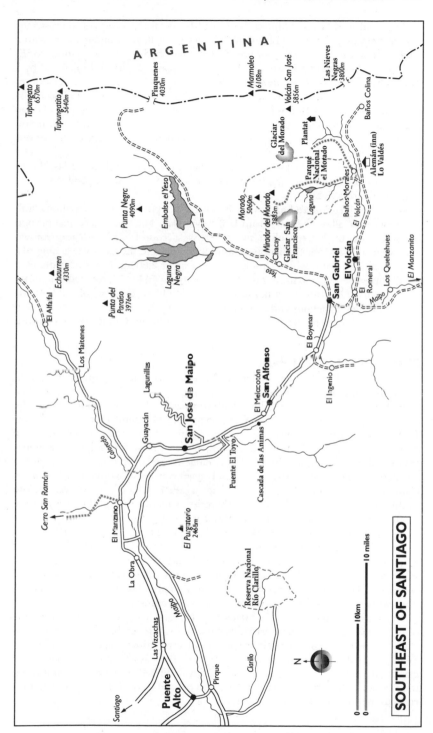

SOUTHEAST OF SANTIAGO

The main road heads south for 3km to El Romeral (1,390m) and then swings east up the valley of the Río El Volcan. The Maipo valley continues south, with a road past a campsite and the Los Queltehues hydro-electric station to El Manzanito. Continuing up the Volcán valley, increasingly dry and inhabited by a rare lizard (*Pristidactylus volcanensis*), you will pass the mining settlement of El Volcán (1,414m, 80km) and then fork left to cross a wooden bridge to Plaza Villa del Valle, the centre of **Baños Morales** (1,950m, 92km from Santiago). Here there are a couple of *residencials* and cafés and basic hot (or at least warm) pools. If you continue along the main road, you will pass Lo Valdés (2,000m), site of the famous Refugio Alemán (tel: 02 850 1773), a popular chalet which is open all year. The road ends after 105km at Baños Colina (2,500m), below the Paso de las Nieves Negras, a closed pass into Argentina; the baths (US$6) are three good small clay pools, with great views!

To the north is **Volcán San José** (5,856m), a very popular acclimatisation climb for Aconcagua; allow five days from Baños Morales. The route starts just beyond the bridge over the Estero Colina, swings left/west around a rock formation known as *El Morro* ('The Moor') and loops around to the right to the Estero de la Engorda, crossed after an hour, where base camp is set up at 2,600m. From here the path climbs up a side valley to the left to the Plantat *refugio* (3,480m), reached in another 3 or 4 hours. The path continues to the east, dipping to the head of the Engorda valley, climbing up a gully and forking left to a campsite at 4,520m, from where it is another 12 hours (requiring another camp) to the summit, mostly on scree, with some snow.

El Morado National Park

From the yard where buses terminate in Baños Morales, head up the hill following signs to camping and then left to cross a footbridge to reach the Park Administration in a couple of minutes. Having paid and received your garbage bag, set off up the steep zig-zags. After about 25 minutes the climb eases somewhat for 10 minutes, before 5 minutes more steep climbing to bring you to the top of the moraine. In a couple of minutes more, at 2,160m, you will find a sign to the Aguas Panimavidas to the right, where yellow/orange mineral deposits have stained the meadows. Here you can enjoy, completely *gratis*, various flavours of *agua mineral*. Camping is permitted here only if bad weather forces you to wait before continuing up the valley. From here there is a superb view up the valley to the Mirador del Morado (3,883m) and behind it the mighty bulk of Cerro Morado (5,060m); its 1,000m south face is a very tough climb.

When returning, be sure to take the left turn on to the Baños Morales path off a four-wheel-drive track (now closed to walkers), that comes in from the southwest at this point. This track continues up the valley to reach the Laguna del Morado (2,380m, 5km from Baños Morales) in about 50 minutes. This is the only place where you are allowed to camp in normal circumstances.

To continue to the foot of the Glacier del Morado, carry on along the east side of the *laguna* and on up the west/right bank of the stream, before crossing it and after 3 hours reaching a small cirque between Cerro Mirador and la Punta Unión. Swinging to the left and climbing some scree, the path reaches the foot of the glacier (at 3,100m) after another hour. Properly equipped climbers can continue up the east side of the glacier to reach the col just behind Cerro Mirador and then turn right to the summit, in another 3 hours or so.

RÍO CLARILLO NATIONAL RESERVE

The **Reserva Nacional Río Clarillo** is a very popular alternative to the Cajón del Maipo for the Sunday excursions of the *santiagueños*. The picnic sites are concentrated near the gate, and if you go a little further you will soon be enjoying some genuine *naturaleza*. Its 10,185ha are dominated by sclerophyllous *matorral* scrub and sclerophyllous woodland (with trees such as litre, peumo, espino, maqui, lingue, canelo, arrayán and quilla); there is also Andean steppe vegetation in the highest parts. The wildlife has suffered greatly from hunting in the past, but is slowly recovering. Most interesting is the Chilean wood pigeon (torcaza; *Columba araucana*), which was virtually extinct in the 1950s.

Getting there

The reserve is 45km southeast of Santiago: from the centre, Providencia, or La Florida metro station, take a bus to Puente Alto and on to Principal Pirque. You will cross the Río Maipo by the Puente San Ramón, turn right at a T-junction at the end of Concha y Toro in Pirque, and then left after about a kilometre. The paved road ends after 5.5km, after crossing the Río Clarillo, at a junction by a small shop where you should turn left onto Calle Nueva. Turn left again onto Camino El Chalaco after a kilometre or so, signed to the Reserve. The reserve gate is about 2.5km along this road, about 500m beyond the turning to the Parque Alemán, where buses terminate. Although the sign says it is another 4km, it only takes 30 minutes to walk to the Administration, where the reserve really begins; the dirt road passes through bushes and cacti, and past fields with cows.

You will have to pay US$4 (US$6 at weekends) at the Information Centre, where there is a display on the SNASPE (the national system of reserves and parks). The park is open 08.00–20.00, with no camping. If you push on through the picnic area, you will find yourself on a well-used path that is easy to follow. After an hour this comes to Rodeo Las Yeguas, where it crosses to the right bank, and then climbs quite steeply away from the river through a dense patch of forest. At the top of this rise, you will join a wide well-worn track. This continues on the north side of the river and after crossing the Quebrada Colihuesi drops back down to cross the river again. After another hour along this track you will arrive at a deep waterhole with its own natural, slippery dip. This is an excellent place to have lunch and cool off, before returning by the same route.

CERRO LA CAMPANA

The chain of mountains that runs to the west of Santiago, parallel to the coast and the Andean *cordillera*, reaches over 2,200m to the east of Viña del Mar and Valparaíso. Cerro La Campana is a sharply peaked mountain rising directly from the Aconcagua valley and dominating the area around it. The national park which protects 8,000ha of this range is named after **Cerro La Campana** even though at 1,880m it is not the highest peak in the park. However, it is the most visible, and folktales describe its jewelled summit guarded by witches. Now a Biosphere Reserve, this is one of the few areas where the flora of central Chile survives. It makes an ideal day-trip if you are getting bored on the beach at Viña del Mar, and it is also an excellent way to prepare for more arduous treks and climbs in the Andes, although it will not help with acclimatisation. As well as offering 1,400m of steep ascent, there are good climbing routes on the 200m of south-facing cliffs below the summit.

The highest peak in the park, on its eastern fringe, is **Cerro Roble** (2,204m),

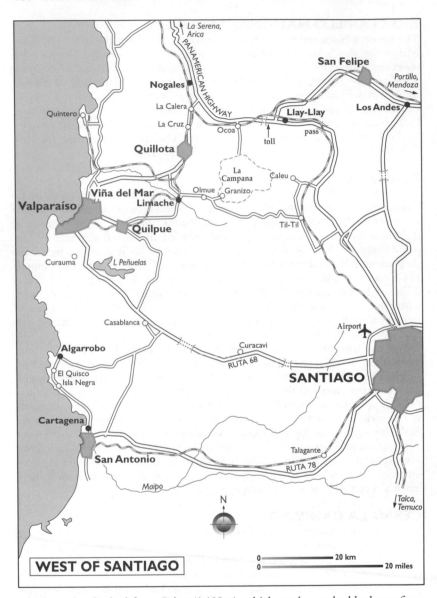

WEST OF SANTIAGO

0 — 20 km
0 — 20 miles

which can be climbed from Caleu (1,100m), which can be reached by buses from Til-Til (just west of the PanAmerican Highway north of Santiago). There is a proposal to extend the park towards Cerro Alvarado and Caleu.

Most of the park is covered by sclerophyllous (hard-broadleaf evergreen) forest of the central Coastal Cordillera; this is surprisingly dense and varied, composed from over a dozen species of small tree such as peumo, quillay, boldo, litre, lingue del norte, canelo, tayú (or palo santo), and belloto del norte. Rare and endangered flowers include *Adiantum gertrudis*, *Alstroemeria garaventai*, *Adesmia resinosa*, *Placea germainii*, and *Rhodophiala tiltilensis*. However, it is best known for the last substantial woodland of Chilean wine-palm (*Jubaea chilensis*), of which 60,000 survive in the park's northern Ocoa sector. These can live for 1,200 years, and can orient themselves to the north. Wildlife includes grey foxes, skunks, Geoffroy's cat, rodents such as the cururo and birds including eagles, buzzards, bay-winged hawk, owls and giant hummingbirds; the endangered lizard *Pristydactylus alvaroi*; and snakes, frogs and toads.

Distance	4km to the summit
Altitude	Between 450m and 1,880m
Rating	Easy
Time	4 hours to summit
Start of trail	La Troya Gate, Cerro La Campana National Park
End of trail	La Troya Gate, Cerro La Campana National Park
Maps	The IGM 1:100,000 map *Quillota y Valparaíso* covers the park

Getting to the trailhead

The Ocoa sector can be reached quite simply by turning off the PanAmerican at km100 (ignore signs to a *Reserva Ecológica* at km 98) and following the road south up the Rabuco valley for 12.5km. From the gate the La Buitrera campsite is 1km east, while following the road on to the southeast for 6km you will come to the La Cortadera waterfalls, 35m high. Buses from La Calera and Quillota run to Hualcapo and Escuela Las Palmas (respectively 4km and 2km short of the gate).

To reach the summits, you need to enter the park from the southwest, as did Darwin when he climbed the mountain in 1836. Buses run from Valparaíso and Viña del Mar to Limache and Olmué, or if you prefer you can even take the suburban train to Limache, 44 minutes from Viña. From Limache or Olmué you need to take a bus to Granizo; most turn right at *paradero 40* (the Valparaíso region does not just run a good train service, it even numbers its bus stops!), but a few go up to *paradero 45* in Granizo Alto. If you have to walk up it takes about 20 minutes to the bus terminal (passing the park administration at 373m at *paradero 43*). Just beyond the Puente La Troya you can walk up a short-cut to the left and turn left at the top to reach the La Troya park gate (Sector Granizo). Here you need to leave your passport, unless you are leaving by another gate. You can camp in the picnic area here and hike up Cerro Campana or to Ocoa.

If you carry on for 3km from *paradero 40*, covered by most local buses, you can also enter the park at the Sector Cajón Grande, where there are two campsites and trails to Ocoa and La Cortadera.

Route description

From the La Troya gate (450m) walk up the rough track and turn left after 5 minutes onto the Sendero Andinista; this crosses the stream and turns right. If you turn left and then right you will come to the start of the Sendero La Canasta, an interpretative path with labelled trees and 12 numbered markers that relate to a leaflet. To the right, you will soon reach the true start of the Andinista path, to the summit of La Campana, while the Los Peumo path, to the right, returns to the mine road, and eventually turns right off it to the Portezuelo Ocoa.

It is only just over 4km to the summit, but it can take 4 hours from here, and you are not allowed to start after midday. The well-maintained path climbs

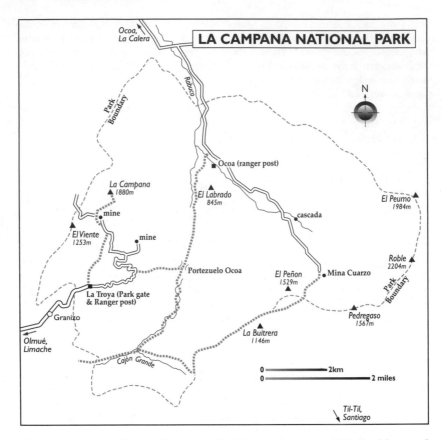

LA CAMPANA NATIONAL PARK

through dense woodland which gradually thins, giving way to thick shrubbery and stunted roble de Santiago (*Nothofagus obliqua* var. *macrocarpa*, at its northern limit), and thorny *Colletia* and acacia. After about 3 hours you will rejoin the mine road just before a plateau. From here the mine road climbs over the northwest ridge (outside the park) and heads north down the Quebrada El Belloto to the road in the Ocoa sector. For the scramble to the top, you should follow the road to the ridge and then pick the best route up the ridge to the right. The rocky terrain is covered in scrub and dead brush, leading to a final 200m scramble. This looks ominous at first, but by sticking to the ridge as much as possible, you should pick up the yellow arrows on the rock that indicate the route to the summit.

The easier main path continues directly upwards through thin woods of false beech and then climbs diagonally below the cliffs, weaving around large boulders to reach the southeast ridge. From here the path climbs above tree level and there is some loose rock and scree to negotiate before reaching the top. The graffiti-covered summit provides an unwelcome splash of colour, but the panoramic view is splendid if there is little haze.

Reserva Nacional Lago Peñuelas

Returning to Santiago on the main highway from Valparaíso, the **Reserva Nacional Lago Peñuelas** covers 9,094ha around an artificial lake created in 1900.

It is now mainly planted with pine and eucalyptus, and suffered a major fire in 1996, but is very popular for fishing. The main gate is at km94, just east of the new town of Curauma; coming from Valparaíso, it is a tricky turn across oncoming traffic. Birds here include partridges, giant hummingbirds, ducks, herons, and eagles, and occasionally black-necked and coscoroba swans.

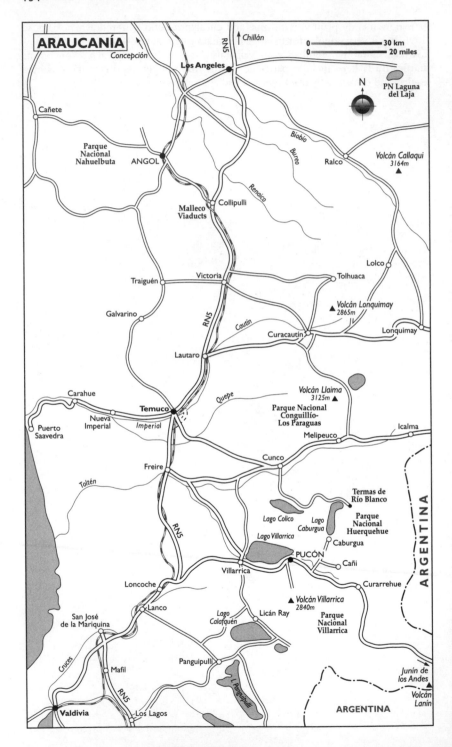

Araucanía

When the Spanish *conquistador*, Pedro de Valdivia, pushed south from Santiago in search of new territory, he was forced by fierce resistance from the Araucanian Indians to stop at the settlement to which he had given his name. In 1554 the Indians, who called themselves Mapuche or 'people of the earth', captured Valdivia and tortured him to death. From 1598 the area south of Concepción, Los Angeles and the Biobío River remained independent Mapuche territory, and it was not until 1881 that it became incorporated into Chile. As Bruce Chatwin put it, somewhat contentiously if entertainingly:

> 'A hundred years ago the Araucanians were incredibly fierce and brave. They painted their bodies red and flayed their enemies alive and sucked at the hearts of the dead. Their boys' education consisted of hockey, horsemanship, liquor, insolence and sexual athletics, and for three centuries they scared the Spaniards out of their wits... The Araucanians are still very tough and would be a lot tougher if they gave up drink.'

Much of Araucanía (now Chile's 9th Region) consists of rich fertile lowlands where most of the country's wheat and barley are grown, hence its reputation as the 'granary of Chile'. To the west, the snow-capped volcanoes of the Andes tower over glistening lakes. Many of these volcanoes are still active; about 2,000 people had to be evacuated from the village of Malalcahuello after Volcán Lonquimay erupted on Christmas Day 1988. Further south you can climb Volcán Villarrica (still in Araucanía, although it is often thought of as being in the Lakes District) and peer over the crater lip into its fiery depths of molten lava. This region also boasts some of the richest temperate forests in the world. Here you will find giant monkey-puzzle trees (*Araucaria araucana*), some over 3,000 years old, whose distinctive umbrella-like profile has led to their local name of paragua. Their edible nuts are traditionally the staple of the Pehuenche, the Mapuche people living in the hills towards the border.

SOUTH FROM SANTIAGO TO TEMUCO

Heading south from Santiago on Ruta 5, the PanAmerican Highway, the first major town is **Rancagua**; to the west, down the Maipo valley near Las Cabras, the Palmas de Cocolán is a small (3,709ha) national park protecting Chilean palms. To the east, 15km beyond the Termas de Cauquenes (35km from Rancagua, and as far as buses get), is the **Reserva Forestal Río de los Cipreses**, which protects 38,582ha of sclerophyllous forest of peumo, quillay and litre, as well as various petroglyphs. The Ranchillo picnic site, start of the Sendero de los Peumos, is 6km from the gate, and it is another 6km to the campsite at Los Maitenes; from here it is another 20km (5–6 hours on foot) along a horse-track up the Cajón Cipreses to the Urriola hut (1,500m), where you will find stands of ciprés de la cordillera (Andean cypress) and olivillo de la cordillera. It is possible to continue up the valley for another dozen or so kilometres to the Cipreses glacier, and to climb Volcán Palomo (4,900m) and the Cordon Granitos. Birds here include the threatened burrowing parrot (loro tricahue; *Cyanoliseus patagonus*), condors, eagles, and, surprisingly far north, Magellanic geese and torrent ducks. Other animals include guanaco, red and grey foxes and vizcachas.

In the Sierra de Bellavista, 40km southeast of San Fernando, the next decent-sized stop on the PanAmerican, you can hike and ride horses around Laguna La Misurina; further up into the hills the 35,000ha **Sanctuario de la Naturaleza Alto Huemul** is a new private reserve set up by Codeff to protect the huemul in its northernmost refuge, as well as 3,000ha of old-growth roble (*Nothofagus obliqua*). Nothing much is in place yet, but there are plans for controlled ecotourism at some point.

From Molina, just south of Curicó on the PanAmerican, the road southeast to **Radal-Siete Tazas** is now paved, due to its popularity as a weekend destination for the *Santiagueños*. The great attraction is the series of granite pools called the *Siete Tazas* ('Seven Cups') and connecting waterfalls, but it is also possible to walk to the higher falls of El Velo de la Novia and La Leona. There is also good kayaking here on the Río Claro. The area is a national reserve because of its ecological importance as a transition zone between the Mediterranean communities of the Central Valley and the moister Valdivian communities to the south; it marks the northern limit of the false beeches raulí (*Nothofagus alpina*), hualo (*N. glauca*) and ñirre (*N. antarctica*). Of the 322 vascular plants, 153 are endemic.

In winter buses run from Molina (Tuesdays and Thursdays at 17.00, returning 08.00 the next morning) as far as the reserve entrance at Radal; in summer they run (up to four times a day) all the way past the Tazas to the administration at Parque Inglés, 65km from Molina. At Parque Inglés there is an Environmental Information Centre, *hostería* and campsite, and there are hikes in the forest, up Cerro El Fraile (1,425m), and also south across country (in 2 or 3 days) to the Altos del Lircay national reserve (formerly Vilches).

The **Reserva Nacional Altos del Lircay** is 65km southeast of Talca, a larger city, also on the PanAmerican, of course, and capital of the 7th Region (Maule); the first 40km are paved, but the last 4km can be difficult in winter. Buses run all year to Vilches Alto, just outside the gate, where there are campsites, a *hostería*, and horses for rent. The road ends at Laguna La Invernada, passing the Administration and Environmental Information Centre, 2km east of the gate. Get as much information here as you can, as the Conaf leaflet has a particularly useless map, with no scale and no paths marked. These do exist, leading to lakes, to El Enladrillado (basaltic columns at 2,300m), to Volcan Descabezado Grande (3,830m), and of course to Parque Inglés. The *Piedras Tacitas* are pre-Columbian bowls for grinding corn carved in rock near the information centre. Seven of the ten Chilean species of *Nothofagus* are found here, more than anywhere else, and it marks the northern limit of lenga (*N. pumilio*). The burrowing parrot is also found here and in Siete Tazas, as is the Magellanic woodpecker; foxes and parakeets have been reintroduced here.

Chillán is the terminal of day trains from Santiago, 408km north. The city is famous for its market and Mexican murals. On the southern slopes of Volcan Chillán (3,212m), the Termas de Chillán (at 1,722m, 82km east of Chillán), is a very upmarket spa resort, with winter skiing and a new five-star hotel, as well as a youth hostel at the Complejo Turístico (tel/fax: 042 243 211) at km73.5. The new **Santuario de Naturaleza Los Huemules de Niblinto** is a joint venture by Conaf and Codeff in the Niblinto watershed, on the northwest side of Volcán Chillán (beyond Coihueco); this is of course a huemul reserve, largely *bosque caducifolia de la montaña* (deciduous montane forest), as well as Andean steppe where vizcachas and other rodents can be found. There are 43 species of birds, and two rare lizards, the lagarto decorbata (in the woods) and lagartija de Chillán (on the higher slopes). On the north side of Volcán Chillán, the **Reserva Forestal Ñuble** already protects 55,948ha, home to huemul and the endangered fish *Nematogenys inermis*. This is reached via San Fabian de Alico, in the Ñuble valley – turn east off the PanAmerican, 25km north of Chillán. It is proposed to protect the whole area as the Reserva Nacional Nevados de Chillán.

The southernmost city in the 8th Region (BioBío) is **Los Angeles**, just north of the Biobío river, from where one route heads east to the Laguna del Laja, and another follows the Biobío to its source. The **Parque Nacional Laguna del Laja** covers 11,600ha around Volcán Antuco (2,985m), on the southwestern shore of the *laguna* (1,459m). Here you can see a few araucarias towards the northern end of their range, and a few *Maihuenia* cacti towards their southern limit. More importantly, there is one of the most substantial forests of ciprés de la cordillera (*Austrocedrus chilensis*) in Chile (in the Chacay area, by the road to the east of the gate). In this same area you can see maitén del Chubut and radal enano trees. There are 47 species of bird, notably condors, Andean gulls and the perdicita cordillerana (Andean quail). The only large mammals are vizcachas, foxes and pumas.

Buses from Los Angeles (five a day, or two on Sundays) will leave you at the junction just south of El Abanico, from where it is 7km to the park entrance at Los Pangues and 5km more (past the Lagunillas restaurant, *cabañas* and picnic site) to the Administration and Environmental Information Centre at Chacay. From here the road continues past the foot of the Antuco ski-slopes (where there is another restaurant) to end by the outlet from the lake; this feeds three large hydro-electric power-stations, fuelling the industry of Concepción. You can visit a couple of big waterfalls here where water from the lake escapes under a lava dam to form the Río Laja.

The park is quite well provided with trails, having been established back in 1958. The longest, from the Administration (1,200m) into the Sierra Velluda, where you will find araucaria trees, takes about 4 hours up and 3 down. It is possible to swing left from this path to continue up the Estero Los Pangues to the 2,054m pass between Volcán Antuco and the Sierra Velluda (far higher than the volcano at 3,585m) and down the Estero El Aguado to the lake; a rough road takes you back northwards along the lakeshore to the outlet. You should allow 2, and ideally 3, days for this. It is also possible to climb the volcano in a day from the north.

There is another fine waterfall right by the PanAmerican Highway where it crosses the Laja at km485, 25km north of Los Angeles; there is an official HI youth hostel here in the Complejo Turístico Los Manantiales (tel/fax: 043 314 275).

Temuco

Temuco currently claims to be the fastest growing city in Latin America, with a population approaching 250,000. It is now the terminus of the overnight rail

THE MAPUCHE

Almost all of Chile's indigenous inhabitants are members of the Mapuche people, estimated at around a million or more in number. Close to half of these are in Santiago, but their heartland is the area of Araucanía around Temuco. Historically the Mapuche people have lived as shifting farmers in the Central Valley, while related groups of Araucanian peoples included the Picunche to the north, who were more settled farmers, the Lafkenche coastal fisher-gatherers, the Pehuenche hunter-gatherers in the fringes of the Cordillera and the Lake District, and the Huilliche, further south and in Chiloé. The Pehuenche are the people of the Araucaria tree (*pehuen* meaning the araucaria nut, which is gathered in March and eaten raw, toasted, or boiled, ground up to produce flour, or made into the sacred drink *chavid*). They are still threatened by loggers seeking to drive them off their lands, as well as by the Biobío dam projects.

Most of the Mapuche and Pehuenche people still live in about 2,000 small and semi-permanent settlements, served by very poor roads, schools and other services, although central governments keep on promising improvements. It is not a straightforward business finding and visiting these settlements, but fortunately there are easier alternatives. Isla Huapi, in Lago Ranco, is a Mapuche reservation, and can be visited by groups organised by the Consejo Inter-Regional Mapuche, at Aldunate 341 (office 401) in Temuco, tel/fax: 045 239 305, or by Turihott at Valparaíso 111 in the village of Lago Ranco (tel: 045 491 201). The Lago Ranco tourist office is also helpful, and the village museum has coverage of Mapuche culture. The Lepun festival is held on Isla Huapi in late January, and visitors are welcome.

In Temuco iself there is a fine museum (see below), and there is another in Cañete, just west of the Nahuelbuta national park. Temuco is the best place to buy crafts, although those in the main market are increasingly made for tourists. It is better to head for the Casa de la Mujer Mapuche at Prat 283, whose profits go to community projects, or the Casa de Arte Mapuche at Matta 25A (where there is live music on Fridays). Things to look for include woollen blankets and ponchos (especially *ikat* – dyed with indigo on a white clay resist), silverware, such as the *tupu* pin used to fasten the *manta* or shawl, basketry, and carvings in horn.

service from Santiago (680km north), and also has good bus (and air) links up and down the PanAmerican, to Concepción, Valdivia and other regional towns, and also to Argentina. However, the PanAmerican will soon bypass the city to the east. Founded (at 107m) in 1881, it is the capital of the 9th Region (Araucanía), and more broadly of the area still known as *La Frontera*, and has the highest indigenous population of any Chilean city. You should certainly try to visit the **Museum of Araucanía**, west of the centre at Avda Alemania 084, to learn about the frontier's original inhabitants and its later settlers. Just to the north of the centre is **Cerro Ñielol** (322m), now made a National Monument, mainly to protect La Patagua, the tree under which the 1881 peace treaty with the Mapuche was signed. There is also a good variety of native plants, notably the copihue (*Lapageria rosea*), a red-flowered creeper which is the national plant. Despite its array of radio aerials, it is a popular urban park of just 85ha, with 65,000 visitors a year, but there can be problems for lone visitors who stray off the beaten track, especially after dark, when the joggers have gone home. By car you should enter by Calle Prat and leave on Lynch. There is an Environmental Information Centre, a restaurant with dancing, and an interesting array of wooden statues. You might be able to visit the Volcanology Centre, which monitors seismological readings from all southern Chile's volcanoes.

There is some fairly cheap **accommodation** on Aldunate, such as the Hospedaje Aldunate at no. 187 (tel: 045 270 057, 213 548) and Espejo at no. 124; the Residencial Temuco (Manuel Rodriguez 1341, 2nd floor; tel/fax: 233 721) is pricier but gives discounts to HI members. However, by far the best place to stay is the Continental (A. Varas 708; tel: 238 973; fax: 233 830), atmospherically traditional and with some affordable rooms with shared bathrooms.

The most convenient **supermarkets**, for hiking supplies, are Las Brisas at Carrera 899, just west of the centre, and Sta Isabel on Rodríguez between Aldunate and Bulnes, handy for the JAC terminal. The Librería Universitaria, Diego Portales 861, has a good choice of **books** on wildlife and the Mapuche; the Librería Alemana, one block south, is similar. Real espresso can be found in the arcade behind the Librería Universitaria, and there is internet access in the basement of the wonderfully named Cibercafé Flipperlandia, across the road at Diego Portales 888. Bikes can be fixed at three workshops on Balmaceda opposite the rural bus terminal. The Conaf offices are at Avda Bilbao 931 (tel: 211 912).

NAHUELBUTA NATIONAL PARK

Altitude	To 1,450m
Rating	Easy
Time	4 hours
Start of trail	Pehuenco campsite
End of trail	Pehuenco
Maps	1:50,000 map G37 'Los Sauces' and Conaf leaflet

Nahuelbuta is a small and relatively little visited park (6,832ha in area and under 4,500 visitors in 1993) but it is one of my favourites the combined effect of the serried ranks of araucaria and the 'soft' (ie: damp) atmosphere. The forest of the coastal *cordillera* has almost entirely been logged and replaced with pine plantations, except here and in Chiloé; technically the dominant species is the araucaria, but you could be forgiven for assuming it is the *Usnea* old-man's-beard lichen that drapes these and all other trees. Other trees include coihue, lenga and roble (all varieties of *Nothofagus*), with *Alstroemeria* flowers in three colours and 16 species of orchid. Insectivorous plants can be found on the El Aguilucho path. The lizard *Eupsophus nahuelbutensis* is found only in the cordillera de Nahuelbuta; an isolated population of the Chiloé fox (zorro chilote; *Dusicyon fulvipes*) also lives here, in the Pehuenco/Piedra del Aguila area. Birds include chucaos, parakeets, Magellanic woodpeckers, buzzards, and huet-huets, with animals such as pudú and puma.

Getting to the trailhead

The base for visiting Nahuelbuta is the town of **Angol**, reached by hourly buses from both Temuco and Los Angeles. From Angol the market bus runs on Monday,

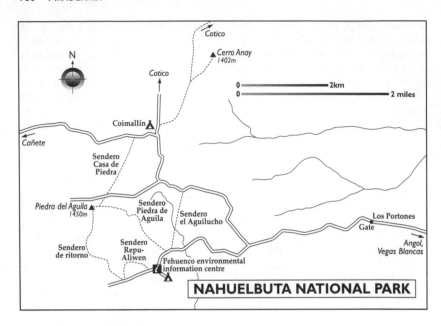

NAHUELBUTA NATIONAL PARK

Wednesday and Friday at 06.45 and 16.00 to Vegas Blancas, returning 2 hours later; also on Sundays from December to March there are day-trips to the park leaving at 06.45. If you have wheels, you can drive through the national park to **Cañete** (home to an important museum of Mapuche culture) on the coast road; coming from Cañete ask for the Fundo El Chacay road. In Angol, Conaf is at Prat 191; tel: 045 711 870; there are reasonable food shops and *hospedajes*.

If hitching from Angol, a Cañon *colectivo* will take you out along Calle Colima up the first steep hill and leave you at the first radio masts; continue westwards, passing turnings to the right to Los Copihues, Los Alpes and Chanleo, and after 20km you will reach the Puente El Manzano, where the Río Picorquen swings over 90° to the right. Just beyond this, opposite a chapel, is a field marked '*baños*', which makes a nice camping spot, with hot springs, rustic benches and fireplaces. Not far beyond, you again need to keep left at an unmarked junction. At the entry to the lovely village of Vegas Blancas, 29km from Angol, you need to ignore the left turn to San Ramon Alto, and continue uphill, through fields fenced by felled trees, for 7km to the park gate at Los Portones, 10 minutes beyond the last farm, Los Corrales. Continuing through forest for 45 minutes, you reach a junction, and taking the left turning drop down to Pehuenco in 20 minutes. To the left is the simple campsite, to the right the rangers' hut and below that the Environmental Interpretation Centre; the road continues across a bridge to a picnic site (with a leaky shelter). From here the Sendero Repu-Aliwen, a 700m interpretative path through forest of coihue, lenga and araucaria, loops to the right by a notice board, while another path heads left by the stream to reach a cascade in 2 minutes.

Route description
This is a circuit that can be hiked in a minimum of 4 hours; therefore if you leave the Pehuenco campsite by 08.00 you will return with time for lunch before setting out at 15.00 for the 18.00 bus.

From the Environmental Interpretation Centre, a path is signposted to the right to Piedra del Aguila, 4.5km away; this climbs to reach some superb millenary monkey-puzzles in about 5 minutes, and continues (past three benches) through fine forest of ñirre, coihue, roble, lenga, and araucaria. After about 50 minutes you will cross some bare rock and pass to the right of a hilltop, reaching the summit (1,450m) at Piedra del Aguila in another minute or so. Near a noticeboard, wooden steps lead up onto this boulder, for views across the forest and the coastal *cordillera*. To the right of the steps the *sendero de ritorno* (return path) leads down the hill to the road beyond the Pehuenco picnic site. Our circuit turns to the left at the noticeboard to reach a car park in 5 minutes. Heading eastwards along the road, in about 7 minutes you will reach the Sendero Casa de Piedra, turning off to the left/north.

This heads downhill to reach the 'Stone House', a rather damp, stone-walled shelter beneath a large boulder, in 3 minutes, and continues to reach the road from Cañete in another 40 minutes. To the right this passes through a lovely open stretch of mature forest, and in 10 minutes reaches a junction. To the left/north it is just a minute to the Coimallín campsite, similar to that at Pehuenco but smaller and without *baño* or ranger; it also seems to rain slightly less than at Pehuenco. Another 5 minutes up the road brings you to a barrier, continuing north, this road would take you to Cotico, in the northern sector of the park, and out through pine plantations. To the right a four-wheel-drive track continues for 4km to Cerro Anay, crossing a more open area of tussocky grass and insectivorous plants; after 12 minutes this route turns sharp left, and after another 10 minutes a path heads to the right up Cerro Anay (1,402m). It takes about 10 minutes more to reach the summit, from where (weather permitting) there is a view to the Andes.

Returning to the road junction a minute south of Coimallín campsite, the road drops to a bridge and then climbs to another junction in under 15 minutes. Turn left there, and in 3 minutes you will reach the Sendero El Aguilucho, a path which heads back to the right into mature araucaria forest. This drops steeply for under 20 minutes, climbs for 30 seconds and heads down the next valley for a couple of minutes to reach the road above the Environmental Interpretation Centre at Pehuenco.

LONQUIMAY

From Los Angeles another road follows the right/north bank of the Río Biobío into the Andes; at Santa Barbara the *Asociación Indígena Akinko Pitril* offers eco- and ethnotourist circuits (with indigenous guides and traditional houses), and 3km north from km 62.7 the Hospedaje Antukelen (tel: 043 326 097) offers horse-riding, camping and vegetarian food. After about 87km, the road becomes unpaved at Ralco, site of the next of the dams which are destroying what was one of the world's great white-water rafting rivers. From here one road turns left to follow the Queuco valley to the Los Copahues crossing into Argentina; it passes the Ñitrao and Chancocó hot springs, which are run by the people of the local Pehuenche communities.

The Biobío valley road continues to the southeast to the Pangue dam (completed in 1998), at what was the Royal Flush gorge (with legendary rapids such as Suicide King, Queen of Clubs, One-Eyed Jack, and Ace in the Hole), squeezed up against Volcan Callaqui (3,164m) to the northeast. This is drowning the entire Ñirreco canyon, 70km long, with a list of great Class V rapids such as Jugbuster, Milky Way, Lost Yak, Lava South, Cyclope and Last Laugh. From the put-in just north of Lonquimay, it is still possible to do a 2-day trip with plenty of Class III and IV rapids, but one senses that the operators' hearts are no longer in it. More seriously, the Pehuenche communities of Lepoy and Quepuca are being forcibly removed to what is claimed to be worse land, despite years of campaigning against the dams.

It is still possible to visit and camp (US$1) at the **Termas del Avellano**, 23km south of Ralco opposite the Malla valley on Volcán Callaqui. South of here, beyond Lepoy, cars swing right for Lonquimay but cyclists and 4WD vehicles can continue along the river, crossing a suspension bridge at Chenqueco and carrying on through Troyo, then crossing back over the Biobío by another suspension bridge to **Lonquimay**, capital of the Alto Biobío. This is 145km from Temuco on a paved road via Curacautín. The Hostería Follil Pehuenche at Carrera Pinto 110 (tel: 045 891 110) is owned by the Mapuche community. From here one road, newly paved, follows the Biobío to the Paso de Pino Hachado (1,884m) to Zapala in Argentina; another runs south to the sources of the Biobío in Lakes Gualletué and Icalma (1,350m), and the Paso Icalma (1,298m) to Aluminé.

To the west from this last a road runs through the Las Raíces railway tunnel, which is used as an alternative route to Curacautín when the main road is blocked by snow. It is the longest tunnel in South America at 4,528m, built for a still incomplete transcontinental railway.

This is very beautiful but harsh country, sometimes called the 'southern *altiplano*', due to the effects of Volcán Llaima's rainshadow. It is bare, high-altitude scenery, but with plentiful araucaria trees, as well as coihue, lenga and ñirre. Swans, ducks, geese and coots can be seen on the lakes, as well as eagles overhead. It is home to scattered groups of Pehuenche, with whom a few ecotourism projects are being developed – 18 families at Laho Icalma are training to work in ecotourism, and the Quinquén valley (near Lago Galletué, now a national reserve) has been bought by NGOs to save it from logging and handed over to its residents. Contact El Clan, which has a base east of Melipeuco (write to Avda Caupolicán 110, oficina 904, Temuco; tel: 045 235 924; fsolis@lazos.cl); or Fundación Instituto Indigena, V Mackenna 779, Icalma (f.i.i@entelchile.net); or ask at ¡Ecole! in Pucón.

In addition to the scenic route along the Biobío, Lonquimay can be reached more directly from the PanAmerican by paved roads from Lautaro (north of Temuco) and Victoria which meet at the logging town of **Curacautín** (400m), northern junping-off point for Conguillío National Park (see below). The bus terminal (in the former rail station, which also houses the best restaurant in town) is served by 14 buses a day from Temuco. The Hotel Plaza (tel: 881 256) is naturally on the plaza, just east, and there are a couple of cheaper *hospedajes* on Tarapacá. You might prefer to continue east for 27km to La SuizAndina (formerly El Encuentro; tel: 09 884 9541, fax: 045 881 892; www.suizandina.com) which offers beds and camping, laundry, horses and bike hire.

Immediately north of Curacautín is the **Parque Nacional Tolhuaca**, just 6,374ha, which surrounds the 76ha Laguna Malleco and is very popular with visitors, owing in large part to the Termas de Tolhuaca and their hotel (1,150m; tel: 045 881164; fax: 881211; www.gochile.cl/tolhuaca; tolhuaca@ctcreuna.cl). There are two access points; from Curacautín it is 34km north to the Termas, then 9km west to the administration and campsite at Inalafquén (by Laguna Malleco at 850m), and another 60km west to the PanAmerican 5km north of Victoria. Buses run from Victoria Mon–Fri only at 16.00, and only to San Gregorio, 19km west of the park. Laguna Malleco is surrounded by mixed forest of evergreens such as tineo, coihue, olivillo and tepa and deciduous trees such as raulí and roble, with an understorey of guindo santo and radal enano; these give way higher up to araucaria forests, and then on the lava slopes of Volcán Tolhuaca (2,806m) to coirón bunchgrass. Animals include pudú, foxes, skunks and coipos, with condors and parakeets the most obvious of the birds.

Continuing east from Curacautín on the Lonquimay road, at km70.9 (from Victoria) you will cross the Puente del Indio, immediately south of this is the Salto del Indio, which we christened the Salto del Indiana Jones; the dramatic falls are surrounded by *Aristotelia chilensis*, *Aquilegia*, *Gunnera*, *Ourisia*, *Guevinia avellana* (Chilean hazelnut) and tree ferns, with hummingbirds. At km74.9 (700m beyond the plush Termas de Manzanar hotel) you will come to the spa village of Manzanar, with camping and cheaper hotels; at km77.8 the Salto a la Princesa lies to the south of the road; and at km83.5 is La SuizAndina (see above).

The Piedra Santa (km84.8) is a huge rock overhanging the north side of the road (the end of a volcanic feeder dyke). On its west side a path zigzags steeply up for a couple of minutes then runs along the ridge and more or less dies out. However, it is easy enough to carry on to a power line which you can follow downhill to a track, and loop left and back to the road; turning sharp right at a fork you can walk back up a valley (directly towards Volcán Lonquimay).

Malalcahuello, 12km east of Manzanar, calls itself a 'pioneer village in integrated rural tourism' – at km87.4 are the headquarters of the Malalcahuello-Nalcas National Reserve, 31,305ha surrounding **Volcán Lonquimay** (2,865m). Just before this, across the disused rail tracks, is the village, with the Hospedaje Rayen-Lo opposite the *carabineros* on Colón. There is camping just east of the reserve headquarters.

At km90.5 you can turn left onto a dirt road at a right-hand bend, and left again at km94.7 (El Colorado) from where it is supposedly 7km to Volcán Lonquimay (or 40km right to Lolco and the road along the upper Biobío. In fact it is 2.6km to a Conaf gate and another 1.4km to a triple junction at the treeline, from where it is 5 minutes walk left to a *refugio* or a couple of kilometres ahead across volcanic ash to the ski station (c 1640m), a simple hut at the foot of a solitary drag. Araucaria gives way almost at once to ash, with a bit of grass but no stunted trees or bushes; you may see hare or guanaco as well as lizards and hawks. From here it takes about 4 hours to climb the mountain and 2 hours to descend – head right to follow a vehicle track well to the right of the ski-drag, which will bring you in 40 minutes to the 'pit stop' (a hollow dug beside the track). From here, depending on snow conditions, you can climb for an hour or so, then traverse right across the very loose volcanic clinker and then climb on snow to the crater edge. Below to the right is Cerro Navidad, created by the eruption of Christmas Day 1988, which scattered ash and spiral toffee-like lava bombs.

If you go right at km94.7 you will cross a bridge at km95.3. just beyond which is a lovely camping spot by the Cautín river, in a grove of araucaria and roble (with *Berberis*, *Fragaria chiloensis*, *Fuchsia magellanica*, *Acaeana* burrs and *Alstromoeria*, as well as Chilean flickers and white-throated tree-runners). A path continues up the left bank, reaching a log bridge over a side-stream in five minutes; here you should go up to the right in a meadow briefly to pick up the road at km96.4 below some steep bends, turning off again after 300m on a dirt road down to a lovely valley with araucaria, roble and some pine.

CONGUILLÍO NATIONAL PARK

Dominating this park of 114,000ha, one of the region's most popular, is the spectacular 3,120m **Volcán Llaima**, whose lava flows have transformed what was a richly forested landscape, and created a number of attractive lakes. The largest of these, Lago Conguillío (750ha), is connected by natural tunnels to the Río Truful-Truful. Llaima is one of Chile's two most active volcanoes, but the last big lava flows date from 1956–7, since when (in 1971–2, 1979, 1984 and 1994) it has been producing pyroclastics (such as the toffee-like material on the beach of Lago Conguillío) and moving to new lower cones, a sign that the volcano is losing its oomph. There are active fumaroles, so keep to the upwind side and clear out if you smell rotting eggs (as a rule what looks like steam really is just steam). On the higher slopes you should also beware rocks falling as the snow softens on warm days. There are superb views, framed by araucarias, of the volcano and also the Sierra Nevada (2,450m).

Wide temperature variations and 2,000–2,500mm of rain produce a rich vegetation here. In winter the snow can be 2m deep, and there is great cross-country skiing – a few rangers spend the winter here to keep an eye on things. There are five species of false beech (mainly coihue or *Nothofagus dombeyi*) in the park; by the lakes there is a mix of coihue and roble, then higher up coihue and raulí, and above 1,400m coihue with araucaria and ñirre, finishing with araucaria and stunted lenga at the tree line, with lots of Quila bamboo, and canelo in the understorey. There is also ciprés de la cordillera (*Austrocedrus chilensis*) and lleuque (*Podocarpus andinus*) at lower levels in the Truful-Truful area. There is also fuchsia, notro, *Solanum*, *Calceolaria*, *Rhodophilia*, *Mimulus*, *Viola reichei*, vetch, and *Usnea* lichen. Wildlife includes pumas, guiña wildcats, pudú, skunks, vizcacha, coipo, monito del monte and red and grey foxes (the last of which come right into the campsites). There is also a wide range of birds, including waterfowl such as torrent ducks and geese, forest birds such as the Magellanic woodpecker, chucao, huet-huet and thorn-tailed rayadito, and the slender-billed parakeet, condor, red-backed hawk and Andean gull. Rare lizards (*Liolaemus chilensis*, *L. pictis* and *L. tenuis*) are also found here, as well as Darwin's frog.

Getting to the trailheads

The easiest access to the park is via the small town of **Melipeuco**, to the south, where you will find cheap *hospedajes* and small shops; bulk food shopping should be done in Temuco. About seven buses a day run from Temuco to Melipeuco (paved for 59km to Cunco, then unpaved for 30km); the occasional bus to Icalma (from Temuco's rural terminus) or to Zapala in Argentina might set you down at the turning to the park 3km further east at km92.2 (from Temuco).

From this junction it takes over 2 hours to drive to the park's Administration on a bad road. You will have to pay US$5 at the Truful-Truful gate (km8.7; 800m), where it is also worth walking the Cañadon del Truful-Truful path, a loop of about 700m to the gorge cut through colourful strata of volcanic ash with excellent views of the surprisingly large Truful-Truful waterfall. There is also the similar but longer Las Vertientes path just north. The road continues through the bare lava landscape known as *El Escorial* (the nose of the 1957 flow) to Laguna Verde (stop at km19.5 for the best view) from where the Sendero Los Glaciares leads 3km west onto the volcano's slopes, and the Sendero La Ensenada leads 800m northeast by the lake. Just beyond is Laguna Arco Iris, formed when a lava flow dammed the river. The road reaches **Lago Conguillío** at **Playa Linda** (1,080m). There is a campsite just west at La Caseta, and three more in the Playa Curacautín sector (12km from the Truful-Truful gate). You will also find the Administration and Ecological Information Centre, just beyond the junction to the beach, where a café, shop, and boat-hire are operated by a private concession. Unless you are in a fair-sized group most pitches are pricey at US$24 each, so be sure to ask for *mochileros* (backpackers') spaces at US$4. Just off the road to the beach you may glimpse some of the ten *cabañas*, each built around an araucaria trunk. By hiring a rowing boat you can reach the Saltos de Conguillío, at the western end of the lake.

Two paths run parallel to the road from Playa Linda to Playa Curacautín, one along the beach to the north and another, the 3km Sendero El Contrabandista, to the south. From the Administration you can loop south on the 1km Las Araucarias interpretative path (which takes about 40 minutes if you read all the 'fotometal panels', which tell the usual 'cycle of life' story).

It is pretty hard to enter the park from Curacautín (see above), to the north of the park, without your own transport. Conguillío is signposted down a dual carriageway from the east end of Curacautín, but this at once turns into a poor dirt road. Turning left at the cemetery, you will come in 2km to the Trahulco bridge, where there is a *balneario* and campsite, go left at about km5, then keep right just beyond a bridge at about km8 and again at a turning to the left to Cañón del Blanco. The road turns sharp right and runs parallel to the river, crossing to its east side by the Puente Blanco Sur and then keeping left. You should keep left at km13 and at about km17.5 before dropping steeply down to the Puente Colorado at km20.3. After about 7km more the road passes the edge of a lava flow before entering the National Park at km28 after about an hour's drive. It takes about 15 minutes more to reach the Captrén gate at km 32.4, where you will pay your fee and can camp. The road continues through thick forest, with tight bends and steep dips. There is a parking area by a bridge at km36.5, just over a kilometre before the administration.

The 1.2km El Mallín trail is a loop around Laguna Captrén, starting out through the campsite and continuing along a track which swings left out of the wood; the path continues over a wooden bridge across a stream, and swings right to the lakeshore, from where there are great views across the water to the volcano. At one point there is quila bamboo to the left and colihue to the right! In addition you will see *Gunnera*, fuchsia, chaura (*Pernettya mucronata*) and frutilla (*Rubus geoides*), and introduced plants such as sheep-sorrel, selfheal, St John's wort, and rose, as well as lizards, and birds such as torrent duck, geese, grebe, chucao, cinclodes, black woodpecker, red-backed hawk, swallow and hummingbird. At the end of the lake is a marsh. It is possible to walk all the way around, or (depending on conditions) to take a short cut – cross a stream on a very overgrown log, then head off to the right parallel to a disused boardwalk (to your left), and cross a stream on very wobbly logs to the far shore. Here you can go ahead and up to the Sendero Los Carpinteros (see below), or take a fishermen's path to the right by the shore to reach the beach by the road in 10 minutes.

To reach the Los Paraguas sector, to the west of the park, you can take a bus from Temuco as far as the village of Cherquenco, from where you will probably have to hike 20km uphill to the end of the road. From here the Cerro Colorado path leads 3km to give wide views of the area. If properly equipped, it is possible to climb Volcán Llaima from here, or to make your way around its slopes to Laguna Captrén or Truful-Truful. There are *refugios* by the ski slopes and two shelters a little way down the road.

Route descriptions

We describe three hikes in slightly more detail, the first from Playa Linda to the Sierra Nevada, the second from the Captrén gate up Volcán Llaima, and the third from Captrén back to the Administration area.

Sierra Nevada hike

Start	From Playa Linda
Altitude	From 1,080m to 1,684m
Difficulty	Moderate
Time	Half day

Volcán Llaima ascent

Start	From Captrén gate
Altitude	1,300m to 3,120m
Difficulty	Hard
Time	8 hours up, 4 down

Sendero Los Carpinteros

Start	From Captrén gate to Administration
Altitude	1,100m
Difficulty	Easy
Time	2 hours
Maps	IGM map 3830-7130 (Volcán Llaima); JLM map 9 (Araucanía)

The **Sierra Nevada** hike is an easy route of about 5km each way to three fine viewpoints, but it also offers access to the Sierra Nevada ridge, where you will normally have to contend with snow and ice. From the Playa Linda parking area, a path leads down to the beach, which lives up to its name by offering fantastic views of the snow-capped Sierra Nevada (also living up to its name!) beyond the lake. The Sierra Nevada hike starts at a noticeboard just above the beach and heads up the valley to the right for 2 minutes before turning to the left. You will climb for 15 minutes through forest with a dense understorey of bamboos to the first *mirador* (viewpoint) over the lake. There is a fairly easy stretch above the lake (with a few views) before crossing to the right/east side of the ridge, where you will hear the waterfalls in the El Blanco valley. The path climbs more steeply to reach the araucarias, and another viewpoint, after another 30 minutes. Again the path swings away from the lake as it rises and the forest thins (giving a view of Volcán Villarrica behind you to the south); after another half hour you will emerge from stunted lenga trees (with *Hebe* and *Rhodophilia andina*) into the open and perhaps onto snow. The highest point of the ridge is less than 10 minutes further on, and most walkers will be happy to halt here, at 1,684m, and return by the same way.

It is, however, possible to continue into the Sierra Nevada proper and indeed across it to descend to the north. Some of the *guardaparques* would like to see this route closed, as it crosses a small glacier where accidents can happen and rescue is very awkward, but really there is no problem for those accustomed to and equipped for Scottish winter conditions, for example. Crampons are not usually necessary, but an ice-axe and rope are advised. You should dip to the col ahead, cross to the Sierra Nevada, then head across a valley to the left and up the minor scrambly ridge to its left (the true right side). After about 3 hours this reaches a pass

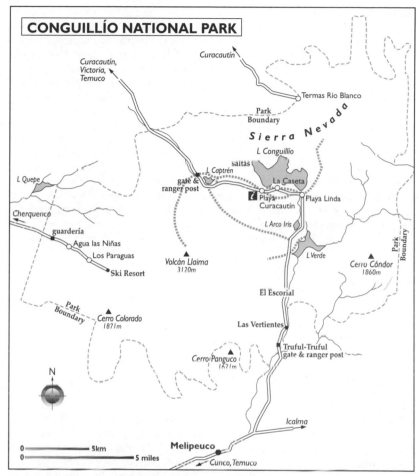

just west of the point where the Sierra Nevada bends from north to southwest. From here you should descend directly on scree or snow to the Río Blanco, and then traverse around the head of the valley to the right. You will find a faintly marked path down a ridge into forest, which leads to the Termas Río Blanco (1,046m), 4–5 hours from the col. It should also be possible to make your way along to the western end of the Sierra Nevada and then down to reach the road just outside the park, just west of Laguna Captrén.

Secondly, the **ascent of Volcán Llaima**: at the Laguna Captrén gate (1,300m), the forest comes to a sudden end, replaced by lava fields, opening up great views of the volcano framed by monkey-puzzle trees. To climb Volcán Llaima (often pronounced 'zhaima' in the Argentine style) cross the road bridge by the gate and turn left to head southwest across the lava field, crossing deep *corridas* or dry watercourses, towards the top of a wood of araucarias to the right, reached in about 50 minutes. From here you should cross a small lava flow (with water at the top of the gully) back to the left to climb a rocky ridge, reaching its top after about an hour. There is a brief dip before you should swing slightly to the right to cross above a volcanic dome (if there is snow, it is easier to climb this, kicking steps, taking about 30 minutes to its foot and 30 minutes to the top). It is best then to keep to the right to reach a rocky outcrop where two ridges meet at about 2,450m, 2½ hours from the dome. From here, following the northwestern ridge, it takes about 1 hour to the top, where you will see that the far side has been blown right out. Crampons and ice-axe may be needed for the final icy section on the crater lip.

Roughly parallel to the road, to its north, the **Sendero Los Carpinteros** leads 5.4km west from Captrén to the Administration. From the lakeside, just south of the gate, follow the sign *sendero* around the head of the lake across a meadow and into the woods. After about 20 minutes you will reach a junction, where the left branch loops around the lake. Going to the right, you will have to cross some fallen logs; it takes about 12 minutes to some benches where the path crosses what seems to be an old forestry track, 12 minutes more to another bench, then 10 minutes more to the highest point of the trail (1,374m), from where the path drops for 12 minutes to the Araucaria Madre Milenaria or Millenial Mother Monkey-puzzle (about 8m in circumference). From here it takes 20 minutes down to more benches, 5 minutes beyond which you cross a stream, and reach the road 5 minutes later just above the Administration.

From Laguna Captrén you could also hike to just south of Laguna Arco Iris by the Sendero Pastos Blancos, passing minor volcanic cones on the slopes of Volcán Llaima.

In 2001 work began to convert the Sendero Los Carpinteros into the pilot section of the **Sendero de Chile**, a high-quality national trail accessible to bikes and horses as well as hikers. This will then be extended from Lago Conguillío across the eastern flanks of Volcán Llaima (reaching an altitude of 1,750m) to the Truful-Truful gate.

VILLARRICA NATIONAL PARK
Pucón
Pucón, at 280m on Lago Villarrica (and below Volcán Villarrica), is the most popular resort in Araucanía and the adventure sports capital of Chile. With trendy bars, cyber-cafés and adventure tourism companies jostling each other on the main streets, there is not much room for anything else. However, there are several superb **places to stay**: ¡Ecole! at General Urrutia 592 (tel: 045 441 675, fax: 441 660; trek@ecole.cl; www.ecole.cl; in the USA PO Box 2453, Redway, CA 95560; tel: 1 800 447 1483; fax: 707 923 3001; www.asis.com/ecole, ecole@asis.com) is the leading centre for environmental activism in southern Chile and is a great source of information, as well as operating its own tours to off-beat places such as Cañi and Valle Cochamó. There is also an excellent vegetarian restaurant, and they give a discount to Hostelling International members. Next door at Urrutia 580 is La Tetera (tel/fax: 441 462; info@tetera.cl), which has nice rooms, a great café and also book exchange. Also recommended are Hospedaje La Casita, handy for the JAC terminal at Palguín 555 (tel/fax: 441 712, lacasita@pucon.com); Hospedaje Irma, Lincoyan 545 (tel: 442 226), which is cheap and simple, with only Spanish spoken; and Hospedaje Sonia, Lincoyán 485 (tel: 441 269). At Camping Los Pozos, between the town and the lake, you can see hummingbirds feeding on the fuchsia, as well as night heron. The main **supermarket** is Eltit, on O'Higgins between Ansorena and Fresia, although there is also a 24-hour supermarket at the east end of O'Higgins. Pucón is reached by JAC bus from Temuco every 15 minutes (alternately express and local) and from Valdivia about half a dozen times a day. There are also plenty of buses from Santiago (it is an easy overnight run), and the

airport is being developed.

The municipal tourist **information** kiosk is at the entry to town, at Caupolicán and Brasil (045 443 338; open daily 08.30–22.30); next to this is another run by the Camera de Turismo, ie: the tour companies and hotels (open 10.00–14.00, 15.30–19.30). On the internet information about the town is available at www.free.cl/pucon (email: pucon@munitel.cl). The Conaf office is on the main road east, at O'Higgins 1355 (tel: 441 261).

Most tour companies will take you to some of the many local thermal pools and up Volcán Villarrica, although only the biggest are authorised by Conaf to operate volcano trips, and others merely act as agents – however, you may get a better price from these (it pays to check the details, see page 171). In addition they all offer white-water rafting on the Río Trancura (from just US$12) and further afield, as well as hydrospeed, 'ducky', rappelling, canyoning, cascading and similar new 'sports' for thrill-seekers. Many can hire you a mountain bike, and sailing is possible on the lake. An increasing number offer trips to Huerquehue (see below).

Aguaventura, Palguin 336 (tel: 444 246, aguaventura@hotmail.com) offer kayaking on the Río Liucura and Lago Caburgua. Most can arrange horse-riding for you, as can ¡Ecole!, or you can make direct contact with Hans through La Casita (rancho@pucon.com); or Wolfgang and Christa (tel: 045 441 575; horsetrekking@netscape.net).

Other operators

Anden Sport O'Higgins 535; tel: 045 441 048; fax: 441 236; andentur@chilesat.net; www.andentur.cl

Aventur O'Higgins 261; tel/fax: 045 442 796; travelaventur@yahoo.com

Turismo Liucura Ansorena 309; tel: 045 441 661

Politur O'Higgins 635; tel/fax: 045 441 373, turismo@politur.com

Sur Expediciones O'Higgins 660; tel: 045 444 030

Sol y Nieve O'Higgins at Lincoyán; tel/fax: 045 441 070; solnieve@entelchile.net; www.chile-travel.com/solnieve.htm

Turismo Trancura O'Higgins 211, 447, 498 and 575!; tel/fax: 045 441 189; turism@trancura.com; www.trancura.com

The **Villarrica Forestry Reserve** was created in 1925, one of the earliest protected areas in the country, and became a National Park in 1940; it now covers 63,000ha between 600m and 3,776m in altitude. It is formed of sedimentary rocks and granite, with vulcanism 15 million years ago and in the last 600,000 years. Most areas receive 2.5–3.5m of precipitation (most between March and August), but the wettest (and coldest) parts receive 5m. Some parts are covered by a very dense, deciduous forest, laden with vines and creepers, while higher up of course there is just Andean grassland followed by bare rock, lava fields and ice. The forest is dominated by coihue (*Nothofagus dombeyii*) and roble (*N. obliqua*), with lingue, laurel, olivillo, canelo, tepa and raulí; in higher parts there is araucaria, with coihue, a *matorral* of lenga and ñirre, and coirón bunchgrass. Guanaco and huemul are no longer found here, but there are still puma and pudú, with red and grey foxes, monito del monte (Chilean opossum), skunks, coipo, vizcacha and smaller rodents such as several types of degu and laucha; there are many birds, notably a dozen raptors (including condors, grey eagles, cinereous harriers, bay-winged and red-backed hawks and peregrine falcons) and waterbirds (geese, grebes, coots and nine ducks, including torrent ducks and flying steamer ducks).

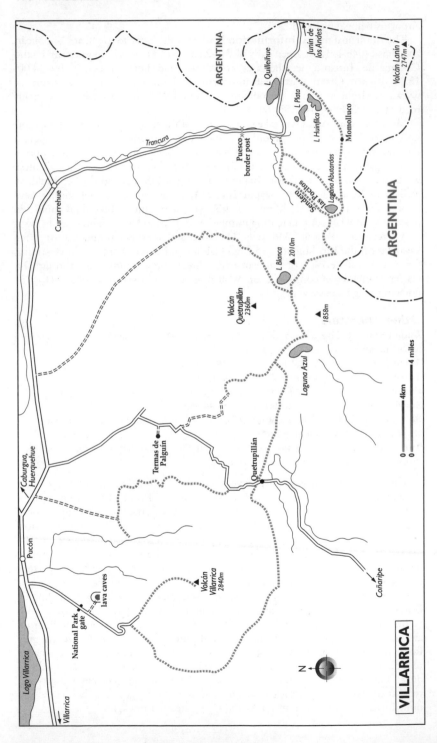

VILLARRICA

Climbing Volcán Villarrica

Distance	4km each way
Altitude	1,450m to 2,840m
Rating	Moderate
Time	One day
Start of trail	Villarrica ski area
End of trail	Summit of Volcán Villarrica
Map	JLM map 7 (Pucón)

Volcán Villarrica (2,840m) is one of Chile's two most active volcanoes, with ten eruptions in the 20th century. In 1971 the village of Coñaripe was destroyed when molten lava melted part of the ice-cap and caused vast lahars (avalanches of hot mud mixed with boulders and trees) to sweep down to the village. The last eruption was in 1984, and the next is now overdue. The crater is active, with lava visible and sulphurous fumes and occasional lava bombs belching forth. The volcano can easily be climbed in 8 hours, up and down, but due to regular accidents and indeed deaths, you must now take a guide unless you can prove, by membership of a climbing club, that you are experienced enough to tackle it alone. Agencies in Pucón operate regular pilgrimages to the summit, and there is enough competition to keep prices to about US$35. However, standards are not high; equipment can be of poor quality – be sure to check the crampons etc, and insist if you want a mask against the fumes; but there is no need for plastic boots. The tour companies treat their clients like sheep, dressing them in identical snowsuits to keep track of them (or even roping them all up). Some companies are less willing than others to give a refund if bad weather prevents an ascent.

If doing it alone, equipment can be rented in Pucón, and transport can be arranged for the 14km trip up to the ski station in the Rucapillán sector (at around 1,500m). There are campsites along the road, such as Huechuntu at km7.2. The Conaf checkpoint, where equipment is checked, or at least discussed, is 8km from the main road. Just beyond this you can head left for 4km to the *refugio antiguo* and caves, in fact a lava tube opened to the public in 1998 (US$6); facilities are good, and you will be given a helmet and lamp for your guided visit, although it is well lit anyway. There is a cafetería near the foot of the lift (US$6) which operates in the mornings to take hikers from 1,450m to 1,850m; alternatively the 45-minute hike, following the ski-lift up the loose volcanic grit, is a good warm-up. The ski-lift was bought second-hand from North America and the stanchions had to be fitted with rubber 'doughnuts' to absorb the volcano's vibrations.

From the top station, near the summer snow-line (where you will probably put on crampons), there is usually a clear trail zigzagging up across the snow, which you should stick to in order to avoid any crevasses. It takes about 90 minutes to reach a small plateau (known as *la pinguinera*) at 2,300m, and 30–40 minutes more to El Tubo (2,410m), which really is just a vertical metal pipe. From here it takes about an hour and a quarter to the point at which crampons come off for the ten-minute scramble (on old lava, which gives a good grip but is quite sharp on the feet) to the crater rim. The summit is to the right, but few people go there, as the unforgettable view into the crater is reason enough for coming here. The snow is not a cornice, so it is safe to go close to the edge. You will also see 'fairy mushrooms', where a stone has prevented snow from melting, leaving it stranded on top of a column. The sulphurous fumes, however, can be quite nauseating – if you do not have a mask, a handkerchief soaked in lemon juice can help.

To the east of Volcán Villarrica the minor road to Coñaripe crosses through the park's **Quetrupillán sector**, climbing first through coihue, then raulí, then araucaria, and then dwarf mañío. It is 35km from Pucón (past the **Termas de Palguín**, perhaps the best in the area, where there are walks to lovely waterfalls) to a junction; turn left for the hike up the Estero Mocho to the southwestern slopes of Volcán Quetrupillán (2,360m), or otherwise keep right to reach the Quetrupillán *guardería* and the Chinay campsite. From here hikers, mountain-bikers and horse-riders can head north along the eastern flanks of Volcán Villarrica and back to the road, and another walk extends south for 15km to Lagunas Azul and Blanca, from where you can continue to Puesco (see below). Further south another path heads off west and then north, right around Volcán Villarrica, a rugged hike that takes two days.

Further east the main international highway from Pucón to Junín (in Argentina) follows the Río Trancura through the **Puesco** sector, which gives easy access to thick rain forest. Local buses run as far as the Puesco frontier post (56km from Pucón), where you will find a *guardería*, a basic campsite and Environmental Education Centre. From Alto Puesco, on the road above Puesco, the Sendero Las Pocitos leads 15km above the right/south bank of the Río Puesco and on to Laguna Blanca and the Quetrupillán sector; and the Sendero Momolluco leads southeast to the west side of Volcán Lanín. To the east of the frontier post the road passes through raulí forest, then climbs through coihue and lenga to Lago Quilleihue, by a *carabineros* post, which is surrounded by araucaria and ñirre trees; from here there is a transition to *pradera andina de coirón*. The Sendero Los Lagos leads south to Lago Huinfilca, and other short paths are planned, but it is quite open country anyway. Camping is not permitted in the zone east of the border post. There are superb views of Volcán Lanín.

Reserva Cañi

The Fundación Lahuén was the first NGO in Chile dedicated to the protection of native forest (*lahuén* is the Mapudungun word for *alerce*); in 1991 it bought 480ha scheduled for logging in the Cordillera de Cañi, which it manages as the Reserva Cañi, the country's first private protected area. It is the caldera of a Pleistocene volcano, with lovely little lakes and araucaria, coihue and lenga, best seen from the summit of El Mirador (1,470m). Wildlife includes pudú, grey fox, puma and other wild cats, Darwin's frog, slender-billed parakeet, black-necked swan, geese, condor, hummingbirds, and Magellanic woodpecker. It is open for sustainable tourism, for guided groups or on a self-guided trail; contact the Fundación Lahuén at Urrutía 477 (tel: 045 441 660) or Turismo Liucura at Ansorena 309 (tel: 441 661) in Pucón, or in Santiago Cascada Expediciones (Orrego Luco 054, Providencia; tel: 02 234 2274, fax: 233 9768; info@cascada-expediciones.com), where there is also a Fundación Lahuén office. CEAL, the *Centro de Educación Aire Libre*, also runs courses here. The similar **Kira-Kira Reserve** is being developed just to the east, and the Sendero de Chile will pass through Cañi.

Although it is currently open only from November to March, there are plans for winter opening, with cross-country skiing. The reserve lies 21km east of Pucón, taking the road towards the Termas de Huife (served by Buses Cordillera) and turning right/south after Villa San Pedro. At ¡Ecole! you can sign up to share a taxi to Cañi for US$7; you will also pay US$6 entry and the same for a guide if required. They have a base hut and the La Loma rustic camp 2km away, with tent space for 24 people. It costs US$2 to sleep in the Aserradero and Pichares refuges.

HUERQUEHUE NATIONAL PARK

Distance	Approximately 26km
Altitude	Between 300m and 1,621m
Rating	Easy
Time	2 days
Start of trail	Lago Tinquilco
End of trail	Cunco
Maps	IGM 1:50,000 3900-7130 (G96); JLM map 7 (Pucón)

Huerquehue offers the best hiking immediately accessible from Pucón, and so is very popular for day-trips as well as longer stays. The *guardaparques* may suggest you simply do the standard circuit of the lakes, but it is possible to go further, although if you choose to leave the park to the north you are likely to have a long, tedious walk out.

The park is a massif of Upper Cretaceous clastic basalts with granitic intrusions, covered by more recent volcanic activity (still a long time ago, so there is more biodiversity than on Volcán Villarrica). It receives less rain than Villarrica, with an average of just over 2m precipitation, 56% of it from May to August. This produces a temperate rainforest similar in structure to that of Villarrica, but with far fewer creepers and epiphytes, but lots of fungi (many poisonous), and huge spiders and snails. At the lower levels there is coihue with raulí and tepa, araucaria is dominant from 1,000–1,700m, with coihue, lenga and ñirre. To the north there is also ciprés de la cordillera. Bushes include taique (*Desfontainia spinosa*), like a scarlet holly, *Lomatia*, *Mitraria*, *Astranthera* and *Pernettya*; and the fern *Blechnum chilensis*. Fauna includes puma, guiña, grey and red foxes, pudú, otter, skunks, coipo, monito del monte, and small rodents such as mice and (above the tree line) tunduco. Birds include raptors such as the condor, red-tailed buzzard, bay-winged hawk, kite and crested caracara, as well as two woodpeckers, ducks, grebes and coots, parakeets, hummingbirds, teros and bandurrias, and typical birds of the Valdivian forest such as rayadito, huet-huet, chucao and tío-tío. Amphibians include Darwin's frog, and fish include the native pejerrey.

Getting to the trailhead

From Pucón JAC buses run to Paillaco at 07.30 and 17.30 (except Sundays), returning 90 minutes later. The buses head east, crossing the Río Turbio (at the junction to Palguín and the border), the Río Trancura (or Pucón) and the Río Liucura, just after the right turn to Cañi and the Termas de Huife, and come to Ojos de Caburgua (where the river flows underground) and, 23km from Pucón, **Caburgua**, at the south end of the lake of the same name, where the swimming is desperately cold. This is a small resort, with camping, *cabañas*, and provisions, served by 9 JAC buses a day. The Paillaco bus turns around and soon (20km from Pucón) turns east onto a dirt road, away from the lake, and 45 minutes after leaving Pucón turns right at the school and shops of Paillaco, where you should get off.

The road straight on from this junction is signposted to Huerquehue National Park (7km); you may get a lift, and in high season buses are apparently met by a minibus – in fact it is worth enquiring at Conaf in Pucón in case it is starting from the town. At ¡Ecole! you can sign up to share a taxi (US$7); or it is easy to take a bus to Caburgua then a taxi.

There is also an enjoyable bike route from Pucón to Caburgua (slightly shorter than the road). Heading east on O'Higgins use the bi-directional bike lane on the north side of the road and turn left after 4km (just after crossing the Río Claro) towards the Pasarela Quelhue. You will cross this suspension bridge (where raft trips on the Trancura end) after 2km, then turn right (the left fork leads to the Trancura delta, where there is good bird-watching) and go up and down for a few kilometres. After about 6km the Salto del Carileufu is signed to the right (there is great *apfelstrudel* at a café by the falls), and it is another kilometre to the Ojos; going on past the shops and turning left at the cemetery you can take a steepish dirt road for half an hour to the Saltos Bellavista and Los Copihues. Otherwise it is 3km to the paved road, 18km from Pucón and 5km short of the lake.

Route description

From Paillaco the road climbs in steep zigzags for almost 3km; you should then fork right at a junction from which Lago Tinquilco is visible ahead, and drop down to a bridge across its outlet stream at km5, just beyond a couple of farms offering *kuchen* (German-style cakes), *once* (high tea), bread, drinks, camping and beds. Following the east shore of the lake, it is another 2km past the park gate (where you will pay US$4), campsite and picnic place to the Environmental Information Centre, from where the 4km Sendero Quincho climbs up to the east, with a short loop at its end. Leaving here you should at once keep right; then you can take the Sendero Ñirrico to the left, a pleasant little 800m interpretative path through bamboo and ulmo trees. This runs parallel to the road to a gate at which it passes into private property (for 1.8km), where you can pay to park or to camp; the Refugio Tinquilco is open all year. Ten minutes down the road is a ford, although there is also a foot-bridge just to the left to a new house (fenced off and marked 'private'). At the end of the road, just beyond, a path enters the forest, just to the left of a large waterfall, and climbs in steep zig-zags for 15 minutes before swinging to the right. After 5 minutes a gate and stile lead to the new Guardería Nido de Aguila in an old field. The path swings sharply to the left and climbs for 10 minutes to a *mirador*, where you should take your photos of the lake and Volcán Villarrica. It is a slightly easier climb for another 25–30 minutes to the pass (at around 1,250m), where you will find the first monkey-puzzle trees.

From here it is just 2 minutes to Lago Chico (1,180m), below massive basalt cliffs. Crossing a good log bridge across its outlet, it takes 5 minutes to reach the north end of the lake and 3 more to a junction, from where it is 100m to the right to Lago El Toro. To the left it is under 500m to the lovely Lago Verde (the largest in the park at 32.5ha). To the left a path follows the shore and then swings left to climb Cerro Comulo (1,621m), for views over the lake. To the right it is possible to cross the outlet stream on rocks and a log, continuing for 5 minutes to a junction from Lago El Toro to the east. If you are doing the shortest circuit, turn right here to return.

Our route climbs steeply to the north from here, and is increasingly strewn with fallen branches and even trees. About 15 minutes from the junction you should swing left at a stream to cross two more streams and reach a pass in another 15 minutes. Here the path (unsigned) swings east, climbing for 3 minutes and then dropping steeply to reach a junction by Lago Huerquehue (1,300m) after another

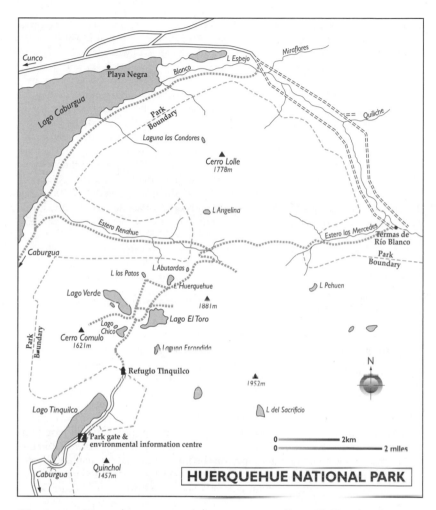

Cunco

Playa Negra

Lago Caburgua

Blanco

L Espejo

Miraflores

Quilche

Park Boundary

Laguna las Condores

▲ Cerro Lolle
1778m

◉ L Angelina

Estero Renahue

Estero las Mercedes

Termas de Río Blanco

Caburgua

Park Boundary

L los Patos

L Abutardas

L Huerquehue

▲ 1881m

L Pehuen

Lago Verde

Lago El Toro

Lago Chico

▲ Cerro Comulo
1621m

Laguna Escondida

N

▲ Refugio Tinquilco

▲ 1952m

Lago Tinquilco

L del Sacrificio

Park gate &
environmental information centre

0 ━━━━━ 2km
0 ━━━━━ 2 miles

Caburgua

Quinchol
1457m

HUERQUEHUE NATIONAL PARK

15 minutes. Here you can turn right to return to Lago El Toro by the route recommended by the *guardaparques*, if you choose. Continuing northwards, the path soon swings inland along a boggy valley, heading straight for a high (1,881m) peak. It passes over an almost imperceptible pass before going down a similar valley and then dropping more steeply. The path emerges from the forest after 30 minutes, just after passing Laguna Abutardas to the left; there is a great view across the Renahue valley to Cerro Lolle (1,778m). This is the centre of a closed 'zone of natural recuperation'.

The path traverses to the right, then zigzags down through pasture to the thick screen of trees along the river. A path does lead to a fallen tree which allows you to cross to a wooden hut (locked), about 30 minutes after leaving the forest. (To the right it is possible to take a track, churned up by cows, over an obvious pass and down the Estero Las Mercedes to the rustic Termas de Río Blanco, where there are *cabañas* with camping; from here a rough road leads northwest to meet up eventually with the route described here.) Heading left/west, you should cross a minor stream, then at once cross another log back to the south bank; after a bit of log-hopping the path improves, leading in 10 minutes to a decent log bridge back to the right/north bank, by a very good cascade. A rough cow track, boggy in parts, leads in 10 minutes to a cowshed and house, from where a better track leads down the hill past a good waterfall. After 10 minutes this crosses to the left bank by a rough footbridge, and passes through pasture and then above some *cabañas*, to reach a gate after 20 minutes. The track continues above the Renahue valley, swinging 90° left after 20 minutes and then 90° right; at the mouth of the valley the track swings left high above the lake, finally reaching a junction after another 40 minutes. Continuing south a lakeside path leads back to Caburgua, and a track joins the road just west of Paillaco. Dropping steeply to the right and then forking right in a field to head north, you will find another, smaller, path traversing back above the lake shore, which reaches the mouth of the Estero Renahue (700m) after 20 minutes. New holiday homes are being built here, blocking access to the lovely beach on the left/south side of the river, but you will still be able to cross to the right side and camp.

Continuing northwards, you should cross the footbridge and swing left on a footpath which is rather more of a switchback than that to the south. After 15 minutes you will pass a house, and after another 10 minutes cross a stream and swing left. The path climbs steeply to pass through two farmyards after 10 more minutes and then forks left, briefly following a streambed downhill before at last running on the level beside the lake. It turns 90° to the right at a fence and climbs straight up to a farm 30 minutes from the last farmyards. It continues as a much better track more or less on the level above holiday homes, and finally after 45 minutes (2 hours from the Estero Renahue) descends to the lakeside at the mouth of the Río Blanco. This is a good spot both for camping and for watching water birds.

To reach the road out of the park, the ideal is to persuade someone with a boat to take you across the river here, but failing that you have a fair distance still to hike. Continuing along the left/south bank, after 20 minutes you will pass some attractive narrows. About 10 minutes beyond this point you will come to a junction where you should keep up to the right on the horse track, rather than the anglers' tracks which are dead-ends, if scenic ones. In another 15-odd minutes you will pass a house, and after 10 more minutes along a good level path you can turn left to cross the mouth of a small gorge on a wooden bridge, about an hour from the river's mouth. There is a good camping spot just ahead as you come off the bridge, while turning right soon brings you to the road along the Río Blanco, at its confluence with the Miraflores.

There is little chance of a lift here, though there are a couple of buses a day to Cunco; you may prefer to keep on hiking. Turning left, the road climbs steeply for a spell, then runs on the level past Lago Espejo to reach Lago Caburgua in almost an hour (passing the Hupanaja guesthouse; tel: 09 822 4005; fax: 02 228 0779). It soon starts to climb again, passing the turning down to the few holiday cottages of Playa Negra after 20 minutes. You will have to keep climbing for another 20 minutes, to a junction with a forestry track from the right. From here the road drops more gradually, turning 90° right after 40 minutes, at a farm virtually by the lake. In 15 minutes you will reach the Lanqui-Lanqui village school at the Puente Trafampulli no. 5 – the Cabañas Río Trafampulli offer *once*, *küchen*, drinks, bread and other provisions as well as accommodation. There is still next to no traffic; the road continues easily down the Trafampulli valley (passing from woodland of laurel and tepa to well-established fields below cliffs and waterfalls), crossing bridges 4, 3 and 2 before, after 2½ hours' hiking, reaching an unsigned junction, at which you should fork right. The road left leads to hotels and houses at the east end of Lago Colico (300m), while the main road crosses bridge No.1 and runs along the lake for a dozen kilometres to Puerto Puma. Colico was the last of the lakes to be discovered, in 1903, and is only now seeing real tourist development.

It is another 12km to **Cunco**, a small logging town on the road from Temuco to Melipeuco, gateway to the Conguillío National Park. There is a slightly overpriced *hospedaje* on the plaza, lots of shops and cafés, and hourly buses on a paved road to Temuco.

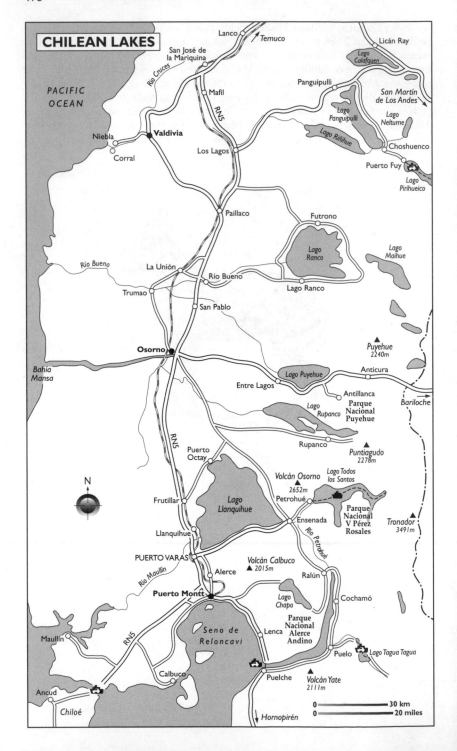

CHILEAN LAKES

PACIFIC OCEAN

Lanco
Temuco
San José de la Mariquina
Licán Ray
Lago Calafquen
Río Cruces
Mafil
Panguipulli
San Martín de Los Andes
Lago Panguipulli
Lago Neltume
RN5
Lago Riñihue
Valdivia
Niebla
Los Lagos
Choshuenco
Corral
Puerto Fuy
Lago Pirihueico
Paillaco
Futrono
Lago Ranco
Lago Maihue
Río Bueno
La Unión
Río Bueno
Trumao
Lago Ranco
San Pablo
Bahía Mansa
Osorno
Puyehue 2240m
Lago Puyehue
Anticura
Entre Lagos
Antillanca
Bariloche
Lago Rupanco
Parque Nacional Puyehue
N
Rupanco
Puntiagudo 2278m
Puerto Octay
Volcán Osorno 2652m
Lago Todos los Santos
Frutillar
Lago Llanquihue
Petrohué
Parque Nacional V Pérez Rosales
Tronador 3491m
Llanquihue
Ensenada
Río Petrohué
PUERTO VARAS
Volcán Calbuco 2015m
Ralún
Río Maullín
Alerce
Lago Chapo
Cochamó
PUERTO MONTT
Parque Nacional Alerce Andino
Maullín
Seno de Reloncaví
Lenca
Puelo
Lago Tagua Tagua
RN5
Calbuco
Puelche
Volcán Yate 2111m
Ancud
Chiloé
Hornopirén

0   30 km
0   20 miles

The Chilean Lakes

Chile's Lakes District stretches from north to south for about 300km; lakes, rivers, waterfalls, thermal pools, volcanoes, glaciers and snowfields combine with an astonishing array of vegetation and wildlife to produce one of the most magnificent landscapes in the world. The lakes are the result of both glaciation and vulcanism, with dams of both moraine and lava. While the Argentine lakes tend to lie at between 600m and 1,700m above sea level and to be cold and wild, the Chilean lakes are mostly below 300m and are much warmer and gentler, making them a mecca for both Chilean and foreign holiday-makers. Some are well developed for tourism, but others can still barely be reached.

The area shows many marks of its colonisation by European (mostly German) settlers in the second half of the 19th century, and a meal of seafood (perhaps the best in the world) may be rounded off with German *kuchen* (cakes) or Swiss-style chocolate. The thatched or red-tiled buildings of the rural north are here replaced by frame buildings of north European design, with unpainted shingle facings, high-pitched roofs and ornate balconies.

PUERTO MONTT

The main cities of the region are Valdivia, Osorno and **Puerto Montt**; you are particularly likely to spend time in the last before taking a boat or plane to Chiloé, Chaitén or Puerto Natales. It was the terminus of the railway from Santiago, over 1,000km to the north ('a very long, strange, wet, windy way from home' in the words of Jan Morris), and is still the transport hub of southern Chile. It is a working port, not a chi-chi tourist resort, but its location between lush rolling hills and islands, and its quaint shingle- and tin-fronted buildings give it a Nordic charm of its own. Incidentally, it also offers the greatest variety of seafood in the whole of South America.

Information, tours and equipment

From the port of Angelmó or the bus terminal turn right/east to follow the Costanera to the centre. The municipal **tourist office** is a kiosk between the Costanera and the Plaza de Armas, while Sernatur is in the Intendencia, O'Higgins 480 (tel: 065 256 999; fax: 254 580; sernatur_pmontt@entelchile.net). Conaf's regional office is at Ochagavía 464 (tel: 254 882); the Patrimonio Silvestre branch, dealing with National Parks, is at Amunategui 500 (tel: 290 711; Mon–Thu 09.30–12.30, 14.30–16.30, Fri to 16.00).

Travellers, Avda Angelmó 2456 (tel/fax: 065 258 555; info@travellers.cl;

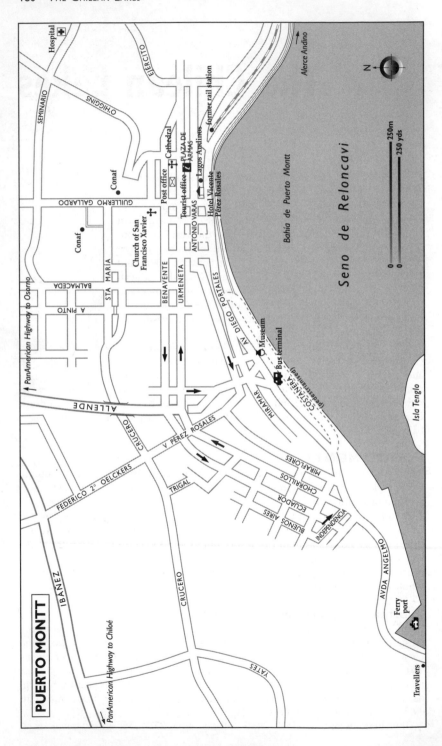

PUERTO MONTT

www.travellers.cl) is a British-run agency which organises bespoke tours and transport. It sells maps and postcards, exchanges money and books, and will also give information with no strings attached; there is also a good café upstairs.

Andina del Sud at A Varas 437 (tel: 065 257 686; www.crucedelagos.cl; crucelag@rdc.cl; adsmontt@chilesat.net; also in Puerto Varas at Del Salvador 72; tel: 065 232 811; adsvaras@chilesat.net) is the place to book the pricey boat-bus trip via Lago Todos los Santos to Bariloche (see pages 235–6). Next door at A Varas 445 (ie: in the town's best hotel, the Vicente Pérez Rosales), the Puerto Varas rafting outfit AlSur has a shop, mainly selling Patagonia gear, and Lagos Andinos (tel: 257 686, fax: 254 988; lagosand@telsur.cl) offers trekking trips. Patagonia Verde, at D Portales 514, offers climbing, trekking and riding, mostly in the Chaitén area. Kayak Austral is at Casa Perla (see below – tel: 254 600; kayakaustral@hotmail.com; www.angelfire.com/mt/kayakaustral).

Where to stay
There is plenty of cheap accommodation up the hill above the bus terminal; particularly recommended are Vista Hermosa (Miramar 1486; tel: 065 268 001), Casa Perla (Trigal 312; tel: 262 104, casaperla@hotmail.com), and Hospedaje Suiza (Independencia 231; tel: 252 640). The official HI youth hostel is Hostal Don Teo, Andres Bello 990 (tel/fax: 251 625), and there is an *albergue* (January and February only) in Escuela No.1, opposite the bus terminal. The nearest **campsites** are 10km west, beyond Angelmó.

Shopping and sightseeing
The Full-Fresh **supermarket** is conveniently sited opposite the bus terminal, with another branch on the site of the rail station; there are also three supermarkets on A Varas. Just east, on the Costanera, is the interesting **museum** (open daily 09.00–12.00, 15.00–18.00) with steam locomotives outside visible at all times. Be sure also to see the wooden **cathedral** (on the north side of the Plaza de Armas) and **Church of San Francisco Xavier** (Gallardo at Rengifo).

Angelmó, in addition to being the port and stuffed with internet places and cheap tour agencies, is also a gourmet's paradise of tiny restaurants serving seafood of every description. It is also a good place to buy handicrafts such as sweaters; they are much cheaper than further north, but quality seems to be falling as the place becomes more touristy. For a few hundred pesos you can be rowed across from Angelmó to the wooded island of Tenglo, a favourite place for picnics. From the cross at the top you get magnificent views of the city and a wide vista of volcanoes and islands, and the island's *curanto* (seafood, meat and vegetable stew) is reputedly the best in Chile.

Excursions
If you are spending a few days here to rest, shop, have your laundry washed or simply wait for a ship, there is a nice day-trip along the rough coastal road to the west; take a Bohle bus (07.00, 12.30 or 17.00) to Calbuco, and return by the PanAmerican (three buses an hour). **Calbuco** was settled in 1604 by survivors of the Mapuche sack of Osorno, and survived the next few centuries as an outpost of Chiloé. It is a small logging and fishing village, with a wealth of seafood restaurants, on an island linked by a causeway to the mainland. On the far side of the PanAmerican from the Calbuco crossroads, a dirt road leads north to Salto Grande, on the Río Maullín. The wetlands downstream of the village are an

SUNNY INTERVAL IN PUERTO MONTT

John Kellie

Puerto Montt is the end of the line, once the terminus of the railway (now disused south of Temuco) that snakes down through Chile. I did not expect much – it has a reputation for dismal weather, and one travel writer I had encountered compared the town to a 'dour North Sea port'. Although the clouds were down when I arrived, I rather enjoyed Puerto Montt.

The following morning sunshine flooded my hotel bedroom, and its unexpectedness filled me with optimism. After breakfast I strolled towards the sea-front, side-stepping yesterday's puddles as I went. I liked the wooden shingled houses that tumbled down the hillsides, painted in simple colours like a child's building blocks. Leisurely gulls were coasting over the bay while a small flotilla of ducks bobbed along the water's edge.

The promenade was busy with elderly gents, dapper in soft hats, chatting animatedly as they chewed over the news. I sat on a sunny bench overlooking the port. The MV *Puerto Edén* had arrived overnight, and her bulk and shiny red paintwork dominated the scene. I called in at the Navimag office. 'Si, señor, board at four o'clock and she will sail at seven'.

At Puerto Montt sea routes take over where the railway tracks give out. The *Puerto Edén* links the northern gates of Chilean Patagonia with the town of Puerto Natales, four days and 1,500 kilometres to the south. A working ferry, she forges along a rugged stretch of coastline where the southern Andes bend their knees and plunge into the Pacific amid a numberless scattering of islands.

I still had a few hours before the voyage. The harbourside at Angelmó was lively with the cries of fishermen, seaweedy smells, boats coming and going, and with boxes of shellfish being carted ashore. I liked the tiny eating-shacks huddled round the port, and I liked the green-eyed girl, scarcely through her teens, who hurried out to lure me in: 'Hey, gringo-man, you wanna eat with me?' In the early afternoon cloud started to build and a light rain fell, awakening new beauty as it veiled the distant hills in a misty opacity. The arms of a rainbow arched over the bay.

Shortly before four I boarded the *Puerto Edén*, but by seven loading was still underway. The quayside bustled with dockers, shouting instructions and gesturing to drivers above the din of machinery. Trailer loads of cargo, stashed under tarpaulins, were being stowed aboard. A brand new Mercedes nosed up the ramp and was hoisted to the upper deck on a giant hydraulic lift, followed by two reluctant horses, whinnying through the dusk and tossing their manes in strangeness. The streetlights of the town were just starting to twinkle, when a shaft of late sunlight pierced the clouds. Beyond the silhouettes of cranes and derricks, the snowy cone of the volcano, Osorno, lit up briefly with rosy brilliance.

At 10 o'clock, the *Eden* pulled out of Puerto Montt to sail with the tide.

important habitat for aquatic birds. At Salto Chico, the Monte Verde archaeological site dates back perhaps 33,000 years, far earlier than South America was thought to be inhabited. There is little for tourists to see, but the site is surrounded by coihue de Chiloé (*Nothofagus nitida*), one of the less common false beeches.

It is 15km north to the **airport**, reached by frequent ETM buses. If you turn right before the airport and go through the new Condominio Lagunitas development, a 3km dirt road leads to the **Parque Provincial Lahuen Ñadi**, protecting more or less the last alerce left unlogged in this area, as well as coihue, ulmo, canelo, tepú, mañío, creepers, epiphytes and fungi; there is a path that takes half an hour to walk.

In addition to the Navimag and Transmarchilay ships, smaller landing-craft-style **ferries** serve most of the islands and small fishing villages in this area, usually coming in to Puerto Montt in the morning and returning in the afternoon, tides permitting. Ask at the office of the Capitán de Puerto, between Angelmó and the bus terminal. If you head out to the marina and yacht club, about 10km west of Puerto Montt, you may find someone looking for crew (*tripulación*) for a jaunt around the islands or further.

VALDIVIA

Valdivia, strategically sited where the Cruces and Calle-Calle rivers meet to form the Río Valdivia, was founded in 1552 and has survived on the same site since then; it was briefly abandoned in 1604 after the Mapuche rising, but was re-established in 1645 as a heavily fortified enclave in Indian territory. In the second half of the 19th century it was a centre of the German colonisation of the Lakes, and still bears many traces of their influence, despite the damage done by the 1960 earthquake. The Germanic Kunstmann wheat beer is still brewed here, for example.

The Sernatur tourist **information office** (open Mon–Thur 08.30–17.30, Fri 08.30–16.30) is at Prat 555, by the dock. There is also a kiosk at the **bus terminal**, which is at Muñoz 360, east of the centre. This is a town that people pass through, rather than a tourist destination in its own right, but even so there is plenty of affordable student accommodation available over the summer. Incidentally, in term time you may notice an abundance of youths with shaved heads and wonder if the city is a centre of the Hare Krishna cult. Apparently the haircut is a result not of religious fervour but of an initiation rite inflicted on new students by their seniors.

The Hospedaje International, García Reyes 660 interior (tel: 063 212 015) rents bikes and does laundry; the official HI hostel is the Residencial Germania at Picarte 873 (tel: 212 405).

The **university museum**, across the river, is well worth visiting (open Tue–Sun 10.00–13.00, 15.00–18.00), as is the MAC (**Museum of Contemporary Art**) next door in a former brewery disused since the 1960 earthquake (open Tue–Fri 10.00–13.00 & 14.00–16.00; Sat & Sun 10.00–13.00 & 15.00–17.00). Other sights are out of town and require an excursion, ideally by boat. The best known are the forts of Corral, Niebla, San Carlos and San Pedro which guard the mouth of the Río Valdivia. In addition to half-day boat tours, there are buses to Niebla and frequent ferries from there to Corral. The **Sanctuario Carlos Anwandter**, on the Río Cruces, is Chile's only Ramsar site, wetlands inhabited by coscoroba swans and other aquatic birds. There are boat tours, but you can also see the wetlands along the main roads to Paillaco and San José de Mariquina. There are plans to extend it to cover side streams and *bosque laurifolio de Valdivia*, although there is also the threat of a cellulose plant upstream. In the hills to the south of Valdivia is the **Refugio Forestal Valdivia** and the **Natural Monument Alerce Costero**, whose centrepiece is an ancient *alerce* with a circumference of almost 4m.

Río Bueno to Valdivia
Nick Cotton

Distance	55km
Altitude	Sea level
Rating	Easy
Time	5 days
Start of trail	La Unión
End of trail	Corral
Maps	4000-7330 (H1), 4015-7345 (H10) and 4015-7330 (H11)

This beautiful walk along the wild Pacific coastline combines vast, sandy beaches with magical forests perched above the sea and has the added bonus of including interesting boat trips at each end. It is probably best to do the hike from south to north so as to be sure of getting transport, as there is only one boat a week to the southern end. However, there are plans to build a coastal road from Maullín, west of Puerto Montt, to Valdivia, which will inevitably bring development and logging. The best time to go is between November and March. Take small change for the boat crossings.

Getting to the trailhead
You start with a boat trip from **Trumao**, a small settlement on the Río Bueno, which has the second highest flow of any river in Chile. Trumao is usually reached via La Unión, 10km west of the PanAmerican, 1½ hours by bus from Valdivia (every 20 minutes) or Osorno (every 10 minutes). Buy supplies at Las Brisas by the La Unión bus terminal, east of the centre, then cross the bridge to the town and turn left for three blocks to the rural terminal for buses to Trumao (except on Sundays). There are also buses at 10.00 and 16.00 on Mondays, Wednesdays and Fridays from the old rail station in Osorno. From Trumao, a motorboat service departs at 09.00 on Saturdays to La Barra at the mouth of the Río Bueno, a breathtaking, six-hour trip through the coastal mountains (US$5; returning the next day). Check at the International Service travel agency in the main square (Prat 662) in La Unión. If you are unable to get a boat to the mouth of Río Bueno, consider shortening the walk and starting at Hueicolla, reached by taxi on a rough track through the Reserva Natural Alerce Costero (in fact mostly raulí forest).

Route description
Ask to be dropped at Venecia, a one-house settlement on the north bank of the river just before it reaches the sea. If, however, the boat will only stop at La Barra on the south bank, you will have to pay someone to row you across. There are no fixed prices for the river crossings, so you will need to haggle before setting out. There is simple accommodation in La Barra.

From Venecia climb the dirt road which leads north towards Hueicolla. You can walk directly to Hueicolla but it is worth taking a diversion to the tiny fishing settlement of Lameguapi. After about 40 minutes turn off left down a sandy path which leads through the forest and reaches Lameguapi in 2 hours. Head north along the beach and about half way along it turn inland to follow the stream which climbs the hillside and joins a path going north. Follow this for about 1½ hours, and after a steep climb you will rejoin the Venecia–Hueicolla dirt road. It is then a downhill walk of 2 hours to Hueicolla, a small coastal village of about 30 holiday houses, where you can celebrate with a fine seafood meal at the *hostería*.

At the point where the road to La Unión turns sharply east at the end of Hueicolla Bay, walk straight on until you reach a small river. Again you will have to find a boat to take you across. Continue for 2 hours along the beach until it ends, then follow the well-worn path which climbs steeply through the forest over Punta Colún. When you come down to the Río Colún on the other side, walk upstream for about 1km, then shout and whistle for a rowing boat. A wonderful *señora* in a most interesting hat rowed us across. Follow the river back along the north bank towards the sea and walk along the next beach past huge sand dunes and cows chewing on seaweed. At the end of the beach, 2 hours from the Río Colún, a path takes you over another promontory, Punta Galera. After another 1½ hours of up-and-down walking you reach the fishing village of Punta Galera where there is good camping beyond the houses.

From here the path stays well above the sea, winding through forest until it reaches the Río Chaihuín. There was a proper bridge across this until some dim timber merchant took his heavily laden juggernaut across. Having been built only to take oxcarts, horses and light vehicles, it collapsed. You can still walk across the remains, however. At Chaihuín there is a small store where you can get basic food.

From here there are two alternative ways of getting to the village of Corral. You can either take the road, which is fairly boring but faster (about 7 hours), or you can walk to the end of the bay and pick up the coastal path which takes about 9 hours to Corral. If you take the road route you will need to stock up on water beforehand as you will not pass a stream for at least 3 hours. From Corral there are about 20 boats a day to Niebla, from where buses leave for Valdivia every 20 minutes.

Note Paradoxically, despite the region's high rainfall, water is a problem so always fill your bottle whenever you come to a stream. It is probably best to camp near streams as there is very little surface water on the sandy, well-drained hills above the sea.

THE SIETE LAGOS

A lovely but little-known area lies not far east of the PanAmerican near Valdivia. **Panguipulli**, the entry point to the *Siete Lagos* (Seven Lakes) is a popular resort, but beyond this things are much quieter. An unmade road runs for 43km along the north shore of Lago Panguipulli to the tiny village of Choshuenco; 15km south is the tinier Enco, from where a rough track (a good mountain bike route) leads west along Lago Riñihue, and a road climbs 9km east up the slopes of Volcán Choshuenco (2,415m) to a Club Andino refuge at Valdivia's tiny ski resort. It is a lovely walk south from Choshuenco for about 3 hours to a farm then up to the east to the *refugio*.

Continuing eastwards from Choshuenco, several buses a day cover the 22km to Puerto Fuy, at the western end of Lago Pirehueico; about 15km along this road is Neltume, where you can visit the 30m-high Saltos del Huilo-huilo, 200m west (with friendly basic accommodation), or take a trail up the north side of **Volcán Choshuenco** (whose only recorded eruption was in 1864). Unfortunately there is talk of damming the Río Fuy for hydroelectricity. In Puerto Fuy (590m) stay at the Hostal Caicahen (casa 40; no telephone), or camp on the beach. To the south a stunning road runs south over the eastern flank of Volcán Choshuenco to Lago

Ranco, but sadly it is private and not open. It is possible to drive to Puerto Pirehueico, at the eastern end of the lake, and on to the HuaHum border crossing (659m) and San Martín de los Andes (see page 205), but it is far better to take the car ferry (Mon–Sat 07.00 and 13.00; US$1) along this lovely lake (aptly named 'Worm of Water' in Mapudungun) and the connecting bus to Argentina. At the moment there is nothing at Puerto Pirehueico but one *hospedaje*, but tourist development is mooted. You can take a hike high on the slopes of Cerro del Encanto (1,890m), to the southwest of Puerto Pirehueico, and take the evening ferry back to Puerto Fuy. The trail along the south side of Lago Pirehueico is also being recut through the dense *bosque laurifolio de Los Lagos* (mainly lingue and raulí); this will make a superb two-day hike.

PUYEHUE NATIONAL PARK

With over 50,000 visitors a year, the Puyehue National Park (pronounced 'poo-yay-way') is one of the most popular in Chile, for a variety of reasons: it is on the main road to Bariloche (in Argentina); this is fully paved from Osorno to the border (and soon throughout); admission is free; and above all, perhaps, many Chileans and Argentinians are attracted by the hot baths. The Anticura sector, giving access to the bare volcanic terrain of Volcán Puyehue, is largely visited by *gringos*. The park's ecology is less of a draw, and indeed it does not protect any particular rarities. Nevertheless the park covers a large area of luxuriant forest, as well as volcanic terrain which is slowly being colonised by vegetation. Evergreen Valdivian forest flourishes in this wet temperate climate, with up to 4m of precipitation a year. In the lower areas huge ulmo trees dominate, with tepa and coihue común, and some mañío, olivillo, tineo, and an understorey of arrayán, quila and fuchsia, as well as lots of creepers. In higher areas, to 1,300m, only species adapted to cold flourish, notably lenga and coihue de Magallanes. In some areas there are also boggy *mallines* (marsh) and low *matorrales* (scrub) of ñirre and ciprés de las Guaitecas. There is the full range of mammals associated with Valdivian forest, such as puma, grey fox, lesser grison, wildcats, skunks, monito del monte, and vizcacha, although there are few huemul. Birds include Des Mur's wiretail, fire-eyed diucon, torrent duck, Magellanic woodpecker, condor and buzzard.

From Osorno and Entre Lagos, the international highway runs along the south side of **Lago Puyehue** (207m), reaching a junction at the Hotel Termas de Puyehue (308m, 76km from Osorno). To the right it is 4km to the Administration and Environmental Information Centre (open daily 09.00–19.00) at **Aguas Calientes** and another 18km to the ski resort of **Antillanca** ('Sun-Jewel'). To the left, the main road follows the Gol-Gol valley to El Caulle, the Salto del Indio (broad waterfalls reached by a half-hour stroll through coihue forest, with signs identifying all the main trees of the Valdivian forest) and **Anticura** (355m), where there is a *guardería* and campsite. It is another 4km (passing two paths, each about 1km long, to more waterfalls on the Gol-Gol, just north) to the Pajaritos border post (450m, 95km from Osorno), and 22km more (now paved) to the border (1,308m).

Eight minibuses a day run from the market in Osorno Mon–Fri, with fewer on Saturdays and Sundays, reaching Aguas Calientes in 1¼ hours; Pajaritos is now served only on Monday and Friday at 19.00 (returning at 07.30 the next morning), but you can also hitch or persuade an international bus to take you. Camping at Aguas Calientes costs just US$2 a head, except in January and February when you

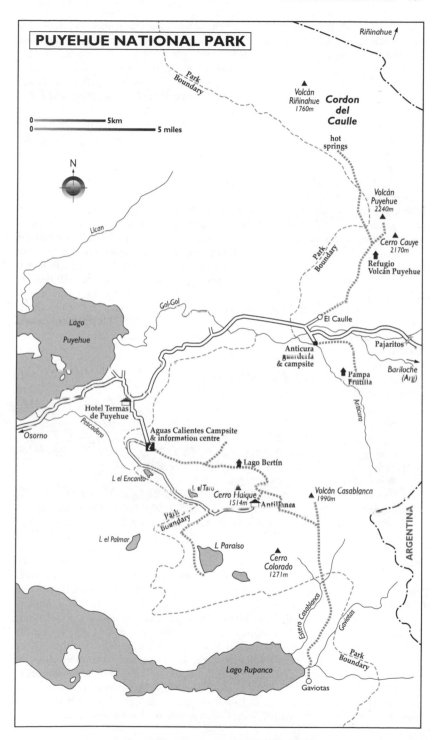

PUYEHUE NATIONAL PARK

Riñinahue

Park Boundary

Volcán Riñinahue 1760m

Cordon del Caulle

hot springs

0 ——— 5km
0 ——— 5 miles

N

Llican

Volcán Puyehue 2240m

Cerro Cauye 2170m

Refugio Volcán Puyehue

Park Boundary

Gol-Gol

Lago Puyehue

El Caulle

Pajaritos

Anticura guardería & campsite

Bariloche (Arg)

Pampa Frutilla

Araucano

Hotel Termas de Puyehue

Pescadero

Osorno

Aguas Calientes Campsite & information centre

Lago Bertín

L el Encanto

L el Taro

Cerro Haique 1514m

Antillanca

Volcán Casablanca 1990m

Park Boundary

L el Palmar

L Paraíso

Cerro Colorado 1271m

ARGENTINA

Estero Casablanca

Gaviotas

Park Boundary

Lago Rupanco

Gaviotas

have to pay US$20 for an eight-person site – however, the rangers do encourage backpackers to get together and share a site. At Anticura sites cost US$7 at all times, and wild camping is permitted and free.

The main hike into the northern part of the park starts opposite a wooden church at El Caulle (where you will have to pay US$7 to cross private land) and heads north across volcanic wasteland to **Volcán Puyehue** (2,240m) and on to Lago Ranco (70m). The decent Refugio Volcán Puyehue is 10km along the trail, at the treeline (1,350m). Check at the Anticura *guardería* whether you need to take the key – you may in fact have to go in a group with a ranger, depending on conditions. It takes 3–5 hours to get here, and under 2 hours more for about 6km to the summit – take the path northwards along the west side of the volcano, and then fork right to follow the prominent ridge after crossing three small streams. The ice-filled crater, which last erupted in 1921, is a couple of kilometres across. To the northwest, the Cordón del Caulle consists of 18 craters along a 4.3km line; this was very active from 1893 until 1960 (when it burst into life 47 hours after the great earthquake). Throughout this region the magma is just 2–4km below the surface, producing many thermal springs and also, in this area, fumaroles. Forking left after the hut, you will reach hot springs, beyond which the path to Lago Ranco is reported as very overgrown and only for tough resilient hikers; you will need to take a tent, of course. From Anticura it is also possible to hike south to the Pampa Frutilla ('Strawberry Flats') hut and on to a bare plateau east of Volcán Casablanca, about 18km from the road. Continuing east from the border into Argentina, you will see a very impressive volcanic plug to the south, and a path to the Cascada Diana.

A hike via the Antillanca ski resort
Route description

Distance	40km
Altitude	Between 470m and 1,500m
Rating	Easy to moderate
Time	1–2 days (stay at Refugio Bertín)
Start of trail	Aguas Calientes
End of trail	Puerto Rico (bus to Osorno) or Aguas Calientes
Maps	4030-7200 (H27) and 4015-7200 (H17), 5-04-08-0036-00 Volcán Casablanca; JLM no. 15 'Ruta de los Jesuitos'

Leaving the Information Centre (470m) and carrying on up the road, you will pass the Chanleufú campsite on your left (and the starts of three paths, the Senderos El Recodo, El Pionero and Los Derrumbes, none longer than 1.8km each way) and then fork left after 2 minutes. Keep straight on at a barrier, then at a wooden turnstile, and likewise at the end of the dirt road, after 15 minutes. Continuing along a muddy path for 30 minutes, you will come to a stream which you can either ford or cross on dead trees just downstream. After another 10 minutes keep right where the Sendero Los Mineros forks left. The path continues climbing steadily, less boggy now, for another 50 minutes to the Refugio Bertín, a minute to the left just before a stream (about 2 hours from Aguas Calientes). It is a real little pioneer cabin, full of character and totally impractical – you are far better off in your tent. It is another 7 minutes up the side path to reach Lago Bertín, but you can barely reach the shore or see anything much; take your water from the stream by the main path.

Continuing across the stream by a footbridge, the path, clearly a former mine railway, rises at an easy grade and passes below some small waterfalls. After 25 minutes you will reach the first hairpin bend, as the track climbs to the right. You should reach the treeline in 35 minutes, from where the track briefly follows the upper edge of the forest. Continuing across the ash slope, it enters a trench, but the going is easier alongside this. You will reach a ridge in 10 minutes, from where the track continues eastwards across bare lava, crossing a gully after another 10 minutes, and reaching a ridge in another 5 minutes, by piles of bleached wood. Here it swings right towards the main ridge west from Volcán Casablanca (1,990m) to Cerro Haique (1,514m), along which you will see marker poles. You can follow the track winding up to the ridge (at about 1,500m) in 15 minutes, or cut straight up the hill without problem. On the far side you will see the ski-drags of Antillanca. There are various ways down, but perhaps the easiest is to the left on the La Loma piste and then by a path under a double chairlift to reach the Antillanca hotel (1,050m) in about 40 minutes. This is just below the tree line in a broad flat valley, at the head of the road from Aguas Calientes. As well as skiing, it is a centre for mountain-biking and parapente.

The road from the ski slopes heads to the left and then cuts down to the right to the hotel. From this junction another road heads on to the east/left, rising slightly, just above the treeline to reach a viewpoint at the edge of the Raihuen crater (1,230m), about 12 minutes' walk away. This is at a gap in the crater wall, giving great views across the crater to the walls opposite and the cone of Volcán Casablanca above. From here it is a fairly easy hike to the summit of Casablanca, taking 2 hours each way. With map, compass, and good route-finding ability it is also possible to descend the lava slopes to the north, to pick up the Pampa Frutilla trail down to Anticura. The road swings right and continues to rise gently, ending in 10 minutes at a barrier by another crater; one track goes into this, while it is possible to walk on beyond the barrier to the hilltop. From here there is a view west to the reddish crags of Cerro Colorado (1,271m), and south towards Lago Rupanco. It is feasible to hike down to the Estero Casablanca and follow the valley to the east end of the lake (just 70m above sea-level) and then follow a trail around to the south side, via Gaviotas (page 194) to Puerto Rico, from where you can pick up a bus to Osorno at 06.00 or 16.00. However, it is not easy to find the overgrown paths, and you will need to be self-reliant and experienced in route finding.

From Antillanca, you can take the road back to Aguas Calientes, but it is quite tough on the feet, so you may prefer to retrace your steps via Bertín. Mountain-bikers may choose to go up on the road and then down the Bertín trail. Taking the road, after 7km (at least a 1¼ hour walk) an unsigned track heads south to Lago Paraíso. Carrying on along the road, you will see Laguna El Toro (750m) on the right after 10 minutes, and reach parking and access steps at its west end in another 5 minutes. Just a couple of minutes further on is the checkpoint where cars are checked for chains in winter. From here (9km above Aguas Calientes) the road continues to drop easily, reaching the falls of the Río Pescador in 20 minutes and the smaller falls of the Río Nauto in another 15 minutes. From here it is just under 7km to Aguas Calientes, passing viewpoints to the left over the small Lago El Encanto (600m) and Laguna del Espejo.

PUERTO VARAS

Thanks to its position as the gateway from the PanAmerican to the Parque Nacional Vicente Pérez Rosales, Puerto Varas is developing into the outdoor tourism centre of the Chilean Lakes, although it is still considerably quieter than Pucón, in Araucanía. It was founded in 1854 as a port through which goods could be transported from Puerto Montt to the German settlements around Lago Llanquihue. Therefore it is much touted as a typically Germanic town, although in fact there is little of interest in its urban fabric. The pseudo-Bavarian church is of note chiefly for its hideous electronic chime (mercifully silent from 22.30 to 07.30). If you want to learn about the history of German colonisation in the area, head north to Frutillar's Museo de la Colonización Alemana. There is no bus station in Puerto Varas, but three of the main bus companies have offices near the junction of Walker Martínez and San Pedro and there are lots of *micros* to Puerto Montt which can be picked up almost anywhere in the centre. Paradoxically, while Puerto Varas is developing into a residential suburb of Puerto Montt, the cheapest accommodation is in Puerto Montt, which is in many ways a better base.

One of the nicest (though hardly cheapest) **places to stay** is Outsider (San Bernardo 318; tel/fax: 065 232 910; outsider@telsur.cl), run by the same people as Campo Aventura in the Valle Cochamó (page 196), and also housing their booking office and a café-bar. Backpackers usually head for either Colores del Sur (Santa Rosa 318; tel: 338 588), or Ellenhaus (Walker Martínez 239; tel: 233 577); slightly classier is Casa Azul at Mirador 18 (tel: 232 904; casaazul@telsur.cl). **Supplies** can be bought at the big Las Brisas and Vhymeister supermarkets in the town centre.

Perhaps the best of the **adventure-tourism companies** here are AlSur (Del Salvador 100; tel/fax: 065 232 300; alsur@telsur.cl; and in Puerto Montt), which offers rafting on the Río Petrohué and trips to Pumalín, and also sells outdoor clothing and maps; and the German-run AquaMotion, San Pedro 422 (tel: 232 747; fax: 235 938; aquamotn@telsur.cl, www.aquamotion.cl), which offers rafting, hiking, riding, and canyoning in the Río León, a short boat trip from Petrohué. Others are Adriazola Expediciones, Santa Rosa 548 (tel/fax: 233 477; cellular 08 888 6664), which offers fishing, rafting, climbs on Volcán Osorno, and trips to the Puelo valley; the French-run Austral Expediciones (casilla 896; tel: 065 346 433; 09 310 5272; richard@whitewater.chile.ms), which does all kinds of water-based activities, including an eight-day descent of the Río Palena; EcoTravel on the Costanera (tel: 233 222), which offers bird-watching, rafting and fishing; Tranco, on the plaza at Sta Rosa 580 (tel: 311 311; trancoaventura@yahoo.com; www.tranco-expediciones.cl), offering rafting, canyoning, horse-riding and ascents of Volcán Osorno; and travelArt, Imperial 0661 (tel: 232 198; fax: 234 818), specialising in mountain-biking down Volcán Osorno.

VICENTE PÉREZ ROSALES NATIONAL PARK

Vicente Pérez Rosales is the oldest national park in Chile, founded in 1926, and it is still one of the most popular, with over 120,000 visitors a year. This is hardly surprising, as it includes the most beautiful of Chile's lakes, and also three stunning, but totally different volcanoes – Osorno, Puntiagudo and Tronador. Boat trips are very popular, as are the park's hot springs. Named after the colonisation agent who supervised the German immigration to the Lakes District in the 1850s, it covers 253,780ha, including Lago Todos los Santos (18,900ha).

With up to 4m of annual precipitation, the park is covered with dense evergreen forest, although not quite as luxuriant as in Puyehue. The dominant species is coihue (*Nothofagus dombeyi*), found from 200m to 1,000m, with ulmo, tepa, tineo and avellano, or in higher parts with shrubs, creepers, nalca, *Blechnum* ferns, and surprisingly little bamboo. Lago Todos los Santos is surrounded by olivillo (*Aextoxicon punctatum*); alone or with coihue, ulmo and tepa. There is some alerce between 800m and 1,000m, and lenga at higher altitudes, and there is plenty of introduced Spanish broom, with its luminous yellow flowers. Animals include puma, pudú, coipo, grey fox, monito del monte, otter, wildcats, skunk, and lesser grison; birds include woodpeckers, hummingbirds, eagles, condor, geese, coot, torrent duck and kingfisher. In December and January the *tábanos* (horseflies) are awful here – cover up and avoid dark clothing.

Lago Llanquihue

Lago Llanquihue (70m), created by glaciation 10,000–12,000 years ago, is the third largest in South America. Its south shore is lined with beautifully kept fields, wooden churches and shingle-faced farmhouses, many now offering accommodation and *küchen* (German cakes) and *once* (high tea). The volcano on the south side of the lake is the heavily eroded Volcán Calbuco (2,015m); from Ensenada you can take horse rides to a waterfall on its north side. Trails also run to the volcano from the Puerto Montt–Lago Chapo road, to the south, and from Río Sur, to the west (reached by Bus Fierro from Puerto Montt via Alerce).

At the crossroads at the southeastern corner of the lake is the settlement of **Ensenada** (46km from Puerto Varas), where the typically Nordic Hotel Ensenada (tel: 065 212 017; fax: 212 028; volcanhotelensenada@entelchile.net) has been run by German-Chileans since the turn of the century, and has a fantastic collection of antiques and bizarre items such as a polyphon that plays the Chilean national anthem. There is a barber's chair in the Gents and a tin bath in the Ladies. Its *ApfelkUchen* (applecake) is… well, out of this world. This is only the best of a wide choice of accommodation here, which also includes the Ruedas Viejas, 3km west, which offers youth hostel discounts. There are also various campsites such as the Montaña, with lovely lakeside views but also sandflies.

Continuing east and forking left, it is 10km to the **Saltos de Petrohué**; look for hummingbirds on the fuchsia by the kiosk where you will pay US$2. It is five minutes walk to the falls, where the outlet from Lago Todos los Santos bursts through a dam of hard basalt from Volcán Osorno. There is some nice woodland of radal, avellano and coihue. The Carilemu trail leads south for 960m, with a loop at the end by a nice little picnic beach. The parallel Los Enamorados trail (620m) has information boards, mainly eco-romantic rather than giving hard facts. Below the falls, which seem set to drain the lake in a day or two, the river is used for rafting (starting by the washed-out section of road at km50), while upstream there is a fenced-off climbing cliff, near which you may see torrent ducks.

Petrohué

The road, unpaved from the Saltos, ends 16km from Ensenada at **Petrohué** (150m), site of the park Administration and Environmental Information Centre; buses come here two or three times a day from Puerto Montt. The Hotel Petrohué is excellent, while the Küschel family owns a cheaper *hospedaje* (with camping) across the river, and has a motor-boat for hire. There is also a campsite on the beach just beyond the carpark.

It is possible to walk from Petrohué to the beach and then up to **Paso Desolación**, where there are great views of the lake and of the volcanoes. This can

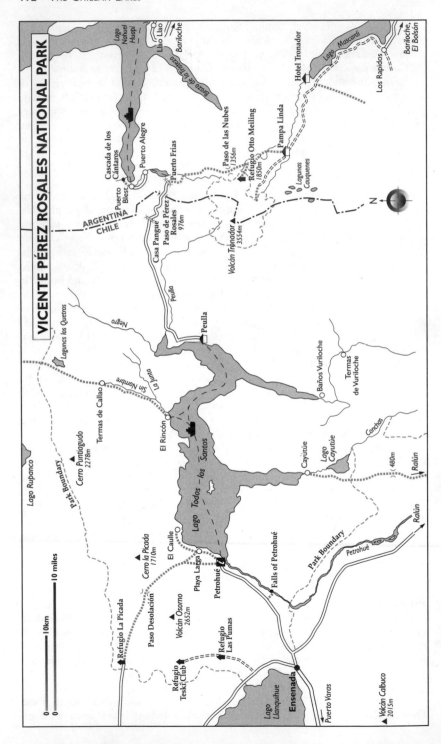

VICENTE PÉREZ ROSALES NATIONAL PARK

be an easy half-day's stroll, or it can be extended by heading up Volcán Osorno or Cerro La Picada. Alternatively you can simply continue along the beach to El Caulle, 5km from Petrohué.

From the Hotel Petrohué cross an open expanse of lava, parallel to the shore, and take a gravel track into the woods. After 5 minutes fork right, pass through a gate marked '*No Entrar*' after 2 minutes and after 2 minutes more fork right onto a path which leads to a small beach in 5 minutes. Here you should immediately turn left and head back into the woods, on a small path which climbs and then drops quite steeply in places, reaching the Playa Larga in another 5 minutes (if the water is low you can stay on the beach throughout, passing rocks created by lava hitting the water and cooling suddenly). Walking along the beach, you will pass some boats under shelters after 15 minutes. About 5 minutes further on, just before a headland, turn left along a riverbed (usually dry), heading straight up towards the amazing bulk of Volcán Osorno. If you continue for about 40 minutes, partly walking along the left bank, you will enter a narrower section, where you will see 'microstylites' or 'fairy mushrooms' – pebbles left poised on pillars of sand (about 5cm high) when the sand around has been washed away by rain. After 5 minutes you will have to clamber over a waterfall (usually fairly dry; it is a lava sill, with an undercut cave beneath), and then another. With a guide it is easy to continue on a path hidden on the right to reach two staircase cascades a little higher up, and then cut across towards the Paso Desolación. On your own, however, it is easier to head to the right from the riverbed about 20 minutes from the beach, on obvious tracks which lead you to the motocross route. From here it should take about 30 minutes to the first obvious viewpoint, and under 10 more to the pass.

It is also possible to head up away from the shore at Petrohué, following the washed-out course of a lahar for ten minutes, then forking right and after 15 minutes going up to the right onto the bank, on a path which becomes a 4WD track climbing gently above the lake for 20 minutes. It crosses a dry watercourse and goes up into thicker taller forest, crossing a stream after ten minutes by a derelict log bridge (or a ford to the left), and two more big washed-out lahars, and after 20 minutes reaching the riverbed which you should follow into the forest to the waterfalls.

There are great views, from Osorno and Cerro La Picada (1,710m), which seems to be almost within reach but is not quite as accessible as it seems, to Puntiagudo (2,278m), the flat-topped El Borracho, and the mighty Tronador (3,554m). Puntiagudo is one of the most dramatic and distinctive mountains in this area, especially since part of its peak collapsed in the 1960 quake.

Longer and more adventurous hikes involve starting by boat from Petrohué. For the hike to Bariloche (page 235) you can use the tourist boat from Petrohué to Peulla (US$25, leaving at 11.00), but for other hikes you will have to hire a boat (about US$40 for a group of four); ask at the park offices at Petrohué. In previous editions we described a hike from Ralún north over an easy 480m pass to the lake at Cayutué, but this has now been ruined by logging and other development, as well as by disputes over access, so that now the favoured option is to take a boat to El Rincón, on the north shore of the lake, and hike to **El Callao** hot springs and beyond.

El Rincón, about 1km east of the mouth of the Río Sin Nombre, is just a jetty, used by local smallholders and by a few hikers. A trail runs from the mouth of the river, so you need to turn right onto this just above the jetty. This heads north for about 1km to the Río Sin Nombre, then follows it upstream to cross first the Río La Junta (or Techado) then the Río Sin Nombre by rickety suspension bridges. From here the trail, well used, and indeed churned up, by horses and cows, follows the right bank northwards for roughly 1½ hours to a small farm, where you should collect the key (and pay US$4) for the *refugio*, if required. The Termas del Callao (*c* 400m) are 5 minutes further north, with the *refugio*, room for tents, and free hot tubs in a shelter by the river.

Here you have various options. In some ways the simplest is to arrange for the boat to collect you in a few days' time, but there are expedition-grade routes east and west, and you can hike out to the north. This last route continues upstream, soon crossing a side stream and swinging to the northeast. After another couple of kilometres, the path turns left to leave the main valley and climb to a pass, in thick rainforest, at about 800m. From here it is not far down to Laguna Los Quetros, 6km from El Callao, where you will find a simple three-sided shelter and space to camp. The trail continues along the west side of the lake and again rises to a low pass. After about 2 hours it emerges from the forest into meadows with views north over Lago Rupanco, and descends for another hour or so to reach the houses of Puerto del Buey by the lakeside (70m). A rough track runs from Las Gaviotas, just north at the mouth of the Río Gaviotas, to Puerto Rico (5 or 6 hours west of Puerto del Buey), from where you can pick up a bus to Osorno at 06.00 or 16.00.

AquaMotion in particular (see *Puerto Varas*, page 190) run a range of trips, hiking or riding horses, using this route; they have several fine places to stay along Lago Rupanco, and will take you across the lake to hike to Antillanca, in the Puyehue National Park. They can also lay on an expedition east from El Callao to the Río Negro, involving a 60m rappel down into a canyon.

Climbing Volcán Osorno

Volcán Osorno (2,652m) is a magnificent Fuji-like cone which dominates virtually the whole of the Lakes District (it is visible from 30km north of the city of Osorno). The ascent to the summit has gained something of a reputation for danger, mainly because inexperienced climbers have attempted it in poor weather conditions and been killed by falling into crevasses. However, it is a magnificent climb if you are properly equipped with crampons, ice-axe, rope (and someone to pull you out). Conaf require you to climb with a guide for every two clients, usually roped up. The day-walk from Ensenada to the refuges on the southwestern slopes gives stupendous views in any case (weather permitting).

At the north end of Ensenada (easily reached by any bus from Puerto Montt or Puerto Varas towards Petrohué or Ralún) you will pass a Conaf gate from where a path leads west for 700m to Laguna Verde, a tiny emerald lake in a clearing from where you can gaze over the vast expanse of Lago Llanquihue; you can continue to rocks overlooking the beach. Continue north for almost 3km towards Puerto Octay, turning right after Puerto Oscuro (campsite) at the junction to the refugios. Soon you will find yourself climbing past meadows and small farms where fruit and honey can be bought. The vegetation on these lower slopes is bewildering in its variety. You will find birch, bamboo, bilberry and blackberry bushes and the chilco plant with its delicate, red, bell-shaped flowers, among lots of others. As you climb, the vegetation thins out and you glimpse the lake. The ascent is steady and gradual on a clear gravel track all the way, and if you get bored with the views, you can test your walking speed against the kilometre posts which have been thoughtfully provided. The first hut is the Refugio Las Pumas (11km from

Ensenada, at 900m), and the second, where there is a Conaf ranger, is the Refugio Teski Club (also known as La Barbuja), 4km further and 300m higher, and 4–5 hours from Ensenada. You can eat and sleep quite cheaply at both, although Los Pumas, which is open all year, seemed cosier.

From the hut the view of the mountain, as with all conical volcanoes, is very foreshortened; at the top of the ski-drag (broken for years) you are only halfway to the foot of the glacier. There are enormous crevasses as soon as you are on the ice, so you must be roped up. The route is fairly obvious, to the left of a bare, rocky area, then directly up, avoiding the crevasses. You should leave at dawn; it takes 2 hours from the Teski hut to the glacier and 3 more to the summit, which is a flat plateau – there is no crater. With fine weather the view from here over Lago Todos los Santos to Tronador and Puntiagudo is superb. It is worth visiting some ice-caves on the northern side of the plateau, where the ice has melted so that you can walk underneath it. Do not stray too near the edge to the east, as there are dangerous crevasses here.

An alternative route starts at Puerto Klocker, by Lago Llanquihue 20km southeast of Puerto Octay, from where a dirt road leads 20km to the Refugio La Picada (950m), owned by the Club Andino de Puerto Octay. This is a good base for climbs to the summit (with guide) or hikes around the volcano, for instance to Paso Desolación (see below).

Guides can be found at La Barbuja, in principle, but it is easier to book one, if required, through Adriazola, AquaMotion, Tranco or travelArt in Puerto Varas, or the Hotel Ruedas Viejas, 3km west of Ensenada, or Hotel Vicente Pérez Rosales in Puerto Montt. Day-trips (for US$100) usually set out at 05.00, but it is better to sleep at a refuge. The IGM map required is 4100-7230 (Las Cascadas), at 1:50,000; JLM's map 15 (Ruta de los Jesuitos) gives good coverage of the whole park.

From Refugio La Picada, a four-wheel-drive track, much used (illegally) by motocross bikers, leads to the Paso Desolación and down to Playa Larga, a fine beach of black sand on the shore of Lago Todos los Santos.

THE COCHAMÓ VALLEY

Distance	23km (to Río Botapiedras)
Altitude	Sea level to 1,450m
Rating	Easy to moderate
Time	2 days to 2 weeks
Start of trail	Río Cochamó bridge
End of trail	Villegas on the Bariloche–El Bolsón road or Puelo
Maps	IGM map 4115-7200 (Río Cochamó), or JLM map no. 15 (Ruta de los Jesuitos)

The Cochamó valley rivals Yosemite in its beauty and its potential for adventure. The only classic U-shaped glacial valley in South America that is easily accessible, it is home to huge stands of some of the biggest and oldest alerce trees yet found. The valley also has a fascinating history. Routes pioneered by intrepid Jesuits in the 18th century led from Chiloé to their mission on Lago Nahuel Huapi in Argentina (allowing them to avoid the dangerous crossing of Lago Todos los Santos), and at the turn of the 20th century another route, known as the Cochamó Road (but now marketed as the 'Gaucho Trail'), was developed to give *estancias* in Argentina an outlet to the sea. Its most notorious users were two *gringos* formerly known as Butch Cassidy and the Sundance Kid, who, with their moll Etta Place, lived in Cholila in 1901–05. A slaughterhouse operated until the 1920s in Cochamó, at the mouth of the river, and inns and farms were dotted along the route. Miraculously, the Cochamó Road still survives as a horse-track – there were proposals recently to build a road, and surveyors started work, but this idea has now been shelved (instead a road is being built along the Puelo valley – page 198). Nor does the area have any legal protection, but its isolation has allowed it to survive unlogged. Although there is no road, there is a surprising number of smallholdings along the valley, some still inhabited. Now it is being discovered by adventure tourism outfits, most notably Campo Aventura which operates horse-back trips to El Arco, a natural bridge over a waterfall, and longer expeditions along the whole length of the Cochamó Road. Other companies such as Cascada (in Santiago), ¡Ecole! (in Pucón) and Cathedral Treks (Redway, California; tel: 1 707 923 2006) come here in conjunction with Campo Aventura, whose address is simply Casilla 5, Cochamó, X Region (info@campo-aventura.com); they also have a booking office at the Outsider *hospedaje* in Puerto Varas (San Bernardo 318; tel/fax: 065 232 910; outsider@telsur.cl). In addition to a base camp near the road at the mouth of the Cochamó Campo Aventura also owns a farm up the valley at La Junta. Very comfortable cabins (US$15) and camping (US$5) are available at both even if you are not using their horses. At La Junta, students have constructed a 6km nature trail, and it is planned to extend this right up into the hanging valley above.

Getting to the trailhead

A paved road from Puerto Varas and Ensenada reaches as far as **Ralún** (32km from Ensenada), at the head of the Seno Reloncaví. There are hot pools here, as well as *cabañas* and a closed hotel. A road heads south, on the west side of the fiord, to Canutillar, in the Alerce Andino park (see below), and a trail heads north to Cayutué and Lago Todos los Santos – you will see signs advertising guides and horses for hire. However, as discussed above, this route is not as attractive an option as it was. There are great views down the fjord to **Volcán Yate** (2,111m), which can be climbed from Puelo by its east ridge. An unpaved road heads down the east side of the fjord to **Cochamó** (16km further), which is pure delight: a quaint fishing village with a few restaurants and shops, although not quite as peaceful as it was before the road from Ralún was built a few years ago. By the water stands an attractive wooden church built in 1909. Two Fierro buses a day run from Puerto Montt to Puelo, and will drop you at the Cochamó bridge 4km southeast of the village (two hours from Puerto Varas).

Route description

The route up the Cochamó valley is used more by horses than by hikers, is pretty boggy in parts, and passes through deep trenches in others. In fact riders too will often find themselves walking and leading their horses through the most awkward stretches. There are several rivers to be forded, none more than knee-deep. The route is unmarked and you may go wrong in places, but the essential is to keep following the valley. There is a fascinating blend of unspoilt nature and human traces along the way.

From the Río Cochamó bridge, where the bus will drop you, Campo Aventura's Valle Concha base camp is 500m east along the left/south bank of the river. The route up the valley runs along the north bank, starting on an unmade road that ends after 2km and continues as a horse-track. After 3.5km (45 minutes) you should keep right at the gate to a farm on the left, and then swing left, parallel to the river. In another 10 minutes you will pass a gate at km4.440, then in 8 minutes turn right and left through a gate. In 15 minutes more you will pass a hut on the right and then cross a big stream on a footbridge and enter the Fundo El Morro, 5 minutes from the hut. Keep left at a gate and go up and along a barbed-wire fence; at km6.5 you will see the last trace of the surveyors. After 25 minutes (1¾ hours from the road) you will leave El Morro at the Río Piedra, which it is usually easy enough to cross. Go a short distance downstream and then head left, just to the left of a hut on a hillock, and into native forest (including thousand-year-old mañío trees, recognisable by their big, ivy-like parasites). After 35 minutes you will cross two streams, head upstream and then up to the right for 5 minutes. The track on is more or less level, as the river rises towards it. After 20 minutes more you will cross a stream and soon find yourself on logs laid in mud. At a second stream go slightly up to the left. After 15 minutes (3 hours from the road) you will pass through a gate into second-growth woodland, with a cliff to the left. In about 10 minutes you will come to the boggiest stretch yet, and in 5 minutes more reach a ruined hut in a field where views to the granite domes ahead begin to open up.

Continuing in more second-growth forest, on logs which could date back to the heyday of the Cochamó Road, you will pass through a gate and turn right, to follow the river – some stretches very sandy, some in muddy trenches. After 30 minutes you will come to a gateway with no gate in it, just before a bend in the river with a shingle bar and a view of two waterfalls to the south. Passing through an abandoned field with a good view ahead, you will pass another gate in 15 minutes and a broken one in 10 more. Between them, just 3 minutes after the first gate, a path leads to a gate on the riverbank; to reach the La Junta Outback Camp (18km or about 4½ hours from the road) you have to ford the river here. If you miss the turning you will see the camp from the second gate, below a good cirque and waterfalls to the south.

Continuing, you will pass a farm on your left in another 5 minutes and ford the Río La Junta; 5 minutes further on you can see another small farm across the river to the right. The track continues much as before, well churned by horses, but obvious enough. After swinging left and right through some big alerces it climbs fairly steeply up rocky steps and then continues pretty much on the level to cross the Río Traidor, 20 minutes further on. After another 20 minutes it drops through a deep trench to a scrubby clearing in a great bowl of mountains (up to 1,833m), and reaches another clearing after another 5 minutes, where the wide Valverde valley suddenly opens up to the left. Forking right, you will have to ford the knee-deep river and head to the right to a gate into a meadow with a hut, about an hour from the La Junta camp. After another 15 minutes you will hear the Saltos del Cochamó to the right. The track climbs in a muddy trench and in 10 minutes reaches a clearing with a hut marked 'Sixto Rojas km22.175', below a rock face that offers great climbing, at the mouth of the Arco valley (371m). Passing a gate, a log bridge over a small gorge, a field with two padlocked huts, and two more bridged gorges, the track reaches another field in 10 minutes. Bizarrely, there is a young araucaria planted in the middle of this field. There are waterfalls just to the right, with whirlpools carved in the pink granite by trapped rocks; it is possible to reach them next to a tall burnt-out tree. This is the Río Botapiedra (aptly named 'stone thrower'), which joins the Río Arco just below to form the Río Cochamó.

I camped here (there *is* a patch of level ground) and returned the same way, but it is possible to carry on for a couple of days past El Arco (where there are hundreds of alerce, up to 4,000 years old) and over a 1,450m pass to Lago Vidal Gormaz (587m) and the Río Manso. From here one one route heads up the Manso to the Paso León (or Cochamó) and down into Argentina, to Villegas on the Bariloche–El Bolsón road. The other option is to head south, down the Manso, to the Río Puelo, and return via Lago Tagua-Tagua (where the ferry can carry horses as well as hikers) to Puelo, on the road south of Cochamó. Campo Aventura offers riding trips along these routes, taking up to 2 weeks.

THE PUELO VALLEY

The Puelo Valley is wider and more populated than the Cochamó, and a road is being built along it, to take advantage of the virtually snow-free pass (225m) into Argentina. Nevertheless it, too, makes an interesting backcountry route, now being opened up by trekking, fishing and horse-riding outfits.

Buses from Puerto Montt (via Puerto Varas, Ensenada and Cochamó) terminate on the north shore of the Río Puelo, opposite the village of **Puelo** at its mouth. A bridge should be open by the end of 2001, but until then a ferry takes you across. A rough track (being upgraded for cars) continues west along the Reloncaví estuary to the Carretera Austral at Puelche. A road runs along the left/south bank of the river, reaching Las Gualas at the western end of **Lago Tagua-Tagua** (43m) in about 3 hours hiking. Just beyond the village is a jetty, from where a ferry sails along the lake to Punto Arena in another hour. You need to make a relatively early start, as by the afternoon it is often too windy to use boats on the lake. There is no regular schedule, so you may have to wait around; if you want collecting by boat on a certain day, the procedure is to have a message transmitted on the local Radio Reloncaví, although this will probably all change when the road and bridges are in place on either side of the lake. It is a two-hour walk along the east/right bank to the mouth of the Río Manso (crossed by boat, although a bridge is being built), which it is possible to follow north to the Cochamó valley (see above). Continuing southeast along the Puelo, past Santo Domingo, it takes 8 hours to reach Llanada Grande, a settlement with a police post and airstrip. A rough road will be completed between Punto Arena and Llanada Grande in 2001; eventually this will be extended to Lago Puelo in Argentina.

From Llanada Grande there are two routes onwards. Start by climbing slightly to the left to pass (through Valdivian rainforest of alerce, coihue and arrayán) along the west sides of Lago Totoral and Lago Azul (4–5 hours). At the sign for a satellite phone (unreliable and expensive – take plenty of coins) you can turn left to climb to the east side of Lago de las Rocas (4 hours; around 300m), before rejoining the river at El Retén (2 hours). Sticking to the main trail at the satellite phone sign, you will reach Lago Las Rocas after an hour, at La Colina farm, the base-camp of OpenTravel Andes Patagonicos. The path crosses the Río Cataratas by a bridge and follows the lake's western shore for an hour to Isla Las Bandurrias, where OpenTravel has its mountain lodge (a cozy cottage). From here you can take a track to the left to El Retén (3½ hours), or go straight on to the hand-powered ferry across to Segundo Corral at the western end of Lago Inferior (195m), where there is also an airstrip. Following the lake's northern shore east from the ferry you can reach El Retén in three hours.

El Retén is the *carabineros* post, where you should show your passport if proceeding to Argentina. A trail runs along the north shore of the lake as a forest of ciprés de la cordillera gives way to *pampa*, to reach the Los Hitos ('Border

Markers') rapids, where water from the Argentine Lago Puelo drops 10m to Lago Inferior, after 5 hours. It is another 2 hours' walk along the north shore of Lago Puelo to reach the Argentinian *gendarmería*, and another 3 hours to the footbridge over the Río Azul, from where a road leads 15km north to El Bolsón (see page 299). The five-star Río Puelo Lodge on Lago Tagua-Tagua has closed and reopened, but more sustainable projects are being developed, such as the Isla Las Bandurrias Mountain Lodge and nearby base-camp of OpenTravel Andes Patagonicos (PO Box 1010, Puerto Montt; tel: 065 260 524; opentravel@telsur.cl; www.opentravel. com.ar), the leading operators for hiking or horseback trips along the Río Puelo. There are also various fly-fishing outfitters in the area.

PUERTO VARAS TO PUERTO MONTT

In previous editions of this guide we described a hike down the old road from Puerto Varas to Puerto Montt via Alerce; this route is now too built-up to be a pleasant hike, while the parallel stretch of the PanAmerican itself is now a dual-carriageway. Therefore cyclists may find the old road a useful alternative, but hikers may prefer to use the railway, now more or less totally disused (steam specials run once or twice each summer). Cyclists should note that the Alerce road, which starts by the Port Captain's office at Puerto Chico, 2km southeast of Puerto Varas, is signposted from the far side but not from the northwest; however, there is a clear sign a short distance south on the Alerce road.

The railway hike (19km long, taking 4–5 hours) starts at the level (grade) crossing on Salvador, the main road northwest out of Puerto Varas, just 3 minutes from the supermarket at Salvador and San Bernardo. Turning left here, 1,047.5km from Santiago, the line can also be accessed from Calles Augusta Schwerter and García Moreno, before it crosses above the main road to Puerto Montt, curves right and rises gently through the fields. At km1053.5, just beyond a level crossing, it reaches its summit (130m) about 1¼ hours from the start. From here there is a long straight stretch, heading almost directly for Volcán Yate, across a heath covered in gorse which is beginning to invade the track, although it is not spiky and is easy enough to pass. Walking on rail sleepers (ties) can, of course, be awkward if the ballast has washed out (giving one 'the gait of a man who could not remember which leg had been amputated', as Nick Crane puts it), but generally this route is in a good state.

After 20 minutes the line curves right and continues over slightly boggier heathland to reach a level crossing at the north end of Alerce in 45 minutes. The rail line bypasses the village to its west side, crossing a bridge to reach the station (km1059.5) in 10 minutes. It crosses a higher bridge, at a popular bathing place, after 15 minutes and again heads out across a great empty space, rising slightly to another summit of 112m. At km1066.5, an hour and a quarter from the bridge, it reaches the new La Paloma station built to replace the one in the centre of Puerto Montt, the line ahead having been blocked by a landslide. Sadly, once the track was laid, it was decided that due to financial constraints passenger trains would not run south of Temuco. You should turn right on to the road here, at the southern end of Puerto Montt's old airport, as the railway takes an immense loop to the east to make its way down to sea level. However, part of it can be walked on the way east to the Alerce Andino park (see overleaf).

Buses from Alerce pass every 10 minutes or so, or it is just a couple of minutes to the asphalt and the first houses, and a couple more to a crossroads where you can pick up a *colectivo* (12, 21, 25, 28) into Puerto Montt.

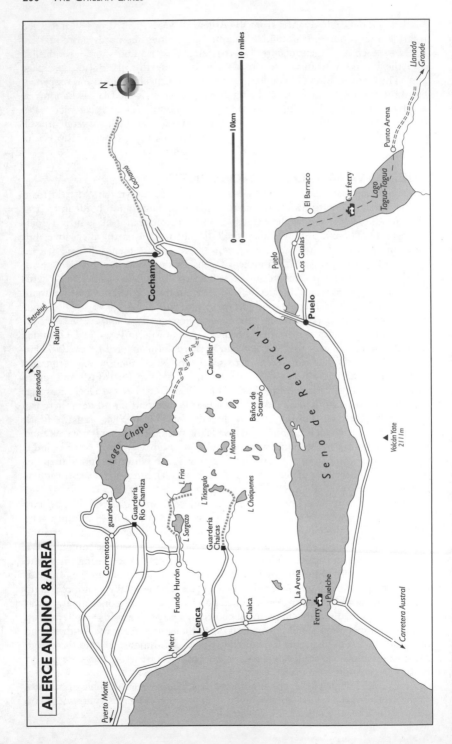

ALERCE ANDINO & AREA

ALERCE ANDINO NATIONAL PARK

Altitude	Sea level to 530m
Rating	Easy
Time	I day
Start of trail	Southern entry to the park from Lenca
End of trail	Southern entry to the park from Lenca
Maps	1:50,000 4115-7230 (H52) (Correntoso) and 4130-7230 (H61) (Lenca)

Given its proximity to Puerto Montt, it is remarkable that this fairly small park (39,255ha) has managed to preserve so many alerce trees, and equally that so few people visit it. It is very hilly, although the maximum altitude is just 1,558m, and it receives plenty of precipitation, up to 4,500mm a year in places, producing forest with a very dense understorey of bamboo and other plants, with over 50 lakes. Half of its area, above 400m, is alerce forest, though not of course uninterrupted alerce trees, but mixed with coihue de Chiloé, tineo, mañío and canelo. From sea level to 900m there is an evergreen forest of tepa, coihue and ulmo, with a tangle of vines, ferns and quila bamboo below. Above this level there is also coihue de Magallanes, especially on the summits, and lenga, stunted at higher levels. Mammals found here include pudú, puma, Chilean forest cat, grey fox, skunk, vizcacha, and monito del monte; birds include condor, woodpecker, huet-huet, chucao, kingfisher, ducks, geese and doves. Fish include the native peladilla and percatrucha, as well as introduced trout.

Getting to the trailheads

There are three access points, but it is now impossible to get from any one to another. The north-south route has been allowed to go wild in its central section, and there has never been a hiking route to the eastern entrance. There are a couple of camping sites and simple refuges, but with such short hiking routes it is quite possible to make a day-trip from Puerto Montt. Perhaps the most popular entrance is to the north, at Río Chamiza, 3km from Correntoso, a village (at 154m) reached by Buses Fierro twice a day from Puerto Montt. Turning off the coast road at km10 (where the asphalt ends at Chamiza, once the base for flying boats to Punta Arenas), it is about 21km to Correntoso, where you should go past the police post, following signs to the National Park on a good gravel road. The road crosses the Río Chamiza at the Puente Cascada, 2km south, with a waterfall to the left, and swings right to the *guardería*; the Pangal campsite is 200m further. The path into the park from here is closed, so you will have to continue 10km (keeping left after 1.5km) along the road to the Sargazo *guardería* (open 09.00–18.00), where you will pay US$2. From here you will have to hike, on an abandoned road, with signs still in place.

Turning right (ie: back to the west) before the Sargazo gate, you will come to Fundo Hurón and the new Alerce Mountain Lodge (tel: 065 286 969; smontt@telsur.cl; www.telsur.cl/alerce) in the private Parque Los Alerces de Lenca. This is luxury ecotourism, with all meals and outings included in the cost.

The southern entry is from Lenca, almost 40km from Puerto Montt on the Carretera Austral, reached by Fierro buses for Chaica at 07.30, 12.00, 12.45, 16.30, or 17.30 (09.00 and 16.00 on Sundays), or for Río Negro (Hornopirén) at 08.00

(except Sunday) and 15.00. There are also *colectivos* at least every 15 minutes to Chamiza (junction to Correntoso), and a dozen a day to Piedra Azul, from where you can hitch. The road runs along the coast, through small villages with Chilote-style wood-shingled churches and edible seaweed drying on net frames, such as Piedra Azul (where there really is a blue-painted rock), Quillaipe, and Metri. **Metri**, 31km from Puerto Montt, has a particularly lovely cove, with an *hospedaje* and camping at its eastern end and a modern, but traditionally-styled, church at its western end, as well as a maritime research station.

The turning to the park is immediately beyond the Lenca sawmill, 37km from Puerto Montt, joining a fairly small gravel track heading into the hills. You should fork right after 7 minutes and again after another 20 minutes. The track climbs gradually up the valley, passing farms and fields, and finally entering native forest almost an hour after the second junction. It is just 5 minutes more to the park gate, at km7.15, where you will have to pay US$2. The road on is closed to traffic, although the road signs are still in place, warning you of the narrow bends.

If you have time, and the inclination, it is also possible to walk along a section of the old railway, through green rolling countryside that seems to have been transplanted from England's West Country. *Colectivos* 4 and 9 terminate at a level (grade) crossing in Pelluco, a suburb (known for its seafood restaurants) just east of Puerto Montt. From here you can walk east for 35 minutes to the next level crossing, where you can hitch or catch a bus on to Lenca. The railway is lined with blackberries, foxgloves, gorse and sycamore, all of course introduced species, and runs near the coast through very Celtic hillocks.

The third entry point is to the east; three Fierro buses a day run from Puerto Montt and Puerto Varas to Canutillar (where there are *cabañas*), opposite Cochamó on the Seno de Reloncavi. A dirt road from just north of the village (92km from Puerto Varas) leads 20km up to the east end of Lago Chapo (240m), now used for hydroelectric power and fish farming. There are great views of sheer cliffs and glaciers, but it is not possible to hike into the park from here.

Route descriptions

From the southern (Río Chaica gate) it takes 30 minutes to reach the Los Chucaos picnic area and campsite, where there is another barrier across the road. This time they really mean it, as 5 minutes further on the road is washed out, although there is a good footbridge over the gap. Just a couple of minutes further on is the start of a loop path to the right to the falls of the Río Chaica, which leads through good gallery forest for 10 minutes to a viewing platform at the impressive falls. From here it is just a couple of minutes back to the track (signed 'Alerce', and indeed there is a tall alerce tree towards the falls), so if you are carrying heavy packs it is easier to hike up the trail to this point and leave your packs here while you view the falls. Continuing uphill, the trail passes some immense nalcas (the local version of rhubarb), crosses a bridge and climbs more steeply before dropping slightly to Lago Chaiquenes (256m, 5.5km from the gate) after 25 minutes.

There is a fine, wooden platform (built by Raleigh International in 1986) with bathing steps jutting over the lake, but otherwise the vegetation is too dense to let you see much of the shoreline. The track ends here but a path turns sharp left and climbs straight up and then down to a new boathouse. From there it follows a valley inland, crosses a single-log bridge and climbs steeply through humid forest. The trail is muddy and rough, involving a lot of clambering over roots and under branches and fallen trunks. You should get to Laguna Triangulo (530m) in 50 minutes to an hour. Again it is impossible to get to the shore without clambering out along branches, unless the water is particularly low, though it is worth trying to get a good view of the great cliffs all around. The path onwards can be followed for a short distance, but it has been totally buried in bamboo over the last few years, so you will have to return as you came.

From the northern (Sargazo) gate, it takes just five minutes to reach the first alerce (only 400 years old), reached by a boardwalk to the right, and another ten minutes to the start of a path to the left to the Rodal Alerce (Alerce Grove) and Laguna Fria (the road carrying on only to Lago Sargazo, where you can take boat trips). This is a muddy path which climbs steeply (through coihue, *Crinodendron hookerianum*, *Lomatia*, *Eucryphia*, filmy ferns, lots of bamboo, huge snails, and birds such as chucaos) to a big mañío tree; it takes another 20 minutes, up and down on slippery logs and roots, to more alerce, two minutes before a viewing platform. There is a steep climb for 25 minutes to a pass, and a steep descent through thick rainforest to a pair of log bridges, then you will go up and down with Lago Sargazo to your right, reaching the start of the loop left to the Rodal Alerce after 35 minutes. As well as alerces roughly 2,000 years old, there are also *Podocarpus* trees here. Go up carefully on the collapsed steps for five minutes, then right to a viewing platform, from where it is another five minutes back to the junction. The path continues to a refuge at the east end of Lago Sargazo, then continues east along the right bank of the Río Sargazo, crosses it by a log bridge, and (passing through more old-growth alerce) reaches Laguna Fría after 4.5km. There is a simpler refuge here, on the west shore of the lake. The path on to Laguna Triangulo (see above) is blocked by impenetrable bamboo.

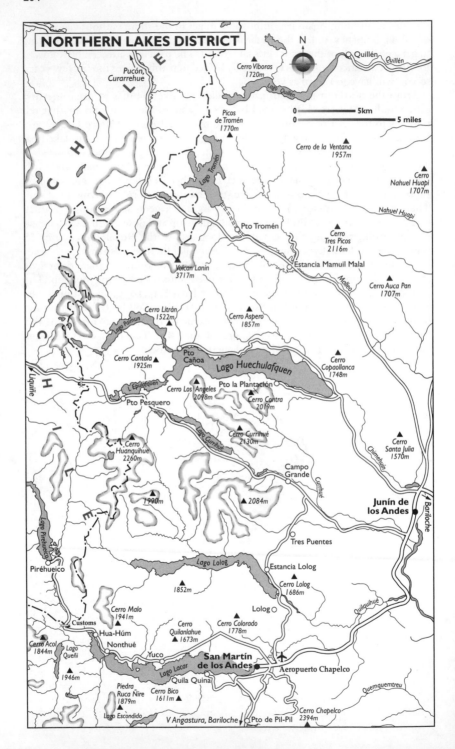

NORTHERN LAKES DISTRICT

N

0   5km
0   5 miles

CHILE

Pucón,
Curarrehue

Cerro Viboras
1720m

Quillén
Quillén

Lago Quillén

Picos
de Tromén
1770m

Cerro de la Ventana
1957m

Cerro
Nahuel Huapi
1707m

Nahuel Huapi

Lago Tromén

Pto Tromén

Cerro
Tres Picos
2116m

Estancia Mamuil Malal

Molleo

Cerro Auca Pan
1707m

Volcan Lanín
3717m

Cerro Litrán
1522m

Lago Pulmun

Cerro Aspero
1857m

Cerro Cantala
1925m

Pto
Cañoa

Lago Huechulafquen

Cerro
Copaollanca
1748m

Liquiñe

L. Epulafquen

Pto Pesquero

Cerro Los Angeles
2098m

Pto la Plantactón

Cerro Contra
2019m

Cerro Currihué
2130m

Lago Currihué

Cerro
Santa Julia
1570m

Chimehuin

Cerro
Huanquihue
2260m

Campo
Grande

Currhué

1990m

▲2084m

Junín de
los Andes

Bariloche

Lago Pirehueico

Tres Puentes

Piréhueico

Lago Lolog

Estancia Lolog

1852m

Cerro Lolog
1686m

Quiluihué

Cerro Malo
1941m

Lolog

Customs

Hua-Húm

Cerro
Quilanlahue
1673m

Cerro Colorado
1778m

Cerro Acol
1844m

Lago
Queñi

Nonthué

Yuco

San Martín
de los Andes

Aeropuerto Chapelco

Quemquemtreu

1946m

Lago Lacar

Quila Quina

Piedra
Ruca Ñire
1879m

Cerro Bico
1611m ▲

Lago Escondido

V Angastura, Bariloche

Pto de Pil-Pil

Cerro Chapelco
2394m

The Argentine Lakes

The Argentine Lakes lie at considerably higher altitudes than those in Chile, producing a colder, starker kind of beauty. There are far fewer volcanoes, but otherwise there is a similar mix of lakes, waterfalls, forests and ski resorts. The district falls naturally into two halves, centred on San Martín de los Andes (gateway to the Lanín National Park) and Bariloche (gateway to the Nahuel Huapi National Park). Between them lies a chain of lakes linked by a scenic road known as the *Ruta de los Siete Lagos*; this is very popular with campers and fishermen, and there are several sites for *camping agreste* (fields for camping with a charge of just US$2 for minimal facilities – tap and outhouse).

SAN MARTÍN DE LOS ANDES

Rapidly becoming an Argentine version of Pucón, with adventure tour companies outnumbered only by trendy bars, this town and the surrounding area are still far less developed and less crowded than the Bariloche area, and it is an excellent base (at 570m altitude) for some relatively little-used trails.

Most **accommodation** is pricey, but there is an official HI youth hostel, the Hostel Puma, Fosberry 535 (tel: 02972 422 443; puma@smandes.com.ar), and a couple of summer-only places for which you will need your own sleeping bag, the Hospedaje Caritas, next to the church, and the Posada del Caminante, Caballeria 1164 (tel: 427 431). **Camping** may be a better bet, at the ACA site a couple of kilometres northeast at the exit to Junín de los Andes (served by city buses), or just west, at the Catritre or Quila Quina beaches on the south side of Lago Lacar (reached by buses in summer, hourly to Catritre and at 09.30, 14.00 and 18.45 to Quila Quina).

There are also **boat trips** to Quila Quina (up to six per day; US$10 return), which is in a Mapuche reservation; once there you can take the 800m El Cipresal interpretative path by the mouth of the Arroyo Grande, or a 500m path to the rapids of the Arroyo Grande. There is also a *guardería* and *camping agreste* (US$2) at Puerto Arturo, on Lago Lolog – buses leave San Martín at 09.30, 11.30, 15.00, and 18.30, returning between 10.30 and 20.00.

The **bus terminal** is near the lake at Villegas 251, and **tourist information** is available at Rosas 790, on the central one of the town's three plazas. The Banco Provincial de Neuquén at Belgrano and Obeld has an **ATM**, and there are plenty of laundries around town. Pura Vida, at Villegas 745, is a good vegetarian restaurant. One **supermarket** is at San Martín 779, opposite the tourism office, another on the 900 block of Villegas, and another just before the ACA campsite. There is a range of **camping shops**, mostly conveniently placed along San Martín.

Flights (with Austral, Dinar and Southern Winds) from Buenos Aires use the Chapelco Airport, midway between San Martín and Junín; buses between the two towns will drop passengers about 200m from the terminal. **Buses** serve Neuquén, Buenos Aires, and Bariloche, with services using the *Ruta de los Siete Lagos* in season. International buses head for Pucón and Temuco at 06.00 except on Sundays, running via Junín and the Tromén pass immediately to the north of Volcán Lanín. An alternative route is by bus (Mon–Sat 09.00) via Huahúm, at the west end of Lago Lacar, to Pirehueico, in Chile, for a boat to Puerto Fuy and then buses to Choshuenco and Panguipulli (see page 185). There is also a boat at 10.00 daily to Hua-Hum (Navigación Lago Lacar; tel: 02972 427 380; US$35 return) including a walk from Puerto Chachín to the 35-metre Cascada Chachín, through dense Valdivian forest with ferns up to two metres long and 90cm broad.

Rafting trips are available on the Ríos Hua Hum, Aluminé and Meliquina, for between US$30 (half-day) and US$70 (full day); riding, gliding, four-wheel drives, hikes (up Cerro Mallo, Cerro Chachín, and Volcán Lanín), and fishing are also available. Ask at El Claro Turismo, Villegas 977 (tel: 02972 428 876), Tiempo Patagónico, San Martín 950 (tel: 425 125; fax: 427 113; tiempopatagonico@usa.net); or Ici Viajes, on Villegas at M Moreno.

To **climb** Volcán Lanín (US$310 for a week's package) contact Tromen Aventura (tel: 02972 491 498, or in Buenos Aires 011 4287 0256); Lanín Trekking (tel: 011 491 637; treklanin@usa.com), or guides such as Gerardo Burgos (tel: 02972 422 190) or Iván Weihmüller (tel: 068 308 515).

It is also worth mentioning San Martín's far quieter twin town of **Junín de los Andes**, 41km to the northeast at 780m altitude; the trout-shaped road signs indicate its main line of business. Even if you are not interested in dangling hooks in rivers, you will have to come here if you want to take a bus to Paimún, on Lago Huechulafquen; the San Martín–Temuco buses also pass through, and you can catch them here at a more civilised time of day, an hour after departure from San Martín. There are very cheap campsites without facilities. The tourist information centre (which includes a Lanín National Park office) is on the plaza (at Suárez and Milanesio, open daily to 21.00). CEAN (*Centro de Ecología Aplicada al Neuquén*) is 8km northwest; it sounds grand, and is a very popular day-trip, but is basically a fish-farm with picnic sites.

Cerro Chapelco

If you happen to be in San Martín de los Andes, do not miss the hike up to Cerro Chapelco. It is an easy 4-hour walk, so you could do the trip there and back in a day. Chapelco is Argentina's second-biggest ski centre (after Cerro Catedral) with restaurants, ski shop, chair-lifts and ski tows – see www.chapelco.com.ar. It is also developing *El Parque de la Aventura*, virtually a theme park, open December–March; in addition to hobbits (the Tolkien variety), huskies, and trips by horses and four-wheel-drive vehicles, you will also find Argentina's first Centro Nacional de Mountain Bike.

The 15km trail climbs through lenga forest from 625m at San Martín to 1,225m at the foot of the ski slopes, from where you can hike or take a chair-lift up to Antulauquen (1,600m) or Silla del Mallín (1,980m, on the ridge). From these points you will have a panoramic view of the *cordillera*, including the snow-capped Volcán Lanín to the north and Lago Lacar spread out far below. Once on the ridge you can walk to the right/south to the summit of Cerro Chapelco (2,394m). A variety of routes, between 4km and 11km in length, take you back down. On

Thursdays a guided hike goes down the far, east, side of the ridge to Laguna Verde (1,100m).

The trail starts at the south end of Calle Misionero Mascardi, five blocks east of the main plaza in San Martín, and one block east of the secondary Plaza Sarmiento. Rough steps lead steeply up to a paved road in 5 minutes. Turn left and skirt the Hotel Sol de los Andes to a fork 200m above the hotel, where the asphalt ends. The road to the right is a back road to Cerro Chapelco (by car you should take the main Bariloche road and turn left) and the road to the left (Calle F F de Amador) winds down to the Junín highway. The Chapelco trail leads straight on from the junction. Zig-zagging at first, it soon curves to the right and straightens out before meeting the road again at a sharp bend. From here you have a choice of walking up the road or following the variety of trails which run parallel to it. The trails are steeper but infinitely more pleasant; take any which leaves the road to the right. You will find they all take you in the same direction, dividing and joining up again and intersecting the road at intervals as it winds its way up.

For those who are not in a hurry, camping is possible all along the way, and the restaurants at the ski centre are surprisingly cheap. There are also buses to Chapelco, currently at 12.00 and 16.00 in summer, returning at 15.00 and 18.00. A lift pass costs US$12 for the day, while a *pasaporte* for all activities costs US$25 (US$38 for 2 days).

LANÍN NATIONAL PARK

Protecting a long strip of the Andes along the border north of the Nahuel Huapi Park (and adjoining Chile's Villarrica Park), the **Lanín National Park** protects its namesake volcano and a whole series of parallel lakes. Created in 1937, the park covers 379,000ha, up to 3,776m in altitude, mostly with a temperate-cold humid climate. Most of Argentina's Mapuches live in reservations along the northern edges of the park. Scenically it is wonderful, and other than a few hotspots it is very uncrowded; but it is also ecologically important as the only place in Argentina where forests of raulí (*Nothofagus alpina*) and roble pellín (*N. obliqua*) can be found, as well as substantial areas of araucaria forest. The northern zone, from Lago Ñorquinco to Lago Tromen, is dominated by araucaria, with lenga, ñirre and colihue bamboo; the central zone, with over 1.5m of precipitation annually, is home to the Valdivian forest of coihue and an understorey of caña colihue, michay, and espino negro, and woods of raulí and roble pellín to the north and southwest; to the south is a transition from forest (ciprés de la cordillera, maitén, radal) to steppe, with plenty of birds. Wildlife is mostly that associated with Valdivian forests in Chile, with puma, guiña, huillín, chinchillón, coipo, monito de monte, foxes, pudú and huemul, as well as introduced game such as red deer. Birds include the chucao, huet-huet, fiofío, rayadito, Magellanic and robust woodpeckers, araucanian dove, torrent and spectacled ducks, grebes, coots, peregrine falcon, red-backed hawk and eagle, and above 1,600m the condor.

Entrance to the park is free except for the road along the north side of Lago Huechulafquen. The *Intendencia* is at Frey 749, on the west side of the central plaza of San Martín (open Mon–Fri 08.00–13.00), and information is also available in the tourist office in Junín.

Volcan Lanín (3,776m) is one of the easiest and safest ascents to high altitude in this part of the world, or perhaps it is one of the highest summits that is also safe and easy to climb, depending how you look at it. It is usually tackled from the north side, starting at the Tromen *guardería* on the international highway, but it can

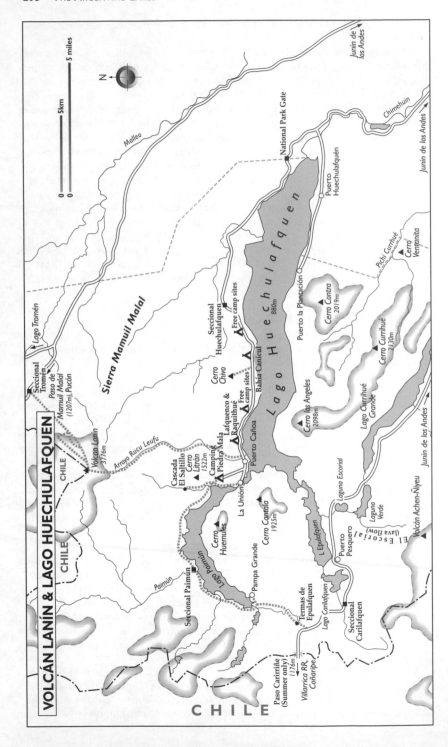

VOLCÁN LANÍN & LAGO HUECHULAFQUEN

5 miles
5km

Junín de los Andes

Malleo

National Park Gate

Chimehuin

Junín de los Andes

Puerto Huechulafquén

Lago Tromén

Seccional Tromén

Paso de Mamuil Malal (1207m), Pucón

Sierra Mamuil Malal

Lago Huechulafquen 880m

Seccional Huechulafquen

Free camp sites

Pichi Currihué

Cerro Ventanita

Cerro Contra 2019m

Puerto la Plantación

Volcán Lanín 3776m

CHILE

CHILE

Arroyo Rucu Leufu

Cerro Chivo

Bahía Cañicul

Free camp sites

Lafquenco & Raquithué

Cerro Currihué 2130m

Cerro los Angeles 2098m

Lago Currihué Grande

CHILE

Cascada El Saltillo

Cerro Litrán 1522m

Camping Piedra Mala

Puerto Cañoa

Puerto Pesquero

Laguna Escorial

Junín de los Andes

La Unión

Cerro Cantala 1925m

El Escorial (lava flow)

Laguna Verde

Volcán Achen-Ñiyeu

Cerro Huemules

L Epulafquen

Paimún

Seccional Paimún

Lago Paimún

Pampa Grande

Termas de Epulafquen

Lago Carilafquen

Seccional Carilafquen

Paso Cariririñe (Summer only) 1176m

Villarrica RR, Coñaripe

CHILE

also be climbed from the south. If you satisfy the rangers that you are properly equipped, there is no problem climbing it alone, in good weather; otherwise trips can be arranged by adventure tourism companies in San Martín (see above). You will need crampons, an ice-axe, a stove, and a sleeping bag, and all provisions should be bought in San Martín or Junín. Above the Arroyo Turbio, water is available only at the huts.

Turning left/west off the Aluminé road 23km north of Junín, the road follows the Río Malleo, reaching the *seccional* (ranger-post) about an hour from Junín, surrounded by araucarias at 1,140m. The Argentine border post is another 2km west, but most bus drivers will drop you at the *seccional*. There are also paths north to Lago Tromen (4km each way) and west to the border (3km each way), through fine araucarias.

Having signed in, follow the signed track south through lenga for about half an hour to the end of the vehicular track, and then take the path across the Arroyo Turbio and on up an obvious moraine ridge known as the *espina de pescado* ('fish spine'). About an hour from the Arroyo Turbio you will come to a junction; the *espina de pescado* continues to the left and forms the *ruta normal* up the north side of the volcano, steep but direct and easy to follow. To the right is a more easily graded track known as the *camino de mulas*, and to the left off this almost at once is a third path known as the *canaleta*, which is recommended only for descending or in very windy conditions. Sticking to the *espina de pescado*, you will reach the Refugio CAJA (Club Andino Junín de los Andes) in 4–5 hours, it takes 5–7 hours by the *camino de mulas*. On the *espina* you will first pass the Refugio RIM (Regimiento de Infantería de Montaña 26) at about 2,400m, reaching the smaller CAJA hut, at 2,600m, 30 minutes later.

From here you should start at dawn, keeping to the right on snow for the first 2 hours, then moving 50m to the right around a rock about 3m high. In summer you should be able to continue without crampons, reaching the summit about 5–7 hours after leaving the hut. You can descend to the *seccional* in 5 hours.

The alternative route to Volcan Lanín is from **Lago Huechulafquen**, to the south, which is the most popular part of the park for camping and general recreation. It is definitely not a wilderness experience, but makes a very pleasant break, even if you do not climb the volcano.

Buses leave Junín for Paimún at 08.45 and 16.00 daily, returning at 11.00 and 18.30. From the junction by the army barracks 4km north of Junín it is 54km to Paimún. It is then 22km (half an hour by bus) to the east end of the lake, at about 880m, with the first wild araucarias, and the park gate, where you have to pay US$5. The road climbs away from the lake and descends to the Huechulafquen *seccional* and the La Tapera and El Vado free campsites and then the Bahía Cañicul organised campsite, which has a shop, laundry, restaurant/tea room and boats for hire. From here you can follow a path through coihue and colihue to the summit of Cerro Chivo (3 hours up, 2 down). The bus continues past the free campsites of La Mesada, Los Coihues, Arroyo Tinticas, El Manzano and Ferri-Corral, close together along one strip of shore opposite the castle-like mountain of Cerro Los Angeles. The organised Lafquenco and Raquithué campsites have shops and showers, and some indigenous homes sell *empanadas*. There is a gap of 2km before the Hostería Huechulafquen, the Arroyo Rucu Leufu, and the Puerto Cañoa *seccional*. Just before this a road turns left to the port (for catamaran excursions), where there is also a café and picnic area, and the El Bosque path, a loop through good woodland with information boards aimed at children. The path up Volcán

Lanín starts 50m beyond the *seccional*, from where it takes 6–7 hours to the Refugio de la Pared Sur (2,300m).

Three minutes' walk further west is the turning to the Hostería Refugio del Pescador, and another 3 minutes' walk on the road splits. To the left it leads 2km to a *gendarmería* at La Unión (the narrows to Lago Paimún) and the Ecufue *camping agreste*. The road to the right ends after 4km at the Camping Piedra Mala. The bus goes to La Unión then returns, taking the Piedra Mala road but turning left and terminating at a few houses; from here you can go through a gate and through a free campsite to rejoin the road (although you will have to climb the fence). From the campsite gate there is a short walk to the Cascada El Saltillo, following the campsite fence and turning right after 5 minutes up an obvious track from the campsite. Turning left after a couple of minutes (following yellow paint markings) and passing through a gate marked, in Spanish, 'Pass and Close' (none of your sensible Chilean gravity-operated gates here), a path continues west along Lago Paimún, reaching the *seccional* in 3 hours (about 7km).

From here it is possible to continue around the western end of the lake and south to the Termas de Epulafquen, 64km from Junín on the road to the summer-only border crossing of Paso Caririñe (1,176m), which is a great mountain bike route. Heading eastwards on the road, you will first come to Lago Carilafquen, where there is a *seccional*, then pass the south side of Lago Epulafquen (an arm of Lago Huechulafquen), and cross El Escorial, a frozen lava flow 7.5km long and up to 2.5km wide. This flowed north about 500 years ago from Volcán Achen Ñiyeu, which can be climbed from Laguna Verde, just east, giving great views of Volcán Lanín.

LAGO QUEÑI THERMAL SPRINGS
Rick Ansell

One of the best hot baths in Argentina! Take the daily excursion boat across Lago Lacar from San Martín to Hua Hum (see above), or the bus at 09.00 (except Sundays). This runs along the north shore of Lago Lacar, passing Yuco (campsite and path to two *lagunas*) and Nonthué (campsite and path up Cerro Malo, 1,941m).

From Hua Hum (*hostería* and *camping agreste*) cross the outlet river on the bridge and follow this dirt road up into the woods, past the *guardaparque*'s house. Ignore the several paths and tracks and after 30 minutes take a road to the south marked 'Cascada' and 'Lago Queñi'. It climbs very gently through the forest, past a farm. After a while the road to Cascada Chachín and Pucará forks to the left. It is about 45 minutes return to the falls, and it is possible to take this road and then hike to the south of Lago Lacar all the way to Quila Quina via Lago Escondido, but for the hot springs you should keep to the right here. You will, almost without noticing, cross the pass and start to descend slightly. The road crosses the Estero Acol on a wooden bridge and continues to Lago Queñi. About 2½ hours (12km) from Hua Hum you come to another *guardaparque*'s house. For the spring, continue along the road for about 500m, when the road fords a wide, shallow river. Immediately afterwards a smaller track marked *Termas* turns left. This path was the most beautiful forest path that we followed, wide, clear and dry, through open forest and bamboo. Five minutes beyond the turning you can camp on the shore of the lake – perfect. An hour and a half (4km) will bring you to a steaming stream, crossing the path. The spring itself is about 20m uphill from the path. You can continue via Lago Venados to reach Lago Lacar again at Pucará (about 3 hours), but we returned the way we had come.

A HIKE IN THE NORTHERN LAKES
John Pilkington

Distance	80km
Altitude	Between 977m and 1,550m
Rating	Difficult
Time	3–5 days
Start of trail	Quillén (entrance to Lanín National Park)
End of trail	Moquehué (Lago Moquehué)
Maps	Argentine IGM 1:100,000 Sheets 3972-29 (Quillén) 3972-23 (Lago Ñorquincó) and 3972-17 (Lago Aluminé) are adequate as long as you do not take them too literally. Crude regional maps are available free from the Dirección Provincial de Turismo in Zapala or Junín.

This walk takes you past some of the remotest and arguably finest lakes in Argentina's northern Lakes District. You will catch tantalising glimpses of the Lanín and Llaima volcanoes as you pass through forests of giant lenga and araucaria (monkey-puzzle) trees. These provide a home to interesting wildfowl and introduced European game animals such as ciervo (red deer) and jabalí (wild boar). You will walk through upland *pampas* where *gauchos* bring their horses, sheep and cattle to graze on the long summer grass. The only other humans are a few *guardaparques* and frontier guards at the *gendarmerías*. Otherwise you will probably have the place to yourself.

The walk, although not long (80km at most), is tough and not to be taken lightly. The trail varies from clear to elusive to non existent, and a compass is vital. Although the hike can be done in 3 days, some of the spots are so good that you will want to linger, and you should take supplies for 5 days or more, since there are none en route. Check in with the *guardaparque* and frontier guards at each lake; apart from being interesting people who can tell you a lot about the wildlife, trail conditions, weather, etc, they are linked by radio and can send a search party if you miss a rendezvous.

Since the lakes are separated by rows of mountains, the hike inevitably involves a lot of up and down. But from the ridges you will see some of the extraordinary highlights of the northern Lakes District: aerial views of the lakes packed in between steep wedges of the Andes; the peaks of the Catan-Lil range (older than the Andes) on the eastern horizon which look as if they are straight out of *The Lord of the Rings*; the strange, vertical outcrops of Cerro Iglesias and the 'Giant's Causeway'; and of course those perfectly shaped volcanoes. The highest point on the walk, at the top of the first pass, is less than 2,000m – mild stuff if you have just come from Peru or Bolivia – but a steep climb all the same. The other passes are both about 1,500m and much easier.

Campsites abound, both by the lakes and in the upland *pampas*. There are also a number of unoccupied rough shelters where you can spend the night. All along the trail there is fresh, clean water and plenty of dead wood for making campfires. You will also see a common lichen which is making dinner of most of the region's timber. You would be doing the trees a favour if you harvested this useless and destructive mould for use as bedding, kindling or toilet paper (admittedly a bit scratchy in the last function).

Like all the hikes in the Lakes District, this is best done in summer (December–March). It is passable in November and April, but the rest of the year is blocked by snow. Provisions can be bought in Zapala or Junín, but tend to be limited and expensive. You can get any last minute odds and ends at the general store in Quillén. It is essential to take a compass.

Getting to the trailhead

The walk starts at Quillén, an entrance to the Lanín National Park. If coming from Zapala, head southwest to Aluminé; on the way you will pass the **Parque Nacional Laguna Blanca**, 15km north of the highway in bleak, eerie desert country. It is important due to the large numbers of birds such as black-necked swans which come to the 1,700ha lake to breed in summer. There are also flamingos, ducks, grebes, peregrine falcons and vizcachas. An endemic frog was thought to be extinct after the illegal introduction of trout and perch which eat it; in fact the frog survives, but only in a few pools. No buses follow this route, but hitch-hiking should be feasible. From Aluminé, head south for 17km to the junction settlement of Rahué, and then 27km west to Quillén on Ruta 46.

If coming from the south, take the main San Martín–Zapala road and turn off 4km north of Junín de los Andes (just after the bridge over the Río Chimehuín) along the road to Rahué and Aluminé. Hitch-hiking from the junction is fairly easy. Alternatively you can take the Empresa Petroleo bus to Rahué and Aluminé, leaving Junín only on Tuesdays at 08.45.

From the village of **Quillén** it is about 1km to the entrance to Lanín National Park and the *gendarmería*, 1km beyond which lies Lago Quillén. Shaped like a broken finger, this lake is a marvel when the sun shines, and positively satanic when it is stormy, as it often is. Straight down the first run of the lake is the pointed white wizard's hat of Volcán Lanín which, flanked by more humble ridges on either side of the lake, makes a magician's court presiding over the magic, transparent table of the lake.

On the south side, above its first knuckle, is a rock formation sitting on a peak, the stones bent so as to resemble a tiny troll sitting on his master's cap watching the mystical proceedings. (The rocks' ethereal qualities, however, seem to have been lost on the Mapuche who gave them the undignified name of 'Pile of Dog Shit'.) Where the road meets the lake is an excellent place for camping, sunbathing and gathering your strength for the walk ahead.

Route description

When you have had your fill of the soft life, go and see the *guardaparque* in the big house overlooking the lake. He has good maps of the area (framed, unfortunately, so you cannot take them away) and the trail starts in his back yard. For the first hour the trail is wide and unmistakable, heading first east and then north to a ranch by the Río Malalco, a tributary of the Río Quillén. Beyond the ranch it peters out for several hundred metres so, if you can, get a *gaucho* to show you where it picks up again. Otherwise, ford the river opposite the ranch and look for two side valleys ahead. The trail goes straight up the spur between the two, through thorn bushes, wild bamboo and then a forest of those amazing monkey-puzzle trees. The trail is steep, but the view which opens up behind is a good reward, especially when Volcán Lanín reappears.

Three hours beyond the ranch, near a pile of rocks, the trail suddenly levels out and for the next hour you more-or-less contour the side of the right-hand valley

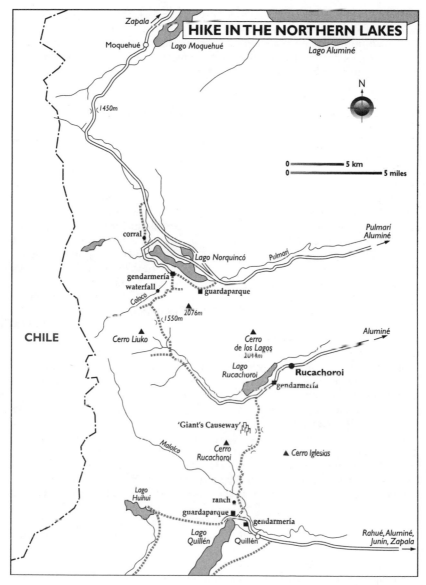

to the cirque at its head. There is good camping here, with plenty of flat grassy spots and splashing, ice-cold streams.

The trail leaves the cirque on its eastern side, at right angles to the way you came in, just right of a large area of scrub. It soon becomes faint again, but the pass is clear enough – just keep heading due east until you reach it. The top is a place to rest and admire, for not only are the snows of Cerro Rucachoroi and Volcán Lanín still in full view behind, but the spires of Cerro Iglesias and the whole of the Catan-Lil range are now visible to the east. You would do well to take breath here: the way ahead becomes difficult to follow and soon disappears in a bog.

From the pass, contour the hillside to your left as far as a spur or headland, which you should reach in about 45 minutes. Now take a long, hard look at the bog ahead. Your route is through the low pass which you can see beyond, about 20° East of magnetic north, but if it has been raining recently the best way to reach it is probably to continue contouring the hillside to your left. If not, strike cheerfully across the bog and say your prayers.

At the second pass you will come across a remarkable pile of granite rocks, whose best imitation (though with inferior materials) is the Giant's Causeway in Ireland. Change course here from 20° East to 20° West and soon you will find yourself following a stream. The valley in which lies Lago Rucachoroi, your next lake, is straight ahead, although you will not see the lake for another hour. Keeping the stream to your right, follow it down through thorn bushes and a grove of monkey-puzzle trees until it veers away to the right. Then strike out on a bearing of 30° West until you see the lake. It is everyone for themselves now. Scramble down the hillside any way you can and follow the lakeside track to the *gendarmería* and *guardería* two-thirds of the way down the lake. About 2km beyond is the tiny Indian village of **Rucachoroi** (or Ruca Choroy, *ruca* being the traditional Mapuche house and *choroy* being a parakeet). There are no shops, so once you have bidden farewell to the boys in blue your best course is to the head of the lake. Here, under a small grove of trees by the lapping waters, is the nicest campsite on the hike.

From Rucachoroi the trail follows the wide valley of the Río Calfiquitra for several kilometres before climbing the 1,550m Cerro Liuko pass to reach the valley of the Río Coloco. For the first couple of hours you pass through flat *pampa*. Then, after fording the river twice in quick succession, you climb through woodland for about an hour until suddenly another wide flat *pampa* opens up ahead. Now you will need all your powers of pathfinding because traffic between Rucachoroi and Ñorquincó seems to have declined and the trail over the pass, being hardly used, is suffering from a severe case of *The Day of the Triffids*.

As soon as the *pampa* comes into view, look for a big rock with a tree on top. The main valley trail passes to the left of this rock, but your route goes to the right, fords the river and heads diagonally across the *pampa* to a point about 300m to the left of a big round boulder on top of a little hill. Where you meet the forest again you will find a clearing with lots of dead wood and a small stream. Cross the stream by the stepping stone and look for the trail at about 75° West. It winds up the hill, disappearing now and again in bamboo thickets and under fallen tree trunks, but keeping all the time between 50° and 80° West. After an hour or so it emerges into another plain, 1km long by 0.5km wide. This is the summit of the pass. The trail re-enters the forest at the far end. Keeping first right and then left of the stream it descends through the woods.

When you reach the main valley you will join another trail from Quillén, more direct though less scenic, and turn northeast. But do not worry if you miss the junction, the correct trail is hardly any clearer than the one you are on, and you will find yourself going northeast in any case. Enticing views of Lago Ñorquincó begin to open up ahead, and you will pass wild apple trees and a huge waterfall on the river below. After walking for an hour in this direction you will come to a small plain and then a large one, the second just after crossing a tiny stream. Now you must concentrate again, because on the second plain two trails invisibly cross. The one you want leaves the *pampa* to your left, and re-crosses the small stream a little lower down before heading for the red-and-white buildings of the **Ñorquincó** *gendarmería* where the main river enters the lake at around 1,040m. Its occupants do not see many backpackers, or indeed any other sort of human being, so you can be sure of a warm welcome. We were immediately presented with mugs of wine and offered a camping place in their garden.

The most difficult part of the walk is behind you now, and those who have had enough can take the beautiful lakeside trail east to the *guardaparque* and the road back to Aluminé. (Incidentally, along this trail you will pass several spectacular waterfalls under which to bathe and recuperate.) Those made of sterner stuff will want to continue to the final lake, Moquehué, and will strike out stubbornly in the opposite direction, first west and then north, along the lakeside track by which the guards get their supplies of wine. The track fords two rivers. At the second, perhaps 1½ hours after leaving the *gendarmería*, you will find a convenient short-cut to the Moquehué road. Just before the ford turn left to a corral. Here turn left again and follow the trail along the left-hand valley for a couple of hours until it peters out in a wide sloping *pampa*. Cut diagonally across it to a deserted ranch where you will find the road to Moquehué.

The road rises gently to 1,450m, providing views of new snow capped peaks, some of them in Chile. Lago Moquehué comes into view, which with its wooded island looks very like Derwentwater in the English Lake District. After 6 or 7 hours you reach the village of **Moquehué** at the head of the lake (around 1,140m). One more *gendarmería* post (no wine here) and you are free to sample the delights of the Hostería Bella Durmiente – hotel, restaurant and shop – with superb views of the lake. But first take the path to the right, 200m beyond the *hostería*, which leads down to the lake edge. Here dip a foot into the smooth, clear water. By doing so you will have completed one of the most difficult walks in the Argentine Lakes District.

LOS ARRAYANES

A small national park that is worth knowing about is Los Arrayanes, at Villa La Angostura, at the southern end of the *Ruta de los Siete Lagos*, just after it crosses the Río Correntoso, perhaps the world's shortest river (linking Lakes Correntoso and Nahuel Huapi). The park exists to protect a 20-hectare wood of arrayán (*Luma apiculata*), an almost unique occurrence (although there is also a small *bosquecito de arrayanes* across the lake, just west of Llao-Llao, and another on Isla Victoria). It is a well-funded and well-run little park, with very informative leaflets and good paths, in a stunning setting.

Angostura developed in the 1930s as a tourist resort, served by boat across Lago Nahuel Huapi from Bariloche; it is the site of the presidential summer residence, a mock-castle known as *El Messidor*. Nowadays the original village lies 3km from El Cruce, the junction on the main road from Bariloche to Chile; it is served by four buses a day from Bariloche (92km, operated by Albus), as well as by international buses and those on the Seven Lakes route. These all halt at **El Cruce**, a stylish resort with a modern bus station, tourist office and cybercafé. It is 40 minutes down a paved road to La Villa or El Puerto, the old village, where the national park office (open 09.30–17.30) is next to an attractive double-deck wooden pier. In fact this is the neck of the Península de Quetrihué, and there is another jetty on the far side, to the west. Turning left between the two you will enter the park and reach a junction. Climbing up steps to the right, you will reach a *mirador* in 10–15 minutes, with fantastic views to the west; it is a rather easier 10 minutes on to a second viewpoint, with less amazing views to the east. This is fine woodland of coihue with ciprés, radal and ñirre, shrubs such as notro, michay and ciruelillo, and creepers such as orange and violet mutisias. Birds include chucao, rayadito, austral thrushes and austral parakeets, as well as grebes and herons in the lake. Turning left at the junction, it is 12km each way to the *arrayanes* at the end of the peninsula. This takes 3–4 hours on foot, or 1–2 hours by mountain bike (easily hired in the village). You can also visit by boat, from Angostura or Bariloche.

You can return to El Cruce by the path past **Laguna Verde**, an attractive lake that is home to native fish such as puyén and pejerrey patagónico, and surrounded by a woodland of ciprés de la cordillera, coihue, arrayán and radal. To the north side of the highway there are other walks, notably to the **Cascada Inacayal**. Starting 1.2km west of the bus station, fork right onto the old road (Calle Cacique Antriao), and after 1km turn right onto the road to the Mirador Belvedere, from where there are great views west over Lago Correntoso. The path to the waterfall starts on the right after 1km. It passes through forest of lenga and coihue, with an understorey of bamboo and then shrubby canelo with two types of *Maytenus*, and reaches the falls in under an hour.

Heading east, towards Bariloche, you can turn left after 3km on the road to the ski centre of **Cerro Bayo** (1,050m), 6km north. After 5km there is a 200m path to the right to the 35m-high Cascada Río Bonito. In summer Cerro Bayo is a centre for mountain-biking (tel: 02944 491 489 to reserve something rather better than the bikes available in Angostura). The chair-lift carries bikes to 1,500m and should be in action all year round, and it is possible to continue to the summit at 1,782m and ride down by various routes. From Angostura the road is paved to Bariloche; it passes scattered arrayans, then after km20 there is a transition from thick low forest to steppe.

BARILOCHE

San Carlos de Bariloche, Argentina's answer to Chamonix, nestles at 760m altitude in a fantastic setting on a narrow shelf beneath Cerro Otto and Lago Nahuel Huapi, the biggest of the region's lakes (560km²). An unashamedly tourist town, its only manufacturing industries are chocolates, jams and woolly sweaters. Its population of 90,000 is almost entirely employed in catering for visitors, a highly lucrative occupation. In consequence the town gets terribly noisy and overcrowded in high summer and it is far better to visit out of season in spring or autumn when the temperature is pleasant.

Bariloche was founded as a lake port in 1895 by Germans from the Chilean Lakes District. Later it became a notorious haunt of Nazi fugitives, but today it is about as likely a haunt for war criminals as Aviemore or Aspen. The railway came in 1934, totally transforming the town's destiny; the Hotel Llao-Llao, 25km west, opened in 1938, and the tourist boom was on (although the hotel was immediately burnt down and rebuilt). Skiing took off in the 1940s, followed in the 1960s by winter tourism from Brazil, and in the 1970s by school groups, now half of the town's business. The **Museo de la Patagonia** (open Tue–Fri 10.00–12.30, 14.00–19.00; Sat and Mon 10.00–13.00), in the Centro Cívico, has good coverage of local history.

Information

The **tourist office** in the Centro Cívico (open Mon–Fri 08.00–21.00, Sat 09.00–21.00; tel: 02944 423 022; fax: 426 784; secturism@bariloche.com.ar) is informative; there are also lots of contacts at www.directorio.bariloche.com.ar.

The best place for all kinds of **trekking information** is the country's leading

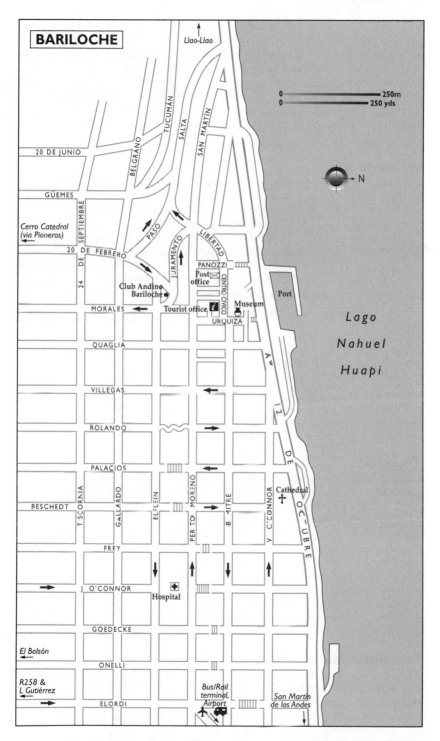

mountaineering club, the **Club Andino Bariloche**, Calle 20 de Febrero 30 (open Jan and Feb Mon–Sat 08.30–14.00, 17.00–20.30; Sundays 08.30–12.00, 18.00–20.00; tel: 02944 424 531; www.clubandino.com.ar); they sell maps and the useful guidebook *Las Montañas de Bariloche*, organise excursions and the Pampa Linda bus service, operate huts, and are generally very helpful. You can also contact the *Sociedad Profesional de Guías de Turismo, Moreno y Villega*s, (8400) Bariloche (tel: 426 802). The Nahuel Huapi National Park's *Intendencía* is at San Martín 24 (open Mon–Fri 09.00–14.00; tel: 423 111). The Fundación Vida Silvestre is at Mitre 727, 4th floor, office B.

Where to stay
The odds are that you will end up spending at least a few days in Bariloche, and if you have just staggered in from several weeks in the mountains you will probably find it a nice change. Hotels are expensive, and in season difficult to find space in, so the best option is to rent a room in somebody's house, or to camp at one of the sites out to the west on Avda Bustillo, the main road along the lakeshore, the Selva Negra (km2.9), El Yeti (km5.6), Petunia (km13.5) and Cirse (km14.5). There are lots of hostels with shared rooms for backpackers, of which the best are the central Albergue Patagonia Andina, Morales 564 (tel: 02944 421861, patagoniaandina@bariloche.com.ar; www.bariloche.com.ar/patagoniaandina), Perigo's, across the road at Morales 555; Bolsa del Mochilero, Palacios 405 (at Elflein; tel/fax: 423 529; bolsadep@bariloche.com.ar); Albergue Mochileros, San Martín 82 (tel: 423 187, 436117; cecilia@bariloche.com.ar); Ruca Hueney, Elflein 396 (at Palacios; tel: 423 132; alec@bariloche.com.ar); Rucalhué, Guelmes 762; Ríos del Sur, Gallardo 950 (tel: 436 454; riosdelsur@bariloche.com.ar; www.riosdelsur.com.ar); and two out west on Avda Bustillo: Alaska, at km7.5 (tel/fax: 461 564; alaska@bariloche.com.ar) and the Refugio Cordillera at km18.6 (tel: 448 261).

Rosán Arko, who rents rooms at Güemes 691 (tel: 423 109), is a member of one of Bariloche's pioneer mountaineering families and is a source of sound information on the mountains.

Transport
The **rail and bus station** is 3km east of the city centre, reached by 3 de Mayo routes 10, 11, 20 and 21, and Codao route 70. Ask at the tourist office for details of services, although it is a safe bet that the train service will be minimal. In addition to buses to most Argentine cities there are also several daily services to Puerto Montt via Osorno. The **airport** is 15km east, with hourly buses from Quaglia 262, near the Aerolíneas office at Quaglia 238 (tel: 02944 422 425) and plenty of flights every day. Most bus services around Bariloche are operated by the Empresa 3 de Mayo, which has offices at FP Moreno 480 (tel: 425 648) and at the bus terminal, and also has email (tresmayo@satlink.com). They have also introduced electronic ticketing, although you can of course still pay as you board. Most services start at the bus terminal and pick up in town at FP Moreno between Palacios and Rolando (westbound)/Elflein and Quaglia (eastbound).

Equipment and activities
There is a **climbing wall** at the Club Andino Bariloche, and another at the Club Los Pehuenes, Pioneros km7.5 (tel: 02944 461 279). **Mountain gear** can be bought at Patagonia Outdoors (Juramento 184; tel: 426 768; omarp@bariloche.com.ar; www.patagonia-outdoors.com.ar); Buenos Aires Ski

(Moreno 60); Scandinavian (San Martín 130; tel: 428 253; fax: 421 777); and La Bolsa del Deporte (Elflein 385; tel/fax: 423 529; bolsadep@bariloche.com.ar). For **mountain-bike hire**, try La Bolsa del Deporte; Pablo Scotti (tel: 467 346; fax: 461 650; mobile 068 308 784); or Bariloche Bike's, Moreno 520 (tel: 424 657, 15 581 898).

Good **supermarkets** are La Anonima at Quaglia 311; Todo at Elflein, east of Villegas; and at Bustillo km3.6; and Red Marka on Elflein behind the CAB (also open on Sundays).

The Librería Cultura, Elflein 74, has some English-language guides, as well as Spanish literature; La Barca, in the arcade at Mitre 131, has second-hand books, some in English. The *Buenos Aires Herald* is sold at a kiosk at Moreno 20.

Tour companies

There are plenty of companies offering various types of adventure tourism: the CAB's Transitando Lo Natural (email: transita/transitando@bariloche.com.ar; www.mercotour.com/transitando) offers day-hikes for US$22–US$56, depending on the amount of transport involved.

Rafting starts at US$65 for a day, far more than in Chile. Specialists include Rafting Adventure (Juramento 75; tel: 02944 432 928; www.mercotour.com/adventure; aventura@bariloche.com.ar); Rafting Limay, Pasaje Urquiza 250 (tel: 424 922); Raft and Kayak (casilla 1433; tel: 427 301; raft kayak@cpsarg.com); Turismo Lauquen (Mitre 86, local 5; tel: 424 854; rafting@bariloche.com.ar; www.nyn-patagonia.com.ar); Randonee, Elflein 443 (tel: 435 813); and Aguas Blancas (Morales 564; tel/fax: 432 799; aguasblancas@infovia.com.ar, www.aguasblancas.com.ar).

For **horses** try Carol Jones (tel: 426 508; fax: 422 996; caroljones@infovia.com) or Tom Wesley (Avda Bustillo km15.5; tel/fax: 448 193, 435 040), or at Pampa Linda the Vereertbrugghen family (casilla 20, Pampa Linda; pampalinda@bariloche.com.ar).

Parapente Bariloche (tel: 441 403, 442 154) fly from Cerro Otto and further afield.

More **general operators** include Aguila Tour, Moreno 126 (tel: 434 598, aguilatour@infovia.com.ar); Andes Patagonicos, Mitre 125 (tel: 431 777); Cumbres Patagonia (Villegas 222; tel: 423 283; fax: 431 835; cumbres@bariloche.com.ar) and Adventure World, Base Cerro Catedral (tel: 460 164, mobile 068 308 603; fax: 422 637; adventure@bariloche.com.ar).

Catedral Turismo, Moreno 238 (tel: 427 143; fax: 426 215; cattur@bariloche.com.ar) operate the Argentinian end of the Lakes route to Puerto Montt; a bus takes you to Puerto Pañuelo for a boat to Puerto Blest, then a bus to Puerto Alegre, a boat to Puerto Frías, and on by the route described on page 237. The whole trip is expensive, but it is possible to pay only for certain segments, eg: US$22 from Puerto Pañuelo to Puerto Blest or US$9 from Puerto Blest to Puerto Frias, or to take a return trip to Puerto Blest, for instance.

Excursions near Bariloche

One of the easiest outings from Bariloche is to **Cerro Otto** (1,405m), the ridge that stretches 8km southwest from Bariloche. A winding road starts at km1 of Avda Los Pioneros (opposite the YPF filling station), and makes a handy 6km mountain-bike ride; indeed you may find it closed for MTB races. There is also a gondola from km5 on Avenida los Pioneros (US$15; reached by a free bus service from

Mitre and Villegas). At the upper terminal there is a rotating restaurant and 1,800m away (at 1,240m) is the **Refugio Berghof**, still operating as a mountain hut (US$6; tel: 15 603 201) and also home to the Museo Otto Meiling (open all year, US$1.50). This is a memorial to one of the pioneers of mountaineering in Bariloche, who lived here and established the first ski school in Argentina, and first ski factory in South America. This is still a base for cross-country skiing, and for rock- and ice-climbing courses on the Piedras Blancas cliffs. There is also a chair-lift up Cerro Campanario (1,049m) from km17.6 on the Llao-Llao road.

Avenida Bustillo leads west for 25km to the chi-chi resort of **Llao-Llao** (pronounced almost as in Zsa-Zsa Gabor), and continues as the **Circuito Chico**, which loops back through stunning scenery to return to Bustillo at km18.3. This is paved throughout, making a very popular drive or cycle-ride, and you can also follow it by 3 de Mayo bus; route 20 runs to Puerto Pañuelo (at Llao-Llao) every 20 minutes, and route 11 continues from here three times a day through Bahía López and Colonia Suiza to Bariloche. At Colonia Suiza (which really does try to look like a bit of Switzerland) you will find the SAC and Goye campsites and the start of a couple of hikes (pages 229–30 and 235); it is reached 13 times a day by route 10 from Bariloche.

From **Bahía López** (km30) a path leads southwest from the road to a viewpoint. This used to continue along the south side of Brazo de la Tristeza, but has long been lost in bamboo. There is a pleasant walk (or bike-ride) back to Llao-Llao from Bahía López. Starting along the road, it is 4km north to Lago Escondido (km34, or 31.6km from Bariloche via Llao-Llao), where a path (marked with blue triangles) goes to the left to the lake, then returns to the road and turns right off it to lead along Lago Perito Moreno Oeste to a small arrayán grove and Puerto Pañuelo.

To the south of Bariloche is the **Refugio Neumeyer** (1,320m; tel: 02944 428 995; refneu@bariloche.com.ar; http://eco-family.com), where you can stay the night but which seems to be more popular as a daytrip for hiking or in winter cross-country skiing and snowshoeing; lots of tour companies run trips here. Head out of town on Onelli and carry on for 1km on RN258 (to km5), from where it is 15km to the left on a dirt road up the Chalhuaco valley.

Parque Nacional Nahuel Huapi

A total of 710,000ha is protected around Bariloche, including a variety of reserves such as Llao-Llao and Los Arrayanes. These include a wonderful range of spectacular scenery, but also cover a significant variety of habitats, from the *altoandino* environment (above 1,600m) through wet forest and transition forest to the steppes. At Puerto Blest there is up to 4m of precipitation a year, diminishing to around 1m at Bariloche and just 600m at the eastern end of Lago Nahuel Huapi.

Above the tree line, *Chaetanthera villosa* is a tiny, almost cactus-like, globular alpine plant; condors and huemul can also be found up here. The *bosque humedo* is dominated by lenga and coihue, with ciprés de la cordillera in drier parts. Animals include pudú, river otter (the main population in Argentina), guiña and monito de monte, and birds include the Magellanic woodpecker, chucao, rayadito, and austral parakeet. To the east, the *bosque de transición* to Patagonian steppe is dominated by ciprés de la cordillera; with radal, ñire and maitén; and the steppe is inhabited by guanaco, puma, foxes, rodents (such as the colonial tuco-tuco) and lizards, with raptors such as cinereous harrier and American kestrel. The imperial cormorant, usually a salt-water bird, can be seen on Lago Nahuel Huapi, as well as kelp gull.

THE CERRO CATEDRAL CIRCUIT

Distance	Approximately 21km
Altitude	Up to 2,090m
Rating	Easy to difficult
Time	1–2 days
Start of trail	Villa Catedral (1,030m) or Lago Gutiérrez (c790m)
End of trail	Refugio Frey
Maps	Ask at the Club Andino Bariloche for a copy of their 1:50,000 map. Although it is rather crude and not 100% accurate, it does show ridges and peaks with 100m contour intervals and certainly enables you to find the way. The Chilean company JLM has also produced a good map of Bariloche (no. 15). You might also look at Argentine IGM 1:100,000 Sheets 4172-23 (Bariloche) and 4172-22 (Llao-Llao), but unless you can lay your hands on editions more recent than 1947, do not bother to buy them.

Although mostly little higher than 2,000m, the peaks of the Catedral range must be among the most rugged in South America. You might expect an excursion to such an area to take a matter of weeks, but in fact a day-trip from Bariloche can take you to the highest parts, while more satisfying longer circuits can be done in 3–5 days. Here we first describe three routes to the Refugio Frey, which can be linked as a circuit either in a day or with an overnight stop, and then the continuation from Frey to further huts.

Much of the landscape is rough and rocky but nowhere are the trails dangerous. They have been excellently waymarked by the Club Andino Bariloche, whose *refugios* provide shelter and make a nice change from camping. The trails are passable from November to April, but at the beginning and end of the season the *refugios* may be closed. Check at the CAB's headquarters before you leave (see *Bariloche* above).

You will find firewood at all the campsites we mention, but it is far better to carry your own stove and leave these unspoilt beauty spots as they are. Drinking water is available throughout this area.

Getting to the trailhead

The main routes described below begin at the Villa Catedral ski village (1,030m), although you can also start from Lago Gutiérrez. The 3 de Mayo company runs buses direct from Moreno 480 in Bariloche to the ski village every hour in high summer (every 15 minutes in the ski season), alternately via Bustillo and Pioneros. The same company's route 50 runs to Villa Los Coihues on Lago Gutiérrez every 20 minutes (every 30 minutes on Sundays). Both routes give you a good view of Bariloche's opulent western suburbs overlooking Lago Nahuel Huapi, before turning south at km8.6.

The 10km road up to the ski village is attractive, with the rocky Catedral Norte looming up ahead, and the gradual climb lets you in gently for the stiffer stuff later. If you choose to walk, you can also take a Los Coihues bus and get off at the junction known as *La Virgen de las Nieves* ('Virgin of the Snows'; km10). The army has a marked climbing cliff on the left just south of the junction. It is not hard to get a lift when you tire; otherwise, turn right off the paved road when you see the buildings of the ski village, about an hour's walk from the *Virgin* and before the top hairpin bend. By following a trail to the left of two electricity lines you will come to the old road to the village and cut 2 or 3km off your walk. However you get to the ski village, you will want to take time to wander round before charging off up the mountain. Set in a natural bowl, the ski schools, equipment shops, *hosterías*, *confiterías* and hotel are housed in an assortment of neo-Tyrolean buildings reminiscent of a Hollywood film set.

Route description

Decisions have to be taken here. You can reach the first main refuge, Refugio Frey, by two routes: one begins at Refugio Lynch near the top of the cable-car and approaches Refugio Frey from above; the other leads south from the ski village car park. The first has spectacular views and some of the wildest backpacking we have ever done. However, the alternative route is good in its own way too.

To reach the beginning of the first route you can ride up in style by the Punta Nevada cable-car (daily 10.00–17.00; US$16), from 1,040m at the rear of the Las Terrazas shopping centre to 1,775m, still 15 minutes' hike below the Refugio Lynch, or by chairlift (Aerosilla Línea Cóndor, until 17.30; US$10) from near the Hotel Pire Hue to 1,785m at the Piedra del Cóndor, along the ridge to the north of the Refugio Lynch.

Alternatively toughnuts can walk up, starting on the path to the right/north of the Cóndor chair-lift, and reaching a surreally placed phone box by a four-wheel-drive track after 5 minutes. A dirt road goes a long way around to the right, but perhaps the most direct of the various permutations is to go left to follow the north (true left) side of the Arroyo La Cascada valley. This track ends after 10 minutes at a small stream, but a small path climbs to the right of the chair-lift, bringing you in 10 minutes back to the dirt road just left/south of a junction. A couple of minutes up the upper road is the intermediate lift-station, with an evacuation platform for the cable-car and the lower terminal of the Militares chair-lift. Continuing up the dirt road, you will head to the left and then zigzag right under the cable-car (passing through some mature forest). Heading on uphill at two junctions you will reach the tree line in 25 minutes (with a view, just, of Lago Gutiérrez). From here the track runs left almost on the level to the Punta Nevada chair-lift at the top cable-car pylon. A steep, 5-minute climb brings you to the upper terminal of the chair-lift from the valley, from where you can continue up to the left on an unuseable four-wheel-drive track, under the cable-car and Punta Nevada chair-lift, up a bare rocky slope, reaching a useable four-wheel-drive track from the right in 12 minutes, just before it takes a sharp zigzag to the right. In 5 minutes this brings you to the upper terminal of the cable-car and chair-lift, from where a better four-wheel-drive track leads up to the left (crossing the cables of an abandoned lift). This then zigzags right, bringing you to another chair-lift in 5 minutes. Heading up a four-wheel-drive shortcut to the left and then sharp right, you will arrive at the Refugio Lynch (1,870m; tel: 02944 424 818) in 5 minutes; this can be reached in 1½ hours without a pack or 2 hours with a lightish one; longer easier routes take 3–4 hours. This all sounds frightfully precise and prescriptive, but it is really a matter of following your nose to find a route which suits you. Refugio Lynch offers breathtaking views of Lago Nahuel Huapi – not to mention tea, coffee, fizzy drinks and excellent meals.

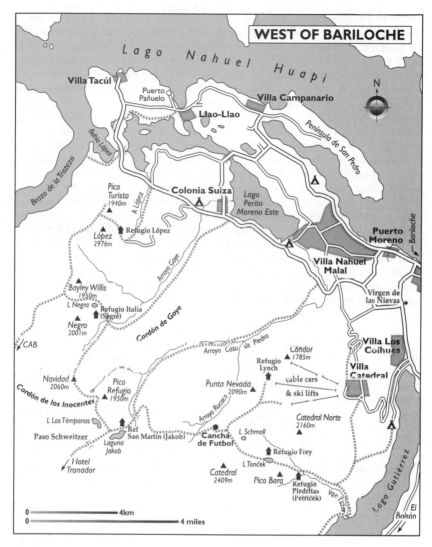

The trail to Refugio Frey follows the ridge southwest from here. It is well marked with yellow and red paint, and although you will scarcely believe the terrain you are crossing, you will be in no danger of getting lost. From Refugio Lynch, you will go below a meteorological station and pass four lift terminals (one ruined). After about 25 minutes the path reaches its highest point at Punta Nevada (2,090m, totally misnamed in summer), then drops down to a saddle between two fierce-looking rocky outcrops. There are other ski-lifts and a four-wheel-drive road in the Robles or Dientes de Caballo area on the south side of the Arroyo La Cascada valley, and you could climb directly to this point. After 5 minutes the path heads to the right across a northwest-facing scree slope, and the next hour is spent negotiating an incredible traverse at about 2,000m, with rocky needles towering directly above and very little for 500m below. Vertigo sufferers beware! It takes under 10 minutes to cross the scree, on a good solid path, and you then have to rock-hop for at least 40 minutes. There is no real scrambling, but hands and a stick are both useful. Finally you will reach a sandy area overlooked by crags and known as the *Cancha de Fútbol* ('football pitch'), where signs painted on the rocks indicate the junction of the paths left to Refugio Frey and right to Refugio San Martín.

For the simple circuit, you should turn left here and pass over the ridge to what really does seem like a football stadium. From its far side the path slices through a narrow canyon in the watershed and drops down steeply to the left beneath snowfields to the tiny Laguna Schmoll. If you do the walk in spring or early summer you will almost certainly have to cross snow, so it is essential to take an ice-axe and to know how to use it. After passing over the lip of the perfectly formed cirque containing Laguna Schmoll, the trail drops down sharply again to the softer shores of Laguna Tonček. At the far end of this tiny lake, at 1,700m, is a little grey house with a bright-red roof called Refugio Frey, reached in 1½ hours at most (3 hours from Refugio Lynch). It does not exactly have all mod cons, but is a welcome sight in such lunar country. It is very popular with climbers (Paul Pritchard rates one route as a superb 7b+), and is one of the few huts that are open in winter. Well-used camping spots can be found to the left (south) of the lake but there are better grassy sites at the far end of the lake. Wherever you camp you should expect rats, so hang your food out of reach. As you cool off with a refreshing dip in the lake you can admire the impressive pinnacles of Cerro Catedral (2,409m).

The easier route from the ski village to the Refugio Frey passes through heath and woodland on the lower slopes of the mountain, though still high enough for spectacular views of Lago Gutiérrez. Sadly this was badly affected by fires in 1996 and 1999; in December 1999 EcoChallenge competitors helped CAB members plant cypress saplings, but it will be a long time before it recovers. Look for a dirt road diagonally across the car park from the bus shelter by a red, iron gate, signposted 'Frey'. It is well marked all the way to Refugio Frey. The dirt road leads in 200m to an old granite quarry, where you should take a signposted track to the left. After 2 hours, in the open then passing through ñirre then lenga, you will meet the trail coming up from Lago Gutiérrez and turn northwest (through dense forest of coihue, lenga and colihue bamboo) along Arroyo van Titter. This is crossed a little further on by a precarious tree-trunk footbridge and then, quite suddenly, you come across the fairytale Refugio Petriček or Piedritas (Little Rocks), a tiny cabin ingeniously built round a giant overhanging boulder at the tree-line. This remarkable little place was rebuilt in 1978 by the Club Andino Esloveno, the climbing club of the Slovene community in Argentina, to replace one destroyed by fire. The ethnic influence is evident in the beautifully painted designs on the window shutters, as well as in the names of the nearby lakes. However, the *refugio* is usually kept locked, so brace yourself and push on. In another hour (4 hours from Villa Catedral) you will be sipping hot *maté* in Refugio Frey.

To return direct to the ski village from Frey takes about 3 hours. The clear, wide trail is steep at first but rapidly eases off into a pleasant woodland walk. A little over half an hour from Refugio Frey you will pass the Petriček refuge. Another 30 minutes and you should fork to the left to contour around the hillside back to the ski village. Towards the end the trail divides once or twice, but all paths lead eventually to the village car park.

The third route to Refugio Frey starts from Villa Los Coihues, the terminus of bus 50, at the north end of Lago Gutiérrez. This is a popular spot for swimming, fishing and windsurfing during summer weekends. There are two good campsites nearby, both with excellent facilities: the Autocamping 'W' (tel: 02944 467 332) at the turning to the lake head; and Camping Los Coihues (tel: 467 481). The bus terminates at the junction of two dirt roads; follow the one to the left for just over 2km to the *seccional*, just before the Autocamping Lago Gutiérrez (currently closed), where you should take the trail to the right, signposted to Refugio Frey. Follow the white markers, which take you through the woods around the campsite and onto a narrow track which climbs steadily. After about 30 minutes you come to the top of a rise. Ignore the path leading right and carry on down the path which crosses a stream. This is a good place to top up water bottles before the hot climb ahead.

The trail continues as a dusty track through open bush country. After 15 minutes you reach a T-junction indicated on a stone. Take the left turning, following the red paint markings and ignoring a path to the left 20 minutes on. Soon the trail enters the woods again and climbs steeply before crossing through a wide expanse of burnt trees. The trail is joined from the right by the trail from the ski village and continues on the level to a junction left (which leads to Playa Muñoz, then south along the lake to the mouth of the Arroyo von Titter, and ultimately along the beach and through the Camping Los Baqueanos to the road at km22.5). A little further up you will cross the Arroyo van Titter and will at last be able to cool your feet in its clear waters. Fifteen minutes on you pass the Refugio Petriček; another hour's walk through lenga forest up the steep and dusty Picada Esloveno brings you to Refugio Frey, 5 hours from the bus terminus.

To continue from Refugio Frey to the *Cancha de Fútbol*, the junction at the watershed, keep to the right of the first lake (Laguna Tonček) and start climbing at the end of the valley, keeping to your left the stream which drops down from the right. This will bring you to the second lake, Laguna Schmoll. By passing to the left of this you will be able to climb up to the cleft in the watershed which brings you to the junction. The path from Refugio Frey to this point is marked by yellow and red paint and will take between 1 and 2 hours.

Day walks from Refugio Frey

A fine morning's outing is the climb up the south side of the valley towards the obvious low point on the ridge to the west of Pica Bara. Several tracks have been worn by rock-climbers gaining access to the peaks, starting about halfway along the lakeshore and winding up the slope through the scrub. At the saddle turn left and continue climbing up the rocky ridge line. Height is gained surprisingly quickly and the views into the surrounding valleys and to the peaks and needles of the Catedral massif are quite stunning. The refuge and tent sites are mere specks on the valley floor far below. Continue as far as you wish – the high point of Pica Bara tends to be more for rock climbers than hikers, though you do not need any special skills to achieve the spectacular views.

Later in the afternoon it is worth climbing to the west to watch the sunset over Tronador. Several gullies lead up between rock outcrops at the very head of the valley. With care some of these can be negotiated without mountaineering skills, and again the reward on reaching the ridge is well worth the effort. You can return by the same route or, especially if the light is failing a little, follow the ridge to your right and pick up the main trekking track. To reach this move along the ridge, keeping to the west of the needles and rock outcrops (ie: keeping the Valle Rucaco in sight on your left) and then drop down to the *Cancha de Fútbol*; turn right here onto the track described above.

A HUT-TO-HUT WALK IN THE BARILOCHE AREA

Distance	Approximately 53km
Altitude	Between 1,600, and 2,060m
Rating	Difficult
Time	4–5 days
Start of trail	*Cancha de Fútbol* or Refugio Frey
End of trail	Refugio López
Maps	See page 221

This challenging circuit takes you through some of the country's wildest and most dramatic scenery via four of the Club Andino's comfortable *refugios*. This allows you to leave your tent behind and travel light. If, however, you want to camp, there are plenty of good spots. Many sections are tough going and from Refugio San Martín to Refugio Italia the route is not waymarked. The walk, which includes a large amount of scrambling up and down steep scree and boulders, is not recommended for beginners. It would be near impossible in the other direction, due to the loose scree. However, an easier variant is possible, leaving the mountains from Refugio San Martín by the Arroyo Casa de Piedra.

The huts are ideally situated a day's walk from each other. The circuit can be done in 4 days, or 5 if the last night is spent in Refugio López. None of the rock scrambling is difficult, but requires care and can be hair-raising at times. The hike includes some scree walking but the trails are all well marked with red blazes.

Be sure to consult the Club Andino Bariloche about snow conditions before setting out. You can buy biscuits, beer and bottled drinks at the *refugios* but you should bring your main supplies from Bariloche. A compass, and warm and waterproof clothing are essential. Gaiters are useful, and an ice-axe is essential if you are doing the walk in spring or early summer before the lower snowfields have melted.

Getting to the trailhead
Follow any route to the *Cancha de Fútbol*, via either Refugio Frey or Refugio Lynch (as described in the previous section).

Route description
Reaching the *Cancha de Fútbol*, you will find yourself on a rocky ledge high above the Arroyo Rucaco. Follow the arrow and sign for Refugio Jakob, painted on a rock. The path doubles back on itself before dropping westwards down steep scree into the Rucaco valley. Many have flunked the hike at this sight, but it is really not as bad as it looks. Slide down as best you can, perhaps going a little to the left to a big red marker on an outcrop just above the first vegetation. The descent takes about 30 minutes. Follow a dry gully, alive with lizards, and swing left into the forest before crossing an area of wet, boggy meadow and re-entering the trees. After about 25 minutes you will reach an ideal camping spot by a good stream, with a waterfall just upstream. From there red paint markings lead you on through the woods across several smaller streams. As you emerge from the trees, do not miss a sign to the left for the Refugio Jakob. The path climbs steadily, and the ridge is in full view all the way up, giving the disconcerting impression of receding as you climb. If you find this too depressing, look behind you at the pinnacles and

flanking buttresses of 2,409m Cerro Catedral rising steadily above the western horizon as you ascend – an awe-inspiring sight.

The path crosses a stony plateau after about 30 minutes, then scrambles up steep scree to the **Paso Brecha Negra**, on the ridge above, another 25–30 minutes on. Here, at 2,025m, you have magnificent views: to the southeast, the towers of Cerro Catedral; ahead below you, Laguna Jakob; and to the northwest, the steep, wooded slopes bordering Arroyo Casa de Piedra. To reach Refugio San Martín, known to many as Refugio Jakob (1,600m; tel: 02944 462 731) you will have to scramble down loose scree for about an hour. Setting off to the left and down the steep slopes, you will eventually enter a rocky gully and follow it into the trees after a bit more than 30 minutes; turning left at a sign you will cross a few boggy patches and reach the outlet stream from Laguna Jakob after another 15 minutes. Cross over to join the path up the Casa de Piedra valley and it is 5 minutes to the hut (about 6 hours from Refugio Frey). There are dusty campsites beyond the hut, and better ones near the southwest end of Laguna Jakob, beside a crystalline stream which flows into the lake from a valley to the north.

The trail down the valley of Arroyo Casa de Piedra is well trodden by feet and hooves; in fact in places it is a mudpath, and there is a new and better track on the other (north/left) bank. However, it is hard to find the start of the track, so you should ask at the hut. Apart from steep zigzags at the start and a short rocky stretch of the old track, negotiated by an iron ladder, it is mostly gently downhill and you should be at the main road in 5 hours. For those not in a hurry, there are some idyllic picnic or camping spots by the bridge just above the confluence with the Arroyo Rucaco, and just before the track swings left away from the river and over a small ridge to the road – soft grassy banks beside clear blue-green waters in a wooded valley-within-a-valley. For those anxious to return to the more sophisticated delights of Bariloche, turn right when you reach the road to Colonia Suiza (15.5km from Bariloche) and in a couple of hours you will reach a *barrio* called Puerto Moreno at km10.5 on Avda Bustillo, where you can pick up bus 20 from Llao-Llao every 20 minutes. Bus 11 passes the trailhead (known as the Picada de Jakob) just three times a day. You may also catch bus 21 in Puerto Moreno just before reaching the lakeside road. Turning left, it is a pleasant enough walk of 1–1½ hours to Colonia Suiza.

The section from Refugio San Martín to Refugio Italia is the wildest and most remote of the circuit, and before attempting it you should consult the warden at Refugio San Martín who will tell you the state of the route and show you maps to help you identify the correct path, and will radio ahead so that you are expected at Refugio Italia, and searched for if you do not make it. Unfortunately the CAB's 1:50,000 map (*Refugios, Sendas y Picadas*) shows an older variant that passes to the west of the Cordón de los Inocentes. The route is deliberately not marked, to deter inexperienced hikers, but in fact there are plenty of cairns, though remember that these may need rebuilding every spring. Even in late December the route can still be blocked by snow. If so, and you do not want simply to hike out down the Arroyo Casa de Piedra, it should be possible to hike from the Refugio San Martín to the north end of Lago Mascardi (on the Bariloche–El Bolsón road), or via the Paso Schweitzer to the west end of the same lake (on the Pampa Linda road).

The route is marked, with red paint arrows and circles, from Refugio San Martín as far as Laguna Los Témpanos, an easy 40-minute walk over ice-polished rock, and this makes a nice morning's stroll before heading back down the valley. It passes through the camping area, to the north side of Laguna Jakob, then to the right over rocks and boulders. About 15 minutes from the hut you will come to a dip where you will see a cairn to the right, then red markers along the route up to a rocky ridge (10 minutes, with one easy climbing move). Here a cairn on the left indicates the path down to Laguna Los Témpanos, a cold and eerie lake with permanent snow right down to the water's edge. There is no need to go down to the lake since the route heads to the right up the rocky ridge between Laguna Los Témpanos and Laguna Jakob and towards the pointed summit of Pico Refugio (1,950m).

The route is unmarked after leaving the path to Laguna Los Témpanos, although the odd cairn shows that you are not the first to have been this way. After about 15 minutes you reach the first of a series of three steep rock faces which can be seen in the profile of Pico Refugio from Refugio San Martín. Go a little way up to the left and then along a level shelf for about 50m until you reach the foot of an obvious gully down which a stream trickles, although it is usually under a snow bank at the foot of the gully. Follow the gully, scrambling up the rock to its right – not difficult but you should tread carefully. Below lies Laguna Los Témpanos and ahead you can see two pinnacles. Follow the gully for about 10 minutes to the point where it opens out and is filled with loose boulders at the base of the twin pinnacles. Move left across the gully to a cairn, then climb a boulder field to reach the ridge in a small col to the right of a third rocky pinnacle northwest of the other two, after another 15 minutes. Go slightly up to the right of this pinnacle, following cairns, before beginning a traverse beneath its east face. Head across the rock basin ahead towards a small scree-filled col in the ridge to the north, identified from the diagram below.

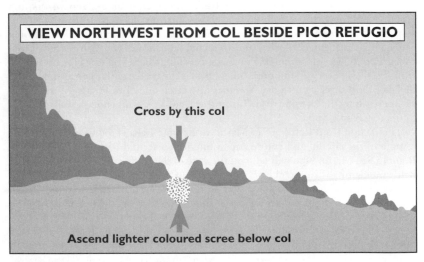

VIEW NORTHWEST FROM COL BESIDE PICO REFUGIO

Cross by this col

Ascend lighter coloured scree below col

Several rocky gullies cut into the rock basin, but they remain hidden until you get close. By keeping fairly high you can easily climb in and out of them and arrive beneath the col in half an hour without having lost too much height. At the top of the col are views of Cerro Catedral behind you, Cerro Negro to the north, Cerro Navidad to the northwest, and just to the left of that, in the far distance, the pointed peak of Cerro Puntiagudo in Chile. It should take about 2½ hours to reach this point from the *refugio*.

The next hour is spent negotiating the screes above Laguna Navidad and requires special care. Losing only a little height, head left (west) around the head of the valley, staying fractionally below the pinnacled ridge top. Pass below the rock buttress about halfway round before turning left and clambering back up the scree to a col, after about 40 minutes. From here you can follow the ridge which leads to the top of Cerro Navidad (2,060m) in 20 minutes, avoiding any pinnacles along the way by keeping left of the ridge.

From the top of Cerro Navidad, continue north across the boulder fields, keeping to the left of the main ridge with Cerro Negro ahead slightly to your left. This will bring you in 5 minutes to the right of an outcrop and to the top of Arroyo Navidad, which you must descend. The path is steep and tough, but if you have got this far on the walk you will be well used to such conditions. We found gaiters useful for keeping stones out of our boots on these descents. At first you will have to slide carefully down scree but this gets easier as it turns into boulders. Even in late February there were also snow fields, which allowed some glissading. As you follow the stream down you will need to pick the easiest route by constantly crossing from one side to the other. After 1–1½ hours you reach the tree line. From here cairns lead you away from the stream to your left, through a 10m gap now overgrown with stunted trees and across a boggy meadow. The path eventually leads back to the stream, and indeed briefly down the stream bed, and half an hour later reaches a good camping spot above a fine waterfall. From here the path is again marked with red paint splashes and a few cairns, but it is still pretty overgrown and winds across the stream in a confusing manner. In particular you have to cross from right to left in an amazing crazy rock fall. Half an hour from the campsite you will reach a dry streambed to the left, and 2 minutes further the T-junction with the main path up the Arroyo Casa de Piedra. Turning left you embark on the laborious slog up a zigzag path to the Refugio Italia (known as Refugio Italia-Manfredo Segré Laguna Negra; 1,650m; tel: 15 605 071), which has been visible since the beginning of the climb down the Arroyo Navidad. If your muscles allow, you can save time by scrambling straight up the streambed left of the path for the first section. It takes an hour to reach the lip of the cirque containing Laguna Negra and the Refugio Italia. You can camp at the southeast end of the lake, but it is usually windy.

Do not forget that someone has to go up to the refuge to announce your safe arrival. That done, you can, if you have had enough, go down the Goye valley to reach Colonia Suiza (14km) in 2½ hours. Just one minute down the path is the Piedra Vivac or Bivouac Rock, which gives the junction its name, and less than 10 minutes further is a campsite, with rough fireplaces and level ground beaten so hard that you can hardly pitch a tent. A good path carries on down the right bank of the stream, in fine mature forest and briefly on boardwalks over a boggy patch. In another 1¼ hours there is a similar campsite, just above a small gorge; the path climbs above this and in 15 minutes joins a logging road from the right. At once you start to see introduced species such as dog rose, broom and firs. After 15 minutes you need to turn right where the road enters private land. You will soon climb to a better path, but this too enters the private land and the same thing happens again. You reach the highest point in 10 minutes and soon begin to drop on a steep and very bad path, reaching the road in 10 minutes. Maps still show the old route down the logging road; in fact you have to walk 200m to the left/west to reach the turning into Colonia Suiza (where buses 10 and 11 pass), 100m more to the end of the old route, the bridge over the Arroyo Goye, and the SAC campsite.

In the other direction, the start of the trail is clearly signed through broom and roses, then there is a very steep and very messy climb for 5 minutes (this is obviously not a path that evolved naturally; it is enough of a disaster without further erosion, so please do not use short-cuts), though it is now well marked by red bullseyes and arrows. It is an easier climb between rocks and a fence, then down to a gate and forestry road. After a couple of minutes on the level, turn right off the road then try not to take the bad path steep down by the fence, but the better one ahead, to reach the trail 30 metres above the gate.

To continue from Refugio Italia to Refugio López, follow the well-marked path which crosses the rocky north side of Laguna Negra. In places you will have to scramble and a rope may be helpful. The path heads north from the end of the lake and follows the stream, which feeds the lake before climbing to the broad ridge to the left of Cerro Bayley Willis (1,950m). Avoiding the summit, follow the path which leads northwest from the mountain's west face to a second col. Pick your way down through the scree and boulders, watching carefully for red paint markings, and then keeping left of the green boggy area before the valley bottom. There are plenty of camping spots in the valley.

The path now climbs steeply in and out of scrub and trees marked with red paint. The trail then levels off slightly as you cross a stony area at the foot of the stone chute, which leads out of the valley to the right of its head wall. It takes 1–1½ hours of careful scrambling up the boulder-filled gully to reach a ridge. Once here, Refugio López is only an hour away so it is worth making a small diversion to the left (north) to climb Pico Turista (2,050m) where you will find a seat from which to admire the fine views of Bariloche and Lago Nahuel Huapi below; the view to the west is also superb, as Tronador does not hide Volcáns Osorno or Puntiagudo here.

Retracing your steps along the ridge top, you will see the path, marked with red and silver arrows, which descends the northeastern side of the ridge. You will pass a rock knoll and a small lake which provides the refuge below with water. After further scrambling down a rocky gully you reach the spectacularly positioned Refugio López (1,620m; tel: 15 604 401), having looped right around the northern side of Cerro López. Although it is no architectural masterpiece (with windows all of different sizes, shapes and levels), it is the largest and most comfortable of the huts in this area, and on summer weekends it is busy with day trippers and has a simple cafeteria service, as well as accommodation. If you wish to camp, the best place is about 15 minutes below the refuge in the woods where there are level clearings. It takes nearly 2 hours to reach the road to Colonia Suiza so depending how you feel, you may decide to descend the same day or linger a little longer in the mountains.

Starting from the hut, the route to Pico Turista starts along the plastic pipeline behind the hut, heading for a small gully. From a distance there seems to be no clear route up the polished rock face, but the way is marked with splashes of red paint; keep looking upwards to locate these markers, as it is easy to lose your way. It is more a hands-on scramble than a well-worn path in places, but no technical climbing is required. When you reach a small lake, pass to its right and start climbing again by the little trickling outlet, again following markers on the rocks to the ridge line, for those superb views. The more adventurous can return by a route over Punta Norte and down the extremely steep scree slopes to the northwest.

To get to Bariloche, take the well-worn track from Refugio López which follows the right/east side of the Arroyo López valley to reach the paved Circuito Chico at km26.8, the junction from Colonia Suiza. Buses 10 and 11 pass here half a dozen times a day (the last at 18.50); ask to be set down at the Picada Cerro López if you want to start the hike here. It is about 2 hours uphill to the hut, following blue and red markers. Halfway up keep left, as the route to the right is very steep. The Camino Cerro López is a rough road of 11km starting about 1km west of Colonia Suiza (2km east of the Picada López junction) – it is a popular mountain-bike outing.

A LAKE-TO-LAKE WALK
John and Christine Myerscough

Distance	Approximately 55km
Altitude	Between 793m and 1,730m
Rating	Difficult
Time	4–5 days (3–4 days starting from Pampa Linda)
Start of trail	Northern tip of eastern arm of Lago Mascardi
End of trail	Colonia Suiza (bus to Bariloche)
Maps	No decent maps are available, although a 1:100,000 map can be bought from the Club Andino in Bariloche, and JLM map 15 covers the area.

This walk, from Lago Mascardi to Colonia Suiza, takes you through a stunningly beautiful and virtually unspoilt area. Here, in complete peace, you will enjoy breathtaking mountain peaks, sparkling blue lakes and cascading streams. The section between Laguna Callvú, nestling between smooth, polished rock walls, and Laguna CAB is perhaps one of the most exhilarating walks in Argentina. Given good weather, which is common early in the year, you will be able to see beyond Volcán Tronador into Chile where the perfect cone of Volcán Osorno rises above Lago Todos los Santos.

Like the Hut-to-Hut Walk above, this tough, challenging hike should only be attempted by experienced walkers. You will need a tent, as there are lovely camping spots beside the lakes or beside mountain streams. You should visit the Club Andino Bariloche before setting out to check on snow conditions and to get their rather basic map of the area.

A tent and compass are essential, as are warm and waterproof clothing. A small machete might be useful for clearing overgrown vegetation.

Route description
The walk starts from the northern tip of the eastern arm of Lago Mascardi, at 793m. From Bariloche take any bus down the El Bolsón road, and get off at the *guardería* at the north end of the lake (km26.5); this is 2km south of the Continental Divide (*División de Vertientes*; 800m), marked by a sign beside the road.

The route starts on a track, about 100m north of the *guardería*, which leads to the lakeshore by an abandoned jetty. You can cross a minor stream on branches, then carry on along the shore or if the lake is too high go inland through very boggy scrub. Before the Arroyo Fresco you will pass through some filthy campsites, but on the far side (it is easy to cross on a log just upstream of the first bend in the stream) there are much nicer sites. Continuing by the lakeside, there are branches

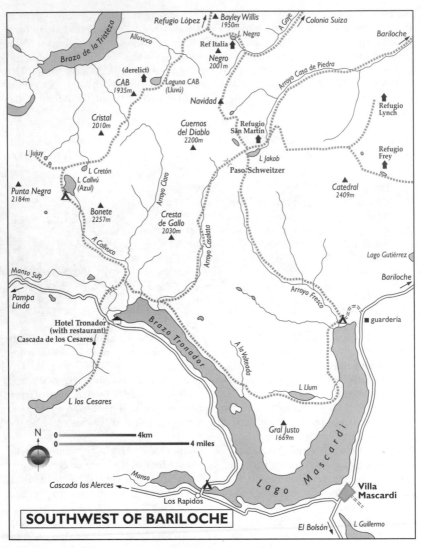

SOUTHWEST OF BARILOCHE

across several streams, and after 10 minutes you will reach drier ground. It takes about 5 minutes to a fenceline, beyond which you are on a vehicle track, blocked by fallen logs; this follows the lakeshore for half an hour and then climbs a steep bank through trees before levelling off again. The path is well defined and wide enough for two people to walk side by side. It passes through a gate after 25 minutes and winds through picturesque woods for 10 minutes, affording occasional views of the lake below, then goes sharply up to the right. After 15 minutes you will drop to a log bridge and the Bahiá Los Leones. Turn right and follow the trail on the right bank. You soon start climbing away from the lake and enter thick bamboo undergrowth. There are useful red markers; horses and mountain-bikes use diversions around fallen trees, but the going is easy otherwise. It takes approximately 20 minutes to reach a clearing, 5 minutes to a ridge and 5 more to a higher one, and 5 more to the eastern end of the secluded and amazingly clear Laguna Llum (pronounced Zhum) at about 870m, about 4 hours from the start.

From here the trail follows the left (southern) side of the lake, initially in attractive forest, then in bamboo scrub, bringing you out at the western end after about 30–40 minutes. Here there is a ramshackle wooden corral enclosing an apple orchard, where you can get water. There is also a dilapidated shelter and plenty of good camping areas; it is also possible to camp in small clearings in the woods along the south side of the lake. The path meanders over fairly level ground but at times you may have to push through vegetation where it has become overgrown. Continuing from the orchard the path is soon climbing fairly steeply through bamboo forest, but eases after 10 minutes and reaches the rocky Llum pass, with fine views of Volcán Tronador and its Black Glacier (*Ventisquero Negro*), in another 20 minutes. Just to the left is a cairn, where you also get a splendid view of Lago Mascardi. It takes a couple of minutes on to a second viewpoint, looking south to Isla Corazón and a very saddle-shaped mountain.

Follow the steep stony track down through thick bamboo, then above an area of trees felled by a storm. Half an hour from the pass you reach a camping spot by a small stream – ignore the log bridge to the right unless the larger stream ahead is in flood. From here the path climbs steeply for 5 minutes to a ridge from where you glimpse Lago Mascardi. The trail is indistinct in places and littered with fallen trees but occasional paint markings reassure you that you are on the right path. After walking for an hour above the lake the path drops down to the small Arroyo la Volteada, just beyond which you can camp, by the lake. Continue for another hour above the lake until you reach a beach at the mouth of the Casalata valley. Follow faded red markings through sandy scrub, turning sharp right to reach the Arroyo Casalata in 20 minutes (about 7 hours from the start). Here the trail meets a path from the right which leads up to the Paso Schweitzer and Refugio Jakob, passing the Castillo Rojo, the triple red outcrop just to the right as you hike inland. Despite the sign, there is no suspension bridge here, but it is easy to cross by a log just upstream, around the bend. Here there are plenty of spaces to camp and you can enjoy views of Cerro Bonete (2,257m) and the obvious cock's comb of Cresta de Gallo (2,030m) to the north, with the snowy top of Volcán Tronador peeping out far to the northwest; across the lake can be seen the luxury Hotel Tronador and its attractive gardens.

Continue following red markings and horse hoofprints, and after 15 minutes you will come to a sign saying *Los Pozones* ('Rock Pools'); after another 10 minutes the path turns 90° right for Cerro Bonete, and 2 minutes later you will reach the Arroyo Claro, the widest river yet. To the right a path leads to the *Pozones*, past a fluviometer where you can ford the *arroyo*. On the far side, the trail to the right continues through the mountains, while that to left leads in 10 minutes to the wobbly suspension bridge which will take you across the Río Manso; this means Calm River, and indeed it is just like the great grey-green, greasy Limpopo and totally unlike all the other streams you will have crossed (*manso* was also the word used for 'tame' Indians).

To leave the park here, go to the left beyond the bridge, by the river, and after 15 minutes turn right by a footbridge at a ford. You will soon pass a gate and go up to the right to reach the Pampa Linda road in 5 minutes; to the left it is under 10 minutes to the Campamento Los Cesares, and the Hotel Tronador just beyond. This is an alternative starting-point for the hike, if it is early in the season and the lakes and streams are high and the fallen trees have not been cleared, or if you simply want a shorter variant.

The Pampa Linda road starts at km36.5 on the paved Bariloche–El Bolsón road, by Lago Guillermo and from a National Park gate (where you will have to pay US$5) follows the south side of Lago Mascardi for 9km to Los Rápidos, where there is a campsite and bike hire. To the left a road follows the Río Manso for 18km to the 20-metre Cascada Los Alerces and Lago Fonck, a nice camping area. To the right it is 14km more to the Hotel Tronador through solid coihue, ciprés, ñire and maitén, with a *mirador* to Isla Corazón after about 6km. Opposite the Campamento Los Cesares, a path leads to the Cascada de los Cesares. It is 15 minutes up a good path to a junction and 5 more to the right to the three-stage falls, with two upper *miradores* and access to the stream (careful!). Carrying on at the junction, it is an easy climb to the Lago los Cesares.

In summer a CAB bus leaves Bariloche for Pampa Linda at 09.00 and returns at 16.00 (US$10 each way, plus the park fee). In addition up to three buses a day run from Bariloche to Los Rápidos. All Bariloche agencies offer same excursion to the *Ventisquero Negro* (US$28 plus the park fee), and you can arrange to be dropped off at the Hotel Tronador on the way back. Above Los Rapidos the road is one-way (up 10.30–14.00, down 16.00–18.00) with a 35km/hr limit.

To the right from the fluviometer, our trail to Colonia Suiza climbs steeply upstream past the Pozones, but soon levels off and veers left away from the river. After 30 minutes the path again climbs gently through the trees along the right bank of another river, the Arroyo Callvú. This flows from Laguna Callvú (also known as Laguna Azul) through a steep-sided twisting gorge. The trail is not waymarked, but it has now been cleared so that horses can pass. The path leads to the foot of Cerro Bonete although the view of this mountain is obscured by vegetation. After following the true right bank of the Arroyo Callvú for an hour it crosses to the left bank and after 15 minutes passes a waterfall trickling down a rocky face on the left.

The trail continues on the left bank of the river which now crashes down in a series of cascades while to your right are the forbidding grey crags of Cerro Bonete. After about 30 minutes you reach a point where the Arroyo Callvú rushes over great slabs of rock (2¾ hours from the hotel). The path is to the right of the slabs, marked by little piles of stones. Soon, however, it crosses to the right bank of the river where it climbs through trees before emerging onto further steep, rocky slabs. After scrambling up these you reach a small level wooded area. The path is marked with cairns and passes through dwarf trees before reaching Laguna Callvú, a deep blue lake situated at about 1,460m in a magnificent rock amphitheatre. Good camping can be found in a grassy clearing left of the lake, close to its outlet stream.

The trail continues along the left/west side of Laguna Callvú and has been cleared through small patches of dwarf trees. It is not waymarked but is easy to follow if you look for the cuts. Cross a stream that comes down off the slabs under Cerro Punta Negra (2,184m) and 30 minutes later you reach the northwest end of the lake where you start to climb the slabs in a northwest direction. The slabs provide good grip and after a strenuous hour's scramble bring you out onto the curved ridge high above Laguna Callvú at about 1,730m. There may be patches of snow up here but these can easily be avoided. Excursions up Cerro Punta Negra and Cerro Bonete could be made from this point but you would need an extra day. From the top of this ridge you can see the small Laguna Jujuy to your left. On the other side of the ridge you can see Brazo de la Tristeza, the southwestern arm of Lago Nahuel Huapi, while to the right the rugged outline of Cerro Cristal (2,010m) is visible. Go right and head east across the ridge above Laguna Callvú. From the shallow col below Cerro Bonete make your way down in a northeasterly direction towards the tiny Laguna Cretón and climb the screes on the south side of Cerro Cristal (ie: to the north of the *laguna*). It should take about 1–1½ hours to reach the ridge from where you have a splendid view of Tronador to the west. Head north along its rocky ridge towards the pointed summit of Cerro Cristal, but before you start the final climb cross the slabs to the right and head towards the northeast ridge coming off Cerro Cristal. It should take about 30 minutes to cross the slabs.

Follow the northeast ridge of Cerro Cristal for about an hour down to the grassy basin below in which there are plenty of camping spots. Head northeast up the scree slopes to the ridge, which is just under 2,000m and looks down on Laguna CAB (or Lluvú). The climb, which is rocky and steep near the top, takes about 1¼ hours. Go right along the ridge that circles Laguna CAB. Below you to the left the closed *refugio* can be seen nestling next to the feeder stream into Laguna CAB. The descent to the right/southeast side of the lake, partly along a dry streambed, should take an hour or so. Here you will find plenty of level ground and fireplaces for camping.

From the outlet stream at the north end of Laguna CAB follow the well-used path down the right side of the stream. The path climbs out of some woods into an area of open mountain. Cross a sandy path eastwards which is waymarked with strips of coloured plastic. The area appears to have been damaged by fire as a lot of burnt trees litter the slopes. This clearing allows you to view your next and final climb, which will bring you out above Laguna Negra. The path turns northeast and goes steeply down a sandy track for 15 minutes towards a tree-covered area. The trail, marked with splashes of red paint on trees and stones, now winds its way down to the valley bottom where you jump or wade across the Arroyo La Chata (or Arroyo Lluvuco). Take the trail to the right/north which climbs gently until you hear a stream to the right. Fifteen minutes from the valley bottom you drop down and cross this stream following the plastic ribbon marker on a tree. The trail now climbs very steeply eastwards away from the stream and up through trees towards the massif of Cerro Bayley Willis (1,950m). After about an hour you reach a cirque filled with small trees. Follow the left hand side of the cirque and climb the scree slopes on the northeast side, directly ahead, which lead to the ridge above Laguna Negra. This takes about 20 minutes. To make your way down, head northeast and after 15 minutes you should reach the eastern edge of Laguna Negra. Follow the well-marked path left of the lake which passes over slabs and boulders close to the shore and leads to the palatial Refugio Italia (1,650m). From here it is 16km downhill to Colonia Suiza. Alternatively you can continue on the route from Refugio Italia to Refugio López.

AN INTERNATIONAL HIKE
Lake Todos Los Santos to Lake Mascardi
Some of the most spectacular mountain and glacier scenery in South America lies on the Chile/Argentina border, between Puerto Montt and Bariloche. Most people travelling the 200km between these towns end up taking the bus via Osorno, or one of the high-priced bus–boat tours (US$120 or more) which afford little time to absorb the remarkable landscape en route. By hiking and hitching you can cover

the route for about a fifth of this price, the only unavoidable cost being about US$28 for the boat across Lago Todos los Santos, and enjoy the mountains, lakes and glaciers of the Ruta de los Lagos at leisure.

The core of the trip is the hike from Peulla on Lago Todos los Santos in Chile to Pampa Linda in the valley of the Río Manso in Argentina, a distance of 50km or 3–4 days of strenuous walking. The remainder, apart from the boat trip, can be walked, bussed or hitched according to how you feel. We found the frontier officials very helpful and not at all put out by scruffy *mochileros* (backpackers) wanting to enter their country. If entering Chile from Argentina you will have to eat up all your provisions of fresh food beforehand as fruits, fresh meat, cheese and other dairy products cannot be taken across the border. Note also that changing currency can be a problem (although the hotel at Peulla does change US$ travellers' cheques to Chilean pesos) so be sure to carry a small quantity of each currency.

Peulla to Lago Mascardi takes about 4 days, but the hike can be shortened by up to a day at either end if you take transport. It can also be combined with the Lake-to-Lake Walk near Bariloche, as a bridge crosses the Río Manso from the Hotel Tronador). The going is sometimes difficult in places because of fallen trees and the trail may be hard to follow.

Distance	50km
Altitude	Between 150m and 1,850m
Rating	Difficult
Time	3–4 days (Peulla to Lago Mascardi)
Start of trail	Peulla
End of trail	Los Rápidos (to camp), Playa Linda (bus to Bariloche)
Maps	Argentine IGM 1:100,000 Sheet 4172-22 (Llao-Llao) covers the most important part of this hike, but the latest edition we could find was not very accurate. Not surprising, really: it was published in 1947. If you are walking east to west you should visit the Club Andino in Bariloche as their hiking maps cover this route and are very helpful. The Chilean JLM map 15 covers the Bariloche area.
Note	For the Chilean end see also map on page 192

Getting to the trailhead

Local buses run two or three times daily from Puerto Montt to Petrohué, at the west end of Lago Todos los Santos, via Puerto Varas and Ensenada (pages 190–1). The 07.00 from Puerto Montt (08.00 at Puerto Varas) will get you to Petrohué in time for the boat across Lago Todos los Santos, leaving at 10.00 Mon–Sat; it takes about 2 hours to Peulla and returns at 17.00. In summer, however, there are often extra sailings so it is worth asking in advance at travel agencies in Puerto Montt, Puerto Varas or Bariloche. Do not start the walk on a Sunday: the border posts are closed, and there are no regular boats across Lago Todos los Santos.

At the end of this hike, there is a risk of the CAB bus and tour buses from Pampa Linda to Bariloche all being full, so you may in fact prefer to start from Pampa Linda – see page 234 for transport options. An increasing number of people now stay wholly within Argentina by hiking from Pampa Linda to Puerto Frías, taking the boat to Puerto Alegre, hiking 3km (or taking the bus) to Puerto Blest, and returning to Puerto Pañuelo (near Bariloche) by boat. Starting with an excursion from Bariloche to the *Ventisquero Negro*, it is possible to spend the first night at Pampa Linda and the second night below the *Ventisquero Frías*, reaching Puerto Frías in time for the boat at 14.00 (US$21).

Route description

You should be sure to stock up with food in Puerto Montt or Puerto Varas before setting off (or Bariloche or El Bolsón if you are doing the route the other way). There are very few supplies en route – other than the luscious blackberries, raspberries and strawberries which you will find all along the hike.

We walked from west to east, that is, from Chile to Argentina, and have described the hike this way. It can equally be done the other way round, but if so remember that you cannot take fresh food into Chile.

The walk begins on the jetty at **Peulla** (150m) where you will disembark around 13.00 from the boat which brought you across Lago Todos los Santos. The village itself is 500m down the road, and consists of about a dozen houses, a campsite and the expensive Hotel Peulla. There are no shops, but you may be able to buy fresh bread at the hotel or at one of the houses.

The dirt road over the **Paso de Pérez Rosales** to Argentina lets you in gently for the first 18km by keeping to the lakeside and then the wide, flat valley floor. You will pass a large *estancia*, then, after about 4 hours, cross the Río Peulla. Half an hour on and you will arrive at the Chilean *carabineros* at Casa Pangue in an idyllic setting with views of glacier-capped Mount Tronador to the south. The incumbents of this isolated post are a friendly bunch, and will probably let you pitch your tent around here if it is getting late. Otherwise, it is another 3–4 hours (11km) over the pass to Argentina and Puerto Frías. From Casa Pangue the road climbs steeply uphill as if forever (about 7km). The pass (976m) is densely forested and only once do you get a really good view of the river far below. But once over the top and into Argentina it is under an hour (4km) down to the Argentine customs and *gendarmería* at Puerto Frías (762m).

Some people prefer to skip this part of the walk, however, and pick up one of the tour buses from Peulla to Puerto Frías. These are very expensive (about US$40) but if you do not fancy the 29km road-hike you have little option as there is no car traffic on this road. It is possible to take a bike on the ferries and along this dirt road, but not on the hike from Puerto Frías to Pampa Linda.

Laguna Frías, from which the port takes its name, is a magical place. Cradled between high forest-covered mountains, its silent waters are an astonishing emerald green (but beware: the minerals that give the lake this romantic look will give you a stomach-ache too). The policemen at the *gendarmería* are very friendly, being only too pleased to have someone to talk to in their lonely post. They will point you to good camping spots in the woods where you can feast on wild raspberries if you are there in summer.

Tours go north from here by boat, at 14.00; from Puerto Alegre it is 3km (bus or hike) to Puerto Blest, on Lago Nahuel Huapi, where there is a good hotel (tel: 02944 425 443) and a university field station studying the *Bosque Lluvioso Templado* – Valdivian forest, with alerce and ciprés de las guiatecas, lenga, coihue, mañío macho, mañío hembra and fuinque (*Lomatia ferruginea*), and pudú.

However, our hike continues south along a trail which winds through the woods just above the *gendarmería* towards the aptly named **Paso de las Nubes**

('Pass of the Clouds'; 1,356m). To find the start of the path, turn left at the shrine behind the *gendarmería*. It is clear and wide at first, but after the first hour or so narrows into an obstacle course of overhanging bamboo and fallen tree trunks. From time to time the *guardaparques* of Nahuel Huapi National Park clear these away and restore the way-marks, which consist of orange plastic strips tied to branches and paint flashes on trees and rocks.

Not far from Puerto Frías you will pass a small monument dedicated to 'Commander Julio Cesar Sagredo and Deputy Commander Pedro Angel Obregón, who fell in this place on 13th April 1952 in the fulfilment of their duty' (two unfortunates who died when their aircraft crashed here). You will soon come to the Río Frías, which you should follow for about 30 minutes until you reach the spot where a huge tree has fallen across the river forming a natural bridge, with a double steel wire for support. (Be very careful crossing this after heavy rain when it will be partially submerged and dangerous.) You will reach small but adequate campsites on the trail about 2, 10 (by a stream) and 15 minutes later. These are the only campsites between Puerto Frías and the *Ventisquero Frías*.

The next 3 or 4 hours are spent scrambling over tree trunks through a thick forest of alerce, bamboo and arrayán. Keep your eyes skinned for plastic or paper strips tied to branches which indicate the way. You eventually emerge at a quite remarkable spot. Directly across the valley, the *Ventisquero Frías* tumbles down from Volcán Tronador in a mass of blue ice, crevasses and glacier-borne gravel (though it has retreated dramatically in recent years); ahead the valley ends in a sheer wall of rock; and below, just across some small rocky outcrops there is a beautiful campsite among the trees beside a stream. The only things likely to bother you, as you listen to the distant thud of falling avalanches which give Tronador (the Thunderer) its name, are the horseflies (*tábanos*) which at certain times of year get extremely fat and troublesome.

When continuing be careful not to lose the path – fighting your way through the bush is almost impossible. After crossing the stream just beyond the campsite, the path almost immediately heads up the bare rock outcrop to your left as you look at the glacier. This is a climb of 500m, marked by red cairns. If you reach a stream running down from the forest to the valley, you have gone too far. The path is marked with red paint, first on the rock and then on trees, and is fairly clear. It climbs steeply for about 1½ hours until you reach the 1,400m pass in an area of thorn bushes. There are incredible views, clouds permitting, in all directions but especially to the north where Laguna Frías can be seen in its hollow among the soaring peaks. If you do the walk in December or early January you are warned that there is likely to be snow on the pass which will make walking tough and route-finding difficult.

The trail winds down through the forest again and after 1¼ hours you will come to a swamp where it all but disappears. Keep your eyes peeled for the white plastic markers. Do not head towards the river but go straight into the swamp for about 50m until you come across a line of submerged logs heading slightly to the right. The next plastic marker is visible from these logs in a tree 30m ahead. From there the trail becomes clearer again, if somewhat boggy, keeping to the right bank of the river. The forested landscape gets better all the time and you can camp almost anywhere.

After about 2 hours you meet the trail from Refugio Otto Meiling and cross over the Arroyo Castaño Overo when you see a grassy campsite on the other side of the river. There is usually a fallen tree positioned here to serve as a footbridge, but if not the crossing is simple enough. The going is easy for the final 30 minutes down the jeep track to Pampa Linda where you enjoy spectacular views of Tronador, not to mention the material delights of the *hostería*.

You will see the **Otto Meiling hut** signposted after crossing the river above Pampa Linda. It is 2 hours through the forest to the tree line (a steep footpath cuts off the curves of the jeep track) and once above the trees there are spectacular views of the glaciers and waterfalls. A further hour brings you to the *refugio* (1,850m; tel: 15 605 404), which is positioned on a rock ridge with glaciers on both sides and condors flying around it. The guardian will guide groups of climbers up to **Pico Argentino** (3,410m) and **Pico Internacional** (3,554m), two of the three summits of Tronador (Pico Chileno is 3,430m above sea level).

The tourist road from the Bariloche–El Bolsón highway to the Hotel Tronador (see page 233) continues to Pampa Linda – see page 234 for transport possibilities. If you want to camp, there are only two viable places because the lakeside is steep and heavily forested: on the beach at the head of Lago Mascardi just before the youth camp; or at the Los Rápidos campsite 12km further on.

From the Hotel Tronador the road (built in the early 1940s) continues for 14km to a *gendarmería*, a bridge over the Manso Superior, and the Pampa Linda hotel (tel: 02944 422 181; fax: 442 038; pampalinda@bariloche.com.ar; www.tronador.com), shop and fully-equipped CAB campsite. The hotel charges from US$20 in a five-bed room (10% less for cash), and the campsite is excellent, with hot showers in season, great food and great views. About 500m to the west a path turns left over a suspension bridge to the Saltillo de las Nalcas, 20 minutes from the road through coihue, lenga, ñire and colihue. Ask at the *hostería* to hire horses (US$20 half-day/US$32 day) and also for a guide (US$100/day for trekking, with a maximum of 10 clients, or US$150 for climbing, with a maximum of 4).

The road splits at Pampa Linda, one continuing for 6km (through lenga and ñire) to the *mirador* of the *Ventisquero Negro* and another 2km to the Hostería Los Ventisqueros (or Hostería Jerman), from where you can walk to the scree on the east side of Tronador. Another trail leads to the Refugio Otto Meiling (see above), about 3 hours from Pampa Linda, and another trail to the Refugio Viejo Tronador, built in 1938, abandoned and reopened in about 1997; there is only room for eight people and camping is not possible. You will need to show your passport at the Pampa Linda *gendarmería*, as the trail passes through Chilean territory; follow the Río Cauquenes to the Lagunas Cauquenes and the Paso Vuriloche on the border (the old *Ruta de los Jesuitas* into Chile), then climb to the right to the hut at 2,270m by a *hito* (border post) between the Manso and Blanco Grande glaciers. It takes about 4 hours to the snowline and another couple of hours on the snow.

Note

If you do the walk to Puerto Frías south to north you should take care at the following points. As you leave Pampa Linda go left when the trail forks; after crossing the bridge follow the jeep road up the hill until you see the trail to Paso de las Nubes signposted to the right.

Chiloé and the Carretera Austral

CHILOÉ

Only a narrow stretch of water separates Chiloé from the Chilean mainland, but crossing it is like stepping into another country. The island, 250km long by 50km wide, is often shrouded in rain and mist, but when the sun shines it is extremely beautiful. The coast is ringed by an emerald and gold patchwork of potato and wheat fields, and all the island's towns. The interior is covered by vast virgin forests, which get higher and denser as you move south and west, towards the ocean.

Chacao and Castro, the oldest settlements in Chiloé, were established in 1567, and the indigenous population, a blend of Mapuches and Chonos, was soon decimated by European diseases. The Mapuche uprising of 1598 drove the Spaniards out of Araucanía and the Lakes region, leaving those in Chiloé cut off and dependent for survival on an annual ship from Peru. This demanded high prices for its cargo and paid low prices for Chiloé's exports, so that the Spanish settlers were as poor as their neighbours and intermarried with them, producing a distinctive and homogenous society, with a vibrant folklore. The road from Ancud to Castro was built only in 1781, and things looked up in the next century, when Chiloé first supplied provisions to whalers heading to the Southern Ocean, and then supplied sleepers (ties) to all the railways of South America. After a collapse of the potato market, many Chilotes left to work on the *estancias* of Argentina, a tradition which continues to this day, due to their reputation for hard work. Indeed, the Chilotes, with their strong Catholic values, their folklore and their large families, can be seen as the Irish of South America; up to half the population lives or works away from the island, but they return often, and there are regular buses to Castro from points as distant as Punta Arenas. Chilote fishermen also established tiny settlements along the coast of the mainland immediately to the east, known as Chiloé Continental. This is now the province of Palena, and like Chiloé Insular it is part of the 10th Region (Los Lagos), rather than the 11th (Aysén), to which it might more logically be attached.

The island is probably best known for its quaint wooden houses or *palafitos*, built out over the water on stilts, perhaps in order to pay less rent (you only pay rent for the bit on land, as no-one owns the water!). The island also has about 150 wooden churches, built by the Jesuits in the 17th and 18th centuries, of which 16 were added to UNESCO's World Heritage List in 2000. The oldest were constructed without the use of a single iron nail. Although not as beautiful as the wooden churches of eastern Europe, they have a strong simple charm of their own. The

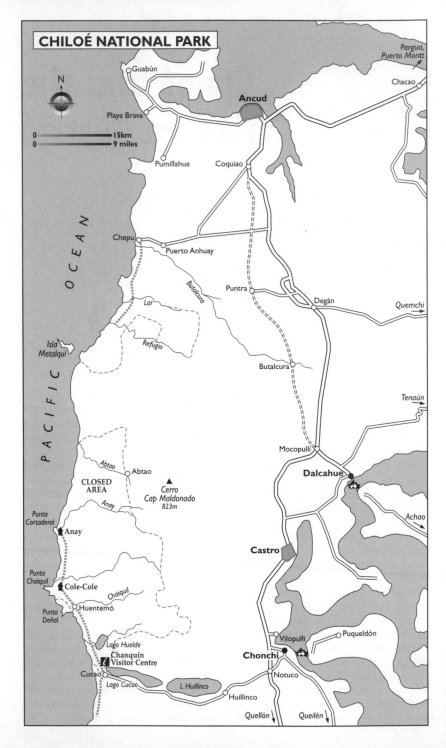

tradition of using wooden shingles on walls and roofs also dates from the same period. If you look closely you will find about a dozen different shapes and styles.

Ancud, in the north of the island, is slightly larger than the capital, **Castro**; these are linked by the PanAmerican (which continues to Quellón, port for Aysén). In Ancud, the Hospedaje Vista al Mar, Av Costanera 918 (tel/fax: 065 622 617) is also the official HI youth hostel; but the nameless place at O'Higgins 6 (tel: 622 2660) is the best of the budget *hospedajes*. At Coquiao, 12km south of Ancud, mountain-bikers could try forking right onto the tracks of the narrow-gauge railway abandoned after the 1960 earthquake; this is now a dirt road passing by Puntra, Butalcura and Pindapulli to Mocopulli, the junction for Dalcahue. The Islotes de Puñihuil, 30km west of Ancud (1.5km offshore) are home to about a thousand Magellanic penguins and some Humboldt penguins, too. Boat trips are available from Ancud, although landing is not permitted. The islands are a reserve managed by the Fundación Otway in Puerto Montt (A Varas 629, 3rd floor, office 5/7; tel: 065 315 494; fax: 278 500; mobile 09 564 7866; otwafund@ctcinternet.cl; otway@telsur.cl).

Twenty-three kilometres south of Castro is **Chonchi**, an attractive fishing village served by buses to the Chiloé National Park, where there are several pleasant places to stay, notably the Canadian-run Esmerelda by the Sea (tel/fax: 065 671 328; grady@telsur.cl) on the waterfront just south of the centre. Black dolphins can usually be seen in the harbour in the evening. The village has a wooden church, begun in 1754, and there is another, dating from the early 18th century, just north in **Vilopulli** (or Vellipulli), which can be reached by a pleasant coastal walk. Heading up Avda Aguirre Cerda, opposite the Hotel Huildin, it takes 10 minutes up and over a hill to the next bay, where you should swing left and then go onto the beach. If the tide is low it takes just 20 minutes to reach Vilopulli; if not you can either climb over a small outcrop, or pass through the fields above.

CHILOÉ NATIONAL PARK

Distance	Approximately 21km to Cole-Cole, 5km further to Río Anay
Altitude	Sea level
Rating	Easy
Time	I day each way to/from Cole-Cole
Start of trail	Cucao
End of trail	Cucao
Maps	1:50,000 4215-7400 (H86) Río Anay and 4230-7400 (H95) Cucao

The eastern side of Chiloé is very attractive and worth exploring at leisure; sea-kayaking with Altué is a particularly enjoyable option (book in Santiago, or through Pehuén Expediciones, Thompson 229, Castro; tel 065 635 254). The western (Pacific) coast is far wetter and wilder, and largely uninhabited. Other than in the island's northwestern corner, only one road reaches this coast, at Cucao, headquarters of the Parque Nacional Chiloé. In summer there are usually three buses a day from Castro, although Saturday can, strangely, be a very quiet day. The Conaf office in Castro is open Mon–Fri 09.00–12.30, but there is a very informative noticeboard outside in any case.

Getting to the trailhead

From the Notuco junction, just south of Chonchi, a 35km road crosses the waist of the island along the south sides of Lagos Huillinco and Cucao, between the hills known as the *Tetas de Cucao* – a route followed by both Darwin and Chatwin. **Cucao** consists of a wooden church, a few *hospedajes* (where you can also camp) and an excellent suspension bridge to the Parador Darwin, the most upmarket place in town, which also hires out horses, although like all the horses available here they are dull plodders. You should cross the bridge and follow the sandy road to the right, and after 5 minutes go to the right to the Chanquín Visitor Centre (open daily 08.30–18.00), set in arrayán trees and nalca plants. This is very informative, and the staff are helpful, too. If you continue along the path you will pass the campsite ('temporarily' closed since 1998) in a couple of minutes, then the Mirador del Sur, looking east over Lago Cucao, and cross a flat boggy heath to reach the start of the Sendero Tepual, 10 minutes further. This is a 770m loop on modern boardwalks that climbs up and down through a tangled wood of tepú (*Tepualia stipularis*), with very good interpretative signs; a path also leads 1km north to a craft shop.

It is also worth mentioning the Sendero Rancho Grande, a 5–6–hour hike to see stands of alerce, for which you need a guide, partly because a boat is needed to reach the start. Finally it is also possible to walk south from Cucao, out of the national park, for 4 hours to Playa Pirulil, where there are sea lions and a cormorant colony. There is a good track, but it crosses private land and has various unmarked junctions, so it is easy to get lost and worth finding a guide.

Route description

The main route into the park starts with the Sendero Playa, beginning at the side of the visitor centre. This crosses the sandy road and dunes covered in introduced plants such as gorse and brambles, to reach the beach in 15 minutes. This stretches for about 15km, and many visitors see nothing else in the park. However, it is worth carrying on, as there is a great deal of variety here. Heading north beside the sea, after an hour or so you will cross a small stream, the outlet of Lago Huelde, and after another 45 minutes (hiking fast) you can turn right to cross the Río Deñal by a wooden bridge. Many people seem to carry on for 10 minutes to the end of the beach and ford the river there, but there is a perfectly good path along the right bank. From the ford at the end of the beach a track heads up and over the rocky headland of Punta Deñal through the scattered houses of the indigenous Huilliche village of Huentemó (or Guantemo), site of a Canadian-backed Model Forest project. In 10 minutes you will be back on the beach, and in 10 more you will cross the Río Chaiquil by another obvious ford. A track passes a soccer pitch then climbs steadily for 25 minutes over Punta Chaiquil, and on for 10 minutes to a viewpoint, rather too high to see any otters or seals. From here it is an easy descent of under 10 minutes to a pasture plateau and houses sheltered behind Punta Huentemó. Go straight across and down to the right, and along the next beach for 10 minutes to the Cole-Cole refuge. This is an old but solid wooden hut in the woods; there are also plenty of camping spots in the scrub along the beach.

You should not miss the continuation of this hike to the north, as it is only beyond Cole-Cole that you will find the true temperate rainforest of the Pacific coast, a wonderfully dense and complex tangle of trees, ferns and creepers. It is about a minute further to a good bridge across the Río Cole-Cole (where you can get fresh water). You should then go slightly to the left, then fork right, continuing on a log corduroy (rows of logs laid parallel) and log bridges through a dense forest of arrayán, with tepú and big epiphytes. It is like a true jungle but without the heat, humidity or insects. However, the path has plenty of mudtraps and other obstacles, especially along the first half. The ground barely seems to rise at all, but there are plenty of watercourses which for the first 50 minutes all seem to be flowing south. After an hour the path follows a streambed for 10 or 20m before continuing on the same side as before; equally in 10 minutes more you should keep to the left to avoid a broken bridge. After another 10 minutes you will emerge into long (usually wet) grass and follow the left bank of the Río Anay to reach the refuge in 5 minutes. This is another solid wooden hut, but it is smaller than the Cole-Cole hut, there is no glass in the windows and no real space to camp here. There is plenty of space on the north bank, but this is the closed area of the park, and it is difficult to cross, except at the bar at the mouth, reached by climbing over the headland of Punta Cortaderal. From the right-hand side of the hut a path leads up as far as a viewpoint. You may prefer to make a day-trip from Cole-Cole.

The park also has a smaller northern area, the **Sector Chepu**, reached from the PanAmerican 25km south of Ancud. From here a road leads 14km west to Puerto Anhuay and 10km further to Chepu (Camping Río Chepu; tel: 622 052), where you must take a boat across the Río Chepu. You then have a walk of 14km (4 hours) south along the coast (on the beach and in rainforest) to the Río Lar, where there is a *guardería* with *refugio*. You can continue another 6km south to the Río Refugio. From Ancud Buses Manuel Mansillo serve Chepu at 16.00 daily.

It is also possible to take a bus (Buses Mar Brava at 06.45 Mon–Sat, 12.00 & 16.00 Mon–Fri and 14.00 Sat) to Pumillahue, which had a mini-gold rush in 1893, and hike south along the coast to the Río Chepu in a couple of days. You can also take a tour: Paralelo 42 (Monseñor Aguilera 755; tel: 065 622 458: or ask at the Residencial María Carolina, Alm. Latorre 558) offers a walk south from Duhatao along the beach via Aulén to the mouth of the Río Chepu, returning by boat on the river. The same company will also arrange other boat trips on the Chepu and Butalcura or horse-riding on the beach at Guabún, and take you to the Caleta Puñihuil penguin colony (see above). Turismo Huaihuén, at Pudeto 1356 2a piso (tel/fax: 623 800) also do a day-trip to Caleta Puñihuil, and (on Fridays) a trip to Cucao, which includes horse-riding. Austral Adventures, at Av. Prat 176–B, Casilla 432, Ancud (tel/fax: 065 625 977; tours@austral-adventures.com) offers the best trips on land and water around Chiloé, while Turismo Suroeste, casilla 635, Puerto Montt (tel/fax: 065 281 490, mobile 09 412 1541; gestorias@telsur.cl) offers cruises in a traditional Chilote sailing boat.

THE CARRETERA AUSTRAL

Until a few years ago the roadless wilderness to the south of Puerto Montt remained virtually unknown and uninhabited except for a handful of isolated fishing villages. Sea travellers caught tantalising glimpses of dense forests through the mist and rain as their ship slid through the channels between the many islands, but only in 1988 was a road opened as far south as Cochrane. This is Chile's *Carretera Austral*.

This wettest of regions (they say that on the coast it rains 370 days a year) also has pockets of sunshine to the east: Chile Chico, on Lago General Carrera and near the Jeinimeni reserve manages 300 sunny days a year. The rugged landscape is dissected by many rivers, and if you want to travel the full length of the Carretera you will have to use a ferry which normally operates only in January and February.

SHIPPING

South of Puerto Montt lies one third of Chile, where under 5% of the population lives. It is a remote region of desolate fjords, channels and uninhabited, thickly forested islands. Even now most traffic to Magallanes, the far south of Chile, goes by air or passes by road through Argentina, but there is also a ferry link through this gloomy, storm-laden archipelago to Puerto Natales, 1,460km from Puerto Montt. It is a route that is the equal of British Columbia's Inside Passage and the Alaska Marine Highway, but until recently its tourist potential was neglected, with only a handful of hardy backpackers joining the truck drivers in reclining seats installed in a container on the deck of Empremar's antique roll-on-roll-off ferry that sailed to an erratic timetable.

In previous editions we included accounts of voyages on this ship, the *Tierra del Fuego*, that ended with her hitting a rock and limping into Puerto Natales at dawn, or damaging her propellor on an iceberg. Nowadays the route is operated by Navimag's Finnish-built *Puerto Edén*, and its tourist potential is being exploited, at least in part, although the voyage has lost little of its adventurous feel. Tales abound on the travellers' grapevine of life in the *claso económico* dorm, deep in the bowels of the ship (close to the anchor chain) as the notorious Golfo de Penas does its worst – but there is also much better accommodation, though still in a large metal box mounted above the car deck. She now sails to a regular weekly schedule – south on Thursdays and north on Mondays – and booking is straightforward. In 2001 a second ship, the *Magallanes*, has been added, sailing south on Mondays and north on Thursdays, and calling at Puerto Chacabuco, too. Prices may seem high to some backpackers, but do include bed and board for three days.

Nor (as a rule) does the ship run onto the rocks. Although passengers' GPS units have been known to indicate that the ship is on dry land, this is due to deficiencies in the charts, which fortunately the officers are well aware of. The standard of seamanship is high, although it can be disconcerting to find the officer of the watch dozing and the ship on autopilot – a helmsman appears only for docking and the passage through the three *angosturas* (narrows) – Inglesa, Guia and Kirke – where there is as little as two metres under the keel even at high tide.

Sailing south, the usual route passes east of Chiloé and the Chonos (or Guaitecas) archipelago, through the Pulluche channel to the Pacific and around the Taitao peninsula and across the Golfo de Penas; then down the Mesier channel to Puerto Edén (where a few Alakaluf board to sell their sad display of souvenirs). Then it passes down the Sarmiento channel and turns sharp east at Monte Burney, on the Peninsula Muñoz Gamero, and into the Golfo Almirante Montt. However, the route is not fixed. The ship may detour to see a glacier if she has to wait for the tide at the narrows.

At other times you will have to fly from Puerto Montt or travel via Argentina or the island of Chiloé. However you get there, the Carretera is one of the world's greatest long-distance mountain-bike tours – in fact it is one of the few roads which are more suited to MTBs than to tourers. However, this will change by around 2005, when the road should be paved from Puerto Montt to Villa Cerro

More popular is the cruise to the **Laguna San Rafael**, to see the amazing glacier, which discharges 2 million cubic metres of ice every day from its 3km face. Not surprisingly then, it is retreating, perhaps by as much as 200m a year. Navimag, Skorpios and Transmarchilay all operate weekly ferries from Puerto Montt to Puerto Chacabuco, continuing to the Laguna San Rafael, starting from around US$200. These both entail sleeping on board; the only way to take a day-trip (other than by flying in) is by Patagonia Connection's catamaran, on Fridays and Sundays in season (US$240); this includes a free bar with 30,000-year-old ice in your *pisco*.

For many centuries canoe-Indians and Jesuits came this way, making a 3km portage across the Ofqui isthmus to the Río Negro, avoiding the lengthy and dangerous circumnavigation of the Taitao peninsula. In 1937 the excavation of a canal was begun, but was abandoned in 1943. This is still a fascinating area to explore by kayak or any other type of small boat. The *laguna* is visited by 18,000 visitors a year but virtually none of them land, so Conaf currently receives next to no fees. Even so there is now 10km of boardwalk, to a viewpoint over the glacier and, soon, to the Glaciar San Quintin, several hours to the south and far larger than the San Rafael glacier.

This is the southern limit of the Valdivian forest, but the 1.7 million hectare national park encompasses a variety of ecosystems; the most common is evergreen coihue forest (with tepa, mañío macho, canelo and chuelillo), but there are also lacustrine and montane ecosystems, Magellanic moorland, and deciduous *Nothofagus* forest. There are no reptiles and few amphibians, but you may see birds such as condor, black-necked swan, cormorants, gulls, ducks, chucao and huet-huet, and mammals such as pudú, red fox, kod-kod and a few huemul to the east and south. Parts of the park are considered to be among the most pristine environments on earth.

Shipping companies

Navimag Avda El Bosque Norte 0440, piso 11, Las Condes, Santiago; tel: 02 442 3120; fax: 203 5025; www.navimag.com – online booking available; also at Angelmó 2107, Puerto Montt; tel: 065 432 300; fax: 276 611; Pedro Montt 262, Puerto Natales; tel: 061 414 300; fax: 414 361

Patagonia Connection Fidel Oteíza 1921, of. 1006, Providencia, Santiago; tel: 02 225 6489; fax: 274 8222; email: info@patagoniaconnex.cl

Skorpios Angelmó 1660, Puerto Montt; tel: 065 256 619; fax: 258 315; email: skoinfo@skorpios.cl

Transmarchilay Avda Providencia 2653, L24, Santiago;, tel: 600 600 8687, 02 234 1464, 234 9635; fax: 234 4899; www.transmarchilay.cl; also at Angelmó 2187, Puerto Montt; tel: 065 270 411; fax: 270 415

Castillo. It runs through dense exuberant vegetation, passing glaciers and snow-capped mountains, lakes of every colour, rivers and waterfalls, with glimpses of hummingbirds and condors. The phrase which perhaps best sums up its nature is 'cold jungle'. Scenically it is a cross between Switzerland, Scotland's west coast and a tropical jungle, with a few volcanoes thrown in; culturally it is like the Wild West, with the land still being tamed by hardy pioneers on horseback or wooden-wheeled oxcarts.

In this region the Andes sink into the Pacific, and the only plains lie to their east rather than the west. Metamorphosed marine sediments have been uplifted and folded three times, allowing intrusions of granite and basalt, as well as the development of many hot springs. Heavy glaciation has produced a fantastically fragmented landscape.

The northern part of this area was known as 'Chiloé Continental', due to settlement by Chilote fishermen. Aysén, to the south, was never more than minimally populated by indigenous peoples. The area was largely explored by foreigners such as the Briton George Musters, the Argentine 'Perito' Moreno, and the German Hans Steffen; from 1903 the Chilean government allocated large areas of land to three agricultural companies, while private settlers began to move in unofficially. Many of these had been working on Argentine *estancias*, and they continued to buy and sell their goods in Argentina due to the total lack of communications in Aysén. A road from Coyhaique reached Puerto Aysén only in 1936; roads south to Puerto Ibáñez and north to Mañihuales followed only in the 1960s. The Colonisation Law, intended to regularise private settlement and undermine the power of the three big ranching companies, led to one of the world's worst ecological disasters. Settlers could freely claim land if it had been cleared, so in 1946–53 huge fires raged across the province, clearing not only potential agricultural land but also inaccessible mountain slopes. Almost 3 million hectares, a third of the province's area, were burnt, and as another third was bare rock or ice, roughly half of Aysén's vegetation was destroyed. Now 1.5 million hectares are affected by erosion, leading to the silting-up of Puerto Aysén and the construction of the new port of Puerto Chacabuco, further downstream. In this cold climate, decay and regeneration move slowly, and the fields are still strewn with logs. At last in 1999 government grants were introduced to help land-owners clear their land, usually by dragging the logs into piles or fence lines. Bamboo and mice, for instance, have benefited from the changes, while the huemul have been badly affected. In the last 20 years in particular the climate has become warmer, drier and windier, and the glaciers are retreating. There are many other environmental problems, mostly deriving from uncontrolled development. Coyhaique has winter smog, but nevertheless much of Aysén still boasts what is claimed to be the purest air and water in the world.

Construction of the **Carretera Austral** began in 1976, with the central section opening in 1983, the 1,028km from Puerto Montt to Cochrane opened in 1988, and the final few kilometres to Villa O'Higgins (212km from Cochrane) in 1999. The Carretera actually begins on the 'mainland', in Puerto Montt, passing the Alerce Andino National Park (page 201); the first ferry crossing is across the Estero Reloncaví, from La Arena to Caleta Puelche. A new road is being completed east to Puelo, allowing a wonderful circuit to Cochamó (page 195), Ralún, Ensenada and Puerto Varas; this also gives access to Volcán Yate (2,111m), one of the snow-capped peaks visible from Puerto Montt. To the south the Carretera passes Contao, the 'Company Town' of the Sociedad Explotadora de Alerces Reloncaví, which spent the 1960s clearing all the alerce trees from the south side of the Reloncaví estuary, and now a virtual ghost town, and (61km from Puelche) reaches Hornopirén (formerly Río Negro), on the fringe of the **Hornopirén National Park**. This protects 48,232ha of rainforest, notably mighty alerce trees, around Volcán Hornopirén (1,572m). A rough road heads northeast along the Río Negro, passing just east of the volcano, to Lago General Pinto Concha (20km). Forking right, a new road leads east to the Río Blanco campsite, from where in a few years time a three-day trail will lead to the Río Ventisquero, from where you will either have to return the same way or take a three-day raft trip down the Ventisquero (Class I) to the Río Puelo (Class III) with AlSur (see page 190).

To continue south from here, you will need a ferry, which operates daily but only from January to mid-March; for all the rest of the year you will either have to drive through Argentina, or take a ferry to Chaitén (usually three a week from Puerto Montt and two a week from Quellón, in Chiloé, with Navimag and Transmarchilay), or a plane. A fast catamaran should soon be operating between Puerto Montt, Castro and Chaitén.

CHAITÉN

Chaitén is capital of Palena province and the only town between Puerto Montt and Coyhaique. It has a superb location and wide streets but somehow fails to be anything more than a place to stay a night. The Pumalín Park has recently opened its Hospedaje El Puma at O'Higgins 54 (tel: 065 731 184); it is not hugely expensive, but there are also plenty of really cheap places for backpackers awaiting ferries, such as the Hospedaje Ancud, Libertad 105 (tel: 731 535). Most buses and tours leave from Chaitur at O'Higgins 67 (tel: 731 429; nchaitur@hotmail.com), which also serves as a tourist information office; B y V Tur, Libertad 432 (tel/fax: 731 390) operates minibuses to Caleta Gonzalo and Futaleufú, and has a cheap hospedaje at the same address. This is near the Entel office, on Aguirre Cerda and Libertad at the corner of the plaza, where (slow) internet access is available.

For **ferries**, Navimag is on Carrera near Riveros (tel: 731 570), and Transmarchilay is on the seafront at Corcovado 266 (tel: 731 272). For **flights**, Aeromet is in the Hotel Schilling, Corcovado 230 (tel: 731 409), and Aerosur at the corner of Carrera and Riveros. Bellavista al Sur, on Riveros between the plaza and Carrera, offers climbing gear and, as Ñuke Mapu Expediciones, courses. There are lots of so-called **supermarkets**, but only the Michinmahuida, on Corcovado at Todesco, is worthy of the name. There is an **ATM** at the Banco del Estado on the plaza.

PUMALÍN

Between Hornopirén and Chaitén is the Pumalín Park, perhaps the most exciting conservation initiative in Chile at the moment. This is a huge area of native forest that was bought (for around US$15m) by Doug Tompkins, the Californian owner of the clothing and hiking gear companies The North Face and Esprit, and donated to the Fundación The Conservation Land Trust, in the face of amazingly virulent opposition. Nationalists and other extreme right-wingers saw it as a foreign plot to cut the country in half (the park stretches from the sea to the Argentine border), to steal its natural resources, and perhaps even create a Zionist colony. Public opinion has gradually come around, however, and the government has accepted that it is a genuinely worthwhile conservation project. Even so, negotiations for it to be declared a *Sanctuario de la Naturaleza* drag on. The governor of Pumalín province did not allow the Chilean flag to be flown at Caleta Gonzalo, and then became mayor of Chaiten largely to obstruct the Pumalín project.

Pumalín covers a total of 270,000ha, an amazingly wild area of fjords, mountains (including Volcán Michinmahuida, 2,404m) and above all untouched temperate rainforest including huge and ancient alerce trees, some as much as 3,600 years old.

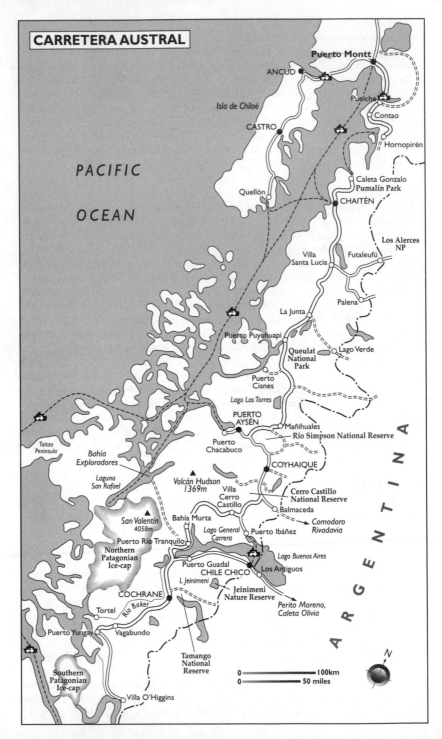

CARRETERA AUSTRAL

Puerto Montt

ANCUD

Puelche

Isla de Chiloé

Contao

CASTRO

Hornopirén

PACIFIC

Caleta Gonzalo
Pumalín Park

Quellón

CHAITÉN

OCEAN

Los Alerces
NP

Villa
Santa Lucia

Futaleufú

Palena

La Junta

Puerto Puyuhuapi

Lago Verde

Queulat
National
Park

Puerto
Cisnes

Lago Las Torres

PUERTO
AYSÉN

Mañihuales

Río Simpson National Reserve

Puerto
Chacabuco

COYHAIQUE

Taitao
Peninsula

Bahía
Exploradores

Volcán Hudson
1369m

Villa
Cerro
Castillo

Cerro Castillo
National Reserve

Laguna
San Rafael

Balmaceda

Comodoro
Rivadavia

San Valentín
4058m

Bahía Murta

Lago General
Carrera

Puerto Ibáñez

Puerto Río Tranquilo

Northern
Patagonian
Ice-cap

Lago Buenos Aires

Puerto Guadal
CHILE CHICO

Los Antiguos

Tortel

COCHRANE

L Jeinimeni

Jeinimeni
Nature Reserve

Perito Moreno,
Caleta Olivia

Río Baker

Puerto Yungay

Vagabundo

ARGENTINA

Tamango
National
Reserve

Southern
Patagonian
Ice-cap

Villa O'Higgins

0 _____ 100km
0 _____ 50 miles

N

This is one of the most productive ecosystems on the planet, thriving on up to 5m of precipitation per year and producing between 500 and 2,000 tonnes of organic matter per hectare.

From sea level to 500m altitude there is an evergreen Valdivian forest, composed mainly of tepa, coihue, tineo, ulmo and olivillo; from 500 to 1,000m is alerce forest (35% of the remaining alerce trees in Chile) and also coihue, with some tineo and mañío. From 1,000 to 1,500m is a mix of lenga and ñirre, both somewhat stunted by the climate. Resident animals include puma, pudú, huillín, coipo, red fox and skunks, and in the sea, dolphins and sea lions. Birds include steamer and torrent ducks, caiquéns, kingfishers, hummingbirds, woodpeckers, species typical of the Valdivian forest, such as chucao, rayadito and huet-huet, and in the higher areas, condors, vultures and eagles.

You can get more information from the Pumalín office at Buin 356 in Puerto Montt (tel: 065 250 079, fax: 255 145, pumalin@chilesat.net), and at O'Higgins 62 in Chaitén (tel: 065 731 341; open Mon–Sat 09.00–13.00,15.00–19.00, Sun 10.00–16.00), opposite Chaitur and next to Pumalín's own Hospedaje Puma and El Puma Verde craft shop. The IGN maps 4230-7230/5-04-08-0101-00 (H101 Caleta Gonzalo; 1:50,000) and 5-02-88-1809-16 (Castro; 1:250,000) do not show any roads or other facilities; JLM's map 17 *Patagonia, Islas de Chiloé* is more useful.

Much of the park is more or less inaccessible, or accessible only by boat, and it is not intended to open it up significantly. Nevertheless visitors are welcome, and various trails and free campsites are being constructed; the most idyllic are at hot springs, reached only by sea. The main entry point to the park is **Caleta Gonzalo**, where information is available (tel: 1812 960 4151). This is 56km north of Chaitén (at km147) – this stretch of the Carretera is to be a Highway of Scenic Value, with carved wooden signs – and Caleta Gonzalo is also a port for the summer ferries from Hornopirén. There are seven simple but comfortable Shaker-style *cabañas* here, as well as a small farm, and great home-made food in the café (07.30–23.00). From 2001 it should be possible to go east to the head of the Reñihue fjord (where there is a campsite), and then south to Lago Reñihue, on the east side of Volcán Michinmahuida, which will be a five-day horseback trip.

Heading south down the road, you will find the campsite signposted at once to the left, across the Río Gonzalo by a fine suspension bridge; to the right/west is the start of the **Sendero La Cascada**. This starts well, but soon turns into a steep and twisty climb through a dense forest of coihue, tepa, canelo and luma, on a path which is largely flooded when it rains. Ignoring the turning to the microhydro station to the right, you will come to a section of several hundred metres of trail being replaced by a raised boardwalk. After about 50 minutes you will reach a bridge that, when I was there, went halfway across the river to some rocks, and left me looking across a raging torrent to an arrow where the trail continued on the far bank. However, the bridge should by now be complete. The path continues to the left for another half-hour to reach a gully with walkways and ladders along the dripping rock walls, leading to the foot of a 15m waterfall at the outlet of the river from a nameless *laguna*. It is intended to build a campsite by the *laguna*; you will have to return the same way.

Heading south, at km158.5 the Carretera crosses the Río Tronador bridge. The **Sendero Río Tronador**, the wildest of the trails along this stretch of the Carretera, starts at a new campsite at this point. Crossing a suspension bridge, the trail heads west to a viewpoint to Volcán Michinmahuida, and a lake where there is a campsite, an hour from the start. Just south at km158.9 you will find the

Sendero Los Alerces, a 700m loop to the east, very well kitted out with boardwalks and a suspension bridge, made of the beautiful red wood of alerce trees felled by a landslide. The signs are very informative, showing how alerce bark was formerly stripped for caulking (sealing the gaps between a boat's planks),. slowly killing the trees. At the north end of the General Manuel Feliu de la R bridge (km160.6) there is a nice new picnic area and campsite (with toilets and plenty of shelters) to the west, from where the **Sendero Cascadas Escondidas** leads left to a new footbridge. A circular route heads off to the right, forking right again in 5 minutes over a small log bridge. After another 5 minutes turn right again down some steep steps to a superb double waterfall. Returning to this last junction and continuing uphill for a minute, there is a viewpoint over the waterfall. From here the path swings left and then down through some superb alerces, returning to the log bridge in 10 minutes. This is a well-made trail, but good footwear is still needed. When I was there it had not yet been signed, so it is possible you will find yourself being sent the other way around the loop. The trail has also been extended for a kilometre to a new campsite and more waterfalls which are said to be much more spectacular.

The road heads south over a low pass of 247m to pass Lago Negro and Lago Blanco, at both of which there are there are new campsites and trails, and then the Michinmahuida Oeste campsite, from where there should in a few years be a trail east onto the slopes of Volcán Michinmahuida. Then the Carretera drops through what seems to be second-growth forest to the coast at Santa Bárbara, the best beach in the area, 11km north of Chaitén. A bus runs from Chaitén at 08.00 on Monday, Wednesday and Friday (daily in January and February), returning at 13.30; with an early start you could do a hike or two and then catch the bus; conceivably you could catch the minibus to Futaleufú the same day.

In the **northern half of the Parque Pumalín** it is intended to provide an entry point similar to Caleta Gonzalo at Cholgo, 31km by road south of Hornopirén (the land is too steep to build at the actual entrance to the Pumalín park, but there is a small campsite at Pichancó, where the road actually ends at the *rampa*). In Hornopirén you can ask for information at the Hotel Hornopirén, Carrera Pinto 388 (tel/fax: 065 217 256), and arrange for a boat to hot springs and a hotel on Isla Llancahue (not part of the park). By boat you can also reach Cahuelmó, at the head of Fiordo Cahuelmó, on the eastern side of Fiordo Comau (or Leptepu), where there are more hot springs and a tiny campsite. This is run by AlSur in Puerto Varas, and you must make reservations through them (tel: 065 232 300) or the Hotel Hornopirén. The 5km path from the springs to a campsite at Laguna Abascal has been rebuilt; it passes through Valdivian forest, with pudú but no alerce.

AlSur also offers five- and ten-day trips along **Fiordo Comau**, with hiking, kayaking, and watching orca and dolphin; ¡Ecole!, in Pucón, and Santiago companies such as Cascada and Altué, organise similar trips, while Travellers, in Puerto Montt, can arrange yacht charters. If you are patient, you could hitch a ride in the *guardaparque*'s *lancha* which sails every 3 or 4 days from Hornopirén to Leptepu. Also on the east side of Fiordo Leptepu is the enclave of Huinay, formerly owned by the Catholic University of Valparaíso, which refused to sell to Doug Tompkins. Instead, it was controversially bought by the electricity company, Endesa, which created the Fundación Huinay (tel: 02 635 0255) to manage it. The Huinay campsite, reached only by boat, is run by AlSur. There is no infrastructure but passing boaters are welcome.

At the southern end of the fjord are the tiny settlements of Leptepú and Vodudahue, where there are more free campsites. From Vodudahue a trail is planned to campsites up the Río Barcelo, to the east. From Leptepú a 12km-long road (built as part of the Carretera Austral but more or less abandoned when the direct Hornopirén–Caleta Gonzalo ferry replaced two connecting ferries) crosses the neck of the Huequi peninsula to Fiordo Largo. This passes Pillán, the park's new operational base, where honey, jam and wool are produced and (of course) there is another free campsite; just south of Pillán the new Mirador trail heads west to a viewpoint. From Fiordo Largo (another campsite and shelters) you can take a boat to Caleta Gonzalo, or to see the 300-odd sealions living in Fiordo Reñihue. The Hornopirén–Chaitén ferry calls in (on Tuesdays southbound and on Mondays northbound) at Ayacara, on the west side of the Huequi peninsula, where community action is seeking to preserve the peninsula's native forest. The Centre for Environmental Education and Training for the Sustainable Development of Rural Communities was set up here in 1997.

FUTALEUFÚ

Heading south from Chaitén, you will cross the grandiose bridge over the Río Yelcho after 46km (km248), straight towards the spectacular glacier-laden *Silla del Diablo* ('Devil's Seat'), and head south along Lago Yelcho, past the Hostería and Cabanas Yelcho and Camping Cavi (km255); at km257 a sign hidden in trees to the right leads to Aguas Minerales. Soon the big glacier-filled bowl of *El Ventisquero* is opening up to the right, and just before the Puente Ventisqueros (where minibuses may stop, to take photos and, in season, nalca) a trail heads west, reaching a glacier in about an hour. At km270 the road crosses the Cuesta Moraga pass, and at km278 (at the northern end of Villa Santa Lucía, where there are a couple of hospedajes) reaches the junction east to Futaleufú.

Turning left again after 31km at Puerto Ramírez (another *hospedaje*), a road follows the Río Futaleufú to the town of Futaleufú (47km) and on to the border crossing to Trevelín and Esquel. This is a little-visited area that makes a handy route to Argentina's Los Alerces National Park (page 303), but it is also worth visiting in itself. There is a lot of small-scale development, such as campsites along the road west of Futaleufú, but little that is too damaging. The **Río Futaleufú** is one of the world's great white-water rafting rivers (see page 74), flowing through great mountain scenery, and there are also lovely lakes which provide some fantastic fishing. The main ecosystem here is *bosque patagónico con coníferas* (Patagonian forest with conifers), unprotected thus far by the SNASPE system of reserves. There are only 64 species of flora, of which six are endemic, and *Elaphoglossum gayanum* and *Gleichenia litoralis* are threatened, as is the fish *Aplochiton taeniatus*. Mammals in the area include the Chilean mountain cat (guiña), huemul, armadillo and otter.

Futaleufú (350m) is a friendly, small town with cheap *hospedajes* and a small supermarket. It can be reached by minibuses from Chaitén at 15.30 except on Sundays. There are services to the border (connecting to Esquel) on Mondays and Fridays at 09.00 and 18.00. Aerosur operates flights from Puerto Montt in January and February only.

The best place to stay in town is the Hostería Río Grande at Aldea and O'Higgins (tel: 065 721 320), base of the Futaleufú Adventure Centre (run by US Olympic kayaker Chris Spelius: office@raftingchile.com; in the USA PO Box 1640, Bryson City, NC 28713; tel: 888 488 9082; fax: 847 400 0790). The

Hospedaje Carahue, O'Higgins 332 (tel: 258 633) is cheap and comfortable, and there is a campsite with *cabañas* just beyond the Puente Espolón. You can catch minibuses to Chaitén (Mon–Sat 07.30) or to the border, connecting to Esquel (Mon & Fri 09.15 and 17.15) at Transportes Cordillera on the plaza (tel: 065 258 633 anexo 249).

Distance	25km
Altitude	Between 300m and 500m
Rating	Moderate
Time	I day
Start of trail	Futaleufú
End of trail	Río Azul
Maps	124/24A Río Futaleufú (5-04-09-0024-00)

Getting to the trailhead

The start of the trail is in the town centre of Futaleufú, see above for details of how to get there.

Route description

From the plaza, O'Higgins leads southeast towards the frontier, past the airstrip. After 25 minutes turn right, just before the new Puente Robert. Follow the track for two minutes to the Puente Gelves, also new, cross to the left bank of the Río Futaleufú, and turn right after 3 more minutes onto a dirt road (after about a minute you can turn left onto the old path in the woods). This climbs for 700m (10 minutes), to a ridge where you will see plenty of ciprés de las Guaitecas and coihue, and then drops – the gravel road ends after another hundred metres, continuing as a simple track. After 10 minutes you will come to a farmed area, predictably dominated by willow and poplar trees, bandurrias and teros. You will pass a lagoon and then, after 30 minutes, along the cliffside high above a spectacular stretch of the river. (This is perfectly safe on foot but perhaps less so by vehicle, as you may notice as you look back.) Descending through a fine wood of coihue and bamboo, in 20 minutes you will reach the start of Las Escalas (300m); in the first house lives a Conaf ranger, in charge of the huemul reserve high on the hills to the left. Continuing past a fishing lodge, then across a stream (there is a footbridge to the left of the ford) you will come in 15 minutes to the *sede* (community hall) built by Raleigh International; there are two more streams just beyond – there is a footbridge to the right at the first one, and to the left at the second. The path follows an irrigation channel back to the track, which reaches a junction 5 minutes from the *sede*.

Here you have a choice. To loop back to the town, swing right past a house, through a gate and then left parallel to the river, crossing it by a suspension bridge after a couple of minutes. Turn right to follow a track through a long field. This eventually swings away from the river and enters forest after 25 minutes. It climbs steeply and then eases, reaching a pass in 20 minutes. Next it passes through spectacularly tall coihues, with a couple of lakes hidden among the trees. After 15 minutes the track begins to descend into fields and after another 15 minutes you should swing right and then left at a farm, and then follow a gravel road for 1.5km to reach the main road from Santa Lucía. Turning right, it takes another 15 minutes to reach the bridge over the Río Espolón, at the entry to Futaleufú.

The longer route continues straight ahead instead of swinging right past the house, on a cart track which rises above the fields. Head left after about 15 minutes, before a farmhouse, to climb gradually up to the left in a field. After another 15 minutes you will enter a fine forest of coihue, and continue to climb gradually for 25 minutes, on a track churned up by cattle. You will enter fields just a couple of minutes after the summit; to the right is the farm of Don Benedicto, who sells fantastic cheese, as well as woolly hats. Descending into forest again, the track turns right below a mountain wall, swinging left after 20 minutes to cross a stream, and then goes down slightly to the right, with the stream parallel but out of sight to the right. Passing a farm after half an hour, it zigzags down in good forest to the river, through the trees to the right. After another 40 minutes it comes to a stony beach just below the rapids known to rafters as El Trono ('The Throne'); Class V+, at the limit of navigability. The most spectacular of the Futaleufú's rapids is La Zeta (Class V), a short distance upstream (about 8km below Las Escalas).

Here you need to ford a side stream, or cross it by a log to the left. The track is now transformed into a rocky cliffside path, but there is still plenty of evidence that horses use it regularly. There is a good view of El Trono, and then of other rapids on either side of an island, before the path descends into fields. About an hour from the beach you will come to a suspension bridge across a good little gorge. On the far (right) bank there is a gravel road which leads up the left side of the Río Azul, past a couple of houses belonging to gringo rafting outfits, to reach the main road from Santa Lucía to Futaleufú in 25 minutes, by a small chapel at km26.5. The hamlet of Río Azul is to the left across the bridge, but it does not even have a shop. There is a minibus from Chaitén except on Sundays, as well as the odd pick-up truck, which should stop for you. The road rises gently eastwards to Lago Lonconau (km33), then drops to the Espolón valley and Futaleufú (km46.5).

Three kilometres west of Futaleufú a road turns north to the south end of the long thin Lago Espolón; tracks run along its shores, but it is easier to arrange a boat to reach the village of Espolón, on the Río Espolón a few kilometres north of the lake. From here it is possible to follow a trail northwest for 3 or 4 days over a 1,200m pass and gently down to the **Termas de Amarillo**, a very rustic spa 5km east of the Carretera, 26km south of Chaitén. This is the original horse route to Futaleufú, and it is still used by the inhabitants of the small-holdings along the trail. Even so it is a rough track which can disappear in a boggy mess of cow tracks, and should only be tackled by experienced backpackers. It is probably easier southbound. The road is now being paved from Chaitén to Amarillo, the junction to the termas, which themselves are now to be managed by the Pumalín Park.

QUEULAT NATIONAL PARK

From Villa Santa Lucía, the Carretera Austral follows the Río Frío downstream for 73km to the crossroads settlement of **La Junta**, a centre for angling. To the east a road runs into a very empty region of Argentine Patagonia (a bus runs four days a week from Coyhaique to Lago Verde, just before the border), while to the west a road, gradually creeping along the south side of the Río Palena, provides access to a very undeveloped area and especially to the northern flanks of Cerro Melimoyu (2,400m). The small fishing village of Raúl Marín Balmaceda, at the mouth of the river, and TicToc, just north, are also owned by Pumalín, and AlSur offers sea-kayaking trips here. You may see pudú, herons, peregrines, black-necked swans, dolphins, seals, sea lions and orca.

Another 30km south (following the Río Risopatrón gently upstream), the

Carretera reaches **El Pangue** (180km or 4 hours from Chaitén), where there is a warmly recommended hotel with *cabañas*, and a campsite just beyond by Lago Risopatrón. Here the road enters the Angostura sector of the **Queulat National Park**, although this sector is best known for fishing. From the south end of the lake the road crosses a low pass and drops to Puerto Puyuhuapi at sea level on the Seno Ventisquero, about 198km from Chaitén and 222km from Coyhaique. It is known for the small settlement of Sudeten Germans who came here in 1932 and after World War II founded a carpet factory, and for the luxury **Termas de Puyuhuapi** at hot springs on the west side of the fjord. This can only be reached by boat from the village or the Embarcadero Río Unión, by a fish farm about 10km south. The road enters the main sector of the Queulat National Park, which covers a large area (154,093ha) of very wild country, high mountains swathed either in glaciers or in dense forest, to which virtually the only access is by the Carretera Austral. Apart from a very few trails, the only way to get far from the road is with serious bush-bashing, taking a great deal of time and energy. With up to 4m of precipitation a year, it is an evergreen forest of coihue, tepa and tepú, with a dense undergrowth of bamboo, fuschia and huge nalcas. The wildlife is typical of Valdivian forest, including Magellanic woodpeckers, hummingbirds, chuaco, huet-huet and rayadito, with pudú and kod-kod; along the rivers there are otters, coipo, ducks, geese, swans, coots, kingfishers and herons.

At km200 (from Coyhaique), south of the Río Ventisquero, you will reach the turning to the park's main sight, the ***Ventisquero Colgante*** ('Hanging Glacier'). The side road leads 2km to the *guardería* (US$3 when staffed), and another 1km through the campsite to parking by the complete but unused Environmental Information Centre. From here you can walk 200m to the *mirador* opposite the glacier. This is vaguely visible from the highway bridge over the Río Ventisquero, but only here can you see the waterfalls coming off it, and a separate smaller glacier to the west. Just downstream is the 200m El Aluvion interpretative trail, winding through and below boulders and other detritus of floods in 1960. Nearby a new suspension bridge crosses to the right/north bank, where a path leads 600m to the right/east to the Laguna Témpanos, mostly through thick nalca and fuchsia. There are now no icebergs on the lake, despite its name, but it offers a great view of the glacier. Turning left from the bridge you can take a 3.3km trail to a higher viewpoint. A few hundred metres back down the road from the car-park another path leads to the south. This takes you up to 6km into the heart of the temperate rainforest, but does not actually lead anywhere. It is very wet, so take your waterproofs but do not bother taking anything else with you. However, there are plans to construct trails to new viewpoints onto the glacier, including a long one from the Carretera to the south, crossing the Cordillera Queulat.

Continuing south the Carretera Austral sees the sea again briefly at the Seno Queulat and then heads inland and starts to climb. At km179 stairs lead 200m east to the Salto Padre García, 30m falls named after the Jesuit from Chiloé who discovered them in 1767, and at km179 the road crosses the Chucao stream three times as it climbs to the Queulat pass (*c*500m) at km172.5. This is the most dramatic stretch of the entire Carretera Austral, with glaciers appearing through clouds on all sides. At km170 there is a short trail to the Río Cascada, and at km167 the superb 40m Salto del Cóndor is visible to the right/west. The road leaves the park at km165, just before the Puente Steffen and the junction to Puerto Cisnes, 35km west, then follows the Río Cisnes upstream, passing spectacular rapids at the Piedra El Gato (Cat Rock).

RÍO SIMPSON NATIONAL RESERVE

The Carretera Austral soon crosses the Río Cisnes and heads south. It passes the scenic Lago de las Torres, centre of a 16,516ha forestry reserve which is also best known for its fishing, and then splits, 97km from the Puerto Cisnes turning and 13km south of Mañihuales. To the left, the eastern branch is officially Ruta 7, the Carretera Austral, but all traffic takes the paved western branch which leads to the highway from Puerto Aysén and Puerto Chacabuco to Coyhaique. There are now paved roads from north of Mañihuales and Puerto Chacabuco to Coyhaique, Balmaceda airport and the Argentine border; soon they will extend south to Villa Cerro Castillo and Puerto Ibáñez, and by 2005 there should be a paved highway north all the way to Chaitén.

The Puerto Aysén-Coyhaique road passes through the **Río Simpson National Reserve**, more superb scenery like that in Queulat, although without the glaciers. Ironically, from the road the only views are to the south, spectacular scenery but not actually in the reserve. Even at its western end there is only a maximum of 2.5m of precipitation per year, but this is ample to produce exuberant vegetation of coihue and tepa, with many smaller trees such as canelo, mañío, ciruelillo (notro), tineo and tepú, and shrubs such as fuchsia, with bamboo, nalca and plenty of introduced lupins, buttercups and dandelions. Animals include puma, pudú, fox, skunk and guiña; birds include condors, parakeets, geese and ducks. A separate sector to the south, reached by the road 16km west from Coyhaique up the Río Claro, is drier and more open, on the slopes of Cerros Cordillerano and Huemules. It is home to one of the most important huemul populations in the country, and is now run by Codeff as a huemul reserve; there are two 3.5km paths here.

There is a bus roughly every 45 minutes between Coyhaique and Puerto Aysén (as well as buses from Chaitén, Mañihuales and Puerto Cisnes, to the north), so it is very easy to visit the reserve. The reserve's administration is at its western end (35km from Coyhaique), with a small museum (open daily 08.30–13.00, 14.15–18.30); if you do not go inside it is still worth seeing the huge stump of a lenga tree, showing events from c1570 until its death in 1970, as well as labelled trees, and a hundred-metre loop by the dirty brown-green river. Five minutes walk to the east is the Cascada de la Virgen (a fine two-stage waterfall, marred by a pipe in the middle); there is also a kiosk, the Cascada restaurant, and a shrine (passing cars toot to the Virgin Mary). At San Sebastian (km33) there is a hostería/campsite, and another shrine; at km26 (the Puente Juan Sepúlveda) the Velo de Novia is a less exciting waterfall; finally at km23 the road crosses the Río Correntoso.

The main hike in the reserve starts a couple of hundred metres east of the bridge (before the Río Correntoso campsite). A track leads up to the guardería, from where there is access only for hikers, horses and cattle. The path heads north up the left/east bank of the Río Correntoso, crossing private land for 4km. Near the headwaters of the Correntoso you may find some petrified trees, and you can also swing west to the Laguna Catedral, on a path which was closed for 30 years until it was reopened by Raleigh International in 1995. Allow two days for this, although shorter hikes are also worthwhile; alternatively you could emerge in the Emperador Guillermo valley to the north.

COYHAIQUE

The largest town on the Carretera Austral, **Coyhaique** has all the services needed for hikers and backpackers, including just about the only **ATMs** in Aysén, and internet access at Entel, Prat 340 (open 09.00–22.30). There is a very helpful Sernatur office at Bulnes 35 (open Mon–Fri 08.30–21.00, Sat and Sun 11.00–20.00), and Conaf's Protected Areas office is at Bilbao 234.

The **transport** situation is a bit unusual, as the only buses to the rest of Chile run through Argentina (to Puerto Montt and Punta Arenas, as well as Comodoro Rivadavia), and smaller planes use Coyhaique's Teniente Vidal airport (5km south) while larger ones (such as Boeing 737s) use Balmaceda, 56km southeast.

There are plenty of *hospedajes*, although they seem to be either a bit too pricey or a bit too basic, and almost none serve breakfast. They include Residencial Puerto Varas, Serrano 168 (tel: 067 235 931); Mónica, Lillo 664 (tel: 234 302); two Hospedajes Lautaro, at Lautaro 269 (tel: 238 116) and 532 (tel: 231 852); and also María Ester at Lautaro 544 (tel: 233 023). The Albergue de las Salamandras, Camino Aerodromo Ten. Vidal km1.5 (tel/fax: 211 865) is recommended but a bit far from town. There are two good large **supermarkets**, both near the junction of Cochrane and Lautaro (open till 22.00). For outdoor gear go to Brautigam at Horn 47 (on the plaza), opposite the Café Ricer, where you can also buy books and maps.

Coyhaique is the base for both Raleigh International and NOLS, who both do outdoor training in their different ways; you should contact them in Britain or the USA (see page 27) rather than here. However, there are various adventure-tourism companies here, and more will doubtless follow. Aventura Turismo, Parra 222 (tel/fax: 067 234 748); 45° Sur (& Turismo Aysen), Lillo 194 (tel: 238 036; fax: 235 294; baguales@entelchile.net) and Exploraciones Lucas Bridges, Campo Alegre Parc 24, casilla 5 (tel/fax: 233 302; lbridges@entelchile.net; www.aisen.cl) all offer canoeing, kayaking, rafting, horse-riding and even expeditions onto the icecap; Expediciones Coyhaique, Portales 195 at 21 de Mayo (tel/fax: 232 300), offers fishing and rafting.

Just to the northeast of town is the **Reserva Nacional Coyhaique**, which can make a pleasant outing for a few hours, although there is an awful lot of pine here. Heading north on the main road, it is about 1.5km to the Puente Coyhaique 3 and another 300m to the junction, from where you have to climb to the right for 1.5km to the *guardería* (around 400m altitude) and pay your US$1.50. The circuit starts anti-clockwise through a very young arboretum and runs largely parallel to a dirt road to a picnic area by the Laguna Verde (4km). Keeping left here, you soon have the choice of following the dirt road back to the *guardería* in another 4km, or following a more pleasant loop path via Cerro Cinchao (1,361m).

CERRO CASTILLO AND SOUTH TO COCHRANE

Continuing to the southward, past Cerro McKay, with its striking volcanic pipes, Laguna Foitzick, known for its waterfowl, and the small ski resort of El Fraile, the Carretera Austral is the road (now being paved) branching right off the asphalt to Balmaceda airport 41km south of Coyhaique. Buses run to Balmaceda to connect with planes, and daily except Mondays to Cochrane. The road climbs to enter the **Reserva Nacional Cerro Castillo**, and at km57.5 reaches the Laguna Chiguay *guardería* and campsite (1,100m).

This easily accessible area of 134,000ha (between 500m and 2,318m altitude) ought to be one of the great hiking areas of southern Chile, but it sadly fails to live up to its potential. Having suffered badly from fires, many of the slopes near the highway are now planted with pines to prevent further erosion, which both reduces their natural beauty and ecological interest and tends to produce overgrown paths. One path is well used, being described in detail in the Lonely

Planet trekking guide, and this has now been marked with paint, though not by Conaf. From Laguna Chiguay the road follows a stream downhill for 8km to Las Horquetas Grandes (km64.9, or km72 by an older series), where it turns left by a couple of highway maintenance huts. The **Cerro Castillo hike**, which takes about 3 days and covers 40km, starts to the right here, continues downstream briefly and then follows the Río La Lima upstream (southwest) to a pass of 1,453m on the east side of Cerro Castillo (2,318m) and descends to Villa Cerro Castillo. The dominant tree (up to 1,200m) is lenga, with coihue, ñirre and notro, and calafate and michay, two types of *Berberis* shrub. Wildlife includes huemul, guanaco, puma, red fox, skunk, condor, eagle, Magellanic woodpecker, owls, parakeets and huet-huet.

The Carretera, meanwhile, continues up a valley, past the Piedra El Conde (km71.5), a rock column in the shape of a human head, to the Ibáñez pass (1,120m; km79.5) and then, leaving the reserve, zigzags down a fearsome hill known as the *Cuesta del Diablo* (now paved) to the Bajada Ibáñez (km85; 672m). This is the junction to Puerto Ibáñez, 31km south, the port for the ferry to Chile Chico, on the northern shore of **Lago General Carrera** (330m; shared with Argentina, which calls it Lago Buenos Aires). This is the second-largest lake in South America, and can be very windy, especially in the afternoons, but the scenery is superb. The Carretera runs 11km west to Villa Cerro Castillo and on through lenga and coihue forest to the 600m Cofre Cajon pass, where it swings left to the west end of Lago General Carrera. East of the pass you will see deep banks of brown ash from Volcán Hudson (1,369m), not far to the northwest, which erupted very destructively in 1991. The debris makes a lovely smooth road surface, but has killed all the undergrowth and some trees.

From km197, where a turning leads 4km east to Bahía Murta (accommodation), the road follows the west side of the lake, from the north side of the Río Tranquilo bridge in Puerto Río Tranquilo, 125km from Villa Cerro Castillo, a road is creeping westwards along the **Río Exploradores** towards the sea not far north of the Laguna San Rafael; within a couple of years this will be the main access for tours to the Laguna and glacier (see also *Shipping* on page 247). It would be well worth exploring this area, on the northern flanks of Monte San Valentín (or San Clemente, 4,058m), the highest peak in Chilean Patagonia, which marks the northern end of the Northern Patagonian Icecap.

Perhaps even better for wilderness hiking is the **Valle Leones**, from the Puente Leones, at km250; there are tracks along both banks, of which most traffic uses the southern one, while the northern one is better for hikers, as the fords are less deep. The Laguna Leones, immediately north of Cerro Nyades (3,078m), is a great base for exploring the glaciers on the fringes of the icecap. You will have to hike south from the track for two hours to get there, or charter a float-plane in Coyhaique. From Puerto Río Tranquilo it is also possible to take a boat to the stunning marble caves (*Cuevas de Marmol*) just south; camping and boat trips are on offer a kilometre south of the village.

The Carretera Austral crosses the *desagüe* or outlet from Lago General Carrera (a contender for the title of the world's shortest river) and at km275 reaches the Cruce El Maitén, junction to Puerto Guadal and Chile Chico, 122km east by a superbly scenic road along the lake's south shore. From Lago Bertrand the road follows the Río Baker, which has the largest flow of any river in Chile, an average 15 million litres/second at its mouth. There is a *mirador* above the Baker's confluence with the Nef; 31km and 8km north of Cochrane turnings to the west lead to a footbridge and a hand-powered ferry across the Baker and new tracks into the semi-wilderness on the eastern flanks of the Northern Ice-Cap.

Seventy kilometres from El Maitén, the Carretera reaches **Cochrane** (106m), a small town which makes a good base for exploring this area. The Hospedaje Cochrane, Steffens 451 (tel: 067 522 377) and Hospedaje Paola, Lago Brown 150 (tel: 522 215) are both cheap and also allow camping; the Residencial El Fogón, San Valentín 135 (tel: 522 240) is better, with the best restaurant in town. There is a **tourist information** kiosk in the plaza near the Banco del Estado, which will change US dollars, but not Argentinian pesos, although they are worth exactly the same. There is a bike-repair shop on the 400 block of San Valentín. There is a good view from the hill with the Hollywood-style 'Cochrane' sign, north of the centre, and a better one from the next hill north.

To the northeast of town on the Río Chacabuco, the **Reserva Nacional Tamango** is an important reserve for about 80 huemul. Raleigh International teams are steadily improving access, with a new path along the north side of Lago Cochrane. From the plaza, go one block east on Teniente Merino, then left on Río Colonia to its junction with San Valentín, cross the Puente Tamango, and turn right (admiring the house like a wooden pineapple to the left). It takes 10 minutes to a junction from where it is 2km left to the Embarcadero, a jetty just east/ upstream of the Río Cochrane rapids, which you cannot quite see clearly; the bank is fenced off in both directions, but it still makes a lovely evening stroll, with incredibly clear water and lots of birds. However, turning left after 1.5km to Tomasin, you can pay US$3 and take the path into the reserve. It is another 11km to the Conaf *guardería*. Beyond this you can head inland to Laguna Elefantita and Laguna Tamango, and eventually back by a dirt road to the Puente Tamango; this takes about 10 hours in total, so plan to camp.

There is a transition-steppe environment in the reserve with 800mm of precipitation (up to 1m in higher parts); there is *matorral* of ñirre, with lenga and coihue; huemul, of course, as well as guanaco, puma, red and grey foxes, skunk, armadillo and hare; birds include ducks, geese, grebes, Magellanic woodpecker, condor and eagle. Feral mink are a problem in the Cochrane area, eating a lot of bird eggs.

To the south of Cochrane, a track branches left after 12km up the Río Tranquilo; this gives access to Cerro San Lorenzo (page 310), and also to a horse track which clips the western edge of Argentina's Parque Nacional Perito Moreno and eventually reaches Villa O'Higgins. A minibus from Cochrane (Wed & Sat 11.00) runs 15km up this track. The Carretera reaches Vagabundo in another 78km. Four minibuses a week come this far, being met by a boat for Tortel (not at the jetty by the A-frame refuge but five minutes away down the track starting 200m to the south). This is a far wetter area; it is a strange transitional zone, with trees typical of Magellanic forest, but Valdivian undergrowth (including lots of bamboo and nalca) and birds. It is a real *Apocalypse Now* experience taking the slow boat down the Río Baker (even slower upstream), but sadly the subsidised boat service will presumably be discontinued when a 24km side-road from the Carretera reaches the outskirts of Tortel in 2001; the same may happen to the San Rafael flights (on Wednesdays) from Coyhaique.

TORTEL

Tortel, at the mouth of the Río Baker, between the northern and southern icecaps, is a wonderful little village of 300 people (known as *Tortelinos*, not *Tortellini*, alas) and no roads; it is tied together by 5km cypress walkways along which friendly dogs follow wherever you go. A road is shortly to arrive at the edge of the village, doubtless to be followed by a hotel; there is a project for catamaran trips to the Jorge Montt glacier, which it now takes five hours to reach. The municipality is poor (living mainly from wood rather than fish – there is *marea roja* here most of the time) and keen to benefit from tourism, while, it hopes, avoiding its harmful aspects. In 1998 there were 500 visitors and in 1999 roughly twice as many (80% foreign). The *lancha* (which takes up to 15 passengers) or faster *chata* (up to 8 passengers) can be chartered to visit the Montt glacier (flowing off the Southern Ice-Cap), or the Steffens glacier (off the Northern Ice-Cap), 2½ hours away.

Boats come and go from the 'Base Area', by the port captain's office, the unique Plaza de Armas (a shingle-roofed octagonal pavilion), and an Artesanía (craft-shop) which may soon house tourist information. To the left steps lead down to the shop (with very limited supplies) and a boardwalk runs at shore-level past a boatyard, the Plaza Orompello and the Hospedaje Familiar and the Hospedaje-Bed-Zimmer (both US$6) to the junction left over a bridge to the beach (15 minutes from the shop), where there are cold showers and an adventure playground, and at its far end a campsite (with *baño*).

Going to the right from the Base Area, it takes 10 minutes to the far side of a bluff topped by a green navigation mark (to enjoy the view here you actually have to step off the boardwalk). You can also take a higher route past a radio station and the Hostal Costanera (US$8). At shore-level again, it takes 10 minutes to the foot of a broad flight of steps, leading up in five minutes to the Health Post (with a public toilet, open 24 hours a day) and the big new school at the end of the village. It takes another 5 minutes to the top of the ridge and the start of the *Senda Turística* which leads to the left to Junquillo. Continuing ahead, it takes 5 minutes to go down wooden steps to a wide marsh and 5 more to cross this on a boardwalk to the *aerodromo*. Crossing the end of the runway you will come to an adventure playground and another campsite (all built by Raleigh International venturers, including Prince William). There is a *baño* by the end of the boardwalk.

The **Senda Turística** (2.5km) is poorly signed and only from the school to Junquillo. Starting on moss (usually springy rather than boggy) it goes uphill for 15 minutes then down a boggy gully and up at its far end. It takes five minutes to the summit (*c*150m), then dips and after 15 minutes reaches a lower hill. When I visited the signs were missing here – go to the left then right down a gully, after which the path is well marked into young cypress, then more secondary woodland with thicker undergrowth. After 22 minutes the path swings left above Junquillo, bringing you down to the boardwalk after another 5 minutes – if you must go the wrong way, it starts beside the first hut east of the junction to the beach, then goes left onto rocks.

It is also possible to climb the peak of *c*600m opposite the village. Carrying on past the steps up to the school, you will come to the end of the boardwalk in 3 minutes; go on up to the left, then up a big natural stone 'staircase', reaching a rocky viewpoint just to seaward of the obvious water-tank in 5 minutes. From here follow the semi-buried water-pipe rising easily up to the right (do not stand on it!). You will have to go up to the left above a small cliff, then when the ground is drier and more open, go up to the left, through moss, clubmoss and holly-leafed barberry. There is no clear path so you will have to improvise a bit. It takes about 1¼ hours to reach the first ridge, beyond which there is a dip and a climb to the peak in half an hour more. To the right is Laguna Tortel, which you could reach by following the pipe all the way, and beyond it some dramatic glaciated mountains.

From Vagabundo it is another 32km to Puerto Yungay, on the Río Bravo, inhabited by Italian missionaries and road-builders. The Carretera Austral was finally completed in 1999 when it reached Villa O'Higgins, 105km further on Lago O'Higgins (Lago San Martín to the Argentines). This is reached by a minibus from Cochrane on Sundays only. It is possible to take a boat into Argentina from Villa O'Higgins, or to walk on trails used to reach prime fly-fishing spots.

It is worth mentioning **Puerto Edén**, at the heart of the Bernardo O'Higgins National Park, to the west of the Southern Ice-Cap. It is known mainly because the last few Kaweshkar live here, and because it is the one stop of the Navimag ships between Puerto Montt and Puerto Natales (indeed their ship is named the *Puerto Edén*). This only pauses for a few minutes, but it is a little-known fact that the *lancha* from Tortel comes here every month (around the 20th). It takes 22 hours and is extremely uncomfortable, but there are plans for a fast ferry from Tortel or Puerto Yungay, which would take just 6 or 7 hours. Already Turismo Yekchal (Eberhard 564, Puerto Natales; tel/fax: 061 412 530; yekchal@entelchile.net; www.patagoniayekchal.co.cl) has opened a *hospedaje* here and is offering ecotouristic trips, which can be booked through Pura Aventura in Britain (see page 24). There are short circuits, such as to Lago Banderas and the cemetery island, but their main offering is a 4–6 day trip to the huge **Glaciar Pio XI** (Pope Pius XI Glacier), flowing west from the Southern Ice-Cap. This involves a 90-minute boat ride, then hiking across the Exmouth peninsula to Bahía Elizabeth, where they are building a refuge. The return is by boat along the Seno Eyre and Canal Messier (7 hours, with dolphins and orcas), stopping at Kaweshkar remains. The village is like Tortel with its *pasarelas* (boardwalks); it has 3.5m of rain per year and an average temperature of 7°C, producing evergreen forest and Magellanic tundra.

TO CHILE CHICO

From Cruce El Maitén it is 122km east to Chile Chico, by a very scenic road along the south shore of Lago General Carrera. There is a bit of traffic over the first 13km to Puerto Guadal, but beyond here there is just a minibus from Puerto Guadal to Chile Chico four days a week (Mon, Tue, Thur & Fri 07.45), and weekly buses from Bahía Murta and Cochrane, and very limited options for hitch-hiking. The best way to reach Chile Chico from Coyhaique is by ferry (see below), but it is worth seeing this road in at least one direction. Just across the border from Chile Chico is Los Antiguos, reached by buses from Río Gallegos and Comodoro Rivadavia, met by minibuses to Chile Chico.

At the eastern end of **Puerto Guadal** there is a campsite built by Raleigh International, but constantly being invaded by wild roses; if the toilets are locked, ask at the *Municipalidad* on the plaza. There is also accommodation in comfortable *cabañas* just east of town. There are pleasant easy hikes to the south of the campsite. Cross the road, follow the dirt track ahead to the foot of the hill and swing left to pass through a gate after 5 minutes; the track ahead leads to an attractive *laguna*, while to the right a path climbs through lenga, some cypress and lots of wild roses. After 10 minutes or less go to the right around a small field and on up for 5 minutes to a rock viewpoint over the village and lake. You can cross the fence and go on uphill, with better views after 5 minutes and access to the rocky rim in about 10 minutes. You can also take a boat or walk along the beach for about 5km to the *Capilla de Marmol* (rock formations carved by wave action), near the mouth of the Maquis stream. Continuing east along the road you cross the Los Maquis bridge, from where you can hike up to the right for 10 minutes to a waterfall, and beyond.

The road runs along two spectacular cliffside sections on either side of a broad plain; 109km from Puerto Guadal it reaches **Chile Chico**. The ferry ramp is at the town's western end, near the Residencial Aguas Azules, Rodriguez 252 (tel: 067 411 320); the cheaper Hospedaje Don Luis (tel: 411 384) is close, by the plaza, but the basic Camping del Sol is right at the opposite end of town. The main street is, as usual, O'Higgins. It has a supermarket (at the corner with Pedro Burgos), the Bianchi bike repair shop, and a museum, recognisable by the fishing boat *Andes* attached to its side. The Conaf office is behind the big green hall at O'Higgins 334.

RESERVA NATURAL JEINIMENI

Distance	Up to 50km
Altitude	Between 834m and 1,839m
Rating	Moderate
Time	2–5 days
Start of trail	Lago Verde
End of trail	Lago Verde
Maps	IGM map J49 *Lago Verde* (5-04-90-0049-00)

Only 60km south of Chile Chico lies the Reserva Natural Jeinimeni, where you will find breathtaking snow-capped peaks, impressive cliffs, waterfalls and small glaciers set around the calypso blue and emerald green Lagos Jeinimeni and Verde. Activities include fishing for salmon and rainbow trout, hiking (or rather trailblazing, as there are few paths), rowing, and just enjoying the tranquillity. Hikes range from multi-day valley walks to tough scrambles on the few accessible 1,800m peaks. The IGM map *Lago Verde* is essential – buy it in Santiago, or ask to photocopy it at Conaf's Chile Chico office.

There is a warm, dry microclimate here, with many species more common in the Argentine steppe to the east, such as a few huemuls, mara, armadillos, guanaco, rhea, martineta tinamou, and the world's most southerly cactus, *Austrocactus patagonicus*.

Getting to the trailhead

The best way to reach Chile Chico from Coyhaique is by the ferry from Puerto Ibáñez; minibuses leave Coyhaique at 06.00 to connect with the boat (except on Mondays), and others leave around 17.00, from El Gran Calafate at Prat and Errázuriz, allowing you to spend a night in Puerto Ibáñez. From the south it is usually easier to take the road from El Maitén.

The road starts 3km east of Chile Chico (330m) and follows the Río Jeinimeni (which forms the border) southwest for 60km, crossing four fords, to the *guardería* and (2km further) a campsite at the east end of Lago Jeinimeni, where a couple of picnic shelters, a rowing boat, and plenty of firewood are available. It is best to continue along the south side of Lago Jeinimeni to the near end of Lago Verde (834m) and make your base camp there. There is very little traffic on the road other than a couple of timber trucks – ask Juan Nuñez at Galvarino 110 (tel: 067 411 541) for a lift.

Route descriptions
Paso Caballo Blanco

From the camp at the northeastern corner of Lago Verde, there is a steep scramble northwest up rock and scrub to reach the 1,257m Roca Huemules in about 2 hours. Here you have views over the lakes and west along the Valle Hermoso to the glaciers of Cerro Jeinimeni (2,600m). Continuing along the ridge of the Cordón Gloria to the northwest you will pass a grassy col which provides an easy alternative route up from the Estero la Gloria to the east, and reach the Paso Caballo Blanco (1,274m), a col which gives views over Lago Verde and up the Valle Hermoso to the glacier. It is also possible to get here by following the Camino Camano, a pleasant wooded path along the Estero la Gloria. Cross the river to its true left/east bank before it hits the cliff, and cross back where the bank rises to form a grassy ledge strewn with dead trees. Follow the path into the wood where it turns sharply up a gully, passing under a cliff before reaching the col, about 1½ hours from the camp.

Glacier trek

This is a 50km trek, taking between 2 and 5 days. There are numerous river crossings, mostly knee-deep. The lakes themselves are surrounded by barren scree and moraine, and technical equipment is needed to climb onto the glaciers.

From the Paso Caballo Blanco, follow the horse track down to the western end of Lago Verde. Cross both rivers to the right/south side (to avoid battling through trees, scrub and bog) and proceed along the valley bottom and through woodland up the Valle Hermoso to explore around Lagunas Escondida and Ventisquero.

Camping spots can be found in the woods, for example at the western edge of Valle Hermoso, the eastern side of Estero Los Ventisqueros and at the bottom of the valley descending from Laguna Escondida. It is possible to hike out to the south through the Río Aviles canyon to the road along the Chacabuco valley from the Paso Roballes border crossing (717m).

Wisdom Peak

This is a steep scramble through trees and up fairly stable scree to the 1,839m peak for views over Argentina, lakes and mountains. From the camp, head a short way up the Estero la Gloria and follow a dry river valley and then a ridge to the summit (6–7 hours return).

An alternative ascent can be made from the northeastern end of Lago Jeinimeni, although this involves negotiating a gully of loose rock near the summit – a safety rope is required.

La Cascada (Waterfall Walk)

This is a scramble at a gentle gradient over boulders and through trees to superb waterfalls falling into clear pools. Cross the outlet from Lago Verde at a shallow point 200–300m downstream from the lake. The crossing is knee-deep, but fast flowing even in dry weather. Proceed south up the stream through the wood on the western side of the valley; 2 hours return.

Chilean Patagonia

'This streight is extreme cold; the trees seem to stoope with the burden of the weather and yet are greene continually; towards the South Sea monstruous hills and craggy rocks do exalt themselves whose tops be all hoary with snow.'

Richard Hakluyt's *Voyages*

It used to be thought that Patagonia took its name from *patagones*, supposedly meaning 'big feet' and possibly a reference to the huge moccasins stuffed with insulating grass worn by the indigenous population. However, it now seems more likely that Magellan named the land after *El Gran Patagón*, a monster in the contemporary chivalric romance *Primaleon of Greece*, due to the Tehuelches' dog-headed battle masks. Either way, the name stuck, and the area has attracted hosts of explorers, outlaws and eccentrics, and more recently, tourists.

The definition of Patagonia is a vague one, but for the purpose of this chapter only, Chilean Patagonia is taken to mean the 12th Region of Magallanes, leaving Aysén aside. Scenically, it is a land of contrasts. Its western fringe has some of the wettest terrain in the world, and some of its most impenetrable forests; the Paine massif must be one of the most beautiful in the Americas; while the eastern side is an extension of the sterile steppes of Argentine Patagonia. The wettest areas are dominated by coihue de Magallanes (*Nothofagus betuloides*), with ñirre (*N. antarctica*), lenga (*N. pumilio*), ciprés de la Guaitecas (*Pilgerodendron uviferum*) and notro (*Embothrium coccineum*). To the south is boggy tundra dominated by *Sphagnum magellanicum*; to the east are dry steppes of coiron (*Festuca gracillima*) with *Chiliotrichum diffusum*, *Stipetum* spp., and calafate bushes.

PUNTA ARENAS

The main settlement on the Chilean side is Punta Arenas, facing Tierra del Fuego on the Magellan Strait. Because of the mountains and ice fields to the north, it can only be reached by air, ship, or overland through Argentina. A penal colony until 1877, it is now a city of 110,000 people, and its flimsy, multi-coloured corrugated-iron houses and their gardens of lupins and marigolds have an air of incongruous impermanence. You will see ample evidence of the hardy European settlers, especially Croats, who moved here at the end of the 19th century and whose descendants still form a significant proportion of the city's population. Founded in 1848, when the population of Fuerte Bulnes was transferred here, the city had a Wild West start, with the governor being killed in a mutiny in 1852 and his successor assassinated by the natives the following year. Things settled down after

1869 when coal-mining began in order to supply steam ships rounding the Horn to and from the Pacific and the Antarctic whalers, and Punta Arenas became a free port. Sheep were introduced from the Falklands in the 1870s, and by 1900 there were a million of them in Magallanes, producing 7 million kg of wool a year. The city's Golden Age lasted from 1892–1914, when the Panama Canal opened and the nitrate trade began to collapse. In 1910 three ships a day were calling, but in 1920 that figure was just three a month. Punta Arenas is an important naval base, and since 1945 oil production has provided more employment, followed by fishing and now tourism.

Punta Arenas has a relatively mild climate, with an average 368mm of precipitation well spread through the year, with typical maximum/minimum temperatures of 14°/7°C December–February and 4°/-1°C in July.

Practical information

Most visitors will arrive at the **airport** 20km north of town; it is 1.5km west of the main road, and buses to Puerto Natales call in (until 20.00 in summer). Otherwise transfer minibuses into town cost US$2. The airport itself has ATMs, car-rental offices and a book stall with an excellent range of wildlife guides.

There is no bus terminal in Punta Arenas, although Buses Fernández, El Pingüino, Queilen Bus and Turibus share premises at Sanhueza 745; at the corner of Colon and Magallanes the Central de Pasajeros is a ticket agency for most companies. **Bus services** run frequently to Puerto Natales, daily to Río Gallegos and most days to Río Grande in Tierra del Fuego. There is also a surprising number of buses to Puerto Montt and Coyhaique, although these are not allowed to set down passengers in Argentina. Buses to Río Grande take the paved Río Gallegos highway to the *Primera Angostura* ('First Narrows'), from where there are frequent **ferries** to Tierra del Fuego. There is also one ferry a day (except Mondays) from Tres Puentes, 5km north of Punta Arenas, just beyond the Free Trade Zone, to Bahía Chilote 5km west of Porvenir. To book a place on the Puerto Natales–Puerto Montt ship, go to Navimag, Independencia 830; (tel: 061 200 200; fax: 225 804; www.navimag.com). Finally, if you are cycling, the inevitable repairs can be handled by Claudio Botton at Bike Service, Sarmiento 1132 (tel: 242 107).

Where to stay

The backpackers' favourite hangouts are the Albergue Backpacker's Paradise (Carrera Pinto 1022; tel: 061 222 554) and Manuel's (O'Higgins 646; tel: 220 567). Rather nicer places (ie: with private rooms) can be found at Caupolicán 169 (Casa Dinka; tel: 226 056), Caupolicán 99 (The Pink House; tel: 222 436) and Caupolicán 75 (Ely House; tel: 226 660); take *micro C* or *colectivo 13* (shared taxi). The Hostal El Bosque, O'Higgins 424 (tel: 221 764; elbosque@patagonian.com) also houses the Centro de Difusión Ecológica, where environmental seminars are held in the winter. In the centre, the Mercurio at Fagnano 595 (tel: 242 300) is a decent mid-range place. There is no shortage of fine hotels, right up to the Hotel José Nogueira, on the plaza in the former *palacio* of sheep magnate Sara Braun (tel: 248 880; fax: 248 832; nogueira@chileaustral.com); this also houses the Club de la Unión, with a bar underneath where you should sample the *licores croatas*.

Information and shopping

The very helpful Sernatur office is at Seguel 689 (tel/fax: 241 300; serna12a @entelchile.net; open Mon–Fri 08.30–17.45), on a corner of the plaza; there is also a municipal information kiosk on the plaza (open Mon–Thur 08.00–17.00, Fri 08.00–16.00 and on Saturdays in summer). For national parks information, Conaf is at Menéndez 1147 (tel: 223 841); its library is at no. 1159 (open Mon–Fri 14.00–16.00).

The Zona Franca is a good place for buying cheap camping gear (particularly Balfer, Módulo 147: tel: 211 267); in addition Camping Sur is at Errazuriz 867. The best **supermarket** is Abu-Gosch, between Magallanes and Bories north of Carrera Pinto (open Mon–Fri, 09.00–22.00, Sun 10.00–21.00).

Tours

For trips south to Laguna Parrillar, Puerto Hambre and Fuerte Bulnes, contact EcoTour Patagonia, at AustroHoteles, Lautaro Navarro 1091 (tel/fax: 061 223 670; ecopatagonia@entelchile.net; www.ecotourpatagonia.com); Turismo Pali Aike (Lautaro Navarro 1129; tel/fax: 223 301); Viento Sur (Fagnano 565; tel: 226 930, 225 167; www.chileaustral.com/vientosur); Polo Sur (Chiloe 873; tel: 243 173; fax: 229 163); or Laguna Azul (Menéndez 631; tel/fax: 225 200). These all do quick trips to Paine, too, as do Arka Patagonia (Magallanes 345 tel/fax: 248 167); Turismo Pehoé (Menéndez 918; tel: 241 373, fax: 248 052); and Inhospita Patagonia (Lautaro Navarro 1013, tel/fax: 224 510; inhospita@chilepatagonia.com; www.inhospitapatagonia.cl) – the last also offers climbing and kayaking. Turismo Yamaná (Colón 568; tel: 221 130, fax: 240 056, yamana@chileaustral.com; www.chileaustral.com/yamana) offers kayaking (for US$70/day), and sailing, with Dynevor Expediciones Marinas (Roca 817; tel/fax: 225 888; dynevor@entelchile.net; www.sailingpatagonia.com).

Sights

It is well worth visiting the **Casa Braun-Menéndez**, another former palacio on the plaza (open daily 10.30–17.30 in summer; entry at the rear on Lautaro Navarro); for stuffed local fauna try the **Salesian Museum** at Bulnes 374 (open Tue–Sun 10.00–13.00, 15.00–18.00 in summer). Further out on Bulnes, the main road north, just before the statue of the First Shepherd, the Municipal Cemetery provides a fascinating viewpoint on local society, and the Instituto de la Patagonia has a superb open-air display of agricultural machinery and vehicles and a basic botanical garden. It has a useful library, but this is closed for the whole of January and February. This is at km4 on Bulnes, more or less opposite the Zona Franca, served by many *colectivos* (particularly routes 2 and 4).

Around Punta Arenas

Immediately to the west of Punta Arenas is a range of hills rising to 620m, where the Club Andino has a ski resort on Cerro Mirador (615m), within the 19,625ha **Reserva Forestal Magallanes**. The chairlift operates in the summer, too, (10.00–19.00 except Mon; US$2.50), and they offer guided hikes on two 2-hour loop paths from the viewpoint at the summit. The hilltop is dominated by TV masts, but there is a good view to the sea on two sides. The radomes on the west side are a radio-listening post, put in and staffed by Britain in 1982, and handed over to Chile once the Falklands/Malvinas War was over. It is worth mentioning also that there are plenty of landmines along the border with Argentina, close to the Puerto Natales highway. This is evergreen forest, of coihue de Magallanes, lenga and ñirre; birds to be seen include upland goose, speckled teal, Chiloe widgeon, austral thrush, rufous-collared sparrow, long-tailed meadowlark and chimango caracara.

Camping is not allowed in the reserve, but there are opportunities for wild camping around it.

To get to the Magallanes reserve, simply head out of town along Avda Independencia, which becomes Avda Allende; a taxi will charge about US$8. For the Club Andino walks, phone 061 241 479 or contact Turismo Pali Aike or Laguna Azul. If you want to hitch or hike, *micro B2* and *taxi-colectivo 100* take you furthest out; others along Eusebio Lillo (heading for Ibáñez and Aguirre Cerda), such as routes 12, 17, 120 and 220, will also drop you on Allende. From here it is 2km to the junction left to Laguna Lynch, where there are picnic facilities. After crossing the Lynch valley, one road goes left to the Sector Andino and the chairlift, and another right to Loreto and the Río de las Minas. This is also known as the *Río del Carbón*, due to the coal mines that operated here from 1867–1914; you may still see traces of the railway that served them, and the remains of a mine lie on the path north from Cerro Mirador. On either road you will pass through a *guardería*, where you will have to pay US$2; the Sendero Las Lengas (3.3km) leads from the north *guardería*, up into the forest and down more or less to the other *guardería*. The roads lead to picnic sites from which there are paths; at the end of the *Río de las Minas* road, the path leads to a viewpoint at the gorge of the *Garganta del Diablo*.

The highway, now being paved, continues south along the coast from Punta Arenas for 58km to Punta San Juan. At km51 there is a double junction and a monolith marking the supposed geographical centre of Chile (ie: the line halfway between Arica and the South Pole). The first road to the left leads in 2km to **Puerto Hambre** ('Famine Port'), where Sarmiento founded Ciudad del Rey Felipe in 1584. By 1587 only 18 men were still alive when the English privateer Thomas Cavendish arrived. Only Tomé Hernández agreed to be taken off, the others staying and starving to death (another man was taken off later but died on the way back to Europe). The ruins of a chapel remain, together with some army huts. The second road leads in 5km to **Fuerte Bulnes**, where Chile established its settlement in 1843. There is now a replica of the wooden fort, visited by daily tour groups. The road ends 7km further south at the Río San Juan, site of the grave of Pringle Stokes, captain of the *Beagle* on her first voyage, who suffered a nervous breakdown and committed suicide here in 1832. Steps lead from the beach to a fibreglass replica of the wooden cross raised over his grave, which is now in the Salesian museum in Punta Arenas. Beyond here, it is possible to continue by mountain bike on a rough track, reaching the lighthouse at Cabo San Isidro in about five hours. It is not possible to hike to Cabo Froward, the southernmost point of the American mainland, but costly excursions by Zodiac inflatable or helicopter can be arranged, though you can see a replica of the huge cross at Cabo Froward (the *Cruz de los Mares*) just north of Punta Arenas. Birds to be seen along this road include kelp gull, upland goose, buff-necked ibis, cormorants, ducks, austral thrush and striated caracara.

At km26, at a police checkpoint, a road leads 22km inland to the **Reserva Forestal Laguna Parrillar**, where the forest has suffered less from logging than the Magallanes reserve. However, beavers from the colony in Tierra del Fuego appeared here in 1998. In addition to the forest of lenga and ñirre there is sphagnum bog and even tundra here. There are paths and picnic sites (but no overnight camping), but the main attraction here is fishing. The 18,814ha reserve can only be reached by car or by tours from Punta Arenas, from late October to mid-April; some agencies include a hike south to Cerro Tarn (830m) or a descent by kayak of the Río San Juan to the end of the coastal road.

The most popular excursion from Punta Arenas is to the **Seno Otway** (Otway Sound) colony of Magellanic penguins. Although this is only 80ha in area it is home to up to 10,000 birds, which move in to their burrows in September and October, lay eggs which hatch in November, moult in March (spending all their time in the burrows) and are gone by April. It is not part of the SNASPE system, but is maintained by the private Fundación Otway. Fences and screens have been installed to keep tourists from disturbing breeding. To get there turn west at the Kon Aike checkpoint, 31km north of Punta Arenas, to cross the neck of the Brunswick Peninsula, follow the coast south and turn right at a T-junction at the rear of the huge opencast Pecket coal mine, 23km from the main road and 4km before the penguin colony. There is useful information in the cafeteria. From here it is 10 minutes' walk south to the first burrows and viewing tower, and 15 minutes more to the far tower, say an hour in all. The dominant vegetation is coirón bunchgrass, with thrift, burrs and lots of jetsam logs, and the fauna also includes foxes, skunks, rhea, geese, skua, ducks and black-necked swans. Most companies in Punta Arenas operate tours here. Some leave at 16.00, because there is most activity before 10.00 and after 17.00; the reserve is open 08.00–19.00. You have to pay about US$8 for a tour, plus US$4 entry fee. People have hiked here from Cerro Mirador, but it is very hard going through dense forest, taking at least 2 days.

This is not to be confused with the **Monumento Natural Los Pingüinos**, an alternative name for Islas Magdalena and Marta, 97ha in the middle of the Magellan Straits which are home to up to 50,000 penguins, and also Imperial and Falkland cormorants and kelp and Austral seagulls, as well as foxes. Turismo Pehoe operates catamaran trips here daily for US$60. Humpback whales can also be seen in these waters, together with some of the world's rarer dolphins (Peale's, Commerson's, Chilean and perhaps dusky dolphins). You may see some of these from the ferries to Tierra del Fuego, but a safer bet is to go out with a fisherman from Caleta Río Seco or Barranco Amarillo, just north of Punta Arenas. Arrange this through the NGO FIDE XII at Fagnano 630; tel: 061 242 142; fax: 226 704; email: fidexii@ctcreuna.cl.

Towards Puerto Natales

The only other settlement you are likely to visit in Chilean Patagonia is Puerto Natales, 247km north of Punta Arenas, and jumping-off point for the Torres del Paine. Ruta 9 is now properly paved, having had to make do with a strip of asphalt wide enough for one vehicle, and gravel shoulders for passing. Along the way you pass through dry steppes dominated by coirón bunchgrass, with calafate and mata verde, and inhabited by what are supposedly South America's largest rheas (mostly in the first 100km to Villa Tehuelches), as well as crested caracara, geese, fox and skunk. As you get nearer to Puerto Natales there are also lenga and coihue trees and waterbirds such as ducks and coscoroba swans.

If you have a four-wheel-drive vehicle, or a mountain bike and lots of stamina, it might be worth knowing about a route that loosely follows the coast to Puerto Natales. Take the *Costanera* north from Punta Arenas through Río Seco, parallel to the highway, then follow Ruta 9 (cyclists may be able to use stretches of the old dirt road alongside). Turn left 43km north of Punta Arenas, and after 42km you will pass the Hotel Río Verde (where a ferry crosses the narrows to Isla Riesco, where there is great mountain-bike riding on *estancia* tracks along Seno Otway and Seno Skyring). At km94, just north of Estancía Río Verde (now rather touristic, with sheep-shearing displays in January and February), turn left along Seno

Skyring to pass El Salto, Estancía Las Coles, Estancía Skyring (45km), Puerto Altamirano, and Río Pérez. The track swings north up the Río Pinto valley, then briefly west and north down to Estancías Río Blanco and María Sofia on Fiordo Obstrucción. It passes inland to the east of Lago Aníbal Pinto to La Junta, from where a better road follows the coast to Puerto Natales.

Just 5km north of the Río Verde turning (48km north of Punta Arenas) the Río Gallegos highway heads northeast, through increasingly arid terrain, although many of the original sheep stations are here, such as San Gregorio, 75km from the junction – you will know it by the two beached ships. It is another 29km to the junction to the *Primera Angostura* ferry, and in 11km more you can turn left to the **Parque Nacional Pali Aike**, which protects 5,030ha of virtual desert (including a huge lava flow) inhabited by guanaco, rhea, armadillos, foxes and skunks. In the park is the Cueva Pali Aike and immediately west is the Cueva de Fell (Fell's Cave); archaeological finds have shown that man lived here 11,000 years ago at the same time as now-extinct creatures such as the milodon.

Continuing by the main road (Ruta 9) from Villa Tehuelches towards Puerto Natales, you will pass other *estancías* now in the hotel business, such as the Río Penitentes (km138), Rubens (km184) and Llanuras de Diana (km216). The Casas Viejas border crossing (to Río Gallegos) is at km230, 5km before the turning to the Villa Dorotea crossing (to Río Turbio). At km239 the *Sendero de Excursion* (hiking trail) to Cerro Dorotea, overlooking Puerto Natales, is signed to the north, and 247km from Punta Arenas (about 3 hours' drive) you will reach Puerto Natales.

PUERTO NATALES

Puerto Natales is a pleasant, small town visited by almost everyone heading for the Paine park (see below). There has been a lot of development in the last few years, with boat trips, horse riding and climbing all on offer now, and even talk of a golf course, but there is still plenty of competition between *hospedajes* to provide accommodation, including cheap shared rooms. Among these are Casa Cecilia (Tomás Rogers 64; tel: 061 411 797), Patagonia Adventure (Tomás Rogers 179; tel: 411 028), Backpacker's Magallania (Tomás Rogers 255 tel: 414 950, magallania@yahoo.com), and Residencial Niko's (Ramírez 669; tel: 412 810; residencialnikos@hotmail.com, www.geocities.com/residencialnikos), which may also have a second house, Niko's II, at Phillipi 528 (tel: 413 543). The HI-affiliated hostel is Path@gone, Eberhard 595 (tel: 061 413 291, fax: 413 290). The best hotel in town is the Costa Australis, at Pedro Montt 262, on the corner of Bulnes (tel: 412 000; fax: 411 881; costaus@ctcreuna.cl; www.australis.com), owned by Navimag and housing the booking office for their ship, the *Puerto Edén*, to Puerto Montt (tel: 061 414 300, fax: 414 361). The town can be a bit full on Sunday and Wednesday nights, before the ferries sail north.

To the north of the Costa Australis along the waterfront Pedro Montt is the **tourist information** kiosk (tel: 061 412 125, www.chileanpatagonia.com/natales, muninata@ctcinternet.cl; open Mon–Fri 08.30–19.30, Sat 09.30–13.00, 14.30– 18.30). South Patagonia Books, at Bulnes 676, is the last place to buy **wildlife books** (such as the photographic bird guide *Donde Observar Aves en el Parque Nacional Torres de Paine*) before going to Paine. You will need to buy **food** – the La Bombonera supermarket at Bulnes 670 is open until 22.00, but has no fruit or vegetables; better bets are on Baquedano and Blanco Encalada in the block north of Esmeralda. A couple of **banks** on Bulnes now have ATMs.

There is not a lot to see in town; the **Municipal Museum** (Bulnes 285) has reopened after rebuilding, and is the best place to buy crafty souvenirs, while the **Salesian College** (Padre Rossa 1456) has a one-room museum full of stuffed fauna.

A plethora of companies offer **tours** to Paine, and road improvements have meant that many also offer tours or bus services to Calafate – it is even possible to visit the Perito Moreno glacier in one of the world's most exhausting day trips. Path@gone, Eberhard 595 (at the corner with Blanco Encalada; tel/fax: 061 413 290/1; pathgone@entelchile.net; www.chileaustral.com/pathgone), is the umbrella organization for three major operators: Andescape (tel: 412 877; fax: 412 592; andescape@chileaustral.com; www.chileaustral.com/andescape); Fantástico Sur (tel/fax: 226 054; info@lastorres.com); and Onas Patagonia (tel: 414 349; fax: 412 707; onas@chileaustral.com; www.onaspatagonia.com), and also houses a hostel and the Evasion café-restaurant. Concepto Indigo, Ladrilleros 105 (tel: 413 609; fax: 410 169; email: explore@bigfootpatagonia.com or indigo@entelchile.net; www.conceptoindigo.co.cl) offers trekking (including the ice-trek on Glacier Grey), kayaking and rock-climbing, and also has a hotel, shop and a climbing wall. Fortaleza Aventura, Prat 234 (tel/fax: 410 595; monofortaleza@hotmail.com; http://membertripod.com/FortalezAventura) does hiking trips and has gear to rent. Most *hospedajes* also rent out hiking and camping gear, but it can be of pretty poor quality. If you are planning to do the full circuit, it is worth taking gaiters, as there are some very muddy stretches, and there can be snow on the pass.

If you want horse-riding in Paine or elsewhere, you could try to contact Blue-Green Adventures (fax: 061 412 911; lian_bluegreen@yahoo.com) or book them in advance through Ride WorldWide (page 26); otherwise there is Baqueano Zamora, who have horses at the Administration in the park.

The asphalt ends 4km beyond Puerto Natales, at the turning left to Puerto Bories (once a massive meat-packing plant, now a luxury hotel), Puerto Prat and Estancia Consuelo; this is an attractive alternative route to the **Cueva del Milodón**, the milodon cave that was the objective of Chatwin's quest in *In Patagonia*. However, the better route is via the road to Cerro Castillo and Paine for 15km, to km263, from where it is 5km west to a striking rock called *La Silla del Diablo*, and 2km more to the cave. At 150m altitude, it is 30m high, 80m wide, and 200m deep (Chatwin claimed it was 400ft (120m) wide). There is a good visitor centre and a tacky plastic model of a milodon (ground sloth; *Mylodon listai*), which lived here until around 2,500 years ago – a scrap of its skin survives in London's Natural History Museum. Every agency and *hospedaje* in town offers tours here.

The road continues along the west side of Lago del Toro and would be the main route into Paine were it not for the obstructiveness of one or two land-owners. At the moment the bridge across the Río Serrano in the park is passable only on foot. There is even talk of a ski resort in the Prat range. You can camp here, once you have paid your entry fee, so it may be a useful stopover.

Another alternative route into the park is by water, with **boats** such as the *Nueva Galicia* taking you up the Seno de Ultima Esperanza at a steady 11 knots, passing cormorant and (in season) sea lion colonies; you should also see quite a few condors. It takes about 4 hours to reach Puerto Toro, a jetty on the western side of the mouth of the Río Serrano, where you are taken on a 20-minute hike to the lake below the Serrano glacier. The boat then crosses to the Hostería Glaciar Balmaceda on the eastern side of the mouth, where day-trippers have lunch and those going on to Paine transfer to Zodiac inflatables to continue up the Río Serrano. It takes about an hour to the confluence with the Río Balmaceda, where walkers can get on or off for a wilderness hike west to Lago Geikle. It is another 40 minutes to the Saltos del Río Serrano (or Cascada Victoria) which everyone has to walk around to fresh boats upstream, for the last 10 minutes to a point just south of the Camping Río Serrano. From here there is a free transfer to the park administration to pay the entry fee. The trip costs US$80 (one-way), through Onas Patagonia. There is a bus transfer to the Hostería Las Torres at 18.00. Kayakers can negotiate to bring their vessels on a one-way trip to the head of Seno de Ultima Esperanza.

The Hostería Glaciar Balmaceda, which opened in 1998, is sited opposite Cerro Balmaceda (2,035m) and the mighty Balmaceda glacier; 15 years ago this reached sea level, but is still mightily impressive. This is the southern end of the immense **Parque Nacional Bernardo O'Higgins**, which covers 3.5 million hectares and most of the southern icecap. All the rest is virtually unvisited, although it can be seen from the ship to Puerto Montt (see p. 262 for trips from Puerto Edén to the Pio XI glacier). The hotel can only be reached by boat or helicopter, but there are routes for horse-riding to the east of the Río Serrano, notably a 12-hour ride north via Lago Bruch to the Hostería Tyndall Cabañas del Paine, opposite the end-point of the Zodiac trip. Stays at the Hostería Glaciar Balmaceda can be booked through Aventour, José Nogueira 1255, Punta Arenas; tel: 061 241 197; fax: 243 354; aventour@entelchile.net; www.aventourpatagonia.com; and Bulnes 698, Puerto Natales; tel: 061 410 253; fax: 410 825: or Turismo Pehoe, José Menéndez 918, Punta Arenas; tel: 061 244 506; fax: 248 052; Bulnes 683, Puerto Natales; tel/fax: 061 411 565; and Antonio Bellet 77, Santiago; tel: 02 235 0252; fax: 236 0917.

TORRES DEL PAINE NATIONAL PARK

The Paine massif is quite simply an unmissable part of any backpacking trip to Chile, and most people would agree that it is one of the highest points of any trip to South America. The granite Towers of Paine thrust up like giant fingers behind the *Cuernos* ('Horns') of Paine, an oddly shaped chunk of pinkish-white granodiorite topped with crumbly sedimentary rock, while the monolithic Paine Grande, covered in snow and ice, rises to the west. These mountains appear suddenly on the horizon after miles of flat, dry, windswept plain: an astonishing sight. Twelve million years ago a laccolith or mass of lava 12km long and 2.5km wide welled up from deep beneath the earth's surface, into the sedimentary strata deposited when the whole area was underwater. Glaciation then gradually removed most of the surrounding calcareous mudstone and exposed the intrusions. The towers took their present shape due to a freeze-thaw cycle (operating 365 days a year up there) enlarging cracks and chipping away at the rock; glaciers in the cirques on either side carried away the debris and deposited it as moraine.

Last Hope Sound and the area to its north were settled from 1892, mainly by sheep-farmers, and the landscape we see now is in many ways the product of this activity. In particular many of the lovely flowers you will see in former pastures are exotic species, mostly brought in with grass seed from the northern hemisphere. Another problem was fire, used to clear large areas near Lagos Paine and Grey; this is still a great danger, but now it is the tourists who light the fires. In 1985 a fire destroyed 12,000ha, and in February 1990 400ha burnt. Regeneration is slow, as the growing season is short, and dead wood rots slowly. The park was established in 1959, under the name of Parque Nacional Lago Grey, covering an area of 5,000ha. In 1962, 25,000ha were added, and the name was changed. In 1975 the climber, Guido Monzino, donated the 12,000ha Estancia Paine, centred on the present Administration, and the park now covers 242,242ha. It was declared a UNESCO

Biosphere Reserve in 1978. It probably takes its name from *payne*, a Tehuelche word for blue – apt to describe the magnificent turquoise of many of the park's lakes – although some say that a woman climber named Paine gave them her name.

The park covers a range of altitudes from 20m to 3,248m, and four main natural floral communities: around the Sarmiento gate there is *matorral xerófito pre-andino*, a steppe habitat of coirón grass and shrubs such as mata negra, mata barrosa and calafate; from Laguna Azul past Laguna Amarga and Lago Pehoé to Lago Grey the dominant community is deciduous Magellanic woodland, primarily lenga and ñirre, with coihue to the west. Elsewhere there is Magellanic tundra, largely of sphagnum moss, and high-altitude desert of stunted shrubs and alpine plants. In spring the woodland and pastures are a blanket of orchids, *Calceolaria* slipper plants, sweetpea-like *Lathyrus* and *Oxalis*, while the hillsides are a blaze of notro, spikeheath and calafate.

The park's great triumph has been the recovery of the guanaco population from around 100 in 1975 to over 3,000 today; they move to the east of the park in spring, and west to the Pehoé area in autumn. Their main predator is the puma, which is also partial to a spring lamb or two. Each ranch used to have a *leonero*, employed purely to hunt pumas, but once the big estates were broken up they could not afford it; puma numbers were rising even before they were protected in 1980, and many ranches switched to cattle. Young guanacos (*chulengos*) form about half of the puma's diet, and a large part of the balance is filled by the European hare (also important to the gato montés or Geoffroy's cat), and red and grey foxes. There are some huemul in valleys to the west of the park, and armadillo, skunk and small rodents. In addition to the 25 mammal species, 115 bird species can be seen here, including black-necked and coscoroba swans, flamingo, coot, grebe, geese and duck by water, and ñandú, condor, buzzard-eagle, peregrine, crested caracara, lapwing, flicker, pygmy owl, swallow, long-tailed meadowlark, house wren, and austral parakeet, hummingbird, blackbird and thrush elsewhere.

Various hikes can be done along the park's 250km of well-marked trails, the most famous being the circuit of about 8 days which will take you right round the Paine massif. The most amazing view is probably the close-up of the Towers of Paine from the glacial lake below, a day-walk from the Hostería Las Torres. You will never forget it. There are also fine walks to Lago and Glaciar Grey and the Valle del Francés, which can be combined with the hike to the Towers to form the 'W', which is now the most popular route (4–6 days in total). Other hikes include those to Laguna Verde (2 days there and back), Refugio Zapata (2 days there and back) and to Laguna Azul and Refugio Paine (about 3 days there and back) – see below.

Whichever you decide to do, allow plenty of time. Some people insist that three weeks is an absolute minimum in such a beautiful park, although this takes a fair bit of planning as you need to take most of your own food. Reserves can be cached with the rangers at most of the *guarderías*.

All hikes are signposted with red or orange paint markings. Do not stray from the trails; quite apart from ecological considerations, virtually all accidents here are due either to getting lost or to the wind. Katabatic winds or williwaws come rushing suddenly off the icecap, usually at around 100km/hr (60mph), but reaching 160km/hr (100mph) at times; they are worst September–January, which is also when the ozone layer is at its thinnest – use plenty of sun protection. Views are best at dawn; Paine Grande in particular is usually covered with cloud soon after.

The number of visitors to the park, most of them foreigners, has risen from

CLIMBING HISTORY

Some of the most difficult climbs in South America are to be found in Paine, and British expeditions have played a significant role in their conquest. The first recorded climbing in Paine was in 1915, when the explorer-priest Alberto de Agostini climbed Cerro Guanaco (1,270m), then in 1937 Hans Teufel and Stefan Zuck climbed Cerro Almirante Nieto (or Paine Chico; 2,640m), just south of the Torres. Punta Bariloche (2,600m), the south peak of Cerro Paine Gande, was climbed in 1952 by the Club Andino Bariloche.

The first attempt on Paine Grande (3,050m or 3,248m, depending on your source) was made in 1954 from the Valle del Francés, resulting in the deaths of two Argentine climbers. The first ascent, by the west face, was in 1957 by Guido Monzino's team, who also climbed the Torre Norte (2,600m) the next year. The first British expedition to Paine was in 1960–1, led by Peter Henry, who tragically drowned in Lago Nordenskjold in February 1961. Chris Bonington returned in 1963 and climbed the Torre Central (2,800m) with Don Whillans, one day ahead of Aste's Italian expedition, who then climbed the Torre Sur (2,850m). The 'Whillans Box' (lashed together from tarpaulin and fenceposts and dubbed the Hotel Británico) evolved here, but was not in fact winched up the face, although this technique was later used in FitzRoy. The 1,200m east face of Torre Central was climbed only in 1974 by Paul Fatti's South Africans; in 1992 a British team including Paul Pritchard, Simon Yates and Sean Smith put up a new route to the left of the South African line in a 5-week siege, sleeping on portaledges, the modern equivalent of the Whillans Box.

In 1968 Chileans led by Eduardo García and Gastón Oyarzún climbed the Cuerno Central (2,600m); in the same year Fortaleza (the Fortress) was climbed by Ian Clough's British team by the left-hand skyline. The 1,500m Fortress Wall, probably the greatest rock face in South America, also succumbed to Britons Keith Myhill, Phil Burke, and Mick Horlov after a 13-day push in 1979. The Aiguilles (Sword, Shield etc) were all climbed in the 1970s, mostly by Italians and Chileans.

8,338 in 1986 to c51,000 in 1996. As a result many of the *refugios* have taken quite a battering and several have been vandalised or destroyed by fires, deliberate or accidental. Now, although the park is still short of resources, a policy of granting concessions for private businesses to run campsites and refuges has led to a considerable improvement. New refuges have been built, and some traditionally free huts and campsites are now subject to a charge. For US$5 campers do at least get a warm shower; full board at a refuge costs about US$35. You still have a choice of free or paying campsites and refuges, with careful planning; camping wild is not permitted. The park is very busy, though not unbearably so, except in January and February, when it would be wise to 'spread the load' by using some of the less popular hikes. In recent years the 'W' route has become even more popular than the circuit, making the Pehoé area especially busy. Fire is a permanent hazard so you must use a stove and make sure cigarette ends are completely extinguished.

There is an entrance fee of about US$16 (half for Chileans). The rangers are friendly and helpful, so do not hesitate to ask for information, and be sure to sign in before hikes. If you want to identify some of the birds or plants you have seen, the administration centre has a moderately informative exhibition of posters. It has no books, however, so serious botanists/zoologists should buy their own before leaving Punta Arenas or Puerto Natales. The best map for hikers is that produced by JLM at 1:100,000 and sold everywhere for US$7; Zagier & Urruty's 1:80,000 map is less complete. There is also a panoramic map which makes a good wall-poster but does not show the 'W' route. For climbing information see page 278.

Getting there

The park entrance is 117km north of Puerto Natales. At least five companies run daily bus services from Puerto Natales into the park, most departing between 06.00 and 07.00 and arriving at the entrance three hours later and at the administration centre about an hour after that. In the last couple of years a few companies have introduced departures at about 14.00, so that it is now possible to travel from Punta Arenas to the park in a day. There is brisk competition – ask at your *hospedaje* what deals they can offer. BusSur often offers the best value, but that can change; Servitur, JB, Gómez and Pacheco are also reputable. The return buses leave between 15.00 and 18.00. With a bit of haggling, you should be able to arrange to be dropped off at Cerro Castillo and pick up a minibus to Calafate there.

Continuing north from the turning to the Milodon Cave, there are views of the Towers to the left from around km290; ahead is the jagged Cordón de los Baguales (Wild Horses Range) right on the border, and to the right there are minefields. Cerro Castillo is at km304, ie: 56km from Puerto Natales; the Chilean border post is right by the café where all buses stop, but it is 7km to the Argentine post at Cancha Carrera. (With the development of the Río Turbio Airport and paving of the road from Río Gallegos to Río Turbio via La Esperanza and Cancha Carrera, this crossing is destined to be more and more important for tourist traffic.) At km311 a road turns left to La Peninsula. This links with the new road along the west side of Lago del Toro which should one day be the main road to the park administration. At km331 a road leads left to Laguna Verde (page 288); and at km334 traffic to Paine turns left off the road north to Cerro Guindo. There are great views of the Paine massif from the top of the first hill, and beside Lake Sarmiento. After 11km buses turn right off the direct route along Lago Sarmiento, to reach the junction right/north to Laguna Azul (page 287) and then the Laguna Amarga gate in another 13km. It is another 37km from here to the national park's administration centre at the northwestern corner of Lago del Toro.

Private vehicles and bikes (both pedal- and motor-) can enter the park along the north shore of Lago Sarmiento. This is a quieter route, with placid guanaco, flamingo, and red foxes hanging around for scraps at the gate. However, buses go via Laguna Amarga (on the far side of which you may see flamingos) where they halt at the *guardería* for all passengers to register and pay their entry fees. There are semi-tame foxes here, too, and it is worth mentioning that guanaco can usually be seen and photographed quite easily from the path south from here to Lago Sarmiento (up steeply for 10 minutes, then 5–10 minutes on) or to the left of the road as it climbs west from the gate. Classic anticline/syncline strata are also visible south of the *guardería*. This is the place for those going to Las Torres or doing the anti-clockwise circuit to get off; the buses continue to the administration centre and will drop you off anywhere along the way. It is a fairly slow 19km to the junction to the free Refugio Pudeto, next to the Lago Pehoé *guardería*, for the boat to Refugio Pehoé (currently at 09.30, 12.00 and 18.00, returning half an hour later;

US$15). For information contact Hielos Patagónicos at Magallanes 960 in Punta Arenas (tel: 061 220 345) or Los Arrieros 1517 in Puerto Natales (tel: 061 411 380).

From here the road follows the east shore of Lago Pehoé; 1km beyond the junction there is a good view to the right of the Salto Grande (see p. 287), and to the left classic dykes (igneous intrusions cutting across the sedimentary strata). The Hostería Pehoé is on an island at km4.5, and the Camping Pehoé is at km6; from the hill on its west there is a view to the Salto Chico and the Paine massif, while to the east a trail leads to a better hilltop *mirador*. This follows a jeep-track from north of the camp for 2 minutes, then heads left to a pole with an orange band (the track carries on toward a hut and radio aerial on another hill). The path runs on between two gravel bands, then goes up to a col south of the peak, passes behind it and climbs (a slightly slippery stretch) to reach the *mirador* after 30 minutes. At km6.8 you can visit the smaller and less impressive Salto Chico (the outlet from Lago Pehoé, by the Hotel explora). The road crosses the Río Paine by the Puente Weber at km13.5, and reaches the Administration at km16 (from the Pehoé junction).

The **information centre** (open daily 08.30–20.00) at the administration is very useful; it has good displays, plus a bird-watching balcony over the lake. Behind it are the remains of the first house here, built in 1911 by the British rancher, Walter Ferrier. A minibus meets the buses from Puerto Natales here to carry passengers on to the Hostería Lago Grey and the Guardería Lago Grey, start of the Zapata hike. Turning off this road almost at once you can continue 6km south to the Camping Río Serrano (expensive except for groups, as you pay per site) and the Hostería Tyndall Cabañas del Paine (reached by boat).

To the east of the Administration is the Posada Río Serrano, a simple corrugated iron building, on the shores of the lake. Before you reach this, the 'Miscellaneous Woodland Areas' path is a 400m loop to the left, with signs in Spanish only, but pitched at elementary school level. Also (if you are killing time waiting for the bus) a path runs left beside Lago Toro from the jetty to a Conaf house, beyond which a rough little path leads to a tiny beach (and beyond). A third walk here is the **Laguna Linda** route (officially for horse-riding) – go up the Puerto Natales road past the stables, turn left past a small wood and then right following horse tracks. It takes 20 minutes to a gate in a fence (with a lagoon to the left), after which you soon climb into some small bare hills. A lagoon will appear on your left after 10 minutes, and the path splits – going to the right, you will see Laguna Linda on the left after 5 minutes. It is quite large, with a sickly smear of reed taking over, not at all the 'Pretty Lake' of its name. Minor paths head right to a *mirador*, but the main path goes straight towards the Cuernos – drop down to the left through scrubby calafate, to the return path, which brings you back to the gate in 20–25 minutes.

Accommodation

While you are out doing the circuit or the 'W' you will probably stay at some point in the refuges and campsites run by Andescape and Fantástico Sur. Andescape run the Lago Pehoe, Grey and Lago Dickson *refugios* and the Camping Los Perros, and Fantástico Sur run the slightly better Refugio Chileno and Refugio Los Cuernos, and the Las Torres and Seron campsites. The refugios all cost US$17 per person (or US$4 to camp) with dinner for US$10, and other meals available. The other huts and campsites are free but pretty run-down; camping wild is not allowed.

When you have completed the circuit, you may feel like splashing out on a room at the Hostería Las Torres (also run by Fantástico Sur), at the former Estancía Cerro Paine (where Cascada clients are housed in high-tech dome tents). Along the road towards the Administration, the Hostería Pehoé is perched on a small island on Lago Pehoé with views of the Cuernos del Paine; here, too, the laundry will return clothes as pristine as if they had never touched a rucksack. The Hotel explora [sic], further along the road, is grander, but is also an eyesore, visible from afar. Cheaper accommodation is available near the administration centre. The Posada Río Serrano (US$90 double), just east by Lago Toro, has a small shop and a quaint, old-fashioned bar/restaurant with white, starched tablecloths where tight-lipped, bow-tied waiters will serve you hot chocolate or bacon and eggs (among other things). Nearby is the Refugio Lago Toro (US$6 per person), and finally the Parador de Mochileros, a picnic shelter next to the administration, used as an overflow when the refuge is full. The Hostería Tyndall (US$132 double) just beyond the Río Serrano has expensive cramped rooms, and no excursions.

Reservations for Andescape, Fantástico Sur, and the Hostería Las Torres can be made through Path@gone in Puerto Natales, and at Magallanes 960, Punta Arenas; tel/fax: 061 226 054; fax: 222 641; info@lastorres.com; www.lastorres.com. Bookings for the Hostería Pehoé can be made in Puerto Natales at Prat 270; tel: 411 390; in Punta Arenas at Colón 782; tel: 244 506; fax: 248 052; and in Santiago at Antonio Bellet 77, of. 605; tel: 02 235 0252; fax: 236 0917. The explora offers packages from US$1,040 for 3 nights (from Punta Arenas back to Punta Arenas, with activities included), book through explora, Américo Vespucio Sur 80, piso 5, Santiago; tel: 02 206 6060; fax: 02 228 4655; or in Puerto Natales; tel: 061 411 247; or via reservexplora@explora-chile.com or www.explora.com; or in the UK through Design Hotels; tel: 020 7348 7040, www.designhotels.com (also for the explora's new sister hotel in San Pedro de Atacama).

Other addresses are: Hostería Lago Grey, 21 de Mayo, Punta Arenas; tel: 061 241 042, 222 681; fax: 241 504; Posada Río Serrano, Prat 258, Puerto Natales; tel: 061 410 684; Mirador del Payne through Turismo Viento Sur, Fagnano 565, Punta Arenas: tel: 061 226 930, 225 167; www.chileaustral.com/vientosur.

Walks in the Torres del Paine National Park

Distance	Walk 1: 104km Walk 2: 133km Walk 3: 71km
Altitude	Between sea level and 1,241m
Rating	Moderate (unless otherwise indicated)
Time	4 days for the 'W'; 5 7 days for the Torres del Paine Circuit, plus a day for each side trail into the Torres or the Cuernos; 4 days (Refugio Paine); 1 day (Laguna Verde); 2 days (Refugio Zapata)
Start of trail	Laguna Amarga
End of trail	Administration/Laguna Amarga
Maps	Mapas JLM publishes the best map, widely available in Punta Arenas and Puerto Natales. Note that the glaciers have all receded from their positions on the maps. The *Guia del Visitante* by Gastón Oyarzún (who made several first ascents in Paine) and the 'Database for the Visitor' may also be of use.

Although the shop in the Posada Río Serrano sells food and drink (but not bread), it is very expensive, so you are advised to bring your food. You can buy most things in Puerto Natales. At least a week's supplies are necessary for the Torres del Paine circuit. Meals are also available at a price in all the new *refugios*. Between late January and March you will be able to supplement this with calafate berries, blackcurrants and giant puffballs. If you have your own transport, fuel and a tyre repair service are available at the Posada Río Serrano.

The weather is almost certain to be cold and windy at least some of the time, so bring a change of clothing and a thick sweater or fleece/down jacket. Completely waterproof anorak and overtrousers are essential. Sneakers (or trainers) are also useful for fording rivers, and, unless you are doing the circuit, you may prefer to hike in them as well. You can get by without a tent by staying in the *refugios* except for the circuit where you definitely need one.

There is some fantastic **climbing** in Paine, and there is next to no problem with altitude or avalanches; however, there are no rescue services. A **permit** from Difrol is essential: see page 73. When you reach the park, you will have to pay US$800 or the equivalent in Chilean pesos (for a group of up to seven). Even Chileans have to pay US$250. You will be given a contract and asked to read, and state that you have understood, a copy of the park's rules. You should present authorisation from your embassy. The climbing fee includes entrance to the park, but you will have to leave all your equipment at the entrance until your paperwork has been completed.

1: The 'W'

The opening of the route along the north shore of Lago Nordenskjold has allowed the creation of the 'W' route (to Las Torres, Valle del Francés, and Glaciar Grey), which takes in all the most spectacular scenery of the park and avoids the duller and tougher parts of the circuit.

Like the traditional circuit, this can be done in either direction, but I prefer to take the bus all the way to the Administration, see the displays, then start the hike with the best views of the Paine massif in front of me, changing as the day goes by. This also means that I am carrying my heaviest load on the easiest terrain. However, if you have good weather but fear it will not last more than a day or two, you may prefer to go first to Hostería Las Torres and go to the Towers viewpoint, to be sure of a clear view.

If starting from the Administration, turn left past the Puma kiosk to the junction south to the Camping Río Serrano and turn right, on the road towards the Hostería Lago Grey. After 5 minutes the path forks right for the Glaciar Grey and Valle Francés, but you can move off the road before this if you want, or stay on the road if the path has been churned up by horses. The path heads across the grassy plain, passing around the left end of a ridge after 15 minutes and then finally distancing itself from the road. It again passes around the left side of another hill, and after an hour approaches the Río Grey (beyond which you will again see cars on the road to the Hostería Lago Grey) and climbs slightly before reaching the **Campamento Las Carretas** (free). You will soon rise above a Z-bend in the river, climbing under an overhang, and then returning to the grassy plain after 15 minutes; the path follows the river for 45 minutes before finally getting away at its right-angle bend to the west.

So far the walking has mostly been pretty dull, although it would be tough in the face of a stiff wind, but after half an hour you will cross a low ridge and see the wonderful china-blue Lago Pehoe ahead, with the magnificent Cuernos rising above. The path drops to the corner of the lake, then passes over a bluff to reach the lake again by some potential picnic sites. It passes below the next two bluffs and

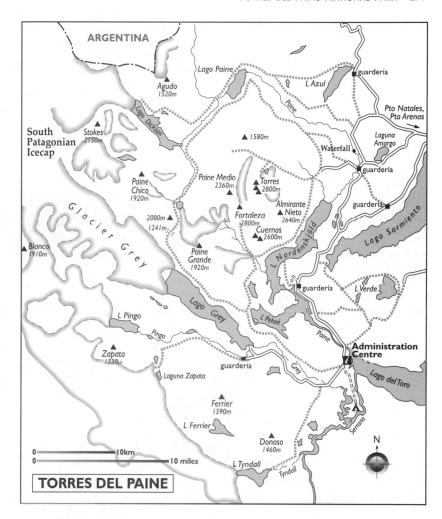

ARGENTINA

Lago Paine

guardería

Agudo
1520m

L Azul

Paine

Lago Dickson

Pto Natales,
Pta Arenas

South
Patagonian
Icecap

Stokes
2150m

▲ 1580m

Laguna
Amargo

Waterfall

guardería

Paine Medio
2360m

Paine
Chico
1920m

▲ Torres
2800m

Almirante
▲ Nieto
2640m

guardería

2080m ▲
1241m

Fortaleza
2800m

Cuernos
2600m

L Nordenskjöld

Lago Sarmiento

Blanco
1910m

G l a c i e r   G r e y

Paine
Grande
1920m

L Pingo

Lago Grey

guardería

L Verde

L Pehoé

Pingo

Paine

Administration
Centre

Zapata
1530m

guardería

Grey

Lago del Toro

Laguna Zapata

Ferrier
1590m

Serrano

L Ferrier

0   10km
0   10 miles

Donoso
1460m

N

TORRES DEL PAINE

L Tyndall

Tyndall

in half an hour reaches the outlet from a small lake. You should cross this stream, ignoring the little-used path around the lake. There is a short climb, and in 10 minutes you will be looking down at the **Refugio Pehoé**, reached in another 5 minutes. This is one of the most scenically situated huts in the park, on the shore of the lake of the same name (*c*60m) and dominated by Punta Bariloche, the southern part of Paine Grande. Rebuilt in 1990 it is now one of the largest and nicest refuges in the park, with good food and pisco sours. The old hut is also still here, as well as a kiosk and camping spaces (US$4, plus US$2 for hot showers in the refuge) with low windbreaks of wood and netting, much needed here. A catamaran links Pehoé with the Refugio Pudeto (currently at 10.00, 12.30 and 18.30), connecting with transfers to the Hostería Las Torres and also the buses to Puerto Natales. This uses a new jetty to the southwest, just below the path from the Adminstration (not the Charley MacLean Jetty to the east).

You can set up camp here and travel light to Glacier Grey and back. The trail

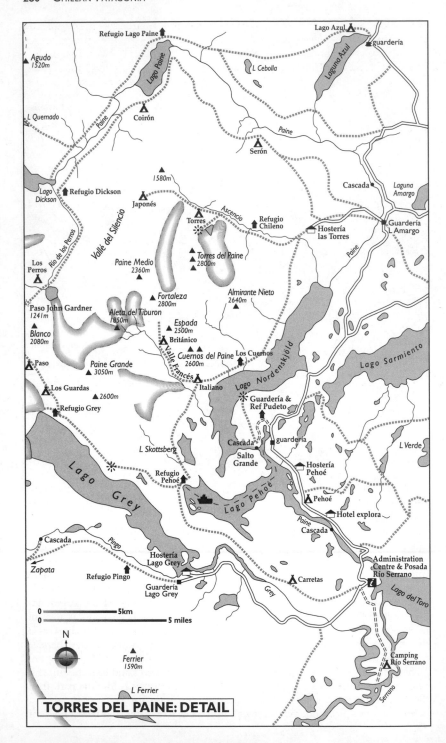

Agudo 1520m

Refugio Lago Paine

Lago Paine

L Cebolla

Lago Azul

guardería

Laguna Azul

L Quemado

Paine

Coirón

Paine

Serón

1580m

Cascada

Laguna Amargo

Lago Dickson

Refugio Dickson

Japonés

Valle del Silencio

Ascencio

Torres

Refugio Chileno

Hostería las Torres

Guardería L Amargo

Río de los Perros

Paine

Los Perros

Paine Medio 2360m

Torres del Paine 2800m

Paso John Gardner 1241m

Aleta del Tiburon 1850m

Fortaleza 2800m

Almirante Nieto 2640m

Blanco 2080m

Espada 2500m

Británico

Paso

Paine Grande 3050m

Cuernos del Paine 2600m

Los Cuernos

Lago Sarmiento

Los Guardas

2600m

Valle Francés

Italiano

Lago Nordenskjöld

Refugio Grey

Guardería & Ref Pudeto

L Skottsberg

Cascada

guardería

L Verde

Salto Grande

Hostería Pehoé

Lago Grey

Refugio Pehoé

Lago Pehoé

Pehoé

Paine

Hotel explora

Cascada

Cascada

Pingo

Hostería Lago Grey

Administration Centre & Posada Río Serrano

Zapata

Refugio Pingo

Guardería Lago Grey

Grey

Carretas

Lago del Toro

0 ————— 5km

0 ————— 5 miles

N

Ferrier 1590m

Camping Río Serrano

L Ferrier

Serrano

TORRES DEL PAINE: DETAIL

starts at the washblock and runs northwest through ñirre trees up the **Quebrada de los Vientos**; note the vertical strata in the cliffs. After 30 minutes you will reach the head of the valley and go down and up for 10 minutes before arriving at a viewpoint to the icecap across the small Laguna Roca (*c*270m), where you may see flighted steamer ducks. It takes under ten minutes to reach the wood at the end of the lake, and a similar time to a viewpoint over Lago Grey; it is worth pushing on for 15 minutes for a better view of the lake and the icecap. Going on up to the left from here past a muddy trench, it takes 15 minutes to reach a large outcrop (on the left) which you should climb for views to both ends of the lake. Here a minor path takes off to the right along the hillside, but you should go down to the left, reaching another viewpoint in 5 minutes. This is an obviously glaciated landscape, with notro shrubs, and bushes such as prickly heath (*Pernettya mucronata*), *Escallonia*, *Baccharis*, *Senecio* (ragwort), and *Festuca* grass. The path goes up and down for 40 minutes to a stream and then drops into an area with more mature trees. After 20 minutes more you will cross the small gorge of the Olguín stream on a good modern bridge, and pass above its right side for a while. In another 10 minutes you will cross a low ridge with a waterfall to the right and enter lenga forest; after 10 minutes the path heads downhill and in 15 minutes more (after passing a deep cleft, made by meltwater from a side glacier, where it found a line of weakness) reaches a triangular junction (under 3 hours net from Refugio Pehoé), where the path to the right leads to the Paso John Gardner and the rest of the Circuit (usually done in the other direction). The path to the left leads in about 5 minutes to the **Refugio Grey**, another Andescape refuge, supposedly 'ecologically sited', but in fact simply on the site of an older (now disused) hut. However, 2 minutes along this path you should turn right, along the moraine of the side glacier (now being colonised by coihue, maiten and canelo), to reach the Glacier Grey *mirador* in 15 minutes. Less than 10 years ago the ice actually reached the rocks here, but now there is 200m of clear water between the *mirador* and the glacier – still a pretty awesome sight (though it has been described as 'like teetering on the edge of a huge gin and tonic'). From the refuge there is a daily glacier trek, run by Concepto Indigo (see page 271).

From here, unless you plan to continue around the circuit, you must return the same way to the Refugio Pehoé.

For the central section of the 'W', heading east from Refugio Pehoé to the **Valle Francés**, go past the camping spaces reserved for groups and gradually climb inland, crossing a stream and a burnt area showing good signs of regeneration. After 30 minutes you will cross a ridge and then a minor one in 15 more; for the next 40 minutes you will have Lago Skottsberg below to the right, followed by a smaller lake. After 20 more minutes you will cross a moraine ridge with no distinct pass to enter the **Valle Francés**. The path descends gradually for 20 minutes to the suspension bridge over the Río Francés, about 2 hours from the Refugio Pehoé. In just 3 minutes more you should turn left at a junction, reaching the **Campamento Italiano** (free) in another minute. There is a *baño*, but drinking water comes from the river; if the first section is crowded, there is another about 3 minutes' walk further up the valley, which is generally quieter. You can pitch your tent here and travel light up the valley, if you choose.

You are very soon rock-hopping through lenga forest, and after 15 minutes reach a good stream with a view to a green *laguna* below the Glaciar Francés. After 10 minutes more there is a steep section, with a loose-ish wire to help, after which the path follows a narrow moraine ridge to some big cascades on the Río Francés.

The path climbs to reach (after 15 minutes) a great viewpoint to the glacier, to the left, and then continues virtually on the level. After crossing two streams and two boggy patches the path climbs by the river, and after 40 minutes reaches a clearing where it turns sharp left. Initially the best route is to the left, by the river, but soon all possibilities are somewhat boggy. If you can get to a mini-ridge to the right, you will reach the **Campamento Británico**, in the woods again, in a couple of minutes more (about 10 minutes from entering the clearing). There is free camping here, and huts used for storing climbing gear. A pipe provides water at the lower end of the site, but there is no *baño*.

The path on is unmarked but clear enough. You are soon climbing the moraine to reach the first *mirador* (viewpoint) in about 10 minutes. To continue, follow the right bank of a small stream in ñirre trees and climb steeply to the second *mirador*, reached in about 12 minutes. From here, clouds permitting, there are great views of this mountain bowl, notably Paine Grande to the west, the Aleta del Tiburon (Shark's Fin, 1,850m) to the north, and the Cuernos to the east. Even here the explora eyesore sticks out like a sore thumb, at the far end of Lago Pehoe. It is possible to continue uphill to the east, to a point at which one could make one's way around the whole basin more or less on the level. If you have time, you can carry on up; it takes at least half an hour to climb the scree of white granite to a false col to the east, and another half hour to the true col, between Espada, the northernmost of the Cuernos, and the mighty bulk of Fortaleza (the Fortress). Beyond this you can see an ice-field, with a big drop to the left and the rear of the Towers to the right.

Returning by the same path to the junction below the Campamento Italiano (1½ hours), the Grand Circuit continues to the left/east. It now follows a new route along the north side of Lago Nordenskjold to the Hostería Las Torres, but it once passed around the west end of Lago Nordenskjold to the Salto Grande. The bridge here was destroyed, leaving the path from Refugio Pehoé as the only access to the Valle Francés for many years. The new path at first takes a rather roundabout route to the right, as if heading for the Salto Grande, but then loops left to cross a ridge after 10 minutes. After crossing a boggy patch and some small streams, it crosses a higher ridge, more or less opposite the Nordenskjold *mirador* (hike No.4), after 20 more minutes. It drops steeply and reaches a shingle beach in 20 minutes, then keeps close to the lake for 10 minutes to a good-size stream flowing from a waterfall. After another shingle beach there is a short muddy climb, and in about 15 minutes the path reaches the new **Refugio Los Cuernos**. The refuge has a striking design, with a high cathedral-style window facing the Cuernos, but the staff seem to have a real attitude problem; this may sort itself out as things settle down. Camping is also possible here.

There is a big stream immediately east, crossed by a simple plank bridge, after which the path climbs, off and on, for 40 minutes to a pass just beyond a dry pond. There is no great view here, and the path soon drops into trees. After 15 minutes it crosses another ridge, with a view of the east end of Lago Nordenskjold, and of the open scrubby scenery ahead. The path drops, reaching a good stream down a big boulder field after 20 minutes, and a gate a couple of minutes beyond. The path turns 90° to the left and climbs, crossing three streams and reaching ridges after 30 minutes and another 10 minutes. From here the path swings away from the lake, crossing a big stream and climbing briefly, before reaching a *laguna* after 15 minutes; on the far side you will see orange markers, which guide you around a boggy area. With a beach and flat grassy areas, this is an ideal spot for minimum-impact picnics! The path follows a line of trees and calafate bushes along a stream, which accelerates downhill after 15 minutes; from here you can see huts and fields ahead. You will cross the stream in 5 minutes, and a smaller one in 10 more, just before the junction of the path to Campamento Torres, to the left up a sandy ridge.

Having got here, you would be crazy not to go up to the Towers, health and other factors allowing, but if so carry on for 1 or 2 minutes to a suspension bridge over the mudstone gorge of the Río Ascencio and turn right. You will arrive at the **Hostería Las Torres** in 15 minutes, supposedly 7 hours from the Campamento Italiano, although it can be done in 4½. The *hostería* is large and modern, and beyond it are stables and the campsite; the fabulous views of the Torres from the campsite are about all that is unchanged since the days when, as Estancía Cerro Paine, this was the base for the early climbing expeditions. The path to Campamento Serón is, of course, the start of the circuit; the road returns to the Laguna Amarga *guardería*, but there is a very obvious short-cut to the left over a ridge covered with stunted ñirre, where the road goes to the right.

To go **up to the Torres**, take the path up the sandy ridge, or if coming from the *hostería* take the path up the cliff to the right immediately after crossing the bridge. It is very steep for 10 minutes, then eases, and then continues as a hard slog (known as 'the grind' to the early British climbers) for another half hour, climbing high above the right bank of the Ascencio as the valley narrows. Five minutes beyond the shoulder of the hill you will see the **Refugio Chileno** below, with the appropriate flag, on the far side of the valley. The path soon drops to reach the good new bridge and the refuge in 15 minutes. This also has a cathedral-style window facing the Towers, and far friendlier staff than at Los Cuernos. Again you can leave your pack here. The path continues up through lenga on the right bank, crossing a stream after 20 minutes, and then climbs for half an hour to a junction overlooking a stream. The **Campamento Torres** is just beyond the stream in the trees.

To go straight to the Towers, head up to the left along the edge of the trees, by the stream and then climb up the boulders for 25–45 minutes. At the top you will enjoy some of the best views in the whole park, across the glacial Laguna Torres (around 1,500m) to the Towers, rising a kilometre above. Fit hikers can get here in under 3 hours, while those fresh off the plane from the northern hemisphere should allow up to 6 hours. The Towers rise out of a glacier set on cliffs, down which waterfalls course into the lake. The reflections of the Towers are best in the evening, while the Towers themselves are superb in the dawn light. This is a perfect place for 'that condor moment', too, but beware of the strong winds that whistle through the Towers: a backpacker died after being blown off a rock ledge up here. The lowest, and easiest to climb, of the Towers is the twin Torre Norte (or Este, or Monzino; 2,600m); to its right is Cerro Nido Negro de Condor (2243m), and to its left the Torre Central (2,800m) and then Torre Sur (or Torre d'Agostini; 2,850m).

Returning down the boulders and keeping to the left of the stream a path leads into the trees and straight into the **Campamento Torres**, an attractive spot with lots of mossy stones and logs, and surprisingly uncrowded. A path continues up the Ascencio to the Valle del Silencio; it is marked by stones aligned along it and then by cairns (the top stone may be a red-painted 'gnome's hat'). After 10 minutes it crosses two outlet streams from Laguna Torres and then crosses a huge rock fall for 10 minutes; following cairns slightly to the left, you will find the path heading into the woods. It follows the river and crosses another windswept rock fall after 15 minutes, and reaches the **Campamento Japonés** in another 15. This is another lovely spot in open woodland, just before the valley turns sharply left to the Valle del Silencio, known for the beauty and of course the silence of its bare crags. At the rear of the Towers and the Fortress, this was the approach for the early climbing expeditions, who knew this as the North Cwm.

2: The Torres del Paine Circuit

This walk, which takes you to the remotest part of the park around Lagos Paine, Dickson and Grey, undoubtedly requires more sustained effort than any other walk here. But it is also the most rewarding, with its perfect combination of tough mountain slogs and lazy strolls through daisy-filled meadows. Unfortunately on the fourth day we woke up to find that the quiet pattering on our tent was not rain but snow. So be warned! The circuit can be walked clockwise or anti-clockwise, depending whether you want the agony first or last. With the opening of the route along the north shore of Lago Nordenskjold, it now seems preferable to hike anti-clockwise, to have a choice of routes (or the boat) with which to finish. You will also have eaten most of your food by the time you tackle the climb to the Paso John Gardner. Some prefer to hike clockwise in order to have the weather on their backs as they climb. However, the stunning revelation of the Grey glacier from this pass is one of the delights of the anti-clockwise route – but then again you will come over the pass into a howling gale, as like as not.

Route description

From the Laguna Amarga gate (*c*75m), where buses halt for all passengers to register and pay their entry fees, you can either start hiking at once, or take a connecting minibus to the Hostería Las Torres (7km; US$3). This allows you to see the Towers before setting off, but it does not save much time on the circuit itself. Starting from the Laguna Amarga, take the road north across the two bridges over the Río Paine and fork right onto the signposted path through ñirre to Campamento Serón and Lago Paine. If you are walking to the Hostería Las Torres, take the obvious sandy track left at the bend 2 minutes north of the bridges. Leaving the Hostería Las Torres for the circuit, turn left/north off the road just east of the campsite, past the refuge, also signed 'Campamento Serón 4 hours'. These routes meet after a couple of hours in the valley of the Río Paine, and pass through buttercup-filled meadows beside the river, where you can watch herds of guanaco leaping on the hillsides.

It takes 4–5 hours to the **Serón campsite** (US$4); there may be a refuge here before too long. An hour or so further on the path swings away from the river to climb to a small lake and over a low pass and down to Lago Paine; it takes 3–4 hours from Serón to the **Coirón campsite** (free) at the west end of the lake. It can be very windy, especially in the afternoon, but the site is among trees and well protected. You have fabulous views of Cerro Stokes (2,150m) and Paine Medio and Grande. The remains of the former Refugio Lago Paine are in a gully: little more than a roof with an earth floor and a few planks for a bed. (There used to be a fine, wooden bridge nearby which gave access to the lake's northern shores and the Laguna Azul/Ventisquero Dickson hike (No. 3), but this has now gone and you are obliged to stick to the circuit path to Refugio Dickson.)

From Coirón the path is boggy in parts as it continues to follow the right bank of the Río Paine; it takes under 3 hours to **Refugio Dickson**, at the southern end of the lake of the same name, dotted with icebergs. This is a modern hut owned by

Andescape and not cheap; you have to pay to camp, too. Those who choose not to camp have a very long hike (30km, about 10 hours) to get here on the first day. As well as the modern refuge, there is a corrugated-iron hut which used to be the home of a shepherd and still has a cast-iron cooking range and a garden stocked with gooseberries, ready to eat in March, and extra fat calafate berries.

Heading south and then west, now following the right bank of the Río de los Perros. The route is on an old herder's track through a sombre forest where you are likely to hear and see flame-crested Magellanic woodpeckers tapping on the tree trunks. Soon after crossing a river on a rickety suspension bridge you will emerge from the forest to the Lago Los Perros, at the foot of the Glaciar Los Perros and dotted with icebergs like blobs of blue detergent. Just beyond this is the **Campamento Los Perros**, about 4 hours from Refugio Dickson. You are pretty much obliged to camp here, as the rest of the terrain is squelchy bog; however, the views are amazing, with glaciers, waterfalls and mountains on all sides. This costs US$4 and has a sheltered cooking area, toilets and cold showers. The path continues over shale and after about 10 minutes you can now use a bridge to cross to the left/north side of the fast-running and painfully cold Río de los Perros. The trail is very boggy and has evolved into multiple tracks; it is like the Pennine Way some years ago, and the same sort of remedial work is urgently needed. Once above the tree line the terrain becomes drier, turning into bare rock. Follow the cairns and orange markings as you climb to the **Paso John Gardner** (1,241m); these are often snow-covered, so tread carefully. You should reach the pass about an hour from the tree line, or 3 hours from the camp. Here your toils will be amply rewarded. Below, **Glaciar Grey** appears as a rippling sea of blue ice, 6km across, which stretches as far as the eye can see towards the Southern Patagonian ice-field. The glacier has been receding for a considerable time; the first nunatak (rock island in the ice) appeared 50 years ago, and a second in the 1980s. For almost everyone this is the highlight of the entire trek, marred only slightly by the fact that a snow blizzard is usually threatening to blow you off your feet.

Again cairns guide you down the slope to the left from the pass. Once below the tree line there is a very tough stretch of trail. When it rains the ground turns to mud and you will spend much of the time clambering over giant tree trunks which seem to have fallen deliberately across the trail to obstruct your way, or else clinging to them to avoid skidding down the slope. You have to climb in and out of several ravines, but there are cables and steps to help you, and there are plenty of side paths to viewpoints over the glacier. After 1 to 2 hours (depending on conditions) you will reach the very poor **Campamento Paso** (free), where there are no facilities and water must be taken from a stream about 50m north. After another 3 hours or so, along a trail which continuously rises and falls by up to 50m, you will reach the slightly better **Campamento Los Guardas** (free), by a clear fast-flowing waterfall, with a sheltered cooking area and toilets. Once the steep descent is over, the path continues through the forest along the side of the glacier. Every now and then it emerges from the trees to take you across scree-filled gullies carved out by rivers which tumble down into the glacier. Crossing these is fairly hair-raising as the scree tends to shift, so you should tread carefully, though in some there are wire cables for you to hang onto. It is easier going after Los Guardas, taking under 2 hours to the **Refugio Grey**, near the head of Lago Grey. You will have to fork right to reach the *refugio*, and right again soon after this junction to reach the *mirador*.

Due to the increased number of icebergs on the lake there is no longer a boat service from here to Hostería Lago Grey, so you will have to hike on at least as far as the Refugio Pehoé. You are now on the 'W' route. Carrying on through the woods, you will cross the Olguín bridge after about 25 minutes; after 20 minutes more you can either climb steeply up to the left on rocks (following an orange arrow on the cliff) or go on a bit to take the horse route. After 15 minutes more you will come out of the trees, go up alongside a stream, and after 15 minutes reach a ridge; the path goes on up and down, passes a higher ridge after 10 minutes, and reaches another, with great views from the rocky outcrop to the right, in under 10 minutes more. Be sure to look back to enjoy the fabulous view of the huge Glaciar Grey, and of the icebergs jamming the lake. Again, it is up and down for a while, reaching another viewpoint after 15 minutes, and a wood at the end of the secluded Laguna Roca in 25 minutes, From here it takes 10 minutes up to the ridge at the far side of the lake, and 30 minutes down the Quebrada de los Vientos to the **Refugio Pehoé**, about 3 hours from Refugio Grey (plus the best part of an hour for photos).

From here there is a choice of the traditional walk out, across rolling grasslands to the administration, the boat to Refugio Pudeto, or the newish route along the north shore of Lago Nordenskjold. This last is recommended, as it allows you to spend a day in the Valle del Francés, enjoying perhaps the park's most spectacular scenery; this can also be done as a side-trip from Refugio Pehoé. See the description under Hike 1, the 'W'.

Turning right to follow the path south along the lake, it takes about 4 hours to the administration centre (12km). The path climbs above the campsite, then drops to a small lake after 15 minutes. Crossing the spit and the outlet stream, the path passes beneath two bluffs and some potential picnic or campsites, then over a final bluff before climbing over a ridge after about half an hour. From here you have to hike across open grassland, reaching the Río Grey after another 30 minutes, where it turns 90° to the south. The path follows the river, out of reach below steep cliffs, and drops below a slightly alarming overhang to pass a Z-bend in the river, and reach the **Camping Las Carretas** (free) in 15 minutes. The path drops again to the grassy plain and passes to the right of a hill where the trees have obviously been killed by a fire. Carrying on across the grasslands (dotted with introduced flowers such as dandelions, clover and cornflowers) it passes to the right of a ridge after an hour and reaches the road from Hostería Lago Grey after 15 minutes more. You can continue to the left of the road if you want, reaching the **Administration Centre** in 5 minutes.

3: Laguna Azul and Refugio Lago Paine

Since the demise of the bridge at the west end of Lago Paine, this path has been relatively little used. Nevertheless this northeastern corner of the park is one of its most attractive areas, being less barren and wild than some of the western and central areas, and supporting lots of guanaco and rhea.

Take the road out of the park from the Guardería Laguna Amarga and fork left at the Estancía Laguna Amarga 1.5km east, re-entering the park at once. The road passes the Cascada Río Paine 5km to the north and then leaves the river to climb northeast into a wooded valley, eventually levelling out into a wide marshy valley where rhea roam. Just before the road swings right, fork left along an little-used old track which is signposted to Laguna Azul (do not take the path a bit further along to the *guardería* at the lake's eastern end). After climbing up through lush meadows you zigzag down once more to the western end of Laguna Azul. This area enjoys a microclimate much milder than the rest of the park and the lake shores are thick with ox-eye daisies and buttercups and a haven for many types of birds. You could camp here.

It takes around 4 hours more to reach Refugio Lago Paine at the eastern end of Lago Paine. Follow the track which leads northwest past the curiously named Laguna Cebolla (Onion Lagoon). Your path will be joined by a track from the *guardería* and campsite at the eastern end of Laguna Azul. You soon reach **Refugio Lago Paine** (free), a comfortable, spacious hut with a good wood-burning stove and plenty of gooseberries, redcurrants and rhubarb in the garden. We also found huge quantities of giant white puffballs in the surrounding meadows which, when fried with garlic, were delicious. This is an ideal place to linger a few days.

From here you can continue along the northern shores of the lake to **Lago Dickson**. This trail is mainly used by horse-riders and so is poorly marked; it becomes quite faint as it winds north towards Lago Dickson but can be picked up again where it passes between two large rock faces before emerging high above the lake. Although you can just about get to and from Lago Dickson in a day, 2 days would be better, and there is an idyllic campsite beyond the rocky pass in the woods beside the small Lago Quemado. It is possible to descend to the shore of Lago Dickson and walk to the glacier at its northern end. Alternatively you can fork left to follow the Río Paine to a point opposite the Albergue Dickson, on the Paine circuit. If you yell loud and long enough someone will pick you up in a rubber dinghy.

On your return journey from Refugio Paine you could take a different route via the **Camping Lago Azul** (US$5) and *guardería* at the eastern end of Laguna Azul. From here a dirt road runs north to Los Glaciares National Park in Argentina, but so far the two countries have failed to reach agreement on its improvement and use for tourism. To the south the road leads in 20km to the Estancia Laguna Amarga; drivers can fork left to reach the road out of the park 11.5km east of the Estancia.

4: Salto Grande and Nordenskjold Viewpoint

If you are taking the boat to or from Refugio Pudeto, you should not miss the nearby Salto Grande, where the Río Paine thunders from Lago Nordenskjold (*c*70m) into Lago Pehoé; it is also well worth carrying on to the *mirador* overlooking Lago Nordenskjold for the spectacular views it affords. A side road leads 200m to the Guardería Lago Pehoé and 500m more to the Refugio Pudeto (free), by the jetty for boats to Refugio Pehoé, and ends 400m further on at a car park. From here a path carries on reaching the Big Falls in under 10 minutes (ie: 2km from the main road) and, twisting and winding over the rolling hills, ends in another 30 minutes at the *mirador*, facing north towards the Cuernos and Paine Grande. Although there are a few interpretative signs along the trail, there is no marker to indicate the end of the trail and thus nothing to stop you carrying on up onto the ridge to the left. However, you will have to return by the same path.

5: Laguna Verde

This walk is less trodden than many of the others in the park. Perhaps because of this, it offers one of the best collections of wildlife in the whole park and you are almost certain to mingle with guanacos, rheas, foxes and maras (Patagonian hares), as well as aquatic birds.

From the administration centre, follow the main road north for 2.5km, to the Weber Bridge, from where there is a great view right up the French valley to the

Aleta de Tiburon. On the far side a short-cut takes you up for 3 minutes and down for 2 minutes to rejoin the road at the sign to Laguna Verde (km12.8).

The path runs parallel to the road for about 300 metres, then begins to wind up to the right below the cliffs (of slate, mudstone and ironstone, with some fossils), before climbing diagonally to the right and reaching a plateau after about 40 minutes. The path rises to a maximum of 800m, with views of the Paine massif to the left, as well as something very like a Peak District edge, then it drops along a nice wooded valley. The trees are mostly lenga, with *Baccharis patagonica* and *Asphodel*. It takes an hour or more to reach Laguna Honda (with a good view to Paine); then the path goes slightly up and away to the right to cross to the next valley, more open and windswept, and drops after about 25 minutes to two (or three, depending on the water level) lakes, where you can see grebes, coots and ruddy ducks. From here the path goes down towards Laguna Verde, with the *hostería* visible on its far side. Making your way through fields of long grass and then woods, with plenty of fallen trees in your way, you will reach the *guardería* and **Refugio Laguna Verde** (free) in about an hour from the lakes (3–4 hours in all from the road). A little further on is an official campsite, but it is very run-down and wind-swept. Just beyond is the **Hostería Mirador del Payne** (formerly the Estancía Lazo), a very friendly and luxurious hotel, with excellent teas. It takes about an hour to walk up to the Mirador Sierra del Toro, at about 600m on the hill to the south of the *hostería*. A 26km road, along which you will see lots of guanaco, rhea and grey fox, leads east to the main road to Puerto Natales. Alternatively, you can return by forking right at the west end of Laguna Honda onto a track that reaches the road just north of the Lago Pehoé campsite, which also takes 4–5 hours; this is used mainly by guided horse-riding groups, so is not well signed.

6: Refugio Zapata

The walk starts near the southern end of Lago Grey. A minibus meets the buses from Puerto Natales at the administration centre to take tourists the 18km to the Hostería Lago Grey; the road has been hugely improved in the last few years so that you have a good chance of hitching a ride, but there is still a 4-tonne weight limit on the bridge over the Río Grey.

The road ends at the Guardería Lago Grey, 1km further north from the turning to the *hostería*. A path leads to the right across a suspension bridge, reaching the beach in 5 minutes. Heading to the left for 5 minutes more you will reach a sandbar lined with icebergs from Glaciar Grey, a sight not to be missed. You can walk to the right along the bar for 20 minutes to an island, and up to a *mirador*. Behind the *guardería* another path leads up to the Mirador Ferrier, at about 600m on the slopes above.

For Refugio Zapata, take the well-marked trail which begins in front of the *guardería* and follows the river northwest past striking folded strata. Along the way there are lenga and ñirre, and calafate, chaura, notro, clubmoss, *Escallonia*, *Baccharis*, *Misodendron*, *Chiliotrichium diffusum*, and orchids. You will reach **Refugio Pingo**, a nice *leonero*'s hut (free) with two beds and a stove, in 30 minutes. The path onwards climbs over a bluff and into low trees, and after 20 minutes crosses a stream on a good wooden bridge. Across the river the forests were badly damaged by fire. There is a short steep climb before the path continues to rise in forest for 20 minutes, then rises and falls and after 40 minutes heads down and into meadow. Again it passes a low wooded ridge and after 45 minutes reaches the junction to the Cascada Pingo. There are cascades just a minute or two down the path to the right, but if you keep going for another 5 minutes downstream you will come to a viewpoint below the real falls.

Back on the trail, in another 10 minutes you will cross a stream on stepping stones and climb in 10 more minutes to a ridge with a good view across a big bend in the Río Pingo. You can see the **Refugio Zapata**, but it takes another 15 minutes to reach it, as the path seems to loop a remarkable distance to the left. This is another former shepherd's hut, rather simpler than the Pingo refuge, and likewise free, if mosquito-ridden. The bridge over the Río de los Hielos which used to take the path on to Lago Pingo has been washed away several times and the park authoritites have given up rebuilding it, therefore the only option for an excursion is to the **Mirador Zapata**.

This path leads through the trees behind the hut and out onto the very flat plain, with the Pingo glacier visible ahead beyond the lake, and the southern icecap to the left. Cairns and orange markers show the way to the left. After 20 minutes you will cross a stream and head into the woods. The climb only lasts 5 minutes, and then you will follow a moraine ridge to reach the edge of the woods in 10 minutes. Go left at the first cairn to reach the *mirador*, with a view across Laguna Zapata to the massive icecap. There are classic moraine terraces and huge areas of rock only recently under ice. The outlet stream, to the north, is usually too big and fast to cross, but if you can get around to the south it is possible to get up onto the ice, or to swing north to climb **Cerro Zapata**, a non-technical peak of 1,530m (unless it is windy). There is also a wilderness route to the south to the Río Serrano, passing over the western shoulder of Cerro Ferrier to Lago Ferrier and Lago Tyndall. There has been talk of opening up a trail for some years, but for now it remains closed. From Lago Tyndall a trail of about 17km follows the north bank of the river to the Río Serrano, then crosses swampy pasture to reach the Hostería Lago Grey road less than 1km west of the Río Grey bridge.

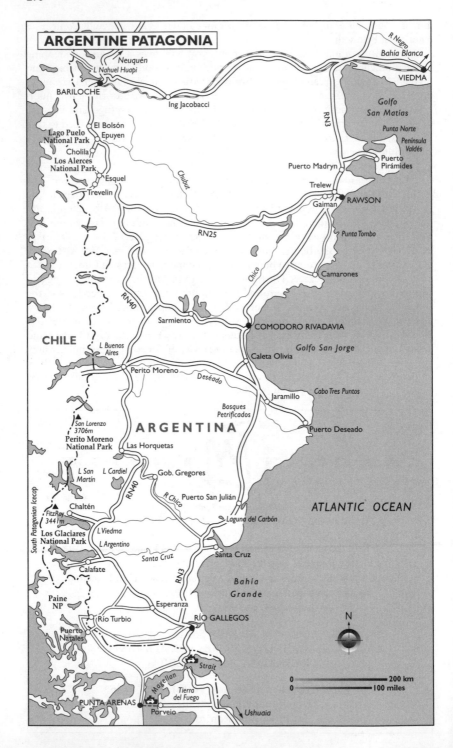

ARGENTINE PATAGONIA

Neuquén

L Nahuel Huapi

BARILOCHE

Ing Jacobacci

El Bolsón

Epuyen

Lago Puelo
National Park

Cholila

Los Alerces
National Park

Esquel

Trevelin

R Negro

Bahía Blanca

VIEDMA

Golfo
San Matías

Punta Norte

Peninsula
Valdés

Puerto
Pirámides

Puerto Madryn

Trelew

Gaiman   RAWSON

Chubut

RN25

Punta Tombo

Chico

Camarones

RN40

Sarmiento

CHILE

L Buenos
Aires

Perito Moreno

COMODORO RIVADAVIA

Golfo San Jorge

Caleta Olivia

Deséado

Cabo Tres Puntos

Jaramillo

Bosques
Petrificados

Puerto Deseado

San Lorenzo
3706m

ARGENTINA

Perito Moreno
National Park

Las Horquetas

L San
Martin

L Cardiel

Gob. Gregores

R Chico

Puerto San Julián

RN40

Chaltén

FitzRoy
3441m

Los Glaciares
National Park

L Viedma

L Argentino

Laguna del Carbón

ATLANTIC OCEAN

South Patagonian Icecap

Santa Cruz

Santa Cruz

Calafate

RN3

Paine
NP

Bahía
Grande

Esperanza

Río Turbio

RÍO GALLEGOS

Puerto
Natales

N

Strait

Magellan

Tierra
del Fuego

Ushuaia

PUNTA ARENAS

Porveio

0   200 km
0   100 miles

Argentine Patagonia

'The country remained the same, and was extremely uninteresting. The complete similarity of the productions throughout Patagonia is one of its most striking characteristics. The level plains of arid shingle support the same stunted and dwarf plants; and in the valleys the same thorn-bearing bushes grow. Everywhere we see the same birds and insects. Even the very banks of the river and of the clear streamlets which entered it, were scarcely enlivened by a brighter tint of green. The curse of sterility is on the land.'

Charles Darwin, *The Voyage of the Beagle*, April 22 1834

Scenically, Patagonia is a land of contrasts. The sterile, featureless plains on the Argentine side, which provoked Darwin's scathing remarks, provide some of the most boring views in the world. The *cordillera* of the Andes and the labyrinth of fjords and glaciers on the Chilean side offer some of the finest. The massifs of FitzRoy and Paine, in the far south, must surely be the most beautiful in the Americas. The area is so rich in wildlife, described in fascinating detail by Darwin in *The Voyage of the Beagle*. Guanacos, rheas and the Patagonian fox and hare are frequently seen in the south, while Península Valdés, on the east coast, is one of the best places for viewing whales, seals and marine birds in the whole of South America, and has recently become famous through television films of orcas hunting here. This is the only place in South America that can rival the African safari experience, with the added benefit of the marine element.

CHUBUT PROVINCE

On July 28 1865, 153 bedraggled Welsh immigrants landed on a desolate beach off what is now Puerto Madryn, in Chubut Province of northern Argentine Patagonia. Led by a Lewis Jones, their dream was to found a New South American Wales, where they would be allowed to speak their native tongue and escape the misery of the cramped mining valleys. But, at first, life in Patagonia was scarcely better than the one they had left behind. One man who climbed the cliffs in search of food disappeared completely, and the rock-hard barren landscape looked as if it would not nurture so much as a blade of grass. Within a few days the sheep brought down from the north were lost on the *pampa* and the semi-wild cattle of the Río Negro refused to be milked. Three weeks later the motley party pushed up the valley of the Río Chubut where they found flat land which they could irrigate, and the colony eventually prospered. The last Welsh contingent arrived in 1911, although nowadays teachers come on exchange from Wales and sometimes marry and settle.

If today you visit **Trelew** (pronounced 'treléo'), 18km inland where the main coastal highway crosses the Río Chubut (or Gaiman), you may still hear Welsh, although the language is slowly dying out as Welsh descendants intermarry with Argentines. However, many still sing in choirs at the Welsh non-conformist chapels, and they even hold an annual *Eisteddfod*. Welsh tea houses, although not authentically Welsh, are now big business, providing delicious cream teas which are quite a bizarre experience in the depths of South America. Try the special *torta negra* (black cake), a delicious spicy fruitcake.

Trelew or **Puerto Madryn** are also the starting points for visits to the Valdés peninsula, an anchor-shaped projection of land jutting into the turbulent Atlantic Ocean which provides a home to the most plentiful wildlife in Patagonia. The plankton-rich Falkland Current washes the peninsula's shores, providing food for the world's largest nursery of the southern right whale (ballena franca austral; *Eubalena australis*). The plankton are also eaten by fish which attract the peninsula's famous sea lions, fur seals and elephant seals, and these in turn fall prey to the carnivorous orcas that frequent the area. Similarly fine wildlife can also be seen at Punta Tombo, 120km south of Trelew. However, a series of natural and man-made disasters have taken a toll on the wildlife populations. In 1991, firstly Volcán Hudson dumped 3km³ of ash over the province, and then a mysterious oil spill off the Valdés peninsula killed at least 16,000 penguins as they migrated to the area from Brazil. In recent years the number of fishing boats plying the area has increased enormously, threatening the delicate ecosystem. The Patagonia Nature Foundation has attempted to create a 30km marine reserve to protect the food supplies of the coastal animals that migrate to the area to breed. The peninsula was added to UNESCO's World Heritage List in 1999.

If you go further up the Chubut valley you come to Esquel and Trevelin, towns founded by the Welsh in the lush foothills of the Andes where you can supplement cream teas with locally-grown raspberries or peaches. From here you can visit the Los Alerces National Park (page 303).

Getting there

The area's commercial centre is Trelew, which is served by all Argentina's main airlines; however, Puerto Madryn is now booming, mainly due to tourism, and its new airport is served by LADE, LAPA, Dinar and Southern Winds. There are also frequent buses along the coastal Ruta 3. Local buses run at least hourly from Trelew to Madryn (64km) and to Gaiman (18km), with a few continuing to Esquel.

Puerto Madryn and Trelew

Puerto Madryn is Argentina's leading centre for scuba diving (and windsurfing), and is rapidly improving its facilities to attract visitors – conveniently, at just the seasons when the wildlife of the Valdés peninsula is least interesting.

Marine parks have been created, such as the Parque Nuevo, 500m off the town's beach, where old buses have been sunk to provide homes for starfish, octopus and grouper. Likewise a fishing boat has been sunk off Punta Cuevas, 4km southeast, and a further 6km along this road towards Punta Loma (see below) there are shallow rock basins, ideal for beginners' first dives, and the Parque Natural Punta Este, 1km offshore.

At Punta Cuevas (El Indio) there is also the new EcoCentro (tel: 02965 457 470; www.ecocentro.org.ar), with displays on the local marine ecosystems, and in

WALES IN PATAGONIA

Hilary Bradt

Trying to find the Welsh flavour of Chubut had been disappointing. We had been ticked off in the Welsh Tea Shop for propping our backpacks against the wall, and there was nothing in Trelew to make us feel we were in Pembrokeshire, or even Cardiff. Gaiman seemed more promising, but hitch-hiking was slow and we arrived in the late evening, irritable, and with nowhere to stay. We walked down the street arguing about whether to sleep in a partly constructed building we had just passed, or to find a field on the outskirts of town to set up our tent (hotels were too expensive). Our raised voices attracted attention and to my embarrassment a man materialised before us and said: 'You need somewhere to stay, then? Come back to my house – I'm fed up with the bloody Spanish.' The accent was strongly Welsh, and we accepted.

Politely masking her surprise, his pretty Argentine wife greeted us then launched into an animated discussion with her husband. I was depressed at my poor Spanish: I could not follow any of the conversation. Gwyn turned to us. 'Sorry you could not understand that. We have to speak in Welsh: it is our common language. María does not speak English and I do not speak Spanish. We want you to come out to her parents' farm this weekend.'

María's family was one of the oldest in the Patagonian Welsh community. The women had always run the farm, and by tradition had been sent to Wales to finish their education and find a husband. Gwyn had not been in Argentina for long. We sat listening to stories of the old days (mercifully María's mother spoke English), how she would watch from the specially built turret for her father's return on horseback from the Big City, the lean years when beef prices were low and there was scarcely enough to eat, the time when the sun was blotted out for 24 hours by a volcanic eruption, and the determination of the tightly-knit community to keep the Welsh traditions alive. 'You know,' she said, 'I think we will still be speaking Welsh in Patagonia when the language has died out in Wales.' She may be right.

At the bottom of the cherry orchard was a one-room adobe building. This had been María's grandfather's retreat, and it was left as it had been when he died the previous year at the age of 89: the hard couch covered with wool ponchos so he could sleep there if the noise of his family became too much, the kerosene lanterns which provided the only light, and his thousands of books lining the walls from top to bottom, several layers thick. He had been fluent in eight languages and conversant with another ten. When he went blind at the age of 80 he wasted no time in learning braille. Leaving the running of the farm to his wife, he immersed himself in his reading. It was he who had built the turret at the top of the house so he could watch out for his daughter as she rode back from town with the latest parcel of books that he had ordered from Europe and which had made their slow way to Buenos Aires by ship.

Our four-day stay gave us an experience that could never be bought: the serendipity of travelling rough.

Madryn (just north of the town centre on Mitre) there is a Museum of Oceanography, housing an eight-metre giant squid, washed up on the beach.

Buses have been moved from the former railway station (which will house a museum) to a new terminal nearby at San Martín and Irigoyen.

The fishing fleet has been moved from the Piedrabuena pier, allowing this to be used by recreational vessels and the promenade to be extended north; cycletracks (*bicisendas*) are planned, as is a windfarm.

Madryn's **tourist office** is at Roca 223 (tel: 02965 453 504, 452 148; sectur@madryn.gov.ar; www.patagoniachubutur.com.ar). There is a full range of **hotels**, with even a five-star place planned; backpackers should head for the youth hostel at 25 de Mayo 1136 (tel: 474 426, madrynhi@hostels.org.ar), a block from the seafront. There are two **campsites** at Punta Cuevas (4km southeast, served by town buses), the ACA site and a cheaper municipal site. Recommended agencies for wildlife **tours** are Causana Viajes, Moreno 390 (tel: 455 044; fax: 452 769; e-causana@causana.com.ar; www.causana.com.ar/causana_viajes) and Eubalena Viajes, Belgrano 175 (tel: 471 568), and in Puerto Pirámides Jorge Schmid (tel: 02965 495 112; puntaballena@puntaballena.com.ar).

Trelew is less interesting, but its **Paleontological Museum** (with 1,700 fossils) has been refurbished. The nearest coast is at Playa Unión (Rawson), where there is surfing, with franciscana and Commerson's dolphins.

Península Valdés

The Valdés peninsula is bigger than people realise, and beyond Puerto Pirámides there is no accommodation and only *ripio* roads; therefore day trips by bus from Madryn, although fairly affordable, give very little time for wildlife viewing, and you may prefer to hire a car. It is easy enough to take a bus with Mar y Valle (Roca 297, Madryn; tel: 02965 450 872; Roca 94, Trelew; tel: 02965 436 223; US$35) from Puerto Madryn to Puerto Pirámides for whale-watching, but once there you will have problems getting elsewhere. It should cost about the same for a group to take a taxi for the day. You can hitch, but it is notoriously difficult. We were reminded of an old saying: 'If you want to see Patagonia, just sit still and it will all blow past you'. In fact it all blew onto us, into our eyes and up our noses. However, many people have hitched successfully, and others have cycled, despite the gales. Certainly this is a place for sitting and watching, rather than being rushed around. You will also have to hitch or hire a car or a taxi to visit the penguin colony at Punta Tombo, 1¾ hours' drive south of Trelew.

Practical information

The best months to visit Península Valdés and Punta Tombo or Camarones are September–November, when all the animals can be seen establishing territories, mating, or giving birth. December–February are almost as good. Between March and July you are unlikely to see any marine wildlife. The birds are here all year, except for the Magellanic penguins, which come to breed between September and March. The whales arrive in around July (seemingly they come earlier every year), and stay till November or December; elephant seals come to breed from early August to October, after which they go to sea for a month and then return to moult. Sea lions breed from December to February, and fur seals from January to March; orcas come to prey on their young from February to April.

You should bring food with you, although there are pricey restuarants in Puerto Pirámides. Water is scarce. Be prepared for constant wind.

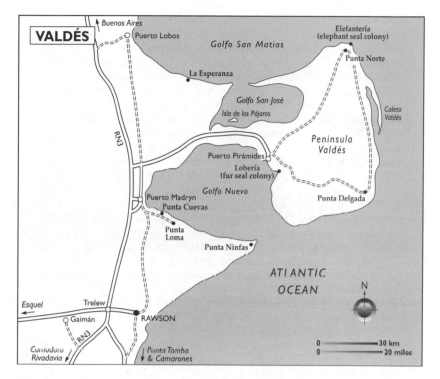

Where to go

Heading north from Madryn, the first whales may be visible, as little as 20 metres offshore, at the El Doradillo (17km) and Las Canteras beaches, which are at risk from a controversial development calling itself a *villa ecologica*; however, coin-operated telescopes have been installed. At the entrance to the peninsula (79km from Madryn), you will have to pay US$10 to enter the nature reserve; there is a visitor centre with very helpful staff. To the south of the peninsula is the Golfo Nuevo, and to the north the far smaller Golfo San José, a deep bay around the aptly named Isla de los Pájaros (Island of Birds). This is home to numerous species of marine birds, such as flamingos, gulls, king and rock cormorants, flightless steamer ducks, terns, herons, egrets and ducks. You are not allowed to land (or to walk across at low tide) but must watch through telescopes from the roadside 400m away (5km east of the visitor centre). Other birds you may see on the coasts of Valdés are the snowy sheathbill, black-browed albatross, and blackish oystercatcher, and on land the elegant-crested tinamou and rhea. The vegetation of the peninsula itself is largely unattractive scrub, with carob, choique and pepper trees growing on saline soils; animals to be seen include guanaco, mara, fox, skunk and armadillo.

The paved road continues across the Istmo Carlos Ameghino (a minimum 7km wide) to end at **Puerto Pirámides**, 103km from Madryn, the only settlement in the peninsula and the only place where you can camp. It is a village of a hundred people, providing restaurants, hotels and *cabañas*. From here you can take boat trips to view whales and other wildlife, and diving is also possible, with visibility up to 70m. The eroded rocks which give it its name are worth a visit, as is the *lobería* (fur

Whale-watching

The Southern right whale (ballena franca austral; *Eubalena australis*) was once hunted to the brink of extinction – the name indicates that these were the 'right' whales to hunt because they moved slowly, floated when dead, and provided plenty of baleen or whalebone. Although they have been protected worldwide since 1935, and have been a Monumento Natural in Argentina since 1984, they are not recovering fast and there are just 1,500–5,000 in all (the Northern right whale is now accepted as a separate species). The 600 or so who come to Valdés are the principal breeding population (with another in South Georgia), and are increasing by 3% per year. Unfortunately it was Argentina which blocked the creation of a South Atlantic Sanctuary for all whales, finally conceding in 1999 as long as this did not reach the coast.

Whale-watching began here in 1983, and has grown so that now 75,000 people participate every year. The whales are at ease with boats full of tourists, and in fact seem to be attracted by classical music. They weigh up to 40 tonnes and are up to 13 metres long, a quarter of which is the head, full of filters to strain plankton from seawater. With rough white growths on their heads they may not be the most attractive of animals, but are certainly among the most intelligent. These callosities, up to 5cm thick, are caused by thousands of small parasites. They have allowed up to 140 of the whales to be individually identified and studied. Probably the best time to visit is in early November when you can watch the females with their newborn calves.

The handsome black and white orcas (known as killer whales, although in fact they are porpoises) are smaller than right whales, but possess a fearsome set of 50 pointed teeth. They feed exclusively on warm-blooded creatures, and have become expert at taking sea lion pups even on the beach. There is a pod of 18 who live here permanently.

For more information, contact **Fundacion Cethus**, Juan de Garay 2861, dpto. 3, Olivos, prov. Buenos Aires (tel: 011 4799 3698; fax: 4823 9739; cethus@houseware.com.ar; www.cethus.org).

seal colony) of the Punta Pirámide Fauna Reserve, 4km away, where up to 1,500 seals come to breed from January.

On leaving the fur seals at Puerto Pirámides, most ecotourists head for the *elefantería* at **Punta Norte**, naturally enough at the northern end of the peninsula (97km from the visitor centre). This is now equally well known for the orcas which specialise in hurling themselves bodily onto the beach to seize young sea lions. This happens only at high tide, mainly in February and March; you can take a boat trip, or hike to the wooden vewing platform at the southern end of the beach (about 4km from the road), where the orcas, particularly a huge male called Mel, come through a channel in the reef. Elephant seals are found all along the coast here (their only mainland breeding grounds), and of course the further you walk from the parking area, the better your chance of watching these marvellous animals in peace – low tide is the best time. Adult males are up to 6m in length and weigh at least 3 tonnes; the females only weigh half a tonne. The pups weigh 40kg at birth, grow by 3–4kg per day, thanks to incredibly rich and creamy milk, and are about 100kg when weaned. Elephant seals can also be seen at Caleta Valdés, 24km south of Punta Norte, and at Punta Delgada; you may also see orcas and, with luck, penguins at both sites.

On the western shore of the Golfo Nuevo, 15km southeast of Puerto Madryn, is the **Punta Loma reserve**, a colony of 400 sea lions whose pups are born in December and January (US$5; free with entry to Peninsula Valdés). Beyond it at Punta Ninfas, the Estancia El Pedral is being developed as a private reserve for southern elephant seals, sea lions and cormorants. At Rancho San Lorenzo Magellanic penguins can be found at their northern limit on this coast.

To the north of Puerto Madryn, the World Land Trust and the Fundación Patagonia Natural have bought the **Estancia La Esperanza**, on the southern shore of the far larger Golfo San Matías, to preserve the steppe ecosystem. Although a sheep station until now, there are still 300 guanaco here, as well as puma, which feed on their young. Accommodation should be available by 2002. For information contact the WLT (Blyth House, Bridge St, Halesworth, Suffolk IP19 8AB, UK; tel: 01986 874 422; fax: 874 425; email: worldlandtrust@ btinternet.com; www.worldlandtrust.org) or FPN (Marcus Azar 760, (9120) Puerto Madryn, Chubut; tel: 02965 474 363, 472 023; www.satlink.com.ar or www.newroad.com.ar/Patagonia). Due to a world crash in wool prices (from US$7 to US$0.60 per kilo), and drought and desertification which mean that in places the land can only support one sheep per hectare, land can now be bought for just £25 per acre, giving a great opportunity for conservation projects. If you are in Viedma, on the north side of the Golfo San Matías, it may be worth visiting the La Lobería and Punta Bermeja reserves, also breeding colonies of seals and sea lions.

Punta Tombo and Camarones

Not far south of Península Valdés is a vast rookery of Magellanic penguins, the largest continental penguin colony outside Antarctica. Nearly a million birds raise their chicks in burrows near Punta Tombo and Camarones during the summer months. Do not bother going after mid-March as the penguins are 'off limits' as they prepare to return to the sea. Visitors are well managed, with well-signposted and -fenced trails, and a big new Interpretation Centre. You may also see snowy sheathbills, skuas, giant petrels, steamer ducks, dolphin, kelp and Cook gulls, imperial and rock cormorants, and oystercatchers.

Punta Tombo is 117km south of Trelew, passing the new Parque Bryn Gwyn, a sort of paleontological theme park 17km south of Trelew, where there are hiking trails and fossil displays. The turning off Ruta 3 to Punta Tombo is well signposted but you are unlikely to hitch a ride, so you will need to take a tour or a taxi from Trelew, or hire a car. The village of **Camarones** is further south (275km from Trelew) and can be reached by bus on Monday and Friday mornings; 35km further south is the **Cabo Dos Bahías** reserve, another large colony of Magellanic penguins. Seals can also be seen here, and as with Punta Tombo, guanaco and rheas can be seen along the road in.

Magellanic penguins are often misnamed jackass penguins (the jackass is a separate South African species) because of their braying call, each one distinctive. After wintering at sea, they meet up with last year's mate at their old nest burrow in September, then indulge in a 'bill-duelling' courtship, trying to shake each other's bill off! The burrow is relined with grass, then the eggs are laid and the parents take turns to incubate and fish. The eggs hatch in December, and January is when the parents are most active; the birds leave in March and April.

Continuing south

The cities in Argentine Patagonia offer little interest, unless you happen to be fascinated by oil extraction and refining techniques. The most important is **Comodoro Rivadavia**, a boom city whose 150,000 inhabitants live almost exclusively off the oil and petrochemicals industries. On December 13 it celebrates Petroleum Day. If you have the misfortune to get stuck here, make sure you have a few novels left unread and head for the beach, Rada Tilly, 5km south of the city (south of which is the Punta Marqués sea lion reserve). On the road to Esquel (156km inland) is Sarmiento, centre of a farming community of Boer origin. From here a gravel road leads south to the Bosques Petrificados José Ormachea (32km) and Victor Szlapelis (72km), petrified forests of proto-araucaria trees buried in volcanic ash 70 million years ago. The similar Monumento Natural Bosques Petrificados (recently expanded from 10,000ha to 56,000ha by adding two adjoining *estancias*) is 82km west from km2063 on Ruta 3 (160km south of Comodoro Rivadavia), just south of Jaramillo on the Río Deseado, which drains Lago Buenos Aires. This is scrubby steppe, with bunchgrass, calafate and cacti; wildlife includes guanaco, Darwin's rhea, mara, red and grey foxes, cats, armadillo, and lizards. There is a 1km path, and no water or camping.

At the mouth of the Río Deseado (on volcanic deposits 160 million years old) is **Puerto Deseado**, a superb natural harbour where explorers such as Magellan, Schouten and Lemaire, and Fitzroy and Darwin, and also privateers such as Thomas Cavendish and John Davis, all stopped to draw breath before tackling Cape Horn. The **Ría del Deseado** nature reserve includes the Isla Pingüinos at the harbour entrance, a colony of Magellanic penguins (Oct–April), and the Barranca de los Cormoranes at the southern edge of the estuary, where you can see three species of cormorants (imperial, rock and grey). Other birds in the area include austral gulls, South American terns, oystercatchers, Antarctic doves, witch herons and ravens. Two tour operators offer one-hour to half-day **boat trips** along the river to see Commerson's dolphins; there are also Peale's dolphins and seals, and shark-fishing is also big here. At Cabo Blanco, 80km to the north of Puerto Deseado, a lighthouse overlooks a fur seal colony, and a bit further north, at Cabo Tres Puntos, there is a sea lion colony.

Ruta 3 reaches the coast again at **Puerto San Julián**, opposite Gibbet Point, where both Magellan and Drake executed mutinous crew members; from December to March Commerson's dolphins can be seen here, and almost 5,000 Magellanic penguins come to breed on an island reserve. Austral gulls, oyster-catchers, Antarctic doves and imperial cormorants can also be seen here. The town is planning to open an information and tourist centre, but until then you should ask at the municipal campsite about boat trips to Banco Cormorán or Isla de los Pingüinos. To the southwest, in the Gran Bajo de San Julián, is the lowest point in the Americas, 105m below sea level. To visit it (a salt pan), turn west at km2287.5 (from Buenos Aires), signed '*Gas del Estado – Planta Compresora de San Julián*' and drive 20km to the Laguna del Carbón.

If travelling overland from Calafate and Punta Arenas or Tierra del Fuego, you are more or less sure to pass through **Río Gallegos**, half the size of Comodoro Rivadavia but equally dull, although it should be mentioned that the **museum** has moved to new premises at Ramón y Cajal and San Martín, and is worth a visit. **Cabo Virgenes** (named on the feast day of the 10,000 Virgins martyred with St Ursula by the Huns) is also worth visiting from October to April, when 80,000 pairs of Magellanic penguins come to breed. Escalatur (Avenida Roca 998; tel/fax:

02966 422 466, scalatur@internet.siscotel.com) in Río Gallegos offers a 5-hour tour for US$60 per person (minimum four people), with a stop at the Monte Dinero *estancia* for lunch and a sheep-shearing show. Enquire also at the tourist office at Roca 863 (tel: 02966 493 011; tur@spse.com.ar) or at the bus terminal and airport.

If you are crazy enough to cycle, the inevitable repairs can be carried out by Galaxi, on Calle Ameghino at Pasteur.

THE PATAGONIAN ANDES
Around El Bolsón
The paved Ruta 258 runs south from Bariloche past Lagos Gutiérrez and Mascardi and after 130km reaches **El Bolsón** (The Sink; 310m), a small town in a beautiful valley with a few palm trees and good fishing. Founded in the 1880s, it became known in the 1960s for its communes of 'hippy' drop-outs. Nowadays many of the same people are providing facilities for ecotourism, of various types, and it is now marketed as the Comarca Andina del Paralelo 42 (the 42nd parallel, just south of town, being the boundary of Río Negro and Chubut provinces). El Bolsón also managed to defeat plans to dump foreign nuclear waste nearby, declaring itself the first nuclear-free town in South America. There is a good microbrewery, which puts on an excellent hop (ie: beer) festival, the *Fiesta del Lúpulo*, in the first week of February.

There are various cheap **places to stay** (most of which can also find horses or mountain bikes for you); the official HI youth hostel is El Pueblito, 3km north in Barrío Lujan (hourly buses, or fork right immediately before the bridge and it is 1km further, tel: 02944 493 560; pueblito@hostels.org.ar), and the Campamento Ecológico (Pagano and Costa del Río; tel: 491 293, 492 954; fax: 492 746), which has rooms and camping space. The Camping El Bolsón (tel: 492 595) is 1km to the north of the centre. The **tourist office** is on San Martín at the Plaza Pagnano (tel: 492 604; http://elbolson.org; open Mon–Fri 09.30–20.00, Sat & Sun 10.00–20.00). You might like to visit the **Ornithological Museum** at Saavedra 2759 (open 10.00–20.00).

There are a couple of **adventure tourism operators**: Grado 42 (Belgrano 406, tel: 02944 493 124; grado42@elbolson.org) offers rafting, trekking, parapente, snorkelling, horse-riding, mountain-biking and boat trips; and, just to their north, Patagonia Adventures (Hube 418; tel: 492 513; fax: 493 280; patago@red42.com.ar; www.patadv.com) deals mainly with rafting. The rafting takes place on the Río Azul, just west of town; there are two possible two-hour runs, Class III from Chacra La Maroma to Camping Río Azul, or Class I from Pasarela del Puelo to Lago Puelo. For bike parts and repairs go to Bicicletaria la Rueda, Sarmiento 2972 (tel/fax: 492 465).

There are plenty of **buses** from Bariloche, with Charter and Vía Bariloche running seven each daily, and Don Otto, Andesmar and TAC also having one or two. From El Bolsón south to Esquel, there are four services daily with Vía Bariloche, as well as TAC (two), Don Otto (one, continuing to Río Gallegos), Andesmar (one, from Córdoba to Esquel) and Mar y Valle (one, to Puerto Madryn). Vía Bariloche is at Roca and San Martín, Charter at Sarmiento 2553 at Roca, Don Otto at Belgrano and Berutti, and Andesmar at Belgrano and Perito Moreno (both near the YPF filling station at the town's central junction), and TAC is opposite the YPF.

Trips

The easiest excursion is to **Cerro Piltriquitrón** (2,055m), 11km to the east, a ski resort which is a good venue for hiking, climbing and horse-riding in summer. From the south end of town, a road reaches roughly 1,000m altitude, and a path continues via the *bosque tallado* (sculpted trees) to the Refugio Cerro Piltriquitrón (1,400m; tel: 02944 492 024; open all year), from where you can follow the abandoned ski-drag and then paint markers to the summit, about 45 minutes from the roadhead.

Otherwise there are various possibilities to the west of town; head north on the main road then turn left on Azcuénaga, signposted to the *Cabeza del Indio*. The dirt road crosses the Río Quemquemtreu then swings left and loops around a long hill called the Loma del Medio (500m). Turn right, then left where the road to the *Cabeza del Indio* heads up the hill to the right, and eventually you will reach the Camping Hue Nain (tel: 15 607 133), from where a 15km trail runs west to a suspension bridge over the Río Azul at 250m and steadily up (following red markers for 6 hours) to the **Refugio Hielo Azul** (1,300m), where you can stay for US$6. There are waterfalls nearby, or you can hike up to the ridge below Cerro Hielo Azul (2,270m) in 3 hours, or to a glacier (1½ hours). From the Camping Hue Nain it is also possible to take a path south along the river's left (east) bank for 4km, to other campsites just off the road.

Heading north out of El Bolsón on the main road to Bariloche, you can fork left after crossing the Río Quemquemtreu (just before km121) towards the Cascada Mallín Ahogado, a fine waterfall 10km from town. Beyond this, the road turns left to a place called Warton (km15) and finally ends at 1,000m at the **Refugio Perito Moreno** (km25; tel: 02944 493 912). There is skiing here, and hiking into the Andes, dominated by Cerro Perito Moreno (2,216m).

From Warton (reached by a school bus at 13.00 Mon–Fri from the south end of Plaza Pagnano in El Bolsón), a 4WD trail leads west to the Camping Arco Iris (tel: 02944 493 142) at the confluence of the Río Azul and the Arroyo Blanco. *Pasarelas* lead over the rivers and then a 20km trail leads above the **Cajón del Azul**, a kilometre-long canyon that is 40m deep and as little as a metre wide in places. There is a kiosk here, selling home-made bread and soft drinks. It takes 4 hours to reach the Refugio Cajón del Azul (600m) and about 3 more to the Refugio Los Laguitos (1,100m); there is also a trail from the Hielo Azul hut to Cajón del Azul (much harder in the other direction!).

Lago Puelo National Park

About 18km southwest of El Bolsón, along a paved road lined with campsites and *cabañas*, is the village of **Villa Lago Puelo**. Here there is a supermarket, pizzeria, YPF filling station, and the administration of the **Parque Nacional Lago Puelo**. This was originally an annexe of Los Alerces, then in 1971 became a national park in its own right, covering 23,700ha, of which 9,600ha is closed as a strict reserve. Thanks to the low altitude (225m) of the lake and the pass into Chile (hence its Mapuche name, meaning Eastern Water), there is a warm microclimate here, allowing the growth of the only Valdivian Forest in Argentina, with trees such as ulmo (*Eucryphia cordifolia*, known here as muermo), olivillo (*Aexotoxicum punctatum*, known here as tique), lingue (*Persea lingue*), tiaca (*Caldcluvia paniculata*), tineo (*Weinmannia trichosperma*), avellano silvestre (*Guevinia avellana*, known here as guevin), which is related to the South African proteas, and colihue bamboo. Two ferns hitherto unknown in Argentina have recently been found here. There is also *bosque andino-patagónico*, with trees such as ciprés de la cordillera, coihue, radal, arrayán and alerce, and bushes such as the poisonous deu (*Coraria ruscifolia*), known as mataratones or mouse-killer, and liana creepers such as voqui blanco (*Boquila trifoliata*). However, much of the more accessible land was burnt for cattle and for orchards, so that following the road to the lake you will see little but introduced willow and apple trees, rosa mosqueta (*Rosa eglanteria*) and lupins, but the nearby trails pass through largely unspoilt woodland. There are 116 species of birds, including grebes, herons, ducks, black-necked swans and austral flamingos on the lake, and the Chilean flicker (pitío; *Colaptes pitius*) and Chilean wood-pigeon (paloma araucana; *Columba araucana*). There are also huemul, pudú, red fox, puma, monito del monte, lesser hurón, and snakes.

From the village it is 30 minutes' walk south along the road (now unpaved, passing lots of campsites) to the national park gate, from where it is 15 minutes to the end of the road at the lake, with a cycle track parallel to the right of the road. After 5 minutes you can fork left to the fine chalet-style building housing the *Intendencia* (tel: 02944 499 232; open Mon–Fri 08.00–15.00, although the park is busiest at weekends), by a Gothic water tower. Quimay Quipan buses run from El Bolsón to the lake every 90 minutes in January and February 08.30–20.00 (from 10.00 at weekends).

At the lakeshore there is a jetty and kiosks selling tickets for boat trips. The *Juana de Arco* (built in 1931; tel: 02944 493 415; juanadearco@red42.com.ar) sails at 11.00 to the Chilean border (US$18 for 3 hours), and then does half-hour cruises for US$5; the *Dadel*, a modern motor-cruiser (tel: 499 043) also offers cruises, and you can hire open Canadian canoes. There is a toilet and phone here, as well as two campsites: to the right/west is the free (*agreste*) site, with the foundations of abandoned washblocks, and on the other side is the organised site (also pretty rustic – typically Argentine, in that barbecue facilities are more important than toilets).

It is a kilometre east along the beach to the *playita*, where swimming is allowed; the 500-metre *mirador* trail starts here, heading inland to a junction then climbing fairly steeply to the right for 5 minutes (following blue-painted pegs), then returning towards the lake for 5 minutes, and dropping to a good rocky viewpoint 150m above the lake. Turning left at the junction, you can follow the 850-metre Pitranto Grande trail (following red markers). This is slow going at first on sand, then easier as you enter a dark old-growth wood of big strange looking pitra trees (*Myrceugenia exsucca*). The path loops around a black pool then continues and after 12 minutes passes over a bridge into a field lined with poplars. From here it takes 2 minutes to reach the road to the *playita*, and turning right here it is 3 minutes to the junction with the Edificio Historico trail, from the *Intendencia* to the beach – turning left it takes under 5 minutes to go through more fine woodland to the road near the kiosks.

The route into Chile and down the Río Puelo (see page 198) runs along the north side of the lake. When the water is low it shold be possible to get there along the beach, but generally it is better to cross the Río Azul by the *pasarela*, turning off the road 1km south of Lago Puelo village. The Camping La Pasarela (tel: 02944 499 061) is by the bridge. The first 10km of the future international road lead through coihue forest as far as the Gendarmería Nacional, where camping is permitted. From here the **Senda Los Hitos** crosses the Arroyo Las Lágrimas and continues west through Valdivian forest to *Los Hitos* (the Border Markers) at the border, just beyond the Puesto de Vargas, with tall non-native trees. About 300m beyond the border is a *mirador*, with a fine view of Lago Inferior beyond the rapids of the Río Puelo. Beyond this you can fork left to reach the lake, or keep right to El Retén, the Chilean *carabineros* post. Camping and fires are not allowed between the two border posts. It takes about 3 hours to reach the *gendarmería* from the *pasarela*, 2 more to *Los Hitos*, and 5 more to El Retén.

It is also possible to hike northwest from the road (a couple of hours from the *pasarela*) to Laguna Huemul, about 4km, taking 6 hours there and back. In its first stage the route is crossed by logging tracks, but if you manage not to get lost it becomes easier and more attractive. Turning right from the *pasarela*, you can follow the Río Motoco to the Refugio Motoco.

South from El Bolsón

Continuing south from El Bolsón (km134), the main road passes through El Hoyo (km145), known for growing organic vegetables, soft fruit and hops. From here a path leads east for 2km through ciprés and coihue to a 90-metre waterfall, and a road runs west for 12km to El Desemboque, on Lago Puelo. From there a path runs south along the east side of the lake to the Seccional Río Turbio (18km, taking 6 hours). You can camp here, visiting rock paintings, and perhaps hike on to the southwest to Cerro Plataforma (15km each way). From Puerto Aguja, just across the Río Turbio (most easily reached by boat from the jetty at the the northern end of the lake) a path leads west to Lago Esperanza (15km each way).

Ruta 268 continues to the village of **Lago Epuyen** (1km west from km172, 37km south of El Bolsón), site of Argentina's only private reserve of native woodland, known as 'Proyecto Lemu' ('forest' in Mapudungun). Contact Lucas Chiappe, Asociación Lihuen-Antu, (9211) Epuyen, who offers guided tours of **Cerro Pirque** (1,792m). There are plans to link the Epuyen forestry reserve with the Cerro Pirque and Río Turbio provincial parks and Lago Puelo national park. More controversially, the German NGO Prima Klima and Ciefap (a public body for the sustainable development of Patagonia) are proposing a carbon-trading deal to preserve 50,000ha of lenga in the basins of Lakes Fontana and La Plata, in the far southwest of Chubut (not far northeast of Coyhaique). Stay at the Refugio del Lago (tel: 02945 499 025), on the lake 8km from the main road, where boating and horse-riding can be arranged. Additionally, a branch of the road from El Hoyo to Lago Puelo leads to Puerto Patriada, at the north end of Lago Epuyen.

Continuing southwards the paved Ruta 258 heads east at km178 to join Ruta 40 to Esquel. The unpaved Ruta 71 runs south to the Parque Nacional Los Alerces, passing **Cholila**, 3km off the road 84km south of El Bolsón, with wonderful views west up the Cholila valley to Cerro Dos Picos (2,550m). This has similar potential to El Bolsón, although as yet there is little development beyond a couple of campsites (to the south in Villa Rivadavia), and fishing lodges on nearby lakes. About 10km north, near a 'Welsh' teashop and *hospedaje*, Te Gales Casa de Piedra (tel: 02945 498 056), signposted to the west, is the cabin built by Butch Cassidy (Robert Leroy Parker) and the Sundance Kid (Henry Longbaugh), who lived here with the Kid's moll, Etta Place, in 1901–05. There is now a charge of US$10 to visit, but that is better than its previous state of total neglect.

In addition to the nine or so buses from El Bolsón to Esquel via Leleque, there is also a daily bus from Villa Lago Puelo to Esquel via El Bolsón, Cholila and the Los Alerces National Park.

LOS ALERCES NATIONAL PARK

Altitude	Between 518m and 1,916m
Rating	Moderate
Time	Up to one day
Start of trail	1. Villa Futalaufquen 2. Puerto Mormoud
End of trail	1. Villa Futalaufquen 2. Puerto Mormoud
Maps	You will be given a map leaflet when you pay the park fee; otherwise there is little alternative to the ancient IGM maps.

Los Alerces is a spectacular park but relatively little-visited, perhaps because it is most easily reached from Futaleufú in Chile. It is not accurately named, but the 'Larches, Mountains, Glaciers, Lakes and Trout National Park' really would be a bit of a mouthful. Most visitors seem to come for trout fishing, or for pleasant days by the river, so the lakes and rivers are lined with a good range of campsites and other places to stay, but as soon as you hike a little way up the hill you will be almost alone. The park has two main areas: to the south is **Lago Amutui Quimei** (508m), also known as ex-Lago Situación, a reservoir which drowned Lago Situación and the rest of a long valley. This sector is visited by guided tours to the hydro-electric station, booked in Esquel or Trevelin. From the dam it is possible to follow a trail southwest to the border crossing at the Río Grande (about 4 hours). To the north Highway 71 runs along **Lago Futalaufquen** ('Great Lake' in Mapudungun; 518m), Lago Verde (520m) and Lago Rivadavia (527m). The main route from Esquel to El Bolsón is the asphalted Ruta 40, and those using Ruta 71 have to pay the US$5 park fee – residents are exempted, while other citizens of Chubut pay half.

The park covers 263,000 largely mountainous hectares with a humid-temperate climate of cold, wet winters and drier summers; in the western parts 4m of precipitation per year produce an exuberant *bosque andino-patagónico* (Valdivian forest), dominated by coihue, ciprés de la cordillera and lenga, with a bamboo understorey. In a few places there are also alerces, virtually the only ones in Argentina, which can only be visited by boat. In the eastern parts with only 300mm of rain, the flora is more scrubby, with willow-like maiten (*Maytenus boaria*) by the rivers. Animals include huemul, pudú, otters, foxes, skunks and wildcats, with birds such as three types of woodpecker, the austral parakeet, austral thrush, Araucarian dove, chucao, huet-huet, flying steamer duck, ducks, herons and grebes, kingfishers, and hummingbirds.

Esquel

The jumping-off point for Los Alerces is the city of Esquel, not particularly attractive but with all services mostly close to the **bus station** at Alvear and Fontana; the **tourist information centre** is at Alvear and Sarmiento (tel: 02945 451 927; open 07.00–24.00 daily in summer, Mon–Fri at other times). The only cheap place to stay is El Hogar del Mochilero, at Roca 1028 (tel: 452 166), which has dormitories and also camping. The Parador Lago Verde, at Volta 1081 (tel: 452 251) runs tours and gives discounts to HI members, but has only twin rooms; the Lihuen, at San Martín 820 (tel: 452 589), is a decent small hotel. Bikes can be repaired at Coyote Bikes, at Rivadavia 887. Adventure activities can be arranged through Trekking & Climbing Patagonia, at Ameghino 98 (tel: 454 140) and Trekways, at Roca 687 (tel: 453 380). Other contacts are the Asociación Argentina de Guias de Montaña (tel: 454 711) and the Club Andino at Darwin 639.

Esquel is base for various other **excursions**, to the ski resort of La Hoya, 15km north, and to Laguna La Zeta, 5km west, where there is a free campsite and the start for mountain-bike routes to Cholila and to Bahía Rosales, on Lago Futalafquen. Additionally there is the *Old Patagonian Express*, known locally as '*La Trochita*', a narrow-gauge steam train (opened only in 1945) that still struggles on despite frequent financial collapse. The train runs, or crawls, from its base at El Maitén to Esquel on Wednesdays, returning on Thursdays, and a *tren turistico* runs from Esquel to Nahuel Pan (an Indian reserve) and back on summer Saturdays. Charters cost from US$15 per person for a minimum of 40 passengers. Contact the Viejo Expreso Patagónico La Trochita, Pellegrini 841, (9210) El Maitén, Chubut (tel/fax: 02945 495 190; latrochita@elbolson.org). The *Fiesta del Trencito* is held in mid-February every year.

To the south of Los Alerces, on the road from Chile, is the smaller town of **Trevelin**, founded by the Welsh of the Chubut valley. Although Welsh culture is heavily diluted now, there is an interesting **museum** in an old mill (open daily 11.00–20.30); in addition Welsh teashops are widespread in this area. Buses to and from the border run from Esquel via Trevelin twice on Mondays, Wednesdays and Fridays, connecting with a minibus to Futaleufú. Just as the American Río Grande is known south of the Mexican border as the Río Bravo, so here the Argentine Río Grande is known west of the border as the Río Futaleufú, one of the world's great white-water rafting rivers (see pages 74 and 253). There is no cheap accommodation, although Casa Verde, on Calle Los Alerces (tel: 02945 480 091; trevelin@teletel.com.ar), gives discounts to HI members.

Getting there

Esquel is most easily reached by air, with Austral, Kaiken, or LADE, which flies from Neuquen to Bariloche and Esquel three days a week (calling at El Bolsón on Thursdays). Otherwise buses come here from major cities.

Transportes Esquel (tel: 455 029) operates buses along Highway 71 through the park. Schedules vary greatly with the seasons, but the most useful and reliable departure (daily in summer, Saturdays and Sundays at other times) is at 08.15 from Esquel to Villa Futalaufquén (09.15), Bahía Rosales, Lago Verde, Lago Rivadavia (11.00), Cholila, the Epuyen turning (13.00), El Bolsón and finally Villa Lago Puelo (14.30); others run as far as Bahía Rosales.

Visiting the park

Turning off Ruta 40 8km southwest of Esquel, you will cross the Punta de Fierro, a very popular picnicking spot made famous by an Argentine film (*Caballos Salvajes*; 'Wild Horses'), and regain the asphalt at the junction from Trevelin. The park's Portada Sur is 37km from Esquel, and you should continue about 10km to the southern end of Lago Futalaufqen and turn left here (rather than at the first, unpaved, turning 8.5km from the gate) to Villa Futalaufquen (49km from Esquel) and the park's *Intendencia* and visitor centre.

The **visitor centre** (open in season daily 09.00–21.00) has a very informative museum, and you can also phone (02945 471 020, interno 26) for information between 08.00 and 14.00. You must register here before starting the Arroyo Cascada, Dedal, Cinco Saltos or Kruger hikes. There is a small, rude and over-

PATAGONIAN STEAM TRAINS

The 760mm-gauge railway from Esquel to El Maitén opened in 1922, and the extension to Ingeniero Jacobacci, on the main line to Bariloche, opened in 1945; it is known locally as La Trochita, after its first locomotive, although gringos tend to know it as the Old Patagonian Express, after Paul Theroux's book of 1979. In 1993 the federal government closed the line, but the province of Chubut kept the 165km Esquel–El Maitén section going largely as a tourist attraction, with local indigenas travelling free.

The railway's base is El Maitén, where you can see its 11 steam locomotives, of which three German Henschels and three American Baldwins are still active. These are oil-fueled 2–8–0 tender locos, built in 1922, as were the Belgian carriages; maximum speed is 60km/hr (40mph).

A similar railway, which does not carry passengers, is the 750mm-gauge Río Turbio Industrial Railway (RFIRT), built in 1956 to carry coal from Río Turbio to the port of Río Gallegos; nowadays diesels haul trains to the new port of Punta Loyola, but steam locomotives, mostly in an advanced state of decay, can be seen by the docks in Río Gallegos, at the end of Calle Mendoza. The original ten 2–10–2 locos were joined in 1964 by ten more, designed by Livio Dante Porta, a pupil of the great French designer André Chapelon, who used a gas combustion system that made the boiler more efficient and produced almost no smoke, despite the poor ashy coal used. These were some of the most advanced steam engines ever produced.

priced shop here and not much else, although it is an attractive spot with beautifully tended lawns and planted araucarias. Coming in from the main road you will pass the free Camping Las Lechuzas and the organized Camping Los Maitenes, on either side of the Río Desaguadero bridge. There are plenty of other campsites, free and paying, along the main road, all detailed on the leaflet you will be given when you pay your US$5 at the Portada Sur (entering from the north or out of hours you will get away without paying).

The visitor centre will also give you leaflets describing walks around Villa Futalaufquen, such as the Sendero Arroyo Cascada, which starts to the left of the visitor centre and takes 3–5 hours for 16km. Another is the Sendero Pinturas Rupestres, 2.5km east of the Visitor Centre (just beyond the Camping Las Lechuzas), which is a 500m loop to the south. It is hard to make out any of the promised rock paintings, but the leaflet is informative about the flora, while you will climb a rock which, while hardly Ayers Rock, still seems to possess some power, and is a lovely place to watch the sunset. Just to the north of the junction with the main road, the Sendero Lo Larga heads east to Lago Larga, and horserides are available to the lake and on to Cerro La Torta.

The most popular excursion in the park is the **Safari Lacustre** or boat trip at 10.00 daily from Puerto Limanao, 3.7km north of Villa Futalaufquen, to Puerto Mormoud on Lago Verde, from where passengers walk to Puerto Chucao on Lago Menéndez, to take another boat (at 12.00) to the Alerzal, where you can walk to alerces up to 60m in height, 3m in diameter and 3,000 years in age. The views as the boat approaches the glaciers of Cerro Torrecillas are stunning. This costs US$55. In summer another cruise sets out for Lago Kruger on Mondays, Wednesdays and Saturdays at 10.00 (US$25).

L Lezama

El Bolsón

L Cholila

Cholila

Carileufú

L Cisne

Alerzal

Lago Rivadavia

Cerro
Torrecillas
2853m

Cerro Alto el Petizo
1790m

Lago
Menéndez

Puerto Mormoud
L Verde

Puerto Chucao

Mina Huemules

L Stange

La Hoya
mountain resort

L Futalaufquen

Percey

L Chico

Cinco
Saltas

Hostéria Futalaufquen

L la Zeta

L Kruger

Puerto Limonao

Cerro Alto el Dedal
1916m

L Larga

ARGENTINA

Intendencia
& Villa
Futalauquen

Esquel

Trelew,
Bariloche

Cerro
Castillo

Portada Sur

L Amutui Quimei
(L Situación)

Trevelin

Hydroelectric station

Cascadas Nant y Fall

Futaleufú

CHILE

Cerro Cónico
2271m

N

L Rosario

0   25km

0   25 miles

Palena

LOS ALERCES

Corcovado

Route descriptions
To the west of Lago Futalaufquen

A road runs up the west side of the lake for 4.3km, giving access to several good hikes and to boat excursions on the lake. Just 2 minutes' walk north of the *Intendencia* the asphalt ends by a chapel, next to which is the start of the Sendero Flora Nativa. This runs parallel to the road for 180m, with signs describing a good range of local plants. It brings you down (ironically through introduced broom and dog rose) to the road by a beach. Two minutes further north you can turn right onto the Sendero Puerto Limonao. This follows the lakeshore, bringing you after 20 minutes to Puerto Bustillo, where you have to return briefly to the road.

On the south side of the Naval Prefecture (ie: the harbourmaster's office) a path heads off up Cerro Alto El Dedal (1,916m), which gives great views of peaks and lakes on three sides; the climb is similar to that to Cerro Alto El Petizo (see below), but slightly shorter (although the summit is higher). You should get permission from the visitor centre, and start by 10.00. It is best to start by the Arroyo Cascada trail, from behind the visitor centre, from which a branch leads to El Dedal, and come down to the Naval Prefecture.

Immediately beyond the port you can return to the lakeside path, but it is less attractive than the first section, with some fallen trees blocking it. It is 1.5km to Puerto Limonao, where you will find the jetty and office for the *Safari Lacustre*, and another 600m to the road's end at the Hostería Futalaufquen, a very comfortable hotel.

Paths continue along the lake and up the hill to the Cinco Saltas, but rather than crossing the hotel lawns you should pick these up by forking left 5 minutes south of Puerto Limonao. A dirt road leads 500m to a broken-down bridge (you should go to the right to a good log bridge) and on around the back of the hotel. It splits at the first hairpin bend into two paths; the one to the right leads in 25km to **Lago Kruger** (sometimes spelt Krügger, and once known as '*Naufragio de Frey*' or Frey's Shipwreck), where there is a *refugio* (US$8, camping US$5, including hot shower). This path is marked with green paint splashes, and climbs steeply to a saddle at 1,085m, with a bone-jarring descent on the far side. Eventually you will reach a camping spot by the lake, at Bahía Blanca (6–8 hours from the start). It is another 4 hours from here to Lago Kruger, crossing two saddles of 650m. From the refuge you can follow the Río Frey south for 15km to Lago Amutui Quimei. The return trip can be done in 10–12 hours if you are fit and just take a daypack. To return to civilisation you must either hike back the same way or haggle for a passage on a tour boat (page 305).

The path to the left, marked with red paint marks, leads to the **Cinco Saltas**. After 3 minutes turn sharp right onto a steep path which leads in 15 minutes to a turning to the first viewpoint, signed as the *Secundo Salto*, 2 minutes to the left. It is just 2 minutes further to the *Primero Salto*. The Five Falls turn out to be one spectacular multi-stage fall, in forest of cypress, coihue and bamboo. The path onwards (starting about 10m before the upper viewpoint) is disused, with the red markings cut out of the trees, but it is worth following it for 5 minutes to a lovely spot to cool off after the climb, with a jacuzzi-like pool and a fallen tree leading across the stream.

Cerro Alto El Petizo

The main road (unpaved from Villa Futalaufquen northwards) heads north along the east side of Lago Futalaufquen, passing various campsites (free and organised), *cabañas* and *hosterías*, and then follows the Río Arrayanes to Lago Verde. Just south of this lake, 34.3km from the *Intendencia*, there is a turning left to a car park and the *pasarela* (footbridge) to the ports on Lago Menéndez and Lago Verde. Just 1km north there are free and organised campsites by Lago Verde, as well as the *seccional* (rangers' house) and Mirador Lago Verde, and to the south, at km32.1, is the free Camping Arrayanes. From this a pleasant path follows the riverside for about 1km northwards (although you have to take the dusty road the remaining kilometre to the *pasarela*), and another path starts behind the *seccional* and leads up to the road. Turning left you will soon reach a red pole to the right and yellow and red marks on a tree at the start of a path up to the northeast. Only after 30m up the path will you come to a sign indicating that this is the trail to Lago Escondido (Hidden Lake); a good but steep path takes you to this peaceful spot in about an hour.

Cerro Alto El Petizo is the 1,790m peak between Lagos Verde and Menéndez; the name is bizarre, meaning 'High Peak the Short One', perhaps because Cerro del Medio ('Middle Peak'), immediately behind, is actually higher. To climb it, cross the excellent *pasarela* and ignore the equally good (pretty much wheelchair-accessible!) trail left to the ferry jetty at Puerto Chucao, 20 minutes hiking away. Turn right from the bridge, turn right after 2 minutes onto a good path along the lake and turn right onto a track from Puerto Chucao to reach Puerto Mormoud, the jetty for boats on Lago Verde, after 10 minutes more. If you head up the slope for about 5m and take a path through the grass below some huts you will come to the wreck of a white boat and an information sign. This warns of the *gran exigencia física* ('great physical demands') required for the climb, and states that ascents must start by 11.00, with return by 19.00, with permission needed from the *seccional* just north of the Puerto Chucao jetty. Heading into the trees, climb steeply for a few minutes, then go to the right on a grassy path and under fallen trees. The path onwards is better, swinging right after 25 minutes to cross a sort of col at the end of a valley and reach a mini-*mirador* to the left. There is a better one, with a view of the lake and more mountains, just 2 minutes further on. Five minutes further on you will enter an area of fine mature coihue, in 10 minutes you will cross a stream, and in a couple of minutes more you will reach a rocky stream bed (about an hour in total from Puerto Mormoud).

Turn right and follow the stream bed uphill. The start of the path is only marked by a couple of plastic bags, so take care you will recognise it on your return. In half an hour you will reach the confluence of two streams, where you will cross the stream from the right almost without noticing it. The path leads straight up the ridge between the two streams, on very loose sand, but after 5 hard minutes the path gets better as it heads into the dwarf ñire, although you will have to clamber over roots and trunks for a spell. After 20 minutes you will reach the tree line, from where you should head up to the right on a very steep slope of loose stones. After about 10 minutes you will pass the first small stick marking the route and carry on through low bushes, passing below a rocky outcrop to the left and reaching the col in 20 minutes more. From here it is 5 minutes to the summit plateau, clambering on big firm rocks, and a couple more to the summit cairn, maybe 3 hours gross from Puerto Mormoud.

You can continue along the ridge, taking about 20 minutes to reach the next top and 20 minutes more to the highest, **Cerro del Medio** (1,820m). You are at the centre of a fantastic circle of peaks and glaciers here, with great views back to the lake and campsites. It is said that you can even see Volcán Michinmahuida, in Chile's Parque Pumalín. You will have to return by the same route.

PERITO MORENO NATIONAL PARK

Continuing southwards, Ruta 40 will eventually bring you to the small town of **Perito Moreno**; virtually no-one comes this way because this is one of the world's worst roads through one of its bleakest landscapes. There is no comparison at all with the parallel Carretera Austral in Chile. The town of Perito Moreno, it should be stressed, is of no great interest in itself, and most people passing by will be travelling east–west between the Atlantic coast and the Carretera Austral. Ruta 40 continues ever southwards to Calafate, but again it is an awful road and virtually everyone will travel via the Atlantic coast, or fly with LADE (southbound on Mondays and northbound on Wednesdays); even so, tourist buses do now use this route at least twice a week (see page 312). Nevertheless, at Las Horquetas, halfway to Calafate, a road turns west to follow the Río Belgrano for 80km to the **Perito Moreno National Park**, on the Chilean border. Created in 1937, it covers 115,000ha, plus 15,000ha adjacent to the park and the Chilean border which were bought by Douglas Tompkins in 1993 as a *de facto* extension to the park. See pages 318–9 for details of tourist *estancias* near and even in this park.

Not surprisingly, the park is little visited, but it offers great hiking in wonderful open countryside, between a network of seven interconnected lakes (Mogote, Peninsula, Azara, Volcán, Escondido, Belgrano and Nansen), which drain to the Pacific. In addition there is Lago Burmeister, to the southeast, which drains via the Río Roble to the Atlantic. A road runs as far as Estancia La Oriental (where you can stay – see page 319), by Lago Belgrano; the Senda Natural Peninsula Belgrano takes a couple of hours, or you can follow a track south for 6km to Laguna del Mié and continue west on a path for 5 hours to a waterfall and Lago Azara. There is also a *pasarela* across the Río Roble to Laguna Roble, a couple of hours south.

The climate is harsh, with hot dry summers and temperatures as low as -25°C

PERITO MORENO (1852–1917)

Who was this Perito Moreno, after whom a town, a national park, a glacier, a mountain and a lake (west of Bariloche) have all been named? Dr Francisco Pascasio Moreno was born in Buenos Aires to a British-born mother in 1852 and first came to Patagonia in 1874. In 1876 he was the first white man to reach Lago Nahuel Huapi from the Atlantic and in 1877 he made the first map of the area of Lagos San Martín, Viedma and Argentina. In 1879 he discovered Lago Gutierrez, south of Bariloche. He founded the Museum of La Plata and was its director in 1884–1905.

His greatest service to the country was on the Comisión de Límites, the commission establishing the border with Chile in 1894–1903. He worked with Sir Thomas Holdich, of Britain's Royal Geographical Society, which gave him its Gold Medal in 1907. For his efforts he was granted 7,500ha of land near Bariloche (which he later donated to the nation as the basis of its first national park, Nahuel Huapi) and the official title *Perito* or 'surveyor'. He also founded the Argentine Scouts in 1908, and was elected to congress, but when he died in 1917 he was apparently poor and forgotten. The debt was at least partially paid in 1944 when he was re-buried on Isla Centinela in Lago Nahuel Huapi.

His books *Viaje a la Patagonia Austral* and *Reminiscencias* are available in Spanish from Elefante Blanco.

in winter. The vegetation ranges from coirón steppe, through transition woodland of stunted ñire and lenga, to forest of lenga (up to 35m tall by Lagos Nansen and Azara) with guindo in less cold areas. The park protects two species endemic to Santa Cruz province, the pilquín or chinchillón anaranjado (the largest of the chinchillas), and the hooded grebe or macá tobiano (*Podiceps gallardoi*), identified only in 1974. There are lots of guanaco, as well as huemul (its most important refuge in Argentina), puma, huiña, skunks, red and grey foxes and vizcacha. The 86 species of birds include rheas, flamingos, geese, grebes, black-necked swans, steamer ducks, peregrine falcons, eagles, condors and the great horned owl (*Bubo virginianus*). Perhaps most unusually, there are no introduced fish. Fossils, particularly ammonites, can be found here, and there are rock paintings and outlined hands at least 9,000 years old in caves below Cerro Casa de Piedra, near Lago Burmeister.

On the border immediately to the north of the park is **Cerro San Lorenzo** (3,706m), the highest peak in Argentine Patagonia (unless you accept that Volcán Domuyo (4,709m), between the Ríos Negro and Colorado, is in Patagonia). Climbers can approach it from Bajo Caracoles via Lago Posadas, or from Cochrane in Chile.

LOS GLACIARES NATIONAL PARK

Covering more than 600,000ha (6,000km²), Los Glaciares National Park offers a remarkable combination of breathtaking glaciers, spectacular mountain ranges, vast emerald-green lakes, and rare plants and animals. Near its southern end is the **Perito Moreno glacier**, which sheds huge chunks of ice into **Lago Argentino**, creating small tidal waves. At its northern end are the granite pinnacles of **Cerro FitzRoy** and **Cerro Torre** (produced in much the same way as the Paine Towers) whose sheer cliffs make them a challenge for any climber. In between is a vast area of wilderness that can only be reached by boat or floatplane.

The climate is cold, with precipitation of between 900mm (to the west) and 400mm (to the east), mainly between March and May. This is enough to support Magellanic or subantarctic forest of deciduous lenga and evergreen guindo (or coihue de Magallanes), in the wetter areas, as well as ciprés de las Guiatecas, notro, ciruelillo and bushes such as calafate, siete camisas (*Escallonia rubra*), and mutilla (*Empetrum rubrum*). Animals include huemul and red fox in the forest, grey fox, guanaco, mara and armadillo on the steppes; birds include condors, Magellanic woodpeckers, austral parakeets, hummingbirds, black-necked swans, torrent ducks, and on the steppe ñandú petizo, known here as the choike.

Calafate

The base for exploring the National Park is **Calafate**, at 250m above sea level on the south shore of Lago Argentino. Existing only as a waystation for tourists, most of whom come solely for a day-trip to the Perito Moreno glacier, it has established a reputation as an unattractive and unfriendly place where tourists pay high prices for everything. There are some decent **campsites**, particularly the municipal site on José Pantin, just north of the YPF filling station, and **youth hostels**, the official HI one being the Albergue del Glaciar (tel: 02902 491 243; glaciar@hostels.org.ar, info@glaciar.com), on Pioneros about 15 minutes' walk from the centre of town. It has dorms, singles and doubles, costing from US$10 per person, and organises tours to the Perito Moreno glacier. Others are the Albergue Lago Argentino, a block from the bus station at Campaña del Desierto 1050 (tel: 491 139;

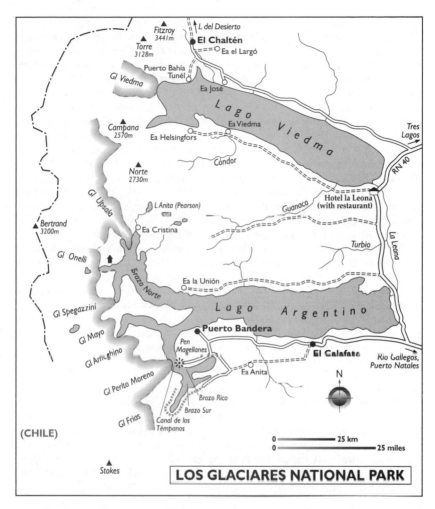

Fitzroy
3441m
Torre
3128m
L del Desierto
El Chaltén
Ea el Largó
Puerto Bahía
Tunél
Gl Viedma
Ea José
Lago
Viedma
Campana
2570m
Ea Viedma
Ea Helsingfors
Tres
Lagos
Norte
2730m
Cóndor
RN 40
Gl Upsala
L Anita (Pearson)
Guanaco
Hotel la Leona
(with restaurant)
Bertrand
3200m
Ea Cristina
La Leona
Gl Onelli
Turbio
Brazo Norte
Gl Spegazzini
Ea la Unión
Lago
Argentino
Gl Mayo
Puerto Bandera
Gl Arricghino
Pen
Magellanes
El Calafate
Río Gallegos,
Puerto Natales
Gl Perito Moreno
Ea Anita
N
Brazo Rico
Gl Frías
Brazo Sur
Canal de los
Témpanos
(CHILE)
0 — 25 km
0 — 25 miles
Stokes

LOS GLACIARES NATIONAL PARK

hostellargentino@cotecal.co.ar), a bit cheaper though with cramped rooms, and the Albergue Calafate, Gobernador Gregores (tel: 492 450; fax: 492 451; calafatehostel@cotecal.com.ar), new, spacious and slightly pricier; they also organise tours and book buses to Chaltén.

There are plenty of **restaurants**, an **ATM**, and a **supermarket**, Los Glaciares, at the corner of Libertador and Perito Moreno (open daily in summer 08.30-22.30). The helpful **tourist information** office is inside the **bus station** at Calle Julio Roca 1004 (tel/fax: 02902 491 090; securelcalafate@cotecal.com.ar, email: info@elcalafate.com; www.calafate.com; open 08.00-22.00 in summer). The national parks office is on the main drag at Libertador 1302 (tel: 491 005; open in summer Mon–Fri 08.00–16.00, Sat and Sun 10.00–21.00).

Just north of Calafate, **Laguna Nimes** offers the best sunsets, as well as horse-riding and, in winter, cross-country skiing. Agencies run 4WD excursions to Cerro Gualicho, a viewpoint about 8km from Calafate where caves and rock outcrops by Lago Argentina are decorated by pre-Hispanic paintings.

Getting there

The easiest way of reaching Calafate for many people will be **by air** – the new Lago Argentino airport, 20km east near Puerto Lara, can take Boeing 737s, so at last there is a decent service from Buenos Aires, with Aerolíneas Argentinas and LAPA. However, you have to pay US$18 tax for the privilege of using the new airport and the Aerobus transfer costs US$6 single, or US$10 return. Kaiken and Southern Winds also fly from Bariloche, Comodoro Rivadavia, Esquel, Río Gallegos and Ushuaia, and soon Puerto Madryn, with luck. LADE has a flight on Mondays from Comodoro Rivadavia via Perito Moreno to Calafate, continuing to Río Turbio and Río Gallegos, and returning on Wednesdays. On Tuesdays the plane flies to Ushuaia and back; there are (amazingly) no buses from Río Gallegos to Tierra del Fuego, so it is handy to be able to fly directly from Calafate to Ushuaia, even with a night in Río Gallegos. Given LADE's amazingly low fares and the tedium of bus rides across the Patagonian steppes it is not surprising that it can be very hard to get a seat.

There are several **buses** per day from Río Gallegos to Calafate, calling at the Río Gallegos airport and taking just 4 hours on a paved road throughout. The other usual approach is from Puerto Natales in Chile. Although little used by anyone other than tourists, the roads are being steadily improved so that it is now a fairly easy journey. Several companies in Puerto Natales offer **minibus** travel to Calafate, and even day trips to the Perito Moreno glacier. However, it is cheaper to take a public bus (very few at weekends) across the border to Río Turbio and then the 08.00 bus from there to Calafate. (Río Turbio is a drab coal-mining town, but its facilities are improving, and there is a decent new hotel at the Valdelén ski station, 4km south near the border crossing.)

From Calafate, Tacsa (tel: 02902 491 843) and Bus Sur Turismo Zahjj (tel: 491 631) run daily to Puerto Natales; Los Glaciares (tel: 491 159) and Chaltén Travel (tel 491 833) go to Chaltén daily at 08.00, with an afternoon departure in peak season. Cal-Tur (tel: 491 842) and Interlagos (tel: 491 179) serve Chaltén and Río Gallegos. Buses head north along Ruta 40 to Los Antiguos at least twice a week. These are aimed at *gringo* tourists and stop at sights such as rock paintings along the way; book through Chaltén Travel at the Hostel Calafate, Gob. Mayano/25 de Mayo; tel/fax: 492 212, in Calafate, or the Rancho Grand in El Chaltén (tel/fax: 02962 493 005; bigranch@hostels.org.ar).

Perito Moreno glacier

Along with the Iguazú Falls, Macchu Picchu, the Angel Falls and Río's Carnival, the Perito Moreno glacier must rank as one of South America's most astonishing sights, so it is no surprise that 70,000 visitors a year come here. Its vast blue front, 5km across and rising 55m above the surface of the lake, is a staggering spectacle. Its drama is enhanced by the constant rumbling noises and the collapse every few minutes into the lake of a slab of ice up to 20 storeys in height, creating a small tidal wave and an echoing boom so loud you could be under artillery bombardment.

It is best known for its habit, between 1934 and 1991, of growing so fast that every 3 to 4 years it would cut Lago Argentino in two by blocking the narrow *Canal de los Témpanos* (Icebergs Channel). This prevented the natural drainage of the Brazo Rico, the southernmost arm of the lake, causing it to rise to as much as 36m above its normal level. Eventually the pressure would cause the ice dam to collapse and the water would flood out creating enormous waves. This last occurred in 1991; this was one of its less spectacular breakthroughs, but a video is for sale in

Calafate and is dramatic enough for most tastes. With global warming the glacier's growth seems to have slowed. By 1998 it had reached the far bank again but water was flowing normally under an ice bridge.

The glacier is 85km west of Calafate and can be reached by tours organised by every agency in town for about US$25 plus the park entry fee of US$5. InterLagos also offers one-way rides for US$10, and it is reported that they take people from the campsites to the glacier without charging. Hitching is possible as well. There are also more expensive tours of the glacier which include a boat trip across the Brazo Rico and a walk through subantarctic forest and onto the ice.

Undoubtedly the best means of experiencing the glacier to the full is to camp in the park. This allows you to avoid the coachloads of tourists who cram the viewing platforms in the day and to enjoy the changing light at the end of the day. Some people find it so hypnotic that they stay for days. Heading west out of Calafate along Libertador, turn left after roughly 45km at the junction to Puerto Bandera, port for tourist boats on Lago Argentino, and head south to the Brazo Rico (the direct road from Calafate to the south side of the Brazo Rico is virtually disused). Once you reach the lake you will have to pay the US$5 fee at the park gate. There are three designated campsites inside the park, at Río Mitre (26km from the glacier), Arroyo Correntoso (10km) and Bahía Escondida (8km). The last two are free (at least until hot water is restored) and the only food available is at the snackbar at the glacier. From the campsites, you can walk most of the way to the glacier along the shore, but before reaching it you will see signs telling you that it is forbidden to view the glacier from the shore, reasonably enough as 32 people were killed between 1968 and 1988, swept away by waves when ice fell into the lake. In 1988 the present viewing galleries were opened, since when there have been no deaths. There is quite a decent range of viewpoints and you should not feel too restricted. I found the best views were to the left, just above the lowest gallery.

Boats from Puerto Bandera cruise along the north side of the Glaciar Perito Moreno, and also offer tours to the other glaciers flowing from the southern icecap to Lago Argentino. The largest and most impressive of these, 60km long, 80m high and 4km wide at its face (and up to 10km wide higher up) is the **Glaciar Upsala**, to the northwest. It has been shrinking for 60 years and is now retreating at over 60m/year. Immediately to its south is the Refugio Onelli, where there is a restaurant and a 1.5km walk to the glacier-filled Lago Onelli, as well as an 800m self-guided trail. Day trips cost US$87, with bus transfer from Calafate at 07.30, and it is possible to camp at the refuge and return another day. Other refuges are near the Spegazzini, Mayo and Ameghino glaciers, and on the Brazo Sur, to the southwest.

At the northmost end of the Brazo Norte of Lago Argentino, just east of the Upsala glacier, the Estancia Cristina has its place in history as the end point of Eric Shipton's north–south traverse of the South Patagonian Icecap in 1961. It also served as base camp to Padre Agostini in 1928 and 1930. Now it has become a tourist lodge, and guanaco are replacing sheep. Guests can hike or ride north to Refugio Pascal, northwest of Lago Anita (or Lago Pearson). This is not to be confused with Estancia Anita, west of Calafate, which was the showpiece of the sheep mogul José Menéndez and the site of the massacre of 120 rebellious Chilote farmworkers in 1921.

CLIMBING HISTORY

Because the Indians respected El Chaltén, they never sought to conquer it. The first ascent of Cerro FitzRoy (VI A3) was only in 1952, by Lionel Terray and Guido Magnone (Jacques Poincenot, one of the great climbers of the period, drowned in the Río FitzRoy), and its second ascent was not until 1965, when the Argentinians Fonrouge and Camesaña climbed the northwest ridge, and also the north face of Aguja Guillaumet. The ascent of Cerro Torre is one of climbing's great controversies. The great Walter Bonatti and Carlo Mauri failed in 1957, as did Bruno Detassis, declaring it unclimbable. Cesare Maestri claimed to have reached the summit in 1959, but his companion Toni Egger was killed during the descent and Maestri was later found in a bad state and unable to recall much of the climb. He returned in 1960 for a vain attempt to recover Egger's body, and his camera which would provide proof that they had reached the summit; and again in 1970 when he reached the top but using a compressor-driven drill to put up bolts. This drew storms of protest, but the bolts are gratefully used to this day. The first ascent is usually credited to another Italian team led by Casimiro Ferrari, in 1974.

The Aguja (or Aiguille) of Poincenot (3,036m) was climbed by Don Whillans and Frank Cochrane in 1962; Fonrouge and Rosasco made the first ascent of the southwest face in 1968, and its west face was finally climbed by Rab Carrington and Al Rouse in 1977. Cerro Torre still attracts obsessive climbers, putting up new routes of grade VII A1 and 6a; Kurt Diemberger describes it as one of his favourite 'smaller' mountains. The Slovenian Silvo Karo is putting up incredible new routes on Cerro Torre, spending many days living and climbing on impossibly steep, blank, loose and dangerous walls. The climbing season is mid-November–mid-March, when it is as cold as a Scottish winter but very windy. The weather comes from the west, and is often very bad for long periods as the icecap creates semi-permanent cloud. A rising barometer means it will clear to the west, but the windows may last for just 24 hours, so it is often necessary to climb all night.

FITZROY

For hikers the major attractions of the park are without doubt the mountains on the northwest shores of Lago Viedma, which include the granite pinnacles of **Cerro FitzRoy** (3,441m) and **Cerro Torre** (3,128m). Perito Moreno named FitzRoy (as the Argentines spell it) after the captain of the *Beagle*, but the Araucanian tribes that once roamed Patagonia saw the mountain as a god and called it *El Chaltén* or 'god of smoke' because of its almost permanent veil of self-created mist. Indeed, until the 20th century it was believed to be an active volcano, and only recently was this proved untrue. The name El Chaltén has now been given to the settlement serving visitors here.

Getting to the trailhead

Branching north 32km east of Calafate, Ruta 40 passes the east ends of Lagos Argentino and Viedma. After 127km (2 hours from Calafate) a side road turns left for El Chaltén, 82km west along the north side of Lago Viedma. The road, though

Altitude	Between 430m and 1,700m
Rating	Easy to difficult
Time	Day trips to a 4–5 day circuit
Start of trail	Chaltén
End of trail	Chaltén
Maps	A very useful and interesting hiking guide *Trekking in Chaltén* (with English translations of the route descriptions) is published by Zagier & Urruty and available in Calafate and Chaltén. The so-called EcoMapa of Los Glaciares is devoid of detail and essentially useless.

still unpaved, has been hugely improved, and several bus companies run daily in summer from Calafate, reaching Chaltén in under 4 hours (US$25 each way). Burmeister operates a direct bus from Río Gallegos three days a week (US$50).

Entry to the FitzRoy sector of the park is free, but you should call at the national park headquarters (tel/fax: 02962 493 004; open daily 08.00–20.00), to the left of the road before the bridge as you arrive. Buses all stop here for passengers to be briefed by rangers on their sensible rules. You will also be given bags to pack your rubbish out, and can obtain climbing permits here.

In **Chaltén** (430m) there is free camping both opposite the park headquarters at Confluenza and at the far (northern) end of the village, at the Madsen site. There are also hotels and hostels, including the Albergues Rancho Grande, on San Martín (tel: 02962 493 005; bigranch@hostels.org.ar), Patagonia, also on San Martín (tel: 493 019; alpatagonia@infovia.com.ar), Los Ñires, on Avda Lago del Desierto (tel: 493 009), and Condor de los Andes, on Río de las Vueltas (tel: 493 101; condordelosandes@ciudad.com.ar). Food can be bought at a couple of shops, although there is a wider, cheaper, choice at the supermarket in Calafate. Cafés in Chaltén, such as La Senyera, are inevitably pricey, but offer far better value than those in Calafate. For more information see www.elchalten.com.

Route description

From the north end of Chaltén you have a choice of two main hikes, which can be linked and will be described here as a circuit. You can also hike to Laguna Toro and over the icecap, both described afterwards.

Cerro FitzRoy and Cerro Torre

The path to Río Blanco and Cerro FitzRoy starts at the northern end of Chaltén, by the Madsen campsite. It heads up into open woodland to the right of a wooden hut with a yellow roof, and climbs steeply for 15 minutes and more easily for 25 more, to a longish (and windy) pass, where you have your first view of the spires of FitzRoy. After 10 minutes it starts to descend easily, and in 10 minutes reaches the junction to Laguna Capri, 5 minutes to the left. There is a campsite here, exposed to wind but with superb views and good bouldering possibilities. The main path continues to drop gently to the broad open valley of the Chorrillo del Salto, which it follows upstream. After 25 minutes you will cross a bridge at the mouth of the valley leading to Laguna Madre (page 319). Continuing mostly in woodland, after 5 minutes you will have to cross the Chorrillo, by a rather

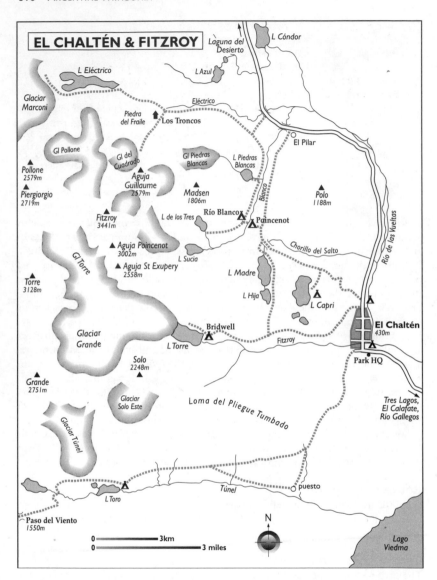

EL CHALTÉN & FITZROY

ramshackle pair of bridges. In another 10 minutes you will reach the Poincenot camp (named after the climber who drowned in 1952 – see box on page 314) in a wood of lenga on the near side of the Río Blanco.

Again there are makeshift log bridges across the various channels of the river. On the far side the main path continues to the right, but the side trip up to the **Laguna de los Tres**, to the left, is absolutely unmissable. After a couple of minutes you will pass the Río Blanco campsite (c780m), reserved by tradition for climbers (you might think that the climbers would use the site named after a climber, but that would be too simple), and climb steeply. In about 40 minutes you will reach a false col; keep slightly to the right to reach a grassy platform for an easy approach up the final moraine, and in 5 minutes you will have a view that is perhaps even better than that of the Torres del Paine. You are at about 1,200m, looking across the Laguna de los Tres (named after Poincenot and his two companions who made it to the top), the tower of Cerro FitzRoy rises over 2km above you. Behind you is Lago Viedma and the Patagonian plain. To the right it is an easy scramble to the peak of Cerro Madsen. You can go down to the lake and walk left to its outlet, where a natural balcony gives you a view of Laguna Sucia, often dotted with ice floes. It is possible to scramble down by the right-hand/western outlet stream, but it would be easier and safer to follow the Río Blanco upstream to Laguna Sucia and scramble upwards.

Once you are back at the Río Blanco, a path of variable quality makes its way along the left bank. After 40 minutes you will reach the outlet of the Laguna Piedras Blancas, between two high moraines. It is aptly named for the large chunks of white granite littering the streambed, up which you can clamber to the lake for more great views. The best place to cross the stream is at the confluence of two streams, about 100m above the Río Blanco, on the far side of which tiny cairns mark the path briefly. Keep to the river bank at first and in half an hour you will pass a sign indicating the end of the national park, into a wide gravel plain. The path meanders a bit, although more cairnlets give some help, and after 15 minutes swings left into the woods in the Eléctrico valley. After about 15 more minutes there is a log bridge across a stream from the left. The path now takes a rather more direct route through lenga forest, passing a gate after another 15 minutes and reaching the Refugio Los Troncos at Piedra del Fraile in a further 40 minutes. Its owner, Alberto Ardillo, was known as an 'interesting' or 'special' character, which is to say that he wanted to be a recluse but had to make money from tourists; anyone who paid to stay the night was welcome, but he would chase anyone else off his land. However, his daughter now runs the place, and it seems far more relaxed. It costs US$5 per person per day to camp, including hot showers; dinner is available for US$12 and breakfast for US$6.

From the top of the rock which gives the place its name (the Monk's Rock – named after Padre de Agostini (1883–1960), the great explorer and mountaineer, who established a base camp here) there is a great view of the north face of the Fitz. You can make a short but steep climb to its foot, up the right/east side of the stream tumbling down the mountain. The path ends at a scree-filled basin below Aguja Guillaumet (2,593m, 2,579m or 2,503m, depending on which source you believe). It is also possible to swing right and onto the foot of the Glaciar del Cuadrado, climbing 200m up to the Paso del Cuadrado (c 1,700m) for the most fantastic views of Cerros FitzRoy and Pollone.

Three hours' walk beyond Piedra del Fraile there are good camping spots on the sheltered beach at the far end of Lago Eléctrico, not far from the base of the Marconi Glacier. On the way you will have to cross the Río Pollone which drains into the Eléctrico lake; look up the side-valley for stunning views of FitzRoy and the spires of Mermoz and Guillaumet. Carry sandals or old trainers and trekking poles for this river crossing. It is possible to climb onto the Marconi glacier and head north (keeping to its right/west side) for about 40 minutes without needing crampons, due to the plentiful stones covering the ice. Beyond this point crampons are required and you are embarking on a serious expedition for which ropes and survival gear are required. Ultimately it is possible to make a circuit of Cerro FitzRoy via the icecap, emerging at the Paso del Viento (see below).

Returning down the Eléctrico valley, you will pass the gate and bridge and in 10

ESTANCIA TOURISM

Until recently *estancia* tourism was mainly to do with tourists popping out from Buenos Aires to some plush estate in the *pampas* to try their hands at polo, while in Patagonia a few locals made *merienda* by a water tank, but nowadays it is an upmarket business in Santa Cruz province, too, even though the idea of ecotourism on the Patagonian steppes is a bit optimistic. There is little wildlife, and the usual ecotourism principle of community involvement does not work, as there is basically no local community. However, it is not a case of the rich getting richer, but the only way to keep the properties going. Whereas the owners used to live in Buenos Aires, they now have to manage their *estancias* themselves, although the wives may stay in the city to look after their children's education.

Some *estancias* have considerable historic interest, such as Harberton in Tierra del Fuego (see page 337), Monte Dinero, near Río Gallegos, or places like Helsingfors, where the early mountaineers based themselves. You can ride with the *gauchos*, perhaps try your hand at shearing a sheep or two (although real sheep stations will be far too busy in January and February to let tourists get in the way), and of course there is always an *asado* (barbecue).

The main *estancias* in Santa Cruz have formed a co-operative with an office in Buenos Aires, at Unión de Estancías de Santa Cruz, Suipacha 1120 (1008 Cap Fed), tel: 011 4325 3098/3102; estancias@interlink.com.ar; www.sectur.gov.ar/estancs/etsc. (See also www.argentina-ranches.com). These include Helsingfors (info@helsingfors.com.ar, www.wam.com.ar/tourism/estancs/helsingfors) on Lago Viedma, founded in 1910 by the Finn Alfredo Ramström and his Danish wife María; naturally the Swede Nordenskjöld stayed here, as did Onelli, Agostini, Lucas Bridges and Tschiffely. This is one of the priciest, at US$200 single or US$360 twin, including a daily excursion. It can be reached by boat (via the Glaciar

minutes more reach a junction where the path from the Río Blanco meets another heading to the left. Here you can choose either to return as you came, or turn left eventually to hike up the right/east side of the Río Blanco valley, a longer route but a better path and with great views of the mountains, as well as an outside chance of hitching a ride to Chaltén or the Lago del Desierto. This path is marked with a few green paint dots and micro-cairns of just four or five stones as it again meanders aimlessly across the gravel plain and crosses a couple of water channels. After 20 minutes you will reach the side of a hill and follow it to your left to reach the road bridge over the Río Eléctrico in 5 minutes more. If you choose to start your trek here, it is possible to hire a pick-up truck in Chaltén to bring you this far, then it is a gentle two-hour walk up the valley to Piedra De Fraile.

To return via the Río Blanco valley and continue to Laguna Torre, turn right to follow the road around the back of the hill, over the Río Blanco bridge, and after almost 20 minutes turn right at a green arrow to pass the El Pilar teashop and hostel. This path follows lines of stones and green arrows, and after 10 minutes climbs up onto the hillside and on in good lenga forest. After 15 minutes it gets steeper, giving you a good view of the Piedras Blancas glacier and the Fitz after 10

Viedma) from Puerto Bahía Túnel, just south of El Chaltén, but this is badly publicised and you will need to contact one of the addresses above for details.

Nibepo Aike (tel: 02902 420 180), at the southern end of Lago Argentino (just north of Paine), offers riding in great scenery. Monte Dinero (montedinero@southern.com.ar) is similar to Harberton, in that it was home to the earliest settlers in the area, and offers the chance to see coastal wildlife.

Stag River (tel: 02966 621 069; fax: 02902 482 830), in the far south just 40km from Puerto Natales, specialises in trout fishing, although there is also horse riding and, March–May, hunting. La Oriental lies inside the Parque Nacional Perito Moreno, and is the best base for the park, with twin rooms at US$70 and camping (Nov–Mar) for US$15, (tel: 02962 452 196; fax: 452 445, in San Julián).

The Hostería Cuevas de las Manos (tel: 02963 432 085), to the south of the town of Perito Moreno, is 20km from the Cave of the Hands, and also has a relatively cheap hostel. La Serena is one of the easiest to reach, on the main road between Perito Moreno and Los Antiguos (casilla 87, 9040 Perito Moreno; tel: 02963 432 340).

Another consortium, more focused on adventure tourism, is Cielos Patagónicos, at Sánchez de Bustamente 2434, 60B, Buenos Aires (tel/fax: 011 4805 1010, 1807 5032; serret@ciepatagonicos.com.ar), which links four estancias with a total of 65,000 hectares. El Cóndor, on the south shore of Lago San Martín, not far north of El Chaltén, covers 43,000ha, where huemul can be found; Chaltén Alto, 20km north of El Chaltén, also has huemul, as well as views of Lagos Azul and Eléctrico and the Marconi glacier; Menelik covers 10,000ha southwest of Bajo Caracoles, just east of the Parque Nacional Perito Moreno, and Veranada de Jones is south of the Perito Moreno park.

minutes more. After another 20 minutes' climb you will reach an open space with great views, from where the path crosses headland for 5 minutes to the edge of the wood hiding the Poincenot camp. Turning left here on the path on which you arrived from Chaltén, in 15 minutes you will be back at the bridge at the mouth of the valley leading to Laguna Madre.

Immediately to the right is a sandy path which goes around the end of a hill. You may have heard that this path, the short-cut to Laguna Torre, is closed, perhaps due to the presence of some rare deer. The situation is in fact that there is a windy pass coupled with some tempting spots for wild camping, producing a serious fire hazard. Argentinians, Chileans and Israelis, who are all pyromaniacs, are told that the path is closed, but there is no objection to responsible *gringos* coming this way. You would not dream of camping illegally, I presume, and even if you do stop for a brew you will, of course, use a stove, *verdad*? Parts of the trail are a bit boggy, but to be ecologically responsible you must stick to the path – no problem in decent boots. In about half an hour you will be at the far end of Laguna Madre (the Mother) and crossing the breezy moraine dam. The path continues along the east side of Laguna Hija (the Daughter), and after 10 minutes you can pass through a gate to the left to a beach at its southern end. The path heads into trees, passes to the left of a boggy area, and after 30 minutes begins to descend steeply. In 15 minutes you will emerge into an open patch, for your first view of the stunning Cerro Torre. It is more or less level for the next 5 minutes to the junction with the main track up the Río FitzRoy.

Turning right, you will cross a sandy ridge in a minute and head up the valley with the river well away to your left. The path brings you to its left bank after 25 minutes, and soon climbs up a steep moraine bank and then down to a log bridge in under 10 minutes more. From here the path follows the river around the end of the next moraine to reach the **Campamento Bridwell** in 15 minutes. This is the base camp for Cerro Torre, with various ramshackle equipment stores, but hikers are graciously permitted to mix with climbers here. There is a bench where climbers sit to plot their route up Cerro Torre, and particularly the surreal ice mushrooms that cap the amazing granite obelisk, but do not be surprised if you see nothing at all; Cerro Torre is notorious for hiding in cloud. It takes 5 minutes more to reach the top of the moraine overlooking Laguna Torre and the Glaciar Grande at its far end. A path follows the moraine ridge to the right and leads onto the ice, which is covered with a thick layer of stones and thus accessible without crampons. It is possible to go all the way to the base of Cerro Torre. To the left you will see a Tyrolean crossing, a single cable across the river designed to be used with a climbing harness but passable without.

Returning down the valley, it takes about 40 minutes to reach the Laguna Madre junction, and another 20 minutes to the top of a low ridge and a dry lagoon, just beyond which a stony path rises to the right, reaching a *mirador* in another 10 minutes. Here the path swings down to the left and follows the right side of a stream. After climbing briefly to the right and passing a lagoon, it drops steeply and after 40 minutes reaches the start of the trail at a sign, about 2 hours from the Campamento Bridwell. From here it is about 100m to the main road, about 100m north of the Albergue Rancho Grande in Chaltén.

Laguna Toro

The other main hike, to Laguna Toro and the Paso del Viento, starts by the National Park headquarters at the southern end of Chaltén; you need to register here, as do climbers – not because it is dangerous terrain, but because the route is largely unmarked. Set off through the unmarked metal gate on the right just before the headquarters and take a track to the left past weather instruments and a stable to a gate and sign. Turn right here along a stream lined with trees which soon curves up to the left to cross the stream on a bridge, just below a good pool. From here you climb steadily through steppe vegetation (with butterflies, grasshoppers and lizards) and then into open lenga forest.

After almost an hour you will reach a clearing with views of Cerro Solo and to its right Cerro Torre and Cerro FitzRoy. From here you should follow a cattle drive slightly up to the left and through two smaller clearings and then straight up through another. Turn left at a tiny arrow at the top to cross a stream and then climb fairly steeply, with fenceposts parallel to the right. This crosses a few small streams and circles around the hill, continuing to rise until it emerges after 40 minutes at the edge of a large pasture. Here you have a choice: the straightforward route goes directly ahead following fence posts (slightly to the left ahead, across a boggy field). The route rises gently through dwarf trees to a cairn at the highest point on the path. Crossing another damp patch you will have the fenceposts about

200m to your right and will then begin to descend on a very nice route on grass, leaving most trees to the right. You can either follow the path down to the *puesto* or farmworkers' hut, or swing right to gradually make your way along the hillside to reach the floor of the Río Túnel valley as far upstream as you choose. The valley bottom can be boggy, while on the hillside you will have to cross some gullies.

The other route goes higher and offers better views, but is far harder to follow. It follows the edge of the forest up to the right and through a gap into another pasture, and continues into the trees slightly to the left (marked by a red and white plastic tag). It is soon very vague. You will emerge from the trees again in under 10 minutes and, following the trees up to the right again, pass dwarf trees to reach the tree line and then very soon the vegetation line, in another 10 minutes. From here there are great views of the ice-cap. You can make your way down and traverse along the hillside, as above.

Heading west along the hillside, it took me an hour to reach the valley bottom and another 40 minutes to the large stream flowing from the West Solo Glacier. Returning, it took 50 minutes along the valley from the stream to the *puesto* and another 50 minutes following the fence line to the cairn.

The stream should be crossed about 30m above its mouth, and carries on westwards in woodland. In about 30 minutes you will reach the **Campamento Laguna Toro**, where there are two small huts at about 600m at the east end of the lake of the same name. It is possible to continue along the north side of the lake for 45 minutes to the foot of the glacier flowing south from Cerro Grande. Again, this is well coated with stones and crampons are unnecessary. Following cairns, you can return to *terra firma* at the far side of this glacier after an hour or so, and climb steeply on moraine for up to 2 hours to reach the aptly named Paso del Viento (about 1,450m), a gateway to the icecap. Descending 200m to the west, you will find the Laguna Ferrari, where it is possible to camp, and an hour (or 4km) to the south is another lagoon with the Paso del Viento refuge of the *Instituto del Hielo Continental Patagónico* (Patagonian Icecap Institute). If the weather changes for the worse you should always head back over the Paso del Viento.

The Icecap Circuit

Altitude	Between 430m and 1,500m
Rating	Difficult
Time	6 days minimum, more days may be necessary for sitting out bad weather
Distance	Approximately 80km.
Start of trail	Chaltén

The South Patagonian Icecap, about 330km long and 13,500km^2 in area, has posed many problems for explorers and remains as the last disputed area of the Chilean–Argentine frontier. The altitudes of the peaks of the Mariano Moreno range, which break through the centre of the icecap and which Argentina claims as the border, are still subject to debate. Chile, or more precisely the Chilean Air Force, which sets up a helicopter base every summer on the ice, claims the area up to the Paso del Viento and Cerro FitzRoy. This is clearly absurd, but the entire area of the Laguna del Desierto (see below) having been awarded to Argentina, the Chilean military feel compensation is due.

It is possible to make a circuit on the ice to the west of Cerro Torre from the Paso Marconi and the Eléctrico valley to the Paso del Viento; you should be experienced and well equipped and of course should not tackle this alone. Guides can be found in Chaltén, and FitzRoy Expediciones (Hostería El Puma, Terray 212, El Chaltén, tel: 02962 493 017; fitzroyexpediciones@infovia.com.ar), Camino Abierto (tel: 493 043) and Expediciones Patagonia (tel: 493 043) offer daily outings on the ice from the Bridwell camp and longer trips on to the ice-cap. For rock- or ice-climbing contact Eduardo Fernández on 011 4982 0203 (in Buenos Aires) or vivmont@elchalten.com.

From the Eléctrico valley, a short but rough walk along the lateral moraine on the south side of the Glaciar Marconi takes you onto the glacier; watch out for landslides on this steep rockstrewn slope. This lower section of the glacier is relatively flat and spread with stone; there are some crevasses which are usually very obvious. After an hour of walking swing north on the ice. Behind you is the sharp granite needle of Gendarme and beyond that Pier Giorgio and Domo Blanco. Continue northwards, ascending gradually with the giant rumbling seracs of Cerro Marconi above you to the west. These seracs are prone to dramatic collapse, so do not get too close. The next, much steeper, section of the glacier requires the use of crampons and takes you up to the Paso Marconi (1,500m). Because of the crevasse danger it is recommended to rope up on this section. From the pass there are impressive views over the wild heart of the ice field and the mountain massifs of the area. You will need to camp on the ice field – it is slightly less exposed close into the slopes of Cerro Marconi. Wherever you camp you will have to build an ice-wall the height of your tent for protection against the tremendous winds that can blow up from the west at any time. Anchor the tent with crampons, snowshoes, hiking poles, skis and whatever else you can find.

Continue southwards, keeping close to the Cordón Marconi; after 5–6 hours' walk, on snowshoes, you will reach the Circo de los Altares. This is a dramatic place to camp, right at the foot of the west face of the awesome granite and ice spire of Cerro Torre (3,128m), flanked by Agujas Egger, Standhart and Biffida.

Carrying on southwards along the edge of the icefield, the peak of Cerro Grande (2,751m) towers above you on the left. After 3–4 hours you will start to descend, keeping left on this heavily crevassed area. Eventually you will leave the ice field by way of the lateral moraine of the Viedma Glacier, and reach the Laguna de los Esquies (or de los Trineos). There is a relatively sheltered camping spot next to this lake behind a huge boulder, but beware of flying grit penetrating everywhere. It takes between 1 and 2 hours from here to reach Laguna Ferrari, at the foot of the Paso del Viento. There are spectacular panoramas over Laguna Toro as you cross the pass. Descend flanking the Túnel glacier and the Río Túnel to camp at the edge of the forest.

If the weather is really poor or too windy to cross the pass, you have the option of continuing to the Paso del Viento hut, approximately an hour from the lake.

For any climbing expedition and any trips on to the ice it is essential to register with the National Park Office in Chaltén. The Park Office can recommend mountain guides and porters as can the two local specialist agencies Camino Abierto or FitzRoy Expediciones.

This trek should only be attempted by experienced mountaineers with a working knowledge of mountain navigation, glacier crossing and crevasse rescue. The use of ropes, crampons, skis or snowshoes is essential. High quality equipment is needed to withstand the ferocious winds so typical of Patagonia.

SUGGESTED KIT LIST

Igloo tent
Rope
Harness
Ice rescue equipment
Ice axe
Snow shovel
Sledges
Compass and map
Torch
Stove
GPS
Crampons
Gaiters
Snow shoes
Ski poles
Thermal underwear
Walking socks
Fleece trousers and jacket
Quick-dry T-shirts and base
    layer micro-fleece

Goretex jacket and trousers
Additional fleece jacket or
    down jacket
Gloves/mitts and waterproof
    overgloves
Well worn-in plastic or four-
    season leather boots
Sandals for river crossings
Sunhat
Sun goggles with full UV
    protection
Lightweight balaclava for sun
    protection
Warm hat/balaclava
Total sunblock
Shorts for walk in and out
3/4 season sleeping bag
Camping towel
Thick camping mat

Some equipment (eg: plastic boots, crampons) can be hired locally at Viento Oeste on Avda San Martín, Chaltén (tel: 02962 493 021). They also sell some second-hand equipment and have a small range of outdoor clothing. Horses to transport heavy kit can be hired from Rodolfo Guerra (tel: 02962 493 020).

Laguna del Desierto

A final possibility is to follow the rough road north from Chaltén to the Laguna del Desierto, which you will hear much of, as it has only been opened up for tourism since the end of this part of the border dispute with Chile in 1996. From the south end of the lake a path follows the east bank for 15km to its north end; boats also make this trip, so you may prefer to cruise north and hike back. There are campsites near the jetties at both ends of the lake, and a police post at the north end. From the south end a short hike (2km each way) leads west up the left/north side of a stream to a moraine ridge with fantastic views of the northeast face of FitzRoy, and on to Laguna Huemul. This and other walks here are on private property (this is outside the national park) and you should enquire before venturing too far. However, new trails are under construction in this area.

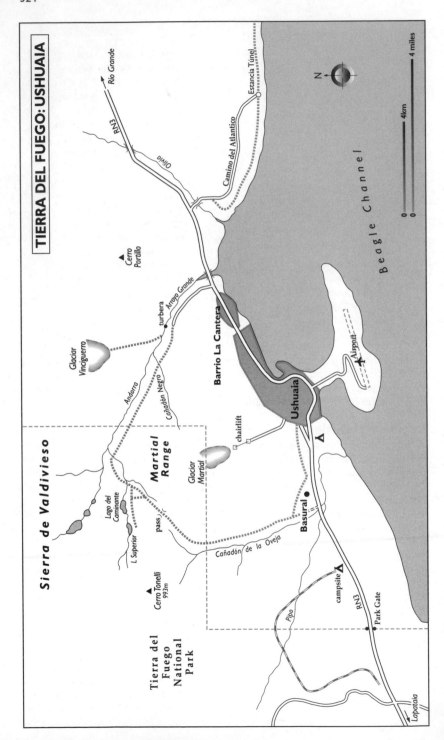

TIERRA DEL FUEGO: USHUAIA

Sierra de Valdivieso

Tierra del Fuego National Park

Cerro Tonelli
993m

L Superior

Lago del
Caminante

pass

Martial
Range

Glaciar
Martial

Cañadón de la Oveja

Basural

campsite

Park Gate

RN3

Pipo

Lapataia

Cañadón Negro

Andorra

Glaciar
Vinciguerro

turbera

Arroyo Grande

Cerro
Portillo

chairlift

Barrio La Cantera

Ushuaia

Airport

RN3

Olivia

Camino del Atlantico

Estancia Túnel

Río Grande

Beagle Channel

N

0   4km
0   4 miles

Tierra del Fuego

'To the south we had a scene of savage magnificence, well becoming Tierra del Fuego. There was a degree of mysterious grandeur in mountain behind mountain, with the deep intervening valleys, all covered by one thick, dusky mass of forest. The atmosphere, likewise, in this climate, where gale succeeds gale, with rain, hail, and sleet, seems blacker than anywhere else. In the Strait of Magellan, looking due southward from Port Famine, the distant channels between the mountains appeared from their gloominess to lead beyond the confines of this world.'

Charles Darwin, *Voyage of the Beagle*, December 17 1832

When, in 1520, the Portuguese explorer Ferdinand Magellan reached the great rugged island at the tip of America, he observed the black smoke from the fires lit by the local Indians to warn each other that a stranger had been sighted. He called it *Tierra del Humo* ('Land of Smoke'). His patron, Charles V of Spain, reasoning that there could be no smoke without fire, renamed the island *Tierra del Fuego* ('Land of Fire').

Just over three centuries later, racked with seasickness after the stormy voyage round Cape San Diego on the island's southeast tip, Fitzroy anchored the *Beagle* a few miles along the coast in the Bay of Good Success. Here he met the island's 'savages' – native Yámana Indians, who were later virtually wiped out by measles and tuberculosis imported by white settlers (see page 327). Today there are no 'pure-blooded' Indians. And the only fires burning are those that flicker from the oil fields, the island's main industry with tourism and sheep farming.

Given its proximity to the treacherous shipwreck-studded rocks of Cape Horn, over 100km south, Tierra del Fuego comes as a pleasant surprise if you want to walk. Although the north of the island is an arid steppe similar to the Patagonian plains, this contrasts with the beautiful southern part where the mighty Andes finally dive into the sea and jagged snow-covered peaks overlook forests of false beech and meadows filled with flowers such as streaked maiden, dog orchid, woods lady's slipper, violets, Fuegian edelweiss and cabbage daisy. Summer can be almost warm. In the west there is up to 2m of annual precipitation, but under 500mm to the east. In the wetter areas there is evergreen forest of coihue de Magallanes, to the east there is lenga and ñirre, and to the north there is coirón bunchgrass (*Poa pratensis*). The treeline reaches 600m at most, and there is also plenty of sphagnum bog. There are no rhea or otters on the main island, although both river and sea otters survive on other islands such as the Isla de los Estados. The Fuegian fox, a sub-species of the red fox and the largest fox in South America, is probably also doomed, as the grey fox has been introduced to deal with the problem of rabbits (also introduced by settlers), and has been all too successful. Similarly, 25 pairs of beavers were introduced from Canada in 1947, by a governor of Argentine Tierra del Fuego, no less, for fur-farming, and were released when this failed. There are now 40–50,000 of them, and they have done great damage, although in a relatively small area. In 1961 they reached Isla Navarino, and in 1998 they appeared at Laguna Parrillar on the mainland. The world's southernmost lizard, *Liolaemus magellanicus*, can be found near the eastern mouth of the Magellan Straits, together with penguins.

Mountaineers will find some of the most beautiful peaks in South America in this area, particularly in the Chilean half of Tierra del Fuego, including the twin-peaked Monte Sarmiento (2,300m), named by early navigators of the Magellan Straits. Although altitudes in the Argentine half of the island are not great, the tree- and snow-lines are so low, due to the cold Humboldt Current, that the mountains have all the drama of far higher ranges. In the northern part of the island are vast sheep *estancias*, usually over 4,000 hectares, and virtually self-sufficient, with a kitchen garden, carpenters' shop and blacksmith.

Tierra del Fuego is divided more or less equally between Chile and Argentina. The Argentine part is more developed; its largest settlement is the oil-producing town of Río Grande, but its administrative centre, **Ushuaia**, is the hub of the island's tourism. Overlooking the emerald waters of the Beagle Channel, Ushuaia claims to be the southernmost city in the world, but the southernmost settlements are Chilean, across the strait on the island of Navarino. The long-running border dispute between the two countries meant that you used not to be able to cross from one side to the other for longer than a day. However, there are no longer any restrictions, other than cost; crossing from Ushuaia costs almost as much as flying all the way from Punta Arenas to Puerto Williams.

The chief town on the Chilean side is **Porvenir**, reached by ferry from Punta Arenas. This is in dull steppe country, and it is difficult to explore the dramatic south of Chilean Tierra del Fuego. From Porvenir a bus runs to Cameron (Mondays and Fridays at 15.00), from where you can continue south along the coast (cycling, hitching or with a car hired in Punta Arenas) to Puerto Arturo, passing the Río Cóndor, centre of the Trillium forestry project (see page 62). Inland, to the southeast of Cameron, you can go via Rusffin to **Estancia Vicuña**, near Lago Blanco, which is very popular with anglers.

From Vicuña a very rough track continues a long way south to Caleta María, on Admiralty Sound, and **Estancia Yendegaia**, on the Beagle Channel; this is being developed for ecotourism by the Fundación Yendegaia (contact Cordillera Darwin Travel in Punta Arenas, at the Hostal El Bosque, O'Higgins 424 (tel: 061 221 764, fax: 224 637; c_darwin@patagonian.com; in Santiago tel: 02 321 5012). The track is being upgraded by the CMT (Military Construction Corps), supposedly to develop tourism, although realistically it must have more to do with logging projects. It is preferable to arrive by light plane or boat. The Río Azopardo is 12km long, linking Lago Fagnano to Seno Almirantazgo, and there is great fishing for sea-run brown trout; otherwise a series of trekking circuits is being developed in the 40,000ha *estancia*, most notably from Yendegaia to Caleta María across the eastern end of the Cordillera Darwin.

The **Cordillera Darwin** extends to the west of Yendegaia, an incredibly dramatic range of ice-capped peaks bisected by glaciers and fjords. Although not high, peaks such as Pico Frances (2,150m), Cerro Italia (2,438m), Monte Darwin

THE FUEGIAN INDIANS
Clare Hargreaves

'The next day we... came to a more inhabited district. Few if any of these natives could ever have seen a white man: certainly nothing could exceed their astonishment at the apparition of the four boats. Fires were lighted on every point (hence the name of Tierra del Fuego), both to attract our attention and to spread far and wide the news. Some of the men ran for miles along the shore. I shall never forget how wild and savage one group appeared: suddenly four or five men came to the edge of an overhanging cliff; they were absolutely naked, and their long hair streamed about their faces; they held rugged staffs in their hands, and, springing from the ground, they waved their arms around their heads, and sent forth the most hideous yells.

It was as easy to please as it was difficult to satisfy these savages. Young and old, men and children, never ceased repeating the word 'yammerschooner', which means 'give me'. After pointing to almost every object one after the other, even to the buttons on our coats, and saying their favourite word in as many intonations as possible, they would then use it in a neuter sense, and vacantly repeat 'yammerschooner.' After yammerschoonering for any article very eagerly, they would point to their young women or little children, as much as to say, 'If you will not give it me, surely you will to such as these.'

Charles Darwin, The Voyage of the Beagle, January 20 1833

Little more than a century ago, the only inhabitants of Tierra del Fuego were Indians. There were four tribes, each with its own language and customs. Living in wigwams, the Selk'nam and Aush were 'foot-Indians', surviving by hunting guanaco with bows, arrows and slings. The Yámana and Kaweshkar were 'canoe-Indians', who lived a nomadic life in the channels of the far south, with a fire kept burning permanently in each canoe.

Contrary to what Darwin believed, human flesh never formed part of their diet; their strict code of customs forbade this. Darwin also did the Indians a gross injustice by describing their language as 'hideous yells'. The language of one of the tribes, the Yámana, was actually rich and complex, with a vocabulary of no fewer than 32,000 words and inflections.

Incredibly hardy, the Indians could go naked even when it was snowing and withstand the toughest physical rigours. Tragically, however, they had no resistance to white men's diseases. With the arrival in 1871 of white colonists – first missionaries, then the navy, farmers and bureaucrats – hundreds died of measles. More horrific still, others met their deaths at the hands of greedy white settlers who saw the Indians as troublesome vermin and offered a bounty for every one killed. Of the 7,000–9,000 Indians who had inhabited this bleak island when Darwin visited, there were fewer than 150 left by 1947. Today there are none.

(2,488m) and Sarmiento (2,404m) provide some of the world's hardest climbing, due mainly to the foul and highly changeable weather and the impenetrable rainforest that fills all the space between sea and ice. This also makes hiking near-impossible; the area is best visited by boat from Punta Arenas. It is protected as the

Parque Nacional Alberto de Agostini, in honour of the priest who explored this area from the 1910s to the 1950s. Eric Shipton undertook four expeditions here, climbing and exploring an area that was still virtually unknown in the 1960s.

USHUAIA

Ushuaia, which means 'inner harbour to the westward' in the Yamana language, is the jumping-off point for all the island's best hiking and natural attractions. Aptly described as a cross between Fort William in Scotland and an Austrian ski resort, the city consists of modern, concrete houses sprawling over the hills overlooking the Beagle Channel. In bizarre contrast, the main street, San Martín, is lined with glossy duty-free shops parading imported chocolates, sound systems, clothes, shoes and alcohol.

Because of its tax-free status and higher wages, Ushuaia has attracted many Argentines in search of wealth, and the city has become something of a boom town. It is also a popular destination for Argentine holidaymakers, and the starting point for Antarctic cruises. It is possible to get an eight-day trip to the Antarctic for about US$600 if there is a cancellation, but you may have to wait a couple of weeks.

Hotels, which are expensive anyway, tend to be packed in high season. The best bet is to stay in one of the numerous reasonably priced private rooms (bookable through the Tourist Office) or to camp. The Dirección de Turismo, San Martín 660 (tel: 02901 432 000, 424 550; http://tierradelfuego.org.ar/ushuaia; muniush@ tierradelfuego.org.ar; Mon–Fri 08.00–22.00, Sat & Sun 09.00–20.00), is very helpful, with plenty of detailed **information**. There is a free information line: 0800 333 1476 (same hours); the province also has an official website: www. tierradelfuego.org.ar.

The official HI **youth hostel** is Torre al Sur, Gobernador Paz 1437 (tel: 02901 430 745; torresur@hostels.org.ar); Hospedaje Violeta de la Montaña, Belgrano 236 (tel: 421 884) is recommended as another cheap place to sleep. There are various good **campsites** nearby: at the Rugby Club 4km to the west is the Río Pipo URC (tel: 435 796); to get there you can follow the main Ruta 3, or take *colectivo 1* or *2* (Ruta 640 indicates the owners, not the route) to Avenida Alem, walk to its western end and then follow Ruta 3 back towards the city for 5 minutes. The Camping Municipal is another 4km west (just 2km before the entrance to the national park) at a golf club, from where the reopened section of the Presidio railway runs into the park. There are also possibilities along Ruta 3 to the east (see page 337).

Ushuaia is really a good base for exploring the surrounding area, but there is also plenty to see in the town. The **Museo del Fin del Mundo** (Museum of the End of the World; open daily 10.00–13.00 & 15.00–19.30; US$5) at Maipú 175 has excellent displays, together with a good bookshop and library. From 1896–1947 Ushuaia housed many of Argentina's most notorious convicts, and you can now visit the **former prison** (*presidio*) to the east of the town at Yaganes and Gobernador Paz, which also houses marine and police museums (open daily 10.00–13.00 & 15.00–20.00; US$3). Prisoners worked as loggers, among other things, with the help of the *Trencito del Presidio* (Prison Railway). This was first established in 1902 as the *xilocarril* or wooden highway (as opposed to a *ferrocarril* or iron highway), with oxen hauling wagons on wooden rails. It was replaced by 1908 by a normal railway of 600mm gauge and extended westwards, reaching the area of the present national park from 1909. It was closed in 1952, and a stretch on the western outskirts of Ushuaia can be walked (see page 331). In addition, despite some environmental controversy, the westernmost 6km have been reopened as a tourist line, with two new steam locomotives and a 1938 diesel (Ferrocarril Austral Fueguino, more commonly known as the *Tren del Fin del Mundo*: tel: 02901 431 600 for information).

There are still various houses built by the early settlers dotted around the town. The tin-sided Merced church (1898) at Maipú 919 is newly restored, and the Beben House (1913; Tue–Fri 10.00–20.00, Sat/Sun 16.00–20.00) on Paseo Antiguos Pobladores houses arts classes.

For camping **supplies** you will find the Supermarket Kelly, at San Martín and Oñas, more useful (open Mon–Sat 09.30–22.00, Sun 10.00–20.00). The La Anonima supermarket is to the east of town on Avda Perito Moreno, relatively convenient for hikes up the Arroyo Grande (page 332) or east along the coast. **Books and maps** can be bought at World's End, San Martín 501, and camping **equipment** at Popper, San Martín 730; more technical **climbing gear** and so on can be found at Z Importación, Gobernador Paz 1537 (open daily 18.00–21.00). **Bikes** can be hired at DTT, San Martín 1258 (tel: 02901 424 424).

Immediately north of town is Cerro Martial, the world's southernmost **ski resort**, with snow from mid-June until October. A good road winds up to the Hotel del Glaciar (perhaps the nicest place to stay in Ushuaia, with great views out across the Beagle Channel), at about 200m altitude, on the lip of a glaciated bowl. From the Punto Panorámico, a *mirador* just west of the centre, it takes 15min to walk to the ring-road, Alem, from where it is 1.8km to the hotel by the road, or less by the path to the right following pylons. The road continues uphill, passing the Club Andino's Refugio de la Montaña and cross-country ski track after 5 minutes, and ending in 15 minutes more at a teashop, at the foot of a chairlift at 385m. The *aerosilla* operates in summer, too (Tue–Sun 10.30–17.30; US$5), taking you to 575m, just below the Club Andino's Refugio del Glaciar Martial (tel: 02901 156 3001; refugiodelglaciar@tierradelfuego.org.ar), which has 12 beds. This gives access to the Martial glacier, a pleasant short walk by a stream. It is possible to climb to the ridge but not down the far side, so unfortunately you will have to return the way you came.

Several **tour companies** in Ushuaia provide minibus services to various hiking venues. These include Eben Ezer (tel: 02901 431 133, 0669 68579) and Pasarela (tel: 424 582, 433 712), leaving from the junction of Maipú and 25 de Mayo, as well as Alvear, at San Martín 146 (tel/fax: 423 303; alvear_ush@infovia.com.ar). The most popular trip is to the national park, with each company offering at least half a dozen departures a day in season, for US$10 return. There are almost as many to the Martial chair-lift (US$5) and to the ski centres (US$10), with one or two per day continuing to Lago Escondido (US$20) and Lago Fagnano (US$25). Pasarela has a daily bus to Harberton (US$20 each – minimum four passengers). For more elaborate Harberton packages, try Pretour (Maipú 237; tel: 02901 422 150; fax: 430 532; pretouushu@arnet.com.ar). In addition Antartur (Gobernador Paz 1569; tel: 423 240; fax: 424 108; antartur@tierradelfuego.org.ar) offers hiking and climbing trips; Ushuaia Extremo (tel: 424 094, 15 562 023; ushuaiaextremo@yahoo.com) offers horse and boat trips; and Canal Fun and Nature, Rivadavia 82 (tel: 437 395, 435 777, 0800 999 6479; canal@satlink.com) offers hiking, kayaking and Land Rover trips.

The **national park office** is at San Martín 1395 (Mon–Fri 08.00–15.00; tel/fax: 421 315). You can also get hiking information at the Club Andino, at Fadul 5 (tel: 422 335, 0669 68626; Mon–Fri 15.00–22.00); they sell a useful but expensive guide to *Trekking y Andinismo en la Tierra del Fuego*. For guides, contact the Compañía de Guías de Patagonia, casilla 147, (9419) Ushuaia (tel: 02901 432 642, 435 557; turil@usa.net).

Getting there

The only land routes to Ushuaia pass through Chile, and bizarrely there are **buses** from Punta Arenas in Chile (08.00 daily) to Río Grande, connecting to Ushuaia, but none from Río Gallegos in Argentina. Therefore, unless you want to get off a Río Gallegos–Punta Arenas bus at the Punta Delgada junction and hang about there, you will have to fly, or hitch as far as Río Grande, from where several buses run to Ushuaia daily.

The main **ferry** across the Magellan Strait is from Punta Delgada to Punta Espora (Bahía Azul), shuttling to and fro across the *Primera Angostura* (the First Narrows) between 08.40 and 23.00 daily, with as often as not a break of a couple of hours at low tide. An unsurfaced road leads from here to the border crossing of San Sebastián, from where the road is paved to Río Grande and most of the way to Ushuaia, over the Paso Garibaldi. From Punta Arenas you can also cross to Porvenir, except on Mondays, from where there are buses (Tue and Sat at 14.00) to Río Grande. Whichever ferry you take, look out for the lovely black-and-white Commerson's dolphins.

Thus the easiest (and sometimes cheapest) way to reach Ushuaia is **by air**. Aerolíneas Argentinas, Austral, LAPA, Southern Winds and Kaiken fly from Río Gallegos, Buenos Aires and other cities. LADE flies twice-weekly from Río Gallegos (heavily booked in summer). DAP flies on Wednesdays from Punta Arenas (and Tapsa Aviacion flies twice-weekly from Punta Arenas to Río Grande). A new airport allows planes as large as Boeing 747s to reach Ushuaia, so the choice of flights may increase.

TIERRA DEL FUEGO NATIONAL PARK

Ten kilometres west of Ushuaia, along the main road beside the Beagle Channel, is the entrance to **Tierra del Fuego National Park**, where you will have to pay a US$5 entrance fee. This is a beautiful area covering 63,000 hectares and combining the clear, blue lakes and snow-capped mountains of the Cordón del Toro with the peaceful shores of Lago Roca and Bahía Lapataia. To the west you have views of the higher and wilder terrain of the Cordillera Darwin, in Chilean Tierra del Fuego. There are few long-distance trails within the park, but it is still well worth exploring, with lots of pleasant shorter walks. At Lago Roca there is a good organised campsite, and others, with fireplaces and fresh water but little else, are available elsewhere for a couple of dollars a head. The national park is remarkably close to Ushuaia, and there is plenty of traffic to and fro. In addition there are buses from town to the campsites in season (see above).

At the national park gate you will be given a photocopy map of the park and surrounding area. This is woefully inadequate for walking, however. A really beautiful map of the whole of Tierra del Fuego has been published by Natalie Goodall in conjunction with her book on the island (see *Appendix 2, Further Information*). This can be bought in Ushuaia, but is not detailed enough for hiking.

The Cañadón de la Oveja

The nearest serious hike to Ushuaia follows the **Cañadón de la Oveja**, just west of town. This clips a corner of the national park, theoretically a closed area, but in practice there is no need for special permission, as it is still used for cattle grazing. However, it would make sense to visit the Lapataia area first, in order to have a park entry ticket. The route then loops right around the north side of the Martial range, returning to the main road to the east of Ushuaia. You will need to camp for one night.

From the centre of town it takes about 20 minutes to walk to the junction to the airport, 20 more to the Rugby Club campsite, and 5 more to the junction with Avda Alem, where the asphalt ends (or take *colectivo 1* or *2* – see above). From here it is another 12 minutes' walk west to a junction by the *basural* (town rubbish tip, now being restored as a recreational area), where you should turn right. This can also be reached by the *senda del Tren del Presidio* (the trackbed of the prison's logging railway): starting from Ushuaia's hospital, take a *colectivo* or follow the paved 12 Octubre, reaching Avda Alem after 25 minutes. On the far side an embankment runs between two small swamps, leading to a good, dry track, which rises gently for 20 minutes, through woodland of lenga and ñirre with calafate bushes. Continuing beyond the track's highpoint for 3 minutes, turn left before a fence to reach the road just before the *basural*, where you will see lots of birds scavenging.

Turning right towards the *autodromo* (race course), go uphill for 5 minutes and then half-right through a gate. In another 5 minutes you will reach a 'car cemetery', where the path through the gate to the left is marked *'Prohibido Pasar'* (no entry). The alternative is to follow a very rough track uphill to cross a stream, after which you can move left to follow the fence. There are lots of fallen logs and boggy patches – this route is much easier for horses than hikers. It takes 20 minutes to the corner of the fenced field, and then 35 minutes along to the left to a gate at its far end. By the direct track through the field, it takes 10 minutes to a gate in a fence of logs, and just 15 minutes more to the end of the field.

If you are feeling slightly adventurous, you could continue along the road for 20 minutes and turn right, just before a road-bridge, towards the golf course. After 10 minutes turn right, away from the Overa stream, to pass the Haras Mathilde (riding stables) and a pile of tyres. Turn left to follow the racetrack (assuming it is not in use) and, beyond a small boggy stream, go up to the left under the fence, over some rocks and through trees into a burnt area, reaching a ridge after 5 minutes. Climb across the gate and go left on the track, past a pool, and fork right after 5 minutes; cross a small stream after 5 minutes, fork left after 5 minutes more, and follow the very boggy track up through forest. After 5 minutes you will come to a fence, where you should turn right, reaching the gate at the end of the field after a couple more minutes.

From the gate, swing right on the track, then take the obvious, well-used path left through a small clearing, reaching a small gate after 3 minutes, at once entering mature forest. The path is soon muddy, with lots of roots across it, but you will soon get the hang of it and will not really notice the steady climb. It takes about an hour to reach the first vaguely decent source of water. After this you need to head uphill (to the right) to reach a path traversing the scree slopes above the trees. This passes below a boulder about 4m long, and drops gradually to the head of the valley; curving right before the green cirque at the head of the valley. About 80 minutes after leaving the trees the path crosses to the stream's right bank, and in another 12 minutes reaches the well-built cairn at the pass out of the Oveja valley (c600m). This is relatively low and easy, but there is nothing but bare scree here, with moss and lichen.

A small pool on the far side is the source of a good stream. The path onwards is visible crossing scree on its left bank, but this is soon lost; keep low to avoid some steep-sided gullies. You can either follow the valley, or take a cow track up to the left. About 30 minutes from the pass you will have your first view of the lovely lakes to the west, and in another 8 minutes you will come to two small pools and a great viewpoint over the lakes and mountains of the Sierra de Valdivieso. From here you can drop in a couple of minutes to join the rough cattle-track up to Lago Superior, about 10 minutes to the west, where there is good camping. Turning right down this track, you are soon high above the white-water stream from Lago del Caminante, just below cliffs to your right. Passing through a cleared strip, you will reach the trees after 15 minutes and rejoin the direct route down the valley.

The path heads into the trees to the left, then diagonally right to cross a clearing, and follows a cow track downhill with the stream from the pass to the right. In 10 minutes it reaches the confluence, where a log bridge crosses the stream from Lago del Caminante; there is also a good log bench just beyond. Continuing, the path is soon descending steeply, with glimpses of waterfalls to the right. After 20 minutes you should cross a log to the right bank, just above the confluence of a stream from the left. Cows can go straight on into the marsh on the right bank, but hikers should keep right to the trees at the foot of the slope, where they will soon find themselves on a decent path. This returns to the bank, but where the river swings left after 12 minutes the path cuts to the right and over a small moraine bank, coming back to the right bank after 6 minutes. Again the main path heads off to the right, returning to the bank after 10 minutes; in another 6 minutes it brings you back to a clearing, with a view ahead to Cerro Portillo. Again the path swings away from the river, but this time if you are not careful you will find yourself heading away up the valley of the Cañadón Negro. After about 20 minutes you will cross a stream, in 10 minutes you will pass a beaver dam, and after another 30 minutes you will come to a meadow and dead trees, due to another beaver dam 10 minutes further on. Keep right by the hillside, and after 10 minutes you will find yourself going upstream. Head to the left across several shallow streams, and you will soon find yourself on a good cattle-track heading east down the main valley again. Crossing two more small streams, in 15 minutes you will come to a slightly boggy meadow, which a track crosses just to the right. In a few minutes you will come to a more solid meadow where you will see a *turbera* (peat bog) to the left. After 20 minutes more keep to the right to avoid a very churned-up section where tractors work and peat is hung on racks to dry. There is a good dirt road immediately beyond this, which ends by the river just to the left, but it is possible to cross a suspension bridge and hike up to the Glaciar Vinciguerra, which you will see to the north.

Following the road to the right down the valley of the Arroyo Grande, you will come to a gate in seven minutes, beyond which every inch on either side is fenced off and claimed, with cabins being built, and lots of German shepherd dogs and Argentine flags guarding them. In half an hour there is a sharp bend to the right. Turning left here it takes 20 minutes to reach a car park at the top of the Cascada de los Amigos, which seems very impressive, but is hard to see properly. Another 5 minutes up the river you will find camping spots, but really you would be better off camping before the *turbera*. Continuing to the right at the bend, it takes 20 minutes to reach Ruta 3 west of the big modern bridge over the Arroyo Grande. You can get here by *colectivo 3*, which runs east through town on Deloqui and turns right off Ruta 3 into Barrio La Cantera just to the west of this junction.

Lapataia

Entering the national park by the main gateway, in 2km you will come to a crossroads, with the terminus of the tourist railway, the Ferrocarril Austral Fuegino, immediately to the right. To the left/south a road leads 2km to Bahía Ensenada (see page 334), while to the right/north it is 4km to the Río Pipo free campsite, which is about 300m below the Cascada Río Pipo. Beyond here the former logging railway continues up the Cañadón del Toro, but this is a closed zone of the park and the trail to Lago Fagnano (Lago Kami) is now disused.

About 8km further west the road splits on the east bank of the Río Lapataia; to the left it is 4km to the end of Ruta 3, at Bahía Lapataia, while the minibuses head right for 1km to the Lago Roca campsite. Heading left/south, you will come in a few minutes to a bridge over the Río Lapataia and the *gendarmería*, where a minor path (the Paseo de la Isla) heads off to the left to follow the shoreline. It is worth taking a short track to the left/east just before this, to a white hut by the falls of the Río Lapataia. The Paseo soon crosses between two yellow posts to the right side of the road, and in about 20 minutes reaches a Punto Panoramico overlooking the Laguna Verde and the very basic Camping Las Bandurrias. From here it is 10 minutes south along the road to one of the nicest **places to camp**, at the Cauquenes and Laguna Verde campsites. The Laguna Verde site, to the right, has a washblock and minimal facilities, while the Cauquenes site, across stepping stones to the left, has no facilities or car access, but has some wonderful spots on a headland projecting into the bay, where geese and rabbits show no fear of mankind.

From here there is a very pleasant circuit of a few hours around the head of Lapataia Bay. Immediately across the bridge to the west bank of the Río Ovando, the **Laguna Negra** path starts to the right. This has the most informative signs of any route in the path, and is very popular with families. It takes under 10 minutes up to a boardwalk, which loops to the right for about 100m, across the sphagnum bog which is gradually encroaching on the lake. The insectivorous sundew *Drosera uniflora* can be found here, although you are unlikely to see any very close to the boardwalk. Continuing along the main road, you can turn left after 3 minutes onto the **Paseo del Mirador**. After 2 minutes this branches to the left, leading in 7 minutes to a junction from where it is a minute to the right to the *mirador* (viewpoint), with a great view along the length of Bahía Lapataia. To the left the path continues below the viewpoint and reaches the end of Ruta 3 in 5 more minutes. Here you are 3,063km from Buenos Aires and a thousand from Antarctica; there is a flagpole and a small car park, and virtually nothing else. A boardwalk leads about 200m to a small pontoon, by a 'do not excavate' sign which seems to indicate that there is something worth digging up. In fact the archaeological site is a midden, where shells and other rubbish were left by the original inhabitants. Turning right halfway along the boardwalk, you can cross the lovely short sward, devotedly tended by thousands of rabbits, and reach a small cove in 10 minutes. Immediately beyond this is a creek and a sign marking the start of the *Reserva Natural Estricta* (Strict Natural Reserve), which you should respect.

Returning up Ruta 3, in 5 minutes you will pass the start of the **Paseo del Turbal**, to the right, and in 2 minutes more cross a bridge. The trail to the left leads in a minute to a field and another reserve sign. You can follow a small path (well marked with discreet metal signs) to the right of the road for 5 minutes, and then cross the road to take an unofficial loop along the right bank of the Arroyo Los Castores (Beaver Creek). This is a good track through good mature forest which in 10 minutes reaches two tables and a fireplace, beyond which it is a minute

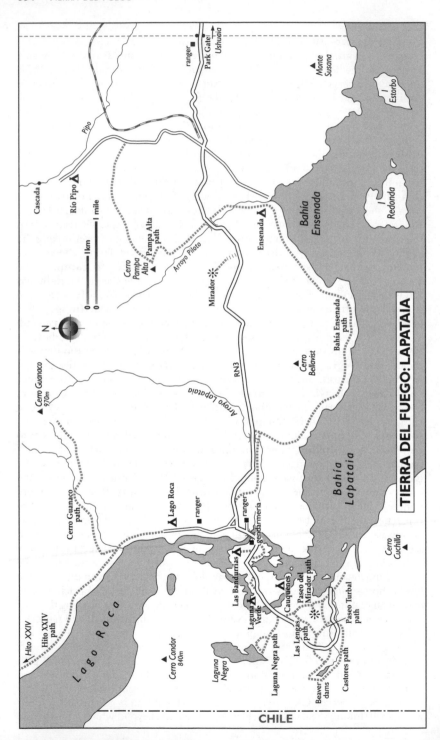

TIERRA DEL FUEGO: LAPATAIA

CHILE

to the river and beaver dams. It is easy to cross here, but, turning right on the far side, in a minute or so you will come to a 'No Entry' sign in the reverse direction. You could cross slightly downstream, where there are plenty of fallen trees, but it is probably boggy; in any case the environment has been permanently changed by the introduction of beavers. On the far side, a *turbera* (peat bog) rises above the path to the left/north; heading to the right, it takes 3 minutes to reach the Paseo del Turbal. Continuing ahead in more mature trees, it takes just a minute to reach a car park, from where the path follows the left bank of the Arroyo Los Castores for 3 minutes back to the road bridge. To the left the Paseo del Turbal runs through attractive forest, crossing the road (slightly to the left) after 7 minutes and splitting after 2 minutes more. To the right the Paseo del Turbal loops back to the end of Ruta 3, while to the left it crosses a stream into more open country.

This area is *en recuperación* after the removal of beavers; the path has been rerouted and you should follow yellow markers. After about 7 minutes you will be back at the start of the Paseo del Mirador, 5 minutes from the Río Ovando bridge.

Lago Roca

Heading north from the road junction, you can take the road or a path by the river, with a few informative signs; in 5 minutes you will come to the burnt-out Hostería Alakush and just beyond it a chapel, the Seccional Fenocchio, and the Lago Roca campsite, the best in the national park. It gets very busy in summer, so is best visited out of season. To the left, where minibuses from Ushuaia terminate, are the shop and washblock; to the right conditions are rather more rustic and half the price (US$2.50). It takes another couple of minutes to reach the end of the road, by the lake (you can also follow the shore all the way here). A path carries on beside the lake to the right, reaching a log bridge across the Arroyo Guanaco in 10 minutes. To the left a sign indicates the path to the Hito XXIV frontier marker. This is an easy walk of 5km each way along the lakeside, which can be done by mountain bike, although you will have to lift your bike over some logs. Do not cross the border even if there is no sign of officialdom; Chilean *carabineros* will probably be watching from a nearby mountaintop and they do not like illegal entry.

To the right at the Arroyo Guanaco the path up **Cerro Guanaco** (970m) is fairly well marked with red metal discs and squares, although it sometimes heads off to the left on the level. It can be very slippery when damp. After 30 minutes of fairly steady climbing you will cross a rough log bridge to the left bank of the Arroyo Guanaco; the path is a bit less clear now, but after 20 minutes you will reach a clearing with great views to Cerro Cóndor and into Chile. Above this it is easy to go slightly astray – the path veers off to the right, across a boggy area, then turns 90° left to cross the stream and a clearing, before swinging right and heading up beyond the treeline. It is about 2km further to the summit. The path disappears but you can continue up the steep scree slopes ahead to the top of Cerro Guanaco. To the west is a superb ridge walk – but make sure you do not cross the border!

Cerro Cóndor

This is not one of the officially marked hikes in the national park, but nevertheless there seems to be no real objection to climbing **Cerro Cóndor** (840m), and you will get some of the best views of the Beagle Channel and Chile's Cordillera Darwin. From the Laguna Negra find your way to the left, around the southern end of the lake. Keep to the high ground, out of the peat bog, and cross the small stream. Although there is a clear path onward, you should take a compass bearing on the summit before entering the trees. After a 2-hour climb through the forest you emerge onto grassy slopes, reaching the scree summit in another 1½ hours.

Bahía Ensenada

This is a delightful coastal hike, and the best way to get away from the crowds in the park. It takes you from the Lapataia area to close to the park gate. From the junction to Lago Roca, head eastwards on the main road for 5 minutes, to a sign reading 'Senda Costera' which marks the start of a new stretch of path parallel to the road. It is rather harder work than walking along the road, taking 15 minutes (rather than 10) to reach the start of the trail proper, but it is more pleasant.

The trail then heads away from the road and swings to the left, on a mostly good path in mature forest of guindo (coihue de Magallanes) and canelo, rising to a ridge and dropping more steeply to a beach after 10 minutes. Here it heads to the left, up on rocks, and along the hillside, reaching another beach in another 10 minutes, and another beach just 2 minutes further on. Continue along this beach for 5 minutes to a red marker at the far end, and return to the forest; after about 20 minutes (passing a few good, rocky picnic points down by the sea) there is a brief tricky descent, after which it takes almost 10 minutes to a cove, and 5 minutes more to a bigger cove, which makes a fantastic spot for a break. Here you are directly opposite the end of the Lapataia peninsula, with a very good view down the Murray Channel, which frames a mountain at the southwest end of Isla Navarino.

The path runs along the back of the beach, rises briefly, and goes on through thick canelo, emerging after 5 minutes over Bahía Escondida, with a view to the jetty used by excursion boats. Following the beach to the left, past the foundations of ruined huts, after 5 minutes you will return into the forest below a big outcrop, and come back down to the beach after another 5 minutes. From here the path runs through the trees just behind the beach, passing another nice cove and then crossing a stream (the only fresh water on the trail) after 10 minutes. The final stretch is nice and grassy, up and down through the trees for 5 minutes, and reaching Bahía Ensenada about 2 hours from the start. From here boats sail to Isla Redonda, just offshore, a 45ha reserve where examples of all the local ecosystems are visible. Yishka Turismo, at San Martín 1295 in Ushuaia (tel: 02901 431 230, 431 535) offers daily tours of 1½ hours for US$15.

Heading up the road, in a couple of minutes you will find a path left into the campsite – there is a car park, but no other facilities here. At the top end of the site cross the stream to find the path to **Pampa Alta**, following red metal markers. After a couple of minutes you will pass a sign at the end of the camping area, and after another 2 minutes turn 90° right. The path is a bit messy, with boggy patches, then a big fallen tree, but improves after crossing the Arroyo Piloto, becoming a good path that rises steadily (by the stream's left bank) to reach the main road after 10 minutes. Here there is parking, and good signs for the path up to Pampa Alta, but not for that down to Bahía Ensenada. The path uphill follows the Arroyo Piloto past beaver dams to the southeastern end of the Guanaco ridge (2.5km) and then heads east for another 2.5km to the Río Pipo road about 2km south of the campsite. Following the main road eastwards, it takes under 15 minutes to the crossroads by the train station, from where it is 12km back to Ushuaia.

GARIBALDI PASS

The only land route in and out of Ushuaia is Ruta 3 to Río Grande, passing over the **Garibaldi Pass**. Heading eastwards out of town, you will pass the end of the hike via the Cañadón de la Oveja and the Valle Andorra. Just east of here the road crosses the Río Olivia, passing the start of the new Camino del Atlantico, which will replace the existing track to Harberton. About 15km down this road is the Estancia Túnel, where riding can be arranged. With a mountain bike you could follow the coastal track to the Río Olivia and on to Punta Segunda, Remolino, Puerto Almanza and on to the present Harberton road. The main road passes the Cascada Velo de Novia (Bridal Veil Falls), just east of km3030, and enters the Valle de Tierra Mayor, a deep glacial trough in which there are several centres for cross-country skiing, hiking and camping, the Solar del Bosque (at km3020, 20km from Ushuaia), with the Albergue Nunatak, then Tierra Mayor (km3019), Xalpen, Las Cotorras (a new ski resort at km3014), and Haruwen (km3003), where Camping Río Tristen has baths, showers, electric lighting, a dining room, fire places, and 8km of signposted trekking paths. Haruwen has an office in Ushuaia, at San Martín 788, local 36 (tel/fax: 02901 424 058); Solar del Bosque is at Paz 620 (tel/fax: 421 228).

After Rancho Hambre (km3000, where the asphalt ends), the highway climbs steadily north to the Garibaldi Pass at km2985, where there are great views north to Lagos Escondido and Fagnano. The latter, named after an 18th-century missionary, also bears the indigenous name of Lago Kami. It is 100km long, and almost forms a continuation of Seno Almirantazgo (Admiralty Sound). For views south, along a huge mountain valley, you need to climb the ridge to the west of the pass. A four-wheel-drive track leads very steeply up to a little saddle only 100m from the pass. From here you can climb down through an opening on the right to a small stream, where you should find some very old red stripes painted vertically on trees. These mark a path that in fact starts from the road by the stream, although it is easier to pick it up here. The path appears to head straight up through the trees towards the ridge-line, but it actually sidles along the south flank of the spur and you emerge high up on the ridge after about 45 minutes. At one point the red markers peter out. Remember that you are not heading straight up the slope but along the flank of the spur.

The pass is 45 minutes from Ushuaia and there are half a dozen buses a day to Río Grande, so you can have several hours for sightseeing before flagging down a later bus. From the pass the old road is still navigable by mountain bike, allowing you to camp near Lago Escondido or go directly to the Hostería Petrel (km2980), now bypassed by the new road. You should see guanaco from the road between here and Río Grande, but not beyond.

ESTANCIA HARBERTON:
The uttermost part of the earth

> 'Coming into Harberton from the land side, you could mistake it for a big estate in the Scottish Highlands, with its sheep fences, sturdy gates and peat-brown trout streams. The house, imported long ago from England, was of corrugated iron, painted white, with green windows and a soft red roof. Inside, it retained the solid mahogany furniture, the plumbing and the upright presence of a Victorian parsonage.'
>
> Bruce Chatwin, *In Patagonia*

Anyone interested in the history of the island's Indian inhabitants – and their subsequent extinction – will certainly want to visit Estancia Harberton, 85km east of Ushuaia. If the name Harberton suggests a village in Devon more than a settlement in one of the bleakest spots of South America, you are right. The place was established in 1887 by Thomas and Mary Bridges, the first white missionaries to settle on the island, and named after Mary's birthplace in England.

Virtually every item on the estate was imported by ship from Britain, from the original wooden frame-house, which was constructed in a Devonshire carpentry shop, to a young South Devon bull, four Romney Marsh rams and a couple of Devonshire pigs. The family's amazing life among the Indians, whose languages they learnt to speak and skills they imitated, was later documented in fascinating detail by their son Lucas in *The Uttermost Part of the Earth* (see *Appendix 2, Further Information*).

The book describes Thomas Bridges' painstaking compilation of a Yámana dictionary with over 32,000 entries. Unfortunately, his business skills did not match his linguistic skills and he entrusted the finished manuscript to a slick American doctor on the Belgian Antarctic Expedition of 1898 who passed it off as his own. Luckily it eventually found its way to the Natural History Museum in London, where it now lies. Today the *estancia* is run by the fourth generation of the Bridges family and a visit, though expensive, is recommended.

Visiting Harberton
Patrick Symington

Bruce Chatwin walked along the coast from Ushuaia to Harberton, and left by the track north to the eastern end of Lago Fagnano, cut by Lucas Bridges in 1900–2. Nowadays, however, visitors are required to arrive by boat or by the main road from Rancho Hambre, from where it is 18km by Ruta J to Puerto Almirante Brown and 17km more along the coast to Harberton, and to confine themselves to the area of the jetty and the tea shop, except for a one-hour tour of the farm (US$6). You are not permitted to walk anywhere else without a guide, or to camp wild. There is, however, a possibility that the track to the Hostería Kaiken, at the east end of Lago Fagnano, may be opened for cars.

The catamaran tours laid on by Rumbo Sur (San Martín 342; tel: 02901 422 441; fax: 430 669; rumbosur@satlink.com) or Tolkeyen (Maipú 237; tel: 430 073) on three afternoons a week (Tue, Thur, Sat) are very popular, and other agencies may also provide tours if they have enough demand. However, these are expensive since they combine Harberton with a visit to a penguin colony and Gable Island – around US$75 per person. The penguin colony is good, with hundreds of Magellanic penguins and a few king penguins, from November to March; you may also see seals, sea-lions, petrels, coromorants, kelp geese and the occasional black-browed albatross. The catamaran comes close to the shore but you do not disembark. At Harberton you land for little more than an hour, and either take a shortened version of the tour or stay near the jetty and tea shop. If you come by bus, you may also be able to negotiate to continue to Moat *estancia* (founded in 1902), further east at the mouth of the Beagle Channel, which is less historic but also less restrictive, allowing more chance to walk around freely.

The tour of Harberton itself is extremely interesting and done in a very friendly style. You see round the *estancia* buildings, including the old and current shearing sheds and gardens. A pretty wood where you can identify local trees and plants has been a nature reserve for a century, and there is a reconstruction of a Yámana hut near an actual Yámana midden. The owner's wife, Natalie Goodall, is a marine biologist who is gathering much new information on the movements of cetaceans through the Beagle Channel; there is a display of skeletons (US$10, not possible

THE FUEGIAN TRIBES
Clare Hargreaves

The Selk'nam

The Selk'nam (or Ona) inhabited the remote interior of the main island (Isla Grande) and its northern and eastern coasts. Their only weapons were bows and arrows, and they lived almost entirely on guanaco meat. They clothed themselves in the skins of these animals as well as using them for their shelters. Having no sense of private property, they simply saw sheep as guanaco which did not need to be hunted, and so were persecuted by the ranchers. The last pure Selk'nam, Angela Loij, died in Río Grande in 1974.

The Aush

The Aush (or Eastern Ona) lived on the boggy southeastern tip of the main island. They lived by hunting and fishing. Very little is known about them, although they seem to have been related to the Selk'nam.

The Yámana

The Yámana (or Yahgan) were the southernmost inhabitants of the earth. Their territory extended from Desolation Bay, along the southern coast of the main island as far as Spaniard Harbour (including Ushuaia) and took in all the islands as far south as Cape Horn. The population gradually concentrated itself on Isla Navarino, where only mixed-blood descendants now survive. Work was divided between the sexes; men gathered fuel and fungi while the women cooked, fetched water, paddled canoes and fished. Fish, seals, limpets, birds and crabs were the main diet. Because of the lack of beaches, the women had to swim like dogs through thick seaweed onto which they moored their canoes. In winter they would coat themselves in animal grease before diving into the freezing sea, but otherwise they lived virtually naked.

The Kaweshkar

Natural adventurers, the Kaweshkar (or Alacaloof) lived in the western parts of the archipelago and survived by fishing in bark canoes. They lived almost entirely on birds, seals, fish and limpets. They were also dexterous in the use of bows and arrows, spears and slings. A dozen or so survive in Puerto Edén, in Chile.

on the catamaran trip), and sei whale jawbones form the gate to the house itself. Cake and refreshments are available (very nice).

The only problem is that if you go on the catamaran day everybody is there at the same time – probably around 50 people when we were there on a Sunday in January. Another option is to hire a car. It would make a nice trip with one or two nights camping, as the scenery is magnificent on the way. There are three places to camp within the *estancia*, which are free if you register at the house, and other free sites on the way. Hiring a car for the day would cost about US$120, but you would see the penguins. Harberton is closed from mid-April to mid-October, and for Christmas, New Year and Easter. You can check by phoning (02901) 422 742 in Ushuaia.

SOUTH OF THE BEAGLE CHANNEL

The Chilean islands to the south of the Beagle Channel never fail to excite interest – principally Cape Horn, of course, but also **Isla Navarino**, which is slightly easier to reach. Its only settlement is Puerto Williams, the world's southernmost town, on the Beagle Channel well east of Ushuaia. The extremely basic *Cruz Australis* ferry (of the company of the same name) comes from Punta Arenas every ten days (US$120 for a great two-day cruise), and DAP flies the same route three times a week (US$65 each way). Presently the only way to get across from Ushuaia is by yacht, although this may change.

There is a helpful tourist office and a decent little museum, but the main sight is, sadly, the hamlet of Ukika, 2km east, where the last descendants of the Yámana survive. A road runs along the north coast. To the east of Ukika it continues to Caleta Eugenia, then south to Puerto Toro, opposite Isla Picton, where five marines and their families live. To the west of Puerto Williams it runs 54km to Puerto Navarino, at the western end of the island (opposite Ushuaia), home to three marines (and their families). About 30km along this road is Caleta Mejillones, where there is a Yámana cemetery. About 5km west of here there was once a trail south to the missionary settlement of Woolya, but this is now lost in the forest.

The best hiking on the island is the **Cordón de los Diente**s circuit (54km, about 4 days), which begins by following a track up the Ukika valley southwest of Puerto Williams, loops inland across the range known as 'The Teeth' and back again, finishing on the road 12km west of town, at a crab cannery. There are some dramatic mountains, but most of the island's interior is a water-logged expanse of pools and peat bogs, with stunted lenga and ñirre. There are lots of guanaco and flightless steamer ducks, without predators, and unfortunately plenty of introduced beavers.

Cape Horn (Cabo de Hornos) is visited mainly by chartered yachts, and, every two months, by a naval supply vessel when the three men tending the lighthouse are relieved. Apart from the lighthouse there is nothing but a wooden chapel, and the sense of being at the very edge of the world.

Chile and Argentina are slowly making progress in opening up the southern channels to tourism. From 2001 three routes have been authorised for tour boats: one to the west along the southern side of the Cordillera Darwin, looping back around Isla Gordon; another around Isla Navarino; and the third to Cape Horn and back. The regulations are very precise about the exact size of vessel allowed on each route. All need a Chilean captain and pilot, but association with Argentinian companies is allowed, so that it should be possible to bring passengers across from Ushuaia.

Appendix 1

LANGUAGE

Chilean Spanish is renowned as one of the fastest and most furious variants of the language, but it is not hard once you get used to it. Above all, consonants, particularly 's' (except at the start of a word), tend to disappear, while 'g' becomes an 'h'. Diminutives such as *ciaoito* are used a lot, even when the locals are speaking English - 'time for some lunchy'.

Argentine pronunciation is more genuinely idiosyncratic, with 'll' (pronounced like 'y' in Chile) pronounced 'zh', so that *cordillera* becomes 'cordizhera' and *valle* becomes 'vazhe'. In the far south there is something like a common Patagonian accent, and the Mendoza accent is more Chilean than Argentine.

Lonely Planet's *Latin American Spanish Phrasebook* is a useful guide to the different forms of the language found across the continent. *How to Survive in the Chilean Jungle*, an English lexicon of Chilean slang and Spanish sayings, by John Brennan and Alvaro Taboada, gives a more focussed, and hilarious, view of the Chilean variant.

Basic phrases

Where is... ?	*¿Dónde está... ?*
What's this place called?	*¿Como se llama este lugar?*
What village is this?	*¿Que aldea es esta?*
Where does this trail go?	*¿A dónde va este camino?*
Where are you from (your country)?	*¿De dónde es?*
How far is it to... ?	*¿A que distancia... ?*
How much does it cost?	*¿Cuánto vale?*
May I.... ? Is it possible.... ?	*¿Se puede ?*
I would like (to eat)	*Quisiera (comer)*
I am English/American	*Soy inglés/norteamericano*
I don't understand	*No entiendo*
Please write it down	*Por favor, escríbalo*
Do you speak English?	*¿Habla inglés?*

Basic vocabulary

bon voyage	*vaya bien, buen viaje*	yesterday	*ayer*
good morning	*buenos días*	sorry	*lo siento*
good afternoon	*buenas tardes*	very well	*muy bien*
goodnight	*buenas noches*	good	*bueno*
goodbye	*adiós*	what	*¿qué?*
yes/no	*sí/no*	when	*¿cuando?*
hello	*hola*	why	*¿por qué?*
please/thankyou	*por favor/gracias*	how	*¿cómo?*
excuse me/	*con permiso/de nada*	here/there	*aquí/ahí*
you're welcome		open/closed	*abierto/cerrado*
today/tomorrow	*hoy/mañana*	large/small	*grande/pequeño*

Food and drink

beer	*cerveza*
bill	*cuenta*
bread	*pan*
butter	*mantequilla*
tea/coffee	*te/café* (in Chile usually *cafecito*)
water	*agua*
wine	*vino*
fish	*pescado*
fruit	*frutas*
beef	*vaca*
milk	*leche*
potatoes	*patatas*
sugar	*azucar*
cheese	*queso*
mushrooms	*hongos*
orange	*naranja*
apple	*manzana*
knife	*cuchillo*
fork	*tenedor*
spoon	*cuchera*
without meat	*sin carne*
enjoy your meal	*buen provecha*

Days of the week

Sunday	*domingo*
Monday	*lunes*
Tuesday	*martes*
Wednesday	*miercoles*
Thursday	*jueves*
Friday	*viernes*
Saturday	*sábado*

Directions

straight ahead	*todo recto*
left/right	*izquierda/derecha*
north/south	*norte/sur*
east/	*este* or *oriente*
west	*oeste, occidente* or *poniente*
northeast/northwest	*noreste/noroeste* (easily confused)

General hiking vocabulary

backpack	*mochila*
boat	*barca*
bridge	*puente, pasarela*
campsite	*campamento, campismo*

(*acampar* or *camping* may mean 'picnic facilities')

cave	*cueva*
cloud	*nube*
crossroad	*cruce, bifurcación*
environment	*medio ambiente*
farm or ranch	*fundo, hacienda, estancia, rancho*
farmer or peasant	*campesino*
field	*campo*
forest	*montaña, bosque, selva*
frontier	*frontera*
gorge	*desfiladero, cañón*
high	*alto*
hill	*cerro, cuesta*
junction	*cruce, desvio*
lake	*lago, laguna*
landscape	*paisaje*
lookout, viewpoint	*mirador*
map	*mapa*
marsh	*pantano, estero, bofedal*
meadow	*llano, llanura*
mountain	*cerro, pico, montaña*
mountain range	*cordillera, sierra*
on vacation	*paseando*
pass	*portezuelo*

(*paso* means frontier crossing)

pasture	*pasto, pradera*
path	*camino, sendero, senda, picada*
peak	*pico*
picnic	*merienda, acampar, camping*
rain	*lluvia*
range	*cordillera, sierra*
ranger post	*guardería* (Chile)/ *seccional* (Argentina)
rent	*alquilar* (Argentina)/ *arriendar* (Chile)
restaurant	*restaurante, comedor*
ridge	*cumbre, cadena*
river	*río*
rock	*roca*
shop	*tienda*
slope	*cuesta, vertiente, ladera, falda*
spring	*fuente, manantial*
steep	*abrupto, escarpado*
stream	*arroyo*
summit	*cima*
tent	*carpa, tienda de campaña*
toilet	*baño*
tired	*cansado*
valley	*valle*
viewpoint	*mirador*
village	*aldea, pueblo, poblado*
walking	*caminando*
wandering	*errante*
wood (material)	*madera*

Numbers

0	*cero*	16	*dieciséis*
1	*uno/a*	17	*diecisiete*
2	*dos*	18	*dieciocho*
3	*tres*	19	*diecinueve*
4	*cuatro*	20	*veinte*
5	*cinco*	21	*veintiuno*
6	*seis*	30	*treinta*
7	*siete*	40	*cuarenta*
8	*ocho*	50	*cincuenta*
9	*nueve*	60	*sesenta*
10	*diez*	70	*setenta*
11	*once*	80	*ochenta*
12	*doce*	90	*noventa*
13	*trece*	100	*cien/ciento*
14	*catorce*	500	*quinientos*
15	*quince*	1,000	*mil*

Appendix 2

FURTHER INFORMATION
Further reading
Below is a selection of books on different aspects of Chile and Argentina, but there are many more. Where only the British publisher is given, the book may be available in a different edition in the United States, and vice versa.

Guidebooks

The South American Handbook, edited by Ben Box (Footprint Handbooks, Bath, England). Particularly helpful for adventurous travellers, and published annually. Each year it gets fatter and pricier, but separate volumes are now available on Chile and Argentina.

Chile and Easter Island, a travel survival kit, Wayne Bernhardson (Lonely Planet). There is also a Lonely Planet atlas of Chile.

Argentina, Uruguay & Paraguay, a travel survival kit, Wayne Bernhardson (Lonely Planet). There is also a Buenos Aires city guide.

Budget Traveller's Guide to Latin America, Marjorie Cohen (Council on International Exchange, New York).

Birnbaum's South America Guide (Houghton Mifflin, US). Updated annually.

Tierra del Fuego, Natalie Goodall (Ediciones Shanamaüm, Buenos Aires, 1979). Bilingual text.

Guía de Excursionismo para la Cordillera de Santiago, Gaston San Ramón Herbage (Editorial Universitaria, Santiago, Chile, 1976). In Spanish.

Traveller's Literary Companion to South and Central America, Jason Wilson (In Print Publishing Ltd, Brighton, 1993). Includes geographical, historical, political and literary comment on each country.

Turistel, in two volumes (CTC, Santiago, updated annually). Spanish-language guide to Chile, also in English reduced to one volume; very detailed and up-to-date, with superb maps.

YPF Guía Patagonia y Antartida Argentina (YPF, Buenos Aires, updated annually). A newer Argentine equivalent to the Turistel guide. Similar is the ACA *Guía Turística Patagonia Norte/Austral*.

Argentina in Focus; Chile in Focus (Latin America Bureau, London). Two guides to the economic, social and political background of Argentina and Chile.

Mountaineering in Patagonia, Alan Kearney (Cordee).

The High Andes, John Biggar (Andes, Kirkcudbrightshire). A comprehensive guide to the peaks of the South American Andes.

Natural history

The Flight of the Condor, Michael Andrews (Collins/BBC 1982). The book of the TV series on the wildlife of the Andes.

Andes to Amazon, a Guide to Wild South America, Michael Bright (BBC 2000). From a more recent TV series, with good lists of sites and species.

Patagonian Wilderness, Marcelo Beccaceci & Bonnie Hayskar (Pangaea, Minnesota 1992). An illustrated essay.

Patagonia: Natural History, Prehistory & Ethnography at the Uttermost End of the Earth, edited by Colin McEwan, Luis A Borrero, Alfred Prieto (Princeton UP, 1997). Combines wildlife and human settlement.

Chile's Native Forests, Ken Wilcox (NW Wild Books, Michigan, 1995).

Naturaleza de Chile, Jurgen Rottman & Nicolas Piwonka (Unisys/WWF1988). Also *Altiplano, Bosques de Chile*, bilingual coffee table books.

Paisaje de Chile, published in Chile in Spanish, English, French, available in bookshops in Santiago. Coffee table reading.

South America's National Parks, William C Leitch (The Mountaineers, Seattle, 1990). Also *Argentine Trout Fishing* by the same author.

Ecological Imperialism: the Biological Expansion of Europe 900-1900, Alfred Crosby (Cambridge University Press, 1986).

Ecology & Biology of Mediterranean Ecosystems in Chile, California and Australia, edited by Mary Kalin Arroyo (Springer Verlag, Ecological Studies no.108, 1995).

Spanish-language natural history

Ecología Forestal; *Bosques templado de Chile y Argentina*, both Claudio Donoso (Editorial Universitaria, Santiago).

Ecología de los Vertebrados de Chile, Fabián Jaksic (Editorial Universitaria Catolica de Chile).

Diversidad Biológica de Chile, edited by Javier A Simonetti, Mary TK Arroyo et al (Conicyt, Santiago 1995).

Ecología de los Bosques Nativos de Chile, edited by Juan Armesto, Carolina Villagrán, Mary Kalin Arroyo (Editorial Universitaria, Santiago 1996).

Ecología y Historia Natural de la Zona Central, Adriana Hoffmann & Malú Sierra (Defensores del Bosque Chileno 1997).

La Tragedia del Bosque Chileno, ed. Adriana Hoffman, Defensores del Bosque Chileno 1998). Superb, big coffee-table volume with graphic illustrations of the rape of Chile by logging.

Soldados de Noé, la conservación de la fauna silvestre en la Argentina, Marcelo Beccaceci (Nuevo Extremó, Buenos Aires 1995).

Flora Patagónica, Maevia Noemi Correa (INTA).

Flora Silvestre de Chile, Grau & Ziska (Frankfurt/Main, Germany, 1992).

Flora y Fauna Patagónicas, Drs Guillermo Tell, Irina Izaguirre, Rubén Darío Quintana (Ediciones Caleuche, Santiago[Bariloche 1997]).

La Region de los Bosques Andino-Patagónicos, Milan J Dimitri (INTA, Buenos Aires).

Aves de Magallanes, Claudio Venegas (Universidad de Magallanes, Punta Arenas 1994).

Los Arboles y Bosques de Magallanes, Orlando Dollenz Alvárez (Universidad de Magallanes, Punta Arena 1995).

Field guides

Birds of Southern South America and Antarctica, Martín R de la Peña & Maurice Rumboll (Harper Collins 1998). The bible.

A Guide to the Birds and Mammals of Coastal Patagonia, Graham Harris (Princeton UP 1999).

Essential Guide to Birding in Chile, Mark Pearman (Worldwide Publications 1995).

Where to Watch Birds in South America, Nigel Wheatley (Princeton UP 1995).

The Birds of Chile, Braulio Arraya & Sharon Chester (Latour/Wandering Albatross 1993). An English-language version (with better illustrations) of *Guía de Campo de las Aves de Chile*, Braulio Arraya M & Guillermo Millie H (Editorial Universitaria, Santiago 1986).

Birds of Argentina and Uruguay, T Narosky and D Yzurieta (Vazquez Mazzini, Buenos Aires). An excellent field guide, in English, which can be bought in Argentina.

Guía para la Identificación de las Aves de Argentina y Uruguay, T Narosky & D Yzurieta (Asociación Ornitologica del Plata, Vazquez Mazzini Editores) is the original; also *Manuel del Observador de Aves*, Tito Narosky & Andrés Bosso (Editorial Albatros).

The Birds of Chile, and the Adjacent Regions of Peru, Argentina and Bolivia, A W Johnson (Platt Establecimientos Gráficos, Buenos Aires, 1967). In two volumes, now dated.

Birds of the Beagle Channel and Cape Horn, E Couve & C Vidal.

Birds of the Antarctic and Sub-Antarctic, George Watson (American Geophysical Union, Washington DC, 1975). Useful in Tierra del Fuego.

South American Landbirds: a Photographic Guide to Identification, J S Dunning (Hardwood Books, Newton Square, Pennsylvania, 1981).

Introducción al estudio de los Insectos de Chile, Luis E Peña G (Editorial Universitaria, Santiago, 4/e 1986).

Las Mariposas de Chile/The Butterflies of Chile, Luis E Peña G & Alfredo B Ugarte P (Editorial Universitaria, Santiago 1997).

Mamíferos Terrestres de Chile, Hugo Campos Cereceda (Marisa Cuneo, Santiago).

Mamíferos de Chile, ed. A Muñoz & J Yáñez (National Museum of Natural History/Centro de Estudios Agrarios y Ambientales, Valdivia 2000). Very detailed.

Batracios de Chile, Jose Miguel Cei (Editorial Universitaria, Santiago).

Flora Silvestre de Chile, Adriana Hoffman (Fundación Claudio Gay); also *Cactaceas* by the same author.

Guía de Campo para identificar los Aves del Neuquen, Ernesto C Gorgoliue 2000, also *Guía de Campo para identificar los Mamíferos del Neuquen*, 1999.

Aves de Santiago, Guillermo Egli (UNORCH 2000).

Donde Observar Aves en el Parque Nacional Torres de Paine, (photographic guide).

Guía de Indentificación de Aves de Ambientes Acuaticos, Jürgen Rottman (UNORCH).

Adventure, exploration and history

The Voyage of the Beagle, Charles Darwin (1839; paperback editions by Penguin and Wordsworth Classics, UK, and NAL-Dutton, USA), perhaps 'the greatest travel book ever'.

On Darwin and related matters see also: *Darwin's Autobiography* (Oxford University Press/Dover 1983); *The Origin of Species* (1859; paperback editions by Penguin, OUP World's Classics and Random House Modern Library); *The Voyage of Charles Darwin*, edited by Christopher Ralling (BBC, London, 1978); *Charles Darwin: Voyaging*, Janet

Browne (the first volume of a biography; Princeton UP/Cape 1996); *Darwin and the Beagle*, Alan Moorehead (Hamish Hamilton 1969, Penguin 1971); *Saddled with Darwin*, Toby Green (Weidenfeld & Nicholson 1999, Phoenix 2000); *Three Men of the Beagle*, Richard Lee Marks (Knopf 1991), on Darwin, FitzRoy and Jemmy Button; *After Darwin*, Timberlake Wertenbaker (Faber 1999). Perhaps her best play.

In Patagonia, Bruce Chatwin (Cape/Picador, London, 1979).

The Old Patagonian Express, Paul Theroux (Penguin, London, 1979).

Patagonia Revisited, Bruce Chatwin and Paul Theroux (Cape/Pan 1986).

An Englishman in Patagonia, John Pilkington (Century, London, 1991).

The Uttermost Part of the Earth, Lucas Bridges (Hodder and Stoughton, 1947; Century Hutchinson, London, 1987).

Beyond the Silver River, Jimmy Burns (Bloomsbury, London, 1989).

Land of Tempest: Travels in Patagonia 1958-62, Eric Shipton (Hodder and Stoughton, London, 1963); also *Tierra del Fuego: the Fatal Lodestone* (Charles Knight 1973).

Mischief in Patagonia, H W Tilman (Cambridge UP, 1957). Sailing and climbing on the Southern Patagonian Icecap.

The Springs of Enchantment, John Earle (Hodder and Stoughton 1981). Climbing and exploring with Shipton.

The Motorcycle Diaries, Che Guevara (Routledge/Fourth Estate 1995). Through Argentina and Chile to Venezuela, with an awakening social conscience.

Travels in a Thin Country, Sara Wheeler (Little, Brown, 1994). The best recent book on Chile.

Bad Times in Buenos Aires Miranda France (Weidenfeld & Nicolson, 1998, Phoenix 1999). An incisive and entertaining account of life in Buenos Aires.

From the Falklands to Patagonia, Michael Mainwaring (Alison & Busby, 1983).

The Cockleshell Journey, John Ridgway (Hodder and Stoughton, 1974). A rubber dinghy journey in Tierra del Fuego.

Trekking: Great Walks of the World, edited by John Cleare (Unwin Hyman, London, 1988). Contains a chapter on Torres del Paine.

Cucumber Sandwiches in the Andes, John Ure (Constable, London, 1973). Describes a crossing on horseback between Chile and Argentina.

The Trail to Titicaca, Rupert Attlee (Hindon 1997, Summerscale Press (Chichester) 1999). Cycling from Tierra del Fuego to Lake Titicaca.

Between Extremes, John McCarthy & Brian Keenan (Bantam 1999, Black Swan 2000).

Tschiffely's Ride Aimé Tschiffely (Heinemann, London, 1934). Describes a 16,000km ride from Argentina to Washington. A classic. Also *This Way Southward* (Heinemann, 1940).

Up, Into the Singing Mountain, Richard Llewellyn (New English Library, 1985). The hero of *How Green Was My Valley* seeks adventure among the Welsh settlers in Patagonia.

Far Away and Long Ago, W H Hudson (1918; paperback editions Eland, Century and Hippocrene). A classic account, written in 1918, of a naturalist's childhood in Argentina. Also *Idle Days in Patagonia* (Dent 1893, reprinted by Dent in 1984) and *The Purple Land* (Dent 1885), which Borges thought the best work of 'gaucho literature'.

Back to Cape Horn, Rosie Swale (Collins 1986/Fontana 1988). A horseback journey down the length of Chile.

Historia del Andinismo en Chile, Gaston San Ramón Herbage (published in Santiago, Chile, 1989). Includes some interesting maps (with routes) of the Chilean *cordillera*. In

Spanish.

Politics and recent history of Chile and Argentina

The Land that Lost its Heroes: Argentina, the Falklands and Alfonsín, Jimmy Burns (Bloomsbury, 1987).

A House Divided: Argentina 1880-1980, Eduardo Crawley (C Hurst, 1984).

A State of Fear, Andrew Graham-Yooll (Eland/Hippocrene Books, 1986). The years of the 'disappearances' by the editor of the *Buenos Aires Herald*.

Chile: Death in the South, Jacobo Timerman (Picador, 1987).

Clandestine in Chile, Gabriel García Márquez (Holt, New York, 1987)

Memoirs, Pablo Neruda (Penguin 1978).

Health guides

Healthy Travel: Bugs, Bites and Bowels, Dr Jane Wilson-Howarth (Cadogan, 1995).

Shitting Pretty, Dr Jane Wilson-Howarth (Travelers' Tales, San Francisco, 2000)

Your Child's Health Abroad: A manual for travelling parents, Dr Jane Wilson-Howarth and Dr Matthew Ellis (Bradt, 1998).

Travellers' Health: How to Stay Healthy Abroad, edited by Dr Richard Dawood (Oxford University Press, 1994).

Wilderness Medicine, William W Forgey (ICS Books, USA, 4/e 1994).

Magazines

Travelling Chile is a bimonthly bilingual magazine with lots of useful information for tourists visiting Chile. Providencia 2594, Office 321, or available from Sernatur.

Adventura is a monthly magazine published by the *Sociedad Chilena de Exploración*, Londres 67, Santiago. In Spanish.

Bookshops
London

Daunt Books, 83 Marylebone High St, W1M 3DE (tel: 020 7224 2295; fax: 7224 6893); 193 Haverstock Hill, NW3 4QL (tel: 7794 4006).

Stanfords, 12–14 Long Acre, WC2E 9LP (tel: 7836 1321; sales@stanfords.co.uk); mail order at this shop; other branches at Campus Travel at 52 Grosvenor Gardens and British Airways at 156 Regent St, and in Bristol (see below).

The Travel Bookshop, 13 Blenheim Crescent, W11 2EE (tel: 7229 5260; www.thetravelbookshop.co.uk).

England

Blackwell's Map and Travel Shop, 53 Broad St, Oxford OX1 3BQ (tel: 01865 792 792). Specialist outlet; also general branches in other cities.

Itchy Feet, 4 Bartlett St, Bath BA1 (tel: 01225 337 987; fax: 337 986).

Stanfords, 29 Corn Street, Bristol BS1 1HT (tel: 0117 929 9966).

Travellers World Bookshop (WLM), 9 Downing Rd, West Meadows, Derby DE21 6HA (tel: 0870 606 2417, 01332 343 332; fax: 01332 340 464; shop@map-guides.com).

Scotland

James Thin Melven's Bookshop, 29 Union St, Inverness, IV1 1QA (tel: 01463 233 500; www.jthin.co.uk). Mail order specialist.

Ireland

Easons Bookshop, 40 O'Connell St, Dublin 1 (tel: 01 873 3811; www.eason.ie).

Fred Hanna's Bookshop, 27 Nassau St, Dublin 2 (tel: 01 677 1255; fax: 671 4330; www.hannas.ie; email: info@hannas.ie

Hodges Figgis Bookshop, 56 Dawson St, Dublin 2 (tel: 01 677 4754; www.hodgesfiggis.com.).

Waterstone's, Queens Bldg, 8 Royal Ave, Belfast BT1 1DA (tel: 028 9024 7355); 7 Dawson St, Dublin 2 (tel: 01 679 1415); 69 Patrick St, Cork (tel: 021 276 522).

USA

The Complete Traveller Bookstore, 199 Madison Ave, New York, NY 10016 (tel: 212 685 9007; fax: 982 7628).

Phileas Fogg's Books & Maps, 87 Stanford Shopping Center, Palo Alto, CA 94304 (tel: 415 327 1754).

Traveler's Bookstore, 75 Rockefeller Plaza, 22 W 52nd St, New York, NY 10019 (tel: 212 664 0995; fax: 397 3984; bill@panix.com).

Canada

Open Air Books and Maps, 25 Toronto St, Toronto ON, M5R 2C1 (tel: 416 363 0719).

Ulysses Travel Bookshop, 4176 St-Denis, Montréal PQ, H2W 2M5 (tel: 1800 748 9171, 514 843 9447; fax: 843 9448; info@ulysses.ca); and 101 Yorkville, Toronto ON, M5R 1CI (tel: 1800 268 4395, 416 323 3609).

The Travel Bug, 2667 West Broadway, Vancouver BC, V6K 2G2 (tel: 604 737 1122; www.swifty.com/tbug).

Australia

The Travel Bookshop, 175 Liverpool Street, Sydney NSW 2000 (tel: 2 9261 8200; fax: 61 2 9261 8481)

Websites
General

rec.travel.latin-america, soc.culture.argentina, soc.culture.cl and
soc.culture.latin-america newsgroups, also www.egroups.com/group/planeta_chile
http://travellatinamerica.com a general travel site
www.cdc.gov/travel medical advice
www.lanic.utexas.edu academic links etc
www.planeta.com environmental contacts
www.samexplo.org South American Explorers

Chile

Chip News: www.chip.cl The Chilean Information Project; also www.chiper.cl Chip
  environmental report, www.chiptravel.cl
www.santiagotimes.cl English-language newspaper
www.elmercurio.cl El Mercurio de Santiago; www.tercera.cl La Tercera - Spanish-
  language newspapers
www.prochile.cl/index ProChile; www.sernatur.cl Sernatur - tourist information
www.travellers.cl Travellers, tourist agency in Puerto Montt
www.amarillas.cl phone directory
www.backpackersbest.cl; www.outdoorschile.cl
www.cipma.cl (database of 14,000 environmental documents)
www.netup.cl/~codeff; www.conama.cl conservation bodies
www.iusanet.cl/conaf/ CONAF - in charge of national parks
www.guardianunlimited.co.uk/Pinochet_on_trial

Argentina

www.buenosairesherald.com English-language newspaper
www.lanacion.com.ar Spanish-language newspaper
www.hotelnet.com.ar upmarket hotels
www.vidasilvestre.org.ar the leading conservation body
www.argentinamenu.com tourist information
www.taventura.com.ar Tiempo de Aventura magazine
www.aventurarse.com www.travelsur.net adventure travel
www.paginas-doradas.com.ar www.paginasamarillas.com.ar phone directories
www.argentina-embassy-uk.org the Argentinian embassy in Britain

Index